Chicanery

From the pages of Cycle News

Chicanery
From the pages of Cycle News

Henny Ray Abrams

Chicanery
Henny Ray Abrams
Copyright © 2014 by Cycle News

Publisher
Cycle News
15 Hammond, Suite 308
Irvine, California 92619
Tel: 949-863-7082
http://www.cyclenews.com
contact@cyclenews.com

Editor, Cover and Book Design Tracy Hagen
Photographs Brian J. Nelson
Copyeditor and Proofreader Larry Lawrence
Printer CreateSpace

This book is set in FF Scala and FF Scala Sans, both from FontShop International GmbH.

Notice of Rights All rights reserved. No part of this book may be reproduced or transmitted in any form by any means, electronic, mechanical, photocopying, recording, or otherwise, without prior written permission of Cycle News. For information on getting permission for reprints or excerpts, contact Cycle News. Unauthorized reproduction may be subject to litigation.

Trademarks This book contains trademarked names. Instead of putting a trademark symbol with every instance of a trademark name, this book uses trademarked names in an editorial fashion and to the benefit of the trademark owner with no intention of infringement of the trademark. All trademarks marks are the property of their respective owners.

Fair use This book contains an excerpt from the song *Pinball Wizard*, copyright Pete Townshend, The Who, Eel Pie Publishing, 1969. The excerpt complies with the fair use guidelines set forth in the United States Copyright Act of 1976, 17 U.S.C. § 107.

ISBN 978-0-9915973-0-7

Version 1.0

Printed and bound in the United States of America

for Bryan, Ronny and Scott

These aren't dumb men; they just make stupefying decisions that show a comprehensive ignorance of the wishes of the race paddock and grandstands, places most of them spend precious little time.

HENNY RAY ABRAMS
1954-2013

Contents

xvii	Foreword - Remembering Henny
xxi	Preface
xxv	Introduction - Memories of Henny
3	It's About Power
7	Very Repairable
12	The Altoona 300
17	It's Legal in Belize
22	The Future of Road Racing
26	Pragmatic Sanction
30	Moving Chickens
35	Making It Up
41	How Not To Win the Daytona 200
46	Recycled Crap
51	Monkey Business
56	What an Idiot
63	Aren't You Worried?
69	The Department of Racetrack Approval
74	It's Good to Be the King
79	Predictions
84	It's Always Something
90	Putting Riders in Harm's Way
95	Common Complaints
101	Mixed Emotions
106	Uncertain Futures
111	"It Was Bad"

117 All Jacked Up
122 Farewell, Randy
126 Meet Mr. Rossi
130 Of Butts and Breasts
134 The Highs and Lows
138 The Little Bike That Could
142 Bungled Again
146 What Next?
150 Incensed!
154 Poker Face
158 Time to Change
162 New Life
166 Rent It - No, Don't!
170 Playing the Percentages
174 All That Glitters Is Not Gold
178 A Joking Matter
182 Where Art Thou, U.S. GP?
186 USGP: When? Where? How?
190 The Roundtable
195 The American Struggle
200 Be Careful What You Wish For
203 Mending Fences
207 The New Daytona 200
211 The Road to Making It Safer
215 Less and More
219 Is It Really Safer?

223	Rainey's Crash-Course Karting School
227	Cover Me Not
231	A Farce
235	The Urgent Need for Urgent Care
240	A Tantalizing Thought
244	Status Quo
249	Laguna Postscript
253	What Now?
257	The Lure of Sturgis
261	Supercross: The Dud
265	Thank You, Roger Lee
269	Last Man Standing
273	Safety First
277	A Motorcycle Movie Worth Seeing
281	The Last Hurrah
286	Doing Things Right
291	"No Comment"
296	What's Next?
300	How Can It Be?
304	Sure, Come and Play
309	The Buell, the Fuel and the Fool
313	Let's Get It Right
318	All Good in Nick Land
322	Standing Up For Their Rights
326	Controlling Traction
331	Just Say No

336 The Way It Should Be
342 Good and Bad
347 New Kid in Town
351 Why Not Kevin?
355 Slingin' in the Rain
360 Where Were They?
365 The Champ!
370 Giving Thanks
374 The Untold Story
378 Who's Next?
383 Love Is In the Air
388 Daytona 200: A Year Later
392 Bring It On
397 Time to Move On
402 Fan Speak
406 Watch It and They Will Come
411 Ding Dong
416 Petcocks and Bostrom
421 Wide Open
426 Rhee-Cluse?
431 Factory or Non-Factory?
436 The Dinger Unplugged
441 Stop the Insanity
446 Merlyn the Magician
451 Doomed?
456 The Shell Game

461	Talk's Cheap
467	Time to Come Clean
472	Rotten to the Core
477	And the Winner Is...
482	Many Questions
487	Good Crank, Bad Crank
491	He Who Makes the Rules
495	Success!
500	Is the Honeymoon Over?
506	Get Smart
512	The Rules, They Are A-Changin' (Again)
517	The Future of *World* Supercross
522	Who Goes Where?
527	A Glimmer of Hope
532	Like Sands Through the Hourglass...
537	The Right Amount?
541	And the Beat Goes On
546	Trouble and More Trouble
551	New Year - Same Old Story
556	The Night the Lights Went Out... In Daytona
561	Fun or Funereal?
565	Listen to Mladin
570	Bottom Line: Go Watch!
575	Lies and Video Tape
580	Cracking into Prime Time
585	Mid-Term Grades

590 The Tutor
595 Safety Car Fights Way Into Top 10
600 Rules? What Rules?
605 Leadership Vacuum
610 Priorities? What Priorities?
616 The Time Is Ripe
621 Happy New Year!
626 Show Me the Money
631 In With the New
637 End of an Era
642 Will He Return?
647 The Ghost of Roger
652 Hall of Shame?
658 Happy, Happy, Happy
662 Secret Champions and Dirty Hogs
667 "Mr. Daytona"
670 The Moment
673 Flirting With Disaster
676 The Welcome Mat
679 Chicanery

Front cover: Henny at the World Superbike Championship race at Miller Motorsports Park on May 31, 2009. Image by Brian J. Nelson.

Back cover: Henny conducting a "roundtable" interview with Eric Bostrom, Miguel DuHamel, Jason Pridmore, Damon Buckmaster and Mat Mladin on May 21, 2004. Image by Brian J. Nelson.

March 5, 2013

Foreword - Remembering Henny

Henny Ray Abrams was a friend, a mentor, one hell of a journalist and photographer. He was also the hardest working person I knew. The amount of work Henny could pump out was simply amazing. The word *prodigious* in the dictionary should have Henny's picture next to it.

He was the king of multi-tasking. He would be sitting at a press conference, recording, picking up snippets of quotes, culling through photos and typing his story on his laptop, sending out and answering texts, often to riders who missed the podium, all simultaneously. When I was media manager of AMA Superbike, I would be amazed to sit down at my computer after conducting a press conference and find that Henny had already posted the race report on the *Cycle News* website.

Henny was the standard by which others in the pressroom measured themselves.

He was a person of integrity. His training as a journalist (Henny was a longtime news service photographer) was evident. He wanted the quotes accurate; he wanted to provide readers with the real story - not PR hype.

Henny's *Chicanery* column in *Cycle News* often got under a lot of people's skin, mainly race organizers. But I knew where Henny was coming from. He'd covered all forms of motorcycle racing for over 30 years and he knew when organizers weren't doing their very best and he'd let his readers know about it. Once when AMA Superbike organizers were trying to peddle the myth that the week-delayed, late Saturday night broadcasts of the races were actually better than same-day delayed, because people would get used to them being on Saturday nights, Henny pointed out in *Chicanery* that if it were such a great idea, that maybe the DMG should let the NFL or NASCAR know about this, so they could find a night to show the Super Bowl and Daytona 500 a week after the event. Henny was the only person in the motorcycling press to question and point out the fallacy in the DMG's logic.

Sometimes Henny's columns went a bit over the line. Not often, but on occasion. Once when his column was killed for being too over the top, Henny was upset enough that he never wrote another. I tried convincing him to start doing the column again and I was going to start working on him again at Daytona in a few weeks. Unfortunately, I never got the chance.

Henny was also one of the most generous persons I ever met. As a freelancer in motorcycle racing, I never made a great deal of money and sometimes it was a struggle to buy the pro photo equipment I needed to cover races. When I came back to racing photography in the digital age Henny sent me a few of his old lenses he didn't use anymore and refused payment. I benefitted from Henny's hand-me-downs for years. One day a box showed up with a like-new Nikon 28-70mm lens. This was an $1800 lens! It was from Henny. I called him up to tell him there was no way I was going to take this without paying him something for it, and he sloughed it off. "That's an old lens I found behind some boxes at the bottom of a shelf," he claimed. I knew if I sent him a check he wouldn't cash it, so my wife sent him a big box of baked goods to show our appreciation. I knew he wouldn't turn that down since cookies were one of his weaknesses.

When I was hopelessly up against a deadline on the Ben Spies book, Henny stepped in at the last minute and saved the project by handling the final edits and photo captions. He was that kind of friend.

Some of Henny's stories about getting race reports into the office in the pre-web days were classic. He carried a portable typewriter with him and would often type up the stories on planes, trains or in the passenger seat of rental cars between races. He would just show up at a European airport with his film and trustingly give his precious GP photos to a passenger heading to L.A. or Atlanta with 20 bucks so someone from *Cycle News* could meet them when they landed to get the photos in before deadline.

In the old days Henny rarely used a tape recorder during press conferences. He took notes. I could never understand how he could get the quotes down on paper so accurately. Once my batteries ran down in the middle of a press conference and I asked if I could see his notes. He handed them to me with a smile. They were written in shorthand.

I once asked highly respected racing photographer Tom Riles who he considered the best racing photographers. He thought about it for a second and the first person he mentioned was Henny. "You can tell by Henny's years of wire service photography," Riles said. "He shoots economically, but always comes up with great results."

Perhaps Henny's most famous racing photograph was the crash he caught of Steve Rapp at Road America, which made a two-page spread in *Sports Illustrated*. Henny also photographed the first American win in the Motocross des Nations in Germany in 1981. In his job as wire service photographer for AFP, UPI and AP, Henny photographed thousands of politicians, sports figures, celebrities and news events. He took iconic images of the 9-11 attacks with people looking at the burning twin towers from the Brooklyn waterfront that ran in newspapers across the globe.

I have to laugh when I think about how organized a person Henny was. He would book a room and flight for a race the day the schedule was released, many times nearly a year in advance. I could almost see him shaking his head on the other end of the phone when a few days before a race I talked to him and he'd say, "You haven't booked your flight or room yet have you."

Even though he was raised in Delaware, Henny was a pure New Yorker. He lived in Brooklyn and had that biting cynicism, often associated with New Yorkers, which was sometimes perceived at being highly critical. But those who knew him best understood he was a person who was highly intelligent, quick witted, and deep down behind the sardonic facade was a deeply caring individual.

Henny loved to read, he was an avid movie goer, a foodie and someone who took pride in his cooking, especially when it came to his signature cookies.

Wendy Black, PR rep for Suzuki and a good friend of Henny's, put it best when she said the press room is just not going to be the same without Henny.

Amen, Wendy.

LARRY LAWRENCE

Preface

Henny Ray Abrams was a skilled photographer, an insightful writer, and a generous friend to many. His interests were many, but above all else he poured his heart into motorcycle racing. Most journalists that report on motorcycle racing are either writers or photographers; Henny was both. In both categories the sheer volume of work he accomplished is unmatched. Moreover, while most journalists specialize in one genre of racing, Henny covered all types of motorcycle racing: road racing, motocross, dirt track, and everything in between.

Though Henny was arguably the most prolific reporter in motorcycle racing, it was his *Chicanery* column in *Cycle News* that he was most renowned for. Henny once told me that *Chicanery* was what he liked writing the most; being a reporter was he had to do to get the insight needed to be an advocate for the sport of motorcycle racing. Henny pulled no punches and his *Chicanery* columns were intelligent, eloquent, and witty.

Chicanery, the column, was written for those that love motorcycle racing. *Chicanery*, the book, was written for those that love Henny. Most of Henny's *Chicanery* columns were written many years ago, and though much time has passed, many of the issues addressed in *Chicanery* are still with us. Not as much time has passed since Henny passed away, yet through reading *Chicanery* you will feel that Henny is still with us.

Henny wrote 144 *Chicanery* columns, plus one guest editorial for *Cycle News* prior to *Cycle News* including an advocacy page as a regular feature. All are included here.

I elected to present the *Chicanery* columns in chronological order rather than group them by subject. The chronological order resulted in a more balanced presentation of Henny's work. Sometimes *Chicanery* was meant purely to generate laughter, other times *Chicanery* took on very serious subjects. The chronological order gave equal time to both in a sort of alternating fashion. Additionally, had I grouped topics together it would have implied that this book should be read from beginning to end. I did not want that, either. This is a pick and chose book. Depending on the time you have, you can spend a few minutes, a few hours, or a few days reading *Chicanery*.

The early *Chicanery* columns ran without a title. Henny probably had a title in mind for each one, but those went with him to his final resting place. For the book I created titles based on a short, relevant phrase from the piece of concern. Henny probably would have written titles better than my synthesized ones. In fact, he often submitted stories to *Cycle News* with whimsical, bogus working titles to see if the long-suffering *CN* editor, Paul Carruthers, was on his toes. An interview Henny did with Eric Bostrom almost went to print in *Cycle News* with the title "Dude, Where's My Karma?"

Since this is a posthumously published book, a few departures from normal conventions were taken in preparation.

First, the dedication page was decided by myself. I'm unsure of who Henny would dedicate a book to: he never wrote a book. Of all who will read *Chicanery*, Henny's brothers will probably enjoy it the most. This book is firstly for them.

Second, the epigraph that appears after the dedication page is usually a quote the author cites from another author, usually as a sign of respect for a related published work. I broke with convention and used a line Henny wrote for the "Status Quo" column. That is about as good as any Henny-ism there is.

Third, the Introduction is normally written by the author. Nobody knew Henny, the moto-journalist, better than Paul Carruthers, and Paul has written the Introduction on behalf of Henny.

Fourth, for a book of this size, one would expect to find a subject index in the back. You will not find one here. If an index was here you would find Mat Mladin referenced 237 times, Miguel DuHamel 92 times, and Ben and Eric Bostrom referenced 137 times, combined. In other words, there are not that many unique subjects in this book and the subjects that are here are referenced over and over and over.

And since Miguel DuHamel's name came up in the previous paragraph, a comment about the spelling of his name: I used the spelling as it was printed in *Cycle News* for that installment of *Chicanery*.

Of the variety of topics addressed in *Chicanery* over the years, the one topic that was clearly closest to Henny's heart was rider safety. Anyone who has spent a few years around the sport of motorcycle racing will attest that they have friends that were seriously injured, or worse. Eventually that aspect of the sport affects you. Some quit and find other things to do, others step up and become an agent of change. Henny was ever vigilant and courageous about holding those with responsible for improving rider safety accountable for their actions, or lack of. Henny was never afraid of standing up for safety.

Given that Henny was a champion for rider safety, Paul Carruthers and I felt that the proceeds of this book should be directed towards a motorcycle racer safety initiative. The initiative that we selected on behalf of Henny is the Asterisk Mobile Medical Center. This was the subject in "The Urgent Need for Urgent Care." At the time of publishing this book the Asterisk Mobile Medical Center is only regularly appearing at AMA national championship supercross and motocross races. Hopefully a day will soon come where the financial support is sufficient for it to appear at AMA national roadracing events.

Finally, the following people deserve thanks for important contributions:

PAUL CARRUTHERS, *Cycle News* editor, for supporting the production of this book.

LARRY LAWRENCE, *Cycle News* contributor, for proof-reading the text.

BRIAN J. NELSON, photographer, for the front and back cover images.

MICHAEL SCOTT, *Cycle News* MotoGP contributor, for the tribute to Henny that appears on the back cover.

HENNY RAY ABRAMS, brother, brother in-law, uncle, family member, friend, writer, photographer, motorcyclist, chef, and chicanerist.

TRACY HAGEN

February 28, 2014

Introduction - Memories of Henny

When Tracy Hagen first came to me with the idea of turning Henny Ray Abrams' *Chicanery* columns from *Cycle News* into a book, my first thought was: "What would Henny think?" And to think I actually believed I was done worrying about such things.

At that point I was torn.

Part of me figured Henny would think it was a horrible idea. The other part figured he would be flattered. And that's Henny Ray Abrams in a nutshell. I was never quite sure how he would react to an idea such as this one.

So to hell with it: Henny's not here to give us grief, so let's do the right thing and make his columns available to those who have never read them. And to those who were fortunate enough to have read them the first time and want another go at reading them again.

I'll deal with Henny the next time we meet.

Coincidentally, I'm writing these words exactly a year after Henny passed away in his Brooklyn apartment. At the time I was in shock, now I'm just sad. I thought I'd miss Henny more from a professional standpoint than from a personal one. Turns out I was wrong. It's the other way around. The work goes on and several people have stepped to the plate to at least try and fill the large shoes (literally and figuratively) left by Henny at *Cycle News*. But I miss him on a personal level. I miss the phone calls, the emails... I miss him at the races. I even miss the abuse he'd give me from time to time, the anger he'd sometimes make me feel. He kept me on my toes on a professional level and I still think of him today and what he'd think of whatever it is I'm doing. Damn it.

I know the motorcycle racing industry misses him, whether they realize it or not. Why? Because he always tried to do the right thing even if it sometimes it wasn't the right thing. He took on the establishment and he showed no fear in his criticism if he thought someone wasn't doing their job (or at least attempting to do their job) - whether that was a top-level racer, a team member, the sanctioning body. And he wasn't above criticizing *Cycle News*, my work, his work. When we did it wrong, he said we did it wrong. That's how he was. And if we argued about *Cycle News*, which we did, it was because we both cared. That's a good thing.

While many people claim to have the sport's best interest in mind, they don't. Henny did.

As I sit and read Henny's old *Chicanery* columns, the memories come rushing back. I can basically recall each column, how they came about. How much grief they caused me when the phone would ring the day after they were published. How good I got at defending him, defending us. Defending good vs. evil.

Now I wonder if I'll start getting the phone calls again when people read columns that are years old. And they're still pissed. Henny knew how to get a reaction. He did so with a writing style that was sometimes brutal but always witty. Even if you didn't agree with what he wrote, you couldn't argue that he had a certain style that made you chuckle at least once a column. Well, unless you were the subject of his disdain.

It was the funny columns that I enjoyed the most (like Sidecars at Road America, for example) as Henny always tried to work in at least a few zingers to keep your interest.

But enough from me. Your time is better spent reading the work that's compiled here... Henny's work. *Chicanery*. Enjoy.

PAUL CARRUTHERS

Chicanery
From the pages of Cycle News

March 10, 1993

It's About Power

In reporting on the 250 GP race at the inaugural AMA National Championship Road Race Series meet at Phoenix International Raceway I found myself somewhat confused by a disturbing turn of events. During Sunday morning's practice a number of riders discovered the unsettling truth about the danger of that otherwise splendid facility. The banked oval turns three and four, dangerous enough in the best conditions to warrant serious consideration, turned somewhat lethal when wet. Riders tiptoed around, aware that at racing speeds they would have little warning and less margin of safety before careening into wet hay bales, or worse, the unprotected concrete wall on turn three's entrance.

Sensing the severity of this situation, some of the 250cc riders, after having huddled privately, got together and took concerns to the AMA referee, who, they had hoped would relay those concerns to the highest authorities Following that, they took a grid sheet through the paddock and asked anyone who agreed with them that the track was unsafe to race on in the rain to sign by their name. If the riders who made the original decision were asked, they would point out that, given their experience, they thought that racing in such conditions was nothing but dangerous. And they were right, of course, though it would take a crash on the very first lap of the Harley-Davidson TwinSports race for the AMA to come to the same conclusion these racers had reached hours earlier.

But a curious thing happened late on Sunday afternoon. The riders most responsible for educating their peers were, in their own words, "called on the carpet, made to feel like an amateur." And for what?

What these riders did was fulfill their contract with humanity. They knew nothing good could come out of an alleged race. They knew people would get hurt, machinery would be destroyed, and the fans, what few braved the elements, would be turned off in their first exposure to the sport we all cherish. Yes, the AMA sold the promoter a package, but it didn't include hourly helicopter rides for the injured, though it may have seemed that way at times. And the package included riders racing, not trying not to hurt themselves or be hurt by others.

No one can blame the promoter for this flaw. From all aspects, he could not have been more responsive or accommodating and the AMA would do well to find more like him to promote their races. While waiting to see a movie in a Phoenix theatre I was pleasantly surprised to see the screen filled with an ad for the race, something I've never seen before anywhere in the world. Following the race he was ecstatic with the photo finish that Doug Polen and Pascal Picotte and Scott Russell provided and gave every indication that he could not stage another motorcycle race soon enough.

But the track is simply not safe, wet or dry, and if there is any question about that you need only ask Donald Jacks, who blew an engine and hit the unprotected wall headfirst at well over 100 mph, "just" breaking an arm, or Larry Pegram, who fell in Jacks' oil shattering a femur and jeopardizing his dirt track season, or Kel Davidson, who escaped mostly unscathed. Jimmy Filice watched the crash at trackside with Jay Springsteen and both were horrified by the experience. It was especially tough on Filice, who'd asked that more hay bales be placed at the entry to the corner, though they never were. Jacks did hit the bales, after first hitting the wall. On a dry track.

If Filice was narrow-minded he would feel vindicated, but instead he just felt sick. He had been one of the 250cc riders singled out by the AMA as a ringleader for the 250cc class and had been told that his actions were the sort of thing that could shorten his career. Chris D'Aluisio had also been threatened and, like Filice, he was dumbfounded, as well he should have been.

Jimmy Filice is a National Champion, a Grand Prix winner, and a former factory rider. He has more experience worldwide than the rest of the 250cc class combined. But the down side to this is that he's been hurt a few times, on the track and off, and has spent more time in hospitals in his relatively young life than anyone should have to. Yet he is undaunted and relentlessly cheerful. If you're looking for a quick smile and a kind word in the paddock, you need go no farther. Chris D'Aluisio races because it consumes him. He would be a far wealthier young man financially if it weren't so: It is only this season and last that he hasn't paid all of the racing bills out of his own pocket. He could afford to race because he makes his living as a mechanical engineer designing mountain bikes on the cutting edge of technology. He is a sensitive, thoughtful man.

So it is difficult for them to understand why the AMA would treat them like pariahs. What, after all, is their crime? They are accused of sedition for doing what comes naturally to them, sharing the wealth of their knowledge with those less aware. The AMA's stand is that they used their influence to organize the field against the best interests of the AMA, that there was a conspiracy, of sorts, which would undermine the program. They say they're interested in what the riders think, as long as it's one rider at a time. The AMA deals with individuals, not with groups, they say. Not surprising since individuals have less power. And that's what this whole episode was about.

This is not about influence or conspiracy, it's about power. It's about who plays God and who must blindly worship at the altar. It's about questioning authority. It's about the inmates running the asylum.

Yet in this case it is the inmates who know the asylum a little better. They've spent more time there, they've examined it more closely, they've put their lives on the line for it over and over again. They know the asylum can be a cruel and punishing place, but they've experienced such joy there that they continue to return. They are not disposable widgets. They are flesh and blood and soul and they should be treated with dignity and not scolded like mischievous school boys. No one with a conscience could allow himself to watch another racer go out ignorant of the risks.

So then, what will come of this? I was told by AMA officials that this wouldn't happen again because the riders were made aware of how it would be viewed. If this is not a threat, and the AMA denies threatening the riders, it is at least a warning. And the riders were scared that the sport that they give their lives to could be denied them.

So the next time, when the riders are told all is well - though they may have doubts - and they look for guidance, there may be none. And that will be a shame. And someone may get to see what the inside of an ambulance looks like for the first time. But that's okay, because that's the way the AMA wants it and it's their asylum.

January 19, 1994

Very Repairable

I am sitting in the east grandstands at Daytona International Speedway on a brisk winter day and I am watching a pickup truck tow Miguel DuHamel and his Harley-Davidson VR1000 less-than-super bike back to the pits for the second time in about an hour, and I am trying to remember when the last time a motorcycle that was towed back to the pits twice, against traffic, won the Daytona 200 by Arai, or by anyone for that matter. And I am stumped. Though, judging from how things are going on the track, it doesn't appear that I'm the most stumped guy at the track this day.

The Daytona 200 is 82 days away as I watch, and if I were a betting man, I would bet that Miguel DuHamel need not worry about smuggling the winner's trophy back to Canada at this point, eh. I would also bet that the Harley will not be on the starting grid when the race starts, not because - as some might fear - it won't be able to qualify for the 80-rider field or will be bringing up the rear of the Harley parade or will have its appeal to field a second rider with a pickup truck denied, but because Harley-Davidson, true to their word, will not introduce it until it can complete more than three laps of a racetrack without the aid of tow rope.

And I am not the only doubter at the track this crisp December day. In the grandstands is a fellow motorhead who has brought a radio to monitor the chatter of various track personnel.

"He's not going to make it," an anonymous voice says as DuHamel goes out late in the afternoon.

He makes one lap and pits, making a liar out of the disembodied voice, though not for long. Soon afterwards he returns to the track on the semi-faired very secret Harley.

"He'll be back," the voice with no name says and, sure enough, he comes to a coasting halt in front of a tour van in the West End Horseshoe. Inside the van, one can only imagine what the tour guide is saying. "Ladies and gentlemen, to our left you will see Daytona's famed banking and on our right you will see Miguel DuHamel hitching a ride back to the pits after his alternator just alternated between working and not working. Anybody hungry?"

Surely there's an explanation for stopping stone cold a mile from the pits. Would you believe low-speed plug chop? That's the best we motorheads could come up with. We would like to have asked a spokesperson for an on-the-record comment, but today did not much seem like a record day for the orange and black, unless, of course, they were trying to set a record for amount of assisted returns to the paddock in one afternoon test session.

After some fiddling, testing continues and twitching fingers grasp digital watches hoping to quantify the ability of the ultra-secret black beast that a group of tourists from Anywhere, USA, has just had a pretty good gander at. There is more at which to gawk. Fritz Kling is riding an equally secret white beast, though with somewhat more success. He hasn't been towed back to the pits at all, though he did make a U-turn once in the International Horseshoe to return to the pits.

You ask: "Has anyone ever won the Daytona 200 by making a U-turn in the horseshoe?" Exactly!

DuHamel's best flying lap is a 1:57.5, a time that sends the pundits rushing for the reference books, which must be misplaced because all the experts can find is a cooler full of beer and some cameras. The reference books will be later referenced. Hmmm, a 57.5 would put him, let's see, second-fastest 250. Certainly if DuHamel had more time to sort out the suspension, gearing, and tires, his times would drop. Then again, so would Harley's profits. They're spending about $3500 per day for the track, and by the time he's sorted everything out, they'll have spent more money fixing this thing than NASA spent correcting the stigmatism of the Hubble telescope, which, by the way, has yet to complete a lap of Daytona.

Lest you think that I am being unduly harsh about this project, let me attempt to dissuade you, the reading public. Harley has a proud history of building great race bikes, and they win nearly every dirt track that Ricky Graham doesn't. Not only that, but they won every H-D 883 TwinSports race as well as every H-D 883 Dirt Track event, not to mention the Harley-Davidson Continental Cup Championship. Every damned one. Looked it up myself.

We know they're serious about winning the AMA Superbike Championship because if they weren't, why would this All-American company, this company that's as American as preservative-enhanced apple pie, liposuction, and drive-by shootings, go out and hire a French Canadian to ride it? Answer me that, ya hoser. The ink on the North American Free Trade Agreement (NAFTA) is barely dry and already it impacts Superbikes. NAFTA, not the ink. And you thought Ross Perot was kidding when he said all the good jobs would go across the border. Wrong border Roscoe. That giant sucking sound Perot spoke of, that's DuHamel's accountants vacuuming out the Harley till.

There exists a rumor that the good folks in Milwaukee were sensitive to hiring a non-U.S. citizen, or the more politically correct "green card-challenged." The rumor has one of the sticking points in his contract being H-D's insistence that Miguel DuHamel change his name to Mike Hammer. Did anyone ask Stacy Keach about this? Remember, this is just a rumor that I'm trying to start. Send your cards and letters to each other.

More likely, they wanted the best rider available because the last thing they'd want to do is put the entire hopes and dreams of

Milwaukee on someone that wasn't up to the challenge of greater heights. And DuHamel is an inspired choice. After all, what other former Grand Prix rider can claim to having put a million-dollar YZR500 Yamaha in a tree? And not a little tree, but a Malaysian tree of many rings, a tall woody plant that you could build a tree house in that could shelter Delaware.

Last year, aboard a very competitive Muzzy Kawasaki, DuHamel managed to stay out of the forest and seemed to gain confidence with every race. (I'm being serious now, in case you hadn't noticed.) His finest was the last of the year, a stirring heads-up win over AMA Superbike Champion Doug Polen on the dangerous bends of Sears Point. It had taken him nearly the entire season to get over his year of racing a Grand Prix bike for a team that's as organized as a food fight. If he brings that confidence and momentum to his new home, DuHamel will bring an excitement to racing heretofore unseen. If not, he'll have found somewhere new to tree-park his bike.

If I may get serious for a minute, and just a minute, I will admit to hoping the best for the VR1000 for a number of reasons. The first is the name. Harley-Davidson knows a thing or two about creating brand loyalty, and their mystique is unmatched in American motoring. Having that attached to the highest level of American road racing has got to be a plus, regardless of its success. Secondly, it will force the rules-makers to treat Harley like it would any other V-twin, say Ducati. Unless, of course, they exempt Harley from the weight rules and apply them only to V-twins or four-cylinder machines that end in a vowel. The multitude of whiners who claim the AMA is Harley-friendly will have a field day keeping all parties honest, assuming, of course, the whiners don't get a life before the season starts.

And, finally, like the ill-fated NR Honda, the initialized VR will spawn a torrent of opprobrium. Very Repairable, Velvet Rattler, Vega Racer. Velocity Reluctant, Vibrating Rock.

Let the games begin.

Note: this was reprinted in the September 12, 2001 edition of Cycle News *following Harley-Davidson's announcement to end the VR1000 project.*

February 16, 1994

The Altoona 300

Hitchhiking on the information superhighway *Chicanery* found a notice from a racing team in Texas offering equipment for the 125cc GP exhibition class to be held at national road race events. Somewhat curious, we gave our cheap correspondent, Henry-Roy Adams, a one-way ticket on a Greyhound bus to find Slick Noodleman, the titular head of Needlessly Irritating Two-Wheelers In Tarmac (NITWIT) a racing-only organization that promotes, yet doesn't sanction, a series of irregular races. Adams caught up with Noodleman at his Jell-O farm in Larry's River, Nova Scotia.

"Why the new NITWIT races?"

"NITWIT firmly believes that racing should be built from the ground up. That's why we're promoting the Junior Educational Racing Championship (JERC)."

"So the class winner will be..."

"The NITWIT JERC."

"I'm sure it will make his family proud. What age group will be allowed to race?"

"We don't want this class to be age-specific. If they can operate a motorcycle, they can race."

"Toddlers, tykes, teens? Anyone can race?"

"Well, not anyone. They'll need a motorcycle, a set of leathers, an approved helmet, and a $600 entry fee."

"Wow! Six hundred bucks. Don't you think that will limit the size of the field?"

"We won't be racing in a field."

"So you'll have two-year olds racing and saying things like 'I just wanted to ride my own race.'"

"They're mistaken. They'll be riding in my races."

"Isn't two years old a little young?"

"Well, not to a one-year-old."

"Why don't you just have fetus racing?"

"Who leaked that to you?"

"You're kidding of course."

"We see it as an enormous opportunity to bring the whole family to the races."

"Mother and fetus?"

"We prefer to think of them, not as fetuses, but as 'incomplete entries'."

"Have you decided on a name for this class?"

"We're going to call it 'Maternity Moto Mamas'."

"And you don't think people will find that politically incorrect?"

"It beat out 'Fat Biker Chicks.'"

"What sort of machinery will they be racing?"

"They won't be racing machinery, they'll be racing motorcycles."

"What displacement?"

"Displacement measurement of volume. Why we talk like this?"

"What type of motorcycles will the women be competing aboard?"

"That's still being discussed. It will either be 1990 Honda Pacific Coasts or 1987 Husky 125s."

"When are you going to decide?"

"Whenever my cousin Filbert figures out which he's got more of in the barn."

"Filbert. Filbert's a nut, right?"

"We like to think of him as two links short of a chain."

"I see. What about having pregnant ladies competing on race bikes? Aren't you worried about their safety?"

"Not as long as the women don't crash 'em too much."

"No, I mean the women."

"We're allowing gas tanks to be modified to be more accommodating, we've looked into footpeg height, and we're not going to have the races too early in the day."

"What difference does it make when they race?"

"Morning sickness."

"Of course."

"Aren't you worried about cheating?"

"You mean, am I worried that the other riders will hit on them?"

"No, I mean is there a mechanism in place to verify that these women are, in fact, pregnant?"

"We ordered the mechanism, but it has to be sterilized first."

"Will you have a licensed obstetrician operating it?"

"We were going to, then he lost his license. Something about three DUI's in a week."

"So who will your new inspector be?"

"We were thinking of Beavis and Butthead."

"You realize, of course, they're completely made-up."

"No, I didn't, but if it makes them look better on TV we here at NITWIT understand."

"Do you have any other new wrinkles this season?"

"No, but you should see my fifth wife. The winter here in Larry's River weren't kind to her."

"I mean, is there anything new we'll see at the races?"

"Well, in order to put some excitement in this year's Altoona 300...

"Excuse me, Altoona is going to be 300 miles?"

"No, of course not. 300 laps. We've extended it slightly to give the fans more racing, but tire changes will be mandatory and at each gas stop the rider has to eat a chicken burrito."

"Why a chicken burrito?"

"Cheaper than beef."

"Don't you think making tire changes mandatory will favor the better-equipped teams?"

"How so?"

"Well, for instance, they're the only ones that would have enough wheels to mount spare tires on."

"We're not allowing spare wheels."

"Let me get this straight. The riders have to use the same wheels for the entire race."

"Correct."

"The only way they could do that is if they changed the tires on the rim at each gas stop."

"Correct."

"Let me get this straight. The rider pulls in, he gasses up, the wheels come off, the tires come off, new ones are pried on, and his crew sends him off?"

"What crew?"

"His pit crew."

"What pit crew?"

"You've eliminated pit crews?"

"Eliminate is too strong a word."

"If they're not allowed to gas the bike up or change the tires, what can they do?"

"Make the burritos."

"The pit stop goes like this: The rider comes in, fills his own gas tank, takes his own wheels off, pries his own tires off, mounts and balances his new tires, puts them back on his bike, and rejoins the race. Is that about right?"

"You forgot one important detail: Tire inflation."

"Don't tell me. They can't use a compressor or bicycle pump, they have to blow them up like a balloon."

"You think that'll work? Let me write that down. How do you spell balloon?"

"Have you considered the danger of so many riders mounting tires badly? Isn't there a safety aspect involved?"

"Not with us. As I was saying, this year's Altoona 300 is going be 'chicane-optional.'"

"Meaning what?"

"Meaning that the riders have the option of skipping the chicane eight times during the race."

"Don't you think they have enough to worry about - tires, gas, traffic, fatigue, debris, burritos, sea gulls, photographers with red T-shirts - that they shouldn't have to worry about counting to eight?"

"As a condition of their credential, photographers will have to wear sandwich boards."

"Advertising what?"

"Husky 125s for next to nothing."

"Aren't you worried that the speed differential between the riders skipping the chicane and those entering the banking will be about 90 mph?"

"No, we were worried it would be 75 mph - 90 mph is more than we could have hoped for. From your lips to God's tailwind. Who does your math?"

"Einstein."

"You think he'll come to work for us? I can get him a good deal on a Pacific Coast."

April 13, 1994

It's Legal in Belize

Of all the photos I shot at Daytona this year, the one you see here will be my most memorable. It's a photocopy of my humble visage, my column title and byline, and it has been enlarged and defaced. De face is mine, de "X" and de "NOT" were added by someone with a dazzling wit in the Harley-Davidson race team garage, a place where a sense of humor is, no doubt, invaluable. It was there that I photographed this art (Art?)[1] work taped to the wall just to the left of the entrance and not far from a naked VR1000 display bike that attracted hordes of the curious, thereby guaranteeing my celebrity.

That Harley made it to Daytona at all is an accomplishment they should be proud of - given how recently a completed lap of the track was cause for giddy celebration. I had prophesied that it would not happen and have been proven wrong. That they are apparently humor deficient is something they should work on once they get the bike running to the point where it can return to the pits under its own power with some regularity.

The cynic in me wants to say that if they had used their time in a more productive manner, instead of thinking up clever ways to sully someone who'd witnessed their pride and joy attached to an umbilical tow rope on these same Florida bends during a

---

[1] Art Gomper, Manager of Racing Promotions, Harley-Davidson

December test, they might be a little closer to the part of the grid where the riders don't use the same bike for their paper routes.

What I would like to attempt with this column is closure. I would like to re-state my position; something that appears to have been misinterpreted by whomever read the column and was inspired to do the photocopying. (I am pitching the idea of "Cycle News on Tape" to the good folks at 2201 Cherry as a way of avoiding this in the future).

My uneducated guess is that some Member Of The Harley-Davidson International Race Team (MOTHDIRT) was reacting to my first stab at *Chicanery*, an effort which garnered me immeasurable praise at Daytona and Phoenix and very little animosity, except for this one unfortunate incident which aggrieved me in ways I hadn't felt since being rejected by the Hair Club for Men. In "Chicanery, the Original" I made some jokes at the expense of the team, the bike, and the rider. Most everyone I spoke to understood them. And just to prove that my sense of humor isn't limited, let me ask: How many AMA officials does it take to screw in a light bulb? None, they'd rather be kept in the dark. (Now if Larry Maiers would pay me the royalties he owes me for repeating that joke, I could quit my day job.)

But before we leave the VR behind, there are a few other points I forgot to mention, which I will add here for the purpose, once again, of closure. For instance, somewhere in the AMA rule book it states that 50 motorcycles need to be produced before the ball drops in Times Square on New Year's Eve and that they be street legal somewhere, anywhere, in the world. Do you know in which country the VR1000 is street legal? Me neither. So I asked someone who should know and was told it was Belize, a Third World country where I'm sure lines began forming months ago to cough up the $49,450 asking price. Though that may seem a scooch high, remember, it comes with an AAA card and a cell phone.

Do you know where Belize is? Me too, and last I looked it wasn't on the AMA Superbike calendar for 1994, though at least one other Third World haven was, and I'm sure that if the Belizeans coughed up the sanctioning fee an event could be added as the "race to be named later." The name could be the "Harley Legal Parking Lot of the Americas Grand Prix." I have also heard the VR may be street legal in Malaysia or Mexico or Poland, but not in the U.S.

So, what happens if there aren't 50 built and no country will license one? I'm told Miguel DuHamel and Fritz Kling will have their points, and/or National Championship, taken away. I have also heard that production of the VR will soon move to an abandoned part of the Harley factory in York, Pennsylvania. I am told that this facility was previously used as part of the Harley defense contract with the U.S. government. Know what they made there? Bombs. Please feel free to take a moment to make up your own joke.

I have heard these things from what journalists like to call unnamed sources, not, as you might think, because the sources have no names and respond only to "Yo, dunghead," but because they would rather it not be known that they are betraying a sacred trust. A tip from one of these sources is a lot like it social disease; you want people to know you're capable of getting it, but you don't want anyone to know where it came from.

Just to clarify my position on *l'equipe* Harley, let me reiterate a few of the points that I made in my first column: I firmly believe that Miguel DuHamel is one of the very best racers in North America. If he had chosen any of the other offers which I'm told he received - from Kawasaki, Honda, or, especially, Ducati - he would have been a contender, if not the favorite, for a title. Period. He is one of the elite and he proved it last year, bouncing back from a dismal Grand Prix year which was no fault of his own, except in his choice of a team.

Harley-Davidson is one of a handful of American brands known worldwide and having them involved in superbike racing can only enhance the sport. The interest the project generated in Daytona and Phoenix far dwarfed that of any other debutante and most of the established teams. It looks different, it sounds different, and it runs different, which is to say, at this time, with some difficulty.

My guess is that prior to Daytona there were two schools of thought in Milwaukee: one which felt that the bike should not be raced until it was more competitive, and a second which probably wanted to get it out there and let it take its lumps. The lumpers appear to have won. It will certainly improve and grow. But going up against established superbike teams in a year that will likely prove to be the most competitive ever - if you discount the Ducatis - is a tough order for anyone, let alone a team with a virgin racebike that seems bent on doing it on their own.

Smokin' Joe's Honda team owner Martin Adams said in a recent issue of *Cycle News* that Harley-Davidson may need to seek outside help, and in the same issue Rob Muzzy of the World Champion Muzzy Kawasaki team wondered aloud about their methods. I am not alone in questioning the ways of the team. In fact, I think I'm in pretty good company. Still, I think the folks at Harley have earned the right to try and fail since that's inevitably the path to progress, and they appear to be succeeding at both.

In the Daytona 200, the VR1000 didn't get all that far before the motor tried to reduce itself to its component parts on the front straightaway. The company line was that it developed a small oil leak, which I would agree to if you consider the Exxon Valdez a medium oil leak and the Kuwaiti oil field fires a large oil leak.

Let me digress, since the 200 wasn't their first competitive endeavor. A third-place finish was carded in one of the 4324 sprints run during the previous AMA/CCS weekend in a race that was suspiciously shortened by - you guessed it - a red flag, but how else could the VR get into the winner's circle? I believe Oliver Stone bought the film rights to that episode. There was also a DNF in the Expert Anything with Decals GP, due, I believe, to a clutch failure.

Phoenix was the next race and the name proved appropriate. "Phoenix" is defined in my dictionary as "a person or thing that has been restored after suffering calamity or apparent annihilation." A report in a local newspaper said that a radar gun showed the top Superbikes doing 141 mph on the front straight, and the Harley doing 127. Still, Fritz Kling, the newest recruit, finished a creditable 14th, scoring the team's first points. DuHamel had yet another unfortunate retirement, though I believe he was running near the top 10 at the time. I'm not sure, but I think he's already retired more times than Sugar Ray Leonard. There appears to be a lingering problem with the fuel delivery system, a problem that another of my "socially diseased" sources told me is easily curable if the regulator were moved to a place further down line and away from the exhaust pipes. I am not a mechanical genius - far from it. To me, the only difference between a valve seat and a toilet seat is that I've never had to call the fire department to pry me off of a valve seat.

The same tipster told me that there appears to be a limitless budget on the project. The original Penske front forks: Guess how much two pair cost? Guess again. Now double that. Then add $4000. I know, I couldn't believe it either.

But those forks have been jettisoned for the more-American [sic] Öhlins forks, a move that shows a willingness to learn. There will, no doubt, be more parts jettisoned - some unintentionally, like valves and clutches. But I will speak badly of the VR1000 no more. I, like you, will watch, glad to have Harley-Davidson around, hopeful about their progress, jealous of their attention, and sad that I now have to find something else to make fun of. Anybody know where the Suzuki pits are?

April 27, 1994

The Future of Road Racing

I have seen the future - and it is in a parking lot in Pomona. Well, I didn't actually see the parking lot. I was about 9000 miles away in Malaysia, sweating in places that can't be shown in an airplane movie and trying to drink enough water to keep my bowels from perforating. It was so hot that if you stood still for more than five minutes the soles of your shoes would melt, and dogs blew up from over-exertion.

On Saturday, while I was watching practice for the Malaysian GP, I suddenly realized I had become planted. Extracting my guidebook, I turned to chapter marked "Stuck in Malaysia." It read: "If you find yourself suddenly immobile, there is no need to panic. The first thing you should do is yell, 'Hey, I'm stuck,' then wait for one of the jumpsuited sneaker-scraping civil servants to come along and liberate you." My scraper showed up within a minute wearing a look of distress normally seen on coroners and Buffalo Bills' quarterbacks in the fourth quarter of Super Bowls. Pointing to my size 14 Nikes he said, "I'm afraid I'll have to send for a snow shovel." I said, "Will this take long?" and he answered, "Probably, since we're nearly on the equator and I don't know what snow is or why I would need to shovel it." Eventually I was freed with the help of a backhoe, but it wasn't so bad. While I was waiting, I saw two poodles and a Shih-Tzu explode.

Getting back to the matter at hand...Thanks to the miracle of long distance and the phone companies' willingness to charge usurious rates that take food out of the mouths of the children I've never had, I was able to keep abreast of the events unfolding in Pomona, as well as relay that information to the burgeoning and anxious American grand prix contingent. (Kenny Roberts, when told there was an AMA National in a parking lot, scratched three layers of skin off his sturdy chin while thinking, "Hmmmm, I wonder if the FIM would homologate the Modesto Bait 'n Bullet Galleria.")

Like me, the rest of the Americans were amused that bridges were simultaneously being moved and burned, and they had thoughtful, probing questions. They wanted to know who the dissidents were and which McDonald's they'd be working at next year. They wanted to know why the Kawasakis could clear the triple jumps over the shopping cart collector and the Hondas couldn't. They wanted to know how the Harleys were doing, but I told them that I had sworn never to mention them again, unless they meant the 883's, in which case I told them no cheaters had yet been caught, but only because the race hadn't been run. They wanted to know if there was a videotape of the riders' meeting, where Michael Barnes, paraphrasing the great American orator Patrick Henry, said, "I know not what course others may take, but as for me, give me liberty and give me my entry fee back," then went out in the 250 GP race and did a divine imitation of a street hockey puck. They wanted to know how many more non-English speaking riders Rob Muzzy would use to file protests in case the race wasn't cancelled. They wanted to know if it was true that the Ducatis were fitted with three-speed automatics and that they hadn't gotten out of "L." And they wanted to know how it came to pass that the pinnacle of American roadbed racing could end up in a parking lot in Pomona, a city established in 1875 and named, not surprisingly, for Pomona, the Roman goddess of fruit.

The goddess Pomona would have been proud of what transpired in her namesake parking lot. She would have looked out over the twisting 13-turn course and said, "Are nuts a fruit? Because anybody that races on this course is nuts. So, technically, I'd be their goddess. And if they're fruits, then, of course, that's no problem. I know bananas are fruit, but nuts are sort of a gray area. I never know how to handle nuts. Nuts are a very sensitive area. I should know, really, after all, I am the goddess of fruit."

But she would be wrong about the riders being nuts or fruits or bananas, the goddess Pomona would. She would be wrong because the future of AMA road racing is in parking lots and I'll tell you why, as if you didn't know already.

Give or take a dozen, there are approximately a dillion parking lots in this country. Every time I go to work I pass about a dozen parking lots and I think to myself, "Wouldn't that be a great place for a grand prix?" (Actually, I take the subway to work and all we pass are large colonies of Collie-sized rats.) There would be corners that would take their place in the pantheon of racing greatness: La Source Hairpin at Spa, the Spoon Curve at Suzuka, the Parabolica at Monza, the Express Lane at Ralph's.

Let's look at the advantages. How many times during a race weekend is the lowliest flunky on the team dispatched to K-Mart for a foam cooler, bananas, beer, duct tape, or mousse? That's right, a dillion. So if all of the races were held in parking lots, the flunkies could put their time to better use - like getting dates for the team manager.

So what I propose is that the races be spontaneous, unannounced, shifty. Secretly, the road-rashers would gather on the outskirts of Deadend, USA. Then, as noon approached, the convoy would sneak into the biggest parking lot, unload the bikes, and start frying their clutches. The first couple of laps would be run behind a pace shopping cart which would decide the course layout as it went along. Sort of like Charlotte. Then, once everyone knew that the finish line was at the drive-through teller, just past the mulch pile but before the Fotomat, the call would go out that would send chills down every racer's spine: "Attention K-Mart Shoppers."

As for the crowd, that's the easy part. A family of four - mom, her second husband, and his two dysfunctional kids from his first marriage to the crossing guard who he found out was a stripper when she got busted for assaulting the mayor when he refused to pay her since she wouldn't pretend she was a giraffe - come out of the J.C. Penney's after an exhausting afternoon of swapping price tags, only to have to dodge Steve Crevier as he flicks it through the chicane created by their Grand Pinto wagon and the recycling bin next to it. Cool, huh? After watching for a few laps, they're hooked. You set up membership booths near the mobile-home surgical station, and give new members a complimentary root canal. Before you know it, the parking lots are begging to be disturbed.

How do you charge admission? You don't - you charge an exit fee. Make them pay to leave, which, I believe, was the thinking behind putting the coma-inducing one-hour Unlimited Team Challenge first on Sunday's seven or eight or nine-race schedule, depending on whether the 80's are running. Whenever a family wants to flee, you take their cash, bring out the pace shopping cart, have the four bikes that are still running line up single-file behind it, and let the heathens escape. A "captive audience" I believe it's called. Guerrilla Nationals: no advertising, no overhead, no need to homologate the parking lot. It's the future. Remember, you read it here first.

May 25, 1994

Pragmatic Sanction

Spring is well upon us and with it comes the annual ritual of de-winterizing your motorcycle. For most people that means cleaning the spider colonies out of the carb inlets, soaking the chain in a winter's worth of bacon grease, and using a magic marker to hide the fabric spots in the tires. Oh sure, it seems like a ton of fun, but for me, this year would be different.

I'd just gotten my contributor's check from *Cycle News* and had $18,000 burning a hole in my pocket. So I went down to my local dealer, "Psyclepaths of Flatbush," to buy the machine I thought would make me the next Carl Fogarty (but without the broken wrist, funny accent, and gap in my front teeth); the machine that has owned the AMA Superbike series this year, the venerable, but ultimately elusive, Ducati 955.

Entering the dealership, the first thing I noticed was that the shop owner looked like he hadn't slept since the last time a Honda won an AMA Superbike race and that his hands were shaking too violently to shave, giving him the outward appearance of an Amish junkie. He was wearing the "I Survived Bike Week '94" T-shirt which he'd put on at Daytona and had yet to remove.

"How ya doing?" I asked innocently.

"Aces, dude, aces. I haven't slept since the last time a Honda won an AMA Superbike race, I'm shaking too violently to shave and I look like an Amish junkie. I've been wearing this T-shirt since Daytona, and today for lunch I sucked on one of the ketchup stains on this shirt. Other than that it's a day at the beach," he replied.

"Well, I think I'm about to brighten your day considerably," I said, my voice filled with hope. "I'd like to buy a motorcycle and I won't take no for answer."

The news brought enough color to his face to cause venal eruption in his distended nose and he nearly knocked over his Pepto-Bismol and Prozac cocktail. Then he issued the salesman's credo: "If we don't have it, you don't need it."

"I would like a Ducati 955," I said, fanning a stack of $1000 bills across the counter.

"You don't need it," he said, his mood suddenly taking a darker turn. It was as if he was about to ask me if I was a playing card.

"What are you, some kind of joker?" he asked, telepathically. "Did that son of a bitch Rob Muzzy send you? I know he sent you. Ever since Phoenix it's been like this every day. I must have had 43 people come through here. If I ever get a hold of him, I'll grab him by the moustache and rip his lips off."

"Who's Rob Muzzy and what don't you like about his lips?" I asked.

"It doesn't exist," the shop owner said. "The Ducati 955 does not exist."

"Sure it does," I said, pointing to a back issue of *Cycle News* (which he was using as a placemat) with that exact model on the cover and a headline which read "Believe it or Not, They Held a Race in a Stinkin' Parking Lot and This Guy Won the Part They Were Able to Finish Before the Starter Tore his Rotator Cuff from Waving the Red Flag so Friggin' Much."

"I would like one of those, please," I said, emphatically.

"I'm telling you, it doesn't exist," he insisted, taking a big gulp of his lithium milk shake.

"So what you're saying, then, is that this guy in this handsome cover shot is on an imaginary motorcycle? Or are you telling me that if I open a Ducati catalog, I won't find it?"

"No, no, no," he said, he said, he said.

"No, it's not an imaginary motorcycle, or no, I wouldn't find it or...what was the third no for?"

"No, you won't find it in the Ducati catalog," he whimpered, now reduced to a quivering mass of subhuman ectoplasm devoid of hope.

"That was the second no."

"No, you idiot, you won't find it here; you won't find it hardly anywhere. There's only one place you can buy it, and if you think I'm going to tell you where that is, you're nuttier than a sperm bank."

"How can that be? How can a bike that you can't buy at your local dealership be winning races? Surely there are rules against that?"

"Hey, I'm no lawyer," he said, as if I'd mistaken him for one. "You want one of these bikes? Find yourself the only guy who can sell one to you, or else find yourself a lawyer."

So I put the $18K back in my pocket, and headed off to visit Laszlo Torts, Esq., chief instigator for the distinguished Wall Street firm Benn, Dover, & Spreddom.

"I'd like you to read this rulebook and look over these documents and tell me why I can't buy that motorcycle in my local shop," I said, pointing to the striking *Cycle News* cover and shouting over the din of ambulance scanners.

"I'm sorry, I can't hear you," Torts said. "Let me turn down the EMS scanners. That's better. Now, let me look. Hmmmm. It's all pretty obvious. That'll be $5000."

"For what?" I asked, incredulous.

"It'll be $4000 to have one of these things FedExed in from Italy and another grand to bribe the guy at DMV to license it," Torts said as he refilled his Oildri seat cushion.

"So what you're telling me is that doesn't exist in the US?" I asked.

"I did not say that, but, as a complete entity in mass numbers, yes. I mean, no. Let me explain in terms that you should be able to understand without seven years of college and a translator. Yes, this bike does not exist, entirely, in quantities of 50 or more - as per the rules - assembled, and though the unassembled machines in question may, under the letter of the law, well be the sum of their various parts at some undetermined point in the future, and therefore perfectly legal for racing under the current guidelines, assuming, of course, that the parts do, in fact, exist and are not invalidated by pre-existing parameters, such as stroke, cylinder head, frame, etc., the legality of their existence can only be determined when, and if, they, or the part kits in question, in sufficient numbers, are presented in good faith in a completed physical form to the unscrupulous inspection of unbiased nondenominational interlopers, or, failing that, they are subject to what is legally known as 'pragmatic sanction.'"

"Which is...?"

"We call it the 'Tough Doo-doo Statute.' Make the rules fit the game after it's already started."

"Wonderful."

"That would depend on which side you were on," Torts said, his eyes suddenly aglow at the report of a 32-car chain reaction rear-ender on Lexington Avenue that was caused when an inexperienced New York City bus driver mistakenly stopped to pick up a fare.

"I can hear whiplash a mile away," he yelled as he grabbed a stack of business cards and ran for the door. "Somebody took it hard in the rear."

"I know," I answered. "Believe me. I know."

July 13, 1994

Moving Chickens

"You bite! You blow! Your skeleton should be removed from your skin one bone at a time until all that's left is a wretched pathetic blood sac that should be punctured and spilled into overflowing outhouses to mingle with higher species. You don't deserve to breathe the same air that fills my tires. Your space on earth could be better filled by Spam. You should be the poster boy for birth control. Will Rogers would smack you silly."

That's the tongue-lashing that Rich Oliver never gave, but should have. At the press conference following his win in the 250cc Grand Prix race at Loudon, his fifth in a row, Oliver said that he'd had trouble with traffic and that he'd lapped one guy four or five times. This someone who he'd pucker passed on other occasions this year and the sort of loser that'd get lapped at a drag race. "I guess I should go have a talk with him," Oliver said, somewhat sheepishly, but he probably didn't. What would he say?

Frenchman Christian Sarron, the gravity-defying former World Champion who still holds the record for suborbital flight by a motorcycle racer, and whose hands look like they'd wrestled a leaf shredder to a draw, often spoke of the constant hazards of "moving chickens," "chickens" being his Gallic pronunciation of "chicanes."

Moving chickens, backmarkers, lappers, slackers, menaces, mouth sores, pus bags: Call them what you want, they are the scourge of racing at every level and far too little is being done about them. That they have been granted licenses to race at the highest levels - 500cc World Championship leader Mick Doohan rightfully complains about them whenever baited - but deserve to be on a racetrack as much as a three-legged poodle, which, by the way, they'd have a hard time passing.

As speeds increase, safety becomes a more prominent and contentious issue. The hazards on the track merit as much discussion as those off the track. It's an area where there can be no excuses, and yet there are no reasonable standards for exclusion. Do we need full fields even if they're fattened up by refugees from the Shriner's parade? In the World Championships there is a cutoff point, however generous, that has to be met if you want to go out and ruin Doohan's day.

So, a few suggestions: If, during qualifying, a rider needs to be timed with a calendar, he's toast; if he has to stop and ask directions in timed practice, juice him; and if the model year of his bike changes during his qualifying run, he's guano.

This may seem unduly harsh, since one of history's most notorious backmarkers became one of our greatest champions. In his very first road race at Laguna Seca, three-time World Champion Wayne Rainey was lapped by no less than his mentor, and tormentor, Kenny Roberts. What did Rainey do after getting lapped? He ran into the back of Roberts' bike, locking the two in an unholy union as they headed for the final turn; nine then, 11 now. They uncoupled just before Rainey was about to send Roberts doggie style into the haybales, but not before Roberts could look back and see Rainey's saucer-sized eyes filling his visor. An inauspicious debut to be sure, but one that Rainey has long since expiated.

Getting lapped once is not a sin; getting lapped five times is. Underachievers have been around in racing since long before the invention of the internal combustion engine. The earliest mention I could find of "backmarking" dates back to the Palio horse race held twice a year in the Tuscan town of Siena, Italy, beginning in 1656. Each of the nearby communes was represented by its best rider. The best of the best raced around a temporary circuit

(Pomona?) in the close confines of the Piazza del Campo, the town's scallop-shaped main square. When the leading rider would lap one of the slower riders he was obligated to slap the slacker on the back with a mace wrapped in the used diapers of the mayor's first-born son. (This became something of a problem as the mayor's son neared puberty.) The slowest rider would be identified by the number of times his back had been marked by the diapers, hence the term: "moving chicken."

How do we adapt this in America? Depends. Maybe Pampers, but I think Depends would pack a bigger punch. Who says there aren't any non-tobacco sponsors out there?

The solution, I think, is quite simple: fines. The first time you get lapped is on the house. It happens to the best of them and could just be a sign you're having a bad day. The fines would start with the second time you're lapped and escalate rapidly.

If you are lapped twice in a race you will be allowed to finish, but afterwards must pay a $1000 fine and buy dinner for the AMA's V.P. for S.M., Tom Mueller. As the S.M. Veep, road racing, or in your case, road blocking, falls under his domain and your career will be discussed with an emphasis on finding out how it is that after racing for 10 years and spending countless thousands of dollars you still suck. You will be asked how you secure your fairing to ensure that it won't be sucked off every time you get passed by a guy going through a first-gear corner three gears higher than you. These, and other issues, will be discussed over a bounteous feast of bulgur wheat tofu, free-ranging schnauzer jerky, and hand-squeezed weasel milk.

If you are lapped three times you will be asked to dine alfresco on a steamy summer evening with Editor Carruthers, who will, I assure you, spend the entire night whining about the heat. "Boy, it's hot. I've never been this hot. My head feels really hot. Did my mousse catch fire? I'll bet hell's not this hot. Do thermometers go this high? I don't think thermometers go this high. Is this like being microwaved? Now I know how David Koresh felt. Did I mention it was hot? Boy, it's hot. I think my zipper just melted." And you'll be fined $2000, though within minutes of being seated with the whine connoisseur you'll conclude that that's the lesser of your punishments. "Look! My iced tea's boiling. Is it still iced tea if it's boiling? At what point does it become tea? Holy **q* is it hot!"

Ride slowly enough to get lapped three times and you have to have breakfast with possibly the only TV broadcaster who prefers anonymity, but whose TV name rhymes with Mary Liars. Mary will share years of broadcast knowledge and lore with you, enlightening you immeasurably, then speak of enjoying the breakfast immensely, even though your conversation will have been held at a decibel level that could fatigue titanium. But forever afterwards Mary will deny ever speaking to you; will deny having enjoyed donuts and coffee with you; will deny repeating any joke you might have told that morning. (Here's a hint Mary: You can't spell amateur without what?) The fine will be around $3000, payable in non-sequential unmarked bills.

If you are so pathetic on a motorcycle that you can actually be lapped four times in a 40-minute race; (and this I find unbelievable, though Rich Oliver swears that it's so and I would never doubt him), you will have to dine with me and the only journalist on the circuit with two first names. No, it's not Sirhan Sirhan, or Boutros-Boutros Ghali, but *American Roadracing's* King of Stuff Larry Lawrence. Larry and I are what is known in the restaurant business as big eaters, and you will have to pay. We will take you to a poultry farm whose gimmick is that you get to visit the coop and pick out your dinner from among the scurrying masses. Larry and I will take turns thinning the herd. While Larry's power-sucking the marrow out of the wishbone, you and I will discuss your technique, your career, your future. I will listen intently, digesting the complexity of your life, contemplating your needs, wants, desires, then tell you: "You bite! You blow! Your skeleton should be removed from your skin one bone at a time until all that's left is a wretched pathetic blood sac that should be punctured and spilled into overflowing outhouses to mingle with a higher species! You don't deserve to breathe the same air that fills my tires! Your space on earth could be better filled by Spam. You should be the poster boy for birth control. Will Rogers would smack you silly." The fine will be $4000; the meal could be twice that. And in the end I can guarantee you there will be no more moving chickens.

April 2, 1997

Making It Up

It's hard to pick the single stupidest thing that was said during the Daytona 200 telecast: There's so much to choose from. This from Mary Reid about Muzzy Kawasaki's Doug Chandler: "He also won the superbike championship back in 1990. Then, of course, had the lay off for a while." "Exactly," his on-air partner, journalist and commentator Nick Ienatsch agreed. Four years racing 500cc GPs, three of them as a factory rider; fifth in the world in 1992, is not a layoff. Where'd that come from? Probably the AMA media guide which doesn't list Chandler's GP years. If that's the case it's the product of sheer laziness.

From Ienatsch about Scott Russell and Chandler: "Both of them are past World Superbike champions." We know that Russell won in 1993. We also know Chandler won the AMA Superbike title in 1990, then, according to Reid, had a layoff for a while, returning on a Harley in 1995. So he couldn't possibly have won a championship, unless he won it before the layoff. In case you're wondering, he didn't.

As the showpiece of the American road racing season, the Daytona 200 gets the most attention and the most television exposure, and deservedly so. With the largest potential audience it deserves the best commentary, and the best production values. Not this year.

According to Mary, the Daytona 200 is "the most prestigious race in the world." The Suzuka 8-Hour is the most prestigious race in the world. Rob Muzzy said that Kawasaki's budget for last year's Suzuka 8-Hour was more than its entire World Superbike budget. After Suzuka comes any of the GPs followed by any of the World

Superbike rounds. The truth is, to most of the Japanese factories, the Daytona 200 simply isn't that important. If it was they'd be there. The Yamaha World Superbike team raced in American colors this year because Yamaha USA paid the bills, according to team spokesman Rupert Williamson.

Fatuous hyperbole is the stock in trade of the grossly uninformed. It's the currency of the knowledge-poor who attempt to subvert the truth with verbal spectacle. (It's called irony.) A certain amount can be forgiven, but not this much, regardless of how dull the race was. On the crowd count Mary said that "250,000 enthusiasts have come to Daytona Beach again this year, most of them on two wheels." It's generally accepted that about half a million people come to Daytona for Bike Week. Since Daytona International Speedway doesn't release crowd figures, no one knows for sure how many attend the race. But if you guessed 40,000 to 45,000 you wouldn't be far off.

More slathering from Nick. Preparation for the race is so intense, according to Ienatsch, that the teams "might give their mechanics one day off some time around Christmas, but probably not." As Eve said to Adam in the Garden of Eden: "Where'd that come from?"

It's not as if these guys are novices. Nick did very good work filling in for Kevin Schwantz on the Grand Prix telecasts last year. Many, including me, thought his work was as good as, if not better than, Schwantz'. But the difference between the GPs and Daytona is this: Daytona was live while the GPs are voice-overs, done on tape in a studio, the Wednesday after the GP. The outcome is known and there's an abundance of research material available. If you say something daffy, you simply rewind the tape and do it again. Last week I caught a season wrap-up Reid did on the World Rally championship and it was very well done, the highlights were outstanding, the commentary informed.

Working on tape you might not say that the riders were "covering the ground at 180 to 185 miles per hour, every lap, for about three hours" at Daytona. In the 56-year history of the race it's been three hours exactly never. In 1961, when it was run on a two-mile infield course and the average was 69 mph, it was 2:53. The closest it's come in the modern era was 2:23 in 1994 and that was due to pace cars which dropped the average to 85 mph. Since it became a superbike race in 1985 it's been over two hours three times. This year, with a pace car, it was 1:55.

Ienatsch said that Chandler's children weren't at Daytona, "They're not here, they're watching on television, watching ESPN's live broadcast." Then Doug's son Jett showed up in Victory Lane, sitting on the second-place Kawasaki, showing very few signs of jet lag after taking the regularly scheduled 9 a.m. Concorde in from Salinas. He'd have come sooner but he heard Nick say the race was three hours long.

Then there was the mention of the Ferracci team showing up with DKNY (Donna Karan New York) Men backing at Daytona. After the Ferracci team encountered problems, Nick said, "That's a tough way to launch a sponsorship." Except that it had been launched at Phoenix three weeks earlier with Mat Mladin romping to a win. Not so tough, really. Another eight tough days like that and they win the title.

"Gary Medley and Rob Muzzy, they've won more Daytona 200s than we could probably count," Nick hyperventilated at one point. Is it really that hard to count to three? He also said that "Chris Carr has, what, 100 million 600 National Championships?" Actually seven.

Early on Mary said that "Ducati had such high hope of making this their first victory." That was simply bad reporting and, later in the broadcast, pit reporter Rick DeBruhl correctly pointed out that "they knew they weren't going to be really strong here. In fact, they had to de-tune their bike." Ferracci told anyone who made the effort to approach him that he just wanted to get through the week and had de-tuned the machine seven or eight percent. Hardly a winning formula. He'd bumped the compression ratio up just to get Mladin up to the third row in qualifying after being two seconds off the pace.

DeBruhl did as good a job as he could - given how little they went to him - except in explaining the dual compound tires. "On the right side they've got a hard compound," he said. "On the left side, it actually comes up a little more than half, and that's the soft side." He got it backwards, but at least he looked into it. And by then Nick had correctly configured the dual compound a few times.

More disturbing was Nick & Mary's cavalier use of speculation and hyperbole. At one point, when Russell turned around and pointed at a rider, Nick's take was, "I think he said, 'You're number one' with his middle finger." So he's accused Russell of flipping the bird when it wasn't so (I re-wound the tape), which one rider acknowledged. Regardless of Mary's assertion that it's the "greatest motorcycle race in the world," it was the weakest international field in years, an AMA National plus two. And for the first time in what - 100 million years? - there wasn't even a full 80-rider grid. Where was the mention that there was no representation from the World Superbike teams of Ducati, Suzuki, and Kawasaki, all of whom were at Daytona in 1996? Or that John Kocinski had asked Honda to run Daytona but had been turned down?

Nick's assertion that the "depth of the field is the who's who of American road racing" ignores Kocinski, Mike Hale, who would have loved to race Daytona, and Kenny Roberts Jr. who will race the 1995 Daytona 200 on the Modenas 750cc four-cylinder Superbike that Kenny Roberts will build as soon as I mention it to him. See, making up stuff's fun.

There were also sins of omission. Scott Russell has never aspired to sainthood and his transgressions have been abundantly cataloged. He ended up spending Friday night in a Daytona Beach jail after being wrongfully collared for a friend's indiscretion. Was this mentioned on the telecast? Not the one I saw. Either they didn't know or they were covering up. Either way it's unconscionable.

You may be wondering why I keep referring to Nick's partner as Mary. Despite having introduced himself at the top or the show as "Marty" Reid, a graphic showing the broadcast team around the 15th lap clearly had it spelled "Mary." I asked a friend in the TV business for the precise technical explanation on how that happens. He said that'd be "the boys in the truck."

Maybe we can blame the boys for the nearly complete lack of information about the race, except for the running order of the top five. It wasn't until the 21st lap that Reid mentioned that Russell was unofficially 13 seconds ahead. Even "the new Mr. Daytona" (Refresh my memory: Who was the old one?) couldn't pull out 13 seconds on one lap, unless maybe he was racing against Dean Mizdal, who, according to Nick, is "one of the quick amateur riders out of California." Quick enough to have finished 30th in the AMA Superbike series last year, a series, I believe, which is not for amateurs.

The great hue and cry will no doubt be that at least it was live on TV. We should be thankful to the gods of the airwaves. That completely misses the point. And is it a good thing that the public is grossly misinformed? "Doug Chandler and Scott Russell, certainly two of the top five riders in the world," according to Ienatsch. So the other three must be Mick Doohan, Alex Criville, Max Biaggi, Troy Corser, Luca Cadalora, Aaron Slight, Carl Fogarty, John Kocinski; does that make five? Okay, that's opinion. Marty Reid saying, during a separate telecast of the 600 Supersport race: "Hacking is the one that impresses me most right now. This is his first time on the high banks." That's simply untrue. A very little research would have shown that Jamie Hacking finished fifth in the NASB EBC Sport Bike race at Daytona last fall. You couldn't expect Reid to know that Hacking had spent three days testing Dunlops at Daytona in the winter. Nick knew, though. He was there.

But, when he wasn't on the verge of exploding clichés, Ienatsch seemed to be pursuing his own agenda. At the end of the race he said that the "eyes of the world are on Daytona." Instead of mentioning the various foreign journalists, with whom he spent time doing research in the press room, he said that "everybody's here, not only news channels, ESPN," then he named the Newport Beach fat-cats for whom he currently free-lances, but not *Sport Rider*, which he once edited, or *Motorcyclist*, where he once worked, or *Cycle News*. "Everybody who's interested in two-wheeled motorsports is here." Not. Any GP press room is filled with three or four times as many journalists as were working at Daytona.

I will gladly admit that no one is perfect. In my Daytona preview I wrote that 1996 was the first season in years that Eraldo Ferracci hadn't won at least one AMA Superbike race. Unless you count the two that Alessandro Gramigni won. My mistake was in thinking about Ferracci's regulars, Larry Pegram and Shawn Higbee, neither of whom won. Hopefully, an editor catches that. Not that one did. If it slips through, as it did, *Cycle News* could run a correction a week later. (Didn't do it, but could have.) If it was on TV, it would have gone out live. In television the mistakes are amplified, which makes it important to get the facts straight. When you start by betraying the truth, you, and the audience, are screwed.

March 18, 1998

How Not To Win the Daytona 200

We all know how to win the Daytona 200: Be like Scott. Scott "Mr. Daytona" Russell won an unprecedented fifth Daytona 200 on Sunday, further adding to his record total and his burgeoning Floridian legend. Long ago, he demonstrated that he, more than anyone before or since, knows how to win the Daytona 200. What is becoming painfully obvious is that his rivals - and the term is used loosely - haven't yet figured out the best way not to win the Daytona 200. This year there was an impressive demonstration of methods employed to defeat success, some never before seen - and for good reason. So if it is your wish to not win the Daytona 200 you should...

...get into a bar fight at the start of the week.

This is a first. According to the official Suzuki press release, Yoshimura Suzuki's Aaron Bates [sic], who could easily pass as the Fourth Musketeer, would be riding "with a broken jaw after being involved in a disturbance in Daytona Beach club on Monday." The semiofficial account of the incident strains credulity and goes something like this: As soon as he walked in the front door of Razzles, a Daytona meat market, Yates was sucker-punched, the victim of mistaken identity. Never saw it coming. The bouncers took him out of the place and put him on the sidewalk. He made his way to a hospital, where he as told to take some pain-killers and come back in the morning. The jaw was plated and wired shut.

"Once I get may helmet on, it holds the jaw tightly and I am not in too much discomfort, but I certainly don't want to risk crashing and aggravating the injury," Yates said. Riding a superbike for 200 miles on a track where your chin spends most of its time bouncing off a gas tank is not conducive to success. Racing is the ultimate pain-killer, and Yates rode valiantly to finish sixth, on the same lap as Russell. Memo to future bar-brawlers: Don't.

...ride a superbike like a 250.

No one is likely to ever repeat what Rich Oliver did in winning 20 250cc GPs over the past two seasons on a Yamaha TZ250. No one is likely to want to repeat what he's done so far on a superbike. In Friday's second qualifying session, the four-time AMA 250cc GP Champion and all-around good guy high-sided going out of turn six on his way to the banking. He was in the air longer than the Wright Brothers and ended up needing a CAT scan. His hand was chewed up and his vision was initially blurred, but he was otherwise okay. He'd flicked it in the same corner during the December Dunlop tire tests, breaking all of the toes on one foot. And, since his inaugural spill in his superbike debut at Las Vegas last year, he's crashed in every test or race but one. In the Daytona 200, Oliver crashed again - this time in turn one. Oliver's time through the final corner onto the banking - one of the two most crucial spots on the track - was faster than anyone's, including four-time Daytona 200 winner Scott Russell. When he made it. Superbikes require more finesse, less corner speed. Once Oliver gets it right, he'll be a force. Until then, keep the Sharkskinz guy's number on the speed dial.

...ride a Harley-Davidson.

Up until Scott Russell gave Yamaha its 18th win this year, Harley-Davidson had won as many Daytona 200s - 17 - as any other brand. Unfortunately, the last time was March 23, 1969: Cal Rayborn was riding, Richard Nixon was president, and Pascal Picotte was just being conceived. Exactly nine months to the day later, Picotte was born on December 23, 1969, in Granby, Quebec, Canada. Another 29 years on and the French-Canadian qualified the VR1000 fifth fastest for the Daytona 200, giving the team good cause to celebrate - something they haven't been able to do for a few lean years.

Picotte was optimistic when he got on the VR last December and he quickly proved his optimism was grounded in reality. Much of the credit, he said, goes to suspension whiz Dale Rathwell, who has worked with most of the top superbike teams and is now with Harley. The Harley wasn't that far off on power, but it hasn't always been able to put it on the track. With a host of changes to the VR that allows for greater adjustability, Picotte was able to flog it the way he'd flogged the Suzuki, Kawasaki and Ducati before it. With due deference to Thomas Wilson and Chris Carr, this is the first time the Milwaukee team has had a veteran road racer since Doug Chandler rode the bike in 1995. Picotte's race was impressive, running as high as third before a Keystone Kops pit stop hurt his chances and mechanical problems killed them, something Yamaha's Jamie Hacking expected: "I was waiting for the thing to blow up."

It didn't, but it was grounded by troubles caused by the first pit stop and eventually retired on the 44th lap. Had this been a regular AMA-length National, around 64 miles, he may well have been on the box. If nothing else, Picotte and the boys from Milwaukee proved that they're a force to be reckoned with.

...try to get away from Scott Russell.

American Honda's Miguel DuHamel pulled the bonehead stunt of the race, crashing into the chicane and out of the race when he tried to pull away from Scott Russell with about 38 laps to go. Up to that point DuHamel had been able to stick with Russell and keep him honest, though Russell later professed he knew he had him covered. Russell wins because he knows the race is 57 laps, knows how to manage his tire wear, and knows that no one can get away from him. It hasn't happened in seven years. When he was beaten in 1993 by Yamaha's Eddie Lawson, Lawson graciously said his day had been carried by horsepower. When

Russell was beaten by DuHamel in 1995, it was because he was on an ill-handling Lucky Strike Suzuki on Michelin tires which he hadn't properly tested - taking nothing away from DuHamel, who has, after all, won the race twice. DuHamel's crash was spectacular, the bike cartwheeling into a very exotic pile of exotic junk, while DuHamel slid, unhurt, along the ground. TV viewers may have been impressed, but his bosses at American Honda, who had guests from Japan over during Honda's 50th anniversary year, weren't. With the surfeit of superbike talent at the top, a single DNF could be the lethal blow to DuHamel's title chances, something at least one Honda honcho posited.

...try to win the race before the first pit stop.

Fast By Ferracci's Mike Hale was my pick to win the AMA/MBNA Superbike title this year. After crashing out of the Daytona 200, he's 19th in the standings. Oh well, at least I picked Chandler the last two years. Hale's crash was *déjà vu*, the Texan tumbling as he exited the infield in the same place he crashed out of the lead of the Daytona 200 in 1995. The difference is that in 1995 he fell on someone else's oil while in the lead on the fourth lap. This year there was no oil, just a front tire that slid out from under him on the seventh lap. Hale later said he was being cautious in that corner and yet he still crashed. The Fast By Ferracci team had access to the same Michelin tires which carried Russell to victory, so you can't blame it on the tire, though Hale and Russell do ride differently and the Ducati V-twin presents different problems for the tires than Russell's inline four-cylinder Yamaha. In Phoenix, where Hale destroyed his number-one bike in a crash during practice, the problem wasn't so much traction as balance, finding a front tire that worked with the rear. Too much traction out back puts too much stress on the front, and makes for a skittery motorcycle and jittery rider. Both Hale and Ferracci have proven that they know how to win: Ferracci won four times last year with Mat Mladin. Hale needs a confidence-builder, and going to Laguna Seca - the first proper road course of the season - may be the answer.

...not bother entering.

As calamitous a race as these riders had, the one constant among them was that they tried. They strapped on their helmets - in Yates' case, gingerly - put on their boots and leathers, and set out on a noble quest. For a while, anyhow. They didn't go to Daytona hoping to get in a bar fight or get high-sided going onto the banking or blow their Harley up or cartwheel into the chicane or low-side in turn six. They went there to win, and they'll come back next year and the year after and the year after, armed with the knowledge, pain and experience from this year. And maybe one of those years, Scott Russell will figure out a way to not win, but I wouldn't bet on it.

April 22, 1998

Recycled Crap

The call from the bossman comes in late on a lazy Friday afternoon, the beginning of the Easter/Passover weekend, a time when no one wants to work, especially me, but he wants to work even less and he's the bossman, so my weekend's shot - not that he's going to let it affect his suntan, putting stroke, or doggy paddle.

"Can you come up with a column by Monday? If I read one more column comparing Supercross to NASCAR I'm going to puke in my snorkel."

"If you do, make sure you get a picture," I asked.

His instructions were succinct: "Write about almost anything. Listen, you took a run at all the teams except Kawasaki in your last one. Now it's their turn."

"Any ideas, Chester?"

"I don't know. I'm going on vacation. I don't want to think about it. That's why I called you, remember? How about... how about a column on Muzzy's mustache?"

"Let me get this straight: You want 1300 words on Rob Muzzy's mustache by Monday? Now, you may think it's silly, but it's really not that silly to have a mustache wide enough for a flock of sea gulls to perch on. Sure I'll write it, but before you go, one more thing: You might want to start cleaning out your desk. It'll save you time on Tuesday."

Note to readers: I don't know how long this is going to be, but you can tell a lot about the writer by the bottom of this page. If the "Looking Back" section runs the covers of the flashback issues, like the one you'll see next year at Daytona, the 13 Years Ago flashback

- the one that'll say, "Fresh from becoming the first rider in history to win the 250cc and 500cc World Championships, Freddie Spencer sets his year off to a really, really crummy start when he gets dorked by Carry Andrew in the 1986 Daytona 200" - it means the guy who wrote the column came up short and they needed to fill the space with copies of the covers. I'm guessing there will be four or five covers at the bottom of this one.

I have two choices: I can either await inspiration from my Muse or practice the time-honored art of environmental writing, recycling old crap from the past. Sounds like Plan B.

If you're going for the minimalist approach - least thought, most response - you can't go wrong with Harley. Until this year, that is. The way Pascal Picotte rode at Daytona should go a long way toward silencing the critics. Granted, he didn't finish, but it was faulty pit work that stopped him, not mechanical mediocrity. For the rest of the AMA calendar, he won't have to worry about pit stops; at least he shouldn't. In any case, for once my angle was less racing-specific, more general.

What made me think about Harley was a joke I recently emailed to a friend living in Tokyo who, because of the usurious rates for parts and labor, is the proud owner of an H-D Fat Girl (that's a Fat Boy without a rod). He said he'd heard the joke a thousand times. It was new to me. Here it is: What's the difference between a Harley and a Hoover vacuum cleaner?

The location of the dirt bag.

It was told to me by an Australian of just slightly less than average height. The editor of this newspaper is an Australian of just slightly less than average height.

(Editor's note: It wasn't me. Honest, Mr. Scheibe,[1] you gotta believe me, it wasn't me. I swear. I love Harley. The thing I most look forward to hearing in life is... let me start over: The thing I most look forward to

---

[1] Steve Scheibe, Manager of Racing at Harley-Davidson

hearing is my son's name in the San Diego Padres starting lineup on Opening Day, 2016. The second-greatest pleasure I would get would be hearing a priest ask my daughter if she "would take Skull - just Skull, no last name - to be her lawful wedded husband, in sickness and in health, for richer or poorer, until he violates his parole...")

That got me to thinking that there must be more humor out there just waiting to be mined. So here's the deal: Send in your favorite motorcycle-related joke to the editor. It'll save him the trouble of calling me again next Friday, and it will also provide limitless mirth to your many fellow readers. The winner will probably get something. One caveat: You cannot just stick a motorcyclist in some lame old joke you heard years ago. If the joke begins, "A priest, a Brahman, and a rabbi on a V-Max are stuck in a lifeboat," it'll get tossed. No way a life raft could hold a V-Max.

My original idea when the bossman called me was this: Eating dinner in Japan is expensive, unless you eat with John Kocinski; then it's really expensive. It was the Thursday night of the season-opening Japanese Grand Prix at Suzuka, when Michael Scott, Motocourse editor and *Cycle News* GP correspondent, and I spotted JK talking to fellow 250cc World Champion Max Biaggi a few tables away.

"You know," I warned Mike, "if we get his attention, he's ours for good." Sure enough, within minutes he'd settled in for the night. Not that that's necessarily a bad thing.

What journalists crave most in the never-ending quest for truth, accuracy, and service to the reader, is information - scads of information, nothing too trivial. Actually, that's a lie. What we crave most is free crap: T-shirts, hats, belt buckles, key fobs, lighters, stickers...nothing's too insignificant. Note to OEMs: An embroidered letterman's jacket will go a long way toward masking the handling deficiencies of your latest wobbler. But you knew that. An old news photographer friend in New York City made a name for himself as a press-conference whore. "I'll take one of those. What is it?"

So the second-most-important asset to a journalist is being able to bathe in the fountain of knowledge, experience and wisdom that the best riders possess. Which means that, even though we might end up paying out the blind spot, we would be enlightened. For instance, did you know that JK hates the individual faucets that are common in Europe? Can't stand 'em. Must have mixer faucets. And he owns nothing. He did say that he wants to finish his career in the United States. Surely inside information like that is worth something.

When it came time to pay, I suggested we split it three ways. But JK decided it'd be easier if we each paid our own. So we go to the cashier, he forages though the seven or eight slips of paper that the incredibly efficient wait staff generated from our modest meal and spots most of what's his - most, not all - pays it, says his good-nights and splits. Mike and I split the rest.

For a bowl of lasagna the size of a knee puck, two Cokes and a small green salad, I end up paying forty bucks. Even in Japan that's hard to do. And Mike's was worse.

We weren't sure what JK forgot to pay for. Might have been the chunks of Parmesan, might have been the breadsticks. Who knows? I'm sure he didn't mean to stiff us. But what I got out of it was this: It helped me understand his race performance that Sunday.

I'm sure he didn't mean to jump the start and get a stop-and-go penalty. And I'm sure that he didn't mean to speed down the pit lane when he came in to serve his penalty, incurring a second penalty. Just an oversight. So it was a small price to pay.

What I don't want to do is give the impression that all World Champions are given to such oversight. At Daytona this year I had the pleasure of having dinner with Kenny Roberts; his lovely girlfriend, Rita; the *CN* editor; and the editor's dad, Kel Carruthers, the man responsible for nearly all of the King's successes, who now works his magic at Chaparral Yamaha.

After a wonderful meal at a rib joint in Ormond Beach, the King gladly picked up the tab.

"I may not have much money left, but I've got enough to buy you dinner," he told Kel after enlightening us with an inventory of the shortcomings of the Modenas KR3 and how they'd be resolved. (Money - lots of it.) I thought it was a very generous gesture.

But, as any of his friends will tell you, if you've got to listen to two hours of KR's crap, you ought to get something out of it.

July 8, 1998

Monkey Business

I was taught at a very young age that if you have nothing nice to say, say it about sidecars.

Sidecars are the answer to the question, what do you get when you mix guys with more money than sense, and too much free time? Normally, hookers, but in this case, oil-puking old piles of fatigued metal, cracking plastic and rotting rubber.

Put another way, they are the answer to the question that was never asked: What do you get when you implant an obsolete motor on a shipping pallet with wheels? Who cares? It'd be like trying to graft a salad shooter on a breast pump. Or putting a Harley motor in a sportbike frame.

This is a recreational activity done by two guys in leather on their knees. I believe that makes it illegal in Utah. To be accurate, women do it, too. (You can quit drooling anytime.)

The passenger is called the monkey, because when this sport was originally conceived, monkeys were the only things dumb enough to sit next to the guy at the controls and hang their bare asses inches above the track. Then the monkeys protested and the ASPCA got involved, which was how it was discovered that monkeys were so smart. To this day, the handrail the passenger holds on to is called the banana, which is, you know, not surprising considering you've got two guys in leather on their knees. Or women.

My consideration of this issue did not start when they began fouling racetracks this year. I have been covering Grands Prix for *Cycle News* since 1981 and have seen the best, Biland & Waltisperg, the British guy and the other British guy, and some Swiss brothers. (Not black guys, but two dudes who actually slid out of the same womb.) They were the best - cutting edge - and still they've been relegated to second-tier status on the world level. If there's no hope for the best, what hope is there for the liquid-barfing artifacts that fester on the AMA schedule like a year-old bedsore? About as much hope as a HyperCycle Suzuki getting through postrace tech without an AMA official saying, "Does he think we're retarded?"

Not that these sidecars don't have a stringent set of technical rules; they do: No electronic devices that could interfere with pacemakers, prescription windscreens, gel-filled seats, and a noise limit of a dillion decibels.

By the way, if you're thinking of scrawling angry letters to the editor denouncing this column, just put the crayons back in the box right now and go back to the shuffleboard court. In a very unscientific poll, I asked a number of people if they could name a single sidecar participant. Not a single rider could name even one, though Yoshimura Suzuki's Mat Mladin answered, "Bob?"

Smart ass.

No one - I repeat for dramatic effect and to fill space, no one - comes to an AMA National to see sidecars - I repeat, sidecars. They come to see the best two-wheeled racers in America doing what they do best - something they're deprived of when these underpowered dollies nuke the track oilier than a sauna full of lawyers. It has happened the last three times they ran.

It happened at Laguna Seca, where a rig greased up almost the entire track. After a few of the riders in the 600cc Supersport class noticed the oil, there was about a 45-minute cleanup. That left a line of Oildri almost everywhere and traction had to be compromised. Even if it wasn't, the perception existed that it was. And because it wasn't visible to the naked eye, it was the riders who noticed the oil, not the corner workers who were not to blame, since they couldn't see the insidious deposit. It happened last week at Loudon, and it happened the week before at Road America. At Elkhart Lake, it happened so often that the corner worker in turn five nearly tore a rotator cuff throwing up more red flags than a HyperCycle Suzuki going through tech inspection.

Unnecessary delays were caused a number of times, and for what? So a handful of nostalgists can justify the expense of owning motorized turtle/skateboards, so they can have an answer for their wives when they're asked, "Why don't you get rid of that pile of crap so we can have room in the garage for something useful, like last year's mulch pile?"

The situation at Loudon could have been tragic on a weekend replete with tragedy. Only dumb luck saved the day.

A light rain fell as the 250s were gridded for their 1 p.m. race. When they finally got going, Erion Racing's Randy Renfrow noticed something was wrong. He alerted AMA officials who relayed their concerns to the corner workers. What they found was oil pretty much everywhere. The culprit was a sidecar which had leaked oil onto one of its tires and then circulated the track, coating the surface with lubricant like a paint roller, only less useful.

On a track which had already exacted a terrible human toll, on a weekend which will certainly bring much-needed reform, the possibility of starting a race on an even more unsafe track is frightening.

Once the oil was discovered, there was another 40-minute delay while the track was cleared, and even then, riders in the Superbike class, run after the 250s, felt the track was still oilier than the publisher of a road racing monthly.

Could this happen with a motorcycle? Of course it could, but belly pans on superbikes make it less likely. The support classes don't have belly pans and there are those that think they should. In the good old days, before Pro Blunder, I can recall seeing an 883 engine explode at Phoenix, leaving not only oil but metal and championship hopes on the track as well. Some of the more modern sidecars have made an effort to fit oil-containment devices, and the movement is growing. But they don't all have them, and the antique class would serve motorcycling better by oiling dusty dirt tracks.

It's also easier to spot fluids leaving a motorcycle than it is a low-capacity hovercraft. And it's less likely to happen to a motorcycle made in the past year or two than to one made decades before HyperCycle Suzuki's first DQ.

Fortunately the AMA is aware of the havoc the chairs have caused on a series which gets better every year. AMA road race manager Ron Barrick said at Loudon, "Obviously, the sidecars are a big issue for next year."

Barrick understands that the promoters should be able to add entertainment, but wonders about sidecars.

"We've got to sit down and, maybe at the AMA Pro Racing board level, decide whether we're even going to negotiate regarding that," he said, adding, "I consider this a serious concern for our two-wheel riders."

If you're a sidecar racer, and you can read between the lines, you might plan your summer vacation now.

If promoters don't think that having the best riders on the fastest bikes is enough, they could always get a stunt rider like Gary Rothwell, whose bargain-basement Suzuki sprayed oil onto the racing line on the front straight at Road Atlanta, nearly causing the live TV broadcast to be delayed. Then the bozos running the water truck couldn't figure out where the "on" switch was, turning the cleanup into a Three Stooges routine - and not a bad one, at that.

I stopped to look at one of these relics at Elkhart Lake. Let me rephrase that: My path was needlessly impeded by one of these relics at Elkhart Lake. It appeared to have a Yamaha 650cc twin engine, an engine which has been not of production since disco died - the first time. The frame had more pipes than a head shop and the rear tire looked like it was lifted from a riding mower - probably in the middle of the night, which is too bad, because a riding mower with three wheels is still more useful than one of these money pits.

Which made me think: Why not have a riding-mower exhibition? Besides building motorcycles, Honda also makes riding mowers. It's a natural fit. None of the other riders have contracts with the mower companies, with the possible exception of Muzzy Kawasaki's Doug Chandler, so you could get them to ride the things, all helmeted and leathered up for action. Semis of works machinery from Toro, John Deere, Cub Cadet, and Honda could sit proudly next to the Honda, Vance & Hines Ducati, and Yamaha rigs. The mowers could be fitted with those sweeper things on the back so they could clean the track rather than oil it during their "race." What's the worst thing that could happen if they ran off the track? They'd mow the lawn. And, of course, it goes without saying that they'd be faster than sidecars.

There would, of course, have to be a rigorous set of technical rules. Is the 36-inch blade legal or can you run the 32 to cut wind resistance? What about pitch? What is pitch? Must reverse gear work? What about functioning grass catchers? The possibility of chicanery is omnipresent. Now I'm hearing that HyperCycle wants to enter the class. Quick, get me some calipers and a jug of espresso - it's gonna be a long night, Chester.

July 22, 1998

What an Idiot

If the AMA takes no action against Anthony Gobert for failing an FIM-administered drug test then the end result of the whole ugly incident is this: He will have admitted to smoking marijuana, been thrown out of an FIM event, humiliated the Vance & Hines Ducati team, cost them untold tens of thousands of dollars, to say nothing of the hundreds of man-hours put into this single race, shamed his mother, who came from Australia to see her son race, and put a black eye on the sport. And he'll walk away scot-free, laughing all the way to the bar, which is where he was on Friday night after getting kicked out of the race, and again on Saturday, because he hadn't been able to sufficiently assuage his guilt the first night. To me, that's unconscionable.

For the record, I, like most baby-boomers, smoked weed at one time. We all did. If anyone in their late 20s to late 40s tells you they didn't, they're either liars or geeks or both. It was what you did in high school, what you did in college. It was wrong, but so was driving drunk, which we have all done at one time or another. Some still do. And the damage to society from drunk driving is well documented. I know of at least two 500cc World Champions who tried cocaine.

I gave up the bong in my mid-teens for a very simple reason: I didn't enjoy it. If I liked it as much as, say, doughnuts, I wouldn't have quit, but I did. In my profession, the only danger from smoking pot is that you might lose track of the keyboard. I can imagine hacking away at a story in yet another strange hotel on Sunday night, stoned to the gills, and crying out to the editor, who's working on the other bed, "I can't find the 'Q,' dude."

What an Idiot

Ours is a low-risk sport, unlike racing. Racing is about a lot of things, paramount among them being trust. You have to trust that the guy going around the outside of you into turn one at Brainerd, on the rev-limiter in sixth gear, has full control of his faculties. The riders I spoke with about Anthony Gobert at Laguna Seca weren't so sure.

In my opinion, Anthony Gobert is an idiot. There's no getting around it. Anyone who would jeopardize his riding career by smoking dope, knowing full well that he was going to be tested, is an idiot - plain and simple.

A bit of history: For those who don't know, the reason Anthony Gobert is racing in the United States this year is that he failed a drug test about this time last year while racing a works Suzuki for the Lucky Strike Suzuki team. The test was administered on behalf of the Suzuki World Championship team. As at Laguna, he was told in advance - when he left the previous race in Brazil - that he would be tested when he arrived for the British Grand Prix. Not that he might be, but that he would be. And he was, and he failed with flying colors.

Much has been made of the fact that it was a team-administered test. The conspiracy nuts would like you to believe that it was all made up, that he didn't fail any test, that the Suzuki team was underperforming and they needed a reason to jettison him. That's crap.

Certainly there was tension in the team. Shouldn't there be if a multi-million dollar operation is relying on a kid who has already failed one urine test? The team had hired a former racer, Stu Avant, a New Zealander, to baby-sit Gobert. It may have been a good idea to them, but to Gobert it was an insult. He didn't need anyone watching over him. He could take care of himself. Apparently not. And the FIM agreed.

At the fall FIM congress in Athens, the Road Racing Commission (CCR), of which AMA road race manager Ron

Barrick is a member, passed a resolution under the heading of "Doping" specifically addressing Gobert. It said, in part, "In order to assure the riders who would be susceptible to run against Mr. Gobert in 1998, in the case where Mr. Gobert participates in an FIM Championship or Prize event, he should be controlled before the event, for the whole season."

In other words, we're protecting our riders from a threat.

Everyone knew he was going to be tested, and yet it came as no surprise that he failed. The unanimous response was, "What an idiot." This is a guy clawing his way back to the top, getting his one big chance to show the world, or at least the World team owners, that he belonged on the World stage - and he blew it. Saddest of all is that he does belong at the next level.

Anthony Gobert is an astonishing motorcycle racer. Even his harshest critics agree that he has a level of natural ability heretofore unseen. He can do things on a motorcycle others can only dream of. Like no one before him, he knows exactly how much he can coax out of a motorcycle, out of a situation. He goes fast and he doesn't crash. And he treats motorcycles well. I, among others, predicted he would win both races at Laguna Seca. If he made the grid.

It's not enough that he's fast, he also has a very engaging personality. In a sport where the recent champions have sometimes lacked charisma, he's the type of rider that people relate to: A beer-drinking yob who says what he thinks, then backs it up on the track. He's exceedingly polite to the fans and will sign autographs until the pen runs dry, then answer every press query politely, and pose for photos until the last camera's run out of film. This combination of personality and ability is rare, though Yamaha's Noriyuki Haga and the Italians Valentino Rossi and Max Biaggi come to mind.

Unlike them (at least the Italians), he doesn't care. He simply doesn't care. His world has nothing to do with our world. By his actions he seems to be saying that he is immortal, and if he gets kicked off the Vance & Hines team, he'll find someone else who wants him. The sad thing is, as long as he's fast, he'll have a job.

Ducati held a press conference the day after Gobert failed the drug test. Sharing the podium with Carl Fogarty, Troy Corser, Pier-Francesco Chili and Paolo Casoli were the owners of the four biggest Ducati teams - Terry Vance, Eraldo Ferracci, and the owners of the World Superbike teams, Davide Tardozzi and Virginio Ferrari. I asked them if they would sign Gobert, knowing he'd failed at least one drug test.

Ferrari was the first of the former racers to answer.

"I like very much Anthony because he's so fast," he said. "I don't know now what's happened about this really bad thing. We have to wait. Today Federico Minoli is there and you have to ask directly to the Ducati factory."

Notice he didn't say "no."

"Sure, I agree with Virginio," Tardozzi said. "Anthony is so fast. I really feel sorry for Terry (Vance). But regarding next year, it's not now the time to discuss about this. Sure Anthony's fast; maybe somebody will take him. I don't know. Ducati will discuss it."

Again, he didn't say no.

Ferracci said: "I have no comment. I'm too old to figure out that kind of stuff. I leave it alone."

And Vance didn't answer, but more than likely he'll do what Ducati tells him.

Is there a chance Gobert could get a ride with one of the Japanese factories? I tend to doubt it.

Even though that's what he lobbies for every time he's on the podium, which, because of his enormous talent, is mostly every race these days. The routine is that he thanks Vance for taking a chance on him, reminds the team of the times the bike has failed him, then says he wants to ride a 500cc Honda next year. I've talked to a number of Grand Prix team owners this year. They say the only way he could possibly get a 500 Honda is to lease one, and even that's speculative. Who'd take the chance of raising $4-5 million to base a team around a rider who has shown not the slightest hint of responsibility? And would Honda even allow him to lease bikes? Could he get a ride with Suzuki? I wouldn't think so. When Wayne Rainey was looking for riders for this year, and he had *carte blanche*, Gobert wasn't on his list. It's doubtful Yamaha would take the chance.

On Sunday afternoon a press release issued by Gobert showed up in the Laguna Seca press room. He said he "was just wrong, just plain wrong. I did have a smoke after Loudon in celebration, which I didn't realize would be considered a serious problem by the FIM.

Can he be serious? The riders think not.

To a man, they were outraged. They don't want to be on the track with someone using a banned, illegal substance. To be fair, smoking a joint 10 days before a race is not going to affect you come race day. You could get high the day before the race and it wouldn't show. That's not the point.

Because the AMA and Vance have chosen not to test Gobert (though both could at any time), we don't know if he has ever raced under the influence. I tend to think not. From what I know of Gobert, he takes the race weekend very seriously. It's the rest of the week he has a hard time with.

Gobert's mother, Sue, was quoted in the release as saying, "All he wants to do is put this behind him and regain the respect of the fans and fellow racers for the excellent rider and person that he really is."

Now it's up to the AMA and Terry Vance. Vance said he would test him this week and if he passed, he'd be on the bike at Mid-Ohio. More than one of his fellow competitors don't think he'll pass another test. He will likely be tested some time before every race.

If the AMA does nothing - which, given the sadly litigious times we live in, is a distinct possibility - then Gobert will have gotten away with one. Can the AMA react based on an FIM test? We don't know, even though the AMA races under the FIM umbrella.

At the very least he should pay his team back. He should ask Terry Vance how much it cost him to bring the team to Monterey and house and feed them, and then write him a check. He should ask Jim Leonard how many hundreds of man-hours he put into building the bike just for this race, building parts that can only be used in World Superbike competition, and in running the bike on the dyno for countless hours to get the most out of the mandated unleaded fuel. Then he should multiply the hours times $100 per, and write another check. He should find a way to make it up to the AMA and the fans, for disparaging the sport in front of the world. That's the easy part.

If he has a shred of common sense, he should seek counseling, and not just for what he may consider an isolated doping incident. He knows better. The team knows better. His fellow riders know better. The most widely abused drug in America is alcohol, and the people I know who saw him on Friday and Saturday nights said he appeared to have made the most of the night.

He is one more mistake away from being banned from racing altogether. As sad as that may be, it actually makes a lot of riders sick. They would give up anything to have an iota of his talent, to be able to do what he does routinely. They find it appalling that he treats his magnificent gift so cavalierly.

The guess here is that I'll see him at Mid-Ohio and every other AMA Superbike National. I also think he has a very good chance of winning the title. Muzzy Kawasaki's Doug Chandler is a few points ahead, but he hasn't won a race yet this year. Gobert's won three and has been on the box every time the Ducati holds together.

How does this sound? 1998 AMA/MBNA Superbike Champion - and drug-test failure - Anthony Gobert. Get used to it.

August 12, 1998

Aren't You Worried?

It's official.

With his latest infraction, HyperCycle Suzuki's Carry Andrew has now been caught cheating more than Frank Gifford, Marv Albert and Bill Clinton combined. Up until now he was the Energizer Bunny of cheaters: No matter how many times he got bent over Merrill Vanderslice's knee and spanked in public, he just kept cheating and cheating and cheating. This time, Suzuki decided they'd had enough and yanked his batteries, along with his bikes and everything else.

His is an impressive rap sheet. The straw that broke Suzuki's backbone was the illegal frame modifications that resulted in disqualifications for both race winner Nicky Hayden and second-place finisher Jason Pridmore from the Mid-Ohio race. Andrew was also fined $4000 for each frame violation. Hayden and Pridmore were also DQed from the 750cc Supersport race at Daytona, because metal had been removed from the cases. The fines added up to $5000. After Hayden won the 750cc Supersport race at Willow Spring, he was found to be using an illegal windscreen. That got Andrew suspended for the remainder of the 1998 season and fined $1000. Last year, Mark Miller was disqualified from both Brainerd and Road America for illegal head modifications. .

In the parlance of law enforcement, Andrew's a recidivist, given to habitual relapse into the dark abyss of mechanical chicanery, always on the prowl for innovative new ways in get caught bumbling. For the AMA tech inspectors, he's a living refresher course, someone they can count on to keep them sharp for the thousands of racers and mechanics who don't like wearing the scarlet letter.

Simple punishment didn't seem to bother him. He'd been banned from the racetracks, been fined thousands of dollars, had his riders humiliated and penalized, more or less had his team's championship hopes sautéed by his fraudulent ways, and shamed his Suzuki benefactors. You can whip him; just don't beat him, he seems to be saying. Not legally, anyhow. Not until he gets to tech. This last time, however, was too much for even Suzuki to pretend not to notice.

What cannot be denied is that his bikes win. Sure they're illegal, but everyone cheats, wink, wink, nod, nod, and he just has this amazing, uncanny, unfortunate capacity for getting nabbed. His bikes are so infused with the stench of cheating that you could blindfold the AMA techies and they could smell the bikes a mile away.

He has certainly cost Jason Pridmore a chance at the 750cc Supersport title this year and the bonus that goes with it. He has cost Nicky Hayden dearly as well. At some point he's going to run out of riders. Guys are just going to get tired of handing trophies and purses back, offering apologies, and making excuses. So he's going to need riders. That's where I come in.

I've never raced a motorcycle in my life. I'm old and slow. I have two choices: I can either race sidecars or I can go to Carry. And given my recent position on sidecars, I'm guessing it'd be hard to get a good sidecar ride these days, if such a beast even exists. On a level playing field, I would have no chance of finishing a race without being lapped at least three times on a normal track, six times or more at Loudon. My only chance is cheating, and there's only one place to go for that.

Getting to that place isn't as easy as it would seem. Since the AMA banned him from the racetrack, to find Andrew you need to scour the hotels near the track where he has holed up, fielding phone calls from the team. I tracked him down and arrived just as he was taking a call from one of his riders.

"What do you mean, when you get on the gas it's stuttering? Mel Tillis stutters. Porky the Pig stutters. Motorcycles don't stutter. Call me back when you know what it's doing."

Before we started talking racing, I asked how devastating it was to be banned from the track.

"Devastating? What, are you kidding me? I love it. I can sit in my air-conditioned room all day ordering room service and watching pay-per-view movies on Spectravision. I've already seen 'Shaving Private Ryan' eight times. 'Arma-get-it-on' starts tomorrow. Do you know how hard it is to get a decent meal at a racetrack? At Mid-Ohio you have to get in line at the crack of dawn just to get a chicken sandwich by noon."

Just then there was a knock on the door.

"Room service," the porter announced, ushering in a lavish spread of shrimp cocktail, vichyssoise, blackened North Sea Salmon on a bed of wilted spinach and fried sweet potato strings, a fine '84 Bordeaux (nutty, but coquettish in a slutty sort of way), a Black Forest gateau, and cappuccino. Like me, he was salivating, but it wasn't the food that impressed him - it was the cart.

Thinking out loud, he said, "I've got enough carbon fiber in the car to replace the trays. We can put 78mm Kryptonics Diablo skate wheels, with BSB ABEC 7 bearings, on it, and shorten the supports by 50mm. You'll be able to get the food to the rooms in half the time."

"Dude," the porter said. "Whatever, dude," he added, staring at the single-digit tip and wondering how he was going to put his future children through college.

With the distractions gone, we got down to business - the business of my racing career. Because I'd never raced before, we agreed that I should start in the 600cc Supersport class.

"Let's start with the engine," I said, "What do we do with the engine?"

"Replace it," Andrew said, making me think he was going to slip in a blue-printed mill direct from Japan. "We'll stick a 750 motor in it."

Suddenly it became clear why he got caught so often.

"Aren't you a little worried about that?" I asked.

"Not at all. We'll pump it up to 840cc with a set of 3mm-over pistons. It'll be one flying son of a bitch."

"What I mean is, aren't you worried about getting caught?"

"Do I look like Alfred E. Neuman? Have I ever worried about being caught in the past?"

At that point the chambermaid knocked, pushing her cleaning cart into the room. His eyes lit up.

Seeing the possibilities, he said to the young lady, "I can chamfer the edges of the wheels, weave a Kevlar bag for the dirty linen, and put a graphite push bar on it. You'll be able to finish your rounds in half the time and your boss will never know."

"Oh, that's sweet. I get paid by the hour and you want to cut my time in half. Are you trying to get me kicked out? Thanks, but no thanks."

"You were saying..."

"The only way I'm going to get caught is if you win. You ain't winning."

"Why not?"

"The nitrous-oxide system has a few bugs in it."

"What nitrous system?"

"The one hidden in the fuel tank. We run the nitrous lines inside the fuel lines to the carbs. If they ask why the fuel lines are the size of a fire hose, just shrug and mumble. It works three times out of 10."

"Does that leave enough room in the tank for fuel?"

"Normally, no, but we have an auxiliary fuel tank in the airbox. Holds about a gallon. Should be enough."

"How does that affect airflow?"

"The blower takes care of the air-flow."

"What blower?"

"The one hidden in the frame rails."

"Doesn't that weaken the frame?"

"Only if you crash."

The phone rang again.

"What do you mean, it's chattering? You think you race on a pool table? Is the little itsy-bitsy bump bothering you? You don't think Kenny Roberts or Mike Hailwood ever rode through bumpy corners? Get a grip, pretty boy!"

Getting back to my problems, I asked, "What about tires?"

"We'll go with slicks."

"Aren't they illegal?" I asked, knowing the answer before the words were out of my mouth.

"We don't start with slicks. We start with DOTs. Then we shave the tread to about an eighth of an inch. You can get rid of whatever tread's left with your start-line burn-out. After that the tires'll be slicker than an outhouse floor."

"And that's a good thing? What about aerodynamics?"

"No problem. Retractable windscreen supports. When you start the race you'll be able to cut the air better than the second runner-up at a chili-eating contest."

"I know that's not a good thing."

"As you're pulling in, pull the cotter pin on the supports and the 3-inch hump in the fairing flattens out like Elvis's EKG."

"Is there anything we're forgetting?"

Just as he was about to answer, the gardener pushed his lawn mower under our window. The lure was too great. He was out the door in a flash.

"First we grind the fins down, then we deck the head to lower the compression, then we stick in a racing plug and fill the tank with av-gas, then we put a Vance & Hines pipe on it, then we coat the underside with Teflon so the grass doesn't stick, then we fill the plastic wheels with helium, then..."

After watching him feverishly work over the lawn mower for half an hour, measuring, calibrating, scheming, I left. I'm not sure when I'll make my way to the track, but I'd be willing to bet good folding green that its going to be a long time before he makes his.

September 23, 1998

The Department of Racetrack Approval

If we learned anything from the recent fiasco at the Joliet AMA Superbike National, it's that whoever approved the track is dopier than a Gobert urine sample (pre-rehab). The place wasn't safe enough for a demolition derby, let alone a road race National, and anyone who thinks otherwise is wackier than the road race points system.

(What must be said up front is that the promoter of Joliet should not be held to blame. No one told him that you couldn't put the start-finish line in the middle of a concrete-lined, fourth-gear kink. You'd have thought someone at the AMA might have mentioned it to him, but they were busy collecting the smoke and mirrors they'd brought in to try to make the place appear race-worthy.)

But with every dark cloud - and this one followed all the teams from Brainerd, Minnesota, and made them sit on their hands for most of a week in Joliet, running up hotel, restaurant, and pay-per-view movie tabs, not to mention exorbitant gambling debts at the riverboat blackjack table, where calculators aren't allowed - there is a silver lining, and the silver lining in this debacle is that I realized that anyone can promote a road race.

It turns out that all you need to get a road race National is a piece of unused land near a big city. Witness the recent additions in the calendar: Pikes Peak, Las Vegas, Road Atlanta, and Joliet. That way, when you cancel the thing - because 90 percent of the corners have less runoff than a bowling alley, the drag strip is covered in traction compound that gets slicker than a president when it's wet, and the entrance to the drag strip is tighter than (take your pick) Thomas Stevens, Terry Vance or Rob Muzzy - you can forever piss off and alienate a much larger group of disgruntled ex-fans than you could in a small market. It's sound logic: Maximize your disappointment.

I found a spot of unused land and I have a phone. Time to promote.

Since all of the AMA motocross and dirt track schedules have already been set, I knew I had to work fast. After all, the road race calendar will probably be announced within months. So I called the AMA's department of racetrack approval. Turns out my timing wasn't great.

Moe was out at lunch, Larry was at the doctor after getting poked in the eye, and Curly was getting a buzz cut. Well down the food chain, I was passed on to Ron Vandermerrill, the AMA's Associate Sub-Supervisor for Asphalt Calamities.

I began by saying that I'd found a piece of land in Eyebrow, Saskatchewan, where I was thinking of promoting a road race.

"What I wanted to know was..."

"Is it near a big city?" the effervescent Ron asked before I could finish my sentence.

"Well, it's about 30 miles from Moose Jaw."

"Close enough. What date do you want?"

"Aren't you going to ask about the facility?"

"Didn't I ask if it was near a big city?"

"Yeah."

"Is it?"

"Well, it's about 80 miles from Assiniboia."

"Close enough. Now let's talk date."

"Before we get started, I think I feel I have an obligation to tell you that the land was recently reclaimed after being sealed for over 30 years as a nuclear waste dump."

"Does it have a drag strip?"

The Department of Race Track Approval

"It's mostly barren wasteland with a few rusted backhoes and some eight-headed frogs."

"Can you put a drag strip on it?"

"I could put all of Delaware on it."

"Because we need a drag strip."

"Why's that?"

"Bracket racing."

"I'm looking to promote a road race."

"But how do you fill the time between races? Not another wheelie weirdo. Bracket racing! Anyone who rides to the track gets to race. We'll have Valkyries against Valkyries, Intruders vs. Intruders, Fat Boys against Fat Girls. We'll have two classes - gas and alcohol."

"But street bikes don't run on alcohol."

"Who's talking about the street bikes? It'll be a class for riders who've had five or more brewskies. We'll urine-test the winner to make sure he's not sober."

"Isn't that unsafe?"

"No, we'll make sure he has a big enough container so he doesn't get any on his shoes."

"Isn't allowing drunks to drag-race unsafe?"

"Describe unsafe."

"Unsafe would be a condition which could conceivably cause harm to the participants."

"They're drunk, they won't feel anything. Besides, didn't you say Smuts was 110 miles away?"

"I didn't, but it is."

"I'm sure they've got a hospital there."

"Can I show you the layout?"

"It's pretty straightforward: a quarter mile, dead straight and level, a short uphill, then sand."

"For the road course."

"Oh."

"This is the tentative layout, pending your approval."

"Looks good to me. Do you want a date before or after Daytona?"

"We're getting ahead of ourselves. You see these? I've drawn the runoff areas. They're marked by waves, indicating raked gravel traps."

"Gravel? Gravel never slowed a bike down. It just tears them up. No, we at the Road Racetrack-Approval Committee commissioned a blue-ribbon panel of experts to do an extensive study on the proper material for runoffs and, after months of exhaustive research, and a not inconsiderable expenditure, they came to the conclusion that there's only one substance which can effectively stop a motorcycle, without doing it, or the rider, any damage, and is environmentally friendly."

"And that would be…"

"Mashed potatoes."

"Mashed potatoes?"

"Is there an echo in here? Yes, mashed potatoes."

"Why mashed potatoes?"

"Well, we considered French fries, but we'd have needed a grease fryer the size of the Astrodome. And, besides, we think there are significant marketing opportunities in mashed potatoes. Each corner will be sponsored by a different company. We'll have the Idaho Spuds Esses, the Hungry Jack Hairpin, the Kroger Kink."

"So if a rider tells me, 'Dude, I went into Betty Crocker so deep I thought I'd never get out,' it means he overshot the corner?"

"Does Betty Crocker make mashed potatoes?"

"I think so."

"Probably. How long's the track?"

"About four miles."

"Sound like you'll need a heap o' taters. Let me do the math. Hmm, that would be 400,000 pounds of spuds."

"Do you have any idea where you can get that many potatoes?"
"Is the track near a big city?"
"Climax is about 150 miles away."
"Can't wait to get there."
"So I've heard."

(The author would like to acknowledge the government of the Canadian province of Saskatchewan for their invaluable help in naming their towns so colorfully. Without them, the author would have had to find some other place to make fun of.)

February 3, 1999

It's Good to Be the King

The King, of course, is the man who holds three 500cc World Championships and two AMA Grand National Championships. He is the team owner with three 500cc World Championships and a 250cc title to his credit. On the days when he is not trying to recapture the 500cc World-Championship, and deciding whether he needs to build a four-cylinder Modenas, he is a World Champion dispenser of wisdom, abuse and crap, depending on the immediate need and company. On this bitterly cold January day, at his ranch in the appropriately named megalopolis of Hickman, California, the crap was piling up faster than Modenas parts invoices.

"You can always tell if Kenny likes you by how much crap he gives you," Randy Mamola, Kenny Roberts' former rival, former rider, longtime friend, one-time ranch regular and current test rider told me recently. Today's target is Mike Hale, but, as always, there was a reason.

Hale, who's made worse career choices than Shelley Long, David Lee Roth and McLean Stevenson combined (yes, I remember that I picked him to win the AMA Superbike title last year), was in the unfortunate position of being the least fast of the fast guys at the ranch. Yet he was happy to be there. The Texan was there because he'd been tapped by Roberts as the potential second rider of the Modenas KR-3, and the King wanted him to be in shape when they went testing in Australia and Malaysia. The tests are something of a tryout, and, if Hale passes, he'll finally reach every road racer's goal of being in the World Championships on a 500cc motorcycle. Or at least a Modenas.

The 160-acre Ranch (with a capital "R"), which Roberts bought in 1985, is the nearly mythical place to which riders of all skill levels peregrinate to learn the subtleties of dirt tracking while simultaneously being humiliated by various members of the Roberts family. They make the pilgrimage so they can shoot at stuff. They go to eat very well, get the royal treatment and bathe in the aura of the Kingdom.

The day before I arrived this year, Steve Crevier was training with Kurtis Roberts and Hale. A day later, the King, Hale and Kenny Roberts Jr. were joined by the latter's Suzuki GP teammate, Nobuatsu Aoki.

"He's probably not going to be sitting up on the seat far enough, putting enough weight on the front, or (he will) have his leg in the wrong position, so he'll push the front and crash," the prescient younger Roberts said.

The TT course, one of several tracks on the spread, is where most of the training on the Honda XR-100s takes place. Among the fast guys, this is as deadly serious as any race anywhere and it's clear who's the best: Kenny Roberts. Junior.

"If my dad spent a serious month riding, he could easily get back to what he used to be, which would be the same as me," Junior accurately says with no trace of conceit.

Junior is the best because he's been doing this since birth, because he's raced the best here, because he's finally training like he must if he wants to win GPs, and because he has good genes. He wasn't always the best, and word is that he broke his arm once trying to keep up with an interloper, but now it's no contest.

Roberts Jr. grew up at the right time, getting the chance to ride with his dad and Wayne Rainey, in his prime.

"I've always hated to think that I couldn't do anything on a motorcycle that they could do better," Junior said. "I was lighter and I was 15 and I knew I was better than Wayne, even though he was World Champion, but I knew I could ride a 100. They would come out and they would always pull me that little bit and eventually get, in five laps, three or four bike lengths. And I could always see my dad and Wayne battle it out there and I never stopped getting faster."

Junior respects and admires his father, but he gives him no quarter and expects none back, and when they go into a corner side by side, his dad treats him like Gary Scott.

"It's a way of life," Roberts the elder said during a break in the action, which Junior interpreted as a sign of concession.

"You're not breathing heavy, are you?" Junior asked insolently, adding, "That thing's so fast that you're rolling out of it on the straights."

Once they get going, they're loathe to stop. A pattern quickly emerges: Roberts, Junior and Hale join up at some point on the TT track. (Forget Aoki – just as Junior predicted, he's busy pushing the front end of the XR-120 into the berms and tipping over like an arthritic stork.) Junior can make any line work and gets the 100 turned faster than anyone. Outside or inside, it doesn't matter. Time and again, Junior would prevail after a number of laps, his dad would never concede, and Hale was left in their wake. Hale took his turn leading, and within one lap Roberts and Junior were on him, he ran wide in the left leading to the TT jump, and the Roberts boys scooted past. In fairness to Hale, this was only his second day at the ranch, he didn't have the best equipment, and he hadn't been racing since July.

Back at the garage, which is filled with enough motorcycles and memorabilia - a proclamation of Roberts' 1978 500cc World Championship hangs on one wall - to fill a museum, and enough mechanical equipment, including a dyno, to outfit a race shop, there was a short break for maintenance. Hale had earlier changed the shock on his bike, replacing the stocker with the de rigueur Works Performance unit, and now he's flopping the rear knobby so that it has a sharp edge.

"You gonna puncture that tube like the other one?" Roberts badgers, later offering that "it's going to make a difference."

"I'm going to start kicking some ass now," Hale answers.

"Not that big a difference," counters the King, and he's right.

They're quickly back at it, a few other friends joining in. Another unwritten rule is that if you go to the ranch, you will be invited to ride, regardless of age, ability or outstanding medical disorder. When Roberts asked if I wanted to have a go, I politely declined by saying that: (a) he didn't have a size 15 hotshoe; (b) I was slower than John Kocinski reaching for a dinner check; and (c) he'd need the "Jaws of Life" to get the XR out of my ass at the end of the day.

Back on the track, Junior lets Aoki go, catches up, then reaches over on the straight and grabs him somewhere high enough on the thigh to get him cited for offensive touching in either Sodom or Gomorrah.

"It's not something you can learn in three or four days," Roberts the elder says.

Aoki rides like the road racer he is, going deep - too deep - into the corner, tracking all the way, nearly stopping, then leaning to get it turned. Too often, he gets on the gas early, the front pushes, and occasionally he goes down. By the end of the day he will have made a small bit of progress and he will have a very sore left leg.

"I try to stay with Junior, but not so easy," Aoki admits with a smile.

When Roberts passes Hale, you can hear the laughter and profanity-laced tirade for miles.

"His bike's got a cam and a head job so he has the torque to keep it stepped out and get through the ruts," Hale says. "Plus, he hauls ass."

With the responsibility of building and racing a new motorcycle, Roberts hasn't been able to enjoy this kind of riding very much lately. He says he's ridden more this winter than he has for the past three years and will keep at it as long as he can. He looks fitter and less haggard than he has for a couple of seasons. This is what he was meant to do. This is what he loves to do. As Junior told me the night before, "If there's one thing that somebody is made to do in life, that was his perfect, ideal situation - not the Modenas, but racing motorcycles and being a team owner."

February 24, 1999

Predictions

When I get old I will leave the house without pants. People will stare, children will point, there will be commensurate embarrassment. The sad truth is that it has already begun.

This past year - rather, the second half of this past year - I left the house without pants. Mechanics stared, riders pointed. Reading lips, I could see them saying, "He's the one who picked Mike Hale to win the AMA Superbike Championship." I have lived with the choice for a year and now it's time to try to explain myself.

The prediction wasn't made using a Ouija board or a dart board. My record speaks for itself. I'd correctly chosen Muzzy Kawasaki's Doug Chandler to win the title the two previous years, in 1996 and '97, the first pundit in the history of the *Cycle News* pickers to accurately choose the champ in consecutive years. Maybe it went to my head. Or my pants.

I should have stayed with Chandler in 1998, but I thought his luck was about to run out. Chandler had had two nearly dream years with only a single failure at a crucial time, that coming at Brainerd in 1997. He was overdue. The first stroke of misfortune struck at the Laguna Seca World Superbike race, where a clip-on - which was built in-house, as opposed to the works item available through Kawasaki - broke entering the Corkscrew. The resulting crash was horrific, though Chandler escaped serious injury. Still, he was beaten up enough that his performance at Mid-Ohio and, to a lesser extent, Brainerd suffered. Valuable points were lost. Then came the engine failure at Las Vegas that truly sealed his fate. That he finished the year in second speaks volumes about his tenacity.

I had thought to choose American Honda's Miguel DuHamel but was convinced he would do something silly. He didn't disappoint. First came the spill while chasing race winner Scott Russell early in the Daytona 200. Then came the awful wet-track crash into the turn-one wall at Loudon. In better conditions, with more concern for rider safety, he would have walked away. As it was, DuHamel severely broke his leg and will still be recovering when the green flag drops for this year's Daytona 200.

Hale had come off a year where he struggled on the Suzuki World Superbike team - not a surprise, given who was running the squad. His results were generally consistent, though not great. He'd included a provision in his contract for a test on the Suzuki RGV-500 Grand Prix bike at the end of the season. The test was in Australia and it went brilliantly. His times were impressive and constant. Garry Taylor, Suzuki's GP boss, wanted to hire him. Having lost Lucky Strike as a sponsor at the end of the 1997 season, Taylor had no leverage and was forced to hire two Japanese riders. The 1998 season was probably the worst ever for the Suzuki 500cc GP team.

In preseason testing, Hale was fast on the Fast By Ferracci Ducati, the team he ended up signing with. He went well at Willow Springs and Las Vegas - impressively well - and, hearing that, I made him my pick. Added to that was the more direct involvement of Michelin, which hadn't looked so good in 1997. Even though Mat Mladin won four races on Ferracci's Ducati, he was let down by tires more than once. Part of it, Mladin is convinced, was Eraldo Ferracci's fault for not asking Michelin for the best World Superbike product. For 1998, Michelin re-dedicated their efforts with their most ambitious testing program ever.

So I chose Hale, and things looked good until he crashed the magic bike in practice for the first race in Phoenix. The magic bike was an ex-works Ducati that went particularly well - vertically, it turned out, as well as in a straight line. Once Hale destroyed that bike in a vicious high-side, his season was irreversibly doomed. He had no faith in the front end of the Ducati and nothing could change that. It was downhill from there, and both sides came to a sensible dissolution after Hale crashed in practice at the midseason Loudon race. Needless to say, he did not make me a three-time winner.

This year, the smart choice is Mat Mladin, at least according to his peers, and who knows better? I had the idea that *Cycle News* should ask the Superbike riders themselves to pick the top 10 this year. Though we didn't get to all of the factory riders, we got to most, and the consensus choice was Mladin, and why not? He's smart, he's fast, he's fit, he's experienced, he doesn't crash, and he works his ass off. His Achilles' heel last year was the team, from which he tried to separate himself by making his own team within a team. Unfortunately, not everyone on the team was up to snuff, which is why he had an engine failure at Loudon that likely cost him the title. That engine builder is gone, replaced by one who is thought of very highly. Also, the team has been making steady progress on the fuel-injected GSX-R750, which can only add to his already-impressive package. So I picked him second.

My choice for the championship is Eric Bostrom. Watching him win at Brainerd and Pikes Peak last year was almost as impressive as the credit he gave to the bike afterward. Bostrom knows he's but one part of a team that is totally committed to winning, and he doesn't take it for granted. He works as hard as anyone, both on the track and off, and is relentless in his quest for perfection. Winning spot races as a stand-in is considerably different from being in a championship chase for the world's largest motorcycle manufacturer. Bostrom knows this. But he's a big-picture rider and sensible enough not to get in over his head. There will be tracks that will confound him. This winter, he struggled in his Superbike tests at Laguna Seca. Over the course of the season, I think he can work through the bad and amplify the good and, at the end of the year, a Bostrom will again wear the number-one crown.

Behind Mladin I put Chandler, because he's Chandler and he'll always be there. He backed the team into a corner this year with the very serious threat of defecting to Fast By Ferracci, and he might have, except that the FBF offer was about half of what he'll make with Kawasaki. In exchange, Chandler got some assurances that things will be better, though neither he nor the team has been more forthcoming with details. Gary Medley, his longtime mechanic, is gone, replaced by Nick Davies, someone Chandler feels will bring new enthusiasm to the team.

I picked the Vance & Hines Ducatis of Ben Bostrom and Anthony Gobert fourth and fifth, respectively, and not because of their abilities, but because of the limitations of the equipment. Of the 10 races in which Gobert competed, he won three. More importantly, mechanical problems took him out of contention in three others - Daytona, Sears Point and Las Vegas. A 30-percent failure rate doesn't cut it in this company, and there could easily have been another failure in one of the three races he missed after he failed a drug test prior to Mid-Ohio. It's not because Gobert's hard on equipment, either. Team owner Terry Vance says that Gobert treats his machinery well.

According to Vance, this year's equipment will be much improved and will come directly from the factory. After some initial problems at Daytona, it's been reliable. On RC45 Hondas, Gobert would be the pick. On Ducatis, there's a question mark.

What has been openly debated is whether Gobert will have a dope relapse. After what Vance has done for him, I can't imagine that he'd do anything so silly and damaging to his career. Knowing that he'll be tested at every race guarantees that Gobert will be constantly reminded of the consequences.

Watching the riders struggle with their picks, especially midpack, reaffirmed my belief in the depth of this year's field.

From sixth on down it's a nearly complete crap shoot, with a few mitigating factors.

How well will Aaron Yates adapt to the Kawasaki after a career on Suzukis. He's always shown bursts of speed, but he hasn't yet been able to sustain it. The health of Miguel DuHamel and Yamaha's Jamie Hacking, a rider not heard from in months, is still in doubt. The new Yamaha R-7s: Are they any good, and how hard will it be for Rich Oliver to develop them during the racing season? They certainly won't be at Daytona. How well will the much-improved Harleys hold up under Scott Russell? And, after a disappointing was season, does the Georgian still have the fire in the belly?

It won't be until the beginning of October that many of these questions will be answered and I'll know whether or not I'm wearing pants.

March 17, 1999

It's Always Something

The saga at this year's Daytona 200 belongs to our friends in orange and black and blue, Harley-Davidson and the man they hired to win the most prestigious race in America, Scott "Mr. Daytona" Russell.

The Georgian came to Daytona with the vision that he could win his sixth Daytona 200 on the perennially troublesome VR1000. He left with blurred vision after what was described by Harley-Davidson in an unfortunately belated press release as an "altercation in a Daytona Beach nightclub" on Thursday night.

The Daytona Beach police responded to the two calls at Razzles, the establishment on Seabreeze Boulevard where Georgians make their annual bar-fight pilgrimage - Aaron Yates was assaulted in the same establishment last year - at 1:24 a.m. and 1:44 a.m., according to the Daytona Beach News-Journal reporter who investigated the incident. So it was more like Friday when Russell joined the peanut shells and bottle caps on the floor.

The first sign that something was amiss was Friday's late-morning practice. Both of the number "4" VR1000s were prepped and ready to go; the same couldn't be said for the rider who didn't make it out in that session, or the one after, or the one after that, or the race.

The first report out of the Harley camp was that Russell had a sore throat, a plausible theory to anyone who'd heard his raspy voice on Thursday, but less plausible to the cynical masses huddled in the press room. As the editor of *Cycle News* posited, his throat was sore because he'd been hit so hard that he swallowed his nose.

Even before Harley finally came clean, the air in the pits was replete with enough rumors to fill an entire road racing monthly, and then some.

It began when an anonymous team owner asked me, "What do you hear about Russell?"

"Haven't heard a thing, Terry," I told him. "What've you heard?"

"Bad things," he said, and nothing more. That tingled my investigative reporter's antennae, and I began my search for the truth.

The best place to start would be the Harley garage, I thought, so I headed straight for the press room, where I was certain I'd find more conspiracy theories than in Oliver Stone's complete oeuvre. And these are a few of the things I was told: Russell had been in a bar fight with either a Yamaha hooligan, who took offense at Russell's switching camps, or his future brother- or brothers-in-law, or a black guy (a rumor which was dismissed before word reached Johnnie Cochran), or just some guy who jumped out of the crowd and sucker-punched him - there were two versions of this story: one had brass knuckles, the other didn't - then belted him a few more times while he was on the ground and his posse stood in mute admiration, not, as the kids say, watching his back.

Since I didn't speak to Russell himself - no one I know has - my best guess is that it was one punch that came out of nowhere and took him down. I'd even heard he was on his way out of the place when had things started happening, precipitated by someone other than the phantom pugilist. This would be the Lone Puncher Theory.

The injuries were described as either a swollen eye or a shattered cheekbone or fluid into or out of the eye or a broken jaw or a detached retina (the last of which would certainly have kept him from racing for a while), or any combination of the above.

He would, it was certain, either be fit to race the Daytona 200 or unable to put his helmet on because it didn't fit that well, or unfit to race in Phoenix in two weeks because of the detached retina, or in need of an operation, or we don't know - what've you heard? Again, the best guess would be that, if he did have a shattered cheekbone and needed reconstructive surgery, 10 days is an awfully short amount of time to squeeze your head into a helmet. In hindsight, what he should have done is strap the helmet on immediately, a move which would have inhibited the swelling and guaranteed that he could race in two weeks. In further hindsight, he should have worn the helmet into the bar.

The gossip continued: He was dragged from the nightclub and taken immediately to the hospital and then back to his hotel room, only to return to the hospital for a CAT scan later in the day, when it was determined that he would need an operation to reconstruct two bones in his face which had been broken.

Some of this was cleared up in the release that Harley-Davidson issued, and more was cleared up by journalists who visited the Harley camp. My best guess here is that they, like everyone else, were being kept entirely in the dark. Given the condition of his throat, the notion that he'd have to visit a hospital was entirely reasonable. Once the facts became clear, the team issued a press release about the incident, which included a quote from Russell wishing his teammate Pascal Picotte well in the 200.

It was not a model response to a crisis. The model had been made by Terry Vance, the owner of the Ducati team for which Anthony Gobert was riding when he tested positive for marijuana at last year's Laguna Seca World Superbike race. Vance issued a brief statement at the time, never ducked the truth, and still doesn't. Neither did Gobert, who, after getting his own less-accurate tests, admitted to smoking pot. What Vance knew, and what it appeared Harley seemed to overlook (even though that likely wasn't the case), is that the truth will almost certainly prevail.

If it's true the team wasn't given the full truth, Russell not only hurt himself, but he damaged the team's credibility.

Regardless of what happened in the nightclub - whether he was sucker-punched or whether it was provoked - one thing which Russell's fellow competitors agreed on is that he shouldn't have put himself in the position for this to happen.

The reason that riders like Doug Chandler and Miguel DuHamel and Mat Mladin and the Bostroms and Pascal Picotte and all the others don't get beaten up in bars is that they know the reason they've been flown to a race is to win the race, and winning the race means being prepared - and being prepared doesn't involve overnight trips to bars.

Not that this was Russell's first run-in during Speed Week. Two years ago, he was involved in a minor incident that clearly wasn't his fault, according to everyone involved. Still, he was forced to spend a night in jail just a few days before the 200. He won that race and he's won from the back row of the third wave and he's won after falling down, but he's never won from an emergency room and he didn't this year.

The Daytona 200 is his season's biggest race - bigger still for Harley, which had worked all winter to give Russell a machine he thought he could win on, spending more time and money than ever before. Harley's most famous son and designer, Willie G. Davidson, was at the race, as always, but more of a presence in the pits than usual, and in the company of Jeff L. Bleustein, Harley's chairman and CEO.

The team was ecstatic that they'd picked up a five-year sponsorship deal from Ford, a commitment that would give them the capital needed to proceed with much-needed development on the rapidly aging VR1000, a motorcycle which has never been very competitive and gets less so with each passing year. Among the many rumors birthed by the Russell incident was that Ford would be sending executives to the race to watch their investment in action. This was among the more-unconfirmed rumors.

The Speedway that has treated Russell so well over the years was excited about his presence. For years they've been wondering how to get the Great Unwashed from Main Street to the grandstands. This year they advertised heavily in the local paper, with photos of Russell on the Harley, on the radio, and on television. Daytona doesn't release crowd figures, but the stands and infield looked a little fuller to me.

Even before Russell's fateful sojourn into the night, things weren't well in the Harley camp. In Wednesday's first 90-minute practice session, he made a total of about four laps - the bike was bedeviled by continuing problems with a new - but unfortunately not yet improved, as it turned out - fuel-injection system. Had he made the race, who knows what might have happened? Judging from the results of teammate Pascal Picotte, nothing good.

The French Canadian, who's been vocally unhappy about the pace of progress, hit a false neutral downshifting for turn one after he'd blown by the Muzzy Kawasaki of Doug Chandler. The ensuing crash left him bruised and battered, but nothing more, and he'll be ready for Phoenix in two weeks, as he was for Daytona. It wasn't his first trip down the road during Speed Week. A stuck throttle had earlier thrown him down.

In a very unscientific poll taken of the riders during the December Dunlop tire test, all thought Russell would put the VR on the podium this year, and a surprising number thought he could win a race.

Who will ride at Phoenix? Thomas Wilson was at Daytona, looking fully recovered from the horrific injuries he suffered in turn one at Loudon about eight months ago. When I asked him if he'd ride Phoenix, before Russell's incident, he answered, "Ask Steve," meaning team manager Steve Scheibe. Now Wilson may get a chance.

Don't expect much. After all, he suffered devastating injuries last year - injuries some thought had ended his career - and he's ridden very little since then. To expect him to come in and race a motorcycle after such a long layoff, let alone win - now that would certainly take a more than superhuman effort.

March 31, 1999

Putting Riders in Harm's Way

"Those who cannot remember the past are condemned to repeat it."
                                                         GEORGE SANTAYANA

When the fifth Medivac helicopter of the weekend lifted off from the infield of Phoenix International Raceway, conveying yet another unfortunate innocent to a distant hospital, I was reminded not only of the Santayana quote, but my first trip to this facility about six years ago, and, sadly, how little had changed.

What should certainly be the final race at Phoenix International Raceway, unless all sense of decency and outrage is ignored - a distinct possibility these days - was a catastrophic mess which put an ugly face on a wonderful though dangerous sport.

Motorcycle racing is dangerous. No one would dispute that. Every racetrack has its glaring faults. If you race long enough you will fall down and if you fall down you will very likely get hurt. The extent of those injuries can be controlled with a little common sense and planning, neither of which was in great supply on an otherwise glorious, sun-filled weekend in the Southwest desert.

By my count there were five incidents that required the use of a helicopter to transport riders. Part of the reason the helicopter was used, I was told by a race official, was simply the distance to the hospital, and not necessarily the severity of the injuries. That may well be, but seeing a chopper fly in over the foothills, accompanied by the eerie silence of a racetrack devoid of activity except for the transport of human tragedy, made an indelible impression on not only the fans - a handful on Saturday and 5000 or so on Sunday -

but also the riders. One rider said there should be a limit: Three Medivac trips and the race is called off.

The reason the helicopter needed to be called is that the racetrack is irredeemably unsafe. Nothing short of a complete leveling and redesign could help the place, though the promoter is on record as saying he's willing to do whatever it takes to get the race back. We'll see how sincere he is. There are inherent hazards that no amount of hay bales and air fence can fix - not that some effort wasn't made.

The first time the race was run was even worse. In 1993, inclement weather led to a wet track, which led to a rider revolt of sorts. Riding, never mind racing, through the banked oval turns three and four on a wet track was undeniably suicidal. A small group of 250cc riders, among them Jimmy Filice and Chris D'Aluisio, made an effort to educate the rest of the class. For his efforts, Filice was "told his actions were the sort of thing that could shorten his career," I wrote at the time in a guest editorial in *Cycle News*. It struck a nerve with the AMA, who responded with a strongly worded letter, then paid a visit to the *CN* headquarters in Long Beach. Ironically, it was their AMA president Ed Youngblood and then road race manager Roger Edmondson, the defendant and plaintiff in Edmondson's recent lawsuit against the AMA, who came calling. What are the odds of that happening again? What were the odds of the race happening again? Pretty good, as it turned out, because we were back a year later.

In the past year, rider safety has finally become a more central issue. That it took catastrophic injuries to riders such as American Honda's Miguel DuHamel and Harley-Davidson's Thomas Wilson at last year's Loudon race is shameful. Loudon has responded by extensively reworking the design of the track, doing whatever if takes to ensure the continued survival of their event. Turn one claimed DuHamel and Wilson last year and has been reworked. Will it be enough? As one rider told me, "So they shortened the straightaway by 50 feet. That means you'll hit the wall at 140 mph instead of 143."

The final verdict on Loudon won't be in for a couple of months, but you can't fault the track for trying. They consulted with the AMA TRAC committee, which is responsible for circuit safety, before making changes. And no one doubts that they'll spend whatever it takes to make certain of the 76th running of the Loudon Classic. Whether all the money and good intention in the world will save the race remains to be seen. Of more immediate concern is what happened at Phoenix.

Everyone at the track, riders and team owners alike, was, or should have been, appalled. Some spoke on the record, others more casually. Among the more outspoken was Jason Pridmore, a rider who teaches rider safety and one who has suffered his share of injuries.

"We're not getting any protection from the people who are supposed to protect us," Pridmore said while watching the Formula Xtreme debacle on Saturday. "Our purses suck and they take us to shit places like this. It's not good. They're going to come out with the standard excuse of, 'Well, no one's ever crashed there before and that's why it wasn't hay-baled.' Now they've got a guy who's getting helicoptered out of here because there's no hay bales. I don't know how many more times it's going to be before somebody gets killed or whatever, but it's sad, really sad. You can't race at a place like this, it's more of a survival thing."

Pridmore said that he'd taken part in an exhibition event at Phoenix prior to a car race back in 1992. Way back then, he made recommendations, none of which were followed, he said. Part of the problem is track ownership. At the time, the track was under different management. It's currently owned by the International Speedway Corporation, the company that owns Daytona International Speedway and a number of other tracks.

Canadian Michael Taylor crashed into an unprotected concrete barrier outside of turn four in Formula Xtreme practice. It wasn't the sort of place you'd expect someone to crash, but safety concerns have to account for the unexpected and in this case the system failed. Why was that? Just beyond where he crashed his way into a helicopter ride, there were three rows of hay bales. Whose job was it to place the bales further down the track?

The short answer is that it's the AMA's job. In this case, however, they'd done a track inspection with a couple of veteran riders and no recommendation was made to make any improvements to that particular spot. Should the AMA be held responsible? Ultimately, yes. But what riders are fond of saying is that no one knows what it's like to go through these corners on a Superbike, so no one can understand their concerns. They had their chance and they failed, and they failed again in the Formula Xtreme race the next day.

Grant Lopez hit the unprotected wall in turn five when his throttle stuck wide open while leading the Formula Xtreme race. He came to a very definitive and sickening halt, according to those that saw the accident, and didn't move for what seemed like an eternity. His injuries turned out to be minor. Not long after the accident, a flatbed truck carted a load of hay bales in the site for added protection. Better late than never?

The most dangerous part of the 1.51-mile track is the bowl, the banked-oval turns three and four leading onto the front straight. You make a mistake there and bad things will happen. As I was standing in the far end of the pits, Ty Piz put his Yamaha TZ250 into the hay bale-lined wall on the exit of the turn, considerably shortening its wheelbase.

Both of Saturday's final events, the Formula Xtreme and the 750cc Supersport, were red-flagged because of accidents. One of the 750cc Supersport incidents happened in the bowl, with the bike catching fire.

There was air fence behind the hay bales in turn four. It looked silly sitting there behind the bales, but that's where the riders had wanted it placed. After winning the race, Mat Mladin said that if you hit the air fence "it doesn't explode, it just deflects you into the racetrack and someone decapitates you from behind."

To try to race here would mean not using the bowl, but changing the track to resemble Las Vegas, a layout which runs parallel to but doesn't use the banking on its run to the front stretch. Right now, there's no room for such a move in Phoenix.

With the recent proliferation of racetracks, is there a compelling reason to put riders in harm's way at a track like PIR? Of course not. Will the AMA board decide they need a race in this burgeoning metropolitan area? Who knows? It's best not to try to figure them out, sometimes there are things they just don't see.

Take the Formula Xtreme race, for example. While fighting for second place, Paul Harrell, claiming he was forced offline, ran straight in turn one, skipped the infield, and rejoined the race without losing a spot on the back straight. The AMA said they didn't see it. How do you not see that? Everyone at the track saw it.

"Our tower didn't call that in as a short cut," AMA road race manager Ron Barrick said. "It's partly our fault for not catching it right away."

After taking part in the podium ceremonies for finishing second, Harrell admitted it - he had no choice - and in due time he was penalized, falling from second place to fifth. Even though he wasn't informed of the penalty until the next day, he accepted the penalty graciously. It took the AMA that long to look over the videotapes and check the times on the transponders before making a call. How's this for a scenario: A game-changing call is disputed in the last minute of the Super Bowl. What does the NFL do? "We didn't see it. We'll let you know tomorrow." Maybe not.

April 21, 1999

Common Complaints

Oh, to be the winner, standing erect, wreathed in garlands, drenched in cheap champagne and garnished with lipstick, effusively thanking every breathing soul from his mechanic to his team to his tire sponsor to his colonic irrigationist to his yoga instructor to his pygmy acupuncturist to his shiatsu masseuse to his aromatherapist to the guy who disinfects his tongue stud to his tattoo artiste to his shaman to Jesus. The rest of the field, they just bitch.

And they usually have legitimate reasons to bitch. The nature of their complaints is diverse, yet certain catchall phrases seem eternal. The most infamous of these I attribute to Jeff Ward, the Indy Racing League star who, in a former life, was a seven-time motocross champion. I think it was Ward who, when asked about a particularly bad night, responded, "I cased it on the triples. My ankles went numb." I hate when that happens.

Numb ankles have been replaced by forearm pump, both in motocross and road racing. The most common complaint in motocross these days is Jeremy McGrath.[1] For the most common complaints in road racing, read on...

Vance & Hines' Ducati's Anthony Gobert complains that, as a consequence of communing with Ganja Bob and firing up a spliff the size of a bratwurst - which ultimately led to a failed drug test and a three-race suspension last year - he has to pay $500 to have his urine tested before every superbike race. Eponymous team owner Terry Vance thinks that's fair, but complains that, in order

---

[1] Jeremy McGrath won seven supercross championships between 1993 and 2000.

to assiduously ensure truthfulness and prevent contamination, he has to hold the specimen container in his bare hands. And what does Gobert's teammate Ben Bostrom complain about? He complains that they keep using his water bottle without telling him. "Dude, check out the side of the bottle. It says 'Ben,' not 'Squirt here,' dude."

Among the other whiners on the V&H team is newest recruit Gary Medley, who complains that he had to spend nearly the entire winter scrubbing the team's transporter clean of former rider Thomas Stevens' mousse residue.

V&H crew chief Jim Leonard complains that he's had to wear the same hat for the past three years since Vance won't give him a new one. Vance counters vehemently that this isn't true. He says he gave Leonard a new hat this year, but hoping to ease the misery of a cross-country trip, Leonard traded it for an upgrade on the Greyhound Vance sent him to Daytona on.

They're not the only Ducatisti complaining. Eraldo Ferracci's riders complain that they can't understand a damn thing the old guy with the white hair's saying.

What else does FBF's Larry Pegram complain about? That his very newest co-ed honey pumpkin sugar muffin is reserving her most amorous delectations until after he's proved himself by winning a race, and that those unfeeling bastards at the AMA won't let him race his Ducati 996 in the Pro Blunder class. "Don't they know a man has needs? How long do they expect me to go on like this?"

What does his FBF teammate Matt Wait complain about? Where to start? In 1997, young Matthew complained his bikes were no damn good - and he was right, they weren't, not after he crashed the crap out of them about 30 times into every immovable barrier, air bag, gravel trap and shrub he could lock his anti-gravity force onto. In 1998, he complained that he didn't have telemetry on his FCC Technical Sports Honda NSR-500V. Good thing, too.

According to Dorna's records, he tied with Juan Bautista Borja for most crashes in the 500cc class. And he also complained about his negative mention in a Kenny Roberts Jr. interview I wrote for *Cycle News*, saying, in so many words, that he and Roberts Jr. were friends and that certain writers had an agenda. And where did he make this complaint? In a column he writes for a road racing monthly which everyone in the English-speaking world considers to be the ultimate paragon, the *ne plus ultra* of virtue, verity, rectitude, decency, honesty, morality, and all that is right and good in the kingdom of Satan.

Harley-Davidson's Pascal Picotte complained in preseason testing that all his bike really needed - I mean if you get right down to it, if you strip it to its barest bones, it's most simplest terms, the two things the Harley VR1000 truly needed, and there really are only two things - let's face it, there could have been many, many more - the only two things the bike absolutely had to have were a new engine and a new trans. That's it. Nothing more. Is that so much to ask? Of course, he said that before flogging the peppy orange-and-black beast to fourth at Phoenix and showing all but three of his fellow factory stars what the ass end of a Harley looks like - well, if they could see it through the blue haze.

What does his teammate Scott "Mr. Daytona's Halifax Medical Center" Russell complain about? For one, he complains that Florida should move their last call up a few hours so he can get in bed before Willard Scott starts wishing "happy birthday" to all the security guards at the Speedway and the guy who did the original design for the bike he was supposed to race before some lout turned his mug into something that looked like it was done by a pissed-off Picasso on acid. And he complains that a guy with as much talent as he has hasn't been able to showcase it for the first two races of the season, but he will.

The unforgotten third member of the Harley wrecking crew, what does he complain about? Thomas Wilson complains he's under contract, but the only thing he's riding is the bench (as they say in baseball) or the Harley push-bike (as they say in England), though that should change once he gets a chance to test.

Some riders have more legitimate complaints. What does American Honda's Miguel DuHamel complain about? That in the Daytona 600cc Supersport race, he was momentarily blinded by the price tag that came off the leathers of the guy he was lapping for the fourth time who'd ridden his bike in from the Wal-Mart - where he was unsuccessfully shopping for a clue - and was sure to crash it, leaving an oil spill the size of the Exxon Valdez. That, and those insensitive bastards in the winner's circle at Daytona who made him climb up and down, up and down the podium on his bum leg, just to please those mercenary photographers who kept screaming, "Just one more, Miguel, just one more, *mun cheri.*" "Don't they know I'm crippled? It was all I could do to win those two races, guys."

His teammate Eric Bostrom complains that he wishes his ankle would heal so that he could go out and win the superbike championship like I said he would.

The Yamaha riders - what are their beefs? They're not allowed to complain. Says so right in their contracts. All is wonderful in the land of the three tuning forks, couldn't be better. Says so right in the contract. Last year, Rich Oliver suggested there might be a small problem - not the problem of tipping over every time he rode the bike, something he fixed midway into the season. No, it was a different kind of problem that he mentioned to the press, and he heard about it - taken behind the team transporter and whipped to within an inch of his life with an unused YZF750 hop-up manual. Actually, that's not entirely true: Chapter 7 - "Replacing Bodywork" - was slightly dog-eared.

His teammate Jamie Hacking complains that espn2 should have muted the microphones on the TV cameras during the

Daytona pit stop when he rightfully asked, "What the f?#$ is going on here?" or words to that effect.

The Yoshimura Suzuki boys have complained for some time about a lack of top speed, something that should be put to rest after their second, fourth, sixth, and cartwheel-through-the-dogleg finishes at Daytona.

When he heard that his team would have more riders than the Tour de France, Yosh's Mat Mladin complained that they were spreading their resources thinner than a Vegemite sandwich.

What do his teammates Jason Pridmore, Steve Crevier and Steve Rapp complain about?

Scratch golfer Pridmore complains that whenever he asks Mladin for advice on suspension or gearing, Mladin reminds him about his recent hole in one, which hole it was, the club he used, how far he took his backswing, the distance to the pin, the number of bounces the ball took, the depth of the hole, the number of dimples on the ball, etc. Crevier complains that once last year's 600cc Supersport title was within reach, Suzuki commanded him to concentrate on scoring points and ride like a girl, when what he really wanted to do was ride like a woman. Steve Rapp has a legitimate complaint. He complains that the walls at Phoenix International Raceway are too close, and he's right, and he's lucky he walked away from his crash to make the complaint.

The Muzzy Kawasaki team has a right to complain about a lack at top speed after their showing at Daytona. The bigger concern was that the team hasn't kept up with the progress the other teams have made.

Aaron Yates is dreading the Northern California races, where he'll be referred to by "Big Bill" Spencer as "Double-A-ron Yates," and he wonders why "Big Bill" doesn't refer to his fellow Georgian as "Sco-Double-T Ru-Double-S-e-Double-L."

Muzzy's Doug Chandler has bigger problems. Where to park the new motorhome? "Does it go where the Impala police pursuit car is, or do I have to move the new Jeep? What about that old thing with the flames on the sides? And how do I get rid of tobacco-juice stains? My wife was asking."

Lest you think that riders are the only ones at a racetrack with gripes...

AMA tech inspector Rob King complains that he doesn't have Carry Andrew to kick around anymore.

Dunlop's Jim Allen complains about having to listen over and over to the joke about his new bosses: What's the difference between a tire and 365 rubbers? One's a Goodyear, the other's a very good year.

What's the Michelin guy complain about? The Michelin guy doesn't come to the races anymore. Something about a memo about dicey tires in the rain.

How about globe-trotting exotic-bike tester Alan Cathcart? Is there anything at all wrong with either the latest one-off factory missile or the newest world-exclusive proddie bike he's testing?

No, apparently.

Webmeister and *American Roadracing* editor Dean Adams - what does he complain about? That he spends so much of his time answering angry e-mails from unpaid contributors that he can't report what allegedly happened at the races.

And me, I'm complaining that I have to share hotel rooms with the editor of *Cycle News*, a guy who moans himself to sleep and keeps me awake all night. The rule I try to live by is, if I'm sharing a room with someone who's moaning, it better not be an Australian dwarf.

April 28, 1999

Mixed Emotions

As I approached the track, the first sign I saw read, "Willow Springs International Raceway, The Fastest Road in the West." Once inside, the second sign I saw read, "Please jiggle the handle, the float slicks."

Like a malfunctioning toilet, Willow Springs evokes mixed emotions: Sure, it'll do, but can't you fix it up just a little? At first glance it appears to be nothing more than an expansive collection of rocks, dirt, tumbleweed and macadam. It is the land where every West Coast road racer cut his or her teeth and which has been anointed the closest place to Los Angeles for a superbike race, and therefore somehow good. It's a place that is so barren, so devoid of life and tormented by weather, that it makes the ground zero of a nuclear blast look like Maui. And yet it's not without its charms.

If the wind isn't blowing in like uninvited relatives, and the temperature hasn't gone down like a three-dollar hooker, it's a truly splendid place to hold a motorcycle race. The not terribly interesting layout is one of the safest on the AMA calendar and the riders like it because of that, and because it takes big hair to master - and it's fast. Runoff seems to go on forever, which is a good thing when you have riders such as Miguel DuHamel turning exquisite one-off machines like his RC45 into cartwheeling, bin-filling parts orders. More on that later.

Of all the tracks on the calendar, Willow Springs is probably the best for spectators, the area outside of turn four, the Budweiser Balcony, affording a generous view of almost the entire track with close up action right in your lap. Whether they know it or not, the crowd is treated well at the concessions, the prices being among the lowest on the circuit, though the attendant lines are some of the longest.

What riders don't like about the place is the place. The pits are cramped and oddly shaped, with team semis seemingly arranged by a blind guy with a sense of a humor and a limp, and the privateers shuffled off to the nether regions like the drooling uncle. With every sort of traffic whizzing through the pits, getting from your truck to the track can be a bigger challenge than the race itself. As a showcase, this falls short.

One complaint the riders had was dust. Through no fault of their own, the track workers driving through the inside of the track kick up dust storms whenever they move, causing some riders to think one of their own had overshot a corner by miles and couldn't get stopped. That isn't possible. If you ran off in turn one full stop in sixth, you wouldn't hit anything but an old pick-up truck or a prairie dog for several miles. Short of paving the inside of the track, which is less likely than seeing an "I Love the AMA" sticker on the back of Roger Edmondson's motorhome, or putting a dome over it, there is no easy solution to this one. Live with it, guys.

The structure of which the track seems most proud is the "House of Charmin'" - I am not making that up. A noble structure, the paddock reading room makes you happy to know that the track would spend time and money not only thinking up a name for the paddock crapper, but putting the energy into painting the name on the brick shi... building. After a trip to the facility, it seems a more accurate name would be "House of newsprint." On the flip side, children can enjoy the playground the track has built near the "house." From what I've seen, that's a unique feature among AMA facilities.

Since returning to the AMA calendar last year, the weekend has been a success, drawing considerable crowds, despite what the locals say was little advance coverage or advertising in the various local media outlets. Those who skipped the Long Beach Grand Prix, held on the same weekend, were treated to sterling racing under optimum weather conditions. Race-day temperature was around 90 degrees - even though a week earlier the high was 46. No doubt the event's success encourages everyone involved in the decision-making process to continue with this one, if for no other reason than that the riders don't complain all that much about it, especially compared to Sears Point, where they'll spend next weekend holding their breath for long stretches of track.

No such problem here. The racing, in three classes at least, was superb, though nothing like last year's Superbike race; when Miguel DuHamel held off a determined Anthony Gobert at the line. That was a two-rider race; this year was five for much of the time, then two at the end, neither being Gobert or DuHamel.

If DuHamel never spoke to me again, I'd understand. Last year, *Cycle News* built their Laguna Seca world superbike preview issue around a boast he made that the AMA regulars could keep the visitors off the podium in both races at Laguna. He also defended his "Win it or bin it" racing style, which, even then, was a cause of visible discomfort to some of the higher-ups at Honda. Not long afterward, he hit an unprotected wall at a wet Loudon and his season was over.

With another road race issue of *Cycle News* coming up, we decided that it was time to talk to Miguel again. His Daytona performance was heroic, and he was right in the thick of the title chase, even with a leg that's at about 25-percent strength. Saturday we sat down with him and he again defended his all-or-nothing approach, Sunday brought all of nothing.

In the 600cc Supersport race he started half a lap back after it was discovered that someone on his team had forgotten to turn his fuel petcock on. Undeterred, he rode like a demon to take 15th and the handful of points that goes with it. I think with the AMA points system, he earned 1347 points. Unfortunately, the winner gets a dillion.

A problem in Superbike qualifying didn't show what he could do on a track which wasn't particularly taxing to his leg. The race would.

Getting away in second, DuHamel chased former teammate Ben Bostrom for the first half of the race before slipping back a few spots to fourth. On the 21st lap he overshot turn three and grabbed a handful of brakes. The rear of the bike came up and stayed up longer than the Wright Brothers, though they didn't have Jamie Hacking in their flight path. DuHamel was sent tumbling through the desert, the parts bill on his bike hitting five figures in a hurry and probably ending up somewhere in six figures. Luckily, he walked away. Hacking continued on his way to the podium.

The day before, Miguel had complained that some riders had picked him to finish sixth (in our poll for the series championship). They made their judgment based on his physical health and not the bonehead issue that strikes too often in a field this deep.

Since his health coming into the season was an unknown, I picked him to finish eighth in the championship, his peers picked him sixth, and *Cycle News* editor Paul Carruthers picked him sixth.

Carruthers picked Anthony Gobert to win, while I chose him fifth, espousing the view that he clearly had the talent to win, but the equipment hadn't proved all that reliable in 1998. After blistering the track in qualifying, Gobert said the Vance & Hines Ducati was the best it'd ever been and the closest thing he'd ever ridden to a 500cc GP bike. The colorful Australian was running up front when he was forced into the pits with an electrical problem which took the top end off of his rev range. Had he stayed out, he probably would've run into the same tire problems the rest of the boys had.

Fast By Ferracci's Larry Pegram won the race because, on this day, his Michelins were the best tires - better than the Dunlops which everyone else was using, and he knew they would be as early as of Friday. On Sunday morning, Kevin Schwantz, who's working with Pegram this year, said they had a tire that could run 1:21s the whole race. Pegram's average lap time was 1:22.648.

Pegram rode a smart race, lurking with intent in the lead quintet before putting Vance & Hines' Ben Bostrom behind him with five laps to go. Bostrom didn't give up, but he didn't have the drive to keep up, and he took second. Yamaha's Jamie Hacking survived his punting by DuHamel to take third, with Yoshimura Suzuki's Mat Mladin a content fourth after two of his championship rivals, DuHamel and Gobert, ended the day in the pits.

The riders we polled picked Mladin to win the title and, three races into the season, it's easy to see why. Fourth was the best he was going to do today and he took it, moving on to two tracks, Sears Point and Laguna Seca, where rider skill weighs heavier than machinery on the balance scales. And where the facilities are maintained in such a way that you don't have to jiggle the handle.

August 11, 1999

Uncertain Futures

Time to cue the music - the game of musical chairs is about to begin. We must start at Honda with Mick Doohan. As this is being written, Doohan is rehabbing his broken body somewhere near Palo Alto, California. He will be there until early next month, after which he'll return to Monaco, where he will be greeted by his girlfriend, Selina, his infant daughter, Allexis with two "l's" (his response to why the baby girl's name has two "l's": "I don't make the rules"), and a slew of rumors.

The speculation the five-time 500cc World Champion will face centers around what he'll be doing next year. His options seem limitless, which is how it should be, given that he's the second most prolific 500cc racer of all time and still nearly unbeatable when healthy.

To this point, he's been cautious in assessing his future. Others, with far less insight and the occasional axe to grind, have been less reticent.

The rumor that wouldn't die at the recent German Grand Prix was that he'd be running - but not riding for - a 500cc team backed by Winfield, an Australian cigarette brand which has been a personal sponsor of his for some time. The irony of the fittest man in the paddock shilling for tobacco money is lost on very few. (When asked about this same conundrum years ago, Kenny Roberts replied something to the effect that he wasn't advocating the use of cigarettes, but please use our brand if you must - an artful dodge, and much better than saying if you'd forsaken your sanity and had to smoke, knowing what we've known for the past so years, then would you please be so kind as to indulge our spikes for all of your emphysema, low birth-weight, lung- and throat-cancer needs? Fair enough.)

Aprilia's Valentino Rossi is the rider Doohan seems to covet, at least according to what Rossi said in a press release in Germany, though the Italian showman equivocates with the unctuous sincerity of a presidential hopeful. He said he had three offers and Doohan's was the least likely. After taking the pole position the day before winning the race, his fifth of the year, he said he preferred to stay in 250s, and little else.

In his Aprilia-approved statement, the colorful and now skin-headed Italian listed his choices in order of probability as: staying with Aprilia in the 250s, something the Italian team will do everything in their power to facilitate, but may have less muscle should he win the title this year; a seat on the factory Repsol Honda team, generally considered the best in the business; or the offer from Mick.

If recent history is any indication, taking Doohan's offer would be tricky. The last multi-time 500cc World Champion to run a front-level 500cc team is now mostly out of racing, having become disillusioned. It made him realize he'd gotten into it too soon and had other things he wanted to do with his life. Concurrently, Yamaha had decided the premium for his name was too high and the sponsorship he brought to the enterprise too low.

Wayne Rainey was as great a champion as we will ever see. But that same drive, that same perfectionism, ill suited him for team management, given the temperament and lack of will of his riders. What he belatedly discovered is that he could not make them him, and that it didn't replace the ineffable joy of riding, and he grew quickly frustrated by the exercise.

Doohan is at least as driven as Rainey, and we don't know what he'll make of the young riders he'll have to employ. Nor do we know what sort of team he could put together, given the limited field of truly competent engineers and mechanics. Since he's been with Honda, the very likable Jeremy Burgess has been Mick's more-than-able crew chief, and also the man behind Wayne Gardner's 500cc World title in 1987. Asked if he would continue to work for Doohan, Burgess, one of the most genial men in the paddock, replied, "I don't work for Mick Doohan," the inference being that he worked for Honda Racing Corporation and had for over a dozen years. He'd certainly be a fool to leave.

If Rossi does move to 500s, and there's no question he will some day, the Repsol Honda team is as good as it gets. But that leaves Doohan without a rider, if indeed he's going to run a team.

Rumors have been rampant that it's not going to be funded by Winfield money but backed by Shell, the same oil giant that currently backs a 250cc GP team in which he has part interest. Don't bother asking him about the Shell connection. Since he rides for Repsol, the biggest oil company in Spain, there's little chance you'll get much of an answer. Judging from one of the more interesting rumors that was floated in Germany, he may have no choice but to go with Shell.

Fellow Aussie and 500cc World Champion Wayne Gardner was said to be exploring the possibility of team ownership, and is said to be chasing the same Winfield money that Doohan covets. But Gardner could have a better shot. The money would be for a World Superbike team, the bikes would be the all-conquering Ducatis, and the riders would be a pair who years ago rode as Winfield Honda teammates in their native Australia, Anthony Gobert and Troy Corser. According to Gobert's Vance & Hines Ducati team, one way or another, the Australian is gone after this season.

Assuming Doohan gets some money, and there are other avenues to explore - he's known to be good mates with the boss of Qantas, the Australian national airline - who would he get, if not Rossi? Daryl Beattie's name surfaced in Germany.

Beattie, you'll recall, quit racing after a horrible few seasons with the Lucky Strike Suzuki team. They were horrible for various reasons; the bike was horrible and Beattie was beaten up too much by spills in testing and the races. After more than a year off, he's keen to get back in the saddle. How good is he? And would you stake your $5 million claim on him?

The next rider whose name is being thrown into the gristmill is Castrol Honda's Colin Edwards II. Edwards has been pining to ride a 500 for years, and the World Superbike tour was the quickest route, he thought. There was a time when it was believed he was the heir apparent at Yamaha. Then he went to Honda and it all changed. It's possible that he, too, may end up at Repsol, but Doohan's team would be a good second choice. Regardless of his occasionally prickly temperament, the knowledge Doohan could impart to a younger rider goes beyond encyclopedic.

Repsol will certainly keep Alex Criville, regardless of whether he wins the 500cc title, which he seems certain to do, though he is the rider Doohan must have if he wants to be as successful a team owner as he was a rider. Aside from Kenny Roberts Jr., who we'll get to later, there is no other rider capable of consistently winning races. Criville will certainly be negotiating from a position of strength, and the dour Spaniard said his relationship with Doohan has improved over the years, and that he's continued to be helpful since his accident at Jerez, in May.

Repsol Honda's Japanese connection Tadayuki Okada is a question mark. This year he's won one race, but there are many who think he's only retained his seat by virtue of birthright, and that there may be someone more deserving in the pipeline.

Yamaha will have the same two riders, Max Biaggi and Carlos "Chubby" Checa. Both are on two-year contracts, which is a very good thing since Chubby has crashed the ill-handling Yamaha 19 times in nine races. Amazingly, he hasn't been badly hurt. A rider for a rival team said he'd heard (can we get more removed from the source?) that Marlboro, as a condition of their Yamaha sponsorship, mandated that the bike have more top speed, which it does - but getting there is another story entirely, especially if you have to go through a corner to do it.

Suzuki will retain Kenny Roberts Jr., who team manager Garry Taylor wisely tied up with a two-year contract. Otherwise, his name would be the most widely bandied about. To those who weren't paying attention for the past three months, he's been the surprise of the season, winning three races and standing second to Criville in the championship. To the rest, his hard-earned success was a just reward for surviving two years on the Modenas. Suzuki's second rider, Nobuatsu Aoki, is in the second year of a two-year deal. This year has been a vast disappointment, the Japanese rider crashing often and taking himself out of the championship early in the season. Suzuki needs a second rider, and possibly a Japanese one, since, in lieu of outside sponsorship, the factory pays all the bills. Whether Aoki is the one is yet to be determined.

The others face uncertain futures. Kanemoto Honda's John Kocinski keeps asking what kind of money AMA Superbike riders make and what opportunities exist in his homeland. There's still something to prove, but he may be running out of time and money, and would justifiably command top dollar on the American tour, where the turnover is expected to be high.

July 4, 2001

"It Was Bad"

The debacle that infested the Pro Honda Oils 600cc Supersport race at New Hampshire International Speedway last week was the most embarrassing, disgraceful episode since, well, last year's Loudon debacle. In the words of Kawasaki's Eric Bostrom, the 600cc Supersport championship leader, "Everyone lost. I'm as disappointed as anybody, but the crowd lost, the organization lost. It was bad." Worse, even, than last year. So why go back?

Rain late in the morning dissolved Sunday's schedule. Track personnel did a commendable job of readying the road course before the start of the 600cc race. The race was called to the line and the AMA regulars were unmoved. They wanted more than a parade lap and a sighting lap; they wanted a 10-minute practice session. The argument was that they were going to be racing on an unfamiliar surface and wanted a few laps at speed. The AMA refused, the dozen Loudon locals took their spots on the grid, many of their mechanics whipping the crowd into a frenzy. The AMA regulars, many of whom are factory racers, were lustily booed and harassed. Meanwhile, AMA officials were besieged, and the owner of NHIS, Bob Bahre, was livid because, for the second year in a row, he watched helplessly as the inmates ran the asylum.

"Who's in charge here?" he asked AMA road race manager Ron Barrick. "You or them?" he said, pointing to the rebellious riders. It was a rhetorical question.

Bahre is the prototypical New Englander - crustier than a week-old baguette. In the movie version, he'd be played by Burgess Meredith. Bahre speaks his mind, often to his own detriment. Meeting with AMA officials on Sunday morning, he made a remark about the riders being "prima donnas," while one of very best of those prima donnas was sitting nearby. Wisecracks like that, once widely circulated, do nothing to endear him to the inmates, or the prima donnas.

Bahre saved NHIS from the disrepair it fell into by the late '80s. The track had become run-down, the facilities Third World class. The previous owner's idea of capital improvements was that every 10 years he'd rotate the zip-ties holding the toilet seats on, whether they needed it or not. Bahre and his son, Gary, made massive improvements, re-doing the oval, adding grandstands, sprucing up the grounds, building garages, generally turning old Loudon into a first-rate facility - for cars. For motorcycles, it's less welcoming. The team manager of one of the Japanese factories once told me his company had spent more money on broken bikes and bodies at Loudon than at all the other tracks combined.

By the late '90s, it was clear the track needed another upgrade for motorcycles. The pavement was coming apart on the road course and the runoff areas, such as they were, needed to be enlarged. Between the 1999 and 2000 seasons, a number of improvements were made, but it still wasn't enough for many riders. Never would be.

The AMA has designated four of the 11 tracks in the AMA/Chevy Trucks U.S. Superbike Championship as dry-weather tracks: Daytona, Brainerd, Pike's Peak and Sears Point. Loudon was on the fence. Last year the Superbike riders decided they couldn't ride in the rain, and they didn't. This year, the AMA's Barrick said, as late as the week prior to Loudon, that no decision had been made about the track's wet-worthiness. There'd been a sealant applied to the road course and Barrick wanted to withhold judgment, and hoped the riders would keep an open mind before deciding the track's fate.

It was a non-starter for two reasons. Firstly, the Bahres claim they weren't told until just prior to the race weekend that this was the case. Certainly the riders weren't: The decision wasn't made until Barrick and a number of riders inspected the track on Thursday. More importantly, to the riders, a wet track isn't the issue. The issue is the lack of runoff, wet or dry, and the lack of progress.

"It just wasn't there," said Kawasaki's Doug Chandler, a voice of reason and one of the few racers to have ridden on both the old and new layouts. "They resealed the oval, but there wasn't anything done to the rest of it."

The resealing, and laser leveling of the oval to a near uniform height, was seen as a reaction to the deaths of two NASCAR drivers in the past few years. "How many riders are going to have to die before they do something?" more than one rider asked. Team Oliver Yamaha/StickerSolution.com's Rich Oliver, a four-time winner here who had one of the most miserable weekends of his stellar career, said, "I love the tradition of this track, I love the people, I love the people behind it, but the bikes are going too fast for this surface. Any size bike. Plus, you've got things like the track disintegrating and potholes. It's just not necessary." (It must be said that not all riders dislike the track, but it is the prevailing sentiment.) Even Barrick wondered aloud, "What's changed? If it couldn't work last year, why would it magically work this year?"

Bob Bahre took offense to those comments, specifically the word "magically," and told Barrick so. It wasn't the last time the two would have words. After the calamity at the 600cc Supersport start, Bahre said: "We've done everything they've asked. We've bent over backwards. The AMA is not running the show, in my opinion. If you go with NASCAR, the drivers do as they're told. In my opinion, they have to get somebody stronger than [Ron] Barrick. That's my opinion."

Bahre makes the point that the AMA didn't ask for any changes for this year. The AMA would likely dispute that. Whether it was requested or not, there was certainly a significant amount of Air

Fence added. In fact, according to someone with knowledge of the issue, the 1.6-mile, 12-turn Loudon road course uses more Air Fence than the four-mile, 14-turn Road America course. Not that it matters.

Last year's fiasco played out under the team awnings on the pit straight, where Barrick, who often tries too hard to be conciliate to all parties, held a tribal council, along with Bahre, the riders, and whomever else would venture an opinion. In the end, the fans were voted off the island and the race was held Monday. This year was less civilized. The tribal council was held in the open, with Barrick and AMA Director of Competition Merrill Vanderslice holding court, and holding off the hordes of dissenters; everyone from the Bahres to riders to team members to other interested loudmouths. In the end, the 600cc race was run with none of the AMA regulars and won by local Scott Greenwood. Greenwood wasn't an imposter. He'd qualified sixth and would have been a top-10 finisher. But he had no competition on this track and spent more time looking over his shoulder than "The Fugitive."

"I support the AMA guys and I support their whole point of view," Greenwood said. "They're Superbike riders and it's their job and their living, they've got to do what they've got to do. But, on the other token, we're here, I spent a lot of money to be here this weekend. I wanted to go out and ride."

Knowing that weather delays are a possibility, and given the last two years, a probability, why does the AMA keep going back? The answer seems to be tradition. This was the 78th running of the Loudon Classic, though records for races in the area only date back to 1940, plus time off for WWII, which would make this 2018. With the benefit of hindsight, we can agree that not going back in 2002 was a good idea.

The race meeting, like Daytona, draws huge crowds to the area, Weirs Beach and Laconia to the north, and a lesser portion to the track. Given the complications of the past two years, it could take some time to rebuild fan faith.

The decision on where races are held falls to AMA Pro Racing CEO Scott Hollingsworth and the Pro Racing Board. How does a track that engenders this much hostility continue to receive a sanction?

"Ultimately it is up to me and the [AMA Pro Racing] board as to whether we put an event on the calendar or not," Hollingsworth said. "And that decision has not been made for any particular event for next year, unless we have a contract already."

Hollingsworth said that he and the board take input from a variety of sources, including the operations and track committees, and the teams. They look at each venue's track design and safety concerns. They look at it from a business and television point of view.

"There's a lot of determining factors to go into whether to put one in or take one off, so we'll take input from all of those sources," he said. As for Loudon, specifically, Hollingsworth was aware of the problems, but was withholding judgment. "There'll be dialogue with Loudon's management over the course of the next several months, and we'll determine collectively what's in the long-term best interest of series."

The first indication of whether Loudon will return will be when the tentative schedule is published in late August or September.

Unless the Bahres are willing to make a good-faith effort to improve the track for motorcycles, motorcycles that have outgrown the circuit, there should be no 79th Loudon Classic. But before cutting them off, they should be given a chance to prove how serious they are. They need to hire an established track designer, someone like Alan Jones, to offer a new design for the track. Even if it takes two or three years, the riders will be placated. It worked at Sears Point, where a huge cash infusion has ensured its impending status as both a first-rate facility and road course, and it could happen at Loudon, if the will is there. Given the amount of time it takes to design a layout and implement them, especially given the harsh New England winters, it's difficult to see how any wholesale changes could be in place next year.

There was a time when the AMA needed tracks more than the tracks needed the AMA. Those days are coming to an end. The boom in racetrack construction gives the AMA more and more options. If Loudon goes away, someone newer, bigger, better and more willing, will take its spot. It's up to them.

April 10, 2002

All Jacked Up

Today, we turn our attention to the ludicrous pit-stop regulations at Daytona and the AMA's whimsical enforcement of the rules.

Though they'd rather it not be made public, the AMA fined all four Japanese Superbike teams for various pit-lane violations during the Daytona 200. American Honda was fined $500 when Dunlop's Jim Allen handled the delaminated rear tire that came off Kurtis Roberts' Erion Honda RC51. Yoshimura Suzuki was fined $500 when a tire that was taken off the back of Jamie Hacking's GSX-R750 inadvertently ended up on the pit road. Yamaha was fined $500 because Tom Halverson was signaling where Anthony Gobert should stop. And Kawasaki was fined $1000 for having their jack-stand man operate from the cold side of the pit wall. That's the short version. The truth, as always, is more enlightening. First, a little background.

Starting in 2001, the AMA mandated that, as a way of leveling the field between the factories and the privateers, they'd allow only four men over the wall during pit stops. They went even farther in 2002 by outlawing pneumatic jack-stands. On closer scrutiny, the folly of this is apparent and, in fact, punitive toward the privateers.

Because they have $30,000 quick-change forks and $12,000 quick-change swingarms, the factory teams can change front and rear tires and dump fuel in around 10-11 seconds. Without such equipment, privateers need more, not less, help to complete their stop. By adding two more men, the factory teams figure they could save 2 to 2½ seconds per stop, five seconds over the course of the race.

"That's cheaper than finding five seconds trying to buy parts off the Japanese manufacturers," one crew chief said.

And, in the end, does it really matter to the privateers? Ground Zero Racing's Woody Deatherage rode well to finish seventh. But he was more than two laps down on American Honda's Nicky Hayden. Would he have been crest-fallen to finish two laps, and five seconds down? The eighth-place finisher, HSA of Stanford's Brian Livengood, was three-laps-plus down on Hayden. That's nearly six minutes. I'm guessing that five seconds more wouldn't have caused him much angst.

Having more personnel over the wall would also be safer. Yoshimura Suzuki would have had someone to catch the tire, instead of watching it bounce away because the AMA pit monitor was in the way.

"They happened to be standing against the wall when I flicked the wheel over to the wall [where a team member was waiting on the cold side to catch it]," Yoshimura Suzuki's Peter Doyle said. "We ended up getting fined."

Honda was fined because Dunlop's Jim Allen grabbed the tire that was taken off Roberts' bike and handed it to a fellow Dunlop employee on the cold pit. Obviously, Dunlop wanted to hide the destroyed tire as quickly as possible. The fine was $500, which suggests one violation. But Allen says that he also handled Nicky Hayden's tire during at least one, if not both of his changes, and wasn't penalized. And why should Honda be fined for something Dunlop did? Anticipating the AMA's reaction, Allen checked with them prior to the race and was told that he would not be counted as one of the four team members over the wall. And yet, the fine was assessed. Allen offered to pay the fine, but Honda declined.

Yamaha was the first to get fined. After signaling where Anthony Gobert should stop for his first pit stop, but not touching the YZF-750, Yamaha's Tom Halverson noticed he was being scrutinized by an AMA official. Halverson pulled him aside before the second pit stop and asked if anything was wrong. "Oh yeah," he was told, "you've already got a Code 2 violation." Told that the rulebook allows a fifth member over the wall for signaling, the AMA rep replied, "I don't really want to discuss that now, but you definitely have a violation and you'll have another one if you do it again."

The rulebook says that four crewmembers are allowed over the pit wall for servicing. A fifth can man the fire extinguisher. The rulebook also states: "Any other crewmembers on the track side of the pit wall above the maximum of five involved with the motorcycle are allowed to perform timing/signaling duties only" - which is what Halverson was doing. Knowing how the AMA operates, Halverson and team manager Keith McCarty had clarified the rule with AMA officials prior to the race and were assured it was legal. Afterward, the AMA's response was that, sure it says that, but by the supplemental regulations you can only signal in the area after the International Horseshoe, which is an entirely separate issue. The AMA kind of blended the two regulations together as a means to fine Yamaha $500.

Kawasaki was fined $1000 and it was the best $1000 they spent in Florida. Prior to Daytona, [Kawasaki] was told by AMA road race manager Ron Barrick that they could use as many people as they wanted on the cold side of the pit wall, as long as there were only four on the hot side. The team built stands and made preparations to have the jack man on the cold side of the pit wall. A week before they left to go to the race, the day before they were loading the truck, they were told by Barrick that no one was allowed to work from the cold side or the pit wall. During the rider's briefing at Daytona, they were told that a fifth person over the wall would bring a $500 fine and a loss of five championship points. Barrick said $500 doesn't affect the factory teams, but five points does. And five points doesn't affect the privateer teams but $500 does. It gets everybody.

The points are the issue. Since the Japanese Superbike teams spend well clear of $60,000 for Daytona, the teams would gladly pay $1000 to save time. It's the points that hurt.

Kawasaki had used a fifth man from the cold side of the pit wall at Virginia International Raceway last year, so they knew how to do it. At the road race advisory board meeting before Daytona, the issue was raised and the AMA's response was that Kawasaki knew it wasn't legal, yet they did it for both of Eric Bostrom's pit stops and were told they'd be fined $1000. No mention was made of points, nor have points been assessed according to the standings on the AMA Pro Racing website. They got away with one.

"They're loose cannons," Yoshimura Suzuki's Peter Doyle said. "They pick and choose who they want to slap fines on and what the amounts are and do it at will."

I asked Kawasaki's Mike Preston about it at the recent Superbike test at Mazda Raceway at Laguna Seca. Preston, who it must be said has always been forthcoming and helpful, wouldn't discuss it. Not only would he not discuss it, he wouldn't say why he wouldn't discuss it. He was polite, but unyielding. The AMA's Ron Barrick was less cheerful.

When Paul Carruthers, the editor of *Cycle News*, called for clarification of the violations, Barrick questioned the news value of it and refused to discuss specifics. Instead, Barrick suggested *Cycle News* should instead write about the safety changes at Sears Point, which instantly exposed him as a non-*CN* web-head. On March 22, editor Carruthers posted Nicky Hayden's glowing review of the Sonoma facility on cyclenews.com under the headline, "Hayden Likes Sears, Does Dirt Tracking."

What Barrick would say was that some of the teams were fined $500 for having too many men on the hot pit during pit stops in the 200, though one team was fined $1000 for "having a person from the cold pit lane actuating the jack." He also said Honda was fined $500 when Dunlop tire technician Jim Allen "assisted" them.

It's easy to understand why Barrick would dissemble. He's the one who said the violations would incur points and he's the one who should dock Kawasaki, unless he spoke to Preston beforehand and told him that he would be fined but not penalized. Technically, Kawasaki didn't have five people over the wall. But, in practice, they're the only ones who demonstrated a clear disregard for the spirit of the rule, if not the actual rule itself.

Kawasaki's slippery escape has the other teams understandably seething. Their violations were all incurred without any attempt to gain an advantage. As one team member said, "You expect incompetence in a group like that, that big, but you don't expect to be bullshitted to."

August 21, 2002

Farewell, Randy

Somewhere, Randy Renfrow was smiling.

It had been a tough weekend for his family, for his friends, for racing. He'd been taken before his time, senselessly, it goes without saying. No more comebacks and no more retirements except for the final one to come shortly. But now two of his friends were swapping stories and laughing and taking a break from a weekend that was tougher than most.

AMA Road Race Manager Ron Barrick and Dunlop's Jim Allen were, it's safe to say, two of Renfrow's closest friends. Barrick met Randy through his brother, Shawn, and he and Randy were soon racing each other. Barrick gave it up to become Renfrow's mechanic, and they were still a team when Barrick took the AMA job. Allen met Renfrow early in his career. "There are two guys that had a lifetime contract with Dunlop: Randy is one and Ski [Dave Sadowski] is the other," Allen said. "Those guys got us where we are today. Randy was just so flippin' loyal. There was never any question. One time he rode the 8-Hours on Bridgestones, and he was so apologetic."

It was one of the few times he'd ever have to apologize.

"Randy was the toughest guy in a sport filled with very tough guys," said photographer and fellow Virginian Tom Riles, and there was no disputing it. Renfrow tortured his body in ways that would make the Marquis de Sade soil his shorts. It was that toughness, that tenaciousness, that was his defining legacy.

Barrick saw it at their very first heads-up race. Renfrow's knees were beat up from motocrossing, and even though he thought road racing was as dull as a banana, he tried it. He and some friends cobbled together a Kawasaki KZ650 out of two wrecked carcasses, and they were off to Summit Point.

"He was out there with his construction boots, his motocross leather pants, and some kind of leather jacket with duct tape around the waist," Barrick recalls. "Some white Bell helmet with the hair flowing out the back."

"Randy was fairly fast straight away, but really out of control. We'd take off, and I'd be ahead of him. Then he'd come blazing by and get to the turn and out of control and off the track, and you go cruising on through again. And three laps later he's on you again and back past again and all out of control. He was pretty into it right from the start. He wasn't going to go out there and play. He was going to do it right and start organizing things."

The organization was another part of his legacy. Renfrow was able to beat Team Honda's Wayne Rainey by being more organized. It happened in 1986, when he won the final Formula One title on a Honda RS500 triple tuned by Barrick and backed by Dr. Bert Bigoney.

"He was hard on people around him for wanting perfection sometimes, but he was no less hard on himself," Allen says. "One thing you had to admire is that he maximized his resources at all possible times. He didn't have as much, but he spent it right - spent the money in the right place."

Or improvised when necessary.

"Before we had tire warmers, at Pocono, the tire wasn't coming in quick enough for us, so Randy put the wheel on top of the van in the sun," Allen recalls. "Every 10 minutes, he'd turn the wheel up there. He was smart enough to figure that out." Adds Barrick, "We even did the same thing on a hot day, empty everything out and put the wheels inside the van."

The work ethic is something Renfrow never lost. "Other than racing, I wish that Randy had spent more time playing in his life, because he was a bit of a workaholic," Barrick said. Renfrow was a vice president at Fitness Resources, a distributor of exercise equipment. "Talking about tenacious, when he was trying to make a deal with a big dealer for a discount on stuff, he was always working and working and working." Allen remembers a tale from Brainerd in the mid-'80s. "Randy was on the ground working on his 250, and Donnie [Greene] may have been number one. And Donnie was pissing and moaning about no support and nobody helping him with the bike, and Randy just looked up and said, 'Donnie, get a job. I got two of them.' He never expected it to be given to him."

In his prime, Renfrow won three crowns, the 1983 250cc title, the 1986 Formula One title, and the 1989 Pro Twins title, times long since forgotten. Allen got an e-mail with an interesting observation: "People in the pits don't know Randy Renfrow. People that are here now don't know him. People that have been around and stuff know, but he was "The Man." He wasn't just an old guy that came to race every now and again."

Renfrow could have quit any number of times. Until his devastating March accident at Daytona, the most memorable came at a Honda test at Willow Springs in the winter of 1990-1991. Renfrow crashed an RC30, severing his right thumb and the tips of several fingers. His left big toe was grafted onto his hand - radical surgery at the time. "Nobody knew if it was going to work," Allen says. "I remember looking at the thing. He said, 'If they put it on with a little rotation, it would have been a lot better.' When he did finally come back, [he had to learn] to ride again with a whole different grip, and you know how important throttle control is at the top level. He said it was difficult, and his fingers were now too short, and the levers and controlling the bike was a whole new experience, almost like being a novice again, trying to learn everything."

But he did it, and in his first sprint race back, he finished third at Daytona on a Honda 600 that Barrick had built in three days in the Two Brothers Racing shop. "I remember seeing him in the winner's circle. I was just crying. He'd gotten on the box," Allen remembers. "That was impressive to do what he did. That was an amazing feat."

The final shock came at Daytona in March. Renfrow was rammed from behind on the warm-up lap of a throwaway CCS race. Even with at least 23 broken bones, he still considered returning. "Ninety-eight percent of the guys in the paddock who had gone through any one of the things he's gone through would seriously consider a career change," Barrick said. Barrick said it wasn't that long after the crash that Renfrow was thinking, "Maybe my knees not that bad." Renfrow was hoping to make it back for Mid-Ohio or Brainerd, tracks he liked. He could afford to pick and choose. But this time, the bones didn't heal quite so fast. He was, after all, 46, and still on crutches five months later.

Even so, he was planning on running a limited schedule in 2003. Barrick hoped he'd get to ride at the Barber track in Birmingham. He won't be there, but his spirit will. He was one of the good guys, one of the few who you never heard disparaged, nor did he disparage anyone. He was tough, but kind. He will be missed.

November 20, 2002

Meet Mr. Rossi

If you want to interview Valentino Rossi, if you want to know what motivates him, what it was like to switch from the NSR500 to the RC211V, what adjustments he had to make to his riding style, what made him successful this year, what he predicts for next year and who his greatest rivals are, you might be granted an audience. Just make sure you have eight minutes to spare. That was the amount of time his multiple handlers were allotting at the final Grand Prix in Valencia, Spain, to the various scribblers of the world if they wanted a glimpse inside the complex world of the man recently voted the most popular sportsman in Italy. Rossi is so popular that Nicky Hayden, in his first GP visit, said watching him traverse the GP paddock was like watching kids play. "They're chasing him around like duck, duck, goose. They never catch him. He never stops," Hayden noticed.

On the first day, the wait for an audience was two hours. A reporter from Britain's *Motorcycle News* and I were told we could go in with the Spanish mob, which we did, only to discover that Rossi was conducting the interview in Spanish. Who knew? The next day was an hour's wait. One of the acolytes tried to talk Rossi into meeting with us late in the afternoon, but he was flat talked out - *domani* (tomorrow). The man himself said he could talk then on Monday, when a group of journalists were riding his bikes. I explained I'd be back in the U.S. "Next time," he said with a smile, as he was whisked off to a meeting of his fan club.

One last chance was offered on Sunday - after the race, understandably. When he crossed the line second to Brazilian Alex Barros, our hopes sank faster than Martha Stewart stock.

Anticipating this might happen, I'd asked one of Rossi's attendants if he could tape a few of Rossi's eight-minute audiences with a pair of German journalists. We'll call them Helmut and Gunther. Amazingly, the request was granted, and for not one eight-minute interview, but two. Surely I could divine his entire being in 16 minutes.

When I listened to the tape, I was incredulous. It was unbelievable. Like nothing I'd expected. Questions you wouldn't have dreamed of. And 16 minutes' worth. Deep, insightful, probing questions? Hardly. Helmut and Gunther were friggin' idiots.

Helmut, I was told, worked for a respected Germany daily newspaper. His interview convinced me the paper's standards were lower than Swedish porn.

First question from **Helmut***: Michael Schumacher said he's more afraid of driving in traffic than on a race circuit. What about you?*

Rossi *(who lives in London)*: *On the streets is more dangerous.*

Second question*: You drive a motorbike or a car?*

Rossi*: I ride a motorbike in the normal traffic when the weather is good, but is more dangerous than in the racetrack.*

Third question*: How many tickets for speeding do you have?*

Rossi*: With the car. With the bike newer, with the car, I don't know. Five.*

Three questions into the interview and we know that Rossi agrees with Michael Schumacher that streets are more dangerous than racetracks and that he has five tickets. That's an average weekend for an AMA dirt tracker.

Now **Gunther***: When you have free time, do you still like to go with your bike?*

Rossi*: Yes, always. I ride the bike in the street.*

Gunther*: Do you have problems with the traffic in London?*

Rossi*: Normally the traffic is a nightmare, also the weather. Very much like bike anyway in London.*

Gunther*: Have you ever gotten a ticket for speeding because you drove too fast?*

(Is there an echo in here?)

Rossi*: With the bike, never. With the car, yes. Sometimes. One per year. Usually when I'm at the motor show in Bologna. When I stay in Italy, I need to start from my home to go in Bologna; always I take the ticket. One time a year, so five or six since '97.*

Right on cue, **Gunther** *asks his Schumacher question: Do you like him?*

Now to me, he's an overrated robot who makes way too much money for loitering in the world's fastest car for an hour and a half every other summer weekend.

Sorry, you want to know what Rossi thinks?

Rossi*: I don't know. Yes, I think Schumacher is the number one, so you need to have respect for him because he's the number one. I don't know him personally, so maybe he's fun. I'm not a Schumacher fan, maybe because in Italy everyone is Schumacher, Ferrari, the flag.*

And then there are the girl questions. ***Helmut****: (Would you prefer) having sex or winning a race?*

Rossi*: Having sex or winning a race is always difficult, but anyway, winning a race.*

Now we're getting to the crux of it.

Helmut*: Would you join your girlfriend if she's driving a motorbike?*

This question was so insipid it required the help of a translator.

Rossi*: Never. With the bike you need to go one, more free, and especially if they don't ride. For sure no, and especially behind a girl, because they're very dangerous. I don't like the girl also with the car. Also with my friends, with the men, if I go inside the car, 95 percent I drive.*

Helmut*: Who are the greatest motorcyclists ever?*

Finally a question with relevance. Not an especially insightful question, but one, at least, that has something to do with the fact that the German is interviewing a motorcycle racer.

Rossi: *For me, maybe Mike Hailwood, Rainey, Schwantz.*
Gunther: *You like the Londoners.*
Rossi: *Yes. Very strange, but anyway I like.*

I think I've got just about enough for my story on the life of the four-time World Champion:

My Eight Minutes with Valentino Rossi

By Henny Ray Abrams

Valentino Rossi may be the world's greatest road racer, but he's undisciplined in a car, getting five speeding tickets, but none on the motorcycle, which he rides around his adopted home of London, where the weather is awful, the people strange, and the traffic hazardous, doubly so if you ride pillion on a motorcycle piloted by a female, which Rossi wouldn't do, because female riders are very dangerous, and, besides, he doesn't want to have sex with her anyhow, he'd rather win a race, like his hero Kevin Schwantz, who might not answer the sex question in quite the same way, at least not now that he's retired, though I could be wrong. I'll let you know in eight minutes.

March 12, 2003

Of Butts and Breasts

Do you know what constitutes 34 percent of a buttock or 26 percent of a woman's breast? If so, you may have a future in law enforcement. That's because the Daytona Beach City Commission, that august group of mouth-breathing brain donors, passed a law in October mandating people cover one-third of the buttocks - it doesn't specify if that's both buttocks, just the left or just the right - and one-quarter of a woman's breast. Break the skin law, and you could find the 15-inch-long eagle-embossed wallet chained to your leather chaps lightened by $106.

The bigger issue, bigger than butts, bigger than boobs, bigger than the boobs who run the city, is why the city of Daytona Beach seems so intent on treating Bike Weekers like used diapers. According to Mark Soskin, an economics professor from the University of South Florida who, at the behest of the local chamber of commerce, performed a study on the economic impact of special events, Bike Week and Biketoberfest generate about $600 million for the local economy. Soskin's study found that during their two annual visits, NASCAR devotees contribute a total of $461 million. His findings were reported on Central Florida Channel 13, who did their own report on the economic impact of the half a million generally law-abiding citizens who come to Daytona Beach for Bike Week. In addition to the big numbers, Channel 13 reported that bikers are better tippers. Except the French, of course.

Soskin was quoted in a recent article in the *Daytona Beach News-Journal*, penned by John Bozzo, as saying, "The benefits far,

far exceed the costs according to our study, but those costs are not trivial."

What the lip-drooling quadrupeds who run the city fail to understand is that without big events like Bike Week, Speed Weeks and spring break, the appeal of Daytona Beach as a vacation destination falls somewhere between Chechnya and Kabul. Under the Taliban.

Bozzo also interviewed Roberts Sheets, president of Government Services Group, a Tallahassee consulting firm who performed a study for Daytona Beach. According to Bozzo's report, Sheets "agrees with the chamber study that special events bring enormous financial benefits to the local economy."

Sheets asked, "Are these special events good for Daytona Beach? That's almost a foolish question. You can't separate events and Daytona Beach. If you take special events away, you don't have Daytona Beach. To me, the issue is how the city, with the help of major benefactors of special events, joins together to meet this financial challenge."

How are they going to balance the budget? On the skin of your ass, that's how.

In addition to the buttocks and breast infractions, there are other fines. Failing to have a muffler on your exhaust pipes provides another $106 to the math scholars who run the city. Carrying an open alcoholic beverage in public will fatten the city coffers by $53. Not having your headlights on, which is different from not covering one-quarter of a breast, is a $44 fine, as is failure to use eye protection. So if you're not wearing goggles ($44) while trolling Main Street on your Fat Boy with open pipes ($106) and the headlight off ($44), and you're wearing a thong ($106) and pasties ($106), you could be docked a sum equal to more than the cost of a Heritage Softail replacement mirror.

Where to start? With the buttock, of course. I think we can all agree where a woman's breast begins. The buttock is another animal altogether. (That the law doesn't specify male or female buttock is a shard of political correctness as transparent as a cellophane bra. Anyone who's been to Main Street or on Daytona Beach will tell you that the last thing they want to see is your average beer-engorged, ribs-filled, shock-busting Harley rider in a thong. Give me a minute while I wash my brain out with soap.)

It's the female buttock that needs to be handled. In order to follow along, you might want to strip to your scants and stand in front of a mirror. Follow the contour of your buttock with your hand. Where does the thigh end and the buttock begin? And how much of it makes up 33 percent? Does the marbled flesh mound of cellulite count? Hard enough to figure when you're standing in the privacy of your kitchen, let alone when your local constable has to make the judgment on the fly.

It's not bad enough that the fine men and women of the Daytona Beach Police Department have to battle the threat of terrorism, anthrax, dirty bombs and cybercrime, now they have to worry about partial buttocks exposure.

Measuring the surface area of a rounded object isn't as easy as you'd think. Quite the opposite. To do it with any accuracy, you'll either need to know the formula for calculating surface area or buy the Uniscan OSP100A 3D Non-Contact Surface Measurement & Profiling system. It can perform noncontact component measurement and profiling of skin, leather (important) and any other application that requires fast, large area, high accuracy, noncontact height measurement. That gadget you think you saw on the passenger seat of the DBPD cruiser, that wasn't a Uniscan OSP100A. It won't fit. That white box with purple and orange lettering, that was the Dunkin Donuts Circular Fat, Calorie, Cholesterol, Jelly, Cream and Sprinkle Replenishment System.

I can imagine the following conversation taking place some time this week.

"Ma'am, do you know why I stopped you?"

"You're lonely, desperate and horny, and this is the only way you could possibly meet chicks?"

"No ma'am. I'm afraid it's your buttocks."

"My buttocks are spectacular."

"Yes ma'am. I couldn't agree more. But the law says you have to cover 33 percent of the buttock."

"I can assure you my buttocks are 34-percent covered. Before I left the house, I made the measurement myself with a Uniscan OSP100A."

"I see."

"Anything else you'd like to say?"

"Care for a doughnut?"

April 16, 2003

The Highs and Lows

It was, in the motorcycle world at least, not a bad weekend for the United States. In their trials by fire, champions Colin Edwards and Nicky Hayden survived a hectic first few laps en route to impressive finishes in their first Grand Prix, at Japan's Suzuka Circuit, showing the world that they more than belong to be in the field when the U.S. GP returns to America in 2004, hopefully at Barber Motorsports Park, a racetrack you could drop onto any European hillside.

The flip side is that it was a tragic weekend for Japan. Daijiro Kato, the quiet yet immensely talented former 250cc World Champion, and Japan's best hope for a MotoGP World Championship, was gravely injured in a senseless and unexplained accident on a track that several of the top riders felt, in the immediate emotional aftermath of more than one serious accident, was no longer suited to host the best road racers in the world.

That he was hastily removed from the track on a stretcher, and that the race wasn't stopped, was a travesty.

"Going into the chicane where [Daijiro] Kato crashed was pretty scary; there was a boot on the track," Hayden said. "There was a lot of dirt. Oh, man. I could not believe it. You know, AMA, there would've been a red flag before I got there."

Neither was the weekend very promising for Team Suzuki, made up of former 500cc World Champion Kenny Roberts Jr. and teammate John Hopkins, now in his second season on the world stage. The concerns they had late in testing proved grounded in reality. The all new GSV-R990 is deficient in any number of areas,

Roberts having handling, transmission and velocity problems. The most speed Roberts could squeeze out of his bike was 187.228 mph, nearly 10 mph down on the 196.673 achieved by Loris Capirossi's Marlboro brand-new Ducati Desmosedici, with Valentino Rossi's Repsol Honda RC-211V second at 196.3, and Nicky Hayden's Repsol Honda third, having run to 196.114 mph.

The speed certainly didn't hurt Hayden in his first race in nearly eight months. After clinching the AMA/Chevy Trucks U.S. Superbike Championship at Virginia International Raceway last August, a heated bidding war for his services ensued at the highest levels, Honda emerging victorious after initially turning its back on its own champion; Yamaha, who'd immediately seen the potential of the 22-year-old Kentuckian, the loser in the high-bucks battle.

The weekend didn't begin well for Nicky. Seven laps into his MotoGP career, he and his RC-211V were sliding and tumbling, his fly-by-wire throttle having stuck open in a fourth-gear corner, the machine triple jumping over a series of trackside barriers. Hayden walked away but was shaken up. When the bell rang for the qualifying session later in the day, he wasn't at his best. Neither was his team. The session began on a slightly wet track that dried for about half an hour before another light rain fell. The tire choice was intermediates; DOTs as Hayden first called them. Not surprisingly, Hayden's teammate, Valentino Rossi, ended up on the pole. The Italian came in when he needed to, his team ready to send him back out on slicks. That would be the key to qualifying. Those with experience would prosper, able to make the most out of the short time they had.

Hayden was watching his pit board. By the time he got the "IN" sign, it was too late. The best he could do was 23rd, the back of the six row grid.

There'd be more dodgy track conditions on Saturday, rain in the morning, half-wet, half-dry in the afternoon. There was no moving up. Then the wind came up on a sunny and chilly Sunday morning, and the meteorological nightmare continued.

"This morning, we had all the conditions this weekend, throw one more in." Hayden said through his million-watt smile.

Edwards has as many miles around Suzuka as almost anyone. This was why the sight of the Texan's sliding along the wet tarmac in Saturday morning's free practice session was so strange, his front having washed out without warning.

"I've got 10-15 hours of rain time here, and that's the first time I crashed, and it took me half a lap," Edwards said.

In the dry he did better, coming within a tenth of a second of the second row. But without the hours of experience that the others had, and with his machine still in the very formative stages, he did well to qualify ninth.

Roberts had qualified seventh, the perfect example of a rider and team being prepared when they had to be. The same approach had earned him his 500cc World Championship. Hopkins was 12th with only two dry laps in qualifying and certain gambles to be taken in tires and set-up for the race.

The first few laps were hectic, riders going everywhere. Edwards and Hayden had never seen anything like it, not at these speeds, at least. Where were the world's best riders?

They were out front and getting away, the trio of Valentino Rossi, Max Biaggi and Loris Capirossi on their way to an all-Italian podium. How did all of the non-Honda teams feel seeing a brand new machine on the podium in its first race?

Edwards and Hayden weren't used to the cut and thrust of the rear guard. The front is normally their domain. Both had to work to move up, and when they met before the mid-point in the race, there was a happy reunion.

"Even though he's been in Europe a while, it still felt like an American style, kind of like I was used to," Hayden said.

Edwards' view was, "We had a good time, and there was nothing really too close."

Edwards got the upper hand, finishing sixth after a setup gamble, which he wouldn't elaborate on, didn't pan out. Hayden made his final play going to the final chicane, losing out by .086 of a second.

Not long after the start, Roberts ran into transmission gremlins, a potentially lethal problem given the speed and acceleration differential. He just wanted to get to the finish in one piece, which he did, one spot behind his new teammate.

"I'm out there realistically trying not to get hit," Roberts said.

Hopkins put the best face on what could well be a very frustrating season. The Suzuki is well behind the others, and the problems may be too fundamental to significantly improve.

"A lot of the manufacturers were here, and they saw the machine and promised us some more effort down at the factory," the soon-to-be 20-year-old Hopkins said. "I'm just going to keep going 100 percent and riding my best and stay positive and hope for better results."

Next year his friends and colleagues will once again get a chance to see him in action. There will be a U.S. GP in 2004, according to those who make the decisions. The choice is down to Barber Motorsports Park, a purpose-built 2.3-mile, 16-turn road race course set in the undulating hills east of Birmingham, Alabama, or Homestead-Miami Speedway, a back and forth road course, tucked inside the speedway's tri-oval, that needs some work to be GP-spec. From a rider's point of view, Barber is the obvious choice, an old fashioned racer's course of the kind that seems to be in increasingly short supply, with safety being paramount. Given the tragedy of this weekend, it's the least the riders are owed.

June 4, 2003

The Little Bike That Could

Whoever said "There is no substitute for cubic inches" never met Tommy Hayden. Nine times out of 10, the fastest bike wins, especially at Daytona International Speedway, the fastest track in racing. So how did Kawasaki's Hayden embarrass a field of Suzuki GSX-R750s by winning the Genuine Suzuki Accessories Superstock final on his little 636cc ZX-GR back in March?

The question arises after allegations of impropriety surfaced at Infineon Raceway. It was after he'd won Daytona and Fontana that rumors of the legality of the Kawasaki first began circulating. Questioned about the reports in Sonoma, team manager Mike Preston said he couldn't comment, that the procedure was ongoing. What he did say was that Hayden would be racing with a different engine at Infineon. It didn't seem to slow him down. Hayden beat Hooters Suzuki's Vincent Haskovec handily, winning by 2.721 seconds.

All along there had been suspicion in some circles that the machine had to be a cheater. There could be no other explanation for a 636 beating a field of 750s.

Given his displacement deficit, Hayden has to utilize other strengths. Tops among them is corner speed. Part of Hayden's success is that with less power he's able to use a softer rear tire, and he's able to get on the gas sooner. The Road Atlanta circuit is one where he was expected to struggle. Aside from the first section, the rest of the track is pretty straightforward, a few corners leading to long, wide open stretches, the kinds of places where his acceleration deficiency is magnified. In the segment from turn one through turn five, the most concentrated collection of corners,

Hayden was the fastest rider. In the timed segment from turn five to turn nine, a section that includes the two longest straights, Hayden fell to 14th.

"It was the backstraight a little bit, and I needed to have the bike working a little bit better, too," Hayden said after finishing fourth in Georgia. "Definitely, they have a little bit more top speed, but I was struggling a little bit in some places where I shouldn't have been. Last year we got 12th, so I guess it's not so bad. I knew this race would be tough."

"Now you see what happens when he's on a legal motorcycle," a senior Suzuki employee said to me in the Road Atlanta press room on Sunday morning. He went on to say that the motorcycle was 10 mms overbored, which anyone with a working knowledge of internals knows is absurd, and he calculated the machine to be 700cc. In addition to a lack of technical savvy, for someone so senior he showed a remarkable ignorance of the rules of the class that his company sponsors, Rule 13 (b) of the AMA's Superstock/Supersport rules says, among other things, that "there is no allowance for overbore."

Hayden's machine was judged to be illegal, not for displacement, but for illegal modifications to the head. What it was, exactly, wasn't immediately disclosed.

After what seemed like a needlessly lengthy delay, the AMA returned the heads from Meiring's and Hayden's machines to Kawasaki at Road Atlanta. Side by side on a workbench, you couldn't tell them apart. Each had valves installed in three of four combustion chambers, the fourth showing the valve seats and ports. Running a finger along the inside edge of the valve seats, you could sense a slight difference. One had been more aggressively cleaned than the other. That would be Hayden's. Without measuring, it was hard to say how much metal had been removed in the cleaning. It doesn't matter. The AMA rules are strict on this point, stating that the "cylinder head ports and combustion chambers must remain absolutely stock with no metal removal." End of discussion. How much performance could be gained by such a minor infraction is open to debate, though the most likely answer is "zip-all."

There was a time, not that long ago, when Suzuki-supported teams were scrutinized more closely than Martha Stewart and found to be much less squeaky clean. I can remember Bill Syfan marching Nicky Hayden to the Sears Point press room in 1998 to explain why he was constantly being disqualified. Hayden's bio in the 2003 AMA press guide states, "His road race season was marred by technical penalties against his team... Rode for HyperCycle Suzuki/Team Suzuki Sport."

What's that line about people in glass houses? More than a few high-profile Suzuki-backed teams have been docked for horsepower violations in Formula USA.

I offered a wager to the Suzuki boss. Would he be willing to bet that Hayden wouldn't win any more Superstock races this year? He grudgingly admitted that there were a few tracks where Hayden could win, beginning this weekend at Pikes Peak International Raceway.

Hayden won the first three races because he's the best rider in the field. He's also the smoothest and the cleanest. He should win at Pikes Peak, a track that favors rider skill over horsepower. Road America, with its long straights out of slow corners, will be a struggle. Brainerd should be interesting. If Hayden can stay close through turns one and two, his run through the rest of the track may be enough, especially with the finish line so close to the final turn.

Mazda Raceway, Mid-Ohio, VIR, Barber, are all proper road courses where the playing field is level enough for Hayden to be a factor.

Ron Barrick, the AMA road racing boss, traditionally presents the number-one plate to the class champion. Since Yamaha's Tom

Kipp won the 750cc Supersport title in 1995, it's been all Suzuki. Kawasaki hasn't won since Scott Russell did the deed in 1992. And when was the last time a machine with a significant displacement disadvantage of similar configuration won the title? Stay tuned.

June 11, 2003

Bungled Again

The first clue that something was hinky came when the AMA timing and scoring monitor showed that Jason Curtis had turned a 4.811-second lap around Pikes Peak International Raceway. Don't get me wrong: Curtis is a good, young up-and-comer, but a 4.811-second lap around a 1.315-mile track averages out to something like 984 mph, and the time couldn't possibly be accurate because I'm pretty sure that a Honda CBR-900RR gas tank is only good for about 900 miles.

Actually that wasn't the first clue. Pretty much from the minute the first bike split the timing beam it was clear that something was hinky. Very hinky. AMA hinky. The times didn't immediately flash up on the screen, and when they did they showed riders averaging 984 mph. On DOT tires no less. Which brings us to Yoshimura Suzuki's Mat Mladin.

Mladin finished the first qualifying session with a time of 53.780 seconds, the best time for a Superbike all weekend. The time was feasible, even though his next-fastest lap was a second slower. After taking the provisional pole, he said he hadn't done the time, but the AMA, in its infinite benevolence, insisted he had. Right up until there were about seven minutes left in Saturday's final qualifying, which was when an AMA official approached Mladin's crew chief Peter Doyle to say something like, "Oh, by the way, that lap we gave Mat yesterday, the one we put on the top of the qualifying sheets we handed out, the one we had plenty of time to think about and question, you know the one; we were just kidding. We're taking it away. Sorry for biffin' it. Stuff happens. Have a nice day."

The reason they told Doyle and not Mladin is that Mladin was already back at the transporter, secure in the knowledge that the AMA had validated a time no one would match. The championship leader had spent the session on a more important task, endurance testing dual-compound tires for the 48-lap slide-a-thon around the PPIR bull ring, rather than trying to beat himself. He already had the pole - the AMA had told him so when it issued Friday's qualifying sheets - so why bother putting on a soft tire to take the pole back from teammate Aaron Yates, who'd just nipped him for the fast time and point that goes with it? Could he have done it? Does a squirrel have nuts?

Earlier in the day American Honda's Chuck Miller had to face the music after three Hondas were found to have illegal parts. Miller admitted the mistake straight up, explained how it happened, never obfuscating; a textbook example of responsibility from a respected team manager that the AMA would do well to learn from.

Director of competition Merrill Vanderslice said. "We're not happy about it," then added, "We'd take the blame for it if it was us, but it's that equipment, and we intend to get satisfaction from the company somehow."

Getting an AMA official to accept blame is harder to find than a nun who can hit a curve ball.

It isn't the technical glitch that irritated the riders; it was how the AMA responded. The riders would have understood the technical problems, though why it took a day to sort out the times from the back-up system seemed odd. Instead, it was standard issue waffling.

Mladin hadn't heard that response when asked for his comments, but he might as well have. "I'm not surprised," he said of the screw-up. "Nothing surprises me anymore. I feel sorry for them [the AMA]."

Mladin has an unfortunate history with the AMA, so conspiracy buffs might speculate there was more to it. They'd be wrong. The AMA botched the times of a number of riders. Pretty much everybody you talked to had a horror story about the way the AMA bungled timing and scoring. Yamaha's Damon Buckmaster had a similar tale to Mladin, though he felt the time the AMA took away from him, which would have put him on the Supersport pole, was legitimate. Like Mladin, he's in a championship hunt and needs every point he can get.

Late on Saturday the AMA issued a release saying there were issues with timing and scoring. This came as a surprise to no one, except, possibly the AMA. Was this a new system they were using? Apparently not. Did they not have time to test it, to see what was obvious to anyone watching the monitors?

There was, of course, a better solution. Since both Mladin and Yates were on the front row anyhow, they should have given Yates the pole, but not the point. That would have been the fair solution. But fairness was never going to be part of this equation.

The qualifying calamity points to a bigger issue than timing and scoring. It goes to respect. How can the riders have any respect for an organization that doesn't show them the same respect? The riders and teams expect the AMA to be at least as professional as they are, to treat racing with the same seriousness, to have systems in place that work consistently, not to make excuses for its errors, and to try to find equitable solutions to unforeseen problems. Which is not to say that the riders aren't the beneficiaries of the AMA's efforts.

The AMA does wonderful things for the riders. Through the diligence of AMA road race manager Ron Barrick and the riders themselves, the tracks are increasingly safer - though they screwed the pooch with the jerry rig at Road Atlanta, and there's work to be done at Infineon Raceway - the television audience continues to grow, both here and overseas, where it can be seen live in Europe, the race weekend is less cluttered, the purses are rising, though not as fast as they should, and the teams have more of a say in the class structure and their own future. All goodwill that is instantly forgotten, not so much when they screw up, but when they refuse to accept responsibility.

UPDATE: In last week's column about a senior Suzuki staffer questioning the legality of Tommy Hayden's Kawasaki ZX-6R, I wrote: "There was a time, not that long ago, when Suzuki-supported teams were scrutinized more closely than Martha Stewart and found to be much less squeaky clean." Comes word at Pikes Peak International Raceway that the Yoshimura Suzuki GSX-R600 of Road Atlanta race-winner Ben Spies was found to be illegal. The machine had a nonstandard oil pressure relief valve. Spies was penalized 20 points and fined $2000. What's that about people in glass houses?

July 30, 2003

What Next?

Have we seen the last of the AMA wild cards at Laguna Seca? More importantly, have we seen the last of World Superbike?

The biggest of the AMA Superbike teams, American Honda, snubbed World Superbike by choosing to showcase its Superbike riders in the Supersport class. That left four AMA wild cards, including the top three in the AMA/Chevy Trucks U.S. Superbike Championship.

Eric Bostrom arrived in Monterey with the best of intentions, surrounded by friends and family, wrapped in a sharp new set of retro leathers, energized by the challenge of racing his standard-bore 750cc Kawasaki ZX-7R against the 1000s of the rest of the world, his charisma a certain draw in a galaxy of stars diminished from last year. Third in Friday's AMA race, Bostrom was headed to the next rounds at Mid-Ohio six points behind Yoshimura Suzuki's Mat Mladin, with five on Yosh's Aaron Yates. Then came World Superbike.

Off the first leg start, Yates tried a low-percentage, high-risk move up the inside of turn two. His front end washed out, he ran through the gravel on the inside, then his GSX-R1000 became the bowling ball that skittled Neil Hodgson, Troy Corser, Frankie Chili and Bostrom. All made the restart but Bostrom.

While Chili was winning the first race, Bostrom was being treated for a thorax compression and dislocated right shoulder, his AMA title hopes damaged, if not shattered.

Less than two weeks after leaving the medical center, he'd have to be in Lexington, Ohio, for the 13th and 14th rounds of the AMA

Superbike Series at the Mid-Ohio Sports Car Course, if his doctor clears him. No one question's Bostrom's determination, but no amount of heart can soften the twists and turns, elevation changes, and hard braking of the hours of practice, qualifying and two superbike races at Mid-Ohio. The first time he brakes from 160 mph plus on the back straight, the pain in his shoulder will be excruciating. Yet there are no regrets at Kawasaki.

"If I don't let him ride, he's off to Australia hanging off a 100-foot cliff," Kawasaki team manager Mike Preston said. "I guess my chances are better letting him ride."

Of the four AMA wild cards, Bostrom was the most enthusiastic. Mladin the least.

"The World Superbike thing is a big pain in the ass to me," Mladin said.

Teammate Aaron Yates was more politic: "I never thought about it. They ask me to do it; I come do it."

Yates restarted in the first leg to finish, then crashed late in leg two while battling for the final podium spot. Mladin had been the fastest rider on the track all weekend, leading the first leg before dropping to fourth. He opted out of leg two because of exhaustion. Ducati Austin's Giovanni Bussei went through two motors after they'd ingested dirt and gravel from first a crash in practice, then another in the AMA race. He finished seventh in the first World Superbike leg, sixth in the second.

Only Mladin left Monterey with a full complement of parts and machinery and with his health intact. The good he did himself and his team will be measured at Mid-Ohio, after which the majority of the teams head directly to Birmingham, Alabama, for a three-day test at Barber Motorsports Park.

"I'm here to try to win the AMA championship," Mladin said after earning the pole for the AMA race. "If I could do a World Superbike race without having to concentrate on AMA, I'd be much happier. I'd be here, ready to go, flat out for World Superbike."

Will there be a World Superbike race in Monterey next year? And, if so, will it be worth watching?

As Gordon Ritchie, *Cycle News*' man on the World Superbike trail, wrote last week, World Superbike is in if not turmoil, at least transition. The Motorcycle Sports Manufacturers Association (MSMA), a group that includes Honda, Suzuki. Ducati, Kawasaki, Yamaha and Aprilia, issued a surprisingly strongly worded statement on Thursday decrying the current and future states of World Superbike technical regulations. "As a consequence, the large majority of the MSMA member companies who were considering entering World Championship Superbike have reviewed their positions and decided not to enter World Championship Superbike at all," the MSMA's release stated.

Is it a bluff? It was known that Yamaha and Aprilia wouldn't be playing in 2004, no matter the rules. Honda hasn't made its plans known, and the signals Kawasaki has been sending don't presage a return to the series. Ducati and Suzuki may return, though tires will certainly factor into their thinking.

On the same day the MSMA fired its salvo, the FIM caught some of the tire companies by surprise by issuing a statement that said next year's World Superbike series would feature spec tires.

"At the request of the Superbike World Championship promoter, FGSport Group, a unique brand and type of tires will be available to all riders and teams to create fair and equitable conditions to all of them and in order to prevent a lack of availability of tires," the FIM release read.

Dunlop supplies tires to the vast majority of the World Superbike paddock. The exceptions are the three-rider DFX Ducati team, which uses Pirellis, and the Foggy Petronas and Fila Ducati teams, which Michelin supplies, though not equally. Foggy

Petronas' Troy Corser complained early in the season about getting two-year-old tires.

Neither Dunlop nor Michelin was aware of the FIM's plans, leading to speculation that Pirelli would be the tire of forced choice, if the regulation flies, making World Superbike an even more Italian championship, run by the Flammini group, raced mostly by Ducatis, possibly to be shod with Pirellis.

None of which would matter to the AMA Superbike teams, all of whom are under contract to Dunlop this year. Suzuki and Kawasaki are signed for 2004, with Honda and Ducati up for grabs, and Yamaha's return to the Superbike class uncertain, though less likely if it doesn't make an attack on the world level. If American Honda and whoever is running AMA's Ducati team go to Michelin, as some have speculated, they'd also be precluded from World Superbike

So maybe the teams won't have to decide whether to allow, or encourage, their riders to pull double duty at Laguna Seca next year.

With the mass defections from World Superbike after 2002 of Ben Bostrom, Colin Edwards, Nori Haga and Troy Bayliss, and with Neil Hodgson almost certain to go to GPs next year, the Laguna Seca weekend is more dependent than ever on the star power of the AMA wild cards, even in reduced numbers. When Yoshimura Suzuki's Mat Mladin took the lead in the first leg, the crowd roared in approval, an unlikely occurrence at AMA races.

"I think for us at Kawasaki, it would be a disappointment if he didn't ride," Kawasaki team manager Mike Preston said of Eric Bostrom. If only he has somewhere to do it.

September 10, 2003

Incensed!

In a single bold stroke, the AMA Pro Racing Board managed to incense nearly the entire AMA Superbike paddock, or at least those who put the most into racing.

The issue was parity and how the Pro Racing Board went about ensuring it. For 2004, V-twins get a break on air boxes, throttle bodies, and gear sets, while the four-cylinders regress to stock air boxes and throttle bodies. Most of those questioned in the paddock were adamant that it would give the V-twins an unfair advantage while slowing down the four-cylinders. The rules even caused Honda to rethink its strategy, according to team manager Chuck Miller. If the four-year-old Honda RC-51 is in the company's model lineup for 2004, it may continue to race it, he said, a position no one seemed to consider even a month ago - not with the imminent arrival of the new inline four.

The rules were pushed through without discussion, more of a fiat than a democratic discussion, which the teams had been accustomed to and expected.

The simple question is why? Why is the AMA Pro Racing Board so interested in giving Ducati, and possibly Honda, an advantage? Because that's clearly what they've done. At Virginia International Raceway there was no easy answer. The only Pro Racing Board member in attendance was Kevin Schwantz, and he initially argued and voted against it. No other board member showed up. Neither did AMA Pro Racing CEO Scott Hollingsworth, who was expected then changed his plans.

The disagreement highlights the disconnect between the Pro Racing Board, made up of industry types, very few of whom spend much time at superbike races, and the road race advisory board, a panel made up of representatives of the major race teams. At VIR, the road race board was left to question its own relevance.

"The advisory board is nothing more than a room to get everybody riled up in a pissing contest. They don't make any sense any more because the AMA doesn't take what's been discussed," Yamaha's Keith McCarty said.

"At the [road race] advisory meeting, a majority of the advisory voting members voted in favor of having one set of rules for all bikes running in Superbike," Yoshimura Suzuki's Don Sakakura said. "I don't know who makes the rules. It's like the advisory board... why are we going to those meetings?"

Kawasaki's Mike Preston said the members of the road race advisory board, "were surprised, because there's stuff happening, some was discussed, some not discussed and the complete opposite of what people said."

So why bother? American Honda's Chuck Miller said they'd requested better communication between the boards.

"Because one thing I've learned in my position, I don't always agree and understand why things go that way, but when you find out all the facts, sometimes it all makes a lot more sense," Miller said. "And we just don't have all the facts all the time. And that frustrates us all."

The new rules are aimed squarely at one rider, Yoshimura Suzuki's Mat Mladin. If not for tire problems at a number of races, Mladin could have won nearly every race since Daytona. When the rules were changed to encourage participation by 1000cc four-cylinders, Yosh embraced it and their results are evident at every meeting. Aaron Yates has had his best year and will likely finish no worse than second in the championship. Jason Pridmore has been able to put the private Attack Suzuki on the box a few times and challenge the factory Hondas and Ducatis.

All of the Japanese companies make a big bore four-cylinder, and all could have raced them, though not with the success of Suzuki. The GSX-R1000 is routinely named as the best large sportbike in worldwide polls. It's certainly the best race bike. And Suzuki thinks enough of it to send it up against the all-powerful Ducatis in World Superbike, the only Japanese factory to do so.

Mladin doesn't believe slowing the bikes down is a bad idea, not with the safety problems at the majority of AMA tracks. But he, and much of the rest of the four-cylinder crowd, doesn't see why the V-twins should be given an advantage.

The argument could be made for inclusion. Two years ago Yamaha had a Superbike, Kawasaki had two, and Ducati supported two teams. Now Yamaha's gone, not to return in 2004. Kawasaki hasn't said what it's doing, though it's hard to imagine it wouldn't market the new ZX-10R. And Ducati is playing the coquettish ingénue, flirting with its suitors until an acceptable gift is proffered. That would be the rules.

Ducati management said as recently as the AMA/World Superbike round at Laguna Seca that it would consider racing if the rules were acceptable. With its sales slumping in the United States and the new 999 not selling in Europe, it's imperative that Ducati markets its newest V-twin by racing in AMA. But it couldn't do it if the costs were prohibitive, not with the amount of money it's pouring into MotoGP. What the rules have done is allow the company to come in without spending too much or working too hard.

Had the Pro Racing Board left the rules the same for the twins while slowing the fours, there would have been less discontent. But to give the twins power while taking it away from the fours defies logic.

One team manager who asked not to be named asked what qualifications the Pro Racing Board had to make those technical decisions, "Show me one guy that's helping you make those decisions that's a friggin' engineer that knows any valuable thing. There isn't any. Is [AMA technical manager] Rob King an engineer? He is. If they consulted him, look at all the bullshit that he's gotten into."

Yamaha's Keith McCarty has the last word. "If you took the money that every company, that the four major companies, take it away, tell me what kind of racing you'd have here? So for them not to pay attention to that is really narrow-minded, I think."

October 1, 2003

Poker Face

A high-stakes game of poker is being played at the highest levels of the AMA and American Suzuki with the final hand likely to determine the look of AMA road racing in 2004.

The AMA Pro Racing board recently issued technical rules for the Superbike class that many feel favor the aging V-twins at the expense of the new inline fours. The vitriol was immediate and forceful, with most of the Superbike team managers incensed that their voices weren't heard and hoping for a change. Now Suzuki's done something about it.

In a strongly worded letter to AMA president Rob Rasor, American Suzuki vice president for motorcycles and ATVs, Mel Harris, has threatened, mildly in his words, to pull out of the Superbike class. "Suzuki feels that under the new proposed rules that there is not parity, not an even playing field," Harris told *Cycle News* editor Paul Carruthers. This isn't Harris talking. He couldn't have issued the letter without the explicit approval of the highest levels of corporate Suzuki.

Specifically he's referring to the rule mandating stock throttle bodies and airboxes for the four-cylinders, while allowing the V-twins an alternate set. What also bothered Harris was that with the elimination of the 750cc Superstock class, traditionally the showcase for Suzuki's GSX-R750, there may be nowhere for Suzuki to showcase its new GSX-R750 since there's talk of banning 750s from the 1000cc Superstock class.

Does he have a point? That depends on your point of view. Will the AMA bend and change the rules? That's the multimillion-dollar question.

"If I was the AMA, I'd call his bluff," a veteran of the race scene said.

The belief throughout most of the paddock is that Suzuki has no choice but to race what is unquestionably the best sportbike line in motorcycle history. That it would choose not to race, and advertise, Mat Mladin's unprecedented fourth number-one plate in the premier Superbike class is a notion many find laughable, especially when it's announced its withdrawal from World Superbike and the MotoGP team runs at the back of the field. With the barons of World Superbike trying to kill that series, the AMA/Chevy Trucks U.S. Superbike Championship could be the pre-eminent production bike series in the world, and Suzuki is not going to allow a pretender to steal its thunder.

Kawasaki, Honda and Yamaha will all have new 1000s next year. Yamaha's committed to Superstock and is likely to develop the Superbike with an eye toward racing it late in the season. Honda will run its new bike in Superbike and likely Superstock, under the Erion Honda tent, though no decisions have been made. It may continue to race the RC-51, though you can bet the crew wants something newer and with more upside potential. Kawasaki remains on the fence awaiting final rules but willing to abide by what's already been ordered. Team manager Mike Preston: "The problem is, I'm hearing some other manufacturers and management are crying the blues that they couldn't get what they wanted and are threatening."

Much of the worry is being fed by the speculation that Ducati Corse is coming with a full factory effort, WSB runner-up Ruben Xaus, and the best of the Michelins. That blue sky combination, given the rules discrepancy, would be potent and more than enough to give the Suzuki crew a few sleepless nights, if Xaus cured his penchant for crashing. It's one thing to spill on the wide expanses of an FIM-homologated track, quite another to hit a tree or scaffold or wall or banking at any number of the considerably more dangerous, yet somehow approved, AMA tracks.

The Ducati Desmo V-twin is nearing the end of its competitive life cycle, with a V-4 based on the MotoGP-winning Desmosedici likely on the horizon for 2005. Ducati wasn't competitive this year, but it wasn't the motorcycle, it was the rider. Anthony Gobert, Ducati Austin's first rider, was asked to leave after Road America. Giovanni Bussei, his genial replacement, adapted to AMA tracks little by little but was never a consistent threat. Nor were the V-twin Hondas a consistent threat after sweeping Daytona, though Kurtis Roberts was better than he's ever been and should only get better, if he sticks around.

Mladin and Aaron Yates ruled because Yoshimura made the smart decision to take advantage of the rules for '03. Mladin makes the point that when he arrived in Daytona for the 200, he had one motorcycle.

"I was told at Daytona, 'Don't crash it, because if you do, you're going to be riding a production bike, full stop,'" he said.

Not race ready for Daytona, Yosh rebounded in the next round at California Speedway with Mladin doing the double, and they didn't stop winning or advertising.

When word of the letter first leaked out, the rumor was that Suzuki was going to pull all of its support for all classes and support teams. Harris' comments to *Cycle News* are vague on the issue, but he seems to suggest that it would abandon Superbikes to concentrate on Superstock.

There are a few reasons Suzuki won't abandon Superbikes; first among them is cost. Many of the bottom-line numbers - rider salaries, travel, testing - are fixed. If you're going to the track, those costs don't change. Certainly it costs less to develop and race a Superstock machine rather than a Superbike, but the return is equally diminished. And though it'd be substantially less work at

Daytona, you'd still have to pay those usurious hotel rates for the week minimum.

But the real reason this won't happen is simple: television.

There is no greater marketing tool than winning races on live television, something Suzuki's done very well this year. Mladin won 10 races and teammate Aaron Yates another three. Superstock racing will not be on live television in '04, and it won't be the feature class, no matter who races in it. Does Suzuki want everyone huddled around the TV on Tuesday night watching the riders they're paying so handsomely race each other?

(There's an unsettled question about who would be allowed to race in the class. One proposal would ban factory-paid Superbike riders from the class, though the vagueness of the early wording invites liberal interpretation. Mladin will tell you he rides for Yoshimura Suzuki, not the factory team, and therefore he isn't a factory rider. Others might beg to differ.)

The question remains, is the AMA going to flip-flop on the Superbike rules? Not if you listen to AMA Pro Racing CEO Scott Hollingsworth: "Everybody is going to have some aspect of the rules that they don't like, so you can't go chasing your tail and try to please everybody because you are never going to do it."

So where does that leave Suzuki? Still with a championship-winning motorcycle and the best rider in the field, for the fourth time, and the desire to let the rest of the world know it.

"Maybe this team's got the best rider, and they've definitely got the best crew. No doubt about that," Mladin says.

But will they be on the Superbike grid when the season opens next year at Daytona? Only if it's on television.

November 26, 2003

Time to Change

In the wake of the tragic death of rising Japanese star Daijiro Kato, a safety committee was formed by various riders and racing officials. The evening before every Grand Prix, the group, which includes Valentino Rossi, Sete Gibernau, Kenny Roberts Jr. and Nobu Aoki, along with representatives from the various governing bodies, takes to the racetrack for a low-speed pass. Circulating in a van, the riders point out areas that need improvement and make notes they hope will translate into changes. Their decisions are guided by a number of factors, including a formula for top speed and runoff. The wrong side of that formula means certain change.

Such is the power of the group that their recommendations for the Honda-owned Suzuka Circuit were so onerous that the 2004 Suzuka GP was canceled while changes are made. Asked at the final race of the year in Valencia, Spain, why it took such a horrific outcome for the riders to become empowered, Rossi said matter-of-factly, "Because we are a little bit dickheads. We need always to wait."

Waiting cost Daijiro Kato his life on a circuit which, though improved for 2003, was still thought to be unsafe by current standards.

At every track the riders visited following the formation of the safety committee, changes have been requested. "We make very good work now," Rossi continued. "Now we wait the good work of the circuit and the organization because the riders are together, and we say, 'This one is okay; this one is not.' Now we need to wait for next year."

What would happen if a group of AMA riders did the same - if the tracks were held to GP standards? The season would either be very short or there'd be 18 rounds at Mazda Raceway at Laguna Seca. Barber Motorsports Park, until given the FIM's blessing, wouldn't make the cut. And it's not likely to receive homologation as currently configured.

Let's start with the first track - Daytona International Speedway. Would the world stop spinning if the season didn't start in Florida? Suzuka provides the answer.

Daytona is a dinosaur that brings out the worst in motorcycles and tires, especially tires. Last month, Yoshimura Suzuki's rising star Ben Spies had his rear tire come apart soon after the Yosh radar gun registered 186 mph. The young Texan suffered severe skin and tissue loss but no broken bones. He was very lucky.

The test had come about because Dunlop technicians weren't happy with the temperatures they saw during a preliminary Daytona test in August. The data from that very selective test is used to build tires for the all-teams gathering in December. Not liking what it saw, Dunlop brought back its engineers from Birmingham, England, along with a new generation of tires and invited Honda and Suzuki. Only Spies and teammate Aaron Yates could make it. Mat Mladin, who could've given the most valuable input, was home in Australia awaiting the imminent birth of his daughter. The Honda riders were all recovering from post-season surgery.

The test was winding down late on a Monday afternoon when Spies' tire blew on the front straight, sending him into a prolonged slide. The tissue on his left buttock was ground away, and there were injuries to his left shoulder and elbow. A skin graft closed the wound, but only after he endured weeks of painful therapy and rehab. But his spirit wasn't broken, and he's ready to come back. And he doesn't blame Dunlop. Neither does anyone on the Yosh squad.

"It's one of the biggest problems that we face with the States with the ridiculous weight limits of the bikes." Mladin said recently in a phone call from Australia, prior to Spies' accident. "With motorbikes putting out upwards of 190 horsepower now and weighing 170kg [374 pounds], that is so much harder on tires than GP bikes; people don't understand. People think GP bikes make so much power and stuff, but the bikes are so light (290 pounds for MotoGP, 356 pounds for World Superbikes), they don't load the tires as much as what our Superbikes do. We're getting all this safety concerns and people wanting to slow down the bikes because they're getting too fast and all that sort of garbage, but you need to lose 20-25 pounds off the bike, and it'll be safer straight away."

Case in point: Mladin's Suzuki makes over 190 horsepower and should be in the high 190s by Daytona. The Kawasaki ZX-RR MotoGP machine makes considerably more power but weighs less and had no significant tire failure this year, despite using many of the same tires. The tires Garry McCoy used showed up in the AMA paddock within weeks.

First a direct quote from *Mechanics of Pneumatic Tires* editor Samuel K. Clarke of University of Michigan, written a long time ago. But the mechanism of failure is put so correctly: "When rolling at high speed, waves are formed on a tire behind the area of contact to the road. The repeated deformation caused by the wave process results in considerable heat build-up, which reduces the strength of the tire and may lead to its ultimate destruction." Think of the tread forming a lazy ess as it comes off the tarmac.

The most dangerous parts of Daytona are the transitions from the banking to the flats, off of NASCAR turns four and two, and into turn one, where the deformation is most pronounced. It's no surprise that where Spies' tire failed was on the flat after the tri-oval. When Kurtis Roberts' tire failed in 2002, it happened going onto the back straight, off of NASCAR two. Mladin's rear tire blew at Road Atlanta just as he straightened up heading down the back straight.

The amount of deformation is due to the amount of load applied and the inflation pressure supporting it (the carcass supports very little load). Load has a large effect, even tougher at Daytona because the bikes operate at close to 2G in the banking, i.e.: considerable deformation.

In round terms, load will increase the proportional amount of energy to the tires. Simply put, a 20 percent increase in weight difference will give 20 percent more energy input.

Will the AMA consider lowering the weight of Superbikes? Not on your life. The AMA has a one big family approach to racing, even at what is meant to be the top level of the sport. Privateers can make impressive horsepower numbers: Witness what Kevin Hunt did to Shawn Higbee's Millennium Technologies/Kaufmann Trailers Suzuki GSX-R1000 last year. But getting weight off is expensive and gets increasingly more so with exotic metals.

With Kawasaki U.S. unwilling to bear the burden of development costs for its new ZX-10RR, the AMA Superbike field will be even smaller this year than last and therefore more dependent on privateers. The truth is that even if Eric Bostrom signs with Ducati Austin, as expected, Mladin is the strongest rider on the strongest team who should win more often than not, regardless of the weight of his machine. If the weight were lowered, would he win by more? Probably. But so what? The other factories could match the lowered weight limits, and the privateers would be self-policing, simply because of budgets.

It took the death of Kato to wake up the GP world. Let's not make that same mistake twice.

December 3, 2003

New Life

What do Eric Bostrom and Valentino Rossi have in common? With deft career moves both injected new life into what threatened to be moribund championships.

All Rossi has said of his move from Honda to Yamaha, an unprecedented defection at the top levels of Japanese racing, is that he needed a new challenge, greater motivation. And that may be true. But there must also be some element of heavy handedness from Honda as well as Honda's finally tiring of Rossi's demands, things like racing with his favored number 46 rather than the number one that Honda spent so much to help him earn. By moving to Yamaha, he's made the world sit up and take notice. His will be the most scrutinized season in the history of racing, which translates to interest world-wide, which is just what the Doctor ordered.

Eric Bostrom has never been shy about his ambitions. Even before older brother Ben went to World Superbike in 2000, Eric's wanted to line up against the best. Kawasaki did its best to accommodate him, but it wasn't enough, and it wouldn't be enough in 2004. Not only couldn't it help him overseas, but its plans for the AMA had him taking a backward step career-wise. Instead of racing in Superbike, he'd be toiling in the far more competitive 1000cc Superstock class, one without live television. He wisely made the decision to leave Kawasaki, though he left it in a bit of a lurch late in the game.

Kawasaki has a brand-new ZX-10R that many expected it to race in Superbike. It made perfect sense but for one major detail: Kawasaki U.S. would have to bear all of the development costs.

Having spent liberally on the aged and overbored ZX-7R in 2003, it knew what fast engines cost. The advantage it had was in the chassis, a proven package. But having to build a chassis and work the engines on the new bike proved too much, and it stepped down for a season, at least.

Bostrom's name was on a short list Ducati had at the final GP in Valencia, but with the notation "too expensive." Others were Nori Haga, who wasn't thought of as serious, John Hopkins, unhappy at Suzuki but under contract and not likely to want to regress to AMA, and Garry McCoy, whose tail-wagging riding style hasn't translated to four-strokes. Others were also considered after Ducati recovered from the sudden shock of losing Shane Byrne to Aprilia. Ducati was sure it had the Englishman locked up until the Saturday of the Valencia GP. Once Ducati saw its options fading, Bostrom's price tag suddenly became irrelevant.

When the chance to move arose, he jumped at it, now with Michelin, who'd been on and off the Ducati Austin project, offering its support.

How serious Michelin is remains to be seen. It's developed the well-earned reputation for picking front-runners and front-runners only. In World Superbike this year, it fully backed only the Fila Ducati team while angering the Foggy Petronas team with second-rate rubber. It was its reluctance to supply more World Superbike teams - which put the onus almost completely on Dunlop - that convinced the barons of FGSport to go to spec tires for 2004. Michelin dropped Suzuki's MotoGP team for 2004, though that may have something to do with commercial arrangements.

The presence of guards will tell if Michelin's serious. The French company is maniacal about chain of custody with its newest tires, forever fearful one might fall into the wrong hands. It hires security to watch the trucks at the world events. The production process is so secretive that virtually none of those involved know what the others are doing. The compound specialist doesn't know how the carcass is built. If one leaves, he can't take all the secrets with him. Case in point: As soon as Fila Ducati's Ruben Xaus finished the postrace burn-out after his second race win at Laguna Seca this past July, a Michelin man was there with a broom and dust pan to collect the smoked rubber. Worried that a simple broom wasn't efficient, a vacuum cleaner was brought in to finish the job.

Michelin's backing of the doomed Dream Team Ducati squad was less than expected, at least from Larry Pegram's point of view. Rightly or wrongly, Pegram claimed the tires he used during a January test at Laguna Seca were the same ones Colin Edwards had won on the year before. He assured one and all that the good rubber would be arriving before long, but it never did, at least not before the Dream Team was euthanized after Road America.

At Valencia, a Ducati spokesman said it wanted Ducati Austin to use Michelins if it had Ruben Xaus, the Spaniard who was already on his way to the d'Antin Ducati MotoGP squad. Otherwise, it didn't have a preference. With Bostrom on board, it appears to have changed its mind.

Ducati's position on AMA racing isn't dissimilar to Michelin's. The last time it was serious about racing was in 2000 when it backed the Vance & Hines team and John Kocinski. The following year its support was fragmented, and the results showed. In the past three years it has been through the Dream Team and Competition Accessories and HMC Racing. This year Ducati Austin was chosen to fly the flag with Anthony Gobert riding. That arrangement imploded after Road America and the genial Italian Giovanni Bussei was brought in to run out the string. Given Ducati's recent level of support, it's made little financial sense to race the V-twins for some time, which explains the high mortality rate of Ducati teams.

Now Bostrom, on the 2003 Ducati World Superbike machines supported directly by Ducati Corse and presumably with some of the better Michelin tires, will be a true challenger for the title, easily the greatest impediment to Yoshimura Suzuki's Mat Mladin winning number one number five.

Before Bostrom's move, the Superbike class looked like a Mladin walkover, as 2003 would have been without his repeated tire problems. Dunlop has already given the AMA series the status of World Superbike but has redoubled its efforts for 2004, promising to bring more senior staff from overseas. The tire problems that repeatedly struck Mladin last year, and prolonged his path to the title, should be eliminated.

Mladin is rightly on the record as detesting the AMA's decision to bend over to give an advantage to the V-twins in airbox and throttle bodies. Privately, the team isn't that worried. Should they be?

Daytona probably won't give us the answer. Ducati's record in Florida is abysmal, and though it would desperately like to win it, the Desmo twin hasn't shown the reliability to finish near the front for years. After that it's on to California Speedway, a track with twists and turns, where experience in setup and tires is paramount. Mladin won both legs in Fontana in 2003, one of the three double wins that made up his 10-race total.

Mladin doesn't like Bostrom, and that's a good thing for the championship. Theirs will be a true rivalry, completely different people on different engines and different tires going for the same goal. Mladin's never lacked motivation in winning four titles; with Bostrom defecting to a stronger position, he won't lack it in 2004.

January 28, 2004

Rent It - No, Don't!

Twenty minutes into the screening of *Torque*, the latest and lamest in a thankfully short string of sportbike-driven testosterone fests, 40 percent of the audience in the Flatbush Pavilion walked out. That left three of us. And I had to be there. It's that good.

Cary Ford, the film's protagonist, played by Martin Henderson, has the honor of delivering the dumbest line: "I live my life a quarter-mile at a time." Replies his thong-wearing mechanic girlfriend, Shane (Monet Mazur), "That's the dumbest thing I ever heard." That's not true. The dumbest thing I heard was the cashier saying, "That'll be $9.50."

You've seen the posters or the ads or the previews. You're drawn in because there are sportbikes and guys in leathers that say "Carpe diem," Latin for "seize the day" as anyone who saw Robin Williams in *Dead Poets Society* knows. And some of the most egregious ad placement you'll ever find for a helmet company. Stay away. Run away. Rent *Dead Poets Society*. Sleep in. Overdose on Twinkies.

We soon find out that Ford is a street racer who's recently returned from six months in Thailand, where he went to hide out after upsetting the Hellions - a local breed of dirty shirts - by stealing their Harleys, which apparently run on test tubes full of crystal methedrine, one of the more effective forms of speed, the irony of which is lost on almost everyone because it's unintentional. The gas tanks full of drugs are a shameless ripoff of the cocaine-filled gas tanks that fueled Captain America and Billy's cross-country odyssey in *Easy Rider*. Rent *Easy Rider*.

Along the way Ford incurs the wrath of Trey, the gangsta leader of the "Reapers," an urban sport bike scourge with their own sweep truck and mascot, a pit bull named Dojo. Trey's face is fixed in a permanent sneer, probably as a result of being in this movie. Ice Cube, an actor of considerable skill who must have been in need of a paycheck between *Barbershop* movies, drew the short straw for Trey and displays a range of emotions ranging from really pissed off to really, really pissed off.

The reason Trey's boxers are twisted is that Henry, the mullet-headed drug-dealing head slimebucket of the Hellions, more of a dirty shirt than sportbike gang, framed Ford for the murder of a Reaper who came to his premature demise in a men's room. Not unlike Elvis. Still awake?

Solving the crime is a pair of FBI agents, one so cartoonish that he'd make J. Edgar Hoover pull his dress over his eyes in disgust. The male wears branded T-shirts under a cheap suit with Converse sneakers, the woman with her hair fixed in corn rows.

Essentially we have a modern Western, a chase movie where the good guy's mistaken for the bad guy by the very good guys because of what the very bad guys did. All in all, 81 minutes of life-sapping drudgery that makes *Gigli* look like *Citizen Kane*. Which would be acceptable if the riding were good or interesting or original. It's not.

On the street, Ford and his posse of two engage in a contest of who can ride most like the 18th-place finisher in the D Superstock race at Summit Point. It was a three-way draw. Mostly they hang off and hold the bikes off to the side as if they were used diapers while using both lanes to remain vertical.

The chase scenes, mostly going after Ford, take place on every imaginable (and a few unimaginable) surfaces.

There's a fairing-banging scene on the street. There's the run through the palm desert on fully-faired dirt bikes, including Trey's Triumph Daytona 955, which flies with the grace of a tarred duck.

But the keeper is the chase scene along the roof of a moving passenger train.

Our hero Ford uses a conveyor belt to jump on the roof - Trey soon to follow. For about 30 seconds, that was the most preposterous stunt. Then Ford jumps down between cars, opens the door with a wheelie, and rides up the aisle, skittling passengers like ten pins until he jumps out the door and off the train. Trey leaps off the front of the train, landing on the tracks, puncturing his tire and landing under the bike, the locomotive bearing down like an avalanche.

There's more on an L.A. freeway. Ford drives a stolen stock car out the back of a semitrailer - don't ask - and drives long enough to catch up to his posse, whom he switches places with at speed. This being as predictable as sticky movie floors, the bad guys can't be far behind, and soon there's another dudly duel - Trey against Ford with lots of bodywork to account for.

That leads to the beginning of the end, a meeting where the drugs are to be returned and everyone gets to ride into the sunset. It doesn't quite end up that way.

Instead we get Y2K, a long, sleek silver beast that's touted as the fastest bike in the world, a carbon-fiber frame supporting a Rolls-Royce helicopter engine with a 0-100 time of less than 10 seconds.

But before we get to the early-'80s video-game-quality, computer-generated chase finale comes the obligatory chick fight. Shane against China, Henry's brooding squeeze with enough metal in her face to make a set of crankcases.

The proper medium for a chick fight is either pudding or cole slaw or both. But these two face off in a stoppie-and-wheelie duel in the middle of a produce market under an elevated highway that ends as predictably as everything else - China getting backflipped into produce. Sadly, not cole slaw.

Hard as it is to believe, Y2K meets its match in Henry's blown Harley, the pair careening through the streets of L.A. like rejects from a 1967 beta version of "Grand Theft Auto."

I'd give away the ending, but I don't remember it, except that the racer/bike thief literally rides into the sunset with his mechanic girlfriend and their two buddies, heading for Mexico, where the laws against committing crimes against movie-going humanity aren't prosecuted.

The movie aims squarely for the treasured 18-34 male demographic. I can imagine the pitch meeting went something like this:

"It's *Easy Rider* meets *Bullitt*, but updated for the new millennium."

"Sounds great. Tell me about the characters."

"We have Ford, a swashbuckling knee-dragger who stole some drug-filled Harleys, then split for six months in Thailand so that his girlfriend, Shane, a thong-wearing mechanical whiz, doesn't get dragged into it by Henry, the knuckle-dragger whose custom Harleys Ford boosted, a maniacal gang leader, drug dealer and murderer, though different from Trey, the leader of an urban sportbike gang who, when he's not petting his pit bull, Dojo, spends the whole movie growling like he has diaper rash mostly because of something China, Henry's lying, sullen, saddle sore who's been pierced more than an archery target, told the Gen-X G-men. Heard enough?"

"So the target audience is larcenous motorcycle racers on the lam, moronic murdering drug dealers, disgruntled urban bikers with pets, body jewelry fetishists, and underwear models with tuning skills?"

"More or less."

"Sounds perfect. Will it be in theaters on Valentine's Day?"

"Ummmm....we can only hope."

February 11, 2004

Playing the Percentages

Qualifying for an AMA Superbike race just got a little harder, but is it hard enough? In a word, no - a view that's shared by at least two of the most likely protagonists for the title.

After years of inaction, the AMA recently lowered the qualifying time to 110 percent of the fastest qualifier from 112 percent. A small difference that should have been greater. The 2 percent solution will do very little to alter the field or the outcome of the race. The mark they should have shot for is 107 percent, the number it takes to make a MotoGP field.

At the 2003 Daytona 200, American Honda's Ben Bostrom took pole position with a lap of 1:48.376. At 112 percent of Bostrom's time, a lap of 2:01.381 was needed to make the field. Theoretically, three of the 77 riders who rode in qualifying were out. (Many were just using Superbike practice to work out setup for other classes and didn't take the grid, which numbered 59.) At the new standard of 110 percent, six would be cut from the back of the grid. Going to MotoGP standards would cut the field exactly in half. Would that be a bad thing? Daytona's traditional 80-rider field is a thing of the past. But should it be half that?

"Not 80 people on that grid. That's crazy," Bostrom said over dinner following last week's Daytona tire test. "That's absolutely insane. It's dangerous."

Ducati Austin's Eric Bostrom agrees. "I think if there are 24 guys on the grid, that's enough guys to go have a race," he said. "There's 20 guys on a Supercross grid, and that's at least five too many. There are 18 guys on a [mile or half-mile] dirt track, and it's probably too many, but it's a big track, so it usually works out."

On a small track, like Pikes Peak International Raceway with its 54-second lap times, Eric Bostrom lapped his first backmarker on the 11th lap of last year's 40-lap race. Why? Because with the 112 percent rule in place, everyone made the main - though six opted not to start. This year's 110 percent mark would have eliminated a measly two riders. At 107 percent, nine riders would be out, and the leaders wouldn't catch the tail-enders until the 21st lap.

The Bostrom brothers are passionate about the safety implications of the all-inclusive Superbike fields. The fields are too big, the standards too low, the back of the grid too slow and unpredictable. It's too easy to get into the main. Their concerns were well voiced, and they offered sensible solutions, solutions they believe will improve the quality and safety of the racing.

For instance, why couldn't the Superbike field be 24 riders, the same number as MotoGP? The World Superbike field at Laguna Seca was 23, with 10 finishers in race two and 13 in race one. No one noticed because the racing at the front was superb. Does anyone come to the racetrack to watch the battle for 35th? They certainly don't see it on television, where only the top handful of riders are ever shown.

"So many of the races end from lappers," Ben Bostrom said. "The last 10 laps are a joke. It's like one guy gets through lappers and then another guy. Pretty soon it's just one-two-three-four. The bikes are spread out."

Ben knows this too well. Taking an inside line that was risky, at best, especially in light of his concerns about lappers, his season ended in a heap outside of turn five at Barber Motorsports Park. Four laps from the end of the year, he rear-ended a backmarker, who was propelled into another lapper, who took out his teammate Miguel Duhamel. Eric wasn't trying to defend Ben, but he offered an explanation. He said it was the unpredictability of the slowest lappers that caused the most anxiety.

Ben's take on big fields is that "the AMA believes more people in a race, better action. That's not true. Less people, more of a race. If you watch any MotoGP or World Superbike, there's only very few riders, and each one of those guys is up front, pretty much. You lap one guy, and it never affects the race, almost ever."

What Ben and Eric think the AMA should do is pay on a sliding scale to many of those who don't qualify for the race. The riders would get about the same purse as if they'd finished in the money, wouldn't burn up equipment and tires, and wouldn't change the outcome of the race. And they'd have something to focus on for the next race or use the qualifying money to fund their Superstock efforts.

"So why not qualify for it and make the same money, go get the money, and then they'll use that money so they can race Superstock?" Ben asks. "Let's go talk to the AMA about how to distribute the money so the privateers get money, and let's make this a strong field, make it good for television, safe for everyone."

These aren't the incoherent rants of a couple of overpaid stars who were born to the manor. Both worked their way up through the ranks of dirt track and motocross. In 1994, Ben finished the 883 dirt track championship in ninth. Eric won the class title in 1996. They moved on to road racing, first on Harley 883s, where Eric won the title in 1997 while finishing 11th in 600cc Supersport and 19th in 750cc Superstock. Ben came in second in SuperTwins in 1996 and was fourth in 600cc Supersport and 22nd in 750cc Superstock.

"Coming from dirt track/motocross background, I can remember guys never making the main event all year long," Eric said. "They would race 40 races in a year and never even make the final, and they'd come back the next year, and they might start making finals or whatever. But if you're a guy that's used to being in the final, how can you all of a sudden not be in the final. You're going to be like, 'This is wrong.' But coming from our background, that's normal. If you're not fast enough, you're not going to make the final."

With only the slowest of the slow not making the main, it's a virtual guarantee that most riders will be in. They've come to expect it as a given, not something they have to earn, unlike in other racing disciplines.

Lack of interest by the factories has left the Superbike field with six works riders. That's who the fans come to see: that's who the viewers tune in to watch. They should be the ones deciding the outcome of the race, not someone getting lapped for the second time.

February 25, 2004

All That Glitters Is Not Gold

So it turns out Honda was fibbing after all. Not a big fib, nothing like "I did not have sexual relationships with that woman, Miss Lewinsky." Nothing that good. No semantic gymnastics. No discussions on what does and doesn't constitute sexual relations. No, it was a little fib, more a change of direction, a kink in the road, a chicane added in the interest of safety. It turns out the vow to provide its six MotoGP riders with identical RC211Vs was less sincere than a hooker at a bachelor party. Two months before the start of the season and it's backtracking faster than a moose in an avalanche and with about as much grace.

The original pronouncement was equal RC211Vs all around, and this was before Honda knew who the riders would be - months before Alex Barros would come on board as Nicky Hayden's Repsol Honda teammate. The first fissure developed during the early December test in Valencia. Of the four riders, only two, Sete Gibernau and Max Biaggi, had the good stuff. Colin Edwards and Makoto Tamada were left out. The main difference was in engine management parts. To Gibernau and Biaggi, the difference was dramatic. Both said they now understood how Rossi did what he did. It put a smile on Biaggi's face.

The official acknowledgement came during a press gathering with HRC development manager Suguru Kanazawa at the recent Sepang test. Kanazawa, known as a straight shooter, said that the factory Repsol Honda team would be the first to get new parts, then the trickle-down effect would take over.

"This season is very important for Honda, because unfortunately Mr. Rossi moved to Yamaha," Kanazawa said.

"Everybody in the MotoGP family is obviously very excited about this, but unfortunately at Honda it means we have to improve our machine's performance. That is why I am here at the tests. Our aim is not to look at our rival's performance, though, but to better our own times from last year's races as a whole by around 2 to 5 percent."

There was no explanation for why Honda was now changing its game plan, but it isn't hard to figure out.

Repsol, the Spanish oil and chemical giant that backs the factory team, couldn't have been happy knowing everyone was getting the same gear. It spends the most, even though it's a fraction of Honda's total racing cost, so it should get the most, was probably the thinking. Not an invalid argument. The Telefonica MoviStar team is backed by rival Castrol, and Camel Honda uses Mobil lubricants.

Colin Edwards didn't really see it coming. In a meeting with senior HRC officials in his hotel room at the Pacific GP at Motegi last year, he'd been told that all six bikes were going to be the same.

"I thought, 'Sweet, sign me up. I'm ready,'" he said.

Not so fast. By the time they got to Sepang, "They kind of backtracked a little bit and said they won't all be the same."

Preseason testing is the time to make yourself heard, not that it paid off.

"What I was told and what I was given were two different things," Edwards said. "I've done just about all I can do, and I just have to take what I can get. From what I understand, I will be on the same as Sete [Gibernau] by the first race. This is what I'm hearing, so I'm a bit happier about that. Obviously, Sete, Max [Biaggi], myself and [Makoto] Tamada, being the only four satellite guys, I can say I'm 99 percent sure we're all going to be on the same stuff by the first race, I think. It's purely my wish, and I think that's what's going to happen."

Edwards has an odd relationship with Honda. He won the company two World Superbike Championships and two Suzuka 8-Hours, and yet Honda treats him, in his words, like "the red-headed stepson." The relationship is all business, unlike his relationship with Michelin, where he's made friends as one of the most prolific and perceptive test riders in its storied history. It was that relationship that kept him from taking the Honda offer last year to ride for the Pramac team on Bridgestone tires, a choice that looks smarter with every passing day. Sure, he had a tough year on the Aprilia, but seeing Kawasaki's Shinya Nakano and friend Kenny Roberts Jr. blow up Bridgestones at recent tests confirmed his decision was the right one.

So for now he'll take what he's given and do what he's always done, ride the ever-loving crap out of it. He was on the phone from Australia, on his way to a three-day test at Phillip Island where there were tires to try and little else.

"That's one I'd say downside of being on a satellite team; the factory team gets to test the new stuff and choose if it's better or worse, where you just kind of have to sit and wait," he said. "That's the game and we'll play it."

The way Honda works is that the hot rider gets the goods. If Valentino Rossi stars applying a little heat, look for the satellite teams to get the good kit quicker. So concerned is HRC about Rossi that it accelerated its off-season testing program. What Gibernau and Biaggi tested in Valencia normally wouldn't show until the first test of the new year.

"I think Honda are sitting back just waiting to see what Valentino does, see how much heat he applies on them and see which one or two of the satellite guys starts going good," Edwards said. "That's Honda's game, and that's how they've always played it, and I don't see why they'd change that."

On the first day in Sepang, Edwards hooked up with Rossi more than once. Rossi may have done his fast lap chasing

Edwards, who ended up with the fourth-best time, three other Hondas in front of him.

The Yamaha works better in some areas, Edwards said, but the Honda is strong everywhere, at every track. Now they're in Australia for a test at Phillip Island, a track where the best Yamaha finished sixth, 28 seconds behind Rossi in the October race.

"I think this week will tell a lot," Edwards said. "The Yamaha didn't go that great here at the race, so it'll be good to see what they do."

For now, Edwards is concentrating on stocking the database that he'll need come race time. He's working with a new crew chief, Fabrizio Cecchini.

"I've been brushing up on my Italian and teaching him some English, well, Texan is more like it, so we're meeting somewhere in the middle."

The communication is already paying off. Edwards ended the first day at Phillip Island with the best time. Looking back, he could see Gibernau and Biaggi and Rossi and Hayden. It was a nice view, one he's known in the past and one he could easily get used to. But it's not what he most wants to see.

In a few days he'll get back on a plane and fly home to Texas to be with his wife, Alyssia, and 13-month old daughter Gracie Kayte.

"I've got almost a month at home to do nothing, get in shape, go do some motocross and hang out with the baby and my wife. She started walking about three days after her first birthday, probably a month ago. She's cruising all over. Everything's good, peachy keen."

Nothing can change that.

March 17, 2004

A Joking Matter

Kudos to AMA Pro Racing for turning the premier class in road racing into a place where, in the sport's most prestigious event, the fourth-place finisher is a credit-card racer who finished two laps down; the sixth-place finisher can crash, remount and finish three laps behind; and the seventh-place finisher spent a grand total of $500 on quick change gear at Sears the night before the race, all this just as the AMA Superbike Championship is being proclaimed as the premier production race series in the world. Well done, lads. Drinks all around.

This year's Bike Week turned into a referendum on the passing of Daytona International Speedway as a suitable venue for Superbikes. May it rest in peace. There was a wide variety of ideas about what to do, ranging from making Superbikes a horsepower-restricted class to building a world-class infield section. Regardless of the fix, the unanimous opinion was that something had to be done immediately.

"Every lap you're out there riding, you're terrified, basically," said Eric Bostrom, shown in the accompanying photo crossing one of the slick tar patches on the banking, after qualifying on the pole with a new lap record. "So you just want to get out of here in one piece, and you don't get to share that love and joy for racing that you typically would have at other racetracks."

No one had or wanted to know top speed times.

"With a 'Q' [qualifying tire], I was going at least 10 mph faster down the front straight," Eric said. Brother Ben did 192 mph on a shakedown run on his Honda CBR1000RR in December.

Tires were the biggest concern coming to Daytona, Dunlops specifically. But the Brummies (those are the poor souls who live in Birmingham, England) did their job, and the Dunlops performed well. As did the Michelins, except for the unexpected appearance of the sock puppet who made a cameo appearance at the tread edge of one of Eric Bostrom's fronts. That a company with the unparalleled MotoGP and World Superbike success of Michelin - the last premier class GP it didn't win was at Donington Park in 1998 - could have a front-tire failure says volumes about the demands of the Speedway. Might have even caused someone to have a heart attack.

But tires aren't the problem at Daytona: the racetrack's the problem; the racetrack causes the tire problems. The racetrack's a dinosaur in need of many things, repaving among them. Did a bit of loose tarmac cause the oil radiator puncture that put Eric Bostrom out?

More to the point, the rules are a bigger problem. There are four classes, two each for two different bikes. Formula Xtreme, the alleged mini-Superbikes on slicks, are slower than Supersport bikes on DOTs. Jason DiSalvo's best Supersport lap was half a second faster than Ben Bostrom's best in Formula Xtreme. Superstock machines were faster than Superbikes after the first practice session. With Honda the only player in Formula Xtreme, the result is as predictable as an hour wait at Carrabba's.

Superbikes and Superstock are essentially the same motorcycle. Same for Supersport and Formula Xtreme. There are differences in brakes and suspension, but a suspension kit gets you close to works spec. Tire size is different, and there are some engine differences. In the end, it's splitting hairs. The Yamaha R1s and Kawasaki ZX10s that filled the Superstock winners' circle would've filled the top 10 in Superbike, dropping riders with career days farther down the pay scale. Jack Pfeifer couldn't believe he'd finished fourth. Maybe because his best in 2003 was 13th.

"Personally, I think that's ridiculous," now three-time Daytona 200 winner and four-time AMA Superbike Champion Mat Mladin believes of the class structure. "They need to get rid of one of those 1000cc classes. Put it in one, even if we race Superstock bikes. They're still going to be 190 horsepower."

AMA Pro Racing tends to be reactive rather than proactive. When news coming out of Daytona of tires blowing up like party favors filtered to Pickerington, someone realized it might be time to get to work on that starter tan. How is it that everyone else in the world knew the bikes were too fast, and they didn't? Are they the custodians of our sport or just custodians?

It must be said; they aren't entirely to blame. It isn't easy to find a way to race what the manufacturers sell. What to do when Honda, Yamaha, Suzuki and Kawasaki sell 170-plus mph motorcycles that a hormone-crazed 16-year-old with no riding experience, bad vision, and the reflexes of a dead cat can pile drive into the side of a Hummer while trying to get to his first chat room booty call. Those are the bikes that Pro Racing has to make work at the increasingly outdated and unsafe tracks it gladly sanctions year after year,

Explain again why we're going back to Brainerd? Did someone in the Pro Racing betting pool pick the snack bar as the next femur-snapping unprotected trackside obstacle? (Congrats to the last year's winners who had tree trunk and TV camera scaffolding.) Or is it the 18 diehard fans? And for three days, no less, allegedly because the crowd likes camping for the weekend. Fine. If they want to lie in the dirt and sleep off a night of binge drinking while having their blood Hoovered by vulture-sized mosquitoes, cool. But why make the teams, and Pro Racing's own woefully underpaid staff, many of whom are volunteers, spend for an extra night of lodging and food and bug spray?

Of the 11 tracks on the calendar, Daytona is the most extreme example and may want to make changes, but not the kind the riders want. The Speedway's rather arrogant and narrow-minded position, as voiced by a Speedway flack, is that the track is the one constant in the equation; ergo, it's not to be fussed with. That, in a very short word, is poo. Changes to the chicane and turn six have shortened the time to reach terminal velocity. More time at full throttle, more tire problems. The surface has degraded so badly and been so patched up that neither race winner Mladin nor American Honda's Ben Bostrom could hold the throttle wide open on the banking. Those few brave souls who went full stick could only do it for a few laps on fresh tires. After that, the rear was jumping around like a barefoot drunk on a lava bed. Erion Honda's Jake Zemke had the rear of his CBR1000RR step out over a foot in NASCAR four at about 180 mph. If that happened to you or me, we'd have to burn not only our underpants, but our leathers, boots, socks, back protector, seat pad, tail section, subframe, and exhaust canister. Maybe the shock reservoir. Zemke got away with changing his thong.

Six factory riders from three teams is too few for the Superbike class. It is imperative that Pro Racing listen to the teams and release technical rules far sooner than it ever has. A crew chief told me Pro Racing had targeted May for next year's rules. Let's see how close to the target it comes.

While we wait, we can hoist a cold one. After all, they're paying.

April 28, 2004

Where Art Thou, U.S. GP?

A mixed bag for the five-strong American contingent in South Africa. On the one hand, they were encouraged by the news that they may be racing in their homeland next year. On the other, it's likely they'll be chasing Valentino Rossi.

Dorna's Carmelo Ezpeleta insisted the U.S. GP will return in 2005. He's said that before, but now there are choices. The options are Barber Motorsports Park in Birmingham, Alabama, or Mazda Raceway Laguna Seca in the idyllic seaside town of Monterey, California.

Ezpeleta can't show favorites. His mandate is to build the championship, which he's done, despite some grousing.

It's becoming clear Laguna Seca is moving to the forefront, as it should. It has hosted World Championship events for 10 years and know how it's done. The sticking point, as always, is money.

The track isn't up to current MotoGP standards. It can be, but it won't be cheap. Kenny Roberts Jr. told them what needs to be done. As a member of the riders' safety group, his knowledge of safety issues is comprehensive. That he lives a short drive from the track won't affect his opinion. Rider safety won't be compromised for any reason, a refreshing stance in a country where safety problems go unchecked for too long.

Whatever it costs, Laguna Seca has to do it, for itself, for GP racing, for the long-term. Ezpeleta said Dorna would share the burden of costs to ensure the economic viability of the event. The irony being that one of the richest countries in the world needs a hand-out. Kenny Roberts lost a pile of money promoting an earlier U.S. GP. When asked how it felt to lose $2 million, the wise-cracking wizard replied. "I didn't lose $2 million: I lost a million; my ex-wife lost a million."

That there isn't a facility and Grand Prix-level racetrack across the breadth of the country where a safe Grand Prix could be held and be profitable is distressing. The Barber facility may be the most beautiful in the world, better in its own way than the racetrack it surrounds. The course is too short and too twisty and not safe for MotoGP though it could be. The 990s wouldn't get much beyond third gear, maybe fourth. It is the greatest lost opportunity in motorcycle racing in America. The truth is that Europeans want to go to Monterey, and who can blame them? Cannery Row, the Pacific Ocean, the Gilroy outlets; it's a busman's holiday. Not so for the riders.

The five-strong American contingent would love to race in front of friends and family. If they have any hope of winning, they need to step up their game.

Rossi humiliated his former employers with his greatest victory ever. Certainly he worked harder than he ever had. As did the team in the run-up to Welkom. The slender Italian was drenched in sweat after fending off archrival Max Biaggi in the brilliant South African sunshine, the two dancing on razor's edge for 28 compelling laps.

Only two of the Americans have a shot at challenging Rossi this year, and both learned hard lessons in Welkom. Nicky Hayden may be the most personable rider in the paddock, little changed from his days as a 14-year-old crisscrossing America with his father and brothers and a van full of bikes. But racing at this level has a way of changing people. It's happened to the best of them: Rainey, Schwantz, Doohan, Lawson. If anyone's immune to the suffocating environment, it's Nicky. Honda may think differently. He's always said that pressure isn't something he feels, but in Welkom he did. Honda has pegged him as its rider of the future and all that goes with it.

For a few laps Hayden hung with the leaders, Rossi, Biaggi and Sete Gibernau. Then the harsh reality: They were simply too fast. Practice and qualifying proved that Hayden didn't have the speed of the others. He knew he wouldn't find it in the race and was smart enough not to try. Pundits who picked him for the World Championship suddenly had to wonder. Mick Doohan wasn't among them. Hayden, he said, had "raw speed." He'll need more to challenge Rossi and Biaggi and Gibernau, and he'll find it, but patience, on everyone's part, will be needed.

Hayden and teammate Alex Barros had the 2004 Honda RC-211V from the beginning of testing. The satellite teams didn't get the machines until later, and by then time was running out. The two Spanish IRTA tests were unproductive. Gibernau and Biaggi raced the newer model, though with reservations. Gibernau sounded defeated on Saturday.

"I had the pace in the whole preseason, and I was very confident of being able to run for victory in every race, but right now, here today, I don't have the pace."

Did Honda get so caught up in beating Rossi that it lost the plot? It certainly looks that way. A senior Honda engineer said that the Repsol team would always get the development parts first. That remains to be seen. Biaggi wears the unflattering title as an unreformed 250cc rider. He can't adjust when the tires go away, the experts say. In Welkom, he proved them wrong. Matching Rossi every inch of the way, he made the case that he might be the one who deserves the better gear.

Honda has a funny relationship with its riders. Some, like Freddie Spencer, are family. Others, like Doohan and Rossi and Edwards, are outsiders.

Edwards won Honda two World Superbike titles and the Suzuka 8-Hours, but he still considers himself Honda's "red-headed stepchild." Weather-plagued testing meant he arrived in South Africa with less confidence in the 2004 machine than the older one. His choice was the more familiar 2003. In the race a front-end hop developed, and it was all he could do to stay vertical. A test after the Spanish GP will help sort out the new bike. By then he'll be two races behind.

The Suzukis are a year behind, but rapidly improving. Upper management finally woke up and recommitted to racing. The GSV-R 990 is vastly improved, and the persuasive team manager, Garry Taylor, along with Roberts Jr., convinced Erv Kanemoto to sign on as crew chief. The transformation has been dramatic. The once hangdog expressions have been replaced with faces of optimism. Bridgestone is supplying first-rate tires, rather than the second-rate Michelins of last year. Response time on parts has been shortened. The aim is to be ready for 2005, while climbing the ladder in 2004.

John Hopkins qualified a career-best 11th. In the race a flash of temper caused him to lose sight of the goal, and he burned up his tire atoning for his sins. The mistake won't happen again.

Kurtis Roberts is also looking at the 2005 season for two reasons. The first is that the Proton KR is two months behind. At the same time, engineers should be designing next year's machine, if only funding were in place.

The current season could be lost. The shoulder Kurtis dislocated trail riding in the mud isn't responding. Rest may help. Kenny Sr. said Kurtis won't be 80 to 90 percent until midseason. Surgery is an unpleasant option. It would put him out for the rest of the season and force his father to find a replacement. I heard Anthony Gobert's looking for work. Anyone have his number?

May 26, 2004

USGP: When? Where? How?

Where to hold the USGP? Rather, what racetrack would produce a better USGP? Should safety be the first concern? Or close racing? And where is the most desirable location?

All questions being pondered by the interested parties in advance of what is expected to be the return of the USGP in 2005. But all secondary considerations. The single most important question: Who can afford it?

The current choices to host the race are Mazda Raceway Laguna Seca, the venerable former home of the USGP and current home of World Superbike and AMA, near the idyllic seaside town of Monterey, and Barber Motorsports Park, the most beautiful racetrack in the world, now completing its second year of hosting AMA Superbikes just west of Birmingham, Alabama.

If you want close racing, it's hard to argue with Barber, at least based on the weekend's AMA races. The largest margin of victory was 2.35 seconds, in Superstock; the smallest 0.011 in Saturday's Superbike race. Without consulting record books, it's a fair guess that this was the closest-ever weekend of AMA road racing. Erion Honda's Jake Zemke missed out on a pair of Superbike wins by a combined 0.388 seconds. Zemke's revenge came in Formula Xtreme, which he won by 0.059 seconds over Miguel Duhamel. Roger Lee Hayden beat his brother Tommy by 0.030 seconds in Supersport.

First impressions of the Barber track were that it was too tight and too twisty. And it is. But it is fun, according to most riders. Challenging, as well, for the riders and their teams, and especially the tire companies. No track in the world chews up fronts like Barber.

The tightness is the sticking point. Spread over its lush and manicured 2.3 miles are 14 turns, according to the AMA count, 17 by others. More per mile than any other track on the AMA schedule. Very little time is spent upright, which explains the tire wear. Eric Bostrom uses the lowest three gears on his Ducati Austin F04 Superbike. Yoshimura Suzuki's Mat Mladin does the same on his Suzuki GSX-R1000. A MotoGP bike would use no more.

"I don't think this is a racetrack you'll see MotoGP bikes at their best," former 500cc World Champion Kevin Schwantz said. "Three gears on a GSX-R1000. I just don't think this is the place."

Mazda Raceway is a more open racetrack, according to Yoshimura Suzuki's Mat Mladin.

Not that he's endorsing it. "I think they're both too small for those bikes," he says, and he's right. But if he had to choose, he'd go with Laguna Seca. "They can stretch their legs there."

Proton KR's Kurtis Roberts is the only GP rider to have ridden both. Roberts won the final Superbike race of the year at Barber last year. His view is that Barber might be the better venue, if changes were made. Changes also need to be made at Laguna Seca, he thinks.

"A Superbike over turn one is scary enough, but MotoGP over turn one might be impossible as far as being safe," he said. "How are they going to make that safe enough the whole race, all the way through qualifying?"

"Laguna Seca with a MotoGP bike, I think in turn one, one of the Hondas or Ducatis might get lift off over that turn."

Kurtis said that for Barber to be more of a GP track, it would have to cut the kink out of the left-right flick on the back straight. It would add two gears and remove one of the more dangerous parts of the track. But it would also create a problem at the end of the straight, where there's already questionable runoff and an errant bike could re-join the track farther along.

"I believe that Barber is a better place for a race, as far as a racing on TV and all that stuff," he said. "I saw the Superbike race in AMA and there's many opportunities to pass. Mladin showed that yesterday."

"Laguna Seca doesn't create the passing possibilities. And in case of bad weather, Barber has grip. Laguna has nothing. It's like running around on ice cubes. If the grip level improved, it'd be better."

Kurtis' older brother, Team Suzuki's Kenny Roberts, made safety recommendations after inspecting Laguna Seca. The fixes are expensive, and therein lies the rub.

Both Barber and Laguna have to look at the bottom line. Can they afford a MotoGP race? Operational costs for Laguna Seca would be in the $3 million range, plus a seven-figure sanction fee and the added costs of safety improvements needed for MotoGP. It's a daunting sum that looks insurmountable in the short term. Barber is still working the numbers, so it doesn't yet know what the costs are. Certainly any track changes would be less expensive, but it would have other expenses that Laguna doesn't, like modular garages for the teams. Dorna desperately wants a race in the United States and is willing to reduce its sanctioning fee. But its recent experience with dodgy financing at the South African GP means it won't move forward without a solid business plan.

Neither would Laguna, and neither would Barber. George Barber, the philanthropist and enthusiast who created the motorsports park, didn't acquire his wealth by making bad decisions. Gene Hallman, who heads the team that promotes races at Barber, said that "Despite the fact that both (Dorna and Barber) have tremendous resources, neither one of them is going to compromise into a bad business deal for themselves." Hallman said he'd know in the next 30 days whether Barber would vie for the GP.

In order for Mazda Raceway to hold the race, it would need help from the industry. A title sponsor would have to assume much of the load, with others coming on board. The more the merrier. If the industry supported it, it can and will happen. Now's the time to let it be known. The fans also need to make their voices heard.

"I think it would be awesome; it would be really special," former Laguna winner and current Repsol Honda rider Nicky Hayden said of a USGP. "It would mean a lot to race a GP in my home country. I think it would help MotoGP in America. If fans could come see a race, it would be good for the sport for the people that follow them. It would be close to home."

Nicky is the only Hayden who hasn't raced at Barber. His choice is Monterey, though he, and many others, thinks the best venue would be Road America, the four-mile track in Wisconsin where the MotoGP bikes could shine. That won't happen without major track changes.

"I haven't seen Alabama," Hayden said. "I would say that's definitely, from what I know, the top choice. I think Road America would have big potential too," though he concedes work would have to be done between the Carousel and the final corner.

Dorna seriously considered Road America several years ago, going so far as drawing up an alternate layout that would have eliminated those sections. The track later invested in a full closed circuit TV system, a requirement in international racing. There was chatter of World Superbike, a companion event to Laguna Seca. It didn't happen. In the end, it comes down to money. As it will this time.

June 9, 2004

The Roundtable

It had never been done, as far as I knew. The idea was to gather the managers from the major road race teams for a roundtable discussion. We would solve the racing world's problems in a day, which would free up a lot of the time that we spend bitching to one another at the racetrack. That idea spawned another: Why not gather the riders? The result is elsewhere in this issue.[1]

It was a rare privilege, opportunity and honor to be able to host this discussion. For whatever faults it has, *Cycle News* has always been a place where riders know they'll be treated fairly, where what comes out of their mouths is what will appear in print. The five riders we approached all agreed without reservation. Only later did a few, but not all, ask that I clean up their language.

Yoshimura Suzuki's Mat Mladin and American Honda's Miguel Duhamel dominated the conversation with Ducati Austin's Eric Bostrom, Yamaha's Damon Buckmaster, and STAR Motorcycle School's Jason Pridmore also contributing. There was a brief discussion about whether an AMA official should have been invited. I thought not for a few reasons. First is that the ones who run the races have little power. The power is in the hands of the Pro Racing Board and CEO Scott Hollingsworth, who has agreed to an interview with *Cycle News*. Secondly, I thought it would turn from a discussion into an attack, which none of us wanted.

What I wanted, and what the riders wanted, was that their voices be heard. Except for the occasional interview, their only printed comments are about qualifying and racing. Years of

---

[1] An image of the roundtable discussion appears on the back cover. Photo by Brian J. Nelson.

listening to their concerns convinced us that it was time we shared those concerns.

It was not an attempt to bash the AMA, as some might think. Duhamel points out repeatedly all the good work the AMA does on behalf of motorcyclists. Whether in the fields of riders' rights or keeping riding trails open at a state level or fighting in Washington, D.C., or the new "Justice for All" program that shines the light on drivers who aren't adequately punished for injuring or killing motorcyclists. But that's a different AMA than the one that administers road racing.

Safety, in a word, has got to be improved, and it's AMA Pro Racing's job to do it. Two tracks, in particular, came under withering criticism. The first is Daytona International Speedway. Daytona has been unsafe at speed for some time. The damage the track has done to riders grows yearly. In response to a column I wrote following Daytona 2004, AMA Pro Racing director of communications Kerry Graeber pointed out that there were no red flags this year. True, but it ignores Bryan Cassell. Cassell was a 28-year-old Floridian who was killed during the October Championship Cup Series weekend at Daytona. It ignores the grievous injuries to Ben Spies when the rear Dunlop on his Yoshimura Suzuki GSX-R1000 blew out at over 180 mph during an October test. It ignores a similar incident with Yamaha's Jason DiSalvo, the New Yorker lucky to walk away. It ignores that Aaron Gobert still isn't 100 percent from his near-death crash in 2002. It ignores the possibility of a catastrophic incident, which is what safety is all about. If there were an assurance that nothing bad would ever happen, that tires wouldn't explode, that engines wouldn't leak oil, that riders wouldn't plow into one another, you could race anywhere - Watkins Glen, Long Beach, even Loudon.

What troubles the riders more than anything else is the lost opportunity. Daytona will be closed for over five months starting in early July, more than enough time to make substantive changes.

AMA Pro Racing announced on April 12 that it would be meeting with officials of Daytona International Speedway. Since then, nothing. Why is that? My guess is that the conversation was one-sided, on Daytona's side: "What can you do for us? We'd like bigger grids, 60 to 80 motorcycles, like the old days." My guess is that the dramatic track proposals various riders have forwarded were not warmly received. I'm guessing, of course, because, as proud as it was of its proposed meeting, Pro Racing is equally reticent about the meeting itself.

Equally worrisome is the lack of tire testing. Last year Dunlop tested four times between August and the March race, each time building new, improved tires. It paid off. Despite Spies' and DiSalvo's testing failures, the race was free of major problems. This year Dunlop and Michelin and Pirelli may only get one chance to test, in late January; too late to react and build new tires with any confidence. In part two of the interview, which will run next week, Eric Bostrom reveals more problems with his tires than previously known. "I can say now, that between testing and the race we chunked more tires than I can count on both my hands," he said.

That from Michelin, a company that has dominated Grand Prix and World Superbike for over a decade.

The riders all understand and agree that they have to race Daytona. They're aware how important it is as a sales tool. But they also agree that, as configured, it's horribly unsafe for not only 1000cc motorcycles, but 600s as well.

"I was chunking fronts on my [750cc] Supersport bike," Pridmore said of his 2003 problems. "You can't come back to Dunlop and go 'What's wrong with the tires?' I didn't even stay around and watch that race. You know why: Physically, I'm sick to my stomach watching the 200. I cannot watch it."

The second-most criticized facility was the Mid-Ohio Sports Car Course.

"Mid-Ohio is a deathtrap." Mladin said. "It's horrible. Full stop. The surface the way that it is, how easy it is to crash there, with the walls so close. It's a death-trap. With the surface being better, it's even worse."

Trackside barriers are too close in too many places, most notably in the far right-hand corner in the back. The guardrail runs hard up against the side of the track, the margin of error nil. In the dry, it's a problem. In the wet, it's lethal. The argument that nothing's happened so it must be safe, doesn't hold. Yoshimura Suzuki's Aaron Yates was trapped under his Suzuki when he fell in the slow up and down left-hand loop just after the back straight. The back straight is laced with track sealant that turns to grease in the rain. The gravel trap at the end of the back straight is built in such a way that, not only do you get air time when you come off the track, but your bike is certain to tumble into its component parts.

What's troubling to the riders is that they believe the track makes money on motorcycle racing. The educated guess is that the AMA weekend is its most profitable especially since it no longer hosts a Champ Car race. Even when it did, its expenses were so much higher that motorcycles were better for the bottom line.

There have been changes - the most drastic being to the front straight after Larry Schwarzbach was killed the day after winning the 600cc Supersport race. But that was in 1992, and motorcycles have only gotten faster. Even the curbing is tattered and dirty. Repaving solves the problem of an irregular track surface - the concrete patches in many of the corners - but it creates others. The walls are that much closer, the back straight that much faster.

"I'm afraid for the AMA, to be honest with you," Duhamel said. "Because we're bringing up situations about safety. And I think it's just a matter of time before somebody gets hurt and somebody doesn't just go home and cry; he goes and gets himself a really good lawyer. If they think Roger [Edmondson] hurt, this guy might really take our series away. If you look at it in that light, we're actually trying to do them a favor right now by improving the racetracks and improving everything."

But do they know that?

June 23, 2004

The American Struggle

You will find them at the opposite ends of the tact scale. One, a polite young Kentuckian with a mop of mousse-matted hair framing a crease-less complexion, the other a slender, buzz-cut Texan with a few lines around the eyes that glint with mischief and quick humor.

Nicky Hayden is likely to be political, the root of which is polite, which he and his family are to a fault, though sometimes you might find Rog on the fringes (see DiSalvo, Jason[1]). Colin Edwards is not. Edwards admits his brashness may not be the greatest career builder, but he's done all right. There are the two World Superbike Championships and the three Suzuka 8-Hours wins.

Honda Racing Corporation (HRC) expected to steamroll its wayward son, Valentino Rossi, in this year's MotoGP World Championship. Leading up to and following his defection to Yamaha, senior staff voiced confidence in the product, the mighty RC-211V. They would flood the grid with the all-conquering machine - there are six this year - and Rossi would do well to finish seventh. It was David and Goliath; the equivalent of bringing a sling-shot to a tank fight. What was missing in this equation was something Honda has misunderstood more than once, the human element.

The key to this year's World Championship is not Valentino Rossi. The key is a wizened crew chief from Australia named Jerry Burgess. Burgess began his GP career under the tutelage of Erv Kanemoto, quickly moving through the ranks. It was he who

---

[1] Jason DiSalvo collidided with Roger Lee Hayden in the Supersport race at Pikes Peak on May 23, 2004, and forced Hayden into the haybales. Hayden vowed revenge.

helped Wayne Gardner to his 1987 500cc World Championship. That winter he told me in a phone conversation from his home in Adelaide that he was thinking of taking on a young Australian by the name Mick Doohan. Five World Championships later, a string that would have continued had Doohan not suffered career-ending injuries at Jerez in 1999, he found his next rider - Valentino Rossi.

Burgess said at Welkom in South Africa that developing the much-maligned Yamaha M1 into a GP winner in a matter of 12 weeks was the hardest thing he and his crew had ever done. Without them, it would not have been possible. Without Burgess and the boys, Rossi's victories in Welkom and Mugello and Catalunya wouldn't have happened. With another crew chief, he would eventually have gotten to the front. But not this quickly and not this often.

Word in the paddock is that Yamaha doubled the salaries of Burgess and his crew. A powerful incentive to be sure, but not one that Honda couldn't have neutralized. What Honda should have done is hand Nicky Hayden to Burgess. It would have accomplished two things: First, it would have accelerated Hayden's learning curve, and secondly, it would have prevented Rossi from developing a winning machine. Maybe Honda didn't want to take Hayden away from his current crew chief, Trevor Morris. But for a company spending tens of millions of dollars on racing to be so sensitive to the feelings of one employee seems down-right human.

With Rossi and Burgess developing the RC-211V, there was a direction, and it was the right one. They refined the best Grand Prix machine in the world. It wasn't perfect, and Burgess got in trouble for pointing out the flaws in the rear suspension. But almost anyone could win on it. Honda's philosophy was to build the perfect machine, one with less adjustability than the others, less chance to go gliding down the wrong path. The Yamaha, on the other hand, is a chameleon, eminently adaptable to the vicissitudes of racing.

For 2004, Michelin designed a fatter rear tire that takes advantage of Yamaha's adjustability. The tire is less of an advantage to the Honda, even though it offers more side grip. The increased contact patch does things to the front of the Honda that riders don't like. Edwards has been outspoken about front-end chatter. Any time championship leader Sete Gibernau is shown talking to his crew chief during qualifying, his hand gestures suggest the same. The cure is a geometry change, something the Honda doesn't allow.

"At the moment we have fixed everything," Edwards bluntly says. "You can't change anything. We have to change. We have to. If we don't, Yamaha are going to win the championship."

Hayden is less strident.

"I'm pretty limited," he says. "HRC, one thing this weekend, basically I got the bike and can change a few clickers, but they basically got their bike and want me to ride it."

Great things were expected from both riders this year. The other Americans were never going to be world beaters. The Suzukis of Kenny Roberts Jr. and John Hopkins are much improved, a lot owing to the influence of Erv Kanemoto, now working with Roberts. But the Bridgestone tires aren't a match for the Michelins. And the GSV-R is 15-20 horsepower down, Roberts says. Kenny's younger brother, Kurtis, is in even more dire straits. He won't discuss the problems of the Dunlops, but his father will, saying the team is "basically out of business until we can come up with a tire that's a lot better." In Kurtis' hands, the Proton KR V-5 has been unrideable and prone to problems. From the side of the Catalunya circuit, it was obvious he couldn't get on the gas without the rear stepping out, though he's always had a heavy throttle hand.

What's keeping Hayden from winning?

"I'd say it's just the pace really," he says with his characteristic honesty. "Some people won't admit it. Other riders I'm sure won't admit it, but the pace has stepped up a lot this year from last year." Hayden says you might not realize it back in America watching on television. "But you go ask [Neil] Hodgson, who was World Champion last year and he's 17th today. I think it's just that the rider talent is really high right now."

Edwards didn't look like himself at Catalunya, hasn't all year.

"You see me on the track, and it looks like I should be in 15th, and I'm winning a race," he says about the smoothness he's shown all these years. That's how Rossi and Gibernau looked at Catalunya.

The bigger Michelin doesn't turn on the same radius as the front on the Honda. The contact patch is moved. They have to figure out how to get the front and rear turning on the same arc.

"Like Yamaha's done, piece of cake, no chatter, everything's beautiful, smells like roses," Edwards said. His machine is quite different from Gibernau's. "From the swingarm pivot back, our bikes are identical. From the swingarm pivot forward, everything you can think of is different. This comes with the territory. You win races, that's what happens."

That said, Edwards says, "Sete's got chatter out the ying yang."

A smaller rear rim boosted Edwards' confidence, though he lost some side grip, and he and Hayden were testing the day after the Catalunya race. It's only a matter of time before they're back in their customary spots at the front.

"I've got to get some front confidence and start being smooth, and when that happens and I start feeling in my element, it comes," Edwards said. "When I'm aggressive and fighting it and I feel like I'm going warp speed, that's not me."

For Hayden, "It's been frustrating. I mean, sure, I'm getting a lot of flak because my results haven't been good, but nobody hates it worse than I do."

HRC is not known for its patience. He says the company has been "pretty cool" but wants results. There've been a few meetings that haven't been the most fun. The Honda execs know he's trying; they know he's learning. They know, whether they'll admit it or not, his problems are of their making.

"It has not been what I wanted," Hayden says. "I've had, essentially, would have had three front rows, a couple of top fives. I crashed out fighting last week [in Mugello], and Le Mans was terrible. Yeah, a lot of flak. That's all right. Put it on me, I can handle it."

August 4, 2004

Be Careful What You Wish For

Words of advice to those wishing to change the venerable Daytona 200 from a Superbike race to Formula Xtreme: That scheme - destined to join New Coke, "Joanie Loves Chachi," and invading Iraq without an exit plan in the pantheon of bad ideas - was floating like a bloated corpse around the pits of Mid-Ohio. Whose idea was it? No one - not the AMA and not Daytona International Speedway - wanted to claim full paternity of the red-headed stepson, and for good reason. It was a collaboration, a two-headed test-tube baby destined to end up in a home for the reality-challenged.

The first question that springs to mind is, "Why?" The first answer would be safety. Rider opinion on the safety of the Speedway is unanimous. It has to be changed, and the Speedway is likely doing so. Construction has started on a tunnel under NASCAR turns one and two and a revamp of the infield roadcourse is in the works. What will likely emerge is a roadcourse that cuts out the west banking. Riders will come through the infield, make a right somewhere near the dog-leg, head toward what is now turn six, then back up that straight toward the second horseshoe, and past, and funnel onto the back stretch.

Eliminating the west banking would reduce the heat-generating-forces on the tires, though not by half. The east banking will not be changed, nor will the chicane, with the highest tire temperatures still being reached on the run from the chicane to the checkered flag. The lighter and slower Formula Xtreme bikes haven't shown the same tire-wear problems as Superbikes, convincing some they should substitute for the premier class at

America's premier race. Between the possible new configuration and the reduced capacity, it's virtually certain there would be less tire problems, given recent experience. It must be said that Dunlop, the company which has had the most recent Daytona problems, suffered no significant failures during Bike Week. Michelin did, though they claim it may have been a puncture and the tires never lost integrity.

Before moving on to why it's such a bad idea, a word about Superbikes. They'll be a support race, maybe on Saturday morning, maybe on Thursday, a plan favored by Yoshimura Suzuki's Mat Mladin. "I could be home on Friday," he said.

The length would probably be in the 19-lap range, similar to one stint in the 57-lap Superbike race and just more than the 100K Supersport race. Mladin and his team realized that his tires wouldn't work very efficiently for 19 laps, so they went shorter and won the race in a romp. Forcing Superbikes to go 19 laps on one set of tires is a bad idea. "So what's the difference?" Mladin asks. "That's no help for safety."

So who would want Formula Xtreme? The answer begins and ends with Honda. With a year's head start on the field, and a proven championship winner, they'd be guaranteed the win that Mladin has denied them too many times recently.

Who wouldn't want FX? Yamaha, Suzuki and Kawasaki. None of those brands would build the mini-Superbikes, with expensive one-time-use quick-change gear, for one race. Honda is rightfully proud of their machinery, but the cost is out of reach for anyone but Big Red. With the other factories on the sidelines, Honda could lap up to the last Honda...twice.

The Speedway is known to like big fields. Nostalgia for the days of 80 Yamaha TZ-750's has them wondering, 'Why not again?' The answer can be found in the FX fields.

At Daytona there were 17 starters and 16 finishers, a fifth the size of their dream field. The largest FX field of 31 came at Laguna Seca. Two weeks later, it was back to 22 at Mid-Ohio.

Privateers have shied away from the class because it provides the worst cost-reward ratio in racing. Building a super trick 600 to race the Honda factory without any chance of winning for the $1700 winner's share of the purse is a certain way to expedite poverty.

Not only can you not win, you won't come very close. Following the Daytona race, very few have gotten a sniff of the winners. Closest was Valvoline EMGO Suzuki's Vincent Haskovec, 8.21 seconds out of second at Brainerd. Often, the gap to the first nonfactory bike is 20 seconds. Erion Honda's Alex Gobert was the third Honda and still 24.3 seconds back at Infineon Raceway.

With none of the other factories supporting the class, and very little interest from the privateers, how do you get to a big number of riders? Change the rules.

AMA rules state that "Motorcycles entered in Supersport are not permitted in Formula Xtreme." Look for that to change. It's the only way to build what's clearly a failure as a class in the short term. If you can't fill the class under the rules, change the rules to fit the class.

August 18, 2004

Mending Fences

"What we've got here is...failure to communicate." That memorable line was delivered by prison captain Strother Martin to Paul Newman, the recalcitrant Luke in the 1967 classic *Cool Hand Luke*. The relevance today is in how AMA Pro Racing interacts with the road race paddock. As you'll read in the second part of our round table discussion with the AMA Pro Racing, there is disagreement on whether the riders, crew chiefs, team managers, etc., have a say in the decisions that govern their livelihood. Road race manager Ron Barrick admits that he'd like to have the time to get the pulse of the paddock, but, given his responsibilities, it's undeniable that he simply doesn't.

Gary Mathers was the man for the job. The most successful team manager in the history of motorcycle racing, the universally respected former Honda and Kawasaki team boss worked as a consultant before taking a full time job. Former adversaries welcomed him for his equanimity and fairness. Finally they had someone who spoke their language, who understood their concerns. There wasn't then, nor is there now, a more qualified individual to work as a liaison among the teams, the AMA, the tracks and the promoters. Smart and experienced, he won titles in the widest variety of disciplines imaginable - road racing, dirt track, motocross, supercross, off-road, desert racing, snowmobile, and others I've probably forgotten. What Mathers has done all his life is build things. Whether its race teams or crown molding, he knows how things go together. And it wasn't long before he realized that the system currently in place in road racing didn't work, and he graciously went back into retirement.

Ever since, there's been a vacuum. The teams, and especially the riders, feel ignored; the AMA feels the opposite just as strongly. Progress cannot, and has not, been made under such an umbrella of antipathy.

What isn't in dispute is that the AMA and the teams and riders want many of the same things. They both want safe racetracks. They want a set of technical rules that fosters close racing. They want to see the sport grow so that everyone can benefit. They want to keep the costs of racing reasonable so that the factories continue to be interested, while maintaining a quality field of privateers. They want to continue to see growth in crowds, both at the races and in television viewing. They want the AMA Chevrolet Superbike Championship to be among the preeminent series in the world. It's how they go about it that differs. That may very well be changing.

Safety is the number one issue among riders. Increasing speeds coupled with marginal safety improvements at too many tracks has proven a toxic mix. Some problems are structural, some are institutional. Few are insurmountable. What the riders want is to know that something is being done, because it is. The problem is that they've been left out of the loop.

Mid-Ohio is the best example. The track came under withering attack by the top riders in a round table discussion at Pikes Peak International Raceway. It wasn't long before the track owner put in what must have been a fevered call to AMA Pro Racing, wondering 'Why the contempt? Where's the love?' Work was ongoing. The worst of what the riders felt was being addressed. The track had a plan, after all.

"What we've got here is... failure to communicate."

Infineon Raceway is the prototype for rider-track communications. Several years ago, the AMA suggested in the strongest possible language that changes had to be made. And they were. The original capital improvement budget of $35 million has since doubled and work continues. When it came time to address the needs of the riders, the riders were summoned. Their opinions ranged from the practical to the whimsical. In the end, the track took the best ideas from the riders and the AMA's Barrick and did the best they could with the space they had. Work is ongoing. Next year's track will be better than this year's track.

Driving the project is track president Steve Page, a former executive with the Oakland A's, and John Cardinale, the track media manager. Page made sure the work got done. Cardinale made sure everyone knew about it. From the first shovelful of dirt, the riders were kept informed and included. The track is far from perfect, but the efforts so far, the communication and the good intentions are what is appreciated.

Mid-Ohio moved a wall that the riders felt was the most dangerous on the track. They also tried to reduce the irregularities in the transition between the rectangular concrete patches in the corners - a holdover from the Indy Car days - to the asphalt. It didn't exactly work out, but they deserve credit for trying. Dunlop and Michelin organized the first-ever Mid-Ohio test prior to Laguna Seca, a move that ensured that there would be no surprises when they arrived a few weeks later. Would they race in the rain? That's for another day.

The difference between Mid-Ohio and Infineon Raceway is communication. One knows how to do it, the other hasn't a clue. That will change.

The AMA, in an effort to improve communications, agreed to meet with the riders on a regular effort. The details are yet to be worked out, but the salient point is that a select group of riders will have the chance to meet with Barrick, and hopefully a track representative, prior to the race weekend.

The purpose will be twofold. Firstly, they'll address the immediate needs of the weekend; where the hay bales and air fence are and where they should be. Secondly, they can hear firsthand what the tracks have in mind. What they're planning. What they can do, what they can't. Imagine the difference if this had been done at Mid-Ohio a year ago. No longer a failure in communication.

"I wouldn't be opposed to putting together some formal process to accomplish that," Barrick said during the AMA round table, adding, "I'd rather it was just a handful of riders that would come to a unified decision. But I'd be happy to gather a group of two or three of the top riders if they're willing to take the time at a specified point in the weekend."

It's a start, and a welcome one at that. Maybe they're calling the riders' bluff, thinking they won't organize, won't take the time. Maybe they want the riders to see how difficult it is to convince track owners of the need for serious changes. It doesn't matter. The two riders I contacted, both Superbike champions, wanted in. As will others. My belief is that it will be hard to choose among the qualified.

The AMA has done the right thing by coming around to the view that the riders need to be involved. Now it's up to the riders.

August 25, 2004

The New Daytona 200

WASHINGTON, D.C. (April 14, 1865) - The White House announced that President Abraham Lincoln thoroughly enjoyed tonight's performance of "Our American Cousin," a three act farcical comedy based on a loutish American's attempt to enter English high society. Judging by his reaction, the president was especially taken by the high-spirited performance of Laura Keene in the difficult role of Asa Tranchard. Additionally, halfway through Act III, Scene 1, during a particularly humorous line reading, President Lincoln was shot to death by a deranged gunman.

That's how the death of our 16th president would have been announced if crafted by the wordsmiths at AMA Pro Racing. It was the only conclusion to be reached after reading the latest dispatch from inside Fortress Pickerington. Having mentioned in its latest bulletin that the class structure for the 2005 AMA Chevrolet Superbike Championship would be unchanged from this year, something it had suggested in an earlier notice, AMA PR tacked on: "Additionally, it was announced that the 2005 Daytona 200 will feature Formula Xtreme machinery." Huh?

What comes to mind is the delusionally optimistic pimple-pocked teenager who springs what he's convinced is a clever diversion by lining the check-out counter with an archaeologist's random cache: toothpaste, a squirt gun, Jujubes, paper plates and, oh yeah, a 12-pack of Trojan Magnums that wouldn't fit if he wrapped the Little General in three Ace bandages and a burrito supreme. Did they think we wouldn't notice? Did they think we'd be so enraptured by the notion of two models of motorcycle racing in nearly identical and redundant classes for the second year in a row that we'd miss the fact that they'd turned the Daytona 200 into a Honda advertising exercise?

I thought the six factory Superbikes in this year's race would be the all-time low. Could you ever have imagined that the 2005 Daytona 200 would have less factory participation than the 2003 Tunica Short Track? Not only will they have reduced the factory field to two - Jake Zemke and Miguel Duhamel - or three - if Honda has the good sense to re-sign the resurgent Ben Bostrom - but they've managed to get rid of at least two more manufacturers and likely a third. Suzuki says they won't take part, and Ducatis run 200 consecutive miles as often as Marlon Brando. We can't expect Aprilia to join the under-sized fun since it's all they can do to get to the races to explain why they aren't at the races. So the premier race's "gorgeous mosaic," a term of inclusion coined by former New York City mayor David Dinkins to describe the ethnic diversity of the greatest city on the planet, is now as monochromatic as a NASCAR beer line.

The change to expensive little Superbikes for one race was pushed through without being discussed by the road race advisory board, the most representative group in the paddock. Not that AMA PR ignores its voice or that of the riders. Riders who want to comment on whether aftermarket fork braces should be permitted or whether pit crews should be required to wear fire suits and goggles during refueling can offer their brief comments on the double secret handshake website. But changing the premier class for what some consider the biggest road race in America? As our esteemed vice president, Dick Cheney, said to Senator Pat Leahy during the Senate class photo, "Go f&%$ yourself."

In an earlier press release, AMA PR wrote: "Scott Hollingsworth, AMA Pro Racing CEO, confirmed that 1000cc Superbikes will remain the premier class in the Championship."

Just not in the sport's biggest race.

The New Daytona 200

The event trumpeted as America's most prestigious motorcycle race will now be run with a small, but undetermined quantity of support-class motorcycles and will be, barring the reversal of the earth's rotation, a walkover for American Honda. Is it any wonder the consensus of the paddock is that Honda runs AMA Pro Racing? Maybe Honda did know some thing when it took its porcine 600 out of Supersport and usurped the new and improved Formula Xtreme class. That it was a year before the Daytona FX 200 was maybe just a happy coincidence, like Clinton's DNA on Monica's blue dress or the blood in O.J.'s Bronco. Or maybe not. If it walks like a duck and talks like a duck and finishes seventh like a Duc...

Yes, they're playing by the rules. But who's making the rules? Certainly not a broad representation of the major manufacturers. The number of senior executives of Japanese manufacturers on the Pro Racing Board numbers one. Can you guess which company he represents? AMA PR is sensitive about this point, as they should be. Perception is often as important as reality and, in this case, the perception is clear.

"I think from a perception perspective, I think it's important that we look at the situation," Hollingsworth said during a roundtable discussion with *Cycle News.*

This year's Daytona 200 will be as predictable as the air quality at a chili cookoff. And probably less noisy. With only 17 FX starters and 15 finishers in 2004 - 13 on the lead lap - it means Daytona's dream of 80 motorcycles droning on as endlessly and meaninglessly as the AMA Road Race Technical Rulebook will remain just that. Imagine privateer 600s going 67 times around the new, safety-first - but you didn't hear that from Daytona or the AMA - configuration. (In their defense, they'd be foolish not to enter the 200 if it offers the biggest purse.) The non-factory 600s - read all but three - will be blowing up like disenfranchised Iraqis or getting passed more often than a fat chick at a nudist camp.

But it will make playing follow the leader a lot easier. First clue: red bikes. Second clue: terminal velocity 25-mph faster than the grid-fillers that make up rows two through whatever. Third clue: lots of raised middle fingers, the preferred form of communication for the chosen few who wish to signal to the grid-fillers that they stop blocking the pre-ordained path of the Red from the green to the black and white checkers. Then a champagne shower, a few group photos, and the post-race press conference where the winners will do their best to ignore the questions and work the less-than-melodic machine name, Honda CBR600RR, into their answers.

Question: When you lapped the fourth-place finisher for the sixth time, do you remember which corner it was in?

Answer: My Honda CBR600RR ran great all day long thanks to my crew: Junior, Beavis, Hitoshi, Homer, Cartman and, of course, Al.

Question: Having built an impressive lead, do you think it was a bit cocky to take a shower and get your blond highlights touched up during your second pit stop?

Answer: My Honda CBR600RR ran great all day long and my hair grows fast, just like my Honda CBR600RR. I really didn't need the shower, but it was as fast as one of my tire changes, thanks to Junior, Beavis, Hitoshi, Homer, Cartman and, of course, Al.

Question: Can you explain why in the Superbike race, a class that has more than three factory entries, you lost sight of the leader very early on and won't see him again until the check-in line for the flight home on Sunday?

Answer: My Honda CBR600RR... I'm sorry. What was the question?

September 15, 2004

The Road to Making It Safer

On the day before the start of the Road Atlanta weekend, Mat Mladin, Jamie Hacking, Tommy Hayden and I spent an hour and 40 minutes inspecting the track with AMA road race manager Ron Barrick. It was educational for the riders and me to witness the difficulties in improving track safety. It was also instructive for Barrick to get input from the riders on what needs to be done and in what order.

But for a few exceptions, riders and teams haven't been involved in the safety process for years. With increasing speeds and diminishing safety margins on outdated tracks, the need for change has become essential. Riders have always said they wanted to be part of the process, and AMA Pro Racing officials, during a roundtable discussion with *Cycle News*, agreed to meet with the riders. This was the first small step.

The plan is simple: Prior to every race weekend, those three riders and Ben Bostrom, the fourth member of the group who wasn't able to join us, will inspect the track with Barrick and a track representative. The purpose is twofold: Making sure the air fence and hay bales are in the right places, and making certain that any planned improvements are the right ones.

The calendar is littered with racetracks whose good intentions haven't been recognized. Two spring to mind: the Mid-Ohio Sports Car Course and Daytona International Speedway. Mid-Ohio was heavily criticized during a meeting I had with a group of riders in June: Walls were too close, nothing was being done. Someone at Mid-Ohio noticed the criticism and got AMA Pro Racing CEO Scott Hollingsworth on the phone. The message was along the lines of "Don't they know we have plans?" My reaction was that I, too, have plans, and they involve Pamela Anderson and a bathtub full of butterscotch pudding, but that was as likely to happen as Mid-Ohio changing. Turns out I was wrong. (Ms. Anderson is allergic to pudding.)

Mid-Ohio did indeed have plans - it would have helped if they'd told the riders - and the first stage of improvements was in evidence during the race weekend. They should be commended for moving a guard rail on the back part of the course. For too long, it stood threatening, guarding with menace the final right onto the back straight. But no one could remember that corner causing a serious accident or red flag. The corner that most needs fixing is the slow, up-and-down left soon after the longest straightaway. Crash there and you will hit the air fence and you may get stuck under it, as Aaron Yates did a few years ago. Though it's a fairly low-speed corner, the runoff is insufficient, and crashes often bring out a red flag, which drives the people in the television truck batty. Fixing that corner is far less complicated than the one on the back straight, where land-ownership issues intervened.

Mid-Ohio is now fixing the up-and-down left, I've been told, in time for next year's race. Had the riders' voices been heard, it would have been the first fixed. And it would have prevented the sort of harsh criticism the track suffered.

The model for communication and cooperation, as I've said many times before, is Infineon Raceway. Faced with losing their date, they instituted massive improvements, spending over $70 million of mostly NASCAR and NHRA money to upgrade the entire facility, not just the track but the physical plant as well. Track president Steve Page has involved the riders, and PR man John Cardinale has kept the world up to date with informative press releases.

The Daytona chicane was built to prevent the sort of mass-bike collisions that plagued the Supersport race two years in a row. It certainly did that, but at the expense of tire life. Dunlop's Jim Allen, the most knowledgeable tire expert in the paddock, said that by lengthening the run onto the turns three and four banking, tire life has been compromised. He believes it contributed to the failure of the rear tire on Ben Spies' Yoshimura Suzuki GSX-R1000 last October. It was another case of good intentions gone bad. Unfortunately, changing the chicane won't be considered until Daytona repaves the entire track, and that's not imminent. The move to Formula Xtreme machines and eliminating the west banking, along with improvements in tire safety, should negate the negative aspects of the new chicane. But Superbikes will still reach their highest tire temperatures in the east banking, though we don't know for how many laps.

The issue of tire safety extends far beyond Daytona. The failure of Hacking's Dunlop at Mid-Ohio, not long after similar tires failed in Canada, was a harsh reminder of a problem everyone thought was fixed following Dunlop's highly successful Daytona Bike Week and virtually every race since.

The riders are sensible enough to know they can't barge in with a list of demands. But they deserve to know what's in the works, and their input can only be a bonus. No one - no track designer, no track owner, no AMA official - knows more about what should be done or has more at stake than the riders. They're the only ones putting their lives on the line.

When I was in Brno for the Czech GP I spoke with anyone who would talk to me about safety - riders' rep Franco Uncini, the 1981 500cc World Champion; World Champion Valentino Rossi; former World Champion Kenny Roberts Jr.; race director Paul Butler; former racer and television commentator Randy Mamola; Nicky Hayden; Colin Edwards; and Peter Ingley, a former tire technician who was the World Superbike riders' rep. The message from all was clear - patience and perseverance. It's possible that the changes the AMA riders suggest won't be implemented during the tenure of the current riders. Uncini told me it took three or four years before people started paying attention. It can't take that long here. It took the death of Daijiro Kato in last year's Japanese GP to spark the formation of the GP rider-safety group - Rossi, Roberts, Sete Gibernau and Nobuatsu Aoki - at the following race in South Africa. Everyone involved in the process takes it very seriously. Rossi singled out his home track of Mugello as being the least cooperative.

Changing the premier class to 600cc-based machines doesn't solve the problem. As Mladin has pointed out, 600s have more corner speed than 1000s, which means they'll hit the walls sooner.

It is in the best interest of everyone - the riders, the tracks, and the AMA - to make this process work. Too much is at stake. The riders, and most everyone in the paddock, have been critical of the lack of progress in track safety. They need to put in the time to make it better. The tracks have the most to lose. As the AMA pointed out in our roundtable discussion, they have taken the sanction away from tracks that didn't provide a safe racing environment. Motorcycle racing is the most profitable event at a number of tracks on the calendar, and the loss of the AMA weekend would be a financial disaster. The worry is that the series would end up with no tracks. Why not give the more cooperative tracks a second date?

AMA Pro Racing is under attack for any number of reasons by fans, teams and riders. Their forceful advocacy of an issue most important to the riders will go along way toward bringing down the level of animosity.

December 1, 2004

Less and More

With a lull in the racing, it's time to offer a few unsolicited suggestions.

The first is that the size of the AMA Superbike field must be reduced. The standard of being within 110 percent of the fast Superbike qualifier is far too lax. It leads to overcrowded fields of unqualified riders who adversely affect the outcome of far too many races. And it's easily fixed. The AMA Pro Racing Board has shown it will act by executive fiat in changing rules - see Formula Xtreme as the premier class at Daytona - so they could easily go to the far more acceptable 107 percent.

"The biggest risk I take all year is passing those guys," Ben Bostrom said of the lapped riders. "That is risk number one and I hate it. I think it's such a joke, and it destroys every race."

Bostrom was responding to a question about the obstacles Brit Neil Hodgson will face in his debut AMA season. Bostrom's opinion was echoed by his brother Eric and American Honda's Jake Zemke, and it's a subject that's brought up at nearly every postrace press conference.

The standard for most all professional racing series is 107 percent. MotoGP, World Superbike, the British Superbike and the Japanese Superbike series all have that mark. Why not here?

What can the argument be for diluting the field with grid fillers? Given how much AMA Pro Racing makes on sanction fees, it can't be for the drippings provided by entry fees. It also can't be for the spectators, for a number of reasons. Fans are sophisticated enough to wait a minute to see a real race, rather than a scrum for 35th. They're not shown on television. They add nothing to the racing. Quite the opposite, in fact. Too often riders find themselves facing the unpredictable late in the race. The safety of the riders, both the lappers and those doing the lapping, isn't being considered.

"We need to get rid of some of those guys off the racetrack because they're spoiling the racing," Yoshimura Suzuki's Mat Mladin said after pulling off the Superbike double at Road Atlanta. "The spectators are not here to see the guy coming 20th. They're here to see the top few guys pushing each other, passing each other for the lead, and see who can win."

The Bostrom brothers offered a sensible solution back in January. What they propose is that riders who don't make the cut get paid in a sliding scale by their qualifying position. It has the added advantage of making sure the slower riders won't be tearing up their bikes, using up their tires or loitering for an extra day, while at the same time improving the racing and giving them some incentive to improve. The only possible notoriety they can garner by being so slow is negative.

Getting noticed by the factories has become increasingly difficult, unless you get bonked off the track by the leaders. The lineups of the factory teams hardly ever change, and when they do, it's a game of musical chairs with riders hopping from one factory to the next. Where's the next Nicky Hayden? The next John Hopkins? And when will they be ready? The answer is that there are a few very good young prospects, but they're not coming along as quickly as the Europeans. Spaniard Dani Pedrosa, the newly crowned 250cc World Champion, is 19. The 125cc World Champion Andrea Dovizioso is an 18-year-old Italian.

How often are riders discouraged by the costs? And where does a rider new to the sport have a chance of standing out or getting noticed for running at the front, rather than battling for 15th behind the factory bikes in Supersport? Production racing.

Valentino Rossi, Mat Mladin, Troy Bayliss, Ben and Eric Bostrom, Jake Zemke, John Hopkins, the Gobert brothers, Troy Corser - all riders who got their starts in production-based classes. In the United States it was the old 883 class, an entry level series where the dirt tracking Bostroms and Zemke got affordable starts.

The 883s are gone, but there are more than a few motorcycles that would be perfect. Tops among them is the Suzuki SV-650S twin. When Kevin Schwantz wants to have it out with the ex and current racers who teach at his school, they do it on the twins, not the much quicker inline fours. Suzuki has provided the bulk of the field for years and would likely get behind a spec class. The SV is reasonably priced and reliable, and it's a blast to ride. At the moment, it's the best option. But other manufacturers may want in, and the model could change year to year.

As for where they might fit into a race weekend, remember it wasn't that long ago that there were six classes. Now there are four and the schedule is almost never the same week to week. Given that flexibility, and the chance to showcase rider ability, it's in everyone's best interest to have a stocker class.

With essentially two displacement motorcycles, 600cc and 1000cc inline fours, making up the grids of all four classes - yes, I know about the few Ducatis and Buells - it's hard to tell them apart. Superbikes are indistinguishable from Superstock machinery on the track and nearly so off of it. There's an easy fix.

When the MotoGP circus comes to Mazda Raceway Laguna Seca this July, the first thing you'll notice is the noise. The decibel limit for the exotic MotoGP machines is 130. The upper limit for all AMA road racing is 105. This is why Superstock sounds like Superbike sounds like Supersport sounds like Formula Xtreme, almost.

The knee jerk reaction to raising noise limits should be avoided. It's anti-social or anti-environment or anti-hearing, all possibly true and completely irrelevant. I'm not advocating 130 db.

But a bump from 105 to 110 would make a surprising difference. You'd take notice immediately. You'd know in an instant that something special was going on. And you'd know that it wasn't just more motorcycles circulating, which is what we have now, especially at the back of the Superbike field.

January 19, 2005

Is It Really Safer?

There's a saying in Florida: "There's the right way, the wrong way, and the Speedway." Never was it truer than at last week's annual winter tire tests.

The new 2.95-mile (measured on a car's odometer) Daytona International Speedway layout was christened by a group of riders anxious to feel better about the Speedway. They'd heard the rumors and seen the photos and wanted the simple truth. They were unanimous in their condemnation of the old 3.56-mile layout last spring and were grateful that someone had finally listened.

The Speedway was rightfully tired of the bad press garnered by the pair of exploding tires in 2003. The solution was slower motorcycles or a slower track or better tires, or all three. They got all three. The Daytona 200 will be run on Formula Xtreme 600s on a layout with one banking removed. Dunlop introduced a new line of stronger tires that showed no signs of failure on the Superbikes or any other class.

Was the track work in exchange for forcing the AMA to change the 200 to Formula Xtreme bikes? Yes and no, depending on who you asked.

It's certain that what made it possible was the track being closed for several months while the new turn-one double-wide tunnel was installed. Would they have done the track work otherwise? Maybe, since it wouldn't have greatly impacted the tri-oval. But a closed track made the decision that much easier.

First impressions of the track were positive, as were later impressions by some. The unanimous opinion expressed about the former track was gone. This time most everyone agreed it was safer, but...

As Yoshimura Suzuki's Mat Mladin said, "When the second banking gets taken out over here, I'll be a lot happier." Then he added, "But for now, it's good they got rid of that banking."

The most destructive segment of the racetrack is the run from the chicane to turn one. That's where the highest sustained speeds are generated, that's where the tires generate the most heat, that's where most of the tires blow up. Barry Sheene's blew up at the end of the front straight in 1975, as did Dave Sadowski's about 15 years later. That's where Ben Spies was sent hurtling down the racetrack in October of 2003. Anthony Gobert had a tire fail coming onto the front straight in the 2003 running of the 200. Two and half years later, Jason DiSalvo, another Yamaha rider, suffered the same fate. Gobert didn't fall; DiSalvo did, but was unhurt.

More than one rider pointed out the abundance of room inside NASCAR turns three and four for a road course. The banking could be re-joined by the old tunnel and in a low enough gear to extend tire life. Daytona wasn't interested. The drafting battles from the chicane to the start-finish line have defined the Speedway forever. There was little chance they'd jeopardize that tradition. They could rightfully argue the quality of the product would be compromised.

An 11th-hour suggestion was possibly the most tire-destroying idea of all. During a meeting attended by American Honda's Miguel Duhamel and track designer Bob Barnard, the idea was floated to lay pavement inside the apron along the west banking. Riders would exit turn six, but instead of climbing the wall, they'd lean over on the left side of the tire and stay there for about half a mile. If they fell, which they'd do when their tires almost certainly failed, they'd slide into the banking so hard it'd be like hitting a wall. All the Air Fence in the world couldn't protect them.

Spending that much time on the side of the tire would be worse than the banking, according to the tire guys.

With that idea sunk, the road-course design that had been circulating for months went forward. With very little room to work, Barnard had to think like a contortionist, squeezing a handful of turns inside the existing track. Safety was the priority, the whole point of the exercise. The irony is that the track may not be safer.

Removing the banking lowered tire temperatures by 10 degrees Celsius, theoretically extending tire life. But tire wear was worse than normal, at least for Dunlop. Why was that? Part of the blame, or praise, goes to Dunlop. Its new N-Tech tires allowed riders to keep the throttle pinned all the way around the banking for the life of the tire. Before, they could pin it for a lap, then feather the throttle and hang on for the next 18 laps while the tire squirmed like a politician under oath. Not only was there more wear this year, but it was on a wider patch of the tire. The good news was that the N-Tech technology provided a stronger carcass and far less chance of the kind of catastrophic failures that plagued the 2003 testing season. The combination of one less banking and the new tires means the big blowout is far less likely. The new infield section offers a different set of challenges.

Riders are notorious for not looking off the track. They don't want to know what they might hit. American Honda's Jake Zemke didn't take a thorough look at the track until the final day of the test. The day before, Mladin had crashed and slid so far that he hit a barrier few thought would come into play. It did, and his bike flipped over the guardrail.

"I rode around today and took a good look at the whole new section and just kind of looking around, and there's stuff to hit in every corner," Zemke said. "Whether it's power poles, concrete wall, Armco, whatever, there's a lot of stuff out there. Hopefully, some of that stuff will be moved before we come back to race in March, because right now, every corner's got issues."

Some of the problems can't be changed. Overshoot the right-hander onto the new section and a number of things can happen, most of them not very good. You could tumble to a stop, as Dan Bilansky did, unhurt, on Tuesday. That's a best-case scenario. Or you could hit the protection in front of a power pole, which will be narrowed before the race, or the drainage culvert. Or you could run across the track and get T-boned by a rider exiting the new turn five. Mladin had overshot the turn-four right-hander and crossed the track by turn five a few times.

"What they're going to do about that, I don't know," he said. "I'm sure they'll have some kind of defense of saying people shouldn't run off."

The corner that bit him came after turn five. Between the pair of first-gear lefts, Mladin spun up his rear and was shot into orbit. When he came down he wasn't in complete control and the barrier was fast approaching. The only choice was to sacrifice the Suzuki.

These were all single-bike incidents on a track that rarely had more than a dozen to 15 riders on it at any one time. Red flags seemed to be needed too often. What happens when the pack of 50 600s hits that turn on the first lap? Or someone tries to move a rider out to the right between the two infield lefts?

Is the track safer? Only time will tell.

January 26, 2005

Rainey's Crash-Course Karting School

Oh sure, everyone thinks Wayne Rainey is a great guy, doting father to Rex, loving husband to Shae, three-time 500cc World Champion, and the rider who changed the way racing motorcycles was approached with his rigid preparation and unwavering commitment. That's the public image. But I know better. The man is a killer, cold-blooded as a copperhead with Slurpee running through his veins. You think he won those 24 GPs and three titles on his surfer-boy good looks alone? Come on. He was as relentless as a bulldog on a mailman, chewing him up and spitting him out and moving on. But why does he want to kill me?

That question was pinballing through my racket-filled skull the first time the 250cc shifter kart I'd wedged my butt into went sideways as I simultaneously downshifted, hit the brakes and let out the clutch entering turn five at Mazda Raceway Laguna Seca. I knew this was a crap idea. After all, how many sports do you know where the first thing you do is get fitted for a neck brace?

I'd put mine on backwards, which impressed the hell out of Rainey and Kevin Schwantz and Doug Chandler and whoever else was watching, and also restricted my breathing. Rainey had invited me to try the kart during media day for the Superstars of Superkarts race that will run on the Saturday of the AMA/MotoGP weekend. I had neither the talent nor desire. But Rainey is nothing if not persistent. Late In the day, I relented.

"Just sit in it, see how it feels," Rainey said as I squeezed into the form-fitting fiberglass tub, my knees sticking up, the shifter digging into my thigh. It was as uncomfortable as a gynecological exam. I half expected a doctor to tell me I was 2 centimeters dilated. Getting in was the easy part. There was no way I was getting out without two bottles of Astroglide and a forklift.

Over the course of the day I'd seen the best at work. Eddie Lawson is a master. The most prolific American 500cc World Champion, with four titles, Lawson has guided his Yamaha TZ250-powered kart around Laguna Seca faster than any motorcycle, but even Lawson's bravery has limits.

"I scared myself in the kart doing that," he said of his 1:23.857, under Troy Bayliss's 2001 mark of 1:24.833. "I don't know if I want to do it again."

Lawson in a kart is as smooth as Lawson on a motorcycle, the kart instantly changing directions like a mechanical Barry Sanders.

Schwantz never stopped grinning.

"It's a lot more fun on a kart than it was on motorcycle," Schwantz, who'd never driven a shifter kart, said. Fearless as always, the 1993 500cc World Champion threw himself into it with volatile neglect, the kart twitching and darting and looking every bit as nervous as a Chihuahua on crack. His times were more than respectable and would've gotten better if the transmission hadn't lunched itself just after lunch.

Rainey only made two laps before pitting with shifting problems.

On Rainey's advice, I took it slowly, gradually feeding in throttle, making deliberate shifts, using roughly the same brake markers as the sweep truck. I thought about weaving back and forth to get heat in the tires, but I didn't need heat. I didn't need tires. My lap times wouldn't have been much different if I was on the rims. By the time I got to turn six, I felt emboldened. I'd been through five corners without spinning or stalling.

The run from turn six up the hill to the Corkscrew was a blur. I was later asked if I thought there was enough runoff on the right side of the track for MotoGP. I have no idea. I didn't look off the track. Pamela Anderson could have been Jell-O wrestling Lindsay Lohan on the side of the track. I wouldn't have noticed.

The last thing I remember before falling off the edge of the earth was a "3" marker. I don't think there was a "2" or a "1." Then I was in the Corkscrew. Kel Carruthers, former 250cc World Champion and crew chief to World Champions Roberts, Lawson and Rainey, thinks it's one of the stupidest pieces of racetrack in the world, and he raced the Isle of Man.

First off, the name is wrong. A corkscrew brings to mind an aged California cabernet savored with a well-marbled filet. It doesn't evoke tsunami-style panic as a two-stroke gargles helplessly while you flail at the steering wheel like you're wrestling an octopus for the last scallop in the bay and plunge in three different directions all the while thinking you should be shifting and wondering what the hell the bridge is doing halfway up the chute between the Corkscrew and Rainey Curve? Corkscrew, my ass; that trap door dead drop should be called "the Abyss."

By the time I got done fumbling with the controls I was through Rainey Curve and into turn 10. Doug Chandler said he went through in sixth, nearly flat out. So was I, in third. Nearly flat out. Then I sputtered up to the final left and the first humiliating run up the front straight. I pinned the throttle as much as my sneakers would allow, racing through the gears as the engine hit the rev limiter - or so I thought. Turns out the engine wasn't screaming toward the redline; it was a cry for help. "There was probably another five grand left," Rainey later told me, shredding the last bit of dignity I might have had.

On my first flying lap, things started going bad entering turn five. Almost before I knew it, the world was suddenly circular and the rear end started to come around, and I was reminded of the time I wrecked the late Dale Singleton's Audi the weekend of the 1981 Belgian GP… but that's another story with a happy ending. Then, just as suddenly, the kart forgave me and I was on my way.

Then, it was to the Corkscrew again. This time I didn't run as far up the curbing or overcompensate quite as much, but I still thought it was a stupid corner.

In the end, I did one out lap, one flying lap and one cool-down lap. Turns out Rainey wasn't trying to kill me, he was schooling me. I came away with an increased appreciation for the better riders - their skills, their concentration, their determination, and their concern over backmarkers. I was a backmarker of the worst kind. Mladin and Duhamel and Ben Bostrom often complain that lappers are unpredictable; the last guys don't know where the grid fillers are going. Hell, I had no idea where I was going. I probably tried more lines than John Belushi. And no two were the same. I was slow in a way molasses could never be. Compared to me, molasses is Valentino Rossi on a qualifier.

The Superstars of Superkarts race is on the Saturday afternoon of the July 9-11 AMA/MotoGP weekend. With three 500cc World Champions, AMA Superbike Champion Doug Chandler and, possibly, multi-time 500cc runner-up Randy Mamola, it will have as much motorcycling history as any race on the weekend. Having survived my adventure, it's a race I wouldn't miss. Neither should you.

March 2, 2005

Cover Me Not

Today you get to be the editor. Today you get to get to make a decision. Today it's up to you to decide whose picture to put on the cover of the Daytona Bike Week issue. Simple, right? You do what you've always done - you put the winner of the Daytona 200 on the front. Not so fast.

The days of the Daytona 200 meaning something are over. There was a time, not long ago, when Grand Prix stars and American globetrotters started their seasons in Florida.

It began, for the most part, in 1973, with a victory by the "Flying Finn," Jarno Saarinen. Saarinen, who died tragically at Monza two months after Daytona, didn't usher in the two-stroke era at Daytona; that honor belongs to 1972 winner Don Emde. But Saarinen, at the time the reigning 250cc World Champion, brought both the excitement of the GP world and a host of fellow world campaigners.

The Yamaha TZ-700 came in 1974, followed soon by the TZ-750, and with them, the level of interest skyrocketed. Giacomo Agostini, the most prolific World Champion ever, won the race in 1974, followed by Californian Gene Romero, then Johnny Cecotto, the 20-year-old Venezuelan who finished the race with cord showing on his rear tire. By now, Kenny Roberts was in the mix and soon to win his first Daytona 200. It came in 1978, with two more to follow, in 1983 and '84. In between were wins by world campaigner, grey market Mercedes importer, and pig farmer Dale Singleton (1979 and '81), and Frenchman Patrick Pons (1980). New Zealander Graeme Crosby won the 1982 Daytona 200, the last time the honor went to a non-North American.

Freddie Spencer kicked off the greatest year of his career by winning all three races at Daytona in 1985: 250cc GP, Superbike, and Formula One. He followed that with the 250cc and 500cc World Championships, a feat that will never be equaled. It also marked the beginning of the end of the two-stroke era in the United States. Superbike took over as the premier race at Daytona and soon after for the rest of the series. The final Formula One Championship was won by the late Randy Renfrow in 1986.

Fellow 500cc World Champion Eddie Lawson followed Spencer's Daytona success in 1986. Then came wins by future champions Wayne Rainey and Kevin Schwantz. John Ashmead won the aberrational 1989 200, with Dave Sadowski getting his lone win in 1990.

The next nine years were dominated by three riders: Scott "Mr. Daytona" Russell, Eddie Lawson (again), and Miguel Duhamel. Russell won five times, Duhamel three, and Lawson his second, in 1993. Russell's final win, in 1998, marked the end of outside involvement in the Daytona 200. By then the foreign interest had dried up. Carl Fogarty's flirtation with success in 1995 being the last hint of international interest. From the lofty heights of the '70s and '80s, it had become just another race on the AMA calendar.

Now comes another step. In which direction is open to interpretation.

The 2005 Daytona 200 will be the first for Formula Xtreme 600s, in a year in which the Speedway will be the only track to feature FX as the premier class.

"I come back and I look at Daytona, the premier event is Formula Xtreme, but then it's not good enough to race here at the GP," Kawasaki team boss Mike Preston said recently at Mazda Raceway Laguna Seca.

With Honda the only factory involved in the FX class, and therefore the 200, Miguel Duhamel should win his fifth Daytona 200 in a 15-year span. No one else has won more AMA road races at Daytona or over a career, and no one ever will. Duhamel's last 200 win in 2003 was a lesson to young upstarts Ben Bostrom and Kurtis Roberts. The veteran snookered both on the final lap, and Bostrom never fully recovered.

As it was in 2003, the race should be a Honda sweep, with Jake Zemke joining the party in Bostrom's absence. After a dismal, injury-filled half MotoGP season on his father's undeveloped Proton KR V-5, Roberts is back with the Erion Honda Superbike team. The circle on his forehead is from the gun that was put to his head to do the 200. Given the choice, it's unlikely he'd race the 200. Then again, given the choice, it's unlikely he'd have left MotoGP. Who can blame him?

It will be very long (68 laps) and exceedingly dull, the only uncertainty being how far up the field they'll lap and how many lappers they'll hip-check out of the way. My guess is they'll lap up to fourth with Attack Kawasaki's Ben Attard likely to be their closest competition and a possible podium finisher if one of the Hondas falters. The Honda CBR-600RR's reliability record is unblemished, and a simple rev-limiter should keep them running for 200 miles. Their pit stops, however many they need, will be models of efficiency that no other team will match.

Will the superbike winner lap up to fourth? Not in 15 laps. Preseason testing suggests that the Suzukis will rocket to the front, but they won't be alone. Ducati Austin's Neil Hodgson went well in his return to Daytona, and even better at Laguna Seca, and he plans to stick with Mladin, Ben Spies and Aaron Yates. Teammate Eric Bostrom has all the motivation he needs in the other half of the Ducati Austin garage to head for the front. Privateers Jason Pridmore and Josh Hayes won't want to see the Suzukis disappear, and now we have the Mat Mladin Motorsports-backed Marty Craggill in the field. The kitted American Hondas haven't developed as quickly as they'd hoped, and testing has been rain-plagued. The project started late and will likely be behind at race time, though they shouldn't be discounted. In 1999, Duhamel got off crutches to win both the Superbike and 600cc classes at Daytona. But heart will only take you so far. Horsepower and traction are what matter, and the Hondas are still searching for both.

So who do you put on the cover? Do you go with tradition and honor the winner of the 200? Or do you go with the premier class in the series, the one the other nine (as of this writing) tracks will feature on the weekend, most of them twice?

The choice is simple. It's called the AMA Superbike Championship, and Superbikes will run at every round, unlike Formula Xtreme, which has a holiday at the Laguna Seca AMA/MotoGP weekend. Daytona chose FX out of fear of exploding tires and riders being injured, though you'll never hear that on the record. They slowed down the track and eliminated the banking for the same reason. These are good things, though half-measures, judging by the reaction of the top riders. Was it a *quid pro quo* for having FX as the premier class? That's an answer you'll never get.

Superbikes, the 1000cc version, remain the premier class and should for years to come. At every other round, the *Cycle News* cover goes to the winner of Superbike - not Supersport, not Superstock, not Formula Xtreme.

Tradition plays a big part in Daytona. With few exceptions, it's been the first race on the calendar. For years, Daytona kicked off the international racing season. Tradition used to bring the best riders in the world to Daytona. That will never happen again. The safety margins, not the speed, guarantee that. The winner of the 200 traditionally has graced the cover. Like other traditions, its time has passed.

March 23, 2005

A Farce

AMA Pro Racing CEO Scott Hollingsworth has two choices: Either he can grow a set of cojones or he should resign.

No other possibilities exist after the charade that was the opening round of the unsponsored AMA Superbike Championship at the continuously perilous Daytona International Speedway.

The first running of the Formula Xtreme Daytona 200, allegedly the most important race of the year and now run on what Superbike series champ Mat Mladin calls mini-bikes - it was the slowest race of the weekend - was an endurance race for anyone who had to endure it. To quote American Honda's Miguel Duhamel, "The Daytona 200 this year, it felt like it was the Daytona 255, because, like Kurtis [Roberts] and Jake [Zemke] mentioned, it never ended."

And he won the race by over 42 seconds, lapping everyone who wasn't on the podium. Not exactly a ringing endorsement. How did we get here? How did we get to a day when the best rider the series has ever known, five-time champion Mladin, was heading for the Orlando airport when the Daytona 200 was run? What sort of knuckleheads makes these decisions?

It begins with exploding tires. As best as can be divined, the Speedway tired of being tarred as a destroyer of youth after two catastrophic rear-tire failures during the 2003 winter testing season. Never mind that Dunlop re-engineered the Daytona dual-compound tires that have been trouble-free ever since. Well down the road, a decision was made to alter the road course, eliminating the west banking. It didn't hurt that the Speedway had to close for months to construct a new tunnel. Why not appease the motorcycle crowd? Possibly in exchange for making the 200 a Formula Xtreme race. No one is jumping up to claim parentage of that crotchet. Forget about the sheer insanity of riding 196-plus mph mere feet from a wall.

During our roundtable with AMA Pro Racing, Hollingsworth was asked if Daytona came to the AMA with the Formula Xtreme 200.

"It's been an ongoing dialogue with Daytona for quite some time about all types of race-operation issues and the Daytona 200 and its future," he said. "So really there have been a number of good ideas that have been put on the table."

Good idea? For whom? Certainly not the fans, who saw an endless procession of mostly slow motorcycles getting in the way of a limited number of very talented riders. The Speedway? You bet. They got their coveted 71-rider grid - there were only 36 Superbikes on the grid for that race - made mostly of filler; hungry Supersport riders looking for a good payday. You want pathetic? Simon Turner, who finished 10th, three laps and 6.914 seconds behind Duhamel, made the same $3000 that Mat Mladin earned for winning the Superbike race. Kudos all around. For American Honda? Certainly. The only factory supporting the class became a very late sponsor of the Daytona 200. In fairness, they've been in the class from the start: Duhamel won last year's title, with Zemke second. It wasn't like they were cherry-picking the race. The class, maybe, but not the race. That discussion is for another day.

Is Formula Xtreme the premier class of the future? I've heard it both ways. Getting a straight answer out of anyone in AMA Pro Racing is about as easy as getting Martha Stewart to breastfeed a baby alligator. Not gonna happen.

As loathe as I am to draw comparisons to NASCAR, this case merits an exception. Racing is business, but more than that, it's entertainment. The Speedway knows that. Which is why Nextel

Cup races run on Sunday, with the best drivers in the best cars. What are the chances that the Speedway would tell Gordon and Earnhardt and Stewart, "Okay boys, y'all can run on Friday or Saturday and we're going to run trucks on Sunday." Because a Formula Xtreme 200 isn't Nextel Cup and it isn't Busch, even if it is bush. At best, it's Craftsman Trucks. It might even be ARCA or Orca, a beached whale very few care about that's rotting in the sun. Of the four races, it was by far the worst. Had it been 22 laps, like 600cc Supersport, it would have been a cracker. Had it been 15 laps like Superbike, you could almost guarantee a photo finish. But it had to be 68 soul-sapping, life-draining, brain-shriveling laps.

 Back to Mr. Hollingsworth and the AMA Pro Racing board. What the hell were they thinking? Somewhere in this mix there has to be someone who can muster up the testosterone to tell Daytona, "We'll decide which races we run. This is our series. These are our races. We do have integrity. Granted, it's fading quicker than the Supermoto series, but still..." It should not be the other way around. And it sets a dangerous precedent. Kawasaki and Yamaha, neither of which are in Superbike, both sponsor races. What's to keep Infineon Raceway from telling the AMA, "Listen, guys, Kawasaki's not in Superbike, so what say we slap Superstock in the live-TV time slot?" Is it any wonder that the Superbike class and the championship have no title sponsor?

 What the entire desperate situation points to is a lack of leadership and vision. There has to be a dramatic change in the nature of the Superbike Championship. Everyone knows it. Two team managers - one whose team races Superbikes, one whose doesn't - and a number of others, including a board member, suggested a very simple solution: one 1000cc class. If Kawasaki and Yamaha can't be convinced to join the top class in racing, and their reasons for abstaining are hollower than an 89-cent chocolate Easter bunny, force them. Grab them by the Pampers and wedgie them over to the sandbox with the other kids, Honda and Suzuki and Ducati, and tell them to make nice. Tell them it's better for all the mommies and daddies if they can all be watched in one place. Tell them that's the only way they'll know if their kids are the best kids. Tell them their kids really do want to play with the other kids. It really is that simple. If that happens, I predict the Daytona 200 will again be a Superbike race in 2006.

One 1000cc class, call it what you want. And while we're at it, make it a Sunday doubleheader with a 600cc Supersport race in between. That would eliminate riders racing two classes. So you'd have the best riders in the country facing each other twice a day on the best machines. Sounds simple, doesn't it? And lower the qualifying requirement from the ridiculous 110 percent to something more sensible, like 108 percent. Former World Superbike Champion Neil Hodgson's take on the back of the Superbike field: "Some of the guys looked like they'd just come from McDonald's." What about the 1000cc riders who don't qualify? Give them a consolation race on Saturday afternoon, along with a second 600cc race. Seems like a good time to run Formula Xtreme. And a starter class, a Suzuki SV-650 Cup for riders who can't afford Supersport. Give them a championship incentive - maybe a Suzuki-sponsored Supersport effort.

What would it take to strengthen Superbike and restore dignity to the Daytona 200? In a word, balls. Which can be grown if the will exists. If not, step aside for someone who has a pair.

May 25, 2005

The Urgent Need for Urgent Care

Jason Pridmore lifted his shirt. An ugly scar ran from below his navel almost to his sternum. There was a row of buttonholes on both sides of the red line and beneath the skin were once 28 surgical staples.

Jason Pridmore should have died. The incision was made by doctors who removed Pridmore's spleen and saved his life. A crash during Superstock qualifying at Barber Motorsports Park sent Pridmore to the track medical center. The diagnosis was internal bruising. Two attending physicians were ready to release him. One nurse agreed, another didn't. And neither did Mark Gallardo and Lincoln James, two of the essential members of Pridmore's Star Motorcycle School. Gallardo and James know their boss. They've seen him suffer. They know he has an abnormally high threshold of pain. They know when he's hurt. They knew he wasn't ready to go home. They insisted he be taken to the University Hospital in Birmingham. Had they not intervened, Pridmore would likely have bled to death of internal injuries.

He awoke in the Intensive Care Unit with a plastic tube down his throat. "I didn't really know how serious it was until I came out of surgery and was on a ventilator," he said. "When you're conscious and you're on one of those, it's a little gnarly."

Three weeks later, Pridmore can talk about it dispassionately. The passion is reserved for the need to guarantee that it never happens again.

"I worry about these kids who thought they might have had internal bleeding," Pridmore said in the Jordan pits at Infineon Raceway. "We really need to get some medical people at the track that are used to dealing with athletes who are used to understanding what we deal with."

Everyone I spoke to agreed that the series should have a dedicated set of physicians working out of a traveling medical center. In AMA Motocross and Supercross, it's the Asterisk Mobile Medical Center. Since AMA Pro Racing is the custodian of the sport, it's imperative that they take the lead in establishing a complimentary unit for road racing. It would go a long way to dispelling some of the anger that AMA PR generates on an almost weekly basis. This week's fiasco is the technical bulletin mandating engine case covers that reads as if it was written by someone in a remedial English-as-a-second-language course.

Tom Carson, director of motorsports of the Asterisk knee brace company, Dr. John Bodnar, and physical therapist Eddie Casillas brought the Asterisk Mobile Medical Center to Infineon Raceway. The race fell during a rare weekend off: Last weekend was the Las Vegas Supercross, next weekend is the first outdoor national at Hangtown. The rig is at 31 motocross and supercross races a year. At Infineon, it was a one-off appearance, but it shouldn't be. "We need to get something like that at the races for all the guys," Pridmore said. "It's something we're going to start pushing for."

Yoshimura Suzuki's Mat Mladin agrees.

"Racing's a dangerous business," he said. "It doesn't matter which way you look at it, but it's the risk we're willing to take to do what we do because we love it. To have a track medical center and staff on hand that knows us and knows our background and everything, I think will be a huge step towards the safety of the riders, for sure. I also think on the overall cost basis, if the manufacturers got involved, it's really not that expensive. Personally, I don't think whatever it costs would be that expensive for the well-being of the factory riders, let alone the other riders that all the manufacturers are looking at."

As much as anyone else, American Honda team manager Chuck Miller knows the value of the Asterisk unit.

"This sport deserves it, these racers deserve it," Miller, whose MX/SX riders have benefited from the unit's care, said. "I can't believe that a professional racing organization would allow it in one area and not another. It's time to bring it into road racing. It costs money, but I think the manufacturers and sponsors, everybody would pitch in to try to make it work, for sure.

"One of the biggest problems with us at the racetrack [is], a rider falls and he injures his elbow or his shoulder or the worst-case scenario, he has a head injury. A lot of time, as a racer, you don't want to say, 'No, I can't race.' But these guys are trained experts, and that's the need. So for us, it's a safety net also that we can go to and ask questions and rely on their expertise to say whether a rider is still eligible to ride or not."

Spend an hour in the road race paddock and you'll discover that AMA Pro Racing isn't doing enough for rider safety. The complaints continue like a bad replay of "Groundhog Day." The horrific injuries suffered by Vincent Haskovec in a single-bike accident at Infineon Raceway reminded all of the need to remain vigilant. And Infiineon Raceway is the most pro-active, rider-friendly track on the AMA calendar. They've poured tens of millions into track and safety improvements.

A proposal to make former 500cc World Champion Kevin Schwantz the riders' safety rep was shot down by the Pro Racing Board. Conversely, they're significant contributors to the Asterisk Mobile Medical Center.

Asterisk's Carson was at Infineon because he wanted to "show everybody what we're able to accomplish in motocross, see if there's any interest in this sport."

Everyone I spoke to, from team managers to riders, agreed that there was more than just interest. There was urgency.

The Asterisk unit is more than a medical center. Dr. Bodnar is the primary care physician for not only the riders, but many in the racing community. They transport medical records for every rider they've treated. Because the staff know their medical history, and what kind of injuries to expect, they can be more effective. Everyone in the unit is a multitasker.

"We have no staff," Dr. Bodnar said.

And 100 percent of the money that's donated goes back to the program.

The start-up costs for a new unit could run to $1 million. A trailer could cost anywhere from $300,000 to $800,000, and the equipment would be about $75,000. The X-ray machine alone costs $40,000.

And then there are the running costs. The current trailer was paid for by Asterisk. The AMA helps pay the driver. The manufacturers and riders donated money for the equipment, the trainer, and the nurse. Clear Channel pays for fuel. The Women's Motocross/Supercross Foundation pays for supplies. Given the millions of dollars the manufacturers pour into racing, a few hundred thousand each is a pittance.

And the savings are enormous. Even a simple injury can run into the thousands of dollars at a hospital. The staff at the Asterisk unit can diagnose and treat the injury on-site, then follow up at the next event. Or recommend a course of therapy. And the rider doesn't have to leave the track or be treated dismissively by jaded ER physicians who too often denigrate our sport.

"If we could have a team of physicians and therapists at the track," Pridmore said, "that would be very beneficial. I think it's time that we start considering taking care of the guys that are at the track. In my case, I had two orthopedic surgeons who were at the track. Twice they looked at it and said it was internal bruising. Had two nurses, only one looking at me like with any seriousness."

As soon as Pridmore was taken off the EKG machine, his blood pressure dropped.

"Once my body shut down, it could have been too late then."

It's a lesson that doesn't need to be repeated.

June 29, 2005

A Tantalizing Thought

Valentino Rossi on a Ducati? A tempting thought for the legions of fans of all things Italian. The greatest racer of his generation, if not all time, racing in the colors of the most passionate motorcycle company on the planet.

Ducati MotoGP team director Livio Suppo has given it some thought. The subject came up during a discussion of Ducati's move to Bridgestone tires. The idea of switching from the all-conquering French tires to the neophyte Japanese brand was his own, Suppo said. As a marketing boss, and someone who has to sell the race team to potential sponsors for many millions of dollars, switching tires was a way of seeking an edge "in a championship in which there is one guy that wins all the f---ing races," he said with a laugh in fluent, lightly accented English before the Catalan Grand Prix. "And that's the reality. It's really amazing. Valentino has won four of five, and I think he's winning seven out of the last eight races. Because the last winner was Sete [Gibernau] in Qatar [in 2004]."

That was the race where Honda made the mistake of pissing off Rossi. The World Champion was forced to start from the back of the grid after six seconds were added to his qualifying time. The punishment was for his team having cleaned his spot on the dusty, desert starting grid. Race officials had been notified of the infraction by a number of teams, including Repsol and Telefonica MoviStar Honda, as well as Marlboro Ducati. The Yamaha team appealed with something of a weak argument - that it was a merely a reference point Rossi could aim for in lining up for the first corner - and was denied. Up to eighth place within a lap, he was fourth on lap six when he crashed.

Since that day in early October, he's won every race but one. He won in Malaysia, he won in Australia, he won in Valencia, plus five of six this year. So he's eight out of nine with one second, to Alex Barros in the dodgy wet of Estoril this year.

Suppo was careful in choosing his words. Whatever chance he might have would vanish if he alienated Rossi's management team.

"I think as well as nobody can say no, I think because Valentino is Valentino, you have to wait until he wants to do it," Suppo said. "At the end of the day his position, you don't change your mind. He's not in a position where money or nice words or whatever can change his mind. If he feels good where he's in, there's really nothing you can do, I think, if I know him a little. Because he's smart enough and intelligent enough to take his own decision."

Suppo made the point that in 2003 Rossi wanted to leave Honda. They'd grown weary of each other. Honda had tired of what they felt were unreasonable demands, and Rossi wasn't feeling the love.

"He was looking for something else," Suppo said. "You remember, he was sending a lot of messages out. He had the motivation to leave. And that's why probably he chose Yamaha for some reason, but at the end of the day, he wanted to leave."

Rossi said the move was motivational, that he wanted a new challenge after serially winning on the Honda. There is, of course, more. Honda is based in Aalst, Belgium, not far outside of Brussels. Yamaha's MotoGP team, run by Rossi's fellow Italian Davide Brivio, is based at the headquarters of Yamaha Motor Italia in Germo de Lesmo, just a few kilometers from Monza.

"Now my feeling is that he wants to stay at Yamaha, and if he wants to come with us, just ring. I think no one manufacturer, if

Valentino is interested in joining, is in a position to say, 'I'm not interested.'"

Rossi has been even more successful at Yamaha than he was at Honda. A comparison of statistics shows that on the M-1 he's winning more frequently and scoring more points per round. Since joining Yamaha at the start of the 2004 season, Rossi has won 14 of 22 races, a stunning 63.6-percent success rate. His 33 wins in 64 Honda starts added up to 51.6 percent.

"Honestly, I think that Valentino is the kind of rider that when he wants something, he's able to show," Suppo said. "So far, to me, it looks like he's really focused to stay where he is. It's understandable. He's winning so much. Reading his declaration, he's really happy with the team and the atmosphere."

And, most importantly, he's not likely to want to change tire brands.

Since joining the premier class, Rossi has known nothing but Michelin. The switch to Yamaha was difficult enough; doing it on different tires would have made the challenge far more difficult. But it would also have given Bridgestone invaluable input.

Ben Bostrom provided an insight into Suppo's thinking. In 2001 there were three factory Ducatis in World Superbike. Bostrom rode on Dunlops with the L&M team while the other two riders, Troy Bayliss and Ruben Xaus, were on Michelins.

"At the end there would be two manufacturers more or less with the same level," Suppo said. "There would be always a track in which Dunlop is better or Michelin is better. So this increases, in theory, the capability to win races,"

Dunlop won more races that year, but Michelin won the championship. Could Bridgestone rise up to the level of the dominant Michelins with Rossi on board?

"I honestly believe that a lot of the rumors about Michelin last year doing more for Yamaha than for Honda are, I think, wrong," Suppo said. "It's not true. I think at the end of the day what they have done is, they have followed the best rider in the world that is racing with Michelin."

Suppo believes Bridgestone is on the right path. They built race-winning tires for Makoto Tamada at both Rio and Motegi last year. Their race tires were clearly the best in the streaming wet of China this year. Suzuki's Kenny Roberts Jr. rekindled his glory days by leading Rossi for several laps until his engine expired. Frenchman Olivier Jacque was a surprising second in his first ride on the Kawasaki. The amount of data Bridgestone has acquired is far less than Michelin's. If they can catch up, Suppo says, "then this could be in theory a very good advantage for the company. Because once you secure this advantage, it's not like a rider, that they'll leave. And if Valentino will leave Yamaha tomorrow, they have won, but they probably have learned something about the bike. If you look with Mick Doohan or Valentino or Carl Fogarty, you have to find another one to replace him."

Rossi moving to Ducati would validate what Suppo believes most.

"Riders make a big difference."

The success Rossi and his team have enjoyed is proof that the challenge of taking a brand other than Honda to the World title has been overcome. What about a third brand on different tires? Now that's a challenge.

July 6, 2005

Status Quo

"That deaf, dumb and blind kid sure plays a mean pinball."
PETE TOWNSHEND, THE WHO,
COPYRIGHT EEL PIE PUBLISHING LTD., 1969

"Forgive me, father, for I have sinned."

"What is your transgression, my son?"

"Father, I've spoken badly of the less fortunate, the visually, mentally, and aurally challenged."

"How was that my son?"

"I made fun of the AMA Pro Racing Board of Directors."

"That's not a sin."

"Yes, father, but I didn't know they were deaf, dumb or blind."

"And what leads you to that conclusion, my son?"

"The very evidence is that I asked all the team managers what they'd like to see in the AMA Superbike Championship in 2006, and the majority favored consolidating the 1000cc classes into one class so that all the top riders would have to race each other."

"And..."

"...and the AMA Pro Racing Board of Directors ignored the wishes of the very teams they're meant to look out for. I can only guess it's because A) They're blind, and they didn't read it when it was written in *Cycle News*; B) They're deaf, because they didn't listen when they were told; or C) They're dumb."

"I'd go with C."

Status Quo

A confession. Confessing isn't part of my tribe's culture. We're more into guilt. So I apologize in advance if I've offended anyone with an inaccurate portrayal of the process.

Can the AMA PR BoD play pinball? Or are they - unlike Tommy of The Who's seminal rock opera - deaf, dumb, and blind... and unskilled in the ways of the flippers and bumpers and high scores?

Anyone with more than a pair of firing synapses in his brain agrees that the unsponsored AMA Superbike show needs to be tightened up. Only a truly committed nitwit would dispute that the best riders need to be in one class, that the fans deserve the best show, that the television audience deserves the best show, that the title sponsor - that whimsical but elusive beast - would mandate the best of the best going head to head. All of which makes it that much harder to get into the minds of the AMA PR BoD. These aren't dumb men; they just make stupefying decisions that show a comprehensive ignorance of the wishes of the race paddock and grandstands, places most of them spend precious little time. A few of them I couldn't pick out if you put them in a police lineup with the Village People.

Last week the AMA PR BoD announced that the status quo would be maintained in 2006: four classes, redundant times two, confusing to all but the most enlightened. How they came to this decision isn't known. What is known is that they don't listen to the men who run the race teams, one of whom is in the employ of one of the board members.

Earlier this year, interviews with the managers of the four Japanese road race teams produced a near consensus: They believe there are too many classes and that they're too similar. The upshot of the decision is that it allows companies such as Yamaha and Kawasaki to duck the Superbike class like a dinner check.

Kawasaki's Mike Preston expects an answer soon on the wishes of his Japanese benefactors. But why should he go to Superbike?

Tommy Hayden is leading the Supersport Championship and within striking distance in Superstock. Roger Lee Hayden is third in Supersport. At the Red Bull U.S. GP his riders will be racing in front of a packed house on Sunday, not on Saturday with the Superbikes.

Still, it's better than Formula Xtreme, the redheaded stepchild that was given the weekend off while being reconfirmed as the headliner in Daytona. How has that decision gone over with the fans? Like a chunked tire, according to the results of a poll done on www.cyclenews.com: "It's whacked," 76 percent said, against the 9 percent who thought the big bikes were too dangerous. I voted with the whimsical 15 percent who believe the AMA should remove Daytona from the calendar. Dream on, my fellow utopians.

Asked what he'd like to see for next year, Preston said, "Two classes, one of them 1000, one of them 600."

And if Kawasaki decides to stand pat, Preston will get the heat. But make no mistake that decision, like the motorcycles he races, is made in Japan. And as long as they're given a choice to stay away, they can.

American Honda's Chuck Miller's preferred structure in 2006?

"I'd like to cut out one class myself. It'd be nice to have three classes." Which one would he cut? "If there was a class to combine, I would probably suggest the Superbike and Superstock class."

Yamaha hasn't said what they're up to in 2006. Team manager Keith McCarty hinted that they may take on Honda in the Formula Xtreme Daytona 200. "Well, we're certainly looking into it," he said back in April. And they could also be in the Superbike class. But how many classes can one company run? More than two is a burden. Yoshimura Suzuki is involved in three this year, though not all successfully. They own the Superbike class, and Aaron Yates is leading Superstock. Ben Spies is a revelation on a

Superbike, but the underdog GSX-R600 makes him look ordinary in Supersport.

McCarty has said his team's decision has been made. It's just a matter of the timing of the announcement. The Daytona FX 200 is looking more likely, according to his comments and those of others on the team, and if they do Daytona why not the whole FX series? Superbike is the real question mark. Pascal Picotte tested a Yamaha Superbike last year with encouraging results before the program was shelved. But for how long?

What would McCarty like to see? After a fashion, he said, "I think in a perfect world, we would do it with two, one 1000cc class of some sort and one 600cc class of some sort, and there would be a variety of support events, where it wasn't necessarily a points thing."

Yoshimura Suzuki's Don Sakakura didn't give a clear answer to the question. He wants to retain Superbikes and said there was a need for an entry-level class, though he wasn't committing to a displacement. Whatever it was, it wouldn't draw factory interest.

"The 600cc Supersport as well as the 1000, I think they're both important classes for the manufacturers to showcase," Sakakura said, without specifying Superstock. Whatever the answer, it doesn't suggest maintaining the current defective structure.

Since the AMA PR BoD thinks so little of the team managers, I called around to find a sympathetic voice. Didn't happen. No one could imagine why a change wasn't made. Nor could anyone think of a reason to keep the current program. Do the promoters think their patrons are mesmerized by endless droning? No fan I've spoken to is in favor of the current approach. And without a title sponsor for the series, a disgraceful condition that shows no sign of improving, there can be no pressure from the sponsor to do the right thing.

"I didn't see any change from what we have now, so all I hear is complaints," Preston said. Unlike the AMA PR BoD, he can see and hear, and isn't so dumb that he doesn't understand the problem. But can he play pinball?

July 20, 2005

Laguna Postscript

The scheduled date of next year's Red Bull U.S. GP is July 23, 2006. Will it happen? Probably, but not certainly - and not without a large infusion of cash. And not without significant improvements.

The 2005 Red Bull U.S. GP was a rousing success. The crowds were huge, the racing was sterling, the weather was *nonpareil*. Could there have been a better result for the home side than a Nicky Hayden-Colin Edwards one-two? Only Edwards-Hayden, if you were in the Yamaha camp. The Red Bull Suzukis were in no position to challenge. Maybe next year they will and the red, white and blue can sweep the podium. Only if Rossi retires.

There was a collective sigh of relief when Nicky Hayden crossed the line on a sun-blessed afternoon with his first Grand Prix victory. Aside from winning the girl in the "Dating Game" on the "Today" show, Hayden hadn't won anything since the AMA Superbike race in August of 2002 at VIR. The next year he moved to MotoGP after being touted by no less than Freddie Spencer and Mick Doohan. Through 37 GPs, their faith hadn't waned.

"His confidence will go through the roof now," Spencer said after Hayden's very popular win. "I think this will really help Nicky get that monkey off his back, and I know how critical it is to get that first win."

Spencer's first came as a 20-year-old prodigy on the daunting Spa-Francorchamps road course.

"Once you get that first one out of the way," Spencer said, "then you know what it takes to win the race, and now is his big chance to really show what he is made of."

Some of that was on display in the race. Having one of the greatest motorcycle racers of all time stalking, spying, studying, has rattled far more seasoned riders. Rossi plays Sete Gibernau like a two-dollar kazoo. He took Assen from Marco Melandri at his leisure. And it would be hard to deny that there was a hint of the inevitable - that Rossi was biding his time, waiting for the late-race push, the lap record at the end.

But in the end he had nothing for Hayden. Nor Edwards, his teammate who could break through with his first win in Donington in two weeks' time. The Texan surprised Rossi in the Corkscrew with a bold inside move that Rossi couldn't answer.

Rossi was asked if safety concerns had kept him from unleashing his full arsenal. His response was that "during the practice, you think maybe some place this track is a little bit dangerous, but in the race you don't think about nothing." Then he gave fair warning, "And, yes, for sure I follow. Is an important race, because with Colin and Nicky I discover some good points, some good lines, and maybe I'm faster for next year."

Maybe?

That Rossi will improve is a certainty. It would be nice to believe that the same could be said for the track.

Rossi was among the minority who decried the lack of track safety. He and fellow Italian Marco Melandri were the most vocal. Were they confusing danger with difficulty? That was the view of many others, including one former World Champion. The track, Rossi admitted, is like no other on the World Championship trail. But it's not far off some of the other tracks in America, where Hayden and Edwards and Hopkins and Roberts grew up.

No one doubts that changes have to be made. But at what cost? Yamaha ponied up $2 million for track enhancements to make this race happen. Certainly the track owners thought they'd done everything they'd been asked to do, and they had. But the changes that allowed the track to be homologated were suggested from drawings, not experience. Wrestling a 990cc four-stroke around the 11 varied turns exposed a few problems. None are insurmountable, according to FIM safety boss Claude Danis, who was on the hook for homologating the track this year and heard from the rider safety commission on Friday night. More had to be done, Rossi and Roberts said after a two-hour tour of the 2.238 miles of tarmac.

A resurfacing for one thing, but that isn't scheduled until 2007. More runoff on the exit of the Corkscrew. A widening of the runoff in turn six. A leveling out of the wavy run up to the Corkscrew. Runway level is the aim. Turn one needs to be addressed. Danis said the changes are possible.

"There are some major works involved, but technically everything is possible - the space is there," he said.

The space may be, but what about the money?

Nicky Hayden joked that, given the size of the crowd and how much he was charged to park his motorhome, Mazda Raceway Laguna Seca must be flush with cash. The truth is that the track charged too little. This won't come as good news to the 150,000 spectators. They can, and should, pay more. And before you start ranting and raving, consider his: The more they make, the more they can put back into the track and donate to local charities. And without it, the race could be imperiled. It's not likely, but it's possible.

Higher prices might shrink the crowd slightly. That's a good thing. Traffic was a mess, as were the public toilets and concession lines. T-shirts were sold out on Saturday. Then a few boxes showed up here and there - but only in selected sizes. The bottlenecks at the Dunlop Bridge into the infield were reminiscent of the Lincoln Tunnel at rush hour, only more civil. And hooker-free.

There were other glitches. Timing and scoring didn't make it to the MotoGP pits on Friday morning, nor to the pit wall until Saturday. The first practice was delayed 25 minutes by marshalling problems. Did I mention the traffic jams? Even Rossi got stuck on his way in.

The good news is that everyone associated with the race wants to make it better. Press officer Ed Nichols solicited suggestions in the pressroom. As did Red Bull's Steve Pegram, who promised a bigger and better race next year.

Which brings us back to 2006. The riders' laundry list will be presented to the track shortly. Costs will be estimated. Decisions will be made. Yamaha was the white knight this year in support of their 50th anniversary. Their presence was as ubiquitous as it was welcome. Expecting another seven-figure check is unlikely. Sete Gibernau's solution: "Get [Michael] Jordan to pay the whole thing."

Jordan and Yamaha aren't the only players in the paddock. Honda's first production motorcycle, the 98cc two-stroke Dream D, was built in 1949. Next year will be its 57th anniversary. There are worse reasons to celebrate.

July 27, 2005

What Now?

What's next for Repsol Honda's Nicky Hayden? Will his win in the Red Bull U.S. GP be the first step toward reaching his destiny, or was it just a blip on the radar? Was it a sign that he's ready to challenge Valentino Rossi, or was it all home-field advantage? Can he build on the momentum of his breakthrough victory, or will his podium drought continue?

A weekend's rest gives way to the ninth round of the MotoGP World Championship at Donington Park. The race will be a severe test for Hayden for several reasons. The first among them is Rossi.

The track in the English Midlands is Rossi's second-home Grand Prix. To escape the pressures of fame, the Italian makes his home in a chic part of London. And he's won six times at Donington - seven if you count 2003, when he was penalized 10 seconds and dropped from first to third.

What effect will Hayden's win have on Donington and beyond? I put the question to a few others with unique insight.

Wayne Rainey won his first GP at Donington Park in 1988. The victory was easy, he said. He'd built up to it for a year and a half. Then, once it was over, he moved on.

"What I learned, though, immediately, is it only lasts for a night, because Monday you're back to square one and you've got to do it again," the famously driven three-time 500cc World Champion said.

But it would take the Californian until the third race of the next year for the second win.

"I think some guys, when they actually win that race, they like to promote it for weeks and weeks and weeks, where I never did,"

Rainey said. "I just said, 'Okay, I did it right there. Let's see what I can do at the next one.' I just think what it does, too, is it gives you confidence knowing that you can beat the guys on your day, early in your career when you're not sure if you can beat these guys. So it was important that you think about it correctly, and hopefully Nicky has and he's going to go to Donington going, 'Okay, it's going to be just another race here.' But Rossi had won eight or nine in a row [actually nine of the previous 10], whatever it is, so he's had it completely his own way. He got third [at Laguna Seca]. And I think if Nicky is really smart about it, he can make Rossi think about getting beat again, if he does it correctly. Who knows what Rossi's going to do? He's so used to winning. Somebody else starts winning, who knows how he'll respond? That's what I'm curious to see. I just don't think he's just going to go 'I'm just going to get second the rest of the year.'"

Hayden gives every indication that the win hasn't gone to his head.

"It still is one race; when I think about it, I definitely still smile," Hayden said. "But Donington is just around corner and I've got to start making plans for that."

What will it take to consistently beat Rossi, touted by many as the best ever?

"Get the lead and hold it," Rainey said, perfectly describing Hayden's Laguna win. "If he charges you, just take it back. And he did it right. Sure, not every race is going to be like that. But you do that to Rossi three or four races in a row, you're going to see some mistakes flying out of that Italian."

In only his third 500cc GP Kenny Roberts won at the high-speed Salzburgring in 1978. Roberts wasn't surprised. He'd have won the previous race at Jarama but for a stuck throttle.

Confidence was never a problem for Roberts. Cockiness, maybe, but not confidence. He knew he had Barry Sheene and Pat Hennen and Johnny Ceccotto covered. For Hayden it's different.

He's watched Rossi attain mythic status with each race. He's watched Rossi make fools of his competition week in and week out. He's struggled just to get on the podium, something he hadn't done for nearly a year prior to the U.S. GP.

"Hopefully, it'll give him a little bit of confidence," Kenny Roberts said. "That's what he's been lacking. A lot of times he's been knocking at the door and so close. Winning in America, for all of us, it just made it better. For Nicky, a win's a win. Of course, I don't know: I never won an American GP. Confidence is something that lets him know he can do it and you can grow into it. I always had self-confidence. I never doubted my ability to ride a motorcycle. I won my third Grand Prix, and I would've won my second one. It was a different era anyway. I hope that it gives him the confidence to stick it in there. Towards the end of the races, mentally he fatigues, and something happens and he falls back another couple of spots. Hopefully, this gives him a little bit of boost mentally."

Former 500cc World Champion Kenny Roberts Jr. knew the race winner before the start.

Junior was talking to Hayden on the grid, and just after the butchering of the National Anthem, Roberts said.

"'Congratulations on your win.' And of course Nicky wasn't really paying attention to me or didn't even really hear me. After the race, I said, 'Hey dude, did you hear me about congratulations before your race?' He's like, 'No, why?' 'I told you during the National Anthem the guy screwed up.' He said, 'You did?' I'm like, 'Yeah, I did.' He's like, 'How'd you know?' 'F--- dude, you're half a second faster than anybody at any given time. That was your race.'"

And it was.

"I knew it was his weekend from basically Saturday morning," said Roberts Jr., the 2000 500cc World Champion.

Junior's maiden victory came in the first GP of the 1999 season in Malaysia. Over the winter, he'd graduated from his father's hand-built Proton to the factory Suzuki, and the difference was staggering. Following Malaysia, he won in Suzuka and would go on to second in the championship.

"I'm not going to say he has to back it up, he has to do this, do that," Roberts Jr. said. "That's just bullshit. That's what you'll hear everybody else say. He's living a dream. The guy won an American GP and all of his fans. It was a low-percentage chance to do it, and he came through. I just say enjoy it and do the best you can the whole race and try and get better to where you can do that week in and week out."

"I can't imagine that he wasn't riding well before," Junior continued. "Sure his confidence will be better. If you're riding well, the lap times are good, fast. If you ride off emotion, like a lot of people, maybe, yeah, the lap times will vary. Valentino [Rossi] doesn't ride off of emotions. If I did I wouldn't be racing around in last again. Some people do and some people don't. I'm not sure what he is. I don't think Nicky rides off of emotions. I think he knew the track well and he got a rhythm going, and the bike was there to give him what he needed, and that was that."

The next two GPs are at tracks that are the closest you'll find to Mazda Raceway Laguna Seca. Donington Park and Sachsenring are among the slower tracks, with few fast corners and a premium on momentum. Does Hayden have it?

"I've always been a momentum guy my whole career," he said. "It's in my family's blood that we're momentum guys. Same for my brothers. I definitely hope this here will be what I need to be here week in and week out."

Stay tuned.

August 24, 2005

The Lure of Sturgis

The woman walking toward me is topless. Except for tiny heart-shaped, flesh-colored pasties that cover the forbidden parts, they are there for all to see. Not that you'd want to see them. Time has not been their friend. They have the weathered look of an old barn, red and dappled by age and neglect and maybe, just maybe, I'm staring a little longer than I should. But I'm convinced she wants me to, as does her husband, who proudly squires his not-so-young lovely down the bustling sidewalk of Main Street, showing her off as proudly as a prized heifer. Pose for a photo? Not a problem. They got stopped more often than an Arab in an airport security line.

And all around, the sun is shining, the potato-potato sound of slow-moving Harleys fills the air, the smell of grilled turkey legs and Indian tacos assaults the senses. This is not a dream. This is Sturgis.

It is said that there are only two things you have to do - die and pay taxes. To that, add a third - Sturgis.

The official name of this year's week-long celebration of exquisite motorcycle riding roads and aberrant behavior was the 65th Annual Sturgis Motorcycle Rally. "Sturgis" is all you need to say. It's iconic and unique. Forget Laconia. Especially forget Daytona - it's a swamp with increasingly irrelevant races and roads with as much character as a planter's wart. The 90 percent of motorcyclists with the good sense to avoid the Speedway spend their days going nowhere and their nights cruising the few blocks of the sclerotic Main Street. Aside from coming up with the $300-

a-night tab to sleep in an overpriced chain crap hole, the right turn onto A1A South will be their most taxing maneuver of the week.

Any motorcyclist who thinks he's seen it all hasn't unless he's been to Sturgis. First and foremost, it's about the riding, which is different from the trailering. The schism that exists between the riders and the trailer trash was best stated in one of the official T-shirts, "Nice trailer pussy," a sentiment left open to interpretation by shoddy punctuation.

Ask anyone what they're riding and they'll tell you a Harley - at least 90 percent - then quickly add, "And I rode it here." Harley-Davidson sanctions a contest that's called the Ride In Show. Riding in eliminates the nouveau poseurs with the choppers whose front end resides in a different zip code from the 14-inch wide rear tire.

It isn't officially a Harley event, but it is vivid testament to the brilliance of their Harley Owners Group (H.O.G.), a group with a membership of over 900,000 worldwide that somehow feels like a small family. It helps that Willie G. is seemingly everywhere, signing T-shirts and admiring his creations gone amok. As were Karen and Bill Davidson, both descendants of the greatest motor company in the history of the internal-combustion engine.

If you're in Sturgis, choppers are for posing, motorcycles are for riding. And why not? The variety of roads within 100 miles of Sturgis is spectacular. Drive east and you'll run into Badlands National Park. Riding its 244,000 acres means navigating a mixture of prehistoric rock formations and the largest protected mixed-grass prairie in the United States. The booklet you're handed upon entering tells you that the "Badlands National Park contains the world's richest Oligocene epoch fossil beds, dating 23 to 35 million years old. Scientists can study the evolution of mammal species such as the horse, sheep, rhinoceros and pig in the Badlands formations."

The greater concentration of roads is to the west and south of Sturgis. The best of them is the Iron Mountain Road, a series of switchbacks, granite pinnacles, tunnels, pigtail bridges, and elevation changes that make Space Mountain seem like a goat path. Come around a blind corner, head through a tunnel, and there in the distance is Mount Rushmore. By the time you're done gawking, it's time to hook a quick left for a descent down the hill. Add a slick surface - the day I went, it was raining lightly - and the skill level of piloting a two-up dresser makes what Valentino Rossi does look like a parlor game.

Iron Mountain Road cuts into the east of Custer National Park, a place where wildlife of two wheels and four legs exist mostly in harmony. It isn't often you see a pack of wild burros watch nonchalantly as a stream of Harleys motors by. Even less frequent is the sight of a buffalo stopping traffic to cross the road, but it happens. And it's best not to loiter. Whether they're rural myths or not, stories exist of buffaloes taking exception to Harleys and stomping them back into their composite parts.

That's just the beginning. There's Deadwood, where you might channel the ghost of Al Swearingen holding profane court at the Gem. No part of his banter can be replicated without more dashes than a Morse Code translation of Ulysses.

There's the Spearfish Canyon Road, where you might see a squid on a sportbike get stuffed up the inside by a middle-aged guy on a Harley with three 500cc World Championships, or his son, the 2000 500cc World Champion, no doubt lamenting the lack of runoff and thinking of ways to make it safer.

The irony is that the majority of riders ride at or under the posted speed limits, even on the Interstate. And the overwhelming majority don't wear helmets, enforcing the maxim that those who don't wear helmets have nothing to protect. Here I am, forced by law to strap into my Korean rental, while in the lane next to me a fat guy on a Fat Boy is cruising at 65 in a wife beater, cutoffs, and Tevas. What's wrong with this picture?

That's a question you're likely to ask repeatedly. There's simply too much to see, too much to do, too many roads to ride, too many demos to try, to fully experience the week in a week.

Days are spent riding, nights are spent relaxing. Those who want to be seen cruise Main Street like unwanted hookers. Better to park and watch or partake in one of the many hospitable establishments. Some of the better ones, like the Full Throttle Saloon, on the eastern side of Sturgis, offer full-service debauchery day and night. Orgasm contests, wet T-shirt contests, bull riding, drinking, lots of drinking, and Angieland, where you can stick your head through a gigantic mock-up of her golden triangle. The line forms to the left and moves quite quickly, I must say.

Former 250cc GP Champion Roland Sands was there, showing off immaculate creations in the Seminole Hard Rock Café compound just off Main Street. Terry Vance brought his Screamin' Eagle drag-race team and a new semi filled with pipes and parts for the cruising set. Vance's riders Andrew Hines and G.T. Tonglet staged exhibition runs at the AHDRA meeting on the edge of town, riding the Screamin' Eagle Destroyer V-Rods down the eighth-mile track after the top-fuelers had gagged those of us stupid enough to inhale their fumes.

That's the paradox of Sturgis. Rational behavior and the true enjoyment of riding a motorcycle rules the day; irrational behavior after parking your motorcycle rules the night.

Words don't do Sturgis justice. If you ride a motorcycle, you should go. It's that simple. And if you see the lady with the pasties, try not to stare. It won't be hard. Ahem...

September 7, 2005

Supercross: The Dud

How bad is *Supercross: The Movie*? So bad that the studio didn't screen it for film critics. So bad that it registered 2 percent among those same critics on rottentomatoes.com. (*Gigli* got 7 percent. *Deuce Bigalow, American Gigolo* got 11 percent.) So bad that if it was showing on an airplane, you'd walk out. And the worst crime is that it doesn't do justice to the sport of Supercross.

You probably want to hear more about *Supercross: the Movie*. Why? Your $10 would be better spent on lottery tickets, gasoline, or porn. This pile is so fragrant that the remaining prints should be chopped up and turned into fertilizer. Sprinkle it over your garden and you'll be growing watermelons the size of Escalades.

The warning to turn off your cell phone is the most interesting part of the movie. The dancing popcorn and Coke were more lifelike than the stick figures who delivered lines like, "Oh, this is awful!" Or did that come from the only other sucker in the theater for the not-such-a-bargain matinee. Probably not. She was in the very middle of the front row, craning her neck like a sword swallower to experience the maximum sensory perception of a few million dollars going up in smoke.

What did I like about the movie? It was short, which is something of a mystery since it took forever to make. When they started making this movie, Steve Whitelock was in diapers. Ricky Carmichael makes appearances on both Hondas and Suzukis.

The story is as simple and linear as a yardstick, but less interesting. It tells the story of the racing Carlyle brothers, K.C. and Trip, a pair of pool-cleaning slackers from Palmdale. There's your first mistake. Nothing against Palmdale, but there are tonier addresses in Southern California. Borrego Springs, East L.A., Rosamond all spring to minds.

Trip, a scruffy, bearded blond, is the impetuous hothead. In a rare moment of clarity, the Tripster wagers the company's beater pickup that his CRF450R can outdrag a dirty shirt's Harley. It might if you didn't spend the whole run on doing a wheelie while Biker Bob hit the boost button. K.C. is the more mature but slower brother, the one doing the slow burn at all of life's injustices. The one who uses a bag of frozen peas - a staple in any rider's cooler - to soothe his pranged knee.

The Holy Grail is the factory ride, with the hot chick thrown in as an added bonus. Only this being a work of fiction, it's not a Yamaha or Kawasaki factory ride, it's the all-new world-beating Nami Bullet. Nam, being a shortened version of Vietnam - the last country the United States unsuccessfully tried to colonize - makes using Nami and Bullet an unfortunate choice. No doubt the bike in the sequel will be the Iraqi Improvised Explosive Device.

In fact the Japanese word "nami" translates to "wave" or "average, medium, common, ordinary." Which means the boys from Palmdale aspire to race an ordinary motorcycle. Sort of like what Junior and Hopper are doing.[1]

The relationships are baffling. True love would seem to prevail when Slow Burn hooks up with a rich brunette law student. The speedy Trip falls for fellow racer Piper Gale (or was it Gale Piper?), a cute young blonde whose brother races and whose father was in the same biker gang as the brothers' late father.

"We're both descendants of chopper trash, I guess," Piper pipes before asking Trip to help her undress.

Rowdy Sparks, the buzz-cut son of the owner of Nami, and the real-life Tyler Evans play the heavies. "That's Tyler Evans, one of the dirtiest riders in Supercross," one of the boys says. Evans has

---

[1] Kenny Roberts, Jr., and John Hopkins finished 13th and 14th, respectively, in the 2005 MotoGP championship racing for the official Suzuki factory team.

more tattoos than the Fresno chapter of the Hell's Angels, which is probably why he was chosen. Evans is, in fact, a nice guy, but the intoxicating effect of show biz is more powerful than the Nami Bullet.

When Rowdy asks Slow Burn to be his wing man, it pits him against his brother, who ingratiated himself to Piper's dad and graduated to Piper's Hog Heaven race team. But nor for long. He ends up with a right-leg-and-hip fracture and a severe concussion. This is when you have to pray for our fallen hero. If he's lucky, he'll be heavily sedated for the rest of the movie. Poor bastard didn't make it. He suffered through the end of it with the rest of us.

Slow Burn nears the end of his fuse as the movie winds down. "I'm tired of playing wing man to that idiot," he says just before his factory ride disappears prior to the Las Vegas Supercross.

Does the movie have a happy ending? Like a $100 massage? No, but I have a better ending that might help save this leaky vessel.

In my version, the movie ends with Slow Burn winning the Las Vegas Supercross. But as he flies through the finish posts, the fireworks trigger an aneurysm and he goes limper than an overdosed crackhead. The super slo-mo shows him leaving the bike, machine and rider hitting the ground like a bag of potatoes, Slow Burn ragdolling like an octopus in a dryer. Tight close up to his goggles that show eyes as empty as the pool of good ideas at the movie's pitch meeting. Which brings us to the sequel.

Flash forward a year later. Through intensive therapy, chronicled in MTV-style slo-mo and fast cut, Slow Burn recovers just in time to make the Las Vegas finale. Nami is long gone. There is a new nemesis. His name is Scooter and he rides for the All Motorcycle Anarchists Pro Racing (AMA PR) team. And it's not a Nami, it's a Mami. (The company slogan: "I want my Mami.") And his posse, a collection of like-minded individuals who've drunk the same Kool-Aid, and who procrastinate before making baffling decisions that only make sense to themselves, calls itself The Board.

The race is neck and neck for 20 laps, bumping and grinding and sweating, all set to impossibly loud techno music; essentially a gay bar on dirt. The Board is jumping up and down like kangaroos on a trampoline. On the final run to the flag, Scooter has a choice: Does he square up Slow Burn on the inside or does he use the berm to rail around him on the outside? At the most critical moment in his career, he's as frozen as Ted Williams' head. He's as helpless as a mime in a straightjacket: Making a sensible decision is his Kryptonite. And for one critical millisecond, he tenses up. Slow Burn brake-checks him into the Tuff Blocks. The checkered flies, Scooter comes in second.

For reasons apparent only to them, The Board is ecstatic. It's a reaction no one saw coming. Their fearless leader has made a bad decision and they're oblivious to criticism.

Naaah, no one would believe that.

September 21, 2005

Thank You, Roger Lee

The savior of racing is sweating. The savior's cherubic face is flush and his hair is matted and he looks like he just outran the devil.

The savior is sweating because he's just done something very foolish and gotten away with it. Which isn't far off what he did to save racing, which needed to be saved from itself. Which has been mishandled and mismanaged for too long. Which doesn't pit the best racers against one another. Thousands of race fans owe him a debt of gratitude. The impact of his decision will do more for road racing than a decade's worth of obtruding by the suits in Ohio.

Today, the savior is sweating because he's just won a race. He did it the hard way. The not very wise way. The way that could have ended his career. The way it had to be done. But now that he's done it, now that he's cheated death and destruction, he's happy. How happy?

"I won't kick the dog when I get home tonight, that's for sure," he said.

For that, the dog's grateful.

Roger Lee Hayden is saving racing from itself. The youngest of the Haydens, with the devilish smile and the curly hair and the quick wit, is an unlikely savior. Aren't they all? Rog gambled by telling his employers he had to ride a Superbike in 2006. What to do? Kawasaki knew he was flirting with rival Suzuki. They knew they could lose him. Or he could end up with nothing. They knew he was one of the ascendant stars of road racing, the increasingly rare combination of speed and personality. They like having him and Tommy and Rose and Earl and half of Owensboro around.

They'd seen him challenge his brother Tommy for the Supersport title two years in a row. They watched as he made an improbable and desperate pass of Jason DiSalvo to win the Superstock final at Road Atlanta. A few inches off line in the disgraceful turn 12, which has less runoff than the gutters on Barbie's Dream House, and he'd have turned air bags and hay bales into pop art. And he wouldn't have walked away.

"He wanted it more today, for sure," DiSalvo admitted.

In the big picture, Kawasaki knew they were getting left behind. They've been getting beaten up for not racing Superbikes. They knew they had a new ZX-10 for '06. So they decided to go Superbike racing - or at least that's what everyone believes. (Officially, no decision's been made.)

So when the Superbikes line up for March's Daytona 44.25, Kawasaki will join Suzuki and Honda and Ducati, and only Yamaha will be left out of the big dance.

And don't think they're happy about it. Instead of the show, Yamaha will spend the year beating itself in Formula Xtreme and taking the heat for it, the way Honda has for two years. They thought they were doing the right thing by joining FX. "Win on Sunday, sell on Monday" is the rule at Daytona. The lure of the Diluted 200.

Then a funny thing happened. American Honda, the team that's won every race in the two-year history of the little FX class, walked away with its 20-race win streak and two titles, leaving it to Erion Honda. "Now they tell us," was the lament from Yamaha. So why did Honda leave?

Beginning with Doug Polen's 1993 Superbike title and right through Mat Mladin's sixth in 2005, only two riders have won the Superbike crown while contesting a second class. As American Honda's Jake Zemke told me at VIR, "There's a guy running around here with that number-one plate, and he's awfully tough to beat, and it's really hard to go and beat a guy like that riding two bikes, two classes."

American Honda knows how hard it is to turn a street bike into a racer. They'd done it with the CBR600RR in Formula Xtreme in 2004 and again in 2005. In 2005, they added the burden of converting the CBR1000RR. Early in the winter word came from on high that they were on their own. No more going to Japan to build bikes out of HRC parts. There was a little grumbling, then they took up the challenge. They worked with what they had. They bought some parts from HRC. They farmed some out. They made some of their own. They started behind most of the field and finished there.

It was to be expected. They were racing and testing on the same weekend and splitting time between two classes. Sure, they made progress, but meanwhile, Mladin was setting lap records, taking pole positions and winning races. And getting stronger with each race. And winning his sixth championship in seven years. Not since 1994 has Honda gone a full year without winning a Superbike race.

The CBR1000RR can be made into a competitive race bike, and it was, but it took time and manpower and money. And everything that crew chiefs Merlyn Plumlee and Al Ludington learned will carry over to the improved 2006 CBR. And they won't be four months behind at the Daytona tire test in December. And the riders and teams will be able to concentrate on one motorcycle 100 percent of the time. Which is what Mladin does and the Ducatis do. And everyone in Superbike should be able to do.

It would have been better if the AMA Pro Racing Board had eliminated one of the 1000cc classes. Everyone would be in the show. But the board abdicated its responsibility by settling for the stagnant quo. Bikes and teams everywhere. The possibility of an even more fragmented paddock in 2006. The grumbling had already begun at Road Atlanta.

At the factory level, Superbike will be strengthened by two to nine, just more than half the number in 1998, the last year Tommy Hayden rode a Kawasaki Superbike. Superstock will pit Yamaha's trio, assuming Eric Bostrom signs, against Yoshimura Suzuki's Aaron Yates, with satellite efforts from Erion Honda, Attack Kawasaki, and a number of Suzuki-supported teams. FX will be Yamaha's exclusive domain outside of Daytona and possibly Laguna Seca, where American Honda may jump in if the program includes Xtreme. And with Yamaha's departure from Supersport, the gutted class will be down to the Kawasakis vs. Yosh's Ben Spies and the new GSX-R600.

The class with the most talent will again be Superbike. As it should be. As it once was. With everyone else in, Yamaha will return in 2007. With Eric Bostrom, with Jason DiSalvo, with Jamie Hacking. And everyone will be there, and the confusion over why there are two big-bike classes will be lessened, though not completely, and even the AMA's meddling won't be able to screw it up. Which puts what Roger Lee started into even greater perspective - and makes him an even more unlikely savior.

For that we have to thank Roger Lee, savior of racing. And his dog thanks him, too.

October 26, 2005

Last Man Standing

The last American to win the premier-class World Championship was Kenny Roberts Jr. in 2000. The next to win will likely be Nicky Hayden. After that, it could be a while.

No longer is throwing around a big Superbike the preferred training ground for advancement. Instead it's the lesser classes and the tinier riders. HRC general manager Tsutomu Ishii said Honda's 800cc machine was being designed for smaller riders, without specifically mentioning the jockey-sized 250cc World Champion Dani Pedrosa.

"The potential rider for MotoGP for the future is quite small," Ishii said. "It's something we have to think of in 2007."

The Spaniard Pedrosa will join Nicky Hayden on the Repsol Honda team in 2006, though that's not official. By then Pedrosa will have raced GPs for five full seasons and won three World Championships - 125cc in 2003, 250cc in 2004 and '05. On September 29, he turned 20.

Southern Europeans are the present and future of the World Championships. First among them is seven-time World Champion Valentino Rossi from Tavullia, Italy. MoviStar Honda MotoGP's Marco Melandri is a short (5 feet 4½ inches) but muscular 134 pounds. Andrea Dovizioso, the 2004 125cc World Champion, started racing in Italy when he was 7. Spaniard Jorge Lorenzo, all 121 pounds of him, became the youngest-ever GP rider when he turned 15 on the second day of qualifying for the 2002 Spanish GP at Jerez. Now in his fourth year, he's all of 18. An exception is Australian Casey Stoner; he turned 20 the day he highsided out of the lead in his home Grand Prix at Phillip Island.

"I see a scenario in three or four years' time where the championship will be fought between Melandri, Hayden, Pedrosa, Stoner and Dovizioso," Yamaha team manager Davide Brivio said.

Can the 103-pound Pedrosa handle next year's 250-plus horsepower? He has no choice. And horsepower isn't what it used to be. The advances in engine management mean riders can pin the throttle without undue worry. The question is whether the 5-foot, 2-inch Pedrosa will be able to use what little weight he has. Mick Doohan notes in this week's Chat Room that one of Kevin Schwantz's great strengths as a rider was his agility.

"When things start to go off or go a bit soft, then they move themselves around like Kevin [Schwantz] used to do," the normal-sized Doohan said. "The Suzuki was not always the best bike. He'd never moan about it. He was always on the podium, if not winning."

Or in the Clinica Mobile.

Schwantz, Doohan, Wayne Rainey, Freddie Spencer all came up through production-bike racing. Rossi started on pocket bikes before a rapid, and well-managed, assent through Italian racing, then into the World Championships. In 1997, his second full year in GPs, Rossi won the 125cc title. Two years later, he took the 250cc crown. Runner-up to Kenny Roberts Jr. in 2000, he won the final 500cc World Championship at Phillip Island in 2001. It had been nearly 30 years since a 250 rider moved up to win the 500cc crown. Phil Read, the 1971 250cc champion, won his first 500cc title in 1973, repeating in 1974.

All eyes are now on Stoner. The 250cc World Championship runner-up is being heavily courted to move to MotoGP in 2006. His boosters include fellow Aussies Mick Doohan and Jerry Burgess. Burgess is the most successful crew chief in history, with 11 premier-class titles. The first came with Wayne Gardner in 1987, then came Doohan's run of five, followed by Rossi's similar streak.

Stoner's slim championship hopes went up in the air with his highside. But such mistakes don't bother Rossi.

"If you are fast but make a lot mistakes, is possible you improve. If you are not fast, you are f--ked," he said. "I think Stoner will be one of the future of MotoGP."

Stoner's ascent hasn't been linear. His family moved to Europe from Kurri-Kurri, in the Hunter Valley of New South Wales, so he could race 125s in the UK and Spain. Twice he started 125cc GPs in 2001 before a full season of 250s in 2002. But it didn't go well and he was back in the smallest class in 2003, winning the final race in Valencia. Last year he was second in the 125cc championship. Now he's back in 250s.

"Of course, Stoner is one rider who is very interesting for us," Yamaha's Brivio said. "What he is doing before his recent run made him an interesting proposition, but his end-of-season results underline how strong he is mentally. It's not surprising, but it's a confirmation of his talent and his potential."

And then there's the issue of money. Racing is expensive and gets more so every year. As Doohan pointed out: "Years ago, it used to be on your results. Now it's more on what sort of wallet do you have."

Where does that leave the Americans? At the end of a very long and growing line. And without the financial backing to jump the queue.

What we know is that there aren't any American teenagers ready to go Grand Prix racing. Ben Spies and Jason DiSalvo, both 21, are the two most often mentioned as GP candidates. Spies knows he isn't ready and has said he isn't in a hurry. Maybe he should be. DiSalvo raced 125s in Europe before moving back to the United States. And he would certainly like to go back. But it's hard to see how he might get the chance. With Yamaha out of Superbikes this year, DiSalvo won't race against the best riders until 2007. By then the next pack of Italians and Spaniards will be ready to graduate.

It isn't just the youngsters who face long odds. Kawasaki team manager Harold Eckl nominated Tommy Hayden as the injured Alex Hofmann's replacement in Australia. His thinking was that it would "show these young riders, hey, if you are good, once you get the chance to move up." But the factory favored injured French journeyman Olivier Jacque. The lack of input in rider choice prompted Eckl to muse, "Sometimes I stay in bed and ask myself, 'What are you doing here?'"

The same could be asked of a number of the superannuated riders. Camel is so enchanted with Max Biaggi, 34, that they agreed to continue with the Pons Honda team after a flirtation with Suzuki. Biaggi will be joined by 33-year-old Carlos Checa, the Spaniard who hasn't won a GP since 1998. Marlboro Ducati has veteran Loris Capirossi, 33, when next season starts, and will have Sete Gibernau, also 33, next year. Alex Barros, 35, could end up at Suzuki. Environmental racing. Recycling the graybeards.

Which leaves the hopes of the United States on the 24-year-old Nicky Hayden. And not just the United States, Hayden has the added pressure and responsibility of being Honda's lead development rider for the 2006 RC211V. Watching how he harassed Rossi to the end of the Australian Grand Prix, Hayden would appear to be up to the job. But he shouldn't expect reinforcements. For the foreseeable future, he's on his own.

November 2, 2005

Safety First

Of the 10 tracks on the 2005 AMA Superbike Championship calendar, all had safety problems. Some were worse than others. All needed attention. AMA Pro Racing knew this. So they formed a distinguished one-time safety committee comprised of Mat Mladin, Kevin Schwantz and Ron Barrick and sent them and their years of collective experience out into the world. The track that AMA PR thought needed the most immediate attention, the one with the most pressing safety issues, the one that was more important to visit than all others? New Hampshire International Speedway.

Huh?

"It was a total waste of time," Mladin, who flew across the country to make the inspection, recently told me. I visited the six-time AMA Superbike Champion and his family at the airy, eco-friendly house he designed on 180 acres in The Oaks, not far from where he grew up, an hour southwest of Sydney. After lunch with Mat, his wife, Janine, their 2-year-old daughter Emily Jean, and Janine's mother, we sat down for an interview. He spoke of the recovery from his foot surgery, about the problems he had launching the GSX-R1000, about his business interests, about how hard he's training for 2006, and about how much he loves living in America. It was an amiable conversation that went on for about half an hour. But when the topic turned to track safety, the tone shifted; now it was from the heart, now there was an edge, and why not? The lack of progress on safety issues could have an immediate and disastrous impact not only on his livelihood, but on his family - which is why, whenever he's asked, he's willing to go anywhere, do anything, meet with anyone to improve racetracks.

Cycle News has twice arranged meetings between Mladin and a track owner, including once this year. Which, I'm guessing, is twice more than AMA PR has done, if you exclude Loudon. As for his input on the Miller Motorsports Park project, Mladin critiqued the plans. Little more.

The $64,000 question is, Why would Loudon, a track that hasn't had a race in four years, that was vilified by the riders for years before it was canceled, that caused grievous injuries to too many riders, including Miguel Duhamel, Scott Zampach, and Thomas Wilson, and whose management publicly ridiculed AMA PR officials, get more attention than, say, Road Atlanta? Or Mid-Ohio? Or any of the other tracks *that actually host AMA Superbike races?* Beats me. And Mladin, too.

Another year has been lost with far too little done for the cause of track safety. The effects of the lethargy were on vivid display at Road Atlanta. A bearded Vincent Haskovec returned to the AMA paddock that he was forced out of by a career-ending injury at Infineon Raceway. The very popular and likeable Czech immigrant was paralyzed when he hit an unprotected barrier during the Formula Xtreme race in May. I asked Mladin if the accident was avoidable.

"Absolutely - everything's avoidable," he said. "From everyone's point of view that I've spoken to - and I've seen the footage quickly - it was an impact accident. That's it. So if the wall wasn't there, big chance that that was avoidable. It's too late to say it now. And we all went and raced on the racetrack and we all did our thing because really that's what we're paid to do. But if the wall wasn't there, I think there's a much better chance he would have got up and been racing that afternoon."

Air bags were placed in front of the barrier after the crash.

"It's the same old deal; if you've got guys, officials of racing, or whoever, out there putting the air bags out and doing this and doing that, they're not always going to go in the right places, because they don't see it as the last guys see it," Mladin said. "Things change. The tires change. They allow you to do different things differently. Technology changes. Corner speeds are up. The lines are different; not that everyone rides the same lines as me - actually not many people do. But even the other guys' lines are different to what they used to take. I mean, things change. Ten years ago, nobody would ever say that they were going to do a backflip on a motocross bike, either. People do things differently. Tires, the bikes, everything. Suspension allows you to do things differently. Even to 10 years ago. So things change."

I asked Mladin if he had any ideas on how it could be improved.

"No, I have no ideas, because personally, I don't think the people that have the power to make it better are really caring about it as much as they should be," he said. "I mean, they're talking [about] slowing the motorcycles."

The problem isn't the motorcycles, it's the impact zones. The first priority should be to move them, the second to protect them. Top riders such as Mladin and Neil Hodgson, who has years of experience on racetracks all over the world, including some of the dodgy British ones, need to be involved.

"I don't know how it should be organized, I just know what needs to be done to the racetrack," Mladin said.

Mladin admits his differences with Duhamel. He vehemently disagrees with Duhamel's position on Daytona, a track he believes Duhamel endorses as a way to enhance his own legacy. But Mladin agrees that the change Duhamel made at California Speedway was for the better (Duhamel suggested to the AMA's Barrick that the kink be eliminated from the back straight. It was, and Barrick wants to take it even further.)

"Absolutely, that was a really good change, no doubt," Mladin said. "But that takes initiative to do something like that. By the way, I didn't know anything about the change. And that's the other problem that you have. I actually went onto the racetrack not knowing about the change."

What Mladin believes is that the AMA needs to take a stance and tell the racetracks, "Listen, we need some improvements done. And when the racetracks decide to do them, get a couple of the top riders there to help, to make the changes right."

If AMA PR had the slightest interest in safety, they wouldn't send Mladin to Loudon. They'd arrange for him, Schwantz, Barrick and some of Mladin's fellow riders to meet with track owners on the Thursdays before the races. They could discuss what needs to be done, which corners need to be addressed, and where the priorities are. Long-term plans. They could place the air-fence and the hay bales. And they could help make sure that what happened to Vincent Haskovec never happens again.

November 23, 2005

A Motorcycle Movie Worth Seeing

The *World's Fastest Indian*, a wonderful tale of passion starring Anthony Hopkins, tells the story of Burt Munro, a New Zealander who made his life's work the perfection of the 1920 Indian Scout and his quest for speed at the Bonneville Salt Flats.

As movies go, this is one worth seeking out when it opens later this year in selected markets, and more widely in 2006. As a movie about a motorcyclist, it's the best to come along in years, maybe decades, *Torque* and *Supercross: The Movie* notwithstanding.

Burt Munro was a lovable rogue, a worldly man from a small town near the bottom of the world whose natural charm was as boundless as his energy. His passion for performance was so far off the charts of what is considered normal behavior that it's hard to fathom in our increasingly impermanent, attention-deficit-disorder world. His commitment to the mechanical perfection of his "motorsickle," as he pronounced it, in a near-pitch-perfect accent, cannot be overstated.

In a letter to a fellow enthusiast dated March 11, 1970, and originally published in New Zealand's veteran and vintage motoring magazine *Beaded Wheels* number 189, Munro writes: "It is almost impossible for me to give you a true picture of the time I have spent on my cycles. The last 22 years has been full-time, and for one stretch of 10 years, I put in 16 hours every day, but on Christmas Day only took the afternoon off."

Makes whining about your mandatory 15-minute coffee break seem a little churlish.

Working out of the brick shed where he lived in Invercargill, a small town on the South Island of New Zealand, Munro was a one-man speed shop - engineer, fabricator, and foundryman. And racer. He cast and poured his own pistons after superheating the metal on a small stove. He built his own four-cam design to replace the two-cam system and converted the Scout to overhead valves. He made his own barrels from iron gasworks pipes that were cast off by the city. Flywheels, rams, followers, an oiling system - he made them all. He built a 17-plate, 1000-pound pressure clutch and used triple chain drive. His streamliner was rare in that it used most of the original motorcycle chassis, though it was lengthened and the suspension altered.

What did it all add up to? The original 37-cubic-inch/600cc 42-degree side-valve V-twin Scout was capable of 55 mph. When it was finished, the Scout, now christened the "Munro Special" and pumped up to 1000ccs, was good for over 200 mph on the Bonneville Salt Flats. To this day, nearly 40 years later, he still holds the 1000cc streamlined fuel record of 183.586 mph.

The movie begins with an affectionate sweep of the spare and discarded parts on the shelves in the shop where he lived in Invercargill. Before long, he's turning molten metal into pistons and waking up the neighbors with the unmuffled rumble of the constantly expanding V-twin.

The first glimpse of speed is shown on Oreti Beach in Invercargill, where he does test runs. Such is his legend that a pack of locals on Triumphs come to take him on in a speed contest. But the big prize is in Bonneville.

Unable to afford the trip - it's never really clear how he supports his speed addiction - the local community comes to his aid, and he's off on a steamer ship to Los Angeles, working to pay his freight.

The quest to get to Bonneville consumes most of the 126-minute running time and is given more weight than the mechanical details, which may disappoint the gearheads in the audience. Like the Scout that keeps getting faster, nothing can stop him. Health problems that would halt a normal man are brushed aside. He cuts through the bureaucracy that's keeping the streamliner in customs.

"What exactly do you intend to do here in the United States?" he's asked by an immigration officer.

"Well, set a land-speed record," he says matter-of-factly.

When it's delivered, with the crate in less-than-pristine condition, he does a quick inventory and is on his way. He barters his mechanical skills for cheap transportation from L.A. to Utah. He fashions a trailer out of spare parts. He befriends a motel clerk who Munro doesn't realize is a transvestite. He gets nabbed by a police officer going 160 mph, and both men walk away with a smile. He has a passion for life, and women, that belies his years, which is something the senior set isn't often given credit for.

Like a shark, he is constantly moving forward, undeterred and unflappable. When a wheel comes off his trailer, he props it up with a piece of wood and drags it on the plank until he can find a solution. Not only does he fix the trailer, at the first available stop, but he gets more than he asked for, in a good way.

As portrayed by Academy Award winner Hopkins, Munro is the eternal optimist, single-mindedly determined, but not selfish. The opposite, in fact. His boundless enthusiasm sweeps up allies along the way. Hopkins portrays this dream as a passion, not a burden, and certainly not an obsession, though that argument could easily be made. At first glance, it's easy to dismiss Burt Munro as an antipodean nutter.

Roger Donaldson, the New Zealand-born writer and director, makes sure that doesn't happen. In 1971, well before he became an accomplished director - *The Recruit, Thirteen Days, The Bounty* - Donaldson, a motorcycle enthusiast, and his collaborator Mike Smith made a documentary about Munro in New Zealand.

The pair accompanied Munro to Los Angeles and then to Bonneville on one of his last runs. The title of the documentary,

Offerings to the God of Speed, was written in chalk on one of the parts-lined shelves in Munro's shed. The documentary was shown on television in New Zealand in 1973. "All my life I wanted to do something big, something bigger and better than all the other jokers," Munro says. "This is it - Bonneville. This is the place where big things happen."

The beaches of New Zealand that constrained the speed were not an issue in Bonneville. Once unleashed to maximum potential, the red streamliner was a wobbling handful of jello.

Counterweights proved useless, even detrimental. Rider skill was the only way to control the beast. That, Munro was able to keep the liner on the black line in the salt cannot be adequately conveyed on film, though Hopkins and Donaldson do a very good job without resorting to special effects.

The 1967 Bonneville record included a one-way run of 190.07 mph in qualifying. Another run was more eventful. Halfway down the line, Munro had to sit up to stop the bike from wobbling. That tore his goggles off, and the wind under his open-faced white Bell helmet threatened to strangle him. He wasn't deterred. When he crashed, just past the eight-mile marker, he was going over 206 mph.

"I did it, Tom, I did it," he tells his once-skeptical neighbor in Invercargill on a transpacific phone call. "She's the world's fastest Indian."

This was a nearly 50-year-old motorcycle being asked to do things its designers could not possibly have conceived of. Certainly it helped that the forks were altered and the wheelbase lengthened. Even so, the quest for speed was as quixotic as it was noble. But maybe that's the point.

"If you don't follow through on your dreams, you might as well be a vegetable," Munro says. Amen.

December 7, 2005

The Last Hurrah

Valentino Rossi should win his sixth premier class championship next year, then move to the rarefied world of Formula One. The vacuum he leaves behind will be cavernous. Promoters will suffer as crowds shrink. The television audience will contract. Concessionaires will lament the days of long lines. But no one will mourn his absence more than Yamaha.

Until Rossi and Honda decided they'd had enough of each other, at the end of the 2003 season, Yamaha hadn't been a factor at the top levels of racing for more than a decade. Their last championship came in 1992, the last of Wayne Rainey's trifecta. In 2003, the year before Rossi resuscitated them, Yamaha's lone podium was a third by Alex Barros in France. Their highest place finisher in the championship was Carlos Checa, the Spanish journeyman who tied for seventh. By contrast, Loris Capirossi, in his first season on the all-new Ducati Desmosedici, had a win and six other podiums, and finished fourth on the year.

Rossi knew this when he signed.

"When I arrive and when I speak with Yamaha, with Mr. [Masao] Furusawa [senior general manager of Yamaha's Engineering Operations], he say to me this, 'Yamaha now wants to change. We changed a lot of engineers and we want to try to win. Our race division start to work harder,'" Rossi quoted Furusawa as saying.

"We need to beat Honda," Furusawa said, and they did. Repeatedly.

Like Rainey before him, Rossi will give Yamaha a trio of championships. His departure won't be as tragic as Rainey's, but the results will be the same: It will be years before Yamaha wins another championship.

As adept and generous as they've been with Rossi and his team, they've been equally clumsy with others. The point was driven home when I read Honda's release from the first day of testing in Sepang, Malaysia. Nicky Hayden, Marco Melandri, Casey Stoner, Toni Elias - all riders Yamaha had either signed or had in their sights - were all quoted on the Honda release.

Hayden was the first to slip from Yamaha's grasp. Following his AMA Superbike Championship in 2002, Hayden had a very public flirtation with Yamaha. Honda's view at the time was that Hayden should go back and do what he was doing for another year, then they'd find a way to fit him in. Hayden looked for another option and found it with Yamaha, whose love was unconditional, Honda woke up. With the looming threat of losing Hayden to their rival, Honda prudently exercised their right of first refusal. The matter was handled clumsily, but no one held it against Hayden, whose surge in the second half of the season vindicated all who'd championed his cause through the lean times.

The only rider more ascendant than Hayden in 2005 was Melandri. In his first year in the cloak of the Gresini Honda team, the former 250cc World Champion prospered. Fausto Gresini, himself a two-time former World Champion, is the model for team ownership. Some team owners want to make money, some to win. Gresini is the latter. And if you win the money will follow. Fortuna cigarettes was quick to jump into the sponsorship hole created when Telefonica MoviStar left in a snit at the end of 2005.

Melandri came to Gresini after two frustrating years on a Yamaha. The Italian rode for the Tech 3 Yamaha team of Herve Poncharal, a satellite team that didn't reap the benefits of the Rossi phenomenon in 2004.

"My Yamaha last year, it was very different than Valentino's bike," Melandri said.

Rossi made the point that Melandri would be better off on a Honda and Melandri agreed. He shunned both Yamaha and Ducati, and better money, to move to Gresini, who saw something special.

"In my opinion Marco has a chance to enjoy a good experience with us in MotoGP," Gresini said.

Brought along slowly, and in the shadow of his imploding teammate Sete Gibernau, Melandri spent most of the season second in the points to Rossi, only losing the spot late in the season. Melandri came through with his first win, in Turkey, in round 16 of 17, and his second victory followed two weeks later in the Valencia season finale. That victory clinched the runner-up spot to Rossi.

Satoru Horiike, Honda Racing Corporation (HRC) managing director, said that Melandri wouldn't be getting the new, smaller RC211V for 2006.

"The policy is only two factory machines next year," he said, but without finality. Could Melandri get one? "Depends on race situation," Horiike said. Either way, Melandri won't be on a Yamaha.

Neither will Casey Stoner. The young Australian had been heavily courted by Yamaha at the end of the season. The factory asked Lucio Cecchinello, Stoner's manager and team owner, to put together a MotoGP team. (Cecchinello also looked into teaming up with Tech 3's Herve Poncharal.) But there were caveats. He'd be on Dunlop tires. And the salary offer was reported to be an insult. Cecchinello had an agreement with Stoner for next year, but when Sito Pons made the offer to ride an unsponsored Honda, that trumped the Yamaha deal. Will the Pons deal fly without a sponsor? It doesn't matter. Dorna, the series promoters who've seen a cascade of sponsor defections, will make sure it does.

Eventually Yamaha relented on the Dunlops - he'd have second tier Michelins - but it was a desperate move that was too little, too late. Stoner moved to the Pons Honda team and Yamaha lost another piece of the future.

In 2005, his rookie MotoGP season, Toni Elias rode a Yamaha for the Tech 3 team with Fortuna backing. It took the young Spaniard some time to adjust: His best finish was a hard-earned sixth when he passed Colin Edwards on the final lap in the penultimate race in Turkey. It was, by far, the team's best finish.

Fortuna is another of the cigarette brands, along with Gauloises, under the Altadis umbrella. Altadis and Yamaha are in the middle of a very public spat over sponsorship of the 2006 team. The most commonly accepted scenario is that Yamaha will run in generic colors and the matter will end up in court. Of course, it could all be worked out and the bikes could again be blue for 15 of 17 races, as they were this year.

When the relationship with Altadis broke down, reportedly over Rossi's insistence that the team not be tobacco-sponsored, Fortuna could have left. But they had a relationship with Elias and Ruben Xaus in 2005 and chose to continue with Elias in 2006. Only now he'll be with Melandri at the Gresini Honda team. Yamaha would like to have kept him, but there was no sponsor and the factory team was full. As of this writing, Edwards and Rossi are the only riders signed to Yamaha. Brit James Ellison is testing at Tech 3 Yamaha backed by Dunlop in Sepang and could join the team. Or not.

Four of the brightest young stars in the MotoGP now ride Hondas when they might have ridden Yamahas. Will the tide reverse? It could. In 2007, when their contracts are up for renewal, Hayden and Melandri will have serious leverage. In 2006, Hayden will be Honda's number-one rider for the first time ever. If, as expected, he continues on his late season progress, and contends for the title in 2006, Honda won't let him go. Same for Melandri, who will continue the rivalry with Hayden that blossomed at the end of the season.

Various reports in the European press put Rossi's salary at $18 million U.S. No one is going to confirm this on the record, I can assure you. But it's probably not far off. That's a lot of money, but it's well spent. Linking racing to retail is a tricky venture, but Yamaha is prospering in the showroom and its newest sport bikes have received rave reviews.

They should enjoy it while they can. It could be a long time before it happens again.

January 11, 2006

Doing Things Right

Gill Campbell would like to sell you a bridge. Not the Brooklyn Bridge, though she could probably sell that as well. Rather she'd like to sell you the bridge that spans the front straightaway of Mazda Raceway Laguna Seca, the one you see every lap of every race. The one that gives you more exposure than a Brazilian bikini wax. And the one that gets you from one side to the other of the only world-class motorcycle racetrack in America and site of the Red Bull U.S. Grand Prix.

The CEO/general manager of Mazda Raceway Laguna Seca sold a number of people on the idea that America should host a round of the MotoGP World Championship. The July 2005 event was a rousing success from most every standpoint. Just ask Nicky Hayden. There were record crowds, great racing, unprecedented fan access to the riders, and enough celebrity wattage to light up Reykjavik on New Year's Eve.

But there were problems. Traffic was hellish, as were the rest rooms, and the concessions were short of clothing faster than a wet T-shirt contest.

And then there was the track. A few of the MotoGP riders complained the track was unsafe, and only after a quick lap on a scooter, Marco Melandri rumbled about a boycott. (Maybe he should have - he crashed twice in the race.)

Lost amid the accusations was the fact that the track had done everything the riders had requested. Everything. Still, it wasn't enough.

The Rider Safety Commission is comprised of World Champions Valentino Rossi, Kenny Roberts Jr., and Loris

Capirossi as permanent members, but every rider from every class is welcome. Following the 2005 race, the commission drew up a daunting set of requests. Move the hill on the right of turn one, widen the runoff on both sides of turn six, and flatten the dip just before the straightaway - none of which are insignificant.

Moving that much earth costs money. Lots of it. Yamaha stepped up in 2005 with $2 million for track improvements. The new price tag was a staggering $7 million. Who has that kind of money? Yamaha and Red Bull and Mazda and Dorna, as it turns out. All pitched in to varying degrees to guarantee the future of the Red Bull U.S. GP.

"It's so cool," said Kenny Roberts, a former promoter of the U.S. GP "I really thought it was just, like, we don't have any money, unless you're a NASCAR track. I just expected that. And to come back with 'We're doing it.' Wow, that's cool."

Laguna Seca wasn't on the schedule when Roberts was winning his three 500cc World Championships. That his son, Kenny Roberts Jr., as well as Nicky Hayden, Colin Edwards, and John Hopkins can race in their homeland, this year and into the future, means a lot to him.

"For a motorcycle racer that's into racing, that's a very nice thing," he said. "America should be the safest country in the world, but racetracks aren't concerned with it. It sort of blows me away as a normal human being. It's like, we can't have a play date at your house without worrying about being sued. For Laguna to stand up and say that and do it, it's cool. Unexpected, let's say. Why in America you can't do anything [without threat of legal action] and the racetracks don't care about safety."

Roberts, like Hayden and others, doesn't agree with all the changes. Eliminating the dip before the Corkscrew wasn't universally welcomed. "Bunch of bloody MotoGP poofs," one rider e-mailed me.

"I thought that some of it was not really needed, but the thing was Laguna stepped up and did it," Roberts said. "From racing in America, where the tracks don't do anything, to standing up and saying we're going to fix this track. I never got to race in America for a GP round. That means a lot to me. When you think about how many racetracks that are Grand Prix approved and there are none in America [except for Laguna Seca]."

Now Roberts says all they need to figure out is the traffic.

"If they can solve the in-and-out problem, Laguna will have a bright future," he said. Gill Campbell is one step ahead.

"There are things in the works," she said. "As soon as I have the plan signed off I'm going to release the entire bloody thing."

Kenny Roberts Jr. says that some of those who complained the loudest about traffic were the very hypocrites who could easily have avoided it.

"The important people, like the riders that are making millions of dollars, they're sitting in their $50 a day rental cars because they don't want to spend $400 on a round-trip helicopter ride," he said. "Give the riders helicopters and it'll be the best race on the calendar."

And he pointed out, try getting out of Mugello after a race, or Jerez. It won't happen. "The traffic's just done," he said.

Kenny Jr. has been a member of the Rider Safety Commission since it's inception in the wake of Daijiro Kato's death in 2003 at Suzuka. With Rossi, Sete Gibernau, and Nobu Aoki, the commission gained instant credibility. The group, of which Gibernau and Aoki are no longer members, meets every MotoGP weekend on Saturday afternoons. Their recommendations are always taken seriously, and almost always implemented. Not always for the better. The turn-one gravel trap the riders added at Phillip Island before last year's Oz GP ended Roberts' 2005 season. Neither did it do any favors for Loris Capirossi, one of the permanent members of the rider safety commission this season.

But overall it works and works well. If the riders say it's needed, and the FIM agrees, the racetracks know they have a respected imprimatur.

Contrast that to this country. Only the most enlightened track owners consult the riders. The best example is Infineon Raceway, where track president Steve Page, and media and community relations boss John Cardinale have an open-door policy. George Bruggenthies, of Road America, invited FIM safety rep Claude Danis to Elkhart Lake for advice on making the track a world-class facility.

Most tracks don't bother to talk to the riders. Do they know better? Of course not. No one does. Certainly not anyone who doesn't race a 200 horsepower Superbike. Are the tracks encouraged by the AMA to talk to the riders? Of course not. There's strong evidence to the contrary, according to one track owner.

For 2006, the Mid-Ohio Sports Car Course is undertaking significant improvements, including a complete resurfacing of the track and pit lane. The changes are admirable and long-needed. Mat Mladin was introduced to Michelle Trueman Gajoch during the race weekend in 2005. They should have met years ago. Mladin was contacted for his advice on the track changes. But he was already home in Australia recovering and unwilling to give advice without being on-site. Not that he's the only rider whose opinion matters. Jason Pridmore, for one, has done enough racing in the U.S. and around world to know what makes a safe racetrack. Pridmore is but one of the many sensible, experienced riders whose knowledge is being wasted by track owners, and AMA Pro Racing. Neil Hodgson, a World Champion, Ben Bostrom, AMA Superbike Champion and World Superbike veteran, Mladin, Pridmore, the list goes on.

The difference between MotoGP and AMA is that in MotoGP the riders are respected by the sanctioning body and the racetracks. They are partners, not adversaries. AMA Pro Racing does nothing to encourage the tracks to meet with the riders, which is both shortsighted and, frankly, asinine. If all you heard were complaints about track safety, wouldn't you solicit the riders' opinions? Will someone please explain the downside to me?

Gill Campbell was blindsided by the riders' attacks at the 2005 Red Bull U.S. GP even before the track was green for the first practice. Gill isn't a racer, so she relied on the racers to tell her what was needed. She complied - $2 million worth of compliance. It wasn't enough. The riders wanted more - $7 million more. Again, she moved heaven and earth to get it done, but ran out of time to sell sponsorship for the new bridge.

Now the riders will have a track they feel safe on, which means the fans will have a better show, not to mention better concessions, better facilities, and better transit times. This is a racetrack that listens to riders and puts its money where its mouth is.

Care to buy a bridge?

February 8, 2006

"No Comment"

Just when you thought things at AMA Pro Racing couldn't get any weirder, our friends in Pickerington screw the pooch in a way that would make Dick Cheney wet his pants, then cloak it in a veil of secrecy that would make Dick Nixon weep with joy. Quite a twofer.

Scott Hollingsworth, the secretive CEO, brought in to turn around Pro Racing's fortunes, was shown the trap door last week. This was initially reported on a website run by a member of the Pro Racing board. In a feat of stunning serendipity, the website's reporter happened to call the AMA looking for Hollingsworth as the whole thing was imploding. What are the odds?

Cycle News editor Paul Carruthers followed up by placing a call to Tom Lindsay, the AMA's public information director, who confirmed Hollingsworth's premature evacuation by reading a statement, then shutting up like a bad clam, thereby directing the public that there would be no information - the guy's good at his job.

When I called on Monday morning, I got much the same response. Lindsay did say, however, that Patty DiPietro, the AMA's executive vice president and chief financial officer, who engineered the palace coup, I think - her silence makes Charlie Chaplin look like Ozzy Osbourne - would be running AMA Pro Racing. Is she qualified? Of course not. Since when did that matter?

The board found out about the shuffle shortly before a competition committee conference call on January 24. When the members rang in, they were told DiPietro and AMA president Rob Rasor would run the meeting. The Rasor story is interesting in itself. An AMA lifer, in the best sense of the word, Rasor is now transitioning to a more expanded role in the FIM, which was announced in late November. The personnel move was given precious little ink in the popular press, but may have been a precursor to the Hollingsworth axing.

Who will be running the AMA day to day in place of Rasor? Patty DiPietro.

Presumably, DiPietro didn't act unilaterally. The move would likely have been approved by the executive committee, a group of five within the 11-member AMA board of directors, then possibly put to a vote of the full board. The AMA website lists only one member as being on the executive committee. But it may not be the best place to get information on this story. The headline on amaproracing.com, as of Monday morning, January 30, was "2006 AMA Hillclimb Championship Schedule Announced," a news nugget of only slightly less import than "CEO Takes A Powder." Nowhere on any AMA website could I find mention of the Hollingsworth departure, and not for lack of effort or a splitting headache.

Since this was their first competition committee phone call, Rasor and DiPietro had legitimate questions, like, "What do you guys normally talk about? Tires, because we have tires. Or hay bales. Got them too. What about noise? You talk about noise? We don't like noise. When's lunch?"

One thing the AMA Pro Racing board has talked about is me. At the AMA Pro Racing board meeting following the Red Bull U.S. GP I was on the agenda. Me. Specifically, what to do about me. And how they could retaliate against *Cycle News* for my random screeds. When I first heard this, I was incredulous. When two board members confirmed it, I was repulsed. At the meeting, one board member suggested that the others should pull their advertising. What this episode illustrates is how someone could abuse his position in the industry to further the cause of AMA Pro

Racing, while trying, in the most desperate way, to silence a dissenting voice. Without getting on too high a horse, that sort of behavior puts our friends at the very top of AMA Pro Racing in league with dictators that suppress free speech, like those in Cuba, Libya, North Korea. Nice company, guys - maybe you'd like to release the minutes of the meeting?

The communications department at both AMA Pro Racing and the AMA are abysmal and getting worse. Al-Qaeda does PR better. And this speaks to what could be the motivation for this whole fiasco.

DiPietro has long been the AMA's chief financial officer. She and Hollingsworth know the numbers and, since AMA Pro Racing is an allegedly for-profit entity, they don't have to open the books. What I'm told by someone familiar with the accounting is that under Hollingsworth's watch, revenues have increased dramatically - on the order of 250 percent. But so did expenses, which made Pro Racing a not-hugely profitable endeavor that generated a lot of negative publicity from people such as myself and others. And generated not a small amount of dyspepsia with their clumsy handling of Supercross that ended up in a court battle between Clear Channel and Jam Productions.

One longtime AMA member said to me, "I genuinely think what we're seeing is the beginning of the end of Pro Racing." Could this be the first stage of dismantling AMA Pro Racing and turning the AMA back into a sanctioning body? Yes. Would that be a bad thing? Not necessarily. Dorna, the Spanish company that runs MotoGP, also runs, among other things, the British Superbike Championship. Could they do worse than AMA Pro Racing at running the AMA Superbike Championship? Can Pam Anderson see her feet?

I remember once trying to differentiate between AMA Pro Racing, which has provided ample evidence of being out of touch with the road-race paddock, and the AMA, which is owed a debt of gratitude by anyone who rides a motorcycle. Why any motorcyclist wouldn't belong to the AMA is a mystery. But the AMA's membership department is at least as confounding as communications. The AMA "newsroom" lists 264,027 members as of January 31, 2005. Sound like a lot? The Harley Owners Group has nearly a million members worldwide, doubling membership in the past six years. The benefits aren't wildly different. The difference is that Harley-Davidson makes you feel like you're part of a family. The AMA makes you feel like you're part of the Addams Family. So who's Gomez?

One rumor was that Steve Whitelock, the motocross boss, was summoned to Ohio and asked to run the show. I'm told that, in a rage of staggering lucidity, he declined.

Whitelock is the most knowledgeable person in the entire AMA Pro Racing department. His experience at the world and national level is unrivaled. He is widely respected and his decisions are informed. He should be put in charge of competition.

The best candidate for the top job - the administrative job, whomever that might be, if they even decide to fill the spot - won't get it. That's the American way. See Bush, George.

I'd nominate Gary Mathers, the most successful team manager in the history of motorcycle racing and a damn nice guy. Gary is currently enjoying retirement in Asheville, North Carolina, with his wife, Denise, the always-cheerful blond who handles registration at the road races. Mathers had one go-around with the AMA, but he didn't like what he saw, so he left on good terms. Which is why they wouldn't have him back. He knows too much. He knows about budgets and personnel. He knows how to form a consensus, how to make people work toward a common goal. He is one of them; he is one of us. Any chance he'll get the job? Are you f---ing kidding me?

And why would I wish such a dysfunctional organization on such a genuinely decent human being? Because I'm a vengeful prick. Just ask the Pro Racing Board.

February 15, 2006

What's Next?

Have we heard the last of Scott Hollingsworth? Probably not. At least not according to someone familiar with the machinations of AMA Pro Racing.

Hollingsworth's contract still had some time to run. When he was terminated, the AMA offered to pay him to the end of contract if he didn't seek litigation. He refused. Which means the AMA is probably looking at yet another lawsuit, which isn't a good thing. The last two most public suits didn't end well.

In June 2001, the AMA agreed to pay former contractor Roger Edmondson $3 million in a case involving the road-race program. Edmondson filed suit in 1996 following his termination in 1994 as the manager of the AMA road-race programs. Coincidentally, the AMA had also offered Edmondson a settlement to end that relationship. Edmondson sued and won, and in 1998 won a judgment that was over $3 million. On appeal, the case was sent back to the lower court and a new trial was scheduled. At that point, the AMA and Edmondson settled out of court, making Edmondson a $3 million man.

At the time of the litigation, Roger Edmondson showed me a document that he considered his smoking gun. While combing through thousands of pages of documents in discovery, he found a letter from the AMA praising his work. How, then, could they have reversed course and decided he was unfit to run road racing? The courts decided they couldn't.

Hollingsworth himself was involved in a more recent suit. In 2001, Hollingsworth approached JamSports, a Chicago-based promotions group with no motorcycle-promotions experience, to take over promotion of the AMA Supercross series. Clear Channel, the promoter of record, and the AMA ended up in court. The matter was settled outside of court, though not before the AMA incurred significant legal expenses. JamSports and Clear Channel also ended up in court, with JamSports winning a $90 million settlement against Clear Channel for interfering with its attempts to promote races. Litigation continued, and JamSports and Clear Channel later settled for an undisclosed amount. AMA Pro Racing had to pay JamSports nearly $170,000 in the case.

Some believe that JamSports never had any intention of promoting a Supercross, that they were simply using the AMA to get Clear Channel into court. If that's the case, it worked.

If Hollingsworth does take the matter to court, he'll have to convince a jury that he was wrongfully terminated. Was he?

The reason for his dismissal hasn't been made public by the AMA, likely out of fear of litigation. His indiscretion, according to someone who asked to remain anonymous, was campaigning for the AMA presidency, a job left vacant when Rob Rasor was shuffled aside and Patty DiPietro, the chief financial offer, was made the interim boss. When DiPietro got wind of Hollingsworth's intentions, she set out on a nationwide fact-finding tour, I was told. When she'd done her due diligence and presented it to the AMA executive board, they agreed, and Hollingsworth was asked to leave.

But consider this view: What if Hollingsworth simply wanted the presidency so he would have a seat in front of the board of directors to explain himself, instead of them sitting in one room and Pro Racing in the other, with neither knowing what the other was doing? Could he have had a greater impact? Could he have done his job better? The job that Hollingsworth was seeking was, and is, still open. The AMA board of directors sees it as a palace coup. Maybe he just wanted to be able to run Pro Racing from the presidency. Would that have worked?

Probably not. More than once, I've been told that Hollingsworth raised revenues by 250 percent. I've also been told it was done through smoke and mirrors. New money wasn't pouring in - for the second year running, the AMA Superbike Championship is unsponsored - and he had to raise sanctioning and entry fees to pay for big salaries at the top, among other things. It was a case of the dog eating its tail. It is inconceivable that anyone in Pro Racing will ever have the same kind of power Hollingsworth held.

If Hollingsworth does seek a legal remedy, he faces the likelihood of explaining his actions in open court. Maybe he has nothing to hide. But he may also want to avoid scrutiny of the business of AMA Pro Racing. So might the AMA.

The more people I talk to, the more I'm convinced that the AMA should go back to being a sanctioning body and that promotion should be left to professionals. Clearly, at least when it comes to road racing, AMA Pro Racing hasn't served the sport well. The factories pour millions of dollars into a sport that has no clear direction, a confusing class structure, and no outside sponsor. And complaints about rider's safety fall mostly on deaf ears.

So what does that mean for the future? Steve Whitelock is part of the troika running Pro Racing in the interim. If they offer him a permanent job as the director of competition, he'll want a very detailed description of his responsibilities and powers - and rightfully so. Same with anyone willing to take on the Herculean task of restoring order to Pro Racing.

Last week in this space I suggested Gary Mathers for the job. I'm told by informed sources that he's the number-one candidate. Like Whitelock, Mathers is too smart to walk into the snake pit without some protection. Like Whitelock, he'd want to know the boundaries of the job. The most crucial element, I believe, would be budget control. Give him a budget, regardless of the size, and he can make it work. He did it well for far too many years to forget how it's done.

Patty DiPietro was close to retirement, I was told by a longtime AMA observer. Her stewardship is temporary, but, while in charge, her passion to do right by the AMA is unwavering. She has no intention of continuing indefinitely in the presidency. That her interim presidency is in its third month speaks volumes about the AMA's plans for succession. With two top jobs to fill, it is a pivotal moment for the association.

Her efforts should center on hiring Mathers and Whitelock as a team. I don't know Whitelock very well, but, when we've spoken, I've found him to be both knowledgeable and reasonable. Mathers I know better, from years of doing laps in the roadrace paddock. There is no one better qualified to run Pro Racing. The question is whether the AMA board of directors would be obstructionist and make him jump through the same hoops they put in front of Hollingsworth. One story making the rounds is that one member of the board of directors suggested selling any property with "super" in front of it. (By the way, what ever happened to Supermoto?)

Whether they do that or not, they still need someone to oversee Pro Racing, to make sure the rules are written in clear, plain English, with no chance of alternative interpretations. That hasn't been the case lately. The next battle may be over the legality of the Buell XBRR for Formula Xtreme.

The Mathers-Whitelock team is as good as it gets. Give them what they want, give them what they need, and dignity and professionalism will be restored to racing for the first time in years. The AMA can invest the money in leadership or they can spend it on lawyers; it's their choice.

February 22, 2006

How Can It Be?

Before Harley-Davidson could begin road racing the VR1000 in 1994, they had to homologate 50 street versions. The story I heard, and I'll be the first to admit I have problems with its authenticity, is about the room with 10 doors.

The story begins with an eagle-eyed AMA inspector being taken into a room in which the composite parts of five motorcycles were laid out on the floor. After a cursory examination of pistons, valves, gas caps, clips-ons, stickers, etc., he declared, "Looks good," before leaving the room briefly. After a short trip down a circular hallway, be was shown back into a room with the parts of five motorcycles laid out on the floor, pistons, valves, gas caps, clip-ons, and stickers, etc. Far too clever to be snookered, he asked, "Aren't these the same five piles of parts?"

The answer came back, "How could they be? They're in a different room."

"My bad," he admitted sheepishly, and so it went until all 50 were present and accounted for. I was reminded of the story because the Buell XBRR that the AMA just gave its blessing to is about as legal as crack and only a crack-pot would certify it. But that didn't stop one of our certifiable friends in AMA Pro Racing from welcoming the big twin into the gorgeous mosaic that is now the Formula "Xtremely Liberal" Daytona 200.

It would be easy to blame this staggeringly wrongheaded decision on the temporary troika running AMA Pro Racing in the wake of the forced exodus of AMA Pro Racing CEO Scott Hollingsworth. But that would be wrong. (Did I say that?) They had little to do with it, though one of them did take the unusual step of issuing a press release saying that the $31,000 bike was legal... and everyone lived happily ever after? Ummmm, no.

The release itself contained a line so precious it made me weep like a gimpy figure skater. It said "that a press release distributed by Buell to announce the motorcycle may have created some confusion as to the bike's eligibility." This from an organization whose command of English is inversely proportional to its deafness to the paddock din. Among my favorites is the November 2005 release heralding the new, final round of racing at Mid-Ohio.

"In addition to determining the AMA Superbike Champion, the Mid-Ohio finale *will* [my emphasis] crown champions in each of the series' support classes including AMA Supersport, Superstock and Formula Xtreme."

Not if Mat Mladin has anything to say about it. And last May's tech bulletin mandating grind-proof engine covers for all motorcycles had Ducati Austin's Gary Medley in such a tizzy that he lost what little hair he had. Ever try buying an aftermarket engine cover for a Ducati F05 from J.C. Whitney? On short notice?

An early disclaimer: Everyone I've spoken to welcomes Buell to the once moribund and Honda-dominated FX class. It will certainly make for a more interesting Daytona 200, since that's the only race that matters in FX and it's the one the Buell factory's been aiming for. Yamaha's entry of Jason DiSalvo and Eric Bostrom added interest at the same time Honda pulled the factory plug - except for Daytona and possibly one more - while leaving the class to Erion Honda. But everyone also believes Buell should be asked to play by the same rules as the rest of the field. Does anyone seriously believe that Harley-Davidson can't field a competitive road racer? (It's been a while; remind me - did the VR in VR1000 stand for Velocity Retarded or Victim Ready or Vanishing Rapidly?).

The Buell XBRR and the Buell XB12R Firebolt, on which it's based, have about as much in common as Brad Pitt and Andrew

Pitt. A 2-year-old, or Angelina Jolie, could tell the difference. Why couldn't the AMA Pro Racing tech wizards?

The XB12R makes 102 horsepower, at 6800 rpm, and the XBRR 150 hp, at 8000, according to specs on the Buell website. And that's the customer model. Can you increase power by 50 percent without a stronger crankshaft and cases? Probably not.

Crankshafts are ungoverned, but if the cases are different does that fall under the open modification rules allowed air-cooled twins in Formula Xtreme? Not unless, as Kevin Erion pointed out, you "put them back in the big melting pot in the sky, melted them down into their raw state, and poured them into a raw casting. And I don't believe that's what the intent of the rule is and I don't believe that's what the intent of the class is."

Erion backed up to this window once before. In 2002, Erion's riders protested the legality of Damon Buckmaster's Graves Motorsports Yamaha R1/R7 hybrid. The AMA tossed out the protest, so he appealed. And on May 21, 2002, an impartial three-member board decided he was right. Graves had to build a new motorcycle and Erion was vindicated. The AMA official who told Graves his bike was okay is the very same person who was quoted in the AMA press release justifying the legality of the Buell - AMA director of competition Merrill Vanderslice. Vanderslice has little support in the AMA road-race paddock. More than a few expected him to be swept out with Hollingsworth. Decisions like this do little to endear him to the paddock.

It also didn't help that he treated the AMA road-race advisory board like the fat guy in the middle seat; he didn't talk to them and, one way or another, he was going to figure a way to get around them when he had to.

The road-race advisory board is comprised of members of the factory and some factory-supported road-race teams, and AMA officials. They discuss a whole spectrum of issues, but the XBRR was never among them. How did that happen? Swingarms on

Superstock-spec Suzuki GSX-R1000s merit discussion, but not a race bike purpose-built by a subsidiary of the most successful motor company in the world aimed at what doddering nostalgists still believe is America's most prestigious motorcycle race? If the matter had been brought up, it would have died faster than a hopped-up XB12R trying to wheeze through 200 miles.

Buell admits they won't have the full run of XBRR's by the March Daytona 200.

"Buell will produce 50 XBRR motorcycles with a short initial run in late February and the balance made in April."

Do we take them on good faith? Or should they be required to build 50 motorcycles before they're homologated?

Time to check the locks on the room with 10 doors.

March 1, 2006

Sure, Come and Play

If I told you that a guy who used to do oil changes in RZ350s at Kenny Roberts' Yamaha in Modesto could pit the two biggest motorcycle companies in the world against each other you'd think I was nuts, right? Wrong.

With the recent departure of AMA Pro Racing CEO Scott Hollingsworth, Merrill Vanderslice, the AMA director of competition and former Roberts' shop employee, is at the vortex of the storm surrounding the legality of the mutable Buell XBRR. It was his name on the quotes insisting that the XBRR is legal. That the XBRR has been homologated to compete in the Formula Xtreme championship, beginning with the Daytona 200, was one of the reasons American Honda cited in a press release for the withdrawal of vice president Ray Blank from both the AMA Board of Trustees and the AMA Pro Racing Board. (The AH press release was issued on Saturday morning, after the Friday Night Massacre of the AMA Pro Racing Board by AMA CEO Patty DiPietro, which makes the AH withdrawal from AMA PR more a case of - You can't fire me, I quit ... you know, a day late.)

The Honda news trumped what was already an eventful weekend for AMA Pro Racing. A series of press releases on Friday night detailed plans for the reorganization of Pro Racing, while leaving too many other questions unanswered. The new racing department will be more accountable to the AMA board of trustees. The days of the all-powerful czar of AMA Pro Racing are gone, replaced - one hopes - by a knowledgeable administrator with a strong racing background, rather than a toady with a calculator. Who that will be, and what staff will run the various racing series, wasn't addressed in the flurry of releases. Nor was the relevance of advisory boards of the various disciplines. Instead, we were introduced to a bloated bureaucracy meant to ensure that the manufacturers who hemorrhage fortunes at racetracks nationwide don't get too uppity.

The mechanism is the make-up of the new rules-making committees. Each committee - there will be one each for road race, Supercross/motocross, flat track, Supermoto, and hillclimb - will include a representative from any manufacturer with a homologated motorcycle, along with an equal number, plus one, to be appointed by the AMA president just to counteract the possibility of the OEM's having too much power. How does that add up? The approved list of motorcycles for the three classes in the 2005 Supermoto Championship included Honda, Yamaha, Suzuki, Kawasaki, Aprilia, KTM, Husqvarna, ATK, Gas Gas, Husaberg, TM, Vor, Vertemati, Service Honda, and Buell. The total comes to 15, plus the 16 AMA counterweights. That's bigger than most Supermoto fields. Hell, that's bigger than most Supermoto crowds. The various other committees will likely have 13-15 members. All in all, you could conceivably have as many as 90 people doing the work of what was eight. Is that a good thing? Maybe, but only if the rules-making committees are stocked with people who attend the races, and not L.A. suits. The goal is to have more direct communication between the paddock and the AMA board of trustees. Crew chiefs should represent the OEMs and as many as possible should come from the paddock. In road racing, you won't find people more knowledgeable than Dunlop's Jim Allen or Öhlins' Jon Cornwell or Arai's Bruce Porter.

The AMA Pro Racing Board was never representative. American Honda was the only company with a senior-management member on the board. The notion that other board members in the employ of manufacturers were the equal of a vice-president is laughable. Former CEO Hollingsworth said in a July

2004 roundtable discussion that the role of OEMs was under review. But in the final 18 months of his reign, he did nothing to make the AMA PR board more inclusive.

In announcing Ray Blank's resignation the AH press release stated that "Recent issues, including the departure of dedicated individuals from AMA Pro Racing," i.e., Hollingsworth, "and its inability to stand by its own rulebook with regard to recent Formula Xtreme considerations, have been particularly alarming."

The irony of Honda complaining about the Formula Xtreme gene pool is more than a little rich. It was Honda who benefited most by the downsizing of the class from 1000s to 600s; though they won the first four FX 1000cc titles, Suzuki swept the next three. And it was Honda who was ready for the inaugural FX Daytona 200 last year, after having won the FX title the previous year. And now they've largely abandoned the class at the factory level, mothballing the FX CBRs after Daytona and allowing Erion Honda to fly the flag. So why are their knickers so twisted?

Is Honda worried that they might get beaten by a Buell? Of all the things that keep American Honda race boss Chuck Miller up at night, I'm guessing that's not one of them. At the Daytona test, Miller gave voice to what everyone else was thinking; with Yamaha joining the party, Honda's got to bring their A game. He didn't mention Buell, but maybe that's because he, and everyone else, knows so little about it.

Buell had tested the previous week at Daytona and, though everyone was sworn to secrecy, the test was leakier than a cheesecloth condom. Word was that the XBRR wasn't breaking any endurance records. Breaking - yes, endurance records - no. Texas World Speedway was the site of more recent secretive testing. Is Dick Cheney the team manager?

Everyone agrees that the Buell XBRR is good for the class. Those same people also believe that it shouldn't have been homologated, but they don't blame Buell. This was an AMA decision made a long time ago, under the reign of former CEO Hollingsworth. With Hollingsworth gone, it's left to Vanderslice to carry the torch that could easily burn him. Buell would have made sure they were playing by the rules, and the rule states that for air-cooled twins, "engine modifications are unlimited." Buell took this to mean that you could melt the cases and re-form them into a new bottom end, complete with new crank and most of the other engine parts as well - an extreme interpretation that the AMA bought into.

Yamaha will likely protest the Buell, and I'm guessing Honda will, as well. The protest will be disallowed by the AMA, since they homologated it. Then it will go to an independent three-man appeals board, probably motorcycle dealers, to determine its legitimacy. If they say it's illegal, the ramifications will be widespread.

The first losers will be any of the customers buying one of the 50 XBRRs, assuming the factory allotment of eight bikes - two per rider - comes out of those 50. A thumbs down by the appeals board would present the AMA with the extraordinary circumstance of having okayed a purpose-built race bike that has no home in AMA racing. It will mean that Buell's years of development and production will have gotten them a whole lot of museum pieces, which would not please Harley-Davidson. What they should do is announce a production model based on the XBRR, sort of a reverse-engineered streetbike with 120, instead of 150, horsepower.

At 1340cc, the XBRR is too big for Superbike. Maybe the ASBA would welcome it in Thunderbike, though I doubt former MotoGP rider Jeremy McWilliams envisioned himself racing at Summit Point and not Laguna Seca. Then again, their rules are clearer than the AMA's, stating that "frame, cylinder heads, and engine cases must be from the same production motorcycle." Though they also say they will maintain a list of "nonstandard" motorcycles and reserve the right to "re-facto" the list at any time.

There is an emerging body of opinion that the AMA should change the rules. They should admit their mistake and state that the XBRR is in, regardless of the fact that it bears no resemblance to anything you can buy in a Buell dealership. There would be a burst of outrage followed by the realization that they'd done the right thing, and finally, resignation. It won't happen. They're not that smart. They're not even as smart as ASBA.

Had the AMA included the ASBA's language that the approved bike list is malleable, they'd have saved themselves a heap of trouble, maybe kept Honda on the board of trustees, maybe kept Harley from worrying that they'd invested in a doomed project, and maybe kept Merrill Vanderslice from wondering whether Kenny Roberts still has a job for him.

March 22, 2006

The Buell, the Fuel and the Fool

Question: How many AMA officials does it take to screw up the Daytona 200?

Answer: The AMA was there?

Yes they were, in all their boneheaded glory and unable to tell two red bikes apart in the showcase event on the AMA calendar.

With a rider down in NASCAR Four and out of view of race control, AMA road race manager Ron Barrick was instructed to pull the pace car in front of the race leader. He thought he did, but he didn't. Barrick pulled out in front of Yamaha's Eric Bostrom and American Honda's Miguel Duhamel, the fourth and fifth placed riders, thinking Duhamel was his teammate Jake Zemke.

Oops.

The fans were confused: The scoring towers showed American Honda's Zemke leading Erion Honda's Josh Hayes. Now what?

The proper procedure, as Barrick had outlined in the riders' meeting, was to wave the riders forward until he got to first place.

That didn't happen. Why? Barrick, amazingly, was alone in the car.

Why? A shortage of personnel, he said.

Honda and Yamaha spend millions on racing, much of it to win the Daytona 200. They spent the winter extensively testing. They enlist the help of their respective factories. They prepare for every eventuality. And the AMA can't find a single warm body with a functioning right arm to wave riders forward? What about the passengers who were in the pace car during the parade lap?

Who makes that decision? Who decides that they can get away with one person in the car when they know full well that person is incapable of following proper procedure? If Barrick didn't make that decision, he should have protested. He should have stood up and said, "It's my race, it's my ass on the line. I don't care what you have to do. I don't care if you have to drag someone kicking and screaming from the bar in the hospitality suite, but I have to have someone riding shotgun."

How qualified do you have to be to wave? How stringent is that test? I'm guessing they could have found a homecoming queen with a free weekend.

But Barrick isn't demonstrative - it's not part of his makeup - and some criticize his perceived lack of urgency in resolving track clean-up issues after red-flag situations, when that may not be the case. In general, the paddock supports him, though some say he doesn't do nearly enough to consistently include riders in track-safety issues.

That said, whoever made the decision to allow Barrick to ride solo should be fired, unless he already has been: This was the last road race for director of competition Merrill Vanderslice, who "resigned" in February.

And why was Barrick sitting in a car on the back straight in the first place? Shouldn't the race director be able to see the entire racetrack, as well as TV monitors, and not just the dashboard of an Accord? Barrick should be in the tower and will in the future, I suspect, if he keeps his job. Given the state of flux in AMA Pro Racing, and the fact that someone needs to oversee all of Pro Racing, it wouldn't be surprising to see a change in his status.

After the race, Barrick should have taken a bullet. He should have said, "I made a mistake. It's my fault. I'm human. I pulled out in front of the wrong rider. Once I did that, there was no easy solution. It won't happen again."

Instead he said the mistake didn't affect the order of the race, a judgment he made based on lap times.

But it's a specious argument. Racing is unpredictable. Who knows what would've happened if Duhamel and Bostrom had gotten a whiff of the leaders? Duhamel is a one-of-a-kind hard-case nutter, plain and simple, a race-grizzled veteran with a very high threshold of pain and an unbreakable will. He throws away a 12-second lead. He goes upside down. He lands on his head. He runs for the bike and picks it up and thinks he's still in the race, which he is, but it won't be easy.

The right side of his faceshield was knocked loose and his windscreen was gone. What's that feel like on 31-degree banking at 170-plus? Duhamel's lap times rose after his crash, but his last lap was among his fastest. Give him a whiff of the podium and he's as voracious as a fat guy at a Mongolian buffet. Bostrom's brakes faded early in the race and he had to back off. But his last lap was his fastest and that was while playing Russian roulette with half-throttle no-hopers.

The pace car should be abolished. Barrick as much as admitted so. The last time it was used, in 2001, was even more of a disaster. The asthmatic Pontiac Aztec, or "Asspack" as Larry Pegram called it, pulled out on the back straight right as the riders were coming off the West Banking full-stick in fourth gear. What followed wasn't pretty. Erion Honda's Kurtis Roberts locked up the brakes and Yoshimura Suzuki's Aaron Yates had nowhere to go. Yates clipped Roberts, then Yates' teammate Jamie Hacking nailed him. Fortunately, Yates wasn't seriously hurt, but he was dazed.

Daytona International Speedway is not a world-class motorcycle-racing facility. It's not even Road America. Tracks homologated for MotoGP and World Superbike, and Road America, have full-course, closed-circuit video systems. They can see the entire track at a glance. When Fania fell in turn four, they could have known there was no danger - if they could have seen him. They couldn't. But there is a firetruck parked above the tunnel turn with a clear view in both directions. Did anyone think to contact them?

The answer that it was chaotic is unacceptable. Chaotic is turn one. Chaotic is entering a corner 30 mph faster than a lapper who's tried more lines than Tony "Scarface" Montana.

AMA Pro Racing has undergone an upheaval in recent weeks. A new regime has swept in, forming committees like mud pies and throwing them at the problems. Good start. How about a committee to investigate how not to screw up the big race?

This was the third major controversy for the AMA in the run-up to Daytona. First was their decision to homologate the Buell XBRR, even though the motor bears only a passing resemblance to the streetbike and the frame/gas tank was altered to allow for more capacity, as the rules allow, sort of.

The rules say that the frame can't be changed, but the gas tank can, so the AMA - read Merrill Vanderslice - went with the gas tank part of the rule. The expected protest never came, possibly because none of the Buells finished. But the Buell showed surprising speed in the hands of Jeremy McWilliams, so the controversy won't go away.

Next came the decision to penalize Makita Suzuki's Ricky Carmichael for illegal fuel. It's an antiquated rule that should have been changed with the advent of four-strokes, but it wasn't. To compound the error, the AMA hid behind the FIM in reversing its own decision, a move that prompted Kawasaki to tear up the rulebook. Now the pace-car debacle.

The Buell, the fuel, and the fool. What's next?

April 12, 2006

Let's Get It Right

Now that Daytona's out of the way, we can get on to the business of racing as it's meant to be. Not by holding your breath for half a lap on a decades-old surface with a very hard wall blinding by a few feet away, but on tracks with corners and elevation changes and escape routes when things go wrong, as they inevitably do in racing. Clearly, there are people who care about track safety, but are they the right people?

The end of the Scott Hollingsworth era gave hope to those who knew that the AMA Pro Racing board never adequately addressed rider safety, i.e., most of the paddock. Unquestionably, track safety has improved greatly over the years, mostly through the efforts of AMA road-race manager Ron Barrick and a few forward-thinking racetracks. But riders have been almost entirely bypassed at a time when their input becomes ever more critical. The old saw that if you get 10 riders, you get 10 opinions just doesn't fly. Look at the collective world-level experience on the Superbike grid: World Champion Neil Hodgson, six-time AMA Champion Mat Mladin, World Superbike veteran Ben Bostrom, World Endurance Champion Jason Pridmore, 500cc GP veteran Miguel Duhamel. To a man, they're intelligent, reasonable, eminently experienced, passionate about the livelihood they've chosen, and willing and ready to help. And yet this abundance of resources is steadfastly ignored.

Steve Whitelock provides a ray of hope. The Supercross/motocross boss understands racing as both business and entertainment. When the three leading Supercross riders - Ricky Carmichael, James Stewart and Chad Reed - all crashed at some point in the opening round of the series, Whitelock mandated safer tracks. The thinking was simple: No one wants to see about $15 million in rider salary laying on the track. Without them, there is no show, and Whitelock understood before anyone else that the four-stroke era had eclipsed current track thinking.

"The goal," Whitelock said in a statement, "Is to build tracks that are as safe as possible and deliver great racing for the fans. That's our objective as we proceed with this process."

Anaheim II, the first race where Whitelock was able to implement changes, showcased some of the best racing of the season.

No one doubts that rearranging a stadium full of dirt is a hell of a lot easier than adding runoff on a road course. You can't just take a bulldozer to the dangerous ones and hope for the best. On second thought...

The costs of road-race safety are enormous and there has to be a return on the investment. That investment must be viewed in human terms, and without riders, the show simply doesn't go on.

Whitelock is part of the troika running racing - temporarily, it's said. Already, director of competition Merrill Vanderslice has announced his resignation, though he seems to be lingering: Now his departure is set for the end of April, I'm told. No word on the status of Michelle Rossi. Even less word on the naming of a racing czar, a position whose vacancy grows more cavernous by the day. And, for those who don't know, in one of many previous and productive lives, Whitelock was the World Superbike technical boss.

The hope here is that whomever takes over the helm of the teetering ship "AMA PR" makes rider involvement in rider safety a priority. Clearly, he or she can't pay less attention to it than their predecessor. And the current fascination with committees could be well served for a change, if that committee consists solely of riders.

A displacement decrease is less than a year away as MotoGP machines outgrow World Championship tracks that are constantly scrutinized and spend millions on safety. There's little doubt that a number of U.S. racetracks aren't keeping up with the constant evolution of the Superbike class. Even the best of them, such as Infineon Raceway in Sonoma, have areas that can be improved; moving the K-wall to add a little more runoff in the right-hand turn seven is one spot riders have mentioned to me. If they'd mentioned it to Infineon management, it probably would have been done by now.

Road America announced a $5 million, three-year capital improvement plan in November. The plan calls for resurfacing five corners and having runoff added at turn five. But the biggest change is the "reconfiguration of the Bill Mitchell bridge at turn 13 to accommodate a greater runoff area," the track said in a release.

The release should have been universally welcomed as good news, but it wasn't. The reason was simple: Instead of consulting riders, the track solicited the opinion of FIM safety boss Claude Danis.

Who better than the man who must give his blessing to a racetrack for FIM homologation? "Us," was the riders' answer, and they have a point. The riders rightfully feel that unless you understand what's happening on a 200-horsepower motorcycle on the 16th lap of a 16-lap race, when the tires are slicker than a Sunday televangelist, the shock's more overheated than the gay-marriage debate, and the front-brake lever feels like an overripe tomato, you shouldn't be the final arbiter. We value your opinion, as you must ours, they believe.

The model to emulate is MotoGP. At the pinnacle of the sport, the Rider's Safety Commission - Valentino Rossi, Kenny Roberts Jr, Loris Capirossi, and others - meet at every GP to discuss all manners of safety issues. An incident very early in the lone qualifying session in Jerez, Spain, proved that even the best tracks aren't immune to the unforeseen. A failure on Alex Hofmann's Pramac d'Antin Ducati Desmosedici had unintended and far-reaching consequences. Rossi was an unwilling victim, as were Roberts, both Kawasakis, and Marco Melandri, of the oil streak Hofmann unwittingly laid down in his own wake. The damage was significant, but it was cleaned up in about 20 minutes and qualifying continued without incident. When was the last time a significant oil spill at an AMA race was quickly resolved? Roberts himself said that the oily track multi-rider pileup would be a topic of discussion at the next Rider's Safety Commission meeting.

One significant difference between the AMA and MotoGP is team structure. The AMA teams are run without sponsor obligations - there are almost none among the factories, except for Parts Unlimited at Ducati Austin - and rely almost entirely on the generosity of the American distributors. Executives in offices mostly in Southern California make the decisions, generate the budgets, pay the salaries, and ignore the grim realities of road racing.

When road racers bitch about track safety and the lack of rider involvement, alarms should be ringing in the same executive suites that pay attention to Supercross/motocross. The factories provide the bulk of the funding for the inestimable Asterisk Mobile Medical Center (the AMA is also a significant contributor).

"Similar plans are being considered by the AMA Pro Racing Medical Advisory Board for the AMA Chevy Trucks U.S. Superbike Championships and the AMA Progressive Insurance U.S, Flat Track Championships," reads a press release issued by the AMA. That was on June 20, 2003. Three years and counting - that's a lot of considering. Maybe it's time for a consideration committee.

American Suzuki is the most generous benefactor in road racing, with a budget I'd conservatively estimate to be in excess of $12 million. They have three factory riders, two of whom sport a number-plate, and a number of satellite teams. When a six-time champion like Mladin voices his opinion, it shouldn't fall on the deaf ears of the people paying his salary. Their investment is enormous and yet their timidity is well documented. Only American Honda had a representative on the now-defunct AMA Pro Racing board, and rider safety was not among the reasons for his departure from all AMA boards. And while it existed, the Pro Racing board made almost no effort to include riders in safety decisions affecting their own lives.

So the next time a rider complains about the frighteningly dangerous final turn at Road Atlanta, an event sponsored by American Suzuki, maybe he should look at the signature on his paycheck. If that guy doesn't care enough to take a stand, why should anyone else?

April 19, 2006

All Good in Nick Land

Nicky Hayden is going to be fine. He's going to earn pole positions. He's going to win races - other than Laguna Seca. He's going to challenge for the 2006 MotoGP World Championship. He's going to do all these things if Honda gets him the tools he needs in time, and that's up to Honda.

Those who rely on internet sites run by the lonely and desperate, slaving away in their "Home of the Whopper" underwear in the darkened basements of their parents suburban tract houses, thought that life, as we know it, ended when Hayden finished a distant third to young teammate Dani Pedrosa at the season-opening Spanish Grand Prix at Jerez. On the strength of one race finish, his MotoGP career with Honda was finished, the digitaliacs posited, without the slightest shred of evidence or truth or understanding of the business of racing. So it goes in a world increasingly dominated by the uninformed clouding the minds of the unsuspecting. Anyone who cuts their own food should know better.

For his first year in GPs, Hayden was paired with one of the greatest racers of all time, Valentino Rossi. It would have been the perfect rookie season but for Honda's choice of Hayden's crew chief. It took two seasons before HRC (Honda Racing Corporation) declared the chemistry experiment a failure.

Hayden had Alex Barros as a teammate for his second season. The Brazilian is a likable journeyman who was slotted into the team after Rossi got angry enough to leave. Hayden was going to learn very little from him.

Last year, Honda turned Hayden's team over to Pete Benson, while adding Erv Kanemoto as an overseer for both Hayden and his third teammate in three years, the mercurial Max Biaggi. Biaggi had long carped that he didn't have the best of everything - the best bike, the best tires, the best support. In 2005, he did, usurping Kanemoto for his own designs and promptly riding himself and Kanemoto out of jobs.

Hayden said at the end of last season that he wished he'd had more time to work with Kanemoto. That wasn't meant as a knock on his own crew chief; rather, he relished the chance to learn from one of the most experienced minds in racing. Why HRC would allow Biaggi to hold Kanemoto hostage, knowing that Hayden is the future, isn't easily explained. So it goes.

Rossi took most of his crew when he left for Yamaha, including the inestimable crew chief Jerry Burgess. Burgess would have leapt at the chance to work with yet another champion, as he'd done previously with Freddie Spencer, Wayne Gardner, Mick Doohan, and Rossi. But Honda let him go - it's believed Yamaha nearly doubled his salary - while insisting, at the time, that they could win by flooding the grid with RC211Vs. A humbling year later, after Rossi took the first of his two Yamaha titles, they admitted their mistake.

For much of the winter testing, Hayden's first job as the new team leader was to test two motorcycles, a smaller version of the RC211V, and a more standard 2006. When the 2005 season ended, Hayden was skeptical that they'd run the small bike, which had a very brief outing in Brno last year. HRC insisted they would. Right to the final test of the season, Hayden was going back and forth, cutting his testing of whichever would emerge as the preferred machine. So when the season began in Jerez, he had less time on the new bike than Pedrosa had on his more standard machine, and than the rest of the field had on theirs.

"The young guys, without a lot of problems with development, testing and some other things in the brain, they are finding it easy to go fast without all the other shit," Rossi said in Qatar. "They can go very fast."

There's no denying the strength of Pedrosa's performance in Jerez. Challenging for victory in his first race in the premier class is something very few riders do. The last rider to win in his senior-class debut was Max Biaggi, on a Kanemoto Honda NSR500 at Suzuka in 1998.

Then came Qatar and a more traditional podium: Rossi-Hayden-Capirossi -Nicky's sixth podium in a row. Sete Gibernau was next, followed by Casey Stoner and Pedrosa, who'd gotten the best of a fight with Marco Melandri, another rider Rossi believes is struggling with development.

Hayden was in position to win the race, but a slight slip on the final lap gave Rossi all he needed to escape. Racing is all about the little bits, and Hayden, at the moment, is missing that little bit to make the 2006 machine a race winner.

"From the morning I got here, we haven't been able to drop the hammer like I need to," he said after practice in Qatar. "On race tires, it's just traction. We get into the corners really loose, and if we get it to where we get some weight to get into the corner, it doesn't finish."

And there were front-end chatter issues as well, an epidemic this season that crosses manufacturer and tire lines.

"It's never easy here in this world," Hayden said. "These guys, it's the top guys in the world, the best riders, the best bikes. Sometimes the speed hasn't been great and we've done a lot of laps and a lot of questions marks. Which bike do I want to use? I'd get on the old bike and be a little bit faster. HRC wanted us to use this new thing. So hopefully we have some new parts coming."

He said he'd hoped for a new chassis for Qatar, but it didn't show. Until then, he'll work with what he has, mostly without complaint. And he wouldn't be drawn into a disagreement with Honda during the postrace press conference.

"I know you guys need something to write about and the press loves to make a big deal about that bike, this bike, swingarm and all that. Yeah, I mean I'm happy, I got..." he said before deciding to end the sentence. "Yeah, my bike is okay." Then came a gentle barb at HRC, delivered with a smile and a laugh, and not a little bit of truth. "When I was trying to draft [Casey] Stoner [whom he passed midway into the race], I was thinking, 'Man, I should be going by this satellite Honda a lot quicker. That's my straightaway.' But it's all good. Yeah, I'm happy. Hopefully, we've got some more stuff coming. There's a few little areas we can still have room for improvement. But HRC, I hope they're working around the clock over there to help me out."

Let's hope they were listening.

Nicky Hayden isn't going anywhere. HRC has too much invested and knows there's no one in America with nearly the talent, charisma, experience or potential to replace him. And they aren't likely to put two Europeans on the factory team, He is, in fact, in a very strong position: If Rossi leaves for F-1, as expected, Yamaha will likely make a run at the "Kentucky Kid," as they did in 2003.

Regardless of what happens in the future, or what gets posted by the pallid netwits of the wireless world, Hayden made one convert in Qatar.

"I am actually very surprised about Hayden today, because for sure he has some problems with his bike this season," said seven-time World Champion Rossi. "I listened to what he said in the press conference and I don't completely understand the situation, but it seems he is having some difficulties, so well done to him. Last season he was very strong at the end, and now he is still here, so I think he is a real rival for me."

Maybe that's who HRC should be listening to.

May 17, 2006

Standing Up For Their Rights

Jamie Hacking finally had his Howard Beale moment. For those of you born before email, Xbox, and Red Bull, you'll remember that Beale was the outraged newscaster in Sidney Lumet's brilliant 1976 social commentary *Network*. As portrayed by the great British actor Peter Finch, Beale came alive as an angry but empowered newsman who'd reached his breaking point. It's Finch, as Beale, who delivers one of the great lines in the history of cinema, "I'm as mad as hell, and I'm not going to take this anymore!"

Like Beale, Hacking's breaking point came gradually. The 2006 campaign marks his 10th year in the AMA Superbike Championship. Like any career, his has had its share of ups and downs; the downs becoming less and less frequent with maturity. There was a time when he fell too often for his own good. And when he fell, he'd hit things. For a long time he was lucky not to get seriously hurt, but that changed few years ago. In 2004 he missed a few races after breaking his collarbone in a practice crash at Mid-Ohio. It was his first broken bone. But it wasn't his own injuries that motivated him.

"I wasn't really close to Vincent [Haskovec]," Hacking said of the Team M4 EMGO Suzuki rider who was paralyzed in a racing incident last year at Infineon Raceway, ironically, the most proactive track on the AMA calendar. "I got more to know Vincent in the last couple of years and to see what happened to him really hit home with me.

"As I get older, you see these things. When I was younger, I didn't even think about walls. I didn't care. It's just something that has to be done. Improvements like these need to be done, and the tracks need to quit overlooking them, and the AMA needs to wake up and see all these things. Whatever I can do - take an hour out of my time on the weekend is nothing to help somebody out."

Hacking knows that AMA has a history of excluding riders from safety issues and he doesn't understand it. When a group of riders were organized - not by the AMA - to look over Road Atlanta at the end of the 2004 season, Hacking wanted in. Months later there was a slight glimmer of hope that the AMA might be coming around. During the 2004-05 winter the AMA Pro Racing Board suggested then-board-member Kevin Schwantz take a more active role in track safety. It was a good choice, but it would be badly executed. Where did they send Schwantz and Mat Mladin last year? Loudon, a track that was booted off the calendar in 2001 after years of rider-safety complaints. Since then, nothing. Which drove Hacking and the others to action.

"We just do our own thing - we've just been doing our own thing," he said.

Yamaha's Eric Bostrom lent his expertise when California Speedway moved the wall on the back straight on the Friday night of the race weekend. Bostrom wasn't invited to the track when the changes were made. Instead, he acted on a tip. And, after what he said was initially met with reluctance from track personnel, "they started being really cool."

And everyone agreed that the change was for the better and long overdue.

"Whatever the case, it's three racetracks in a row, actually four - Infineon too - that said they had no direction and no communication with anybody from the AMA," Bostrom said.

Bostrom isn't entirely right. AMA road-race manager Ron Barrick talks to all the tracks about safety issues. He met with the California Speedway personnel during the February test and came early to the track to implement changes. But nothing was done before Friday night. And riders weren't asked to participate, even though last year American Honda's Miguel Duhamel had gotten the back stretch kink straightened out.

On a bad weather day during a mid-March test at Infineon Raceway, Hacking gathered a few of his colleagues and met with general manager Steve Page, and media and community relations director John Cardinale.

"When we tested there, we had a bum day," he said. "I'm in pretty good with the track people there, John [Cardinale] and Steve [Page]. And I always give a lot of stuff for the charity event. And they always come by to see what I've got. And I told them, I said, 'Look, since today's a crap day, we definitely need to sit down and go over a lot of things.' And they were, like, 'Yeah, let's do that. We'll be more than glad to do it.' I gathered everybody up. Me, Mat [Mladin], Jake [Zemke], Ben [Spies] and just went around the racetrack and just pointed things out and prioritized things - kind of like we did at Barber. We put one, two, three, and so forth. And we'll go from there."

American Honda's Zemke and Yamaha's Bostrom credited Hacking with taking the same initiative during a late-March test at Barber Motorsports Park.

Bostrom said that Hacking had organized a meeting with track officials at the Barber Motorsports Park test, prior to the race.

"Jamie got us all together and it was killer," Bostrom said at California Speedway. The riders prioritized the concerns and changes were made before last month's second round of the championship. "Turn one is such a huge improvement," Bostrom said. "They said we have plans to redo turn 11, which is going to be expensive. They're totally supporting us and yet everything I hear [from the AMA] is they won't do it, they won't do it."

Hacking said the changes at Infineon, which has spent millions over the years to improve safety, will be immediately obvious.

"When we go to Infineon, you're going to see some improvements there that I got started," he said. "Turn one's going to be different. Turn three down in the dip - that wall's going to be gone. The corner where Vincent hit [turn five], we've got real big plans for that. They use the backside of that for NASCAR parking. There's no reason the fence has to be there. The fence is there to separate parking from the racetrack. Well, if they moved the fence back, they can still use it as parking, no matter where the fence is. I don't know how soon that area will be done, but some areas will be done when we get there.

"We'll go to the next track after Sears Point and we'll go to Road America and there's definitely some improvements there that needs to be done," Hacking said. "I'll be definitely gathering up some guys and going through that."

The riders feel empowered. Now that they know the tracks appreciate their input, they won't be stopped. Without them the show doesn't go on, and if too many are hurt, there is no show.

The AMA has a very simple choice to make; they can discard their historic reluctance to engage the riders in the decisions that affect their lives and make a difference in the quality of the racetracks, in the quality of the racing, in the quality of the racers lives, or they can get out of the way. The riders are not going to take it any more.

June 7, 2006

Controlling Traction

Ever wonder about the lack of on-bike cameras on the front-runners of an AMA Superbike race? Me, too. So I asked. And I discovered that at one point Yoshimura Suzuki agreed to run a camera on Ben Spies' Suzuki GSX-R1000. But there was one caveat - no audio. Why not? The short answer is traction control. The long answer is, well, longer.

Stand in a corner and listen to the sound coming off the motorcycles of Spies or Mat Mladin. The engines burble, like they're misfiring or on the rev-limiter, then miraculously clear up on the corner exit. Lap after lap. What's going on?

Simply put, Suzuki is the best in the paddock at programming their engine control unit (ECU). The ECU can legally measure crank speed and rear-wheel speed and engine temperature and airbox temperature and a bewildering number of other parameters. A gyroscope can help tell the ECU when the bike is leaned over, and on the side of the tire, and when it's upright, and on the fat part of the tire. And at some point the ECU is made aware of wheelspin or a wheelie, both of which are sometimes useful, sometimes not.

The trick is figuring out what happens next. Do they retard the ignition? Do they cut a cylinder? Do they cut the spark? Do they cut the fuel injection? Probably they do a little of each in differing amounts. The net result is that they're modifying the map around legally monitored parameters.

"It's not traction control, it's a map," one crew chief told me.

And mapping is not illegal. And that has the AMA bouncing off the rev-limiter. Legally.

Rule 23 a. of the AMA Road Race Rule Book General Equipment Standards reads: "Electronic devices specifically designed for traction control are prohibited. This includes sensors that can determine front-wheel speed, and any electronic control of the brake systems."

In the final corner of Sunday's Superbike race at Barber Motorsports Park, Mladin had a slight edge before American Honda's Miguel Duhamel surged forward to take second by .050 of a second.

"I think they're having a problem with their fuel injection; the bike was popping a lot," Duhamel said with a straight face and tongue firmly in cheek. "And it went pop, pop, pop. And when it did that, I just went by him. And after that, it was a heat race all the way to the line. That problem they had with the injection finally caught up with them."

Is American Honda innocent? They agreed to run a camera on Jake Zemke's CBR1000RR but ran into problems trying to power it off the motorcycle, rather than with an auxiliary battery. And there was no restriction on the audio. But they aren't complete innocents. There was suspicion they had some form of "traction control" back in 2004, the last year they had full factory bikes, and the last time they won a Superbike race. Hondas won nine of 18 races that year, and Duhamel finished second in the championship. And the more people you ask, the more you will be led to believe that everyone is desperately tinkering with their ECUs like mad scientists trying to decode the Colonel's Secret Recipe.

The Suzukis are the most obvious by their distinctive sound. Some believe Spies has been successful this year because he finally has faith in the system, that he can open the throttle before the apex and know he won't be put into a low gravitational orbit. Aaron Yates doesn't seem to like it.

Kawasaki began its ZX10R Superbike project with Magneti Marelli, the masters of ECU wizardry, before switching to Mitsubishi. When Yamaha hired electronics engineer Vittorio Bolognesi away from Parts Unlimited Ducati, it was widely assumed it was because of his knowledge of the Magneti Marelli system. Parts Unlimited Ducati hasn't replicated their World Superbike effort because the factory system uses a front-wheel sensor, which would draw immediate attention. They could develop a sensorless system, but the cost in time and money rules it out. They have run a front-wheel sensor in tests.

The best way to get a rise out of Neil Hodgson or Ben Bostrom is to ask why Troy Bayliss and Gregorio Lavilla can win in their respective series, World Superbike and British Superbike, where traction control is legal, while they can't hope for a sniff of the podium without the misfortune of many. It's true that the Suzuki GSX-R1000 is the best chassis in the field. It's also true that Yosh has two of the best riders. But is that enough for everyone else to be racing for third?

What would happen if Bostrom and Hodgson had it? And do they? Was Bostrom's fast lap at the recent Miller Motorsports Park test assisted by traction control?

Everyone admits Suzuki has the finest system in the paddock. Their bikes are fast, but they're not doing anything illegal. Rival crew chiefs I've spoken to don't begrudge them their success. They're allowed to have data acquisition, they're allowed to change their ECU. The rocket science is knowing when to apply it.

What if the AMA asked to look inside? What would they find? Maybe nothing, if they didn't have the proper software to read the data. And even then they might not know what they were looking at. And if the software is proprietary, Suzuki or any other factory would be well within their rights to refuse to give the AMA a copy.

Formula One got so fed up trying to enforce traction control that they gave up the fight. Not surprising, when you have budgets that run as high as half a billion dollars.

The AMA is aware of the issue. It has been repeatedly discussed, most recently at a meeting on the Friday night of the Infineon Raceway weekend. But it was put into a state of suspended animation pending a June 6 meeting in Rome, where representatives of many national series, inducing the AMA Superbike Championship, are to meet with the World Superbike brass and the FIM to unify a worldwide series of technical standards. Much of the discussion will center on Ducati's desire to raise the displacement for twins to 1200cc.

What will the AMA bring back? At the moment they're powerless, since no one is doing anything illegal. The only intelligent thing to do is legalize full traction control.

Ask why they don't, and the AMA will dust off the old canard that it's unfair to the privateers. Which is crap. The cost wouldn't be great for a clever technician with the right software and, most importantly, a front-wheel sensor. A privateer could buy a third-party system that would improve the performance of his machine it ways that hours on the dyno never could, at a much lower cost, and without stressing the engine, which leads to greater cost. And it would be easier or tires, which makes it safer and cheaper. And, as much as racing relies on privateers to fill the field, no one has ever forked over folding green to watch a steel cage death match for ninth.

Most importantly, if it was legal and everyone had it, the racing would improve, which is better entertainment, which might make someone outside the industry take notice, which might lead to a series sponsorship. Which, I admit, is a stretch, given the rudderless state of AMA Pro Racing, but we can hope.

What isn't a stretch is that the quality of the television broadcast would improve. True, if it was mounted on Spies' bike, you'd want a rear-facing camera. But, instead of just Mladin, you might see a few different bikes fading in the distance... or not.

June 21, 2006

Just Say No

If your elephant has hemorrhoids, you don't fit him with a training bra. At least most people wouldn't. But our friends in AMA Pro Racing in Pickerington, well, they're a different story. The AMA Superbike Championship has more problems than a hemophiliac with a porcupine fetish, but that isn't stopping them from trying to fix problems that don't exist.

By narrowly focusing its wave band to a station that plays "All Me" radio, the somewhat fluid Pro Racing hierarchy is receiving bad broadcasts about the state of the Superbike paddock. What's wrong? Where to start? The schedule, class similarity, track safety, the leadership's tin ear, traction control, etc. So what's their response? Spec tires!

The gruel they're being fed, is that it must be a good thing because it works in World Superbike and it works in Canada. Canada? The argument misses one salient point - the AMA doesn't need it.

Spec tires were introduced to World Superbike for one very good reason; Michelin was winning everything on their own very narrow, very selfish terms. In 2003, the year before the advent of spec tires, Michelin supplied two riders, Neil Hodgson and Ruben Xaus. Between them, they won 20 of 24 races and would have won more if not for a crash by Ruben Xaus at Laguna Seca. Hodgson won the World Championship.

At the time, Dunlop was supplying tires to 20 riders. Pirelli fitted three or four and they were back of the packers.

The spec-tire debate came to a head at the U.S. round of the World Superbike Championship when World Superbike organizers FGSport announced that the 2004 season would be run with spec tires. In Monterey, they said they had the outline of an agreement with Pirelli and a bid from Pirelli that they had not accepted, and were waiting for bids from other companies. Before the following round at Brands Hatch, Pirelli sweetened their bid, and, as there was no counter bid, FGSport signed and announced the deal in England.

Michelin wouldn't have been interested - going from two riders to an entire field isn't something they do - but Dunlop would have been. The Brummies claimed at the time that they were not invited to bid. FGSport say that they had meetings with all tire companies - denied by some - all of whom except Pirelli told them they weren't interested. Legal action may still be ongoing, but after nearly three years of spec tires, it's a moot point. The contract expires at the end of this year.

For races and officials tests, Pirelli tires and support are supplied by FGSport at a cost per rider of 45,000 Euros (about $57,000) for the season. It is believed that the top six teams from the previous year's points standings didn't pay the first year, but as to who pays now, that's up to FGSports. Pirelli supplies tires, FGSport determines who pays what.

One team from each supplying bike manufacturer is designated as a test team, which is unsatisfactory to both the teams and Pirelli. With Winston Ten Kate, the official Honda team, Alex Barros's Klaffi Honda team doesn't get test tires.

The FIM rulebook says that at each event, 13 rear and nine front tires will be allotted to each Superbike rider for practice, qualifying, Superpole, and warmup. In Supersport, it's 10 rears and eight fronts.

So how has it worked? Three years on, Hodgson still holds the lap record at Valencia. Hodgson's race lap in 2003 was a 1:35.007. Troy Corset ran a 1:35.374 in the second race this year. Troy Bayliss' race record, Superpole, and best lap still stand at Misano from 2002. Shakey Byrne's Brands Hatch fast lap remains a record. And much of the improvement in World Superbike times comes from the engine and, mostly, engine management, not rubber.

Compare this to MotoGP Valentino Rossi's pole in 2006 was nearly three seconds faster than his 2003 pole. The fastest lap was a 1:52.623 run by Loris Capirossi. In 2006, Capirossi again had the fast lap, a 1:50.195, a time that didn't match the exiled Max Biaggi's 1:50.117 from 2005. Tires are the reason, according to Repsol Honda's Nicky Hayden.

"That's where a lot of time comes from," he said.

In the United States, Mat Mladin's pole time from this year's Road America was over three seconds faster than his 2003 time. His fastest race lap, which was faster than his pole time, was 3.5 seconds better than his best of 2003.

The difference is clear. Progress is being made here and in MotoGP and to a much lesser extent in World Superbike.

Essentially, they're trying to break even after three years of development.

The improvement in Mladin's times has much to do with tires, as well as engine and engine mapping. When Michelin came in to support the Ducati Austin team in 2003 and 2004, Dunlop stepped up. Two technicians and an engineer commuted from their headquarters in Birmingham, England. Dunlop developed the NT (New Technology) line of tires, which continue to be the standard. And they continued to win nearly every race in every class. Having been soundly defeated, and with very little to show for their two-year stint, Michelin retreated. The lesson is that you don't improve without competition.

Because of Dunlop's support of racing - they supply all the factory teams and most of the factory-supported teams - a spec-tire class exists. It's Dunlop. Pirelli supplies one of the factory-supported teams and they've been moderately successful. But they also withdrew from the Daytona Superbike race because of concern over tire wear in the earlier Superstock race. Imagine if they were the sole supplier. Does last year's Indy F-1 race ring a bell?[1]

Dunlop supplies an allocation of tires and service to all of their teams, and many others. HotBodies Racing's/Mat Mladin Motorsports Marty Craggill gets NTs, as does Hooters Suzuki's Eric Wood and Doug Chandler in his return. If the teams go over their allocation - all of them do - they have to pay. So it's conceivable that, depending on the fees charged, the factory teams could spend less on tires than they do now. They'd also get less. And imagine what would happen if the private teams were asked to pay $50,000 for tires? Or the backfield support teams, who would also have to pay. The grids would be much smaller. And this is regardless of which tire company won the contract.

And what of the occasional privateers? Part-timers would have to pay thousands of dollars for tires. You want small fields? There's your solution.

Count Michelin out. Same for Bridgestone. It would be between Dunlop and Pirelli. Dunlop, if given the chance, would be an active bidder. They've supported racing for too long, had too much success, and developed too many tires for both racing and street use to give up without a fight. But if they won the bid, the quality of the tires would suffer; they certainly couldn't supply every Superbike and Superstock bike with NTs.

Ben Bostrom is the only rider in the paddock to experience all sides of the argument. He's been both a Michelin and Dunlop-supported rider in World Superbike, he raced Pirellis last year for a downmarket Honda team, and he's back on Dunlops this year.

---

[1] The 2005 United States Grand Prix was controversial for the fourteen cars with Michelin tires withdrawing from the race following the parade lap and not starting the race.. Only six cars, all with Bridgestone tires, comptseted in the race.

"Dunlop's been the one that's supported the sport so hard, it wouldn't be right [if Pirelli was chosen]," he said. "Right now we have a spec-tire rule, so it wouldn't make any difference because everyone runs Dunlop and it works great. If everyone runs Pirelli it would be the same situation, just on Pirelli. Right now it's like we have a spec-tire rule. I got to admit, it's pretty nice. It's pretty nice because you kind of know, this is what I'm given. You're not going, 'What's that other guy got up his sleeve?' You don't know."

Who stands to benefit? Pirelli, if they won the bid, would significantly raise their American profile. They would also raise their profits; this would have to be a money-making deal. And it would surely make money for the AMA, who would administer the deal.

And where would that money go? More elephant training bras.

July 19, 2006

The Way It Should Be

The two series that will converge at the Red Bull U.S. GP the third weekend in July could not be more different. MotoGP is a thriving international series playing to mostly huge crowds on the safest racetracks in the world. The AMA Superbike Series plays to much smaller crowds - official numbers are rarely released - on racetracks, with few exceptions, that have been historically reluctant to embrace change. MotoGP has a set schedule that's changed only rarely and then with much advance notice. The template for an AMA race weekend has yet to be written. MotoGP limits their fields to the best of the best with strict qualifying standards. The AMA series also has qualifying standards; in Superbike it's close to MotoGP, in the support classes it's much more inclusive. MotoGP has three very distinct classes that provide a clear career path for riders. The AMA series has two classes for 600s - Buells and others welcome - and two for 1000s, which is nothing if not confusing for the casual fan. The differences could fill up the rest of this space. But the biggest difference is leadership.

In the recent round-table discussion we held with the managers of the five factory Superbike teams, leadership and communication were the two biggest concerns. What they said was that there is no leadership and there was little communication. First, a bit of history. AMA Pro Racing CEO Scott Hollingsworth was ousted at the end of January. No reason was given and Hollingsworth has issued no public statements. Less than a week later, interim AMA CEO Patty DiPietro announced that a new three-member management team would run Pro Racing on an interim basis. That's a lot of interims.

But the real changes came following the AMA board of directors meeting at the Indy Trade Show. The Pro Racing Board was unilaterally dissolved. Such was the outcry from the dissolution of the 12-year-old board that the AMA got into a very public squabble with American Honda, which highlighted the schism between the AMA and those it's meant to serve.

New rules-making committees were to be formed for the various disciplines. Nearly five months later, these committees still don't exist.

So who's running racing now? More importantly, who's running the AMA? Those questions are inextricably interlinked.

At the moment, DiPietro is both the chief executive of the AMA and the head of Pro Racing. Her background is not in racing - she comes from the financial side - and this is very much on-the-job training. And it's clear that one person cannot, and should not, run both. The AMA is actively recruiting a new CEO.

DiPietro is currently being advised on racing issues by what's become a fluid board that currently consists of six members. The board lost a valuable resource when Don Emde quit, but there are signs of hope from the two most recent additions - legendary dirt-track tuner Bill Werner and longtime motocross fixture Bevo Forti of Scott Goggles.

So what we have is very much an interim government with three key positions - AMA CEO, AMA Pro Racing CEO, and AMA Pro Racing Director of Competition - in need of permanent solutions. The power vacuum is enormous and it shows. Whatever they're doing simply doesn't work. With no rules-making committees in place five months on, the chance of any substantive work getting done for the 2007 season is rapidly fading. The unofficial start of the 2007 road race season is the annual early December Daytona tire tests, now less than six months away.

Nothing major will change, but some pet peeves may be resolved. Maybe a dress code for umbrella girls?

All of the team managers expressed interest in taking part in the rules-making committees, which raises the question about why they haven't been formed. One reason is that they're having a hard time finding people outside of the paddock and the reason for that is communication. To the best of my knowledge, they announced the committees on the AMA's own web site for about 45 days. Other than that, it was a secret.

Which is appropriate because their communication skills are limited, at best. Paranoia and secrecy drives too much of their decision making. One example: At the end of May the decision had been made not to enforce traction control in the Superbike class for the 2006 season. All that was left to work out was the wording of the press release, which was discussed during a conference call. The next day it had all changed - enforcement would continue - but why? Either they'd read the posting and realized the firestorm it would create, which is in itself a lame reason, or they didn't like being scooped, an even lamer reason.

Leadership and communication are two very large problems. A close third is that the AMA tries to do too much with too few people. They are the sanctioning body, they set the rules, they promote the races. In MotoGP, the FIM is the sanctioning body, the MSMA (the GP manufacturers association) sets the rules, and Dorna, which has 150 full-time employees and another 200 during race peaks, promotes the series, along with a host of other tasks, all of which they do well and openly.

Carmelo Ezpeleta is the very engaging CEO of Dorna. The Spaniard has been in charge since Dorna became the commercial rights holders in 1992 and remains as enthusiastic and engaging as he was in his first day on the job. Unlike his AMA counterpart, Ezpeleta is open and communicative, so much so that he sometimes surprises his own staff with his frankness when speaking to the media. More than once they've been surprised to read something in print or online that they knew nothing about.

Ezpeleta has made a U.S. GP a priority for some years and he once showed me blueprints, complete with needed improvements, of Homestead Miami Speedway, one of many U.S. tracks where he'd sent five-time World Champion Mick Doohan on fact-finding missions. Never have I been turned down a request to speak with Ezpeleta, which I can't say is the case with the AMA. And he has always exceeded the amount of time his very busy schedule allows.

Ezpeleta speaks fluent English, though with the heavy accent of his native Spain. At times his enthusiasm is so great that his mind gets ahead of his tongue, but he always makes his point and usually with a smile. And he believes the most important part of his job is communication, keeping in touch with all the various parties and making sure they're all happy when a decision affects more than one of them. He sees himself as a catalyst, whether it's the FIM, the MSMA, the tire companies, the riders, or the teams. It's only when all are happy that they can have one voice.

Ezpeleta speaks to the principals on a regular basis, whether it's FIM safety boss Claude Danis, who recently gave Mazda Raceway Laguna Seca its homologation, or any other members of the Grand Prix Commission, which includes IRTA (the teams association), MSMA, or other members of the FIM. He meets with the GP Rider Safety Commission - currently Valentino Rossi, Kenny Roberts Jr., and Loris Capirossi - on the Saturday evening of every Grand Prix. And all that is apart from what he gathers while constantly strolling through the paddock, always willing to engage anyone with a question or need.

When asked if he saw himself as a benevolent dictator, a term often used for what's needed in the AMA, he laughed. He certainly doesn't see himself as a dictator, benevolent or not. Dorna has the MotoGP contract, and he sees himself as an intermediary, someone who needs to make agreements with everyone in the best interests of the sport.

Nor is he closed-minded. He has his ideas and opinions, but he's open to suggestions. And the door to his office is always open.

"The sport needs someone who can make decisions, but most importantly they need someone who understands the sport," Ezpeleta said.

Ezpeleta maintains his enthusiasm for his job because "the sport is so enjoyable. It's still enjoyable and I still enjoy it, but also because the sport keeps improving and I can have a positive influence and can still work on it and improve it further."

Anyone who's been to a Grand Prix, especially in Italy or Spain or Holland, can't deny that he's on to something.

MotoGP is in its boom years, thanks to his stewardship and a number of personalities, led by Rossi and including Nicky Hayden. Hayden won last year's Red Bull U.S. GP, an event that Ezpeleta singled out in his end of season statement.

"The return to Laguna Seca was hugely successful, with a sell-out crowd for race day and enormous interest in the event from all over the world," he said in his statement. "From a personal point of view this was probably the highlight of the season because it was something we had worked on for a long time and to see the dream finally become a reality was very satisfying."

Ezpeleta didn't deny that there were problems last year, but he was encouraged because the track was full every day and the "atmosphere was fantastic." He understands that there's work to be done to please the fans, but he saw the 2005 race as "a really welcome start back to life in the U.S. and good base to move on from."

Ezpeleta will be a fixture in the Laguna Seca paddock. He'll see the improvements and he'll ask what else needs to be done. He'll talk to anyone and everyone and consider their counsel. That's what a leader does. Wonder if Carmelo wants to move to Pickerington?

August 2, 2006

Good and Bad

The Red Bull U.S. Grand Prix was a rousing success. The Red Bull U.S. Grand Prix was an embarrassment. Both statements are true, but for very different reasons.

The success came out of the problems in last year's race. The 2005 version was a mess from top to bottom, saved only by Nicky Hayden's fairy-tale maiden victory on the Repsol Honda.

But that would have been little comfort while you were sitting in your car for hours or waiting in line at the concessions/toilets/souvenir stands/track crossings. Take your pick.

Given the constraints of the geography both leading to and inside Mazda Raceway Laguna Seca, and some financial issues, those problems were mostly fixed. The track crossings were ameliorated somewhat by using the track itself. But much of the time you felt like a sperm cell, wriggling uncomfortably among scores of your peers in an ultimately failed bid to be first to the holy land. A new bridge across the front straight should be up in time for the 2007 race. And, yes, there were still traffic delays. But it's a little like childbirth. It's bound to be messy when you push that much through that small a space. And, like childbirth, you forget about the pain after a while, which is why more than 51,000 race fans endured record, searing heat to watch Nicky Hayden win yet again.

Nicky's measured ride was brilliant, and it moved him closer to his lifelong goal of becoming the first American premier-class champion since Kenny Roberts Jr. won the 500cc World Championship in 2000. With much of Modesto, Turlock, Manteca, Oakdale and Hickman looking on, Junior continued his resurgence, proving wrong all those who'd written him off after his down years with the second-tier Suzuki team.

Camel Yamaha's Colin Edwards was less than his usual cheerful self. The victim of a flu bug, the Texas struggled in the race, losing a strip of his rear Michelin near the end, but he forged on to the end to collect a handful of points for the Conrovians (residents of Conroe, Texas) in attendance.

Not so for his teammate. Like Edwards, Valentino Rossi lost a strip of rubber off his the left side of his rear tire before his motor decided the heat was too much. But others took his place in the sun.

The diminutive giant-killer Dani Pedrosa survived the bumpiest track and hardest race of his young career to finish an impressive second to Hayden. He'd never seen the track, which had more whoops than Unadilla and more potholes than John Kerry's presidential run. Fellow Laguna Seca debutante Casey Stoner did what he's done too often this year. The fiery Australian found the gravel trap after tucking the front. It was his ninth crash of the season.

Australian Chris Vermeulen relived the glory days of his 2004 double Superbike win here on the Winston Ten Kate Honda by leading the first half of the race before gradually dropping back with machine problems. Teammate John Hopkins never got going and finished behind Vermeulen at a race he thought would end with his first MotoGP podium.

MotoGP wasn't the only race on the weekend. The AMA wrong-headedly decided to cram all four classes into a very limited schedule. The Superbike riders got less than half an hour of practice on Friday - various problems cut it from the original 45 minutes - and another 30 of qualifying before Saturday's race. It wasn't enough time to adjust for the new surface and the bumps, and tire choice was a crapshoot.

The bunched-up schedule, and problems with getting the corner workers up to speed for the first MotoGP practice (now a Laguna Seca ritual), had people talking about bringing the 125s and 250s next year, just to get the AMA out of the paddock. But it's simply too expensive. Instead they should run two classes, Superbike and Supersport, and give them proper respect by slotting them into the traditional 125 and 250cc time slots. With three hours of track time before Saturday afternoon, they could easily make it a Superbike doubleheader.

The MotoGP riders were as disgruntled as the fans last year. Track safety was abysmal, far below that of any other track on the calendar, despite $2 million worth of work that they'd asked for. To come back, they needed a lot more work done - $7 million worth, it turned out. Track boss Gill Campbell somehow found a way to raise the funds, with help from Yamaha, Mazda, Red Bull, Dorna and others. And she complied to the last detail with the requests of Rossi, Roberts, Capirossi and the rest.

When they arrived on Thursday, the riders were impressed by the improvements. But the track was bumpy on a scooter and it wouldn't get any better on a 250-horsepower MotoGP bike. There was buckling pavement, with whoops out of the Corkscrew, and a pothole formed near a patch job in the fast downhill Rainey Curve. The best analogy was that it was like someone had put down the beach blanket without smoothing the sand. Roberts Jr. said it was the bumpiest track he'd ever ridden on. And he'd raced at Loudon in 1992.

"It's bad, it's really bad," Roberts Jr., a member of the GP Rider Safety Commission, said after Friday practice. "I can't believe it's that bumpy. I don't know what to say."

The surface began to crumble so badly on Saturday afternoon that it was decided no other motorcycles would take to the track until the MotoGP program was finished. From 10:20 a.m., when the Sunday morning warmup finished, to the start of the 2 p.m.

race, the track was mostly quiet, save for some stunt riders, two-seater rides, and parade laps. But much damage had been done during the AMA Superbike race.

"News break," Miguel Duhamel said after finishing fourth. "I don't know if they're going to be racing this weekend; the track's coming apart."

Loris Capirossi, a member of the GP Rider Safety Commission, summed it up like this before the race: "I think this is the problem is coming from the company, not the problem from the track. The track coming to this company, say, 'F---ing hell, you have to do again the work because it's s--t.'"

After the race, the normally voluble Edwards was nearly at a loss for words: "I don't know what I should say. The fact that we actually had to come here and endure it for a year, this weekend is, in my opinion, ridiculous. It just shouldn't have happened. It's bullshit."

The work was done by the Pavex Construction Division of Graniterock construction company. This is no fly-by-night outfit. Graniterock is an award-winning Northern California firm with an impressive resume of high-profile projects - everything from Pebble Beach to San Francisco International Airport. Yet those projects are fairly straightforward compared to a racetrack, especially one like Laguna Seca, with its elevation changes. The stresses of a racing motorcycle are some of the greatest an asphalt surface endures. Two hundred-fifty horsepower in a contact patch the size of an orange does nasty things to bitumen, especially on the seams. Proper cure time can impact the long-term health of a track surface and Laguna was operating in a very narrow window. Even the best-intentioned projects go awry.

What went wrong at Laguna Seca isn't yet known, but it will be and soon. And well before next year's race, or there won't be a race.

At the end of the day, the loser is race organizer SCRAMP, the nonprofit organization that donates proceeds to local charities and civic organizations. Because the Laguna Seca Recreation Area is a Monterey County Park, it's the county that is responsible for the paving. But the track loses valuable revenue every day that the track's closed, and this year it was shut for 45 days for the safety improvements and paving.

The hope here is that it's done right the second time and well in advance of the race. So that when we reconvene on the Monterey Peninsula next July, for Nicky's hat trick, and for years to follow, the sounds we'll remember won't be the shrill voices of the riders, but the sweet strains of 800cc prototypes. Now that's something to look forward to.

August 23, 2006

New Kid in Town

Can Keith Kizer save road racing from the AMA? The hope here and in the paddock is yes, but with equal doses of optimism and skepticism.

Kizer comes to road racing with the blessing of, among others, Kevin Schwantz. The Schwantz and Kizer families have a long history, and Kevin believes Keith is the right man for the job. He's not alone. In talking with a number of people in the paddock, there was only one note of dissent, and that was from someone with severely compromised credibility.

In a gathering Kizer had with reporters on Saturday, it was clear that he'd either read the recent roundtable discussion that *Cycle News* hosted at Miller Motorsports Park or had been briefed on it. His central issues were some of the same shared by the Superbike team managers: safety and communication. He didn't mention leadership, but he didn't have to. If he does the job that's been created for him, the question will answer itself. There's no reason to believe he won't, if his bosses at AMA Pro Racing let him. Their history of kneecapping series managers is well known - ask Steve Whitelock - and nothing they've done recently suggests a change of policy.

In fact, if he succeeds, it will be in spite of the AMA, not because of it. A day after his appointment was greeted with optimism by the paddock, AMA Pro Racing proved themselves incapable of sustaining good news. At Saturday's riders' meeting, an AMA vice president showed an alarming range of ignorance that culminated with him making an ass of himself and AMA Pro Racing.

Doug Neubauer had no reason to be at the riders' meeting: He's the vice president of AMA Sports, the AMA's Amateur and Pro-Am competition division. But that didn't stop him from asking for the opportunity to spew venom about something he knew nothing about to riders he didn't know, including Ben Bostrom.

But first, a little history.

As I've pointed out many times in this space, the AMA has a sad record of soliciting rider opinion on safety issues, though Ron Barrick did organize a group of riders at Road America this year. (Road America track president George Bruggenthies was originally credited with organizing the meeting.) Barrick, for his part, has done a great deal for rider safety but, aside from Road America, has refused to formalize rider involvement. This year the riders, often led by Yamaha's Jamie Hacking, took issues into their own hands. They met with track officials during early-season tests, and the results are impressive, with improvements everywhere. Infineon Raceway has long been the standard for soliciting rider input.

During an early-June Mid-Ohio test, new members of the track-management team asked to meet with the racing community. After the meeting, the group did a lap of the road course, noting everything that could be improved. The number-one issue was the horrendously high curbing.

"We knew that time was really short, but we said if you can get these curbs fixed for the race, that would be the number-one goal right now, because we can't race with it as it is," American Honda's Jake Zemke remembers.

Mid-Ohio agreed to fix the curbs in time for the race and they did.

No one from the AMA was at the test. This was an initiative of the riders and teams, and the track improvements would not have gotten done without them. How could it have? For anyone in the

AMA to suggest otherwise is a lie. For someone in the AMA to chastise the riders for nearly screwing up the process, which Neubauer did, is disgraceful. That an uninformed interloper, who should never have been given the platform to spew his nonsense, was allowed to is the sort of stupidity that Keith Kizer may have to deal with. The bet here is that Kizer won't be allowing guest hosts at riders' meetings in the future.

"We want to funnel it into one place, to where the AMA, the racers, the tracks, everybody's on the same page," Kizer said. "So, if we can communicate through one avenue, I think we're going to have a lot better chance of getting results."

That's what the riders have wanted all along. It's depressing that it's taken a new face at the AMA to finally recognize the value of the riders they're meant to protect.

Nothing will get fixed without the riders. Nothing should get fixed without the riders. But it has to be the same riders.

"There are going to be rider committees that are put together, and what's going to happen is that at each race, it'll be a different set of riders, so that you're not just always going to the go-to guys - it's not always Mladin or Hayden - it's going to be a different group of guys, which will include the privateers," Kizer said. "Because there's obvious issues with the backmarker guys - well, maybe there's issues with them, too, that we need to talk to them. There will be definitely be communication between everybody."

No disrespect to the privateers - I'd put Jason Pridmore or Josh Hayes on a safety committee any day of the week - but the speeds the factory guys are going gives them a perspective others don't have. A wall that the guy in 28th isn't worried about could be lethal for the fast qualifier.

AMA communications boss Kerry Graeber said that work was already proceeding on a rider-safety delegation, but that nothing had been settled.

"Is it the same five guys? Is it a rotating group of three guys? Those are some of the details we're sorting out," he said.

Here's one detail you don't need to worry about: rotating riders. You rotate tires, you rotate pitchers - you don't rotate members on a safety committee. They don't do it in MotoGP; they shouldn't do it here. Mat Mladin, Jamie Hacking, Jake Zemke, Tommy Hayden. That's your committee. Every all-teams test, every race, those are the guys to make the decisions. All riders should be encouraged to attend the safety meetings - as they are in MotoGP - but for consistent results, the core has to remain the same.

Kizer will have to navigate any number of minefields, none more likely to be lethal than the road leading to Pickerington. An example: Last week, AMA Pro Racing announced expanded eligibility for the 2007 Formula Xtreme class. In a press release they said, "The changes to the eligible model list are the result of actions taken by the newly formed AMA Racing Committee created earlier this year as part of a reorganization of the AMA and AMA Pro Racing." The AMA Racing Committee is separate from the rules-making committee. The newly formed rules-making committee is comprised of one representative from each of the participating OEMs, plus an equal number, plus one, from within the industry. The FX rules were discussed in the one rules-making committee gathering, but not voted on. Which means their input was bypassed, ignored, or marginalized; not a good sign, but also not a complete surprise.

Welcome to AMA road racing, Keith.

September 13, 2006

Why Not Kevin?

Kevin Schwantz wanted to ride Ben Spies' Yoshimura Suzuki GSX-R600 at Road Atlanta. Spies, you'll recall, broke a metacarpal in his right hand in a 10.0 highside during Superbike qualifying at VIR a few weeks ago. The injury allowed him to end his half-hearted Supersport campaign three races early.

"I put my 12 minutes in," he said with a mischievous grin as the crew pushed the bikes back early in the VIR Supersport practice prior to the Superbike crash. The very sensible decision was made to allow Spies to park the 600 and concentrate on the Superbike Championship, which he's controlled since the second race of the year. Who then to ride it?

The obvious candidate was Danny Eslick. The enthusiastic and sometimes overly aggressive Oklahoman arrived in Atlanta second in the Supersport Championship. This was, if not remarkable, certainly admirable for the Mamushima Performance team. The team is a much more humble operation than that of most of the riders Eslick has humbled over the course of the year. At 20, Eslick could be the Suzuki rider of the future.

Kevin Schwantz represents Suzuki's past. He isn't the most recent Suzuki premier class World Champion - Kenny Roberts Jr. won the 500cc World Championship in 2000 - but Schwantz is the one that people remember and with good reason. What he did on the most evil-handling Grand Prix hand-assembled motorcycles ever defies belief, and common sense, which is why he only won one title. The RGV500s of the late '80s, and, to a lesser extent the early '90s, with powerbands peakier than the Rockies and frames as flexible as celery, required something above the ordinary to keep upright. Often enough, even Schwantz wasn't up to the task.

Retirement isn't easy on elite athletes. The evidence is most apparent in boxing, where the danger of loitering couldn't be starker. Motorcycle racers tend to find out their careers are over by different means - they can't find work. Not so for Schwantz. The Texan is one of the great 500cc World Champions of the '90s, all of whom were forced into retirement by injuries. For Schwantz, there were too many falls. More to the point, there was no great rival.

Once Wayne Rainey was paralyzed at Misano at the end of 1993, the motivation that made Schwantz a hero to a generation was no longer there. He retired in a tear-filled ceremony at Mugello in 1995 and his number 34 was retired. It was the first time that had ever been done and it hasn't been done since.

Schwantz didn't fade away. He tried his hand at car racing, but found it expensive and dishonest. Motorcycles were his and his family's life and he never lost that passion. He began the Kevin Schwantz Suzuki Schools at Road Atlanta. And he signed on as an advisor to the Yoshimura Suzuki team, not to be a figurehead, but to make a contribution.

It wasn't just the team that benefited. Schwantz served on the AMA Pro Racing board before it was summarily disbanded in last winter's purge. And he wanted to serve all the riders as their safety rep, though there was little support for that in halls of Pickerington.

Since his retirement, he's dabbled in motorcycle racing. He faced off against fellow GP stars Randy Mamola and Luca Cadalora, among others, in a BMW BoxerCup race in Italy. He raced much of the first season of the AMA Supermoto Championship. He did the Bol d'Or 24 Hours with a pair of French journalists. He did an endurance race at Road Atlanta. But he'd been absent from an AMA event for years.

That changed when he took over the EMGO Taiwan Suzuki GSX-R600 Formula Xtreme bike for Opie Caylor last year at Road America. Caylor, one of the KSSS instructors, had to be home with his expectant wife.

In practice he was well off the pace.

"I was like, 'How fast do you need to go?' They're like. 'Low 2:20.' I'm like, 'Where the f--k am I going to find eight f---ing seconds at?'"

He found more than half of it, qualifying with a lap of 2:23.877, less than four seconds off the 2:20.097 pole time.

Road Atlanta would have been perfect for a Schwantz cameo. He knows the track as well as anyone. He had plenty of time to get the Spies' 600 setup, including Thursday's promoter practice.

Most importantly, he wanted to do it and let Suzuki know it well in advance. There were two Spies' GSX-R600s to be ridden. Why not give one to Eslick and one to Schwantz?

Could he have won? Of course not. No one was going to beat Yamaha's Jamie Hacking - only one rider has on a Supersport bike this year. But the class isn't as deep as it once was. I believe Schwantz could easily have finished in the top 10, maybe as high as sixth if the stars lined up properly.

More importantly, it would have generated more publicity and good will for Suzuki than they seem to understand. Schwantz wasn't going to embarrass himself or his company. He knows his limits, something that couldn't be said during his glory days. And he wouldn't have asked if he didn't think he could fly the flag proudly.

Another reason to put him on the bike is that the AMA Superbike Championship isn't very exciting these days. Blame it on Mat Mladin and crew chief Peter Doyle. Between them, they've developed the Suzuki GSX-R franchise into the most prolific race winner in the history of AMA Superbike racing. Ben Spies is but one beneficiary of their efforts. Troy Corser is another. Suzuki is lucky to have them. Attempts by AMA Pro Racing to even the field - legalizing traction control, for example - have made little difference. The other factories haven't shown they want to win as badly as Suzuki. Or they've forgotten how.

No matter. The point is that they make it look easy; which it's not, and they're expected to win; which they've done with stunning proficiency; 17 of 18 Superbike races, 16 of 18 second places.

Which brings us back to Schwantz. Those of us lucky enough to watch him in his prime never quite knew what was going to happen. Would he win or would he crash? Either way, you wanted to be there. Either way, Suzuki was going to get noticed. Either way, we were going to get our money's worth.

There is a certain amount of nostalgia at work here. The 500s were unpredictable, evil beasts that required an often painful apprenticeship. Kevin Schwantz on a Suzuki GSX-R600 at Road Atlanta in 2006 isn't Kevin Schwantz on a Suzuki RGV500 at Hockenheim in 1991. (Check out the video on youtube.com.) But in a season mostly bereft of excitement, why not give us a glimpse of greatness past?

October 11, 2006

Slingin' in the Rain

A MA Pro Racing's policy on racing in the rain at Mid-Ohio is simple: "We won't race in the rain... unless it's raining." Makes perfect sense. You wouldn't want to race in the rain if it wasn't raining. Damn near impossible. But if it's raining, sure, we can do that. Look at other options. A policy so simple that it once again proves that you can't spell "amateur" without AMA (thanks, Pete).

This bit of wisdom can be attributed to Keith Kizer, the AMA director of road racing who managed to ram a Hummer full of built-up goodwill right into the side of a flaming outhouse at the Mid-Ohio Sports Car, not Motorcycle, Course.

The matter of racing in the rain came to a head - not the flaming one - just prior to the inaugural AMA Superbike Shootout season finale. Back on the weekend he was appointed in August, the AMA official formerly known as "Scooter" declared M-O unsuitable for rain racing after a tour of the road course with six-time Superbike champion Mat Mladin. He repeated that belief a month later at Road Atlanta. Then the tire companies were told to bring rain tires. Then came a change of heart. Then a statement at the Friday riders' meeting that there wouldn't be any racing in the rain unless it was going to rain all weekend - then it's okay.

The issue here is not the track's wet worthiness, but it's until recent aversion to rider input.

During a testy meeting among various interested parties, track owner Michele Trueman-Gajoch made the point that she'd done everything the AMA had ever asked and they still couldn't shepherd their riders onto the wet track. She made the point that all of the changes to the track, including the repaving, were done at the request of the two-wheel crowd. And it still wasn't good enough. She had one valid point, but she missed another.

The fact is she was discouraged from talking to the riders by at least one former AMA employee. Had she listened to the riders years ago, when she was wasting money moving the wrong walls and installing the wrong curbing, not only would she have saved countless thousands of dollars, she'd have had a racetrack you could race on any day of the year. Common sense seems to have prevailed after riders got together with track management during a test earlier this year. Two attempts to reach Trueman-Gajoch through the track PR department were unsuccessful.

Paving the track certainly helped in the dry and gave more traction in the wet, which meant higher speeds, and closer walls. The issue isn't the track surface, which already has more patches than a room full of Hell's Angels, but the walls - specifically the guard rail to the riders left on the back straight and another in turn nine. That one is particularly problematic since Mid-Ohio doesn't own the land on the other side of the fence and the owner has an inflated view of its worth.

"For me, it's always the walls, before anything else," Mladin said, "and it's been like that for a number years, that I've said it's more important to move walls than spend your money paving the racetrack. But they've paved the racetrack anyway. The walls really haven't been hardly moved."

Said Yamaha team manager Keith McCarty, who had a championship on the line, "I think the situation is, we all knew before we got here what we should and shouldn't be doing."

With Saturday wiped out by rain, the AMA rejiggered the schedule, keeping in mind Speed TV's four-hour window, and the promoter, but not the riders. At least that was the perception at a contentious riders' meeting held late on Sunday morning. AMA road race manager Ron Barrick tried to explain his point, that the schedule was inviolate - it wasn't - but instead found himself under attack by at least a few riders who should never have been given a voice. What should have happened, and what eventually did happen, was that the situation should have been worked out in private, away from the noise of the crowd.

The AMA, under orders from the promoter, was adamant that the heat races go forward. And the AMA insisted that the AMA Sports race, for amateur riders who'd qualified the weekend before, get plugged right into the middle of the day. With the exception of the 20 riders, their friends and families, no one, except possibly the AMA, believed they were worth jeopardizing the Superbike race over.

The reason the AMA wouldn't move the Sports race until the more sensible end of the day was because they wanted three minutes included in Speed's Supersport broadcast. For that, they were willing to scuttle the Superbike race. And they didn't get their three minutes.

The AMA's Kizer stood by Barrick's side and bluntly said that the schedule had to go forward, a decision he later regretted. But by then, the damage was done. The track would get its cherished heat races - two, not three, and no LCQ - and the fans would be treated to a breathtaking display of speed by six riders in one heat and four in the other. Which is not a knock on those privateers. They didn't have the luxury of a provisional start if they skipped the heats. Neither did the factory riders; at least they shouldn't have, according to the AMA rule book, which says that "In programs that require heat races, a rider must attempt to start a heat in order to qualify for the main event."

Furthermore, the supplemental regulations state that if the heat races didn't run, the grid would be set "based on the timed laps from all previous practice sessions run." Selective enforcement.

The heat races provided a peak into the future, a 10-rider Superbike race fought among much lesser-known riders. Would anyone care? No one had come to see them. No one was going to watch them on Speed.

Once the promoters got their heat races, and they realized the riders were resolute in their decision, a solution was devised. The Superbike riders, who were holding out for a dry track, would get 15 minutes of practice before their race. And the Supersport and Superstock riders would get a few extra laps before theirs, in addition to the laps they were previously promised. All that was left was for the top 10 riders who were permitted provisional starts to express their desire, and the field was set. But the damage was done.

"We had to fix this," Kizer said on Sunday night. "No matter what, we had to make this right. We had to make these guys feel comfortable that they could go out and run the race. We had an obligation to those fans to put on a show. I think in the end we did the right thing. I hope the riders will understand that I will state my original position when we were here in August that safety is the first concern, and that means a tremendous amount to me. I never want to put a racer out there on an unsafe racetrack. Let us go forth from here and we will make things a lot better than they were this weekend."

In his defense, Kizer is the most proactive AMA official when it comes to involving riders in issues of their own safety. Shortly he'll announce the formation of a rider safety committee, which will be tasked with inventorying the racetracks and deciding which ones are worthy of wet racing. At the moment, the list is depressingly short.

The Shootout turned out to be quite entertaining. Alaskan Ben Thompson, winner of the faster heat, comported himself well in mixing it up with the factory guys for the first several laps. And after the Shootout was red-flagged and restarted, the grid looked like a proper Superbike race - 22 riders, with the best at the front. Do we need more than that? No, but we all - riders, spectators, promoters, television - need a consistent track policy. Is that to much to ask for?

October 25, 2006

Where Were They?

If only there were grown-ups from Honda Racing Corporation (HRC) in Estoril. If only they'd have sat down young, impetuous Dani Pedrosa for a chat. If only they'd have explained how close Nicky Hayden was to the 2006 MotoGP World Championship. If only they'd have explained how many millions of dollars and thousands of man hours they'd poured into the team. If only they'd have explained the prestige that comes with winning the most prestigious crown in the motorcycle kingdom. If only they'd have explained how many hours, days, years that Hayden has dedicated himself to the single-minded pursuit of motorcycle racing's greatest prize.

But there were no grown-ups in the HRC camp in Estoril and Pedrosa was at his most selfish, which is why Nicky Hayden ended up in a gravel trap, railing obscenely at the injustice after his dream went down in a heap and Pedrosa slinked off in fear. And now HRC is facing the very real prospect of yet another humiliation at the hands of a brilliant rider they once drove away.

The difference between the Yamaha and Honda teams is striking. Pedrosa and Hayden are on two separate teams; Rossi and Edwards are teammates and friends. Can you imagine Hayden taking Pedrosa to a Las Vegas strip joint, as Edwards did with Rossi?

"I think the atmosphere in our team is great," Rossi said after finishing second to Toni Elias. "Is just one big team, not two, and Colin today have the chance to help me and he help me a lot, so I need to say thank you to him."

Last month in Japan Rossi told me that Yamaha was "Not just like a family, human. In Yamaha is always very good."

And on technical matters they trust the judgment of seven-time World Champion and crew chief Jerry Burgess, who's won 10 World Championships. "Sometimes Yamaha makes some work and they say, 'Okay, good work.' In Honda, never."

I found Nicky on Instant Messenger at close to 11 p.m. Sunday night. "It ain't over till the flag at Valencia," he wrote, and he's right. But he should be going to Valencia with a surplus of points, not the deficit he was levied by Pedrosa's astonishing blunder.

Assuming Rossi finishes, Hayden has to win the race, Pedrosa has to finish second, and Rossi third or worse. A week ago I wouldn't have believed it possible. Now I do.

Hayden proved in Portugal what I've said all season; if Honda gives him what he needs, he can win. They did, in the form of a clutch that worked at the start and throughout his brief race.

That the clutch would be problematic was something of a sad running joke, yet another sign of a lack of leadership. The problem, it turns out, wasn't the strength of the clutch but the spine of a test rider so eager to please that he was spineless. Maybe it was fear of job security. Hayden joked the guy might be angling for a raise. The murmuring inside Honda, based solely on the test rider's reports, was that there was nothing wrong with the clutch. As a former World Champion told me in Estoril, "Who do you think they're going to believe, Nicky or their test rider?"

A grown-up would believe they'd listen to the kid leading the World Championship.

There are, it must be said, some very good people at HRC. The belief in the press room was that if the avuncular Satoru Horiike, the HRC managing director, had been in Portugal, he'd have made it clear what was at stake. Horiike said in Motegi that there were no team orders. Hayden understood. Pedrosa had a mathematical chance to win the title. But team orders and common sense are two different things.

Horiike wasn't in Portugal. Neither was HRC boss Suguru Kanazawa, another racing man through and through and a supporter of Hayden's and of winning. Likely they were waiting to bask in the glow of Hayden's success in Valencia. Now they'll travel to Spain hoping that the rider HRC nearly rejected pulls off the upset of a lifetime over a rider that did reject them.

Camel Yamaha team manager Davide Brivio lauded the experience and common sense of Edwards after the race.

"The atmosphere is, like, really - every single member of the team wants to see Valentino win the championship, including Colin, so this makes things much easier," he said.

"For sure, for sure. That's what a team does. I know next year he's going to help me out to win it," Edwards said with a Texas twinkle in his eye.

Nicky Hayden very nearly cost Edwards his job. The night before he signed his Honda contract in Japan, Yamaha had the upper hand. Then someone woke up and realized what they were about to lose. Suddenly they'd hit the lottery. The penny pinchers cracked the piggy bank and found enough to approach, but not equal, either the Yamaha offer or one from Ducati that nearly came to fruition in Phillip Island.

Why the delay? The truth is that Honda never thought Nicky could win the title. Back at the Chinese Grand Prix, I asked HRC general manager Tsutomu Ishii about the evolution RC211V Hayden was pressured to ride. Was it capable of winning races at the start of the season?

"I don't think so," he said.

Do you think Yamaha's racing boss said the same thing to Valentino Rossi? Do you think anyone told Dani Pedrosa his bike wasn't capable? But they were willing to put Hayden in a position to not succeed. I asked how many races it would take for the evo-RV to win.

"How many? How many? Difficult to say," he said. "My feeling is soon coming. Because not only machine, but also his heart, mentality. Now I believe is so strong, can concentrate every race. Compared with last year, incredible change." A very nice thing to say about someone you've handicapped from the start.

Hayden refused to believe the bike wasn't capable of winning. Every time he was asked about the bike, he'd hesitate, say the right thing, and end with "It's all good." It wasn't good then and it's no good now. And no one could remember the last time they heard it was "all good."

A few hours after the Pedrosa debacle, Hayden faced the press. Mostly, he didn't need to be asked questions and a few were inane, as expected. He was resolute and forward thinking while railing at the injustice and choosing his words carefully. He didn't say Honda was to blame, but he wondered why there was no plan. The only time he came close to breaking down was when he talked about how much he poured into it. No one sees him when he's in the back yard with Earl on the stopwatch. No one seems him on his bicycle or in the gym. All they see is the million-watt smile and the umbrella girls and the eyes peering through the face shield and the champagne.

"He did come and talk to me," Hayden said, though he initially didn't want to let Pedrosa into his motorhome. And when he did, the conversation was very brief, very vocal, very one-sided, and very close up. Pedrosa likely feared for his safety and no one would have held it against Hayden if he'd have bitch-slapped his "teammate." But he didn't. That's not how he and his siblings were raised. He continued. His voice began to crack. This was from the heart.

"And, I mean, I'm sure he hates it. I mean he sincerely hates it. I'm sure he hates it for himself because it makes him look terrible.

But, I mean, I honestly would like to think the guy seen how much I put into it - knows what this means to me. Tuesday, when everybody else has went home, I was still out there testing. I mean, a guy with any kind of heart's got to know - World Championships - you don't get these opportunities all the time. It's not like I'm going to just brush it off, come back next Sunday. It could cost me the championship. That's something I couldn't live with the rest of my life."

If only there was a grown-up to tell that to Dani Pedrosa.

November 8, 2006

The Champ!

Nicky Hayden deserved to win the 2006 MotoGP World Championship more than anyone could imagine. He pours his heart and soul into his racing. He's humble in victory and gracious in defeat. This season he's become more animated, more open, and more of his personality has come through. He has a wicked sense of humor. And when he was introduced as the 2006 champion in the best-attended postrace press conference of the year, he got an ovation that would still be going if he didn't break in to stop it by thanking everyone.

In return, he asks for very little. A competitive bike, good tires, the support of the factory, and "It's all good."

Odd as this may sound, Nicky Hayden's championship wasn't in Honda's plans when the season started. The plan was to use Nicky as a test rider for next year's 800. The bike that he rode was a larger, 990cc version of the bike he'll test a few days after his championship. The figure of 80 percent was given on the similarities of their concepts, though very few parts were shared.

The bike made a very public debut at Brno in 2005. So we know it was on the drawing board well before that. Which means as early as the beginning of last year Honda had decided on the configuration of the 800. Lop one cylinder off the 990 and it's good to go.

How to test it? No amount of riding around a test track in Japan can replicate the demands of racing. If for no other reason than you have access to some of the best riders in the world, Nicky Hayden among them, racing a test bike would be efficient.

For the first several races, Nicky was bombarded with questions about whether he chose the evolution RC211V (Pedrosa rode the traditional model) or not. Mostly, he deflected the question and ended with, "It's all good." But it wasn't.

Honda Racing Corporation (HRC) was adamant that Hayden chose this bike. Hayden didn't contradict them. They contradicted themselves. The position that there was no pressure morphed into "it was strongly suggested" - another way of saying that the pistol being pointed at his temple had one empty chamber.

Hayden didn't complain; it's not in his nature and it wasn't how he was raised. But he did get frustrated, both by the endless and repetitive questions and by technical matters.

Even when he left the Red Bull U.S. Grand Prix with a 21-point lead on Rossi, and 34 on Pedrosa, there were concerns. The clutch was dysfunctional and immune to improvement. And the most grueling part of the season was about to come. Following the stand-alone Czech Grand Prix in Brno came the fly-aways, three races in three weeks on two different continents.

Hayden hemorrhaged points at Brno and in the fly-aways - Malaysia, Australia, Japan. Brno was his worst race to that point. Malaysia netted him a fourth, and then he got a pair of fifths in Australia and Japan.

Luck was on his side in Australia. Sixteenth on the first lap, it was clear the clutch wasn't any better. But changing weather produced the first flag-to-flag race, and Hayden had much better luck with his second bike. In Japan, he was again frustrated by the clutch. Not only does it prevent proper starts, but it hinders corner entry, which has become the most crucial element of a fast lap on a MotoGP race bike.

While he was struggling, Valentino Rossi was ascendant. In the four post-Laguna races he won a race, finished second twice and third once. By the time the series returned to Europe, he was upbeat and confident. And why not? The 21-point deficit had been reduced to 12. Next on the schedule was Portugal, a race Rossi had won many times that wasn't kind to Hayden. As unkind as it had been, Estoril 2006 would be the nadir.

When teammate Pedrosa punted him off the track on the fifth lap, it looked like his world had collapsed. Hayden retreated to his motorhome and cheered on Toni Elias, the Spaniard who's had little luck in the MotoGP class. If he was going to get his maiden win, now would be a good time. And it was.

Elias edged Rossi at the stripe in the closest-ever finish in MotoGP, .002 of a second. More important were the five points he denied Rossi, points no one would forget.

The victory by Elias gave Hayden hope at a time when very few thought he had any. Hayden himself admitted that Rossi isn't a "choke artist," that you can't spot the fastest rider in the world eight points with one race to go.

The clutch and the Pedrosa incident gave Hayden license to speak his mind in new and refreshing ways. He wished Honda had a plan before Estoril. He wished progress would be made with the clutch. But his comments were restrained.

A few days earlier, Rossi pointed out what Hayden wouldn't.

"Usually, in the past, or in everything, the good parts and the best treatment is for the rider that is in first position or is in front. In Honda this year, maybe it's the opposite. And this is, I think, the problem."

Hayden's initial reaction was telling.

"I mean, at times I got frustrated, because, I mean, you know, I probably should be the number-one rider - not, you know, the test rider," he said. As he continued, his comments softened, but he didn't entirely abandon the theme. "I know Rossi - I mean, you know, he loves to get stuff stirred up. He's good at it. And that's how he feels. I definitely feel at times that I did test too much and hurt myself. But I feel like I've learned a lot from it. I feel like I'm so much smarter as far as development, understanding the bike. I think we've made some mistakes. I can't blame Honda, by no means. I made some mistakes this year on my own."

His lone mistake in a race came when he ran off the track in Donington Park. That he'd wasted Friday testing a new chassis, while in the thick of the championship, was irrelevant, he said.

Rossi's original point is salient. Hayden has changed very little over the years. Once he'd clinched the title, he forgave Pedrosa for his bone-headed stunt, something many lesser men wouldn't consider.

"Dani... me and him are straight up," Hayden said. "We can just let all that die now. That's over with."

Racing is his life. Racing is his family's life. Racing is all he's ever wanted to do. What does the championship mean to him, his older brother Tommy was asked.

"I know what it means," Tommy replied. "It's as much as possible. It's as much as most people's next breath is what it means to him."

Rossi pointed out that four years in the cauldron of Grand Prix racing haven't changed Nicky Hayden.

"I'm very happy about Nicky winning the title," Rossi said hours after being denied an eighth title. In fact, Rossi would have liked Hayden as a teammate in 2007. But Hayden knew that he wouldn't get equal treatment, which was among the factors for his decision to remain with Honda.

"In my personal ranking, if I don't win, Nicky is my favorite, because is a great guy, apart of a great rider," Rossi said. "We fight a lot this year on the last race for the championship, but our relationship out of the track is exactly the same as 2003 when Nicky arrive in Honda. This is not easy for this sport, for this type of sport, this type of riders. I like him, I like his family. For example, his father come personally to my motorhome after Portugal to make congratulations after Nicky crash. So I say, f---, is very much a gentleman. He's a gentleman when Pedrosa touch him always. I think he deserves the championship."

Nicky Hayden does deserve the championship, but does Honda?

December 6, 2006

Giving Thanks

Sated and stuffed and slightly sedated by the tranquilizing tryptophan in too much turkey, I offer my reasons to give thanks for the coming year and years past, and apologize to the many deserving others who I wasn't able to include.

Terry Vance is living proof that good things happen to good people. The first time I met Vance I knew immediately this was no ordinary racer. The pair of us had taken refuge from the rain in the timing tower of Atco Raceway in South Jersey. He had as many questions for me as I for him. The difference was that he knew more about my business than I knew about his. And he was better at his job than I was at mine, and continues to be. From humble beginnings he and Byron Hines built the Vance & Hines name into one of the most respected businesses in the world of motorcycles. He was winning championships when I met him and hasn't stopped. His departure from the road-race paddock created a vacuum that hasn't been filled and probably never will be. Now if only someone could talk him into coming back.

Dunlop's Jim Allen is the most trusted man in the road-race paddock and for good reason. The "Vindictive Tire Baron," as an extremely misguided nitwit once labeled him in a publication, may be the lone individual whose lifetime of discretion, decency, and integrity allows him to be welcome in the transporter, garage, or pit of any Dunlop team. Racing is not an exact science and tires can be the most maddeningly frustrating piece of the puzzle. Dunlop's record in AMA Superbike racing is unmatched, mostly due to Allen's efforts. And when they fail, sometimes with spectacular destruction to both man and machine, Allen doesn't hide. Rather, he works that much harder to make sure it never happens again. And for that, most of the paddock should be thankful.

We haven't seen enough of American Honda's Merlyn Plumlee this year. Merlyn was at California Speedway, the closest race to his home, but illness prevented him from making any other races, and that's too bad. Merlyn is that rare individual you don't notice, but whose work is noticeable. He does his job quietly and brilliantly and let's others take the credit. He was instrumental in Nicky Hayden's formative years with American Honda and the two remain close, which seems about right, because Nicky has a habit of surrounding himself with good people and they don't get much better than Merlyn.

It's hard to mention one without the other, Rainey & Schwantz, Schwantz & Rainey. Long after their bitter rivalry ended, the two forged a friendship based on mutual respect. Only they knew how much they'd elevated each other's greatness. Rainey doesn't travel much, but he's a critical observer of the race scene, watching MotoGP races on "SPEED" as if they were live; don't even think of calling or e-mailing him with results on Sunday morning. Schwantz is Suzuki's ambassador to the world, a job which never seems to tire the tireless Texan. (Note to Suzuki: The next time he asks to race in the Supersport class, say, "yes" - Jim Allen says it's okay). I saw him last at Valencia, the first stop on a worldwide tour that would take him to Barcelona, the Canary Islands, and the Macau Grand Prix. If you could mix Rainey's single-minded determination and laser-like focus with Schwantz's sheer love of racing and "How'd he do that?" style, you'd have...Valentino Rossi.

Valentino Rossi may go down in history as the greatest road racer of all time. In Motegi, as his run at championship leader Nicky Hayden was gaining steam, I asked him if there was pressure to win an eighth title. "For me, I don't have to win. I won a lot: I am seven-time world champion. I am 27. If I don't win this year, I try another time next year." He will try in ways very few among us understand, and for that, we're all very lucky.

"Canceled because of poor lighting" is how the debacle of the Syracuse Mile is described in the results section of the Harley-Davidson media website. This is not an aberration. Dirt track, which remains the most exciting form of two-wheeled racing on earth, especially the Miles, is a very hard way to make a living, which is why we should appreciate champions like Jay Springsteen and Chris Carr. That they can not only stay motivated but continue to excel is a testament to their determination. Springsteen is an American original, easily the most popular rider at any dirt track, as well as the Daytona vintage road races. When he wasn't setting a new land-speed record, Carr took the Grand National Championship title chase to the last race before being knocked out with a mechanical. But he remained utterly professional, which is why he has the best outside-the industry sponsorship in the sport. And why he will take the title chase to the last round in 2007.

It's too bad James Stewart wasn't born a few years earlier. Seeing him and Ricky Carmichael both in their prime of their careers would have set a new standard for rivalries. Watching the pair square off in the deep sand on a sweltering day at MX 338 in Southwick, Massachusetts, was clear evidence of how much better they are than the rest of the field. Without Carmichael to push him, Stewart could become the next in a short line of very dominant motocross and Supercrossers led by Jeremy McGrath. But with Carmichael moving part-time to four wheels and the same possibly in Stewart's future, the rivalry may soon continue well into the future.

What would we do without "SPEED?" The racing channel allows us to channel our inner racers all day Sunday and beyond, thanks to DVRs and the like. That they've stuck with the AMA Superbike Championship through years of interminable red-flag delays and puzzling scheduling is something we should be grateful for. To say nothing of the MotoGP broadcasts, voiced by the very excitable Englishman Nick Harris and his soporific sidekick, Mark Bracks. Now if they could only dose the tea pots of the screaming World Superbike announcers with Ritalin, I might turn on the volume.

All things Hayden. Nicky won the MotoGP World Championship with the support of his parents, Earl and Rose, and siblings, Tommy. Roger Lee, Kathleen, and Jenny, as well as the American motorcycle racing community, and anyone who's ever been converted by the million-watt smile and homespun charm. Earl "the Squirrel" very cheerfully does the heavy lifting, leaving 2nd Chance Auto Sales in the OWB to jet through time zones, living airport to hotel to motorhome, and spreading Kentucky wisdom along the way. He doesn't go to all the races; Rose goes to a few, as does Nicky's trainer Aldon Baker, and Reynolds Wrap might make the occasional trip. But on the rare weekend when Squirrel's not at a grand prix, he's probably watching a monitor and holding a clipboard and keeping tabs on Tommy and Roger Lee in Ohio or Wisconsin or Alabama or California. During the news conference following his MotoGP World Championship, Nicky put it best when he said, "Honestly, we grew up in Kentucky at the end of a dirt road, and just - our family - we race motorcycles. And motorcycles have been really good to my family."

And for that, we should all be very thankful.

January 24, 2007

The Untold Story

Twenty-five years later, Rob Muzzy thought it was okay to talk. I called Rob to talk about his drag-race plans last week, and I could tell he was busy. After a few years struggling with Buell motors in the NHRA Pro Stock Bike class, he was back with Kawasaki, the factory where he had his greatest success. It was also where he was working when he had one of his greatest frustrations. It is one of the greatest stories never told.

Eddie Lawson wasn't going to beat Freddie Spencer in the 1981 Daytona Superbike race. The KZ1000 was too slow compared to the Honda. Kawasaki had only one hope: If they ran one pit stop instead of two, they might save enough time to stay close. Even that would probably only gain them second place. They knew they weren't going to win unless Spencer ran into trouble.

"Back in those days we'd probably gain about 20 to 30 seconds by skipping a pit stop," Muzzy said on another busy day at his shop on Monday morning, January 15. "Everybody had to stop [twice] except us."

The trick was finding a way to get more fuel into the system. The standard ZX1000 tank didn't hold enough to make it to the finish with only one fuel stop. They didn't need a lot more, just enough for a few more laps. So the team put their heads together and came up with a simple - but effective - solution.

AMA rules mandated that an overflow tank be connected to the fuel tank. Normally, this tank would be empty when the race started. But what if that tank was filled with fuel also? And if so, could that fuel reverse course to feed the fuel tank? The answer was yes, and the mechanics involved are simple. Fuel from the overflow tank would be sucked back into the gas tank if the tube from the gas tank to the overflow tank reached the bottom of the filled overflow tank.

"If you put the tube to bottom of the catch tank, it will suck it back in," Muzzy said, adding that that's how the overflow tank on a radiator works. "Fundamentally, we made a rather large catch tank. For it to do any good, we had to fill the tank up, but by filling that tank up, it used that gas first; then the gas tank would work."

What they were doing wasn't, strictly speaking, illegal, he says.

"We figured we'd get away with it one time," he said. "Then if they figured it out, they'd outlaw it. We weren't breaking the rules, we were just finding the way around it. I'm sure Honda would have thought we were breaking the rules."

"We had this really neat plan," Muzzy continues, "but like all things like this, you have to worry about who knows about it. What I'm saying is, nobody knew about it other than very close people on the team."

He can't remember how many people were in the garage, but four at most, one of them being team manager Gary Mathers. Lawson, obviously, was in on the fix.

For the system to be pressurized the overflow tank had to be filled through the overflow tube; the fuel couldn't be poured directly into the overflow tank. Now comes the hitch: As they were in the final minutes of preparing to head to the grid, with the garage door down, they received an unwelcome visitor, in the form of one of the managers from Kawasaki. Not wanting to cause suspicion, and also not wanting to be inhospitable, the team had to wait until he left, not letting about on the plan they were hatching.

"What happens is, we flat ran out of time," Muzzy said. "We don't get the tank filled well, but Eddie [Lawson] doesn't know that. He doesn't know."

The team made it to the grid just in time for the warmup lap.

As expected, Spencer was in charge of the race, but Lawson was able to stay near the front. The first pit stop went as planned. Lawson thought that was it.

"Eddie thinks it's okay, and he thinks he can go with only one stop," Muzzy said. The team signaled for him to pit. He ignored it. "We're trying to tell him to come in. He's shaking his head no. Any gas that spilled out or poured out got sucked back in and he could see it was a clear tank. He made the choice not to come in. And he thought he knew something we didn't know, and we knew something he didn't know, but of course you can't write on the pit board, 'We didn't get the gas in, hey, come in.'"

The *Cycle News* race report that day, written by Gary Van Voorhis, noted that Lawson coasted to a stop about two miles - half a lap - from the finish. He ended up sixth. Still, he went on to win five races that year and the 1982 Superbike Championship. That was the springboard to the World Championships, where he became America's most prolific champion, with four 500cc titles.

None of which mattered on the day. Mathers, at the time, wasn't happy.

"I really don't know what was going through Eddie's head," he said in the *Cycle News* report before hearing Lawson's explanation. "It was a mistake to do that. If he had been able to draft one of the fast guys for as little as five laps, he probably would have saved enough gas to have made it, but he lost that chance when he smoked the tire on the start and lost the lead group."

Van Voorhis wrote: "Mathers left the Kawasaki pits soon after the finish, preferring to cool down a bit before talking to his star rider."

It was Mathers who first told me of the incident, about five years ago.

I asked Muzzy about the mood in the garage when Lawson returned.

"I don't remember; obviously we were all frustrated," he said. "It would have worked, had we have been able to get the fuel in it."

As to how they were able to keep it a secret for so long, Muzzy wasn't sure. For at least 10 years, no one knew, he said.

"So nobody, as far as I know, ever let that out of the bag."

I told Muzzy I'd heard another story. It was about a motorcycle that was underweight at the end of the race. But the team manager convinced the AMA tech inspectors that it hadn't made weight because of the oil it had burned. So they were allowed to add a quart of oil that somehow weighed several pounds more than a quart of oil should have. Turns out the oil bottle contained more than oil; it was filled with buckshot.

"I can't believe the AMA didn't catch that," Muzzy said, but added, "That wasn't me, that was... ," he said, before naming someone currently involved in racing. That story is for another day.

February 7, 2007

Who's Next?

The future of American road racing is bright, contrary to what I wrote in this space not long ago. There are boys and at least one girl eager to continue the legacy of Roberts, Spencer, Lawson, Rainey, Schwantz, Roberts Jr, and Hayden.

For some, their single-minded commitment echoes that of past champions like Rainey and current ones like Hayden. They are consumed by racing and have but one ultimate goal. And you may not have heard of any of them.

The next American World Champion probably isn't old enough to drive, attend college, or surf for porn. He or she lives at home with their parents and attends high school, maybe a senior, maybe a junior. He or she isn't eligible for an AMA pro license, but that doesn't matter. He or she may never ride in an AMA-sanctioned professional road race.

The path to MotoGP is no longer through the AMA Superbike Championship. Quite the opposite, Englishman Chaz Davies will race the Celtic Racing Yamahas next year precisely because he couldn't get a MotoGP ride. And because of his size - he's nearly 6 feet - some believe he's simply too tall to ever race MotoGP.

The future is in the hands of jockey-sized adolescents who by the time they're 16, the legal age for an AMA pro license, will be well on their way to greater ambitions. They will have honed their craft in club races before bypassing the AMA and going straight overseas. And because they'll grow up away from their parochial American colleagues, they may be hard-pressed to develop a following in their home country.

Who's Next?

Dani Pedrosa is the poster child for the less-is-more set. The elfin Spaniard is the protégé and glamour project of Alberto Puig, a man who smiles as often as Pedrosa wins slam-dunk contests. Puig knows something about suffering. He shattered his left leg in the 500cc French GP at LeMans in 1995. The crash was so bad that the track was taken off the calendar for six years while safety was upgraded. The accident has left Puig in considerable pain, despite repeated visits to the famed Mayo Clinic in Minnesota. This is a man who knows something about sacrifice.

Pedrosa won three championships in a row before making an impressive MotoGP debut in 2006. The MotoGP website lists his weight as 112 pounds, which is about right for a 14-year-old. But rather than being a handicap, it's thought to be an asset in the increasingly corner-speed- and electronics-driven world of Grand Prix racing. (The recent tests in Sepang, where Pedrosa was fourth behind Rossi, Hopkins, and Capirossi, may contradict that.) Pedrosa made short work of the smaller classes, winning the 125cc World Championship in 2003, then the 250cc crown the next two years. His rapid ascent was paralleled by an increasing emphasis on corner entry and engine management in MotoGP so by the time he arrived, backing into corners and sluing wildly on the exit was both out of fashion and inefficient. Rather, they resemble slot-car racers with both wheels in line. And the move to 800cc seems to amplify this tendency.

The longer a rider stays on a big production four-stroke, the more difficult the transition. The only AMA Superbike rider who may have a chance of going overseas with a good team is Yoshimura Suzuki's Ben Spies, but even he admits there's no hurry. The tall Texan has no raging ambition to walk away from a very comfortable lifestyle and paycheck for a more rigorous, less remunerative nomadic existence. And from a riding standpoint, he's smart enough to know he's not yet ready to face the world's best.

There's also the question of machinery. Suzuki hasn't exactly bathed itself in glory the past six years. No one will forget the spectacle of Rizla Suzuki's John Hopkins kicking his GSV-R990 after it blew up in Qatar, one the team's eight engine failures on the weekend. There are, however, recent signs of hope. Hopkins was a revelation at the Sepang tests - first place the initial two days and a close second to Rossi on day three.

While Hopkins battles Hayden and Rossi and Pedrosa, the next American World Champion will be racing against riders most of us know little about, on tracks that are mostly absent from the AMA calendar. The pool of riders from which the next champion will likely emerge includes New Yorker P.J. Jacobsen, the 125 USGPRU and Can-Am champion; Red Bull rookies Cameron Beaubier, J.D. Beach, and Kris Turner; Elena Meyers; and 2005 Horizon Award winner Steve Bonsey.

Bonsey has been taken under the wing of fellow northern Californian Kenny Roberts. We know how a few of his projects have turned out; Rainey and Roberts Jr. spring to mind. We also know about Kurtis Roberts and John Kocinski, who somehow managed to control his idiosyncrasies long enough to win two World Championships.

Bonsey has virtually no road-racing experience and is by far the biggest challenge. He's road raced a few times, done some track days, and has taken part in a Freddie Spencer school. He appears to be a quick study. Those who've seen him have come away impressed. Suzuki Sport showed interest last season. According to the current AMA licensing rules, he wouldn't qualify for an AMA Superbike license. And yet, in 2007 he'll be racing in the 125cc World Championship. To paraphrase Jerry Seinfeld, "Let me get this straight; he can't race an AMA Superbike, but he can race against the best 125 riders in the world?" Somewhere, somehow the King must have photos of an FIM or Dorna grandee with a bull, and not a red one.

The greatest irony of the move is that Bonsey is being fed to the angry tiddlers aboard a Red Bull KTM, the Austrian company with which Roberts has some recent unpleasant history. In 2005, KTM and Team Roberts entered into an agreement - there's some question whether it was ever signed by Team Roberts - that had KTM providing engines for the Roberts MotoGP machine. But the wheels came off and the engines were removed just past midseason. What followed was a period of acrimonious back and forth and finger-pointing, and the threat of legal action. Less than two years later, they're spooning in the same sleeping bag. Likely this is because the 125 program is run by KTM race director Harald Bartol, a longtime friend of Roberts who runs the program autonomously.

Bartol and Puig are the principals behind the Red Bull MotoGP Rookies Program, the one that produced Pedrosa. Turner, Beach, and Beaubier were three of the very lucky and talented riders among the 1100 who fought to get into the Red Bull Rookies Cup. Their reward is the chance to face off against 20 others from around the world on identically prepared 125cc KTMs as a support class at seven of the European MotoGP races. They'll be racing in front of their potential future employers, a luxury not available to AMA riders. The best of that crop will advance to the Red Bull Rookies Academy or straight into the 125cc World Championship.

Jacobsen was two weeks shy of qualifying for the Red Bull program. The 2006 season was his first in road racing. In his third-ever road race, and first in the wet, he finished third at Shannonville Motorsports Park riding with an injured hand. Then he got hot. He won every other 125 USGPRU event that he entered, including the finale at Miller Motorsports Park, plus the AMA Grand National Championship 125cc finale at Mid-Ohio. Now that he's 13, there's talk that he may get a tryout with Puig. What that means, no one really knows. And if it doesn't happen, he'll spend another year beating everyone in his path, which he's already done.

Only time will tell which of these speed prodigies emerges as the best of their generation. It is worth our effort to seek out their exploits. The battle has already begun. The legacy will continue.

February 21, 2007

Love Is In the Air

Valentine's Day is quick upon us, which makes it appropriate to ask, "Where's the love?" I'm not the only one who's curious. The allegedly influential Road Race Committee wants to know where the love is after being marginalized by the wizened wizards of Westerville. The love, the spurned committee members should know, is still in the air, but that air is only to be breathed by AMA Pro Racing's newest valentines.

Decisions that affect everyone in the paddock, mostly negatively, though notably not so in one glaring case, are being made by a group whose time in office can be measured in months. Years would be better, but just barely, and nothing like the decades of accumulated wisdom represented by the Road Race Committee. If only they'd told Gary Mathers.

Mathers, you'll remember, is the most successful team manager in the history of motorcycle racing, with serial success that stretched across brands, disciplines, and platforms. It is the belief of myself and many others that he's the person to run AMA PR. But it was made clear that if he took the job, he wouldn't be running AMA PR - he'd have to answer to committees. That was a non-starter. That also turns out to be scat.

The most recent evidence was unilaterally imposed on the road-race world without the benefit of discussion. One fiat has no support among the factory teams, the very same that enthusiasts come to watch, and the other has very little support. Given the reception they've gotten - think incontinent hunchbacks with genital warts crashing an orgy - I asked one of the committee members at a recent California Speedway test why he bothered. His answer, "I don't know."

What he and everyone else knows is that someone in Ohio thought it only fair that everyone be allowed to practice on Thursdays. The argument is that the privateers can't afford to rent tracks and take part in tests, as the factory teams do. And if the factories did ride on Thursday, imagine the disparity in speed between the fastest Superbike and a wide-eyed Supersport rider on a track that may not have hay bales or an air fence properly placed. The flip side is that everything you hear out of Ohio is that they need to bring costs down, especially for the privateer. So how do you save privateers money? I know! Let them spend a day wrecking their bikes and using up their tires on Thursday, while having to spend more money on hotels and meals.

The AMA rulebook states that "At facilities where road races are to be held, exclusive track rentals by participants, including manufacturers, teams or individuals, within ten days preceding the first day of official practice, are not allowed." How to get around it. "Regional race meets, promoter/racetrack organized open practice and open schools are not restricted," the rulebook says.

Factory riders were banned from testing in the past, leading many to ask "What's a factory rider?" That question came to a head last year when Yamaha's Eric Bostrom and Erion Honda's Josh Hayes were pursuing the Formula Xtreme title. Hayes was allowed to ride on Thursday, Bostrom wasn't. Did it make the difference in Hayes winning the title?

Instead of calculating some porous formula that disallows factory riders, riders in the top 10 in points from this year or last, or any other, there's a much easier solution - make a list. The riders on the list can't practice. End of discussion.

The factory teams are hopeful they can come to a gentleman's agreement that will protect them from themselves, hopeful being the key word. Asked if they'd stick to it at the final race with a championship on the line, the answers were more equivocal.

The main beneficiary of Thursday practice at several tracks last season, and at three AMA Superbike venues this year, is the Team Hammer School. In order to ride on Thursday, you have to sign up with the school, which falls under the "open school" language of the rulebook. The charge is $175 if you pre-register, $225 on-site, according to the team website. The school is run under the umbrella of Team Hammer, whose principal owner is John Ulrich. Ulrich, who twice worked for *Cycle News*, wears a number of hats - team owner, publisher, AMA board member - which means that on far too many matters, he's conflicted.

There is no evidence that Ulrich had anything to do with the decision to open Thursday practice, but more than one person pointed out that he had the most to gain. In any discussion of the matter, it would be essential that he recluse himself. And no one denied him the right to profit from the AMA decision, only that Pro Racing have the (apparently lacking) good sense to allow the Road Race Committee to have its rightful voice.

The other hot-button issue is pit-lane speed at Daytona International Speedway. Unlike every other track on the AMA calendar, there has never been a pit-lane speed limit at the Speedway. Has this been a problem? Apparently not. No one I spoke to at the Fontana test could remember a pit-lane accident of any kind during practice or the race. (One consistently over-exuberant rider was singled out, but that's for his team to discipline.) Now we have a 50-mph pit-lane speed limit. Where does it start? It would have to be prior to the beginning of the pit box closest to the banking. Which means when the 200 leaders come off the banking at over 180 mph, veer down to the dirtiest patch of the track and clamp on the brakes, they can only pray they won't get Brokebacked by a rider with less talent, less brakes, less tires, and less to lose. At least twice during the race. Remember the first year of the pace car, the tortoise-like Pontiac Aztek, and the carnage that was strewn over the back straight when everyone had to make sudden stops? Day at the beach.

Pit-lane proficiency is among the reasons Miguel Duhamel has five Daytona 200 wins. Teammate Jake Zemke figures Miguel is about four or five seconds quicker per stop. Yoshimura Suzuki's Mat Mladin used his expertise to make three pit stops and still win in 2004, the last year of the Superbike 200.

Much of the excitement of the otherwise interminable 200 comes during the pit stops. Watching the riders parade down the pit lane at 50 mph will do little to keep the crowd from lining up for another $6 beer.

The counterargument is that it should be safer, which might be true, if you don't get run over first. More than that, it's a solution to a problem know one knew existed. What about the real problems? Regardless, it's important enough to be put to the Road Race Committee.

So who has AMA Pro Racing caressed to their collective bosoms? What previously ignored group has suddenly been elevated from the status of leper? Who have they quixotically allowed a happy ending, after years of playing the role of fluffers?

Decades of treating the riders - the most important element of the show - like toilet brushes, has, I think, come to an end, with the formation of the Rider Safety Committee. I say, "I think," because at the top reaches of the reliably-unreliable communications department, no one has deigned it necessary to make this announcement, even though it's the sort of positive news that they complain is never reported. For anyone paying attention, start typing, then hit "Send." If you need help, let me know: I think I could whip something up in the almost two weeks since I got wind of it. Or you could just lift what Mladin said off of the *Cycle News* site. You wouldn't be the first.

In separate phone conversations following the first of two recent Fontana tests, Mladin and Jake Zemke both told me that they, and three others, had been asked to be part of the committee. Mladin had told me at the Dunlop Daytona test that he would have no part of it, but we both knew otherwise. The six-time Superbike champion, his team manager, Don Sakakura; and most of the paddock feel that safety is the number-one issue.

Mladin would like to see the day when every track is suitable for wet-weather racing. It won't happen during his career, but he's committed to ensuring those who follow will have safer tracks. He is an asset of the first order, as is Zemke, Jamie Hacking, Tommy Hayden, and Ben Bostrom - the other committee members. Now is their moment; they're the ones feeling the love. They should embrace it. Because as we know, when it comes to the wizards of Westerville, love is fleeting.

March 7, 2007

Daytona 200: A Year Later

A year has passed since we first lived through the not-very-touching tale of the "Little Pace Car That Couldn't." The little pace car that couldn't was a white Honda Accord that couldn't find its way on the 2.95-mile road course at Daytona International Speedway. And because it couldn't find its way, it couldn't find the leader of the Daytona 200. And because it couldn't find the leader, the sun-baked spectators who forked over a good amount of folding green to watch a field of racers whose talent levels ranged from very good to "What the hell is he doing out there?" were denied the chance to see what might have been a memorable race. As it was, the race will forever be remembered for AMA Pro Racing's less-than-competent performance of the pace car procedure. (Almost unnoticed was that a very deserving Jake Zemke won the race by 1.562 seconds over a charging Josh Hayes.) It will also be remembered, one can only hope, as the last time AMA Pro Racing ran a pace car with one occupant.

Ron Barrick drove last year's pace car with no one riding shotgun. He didn't know it at the time, but the Daytona weekend marked the beginning of his final year as the AMA Road Race Manager. (Morgan Broadhead, formerly of American Suzuki, replaced Barrick late last year: Barrick remains with AMA Pro Racing.) Barrick admitted in a postrace news conference that the reason there was no one else in the car was that "just basically we were short on personnel." This stunningly dunderheaded display of penury infuriated many, including the riders and especially Miguel Duhamel.

Duhamel had dug himself a hole with a gymnastically inspired handstand/crash in turn one with about a 12-second lead. A record-setting sixth victory in the 200 was well within his grasp when the Honda CBR600RR went out of his grasp, just barely. Duhamel did an admirable job of hanging on longer than your average bull rider before his Shark[1] took a bite out of the tarmac. Unfazed by the get-off, and protected by his lid, Duhamel picked up the wrecker and began to redress his mistake. But any chance of victory ended when he and Eric Bostrom were the victims of mistaken identity. Rather than putting the Accord in front of Jake Zemke, the race leader, Barrick brake-checked Bostrom and Duhamel. Once the mistake was made, neither Barrick nor anyone in race control did anything to correct it.

"The bottom line," Barrick said after the race, "is they finished in the same order at the end as they were in before the pace car came out."

Mention that line to Miguel at your own peril. He admits to having made a mistake, though now with speculation that he might have run over someone's tear-off or leaking fluids. Well back when the pace car came out, he would have been in the thick of the pack had he been in his proper place, rather than nearly a lap behind. And if the same thing happens this year, watch closely: That lone red streak on the banking will be Miguel taking matters into his own hands.

Duhamel is one of three factory riders taking part in the 200; Jake Zemke and Jason DiSalvo are the other two. Eric Bostrom has no interest. DiSalvo's interest in the 200 forces Yamaha to contest all four classes at Daytona, a form of madness worthy of analysis. Team manager Tom Halverson said the Graves Motorsports crew would be able to help out in Saturday's Superbike and FX races.

---

[1] Shark is the brand of Miguel Duhamel's helmet.

Supersport and Superstock are on Thursday. Halverson also said that it had always been a goal of DiSalvo's to win the 200.

"Eric [Bostrom] wants to focus on the Superbike," Halverson says. "Jason [DiSalvo] thinks he can do both, it's just an important goal for him. We said yes and we're going to support him in full for this year."

The cost of running the 200 dwarfs that of any other race. The tab runs higher for Yamaha, which is building a very highly modified and expensive motorcycle for one race. This is not something they would want to make a habit of.

Duhamel was credited with a time of 1:39.726 at the December Dunlop Daytona tire tests. The time was two seconds faster than DiSalvo's best. It was four seconds quicker than Zemke. It was half a second quicker than his own best Superbike time. It was also total fiction. The transponder wasn't on his CBR600RR, but on his second CBR1000RR Superbike, which means that the times were actually quite close for the first several riders. But those were different motorcycles than will show up in March, and Duhamel was encouraged by the progress of his one-off FX weapon when he tested it again at California Speedway in early February.

"We will be extremely competitive with this bike," he said.

He also said that the race would be among him and the three J's - Jake, Josh and Jason - before throwing in the second Erion Honda of Aaron Gobert. There might be one other rider who can finish on the lead lap. Mostly the leaders will spend a few hours muttering to themselves, "Didn't I just lap that guy?" One rider was lapped 10 times last year.

That doesn't happen in the much shorter Superbike race, but if it did, the riders doing the lapping would be Ben Spies and Mat Mladin. Spies has the confidence of beating Mladin repeatedly en route to last year's Superbike title. If it again comes down to the final lap, as it did in 2006, he won't be snookered. Spies has been the fastest rider in every preseason test. Mladin knows what went wrong last year and plans to fix it. Winning Daytona, a race he's won four times - three times when it was the 200 and again in 2005, the first year of the shortened Superbike race - would be a bold statement.

Suzuki has won for many years by having the best riders on the best bikes. That isn't changing. Long accused of using traction control, this year they finally can. And they're light-years ahead of the competition. Not only do they have a brand-new GSX-R1000, but they've fitted it with a Mitsubishi traction-control system that's been battle-tested in MotoGP. Fine-tuning will be an ongoing process, but they have the luxury of starting well ahead of their rivals who have little or no cooperation at the world level.

American Honda will be throttling the oldest machine in the field for another year. The CBR1000RR is a graying 4-year-old, now fitted with Magneti Marelli traction control. The gap to the Suzukis will close, but it won't evaporate. Miguel or Jake could easily fill the podium if Tommy Hayden hasn't come to grips with the Suzuki by race time. Otherwise, it could be the first of many Suzuki sweeps.

What of Yamaha and Kawasaki? Yamaha began working on its Superbike project last June. It has been a much more difficult task than Yamaha envisioned.

"We knew it would be a lot of work," Yamaha's Halverson began, "but now, with this traction control, it seems like it's going to be constant development and learning."

Kawasaki has been behind since the start of the testing season. To expect a huge leap at Daytona is a huge leap.

And no one makes huge leaps at Daytona, if you exclude Miguel, who leaped out of his saddle and onto the ground before taking up the fight, only to be denied by the "Little Pace Car That Couldn't."

April 4, 2007

Bring It On

Great minds think alike. Or at least I can flatter myself into believing that when the other mind belongs to one of the greatest dirt trackers of all time.

"How cool would it be if someone could resurrect the Indy Mile on the same weekend of a U.S. GP in Indy if they run one in 2008?" I asked a rider with a history of success in the Indy Mile in the pits of Wednesday night's Daytona short track.

"I'm already working on it," was the answer.

Chris Carr knows a thing or two about dirt-track racing. He has seven Grand National Championships and six runner-up finishes in a career spanning more than 20 years, and there might have been more had he not taken a two-year detour into road racing. He was mostly new to pavement and Harley-Davidson was very new, and the combination didn't produce the results either is accustomed to.

But it's road racing that may provide a boost to what he and many others believe is the most exciting form of motorcycle racing in the world. During the February Indianapolis trade show, Carr was introduced to the decision makers at Indianapolis Motor Speedway. IMS is actively considering hosting a second round of the MotoGP World Championship at The Brickyard in 2008. The race would be a godsend for the legions of Nicky Hayden fans in the Midwest, including those in his neighboring home state of Kentucky. And it would also be the perfect opportunity to show the world what made Nicky and Kenny and Freddie and Wayne and Eddie and Junior the champions they became.

"If that came about, it would be the perfect opportunity to showcase flat track to the European contingent that have all heard about it but never had a chance to see it," Carr believes and, after a few minutes talking to him, it's clear he's given it a lot of thought.

Carr has a history at the Indy Mile. He won in 1992, again in '94, and took the final race held there in 1999. He remembers it being a fairgrounds race. You'd come in on Saturday afternoon and park in a remote lot, half a mile from the track in a field you'd share with livestock.

"We would be staged out there in our box vans and trucks and rental cars," he recounts, "and at three in the afternoon we paraded in, after horses got done running. They'd shoot a load of calcium chloride on the track, start practice at 6 o'clock and run through practice, time trials, heat races, and the main. It was always a decent show. The track was pretty good. It didn't take a ton of prep. We'd end up coming back on Sunday as well, a doubleheader."

Carr remembers scheduling problems leading to the demise of the race. The race dates got changed and the fair changed weekends, so another race got scheduled in its place. There were a few attempts to resurrect it on a non-fair weekend, but none were successful.

"One weekend was July 4," he remembers, "and everyone was scared to death. On that side of town, everyone was shooting off guns. You needed a police escort to get out of town."

Much has changed in the past eight years. Dirt-track racing has suffered a precipitous slide from the public consciousness while other forms of racing have risen to greater prominence. The dirt-track demographic skews close to the Harley-Davidsons, which means the fans are older. Carr, for whom age is just a number, would like to expose a new generation to the wonder that is dirt-track racing. Anyone who's seen a mile close up becomes an acolyte. There is nothing more visceral than a pack of Harleys thundering down the front straight and into turn one. You feel it in your bones and it resonates in a way that you'll find nowhere else. There is nothing more exciting than the final turn of the Springfield Mile, eight riders lined up in a row like they'd just come off the starting line, all aiming for the magical chalk line less than a quarter-mile away.

"There's no doubt that the tension level the last five laps of the Springfield Mile ratchets up pretty intensely compared to the first 20 laps," Carr says. "From a competitor's standpoint, you're just trying to put yourself in a position to try to win. It's not like watching Bristol [NASCAR Nextel Cup] yesterday, where the only way to get by a guy is a bump-and-run. In our deal, you do stuff like that and people get hurt. It's a strategic thing - an art form in a sense, kind of hard to understand... unless you're in the saddle. You can win races from a different position if you're in the right place at the right time. There's some luck, some skill, some plain courage."

MotoGP owes a debt to dirt-track racing, Carr thinks, because of the American champions it's produced.

"It's mostly a historical connection to their champions in the upper echelon of MotoGP and going back to 500cc GP before that," Carr says. "If they were given the opportunity to witness where these guys came from, it may open the doors to some type of racing in Europe as well.

"I think it's part of their history in a lot of sense when you consider the majority if not all of the American GP champions have some dirt track roots. [Kevin Schwantz is the exception.] The one with the least amount is Kenny Jr. He's been dirt tracking all his life; it's just been mostly in his back yard."

Carr points out there are already amateur pockets forming in Europe. There's a nascent dirt-track scene in England and Italy. The recent Daytona short track Grand National Championship season opener had an international field, with riders from Europe,

Japan and Australia. The irony is that dirt-track skills are mostly antithetical to what's needed for success aboard the new generation of MotoGP 800s.

"There's some interest worldwide in AMA dirt track, and if we bring the world here, there's no better place to show the motorcycling world what we're all about," Carr says.

More importantly, Carr believes, "We need to reintroduce flat track in a lot of senses to new people, and here you have the opportunity; if Indy runs a big motorcycle race like MotoGP or World Superbike, you have the opportunity to work with the main group."

He also believes it should be on Saturday night.

"By running a night race at the Indy Mile, we're not in competition with what's going on at the Speedway. There is an opportunity for the MotoGP riders, along with 150,000 others who are at the race, to come out and watch us. They're there to watch races. You go to a NASCAR event and they have racing from Friday to Sunday, and the dedicated fans are going to see all of it or most of it. And to have a dirt track in the vicinity of a major motorcycle race is better for the industry as well as flat track.

"We would love the opportunity to watch MotoGP, but were always racing that weekend. Here you have the opportunity and a facility that's capable of running our event in conjunction with MotoGP. I think it's a good opportunity for the fans and a good opportunity for MotoGP, because they've heard about it for years and we as fans get to see Nicky [Hayden]. We'd all love to be able to cheer Nicky on, because he's one of us."

Carr raced against Hayden a number of times, including in Nicky's final shot at the Grand Slam. It was the Du Quoin Mile in 2002, and Hayden was riding one of Terry Poovey's Honda RS-750s.

"I recall him going pretty good, but struggling a little bit. I think he just needed more time on the Honda. For those younger riders, it's little tougher bikes to get used to. They rev about 1000 to 1500 more rpm than the Harleys did.

"Du Quoin at nighttime, the few times that we've run there it is typically a slicker racetrack, and that made it harder for the Honda to come forward coming off the corners. I remember him not coming off the corners that well. He was nowhere near in the hunt completing the grand slam on that day."

And he probably won't be if IMS hosts MotoGP, though if Honda said it was okay, he'd have Earl looking for the steel shoe and two-piece leathers in a New York minute. Carr's willing to wait on a rematch.

"I told him a few years ago, before he was getting ready to go over the pond. 'Go make your millions, accomplish what you want to accomplish, and come back and play with us.'"

Hayden would certainly be a railbird if the Indy Mile runs. And he wouldn't be alone. He'd bring friends, friends like Rossi and Melandri and Capirossi and Checa and hopefully tens of thousands of others. And he'd take them down to turn one and listen for the whistle of the wind going through the rear-brake caliper and show them Carr and Coolbeth and Kopp backing it in, Then he'd take them to turn four and point out Murprhee and Schabel and Smith feet up and sideways, right hand powered on, left hand gripping the left fork tube, And the place would be lit up by Hayden's smile and, inside his helmet, Carr would be smiling, too.

May 16, 2007

Time to Move On

The experiment has failed. Running the Daytona 200 without all of the factory stars turns out to be as clever as driving solo in the pace car. And it's magnified when the factory Hondas end up on a Chevy pick-up truck after simultaneously expiring of not being able to respire.

Exploding tires caused the race to be downgraded from Superbike to Formula Xtreme in 2005. The movement began when Ben Spies left too many chunks of his teenage flesh on the front straight when his tire exploded at 186 mph during an October, 2003 test. That he survived is a miracle. But his suffering was enormous and he was scarred for life. Jason DiSalvo had his own catastrophic tire failure during the winter Dunlop test two months later. That prompted AMA Pro Racing to convene an extraordinary test to confirm the integrity of the next batch of Dunlops. Since then, there have been failures - Mladin and Eric Bostrom chunked fronts in this year's Superbike race - but nothing calamitous.

So a deal was struck between Daytona International Speedway and AMA PR. In exchange for long-needed track-configuration changes, the race bikes would lose 400ccs. Honda, alone among the factories in campaigning the FX class with Miguel Duhamel and Jake Zemke, was the big winner. Duhamel won in 2005, Zemke in 2006. Neither made the first gas stop this year. The only other factory to step in this year was Yamaha, and then half-heartedly - or rather "half-teamedly," if such a word exists, because Eric Bostrom had no desire to run the 200 or any other race at Daytona. Jason DiSalvo felt otherwise and Yamaha built him two one-off motorcycles. Which meant Yamaha was entered in every class at Daytona, aging Tom Halverson by dog years.

DiSalvo finished fifth, 42 seconds behind Attack Kawasaki's Steve Rapp, the unexpected winner. Rapp's win wasn't the fluke many saw it as. He'd kept the Hondas in sight during the brief time they were running and his pit stops were sterling.

But Rapp is journeyman, not a star, and running the Daytona 200 without the factory riders is like running the Daytona 500 without Junior, as one Florida sportswriter put it. And Honda could not have been happy at spending several hundreds of thousands dollars to be reduced to the role of spectator in a race they sponsor.

The idea of restoring Superbikes was discussed in a postrace conference call between the Speedway and AMA PR. At some point, the riders may be consulted. But they weren't immediately. So it was news to them that such a change was being discussed.

"I don't think it'd be a great idea at all," Spies said. "Now, you know the tires are getting a lot better, but they're still chunking here and there. Riding a Superbike on the banking, I can't even explain it. It's pretty scary, honestly. They're fast, man. We're going 200 mph and there's a wall right there. I've touched my elbow right on the wall before."

Teammate Mat Mladin was even more concise.

"That's a bad idea - it's too fast," he said, and he's won the Daytona 200 twice and the much shorter Daytona 44.25, also twice.

This year Mladin chunked a front tire, crashed, and then remounted. He'd worked his way back up to eighth before a front-tire vibration got so bad that he had to back off. He finished 10th.

Which was 11 spots better than Eric Bostrom, who, like Mladin, had led two early laps, His front tire required a 12th-lap replacement.

"They asked me on a few interviews before Daytona, 'Hey, now that Daytona's 15 laps, you're not going to have any tire trouble, right?' And we saw where that went," Bostrom said. "It's a bummer, because I know, fanwise, everyone would like it to be a Superbike race. But the fact is, it's a disaster. You put 80 motorcycles on a dodgy racetrack and there's going to be tire failures and you've got to do 68 laps. It's not fit for Superbikes. It's not fit for a 15-lap race, in reality. I hate to say that. They need to get their ass on one of these bikes and feel what it's like for the front end to push at 186 mph."

Last year's winner, Zemke, thinks bringing back 1000s would be pretty dangerous. He said the closing speeds in the 200 "are unbelievable the way the track is [with an 80-rider field]. The old track layout provided far more chances to pass. "The way it is now, it's really hard. There's a couple sections there in the new infield section where if you get stuck behind a guy, you're not gonna get him for a couple of corners."

Duhamel is tied with Scott Russell at five 200 wins each. His take on bringing back Superbikes evolved in a matter of minutes: "As long as everybody's good with it, it doesn't bother me too much. I'll know a bit more what to expect having ridden for 200 miles on the 600."

When it was pointed out that he'd be racing a 1000cc Superbike against 79 other riders for 68 laps on a smaller track with a gas tank that will require at least three top-ups, his view changed.

"Like you pointed out, it's going to be quite an issue," he conceded.

Superbikes won't return to the 200 before 2009, the year new Superbike regulations take effect. The super-secret road-race rules committee met at Fontana and the discussion centered on Superbikes. Regardless of what they come up with - early indications are Superstock motor, Superbike chassis, and allowing Ducati to go big - the 1000s will continue to be too powerful for Daytona. And other tracks will soon be overpowered.

"If you look at the Superstock class right now, they're only a second off of the Superbikes anyways, so what's the difference?" Zemke asks.

What, then, is the answer? Zemke believes it's in 600 Supersport, an idea championed by his boss, Chuck Miller. Zemke said it would be "a lot more affordable for all the manufacturers, or even for the guys who do Superbike only, to build a Supersport bike just for Daytona, rather than trying to build a Formula Xtreme bike, which we all know costs an arm and a leg to do that." Zemke said it would bring more of the top riders back into the class, because every manufacturer at that point could say, "Okay, here you go guys, go out there and run it."

And, he added, Supersport usually produces close racing at Daytona.

Duhamel agrees: "I think the best setup is with the 600s. I think it's the easiest setup. Unfortunately, [Formula Xtreme] is very expensive for all the teams, and not everybody wants to do it.

It's obviously also disappointing in the 200 not to have the best riders in there. Until somebody comes up with a better solution, I don't know what to do. It's Daytona, so I'll do whatever needs to be done as long as it's safe and we can go out there and do it."

Spies also agrees: "I think it should stay 600s. Until we figure something out, I just don't think it's a good idea."

Mladin believes that all the top riders need to be in the 200, but not on these motorcycles. He suggested restricting the bikes to 150 horsepower: "Everybody can ride a 150-horsepower motorcycle."

Any of the stock liter four-cylinders make well in excess of that. But, as the Daytona 500 proves, the Speedway is familiar with restricting horsepower. Duhamel also thinks it's time to take another look at the layout.

"Unfortunately, I was not involved with the track design," he said. "I wish we had more time and then, depending on the limitation - and there are some limitations, but I'd like to see a better infield track that would facilitate the Superbike running for 200 miles. On that track, it's going to be a handful. If that would be an option on top of it for 2009, and that's the truth, and we have 'til 2009 to come up with a good setup, then that could be something really interesting and finally put our concerns about the Daytona 200 to rest for many, many years."

At the end of the day, displacement isn't the problem. Horsepower isn't the problem. The infield isn't the problem. It's the speed and G-forces generated on the east banking and the run to the flag, and an unforgiving and far too close wall. It could easily be fixed to make it less dangerous for all bikes, but it won't be. And the next experiment, whatever it is, is doomed to failure.

May 30, 2007

Fan Speak

It wasn't one of the dullest weekends of motorcycle racing that drove me to distraction. That Mat Mladin was miles above the field wasn't the deciding factor. Nor was his teammate's mastery of the Superstock class. And it wasn't enough that the little bikes saved the day, with Josh Hayes showing that he deserves the chance to upgrade by 400cc with yet another double 600cc victory. Suzukis win the 1000cc races, Hondas more often than not win the 600cc classes. So it goes.

Mladin shouldn't be blamed. He's doing the job he's paid very well to do and doing it better than he did last year, and he has the support of a sterling team, probably the best in the paddock. This is vintage Mladin, the one that won six championships in seven years, the one who not only wins, but demoralizes. Five of seven wins this season, and 10 of 12 going back to last year, has knocked back the confidence of teammate Ben Spies, who, at this time a year ago, was enjoying a similar streak of his own. But that seems so 2006, and the Mladin train could easily steam to an early championship. Not that he cares. He continues to repeat his mantra: Championships don't matter, I just want to win races. (I wonder how American Suzuki feels about that?) But one begets the other, which means that if he continues on this path, an unprecedented seventh championship is a likelihood whether he wants it or not.

The class structure of the AMA Superbike Championship has been faulted by virtually everyone in the paddock. New rules are expected for 2009. The number of similar classes dilutes what is becoming an aging talent field. The championship is almost a closed society, with the principals playing musical chairs and very little new blood infused. But that's not all bad. The positive effect is that riders who make their career in the United States can establish loyal fan bases. And others can make an impression. This year, Englishman Chaz Davies has been a breath of fresh air, racing near the front for the scrappy Celtic Racing Yamaha team. Davies didn't make a friend of Roger Lee Hayden at Fontana, but Larry Pegram marveled at how closely they could race on a track with less runoff than a Skee-Ball alley.

Most, but not all, of the best riders are finally in Superbike, now that Yamaha has made the leap back in. But Ducati left, and with it went Neil Hodgson. Ducati would like to rejoin the fray in 2008, if its 1098 is approved in short order. Too much time and the window will close. The AMA series is the most prestigious National Championship and certainly the best-paying, which is what continues to make it an attractive destination. Ducati is enjoying record sales and needs to race.

But what of the races themselves? What do the fans think? To answer that, I cruised the pits and concession areas of Infineon Raceway, looking for answers. Out of sheer laziness, I spoke mostly with couples (two for one) or at least fans traveling in pairs. I tried for a broad cross-section of ages, ethnicities, and fan interest. There were track-day racers mixed with first-timers, families, couples and singles, and one tattooed and pierced female first-timer with a buzz cut. Their common interest brought them all together in Sonoma on a beautiful Sunday morning. What emerged was a thoroughly unscientific poll of what the AMA, track promoters, and riders should consider if they understand that racing is, first and foremost, entertainment.

Infineon Raceway may be the best venue to survey. Track president Steve Page and PR man extraordinaire John Cardinale are constantly experimenting with new ways to make fans happy. This is a track with a wealth of knowledge. The AMA race is their fourth-biggest event, after NASCAR, NHRA and IRL. What they learn from far larger crowds, they apply to their AMA visitors.

This was the first race for Hunter Van Dalen, 14, whose father, Greg, a longtime fan, was wearing a Nicky Hayden ball cap. What Greg would like to see is a more competitive weekend. "I think it's a little dull," he said, echoing the complaint of many, and not just fans. "Just do the same thing as World Superbike. It's baffling to me. One series can make it so competitive and the other is so dull." Van Dalen was among the fans who didn't like the current class structure. "It's so confusing. What is Supersport? What is Superstock? You've got Formula Xtreme. They're dividing up all the great talent among too many classes. It's like glorified club racing. They're into backmarkers by lap five."

Randy Cobb of Nipomo, near Pismo Beach, California, agreed. Cobb, who was keeping the sun at bay with his Dunlop hat, rides his Honda CBR600F4i on track days. He thinks the number of riders needs to be limited. "When you end up with 45 riders, that's insane," he said. He likes the 110-percent rule in the support classes, but thinks the maximum count should be 30, which would make for less lappers. Not long after Cobb spoke, Team M4 EMGO Suzuki's Geoff May spoke at length about the problem with lappers at Infineon. But Cobb likes all the classes, even Superstock, which is soon to go away. Cobb's friend, Gary Keltz of Atascadero, had a different view. "Maybe a better explanation of the classes," he said from under the brim of his 2006 Red Bull U.S. GP hat. "I'm still confused, and I've been doing this a long time." As we spoke, both remarked on the volume of the heavy-metal band entertaining on the Jagermeister stage in the late morning. "It doesn't need to be that loud," Keltz said, and he was right.

The entertainment they and others would like to see is more big-screen TVs. "That would be nice," Keltz said. "It'd be nice to have some screens for the areas you can't see." Back in February,

Fan Speak

AMA Pro Racing issued a press release that they would bring JumboTrons "to all rounds of the AMA Superbike Championship," adding that "up to six units will be positioned at high-visibility locations around the track." The screens showed up at Daytona, skipped Barber, and were back at Fontana. Now they're gone - yet another broken promise.

One of the attractions the fans endorse is rider interaction. Many attended the Red Bull U.S. Grand Prix at Laguna Seca and remarked how difficult it was to see the MotoGP riders. The autograph sessions, new this year at AMA races, were well-received, though some wanted more. Lori Burleson, visiting with her husband, David, and son Broc, 6, would like the riders to be more interactive.

"Are you allowed to do wheelies here?" Broc wanted to know. "I love the wheelies." "Fans love wheelies," said his father, a Miguel Duhamel fan and before that a Freddie Spencer and Kevin Schwantz fan, and a former AFM racer. "When they wheelie, you stand up. I think the wheelie is a lost art."

One fan wanted more Supermoto, another wanted the World Superbike format - two races on Sunday, plus Supersport, and practice and qualifying on Friday and Saturday. Kevin Chavez of San Jose wanted to be able to do more than one lap of the track.

The races could start earlier, more than one fan said, especially on Sundays. The 3 p.m. Superbike start wasn't very popular, nor was Saturday's 4:45 p.m. Formula Xtreme race, which started closer to 5 p.m. "Half the spectators left after the first race," Gary Keltz said. "They're leaving Formula Xtreme, and that's going to be a good race."

It was, thanks to Josh Hayes and his teammate Aaron Gobert, whose return to form is one of the better stories of 2007. Now if only Spies could return to his 2006 form. As a fan, it's the least you can hope for. That, and big-screen TVs. And wheelies.

June 13, 2007

Watch It and They Will Come

If you want to see more motorcycle racing on TV, it's simple - just ask for it.

That's the proposition behind MavTV, a nascent website/network that has the rights to broadcast eight disciplines of AMA racing, both professional and amateur.

But MavTV needs your help. They need you to ask your satellite company or cable provider to add them to your menu. You've already got 500 channels that you don't watch - why not one you would?

MavTV is run by passionate guys who are passionate about motorcycle racing. And what they've found is that if you can get motorcycle racing on television, it will get watched. The racing that's being streamed on the website (www.mavtv.com) draws viewers and keeps them.

"There's a great opportunity for the motorcycle community," said Chet Burks, one of the MavTV principals. Burks' company produces the AMA Superbike Championship telecasts for Speed. They also produce the AMA Motocross Championship and bring in the feeds for MotoGP and World Superbike, cutting them to fit Speed's format. This year they took on MotoST and have a number of motorcycle specials on Speed, including the *World's Fastest Motorcycle* - the documentary on Chris Carr's recording-breaking Bonneville run.

Now they want to add AMA Flat Track, Supermoto and Hillclimb, plus trials, ice racing, AMA Prostar drag racing, the flat-track Amateur Nationals, the amateur hillclimbs, the Road Racing

Grand Championship, the Motocross Grand Championship, and speedway.

"Speed stepped up with Supercross and road racing," Burks said. "Outside of that, it doesn't fit into their plans."

But it's the perfect fit for MavTV

"The bad news is that the venues are too small [to attract Speed or other established networks]," Burks added. "The good news is that there's a network willing to take a chance."

Half of the racing will be shot in HDTV and, if it gets distributed on DirecTV, all of it will be in HDTV.

"It's a long-term commitment," Burks said of the three-year contracts. "We're not going to go away."

The biggest issue facing MavTV is distribution. They aren't seen by enough eyeballs.

"Now's the time if they want to see this in HD on DirecTV or Echostar," Burks said. "They just put up a bunch of capacity to add networks. If we can show DirecTV that there's a demand for this, they'll all do it. It's like the airline industry; once one does it, they all fall in line."

The motorcycle industry is starting to get behind it. Suzuki is on board. Erion Racing is on board. Burks recently met with Yamaha and expects them to come on board. Microsoft called to say that they'd like to import it into the Xbox.

"Once we've gone after the big guys, the smaller guys will come in," Burks said.

There will be a minimum of 100 hours of original race broadcasting, and this is where your help is needed.

If you want to see the broadest menu of motorcycle racing in the world, take a minute to write an e-mail. The people who need to be convinced are DirecTV and the DishNetwork. Their contact information is provided below.

DIRECTV

http://directv.com/DTVAPP/customer/HowToReachUs.asp
(Phone: 888/777-2454)

DISH NETWORK

http://www.dishnetwork.com/content/customer_service/contact_us/email/index.asp
(Phone: 888/825-2557)

You can also do it directly from the MavTV website at http://www.mavtv.org/pages/public_request.asp.

The emails need to say you want to see MavTV and, if you're not already a subscriber, are willing to switch to Dish or Direct if they add MavTV.

If you're leery about e-mailing the satellite companies, drop an e-mail to MavTV's Steve Smith (steve.smith@mavtv.net) and he'll make sure it reaches the right person. MavTV will soon broadcast the Springfield Mile. What you'll see is class champion Kenny Coolbeth winning by 4.71 seconds. The next four riders, led by Chris Carr, finished within two-tenths of each other, a more typical Springfield finish.

But the race didn't end there. Coolbeth's factory XR750 failed the post-race tech inspection for being under-weight. Earlier in the day, AMA officials admitted their scales were off. So they took Coolbeth's XR back to Ohio to be weighed on certified scales, but not at the AMA. And, miraculously, it porked up and Coolbeth was declared the winner.

There is no suggestion that Coolbeth did anything improper - quite the opposite. He would have won if the bike was 10 pounds overweight. It was one of those days where he hit the perfect setup and no one was going to beat him. So suspicion turns to AMA Pro

Racing and how the AMA scales, or the officials operating them, could be so utterly and completely wrong.

Dirt track deserves better. Dirt track deserves to be exposed to a larger audience, an audience that would normally see the Springfield Mile decided by inches, not seconds. (Last year's Memorial Day race was won by sixth-thousandths of a second - Carr over Jay Springsteen. Coolbeth was a distant twelve-hundredths of a second behind Springer. Brian Smith won the fall race by eighteen-thousandths of a second over Rich King, with Coolbeth third by twenty-six-thousandths of a second.)

Carr came second at Springfield. I was told he wasn't happy with the outcome, so I gave him a call. To his credit, and to the surprise of anyone who knows him, he was taking a wait-and-see approach.

"Kind of how I look at the whole situation right now is, I'm not going to comment on the situation other than to say I've won 75 Nationals in my career and I've never won one of those because the winner of the race was DQed," he said. "Until I get a better idea of how this happened and why his bike was impounded in the first place, I'm going to kind of suspend my thoughts."

Carr said he was "trying to keep a cool head," but it was clear he was thinking about how it could have happened. Through a stellar seven-Grand National Championship-winning career, Carr has never failed a tech inspection.

"I'm trying to give everybody the benefit of the doubt about how this happened in the first place," he said, adding about his bike, "My bike weighed about the same as it always has."

As did the third- and fourth-place finishers.

The minimum weight for a 750cc dirt tracker is 310 pounds dry, 314 pounds with fuel. Coolbeth's was 309 with fuel, according to someone who witnessed the weigh-in. Yet when the bike arrived in Ohio, suddenly it had Jenny Craiged in reverse. Maybe it stopped at a Stuckey's along the way and loaded up on Pecan Log

Rolls. Maybe it was the Wendy's Triple with Cheese. Maybe it was the Denny's Lumberjack Slam. Whatever it was, the Hog got hoggier and the stink coming off the whole fiasco was positively porcine.

AMA Pro Racing then issued a press release that gave very few specifics. Nowhere were any of the weights mentioned. That would have gone a long way to cooling the flames and calming the tempers. But history tells us that AMA Pro Racing is fundamentally incapable of communicating even the most basic facts, so the stink lingers. It didn't help that the findings were blessed by Doug Neubauer, the blowhard who made an ass of himself with an ignorant tirade at riders he knew nothing about last year at Mid-Ohio.

We need more of the mainstream providers to put dirt track and everything else on two wheels on the air, which is why you'll help in the campaign to get MavTV on DirecTV and the Dish Network. And while you're at your keyboard, you might also drop the magicians at AMA Pro Racing an e-mail. It would be enlightening to find out how they can create matter out of thin air and inflate it with dead air.

June 27, 2007

Ding Dong

Baseball fans know "the dinger" as a home run, a glorious stroll around a sun-splashed diamond that's been elegized in books, in song, and on screen. For a batter, it's the apogee of achievement, the crowning glory, the *ne plus ultra*, sweetened only by timing or runners on base.

The dinger means something else to AMA Pro Racing employees. "The Dinger" is Rob Dingman, the new AMA CEO with no background in racing who's been thrust into the job of cleaning up a dysfunctional department that has the respect of few and the enmity of many. You need only look at dirt track, where the scales of justice are even more out of whack than the official scales. Given the tumult in AMA PR over the last 17 months, it's hard to imagine anyone sorting out the mess.

The Dinger is relying on "Scooter" to help with road racing. Scooter is the nick-name Keith Kizer enjoyed during his mostly successful stewardship of AMA Prostar drag racing. Mostly successful, because, as he's admitted, the splintering of drag racing into so many pieces made the business less viable. So he moved to a form of two-wheeled sport where motorcycles are asked to do more than go in a straight line for eight or nine seconds.

The Dinger and Scooter have their hands full. Road racing is ugly and getting uglier. They may be able to fix it, but do they have the stomach? With the bad advice the Dinger's getting (not from Scooter), and the historically hysterical nature of AMA PR, it isn't easy to envision either hitting a home run. And if by some celestial eruption they did, there is little hope it would be properly communicated.

The ugliness is on the racetrack and off. The fields are horribly inflated with wobblers who should be honing their skills one step below what's meant to be the pinnacle of AMA road racing. Instead, because of a laxity of standards and a perverse view of "pro" racing that's allowed to fester, too often the undeserving determine the outcome of the race by stumbling into the path of the leaders as they go a lap down. Or two laps down or three laps down. The standard of 110 percent for all classes but Superbike allows too many who aren't ready and don't deserve to be on the same racetrack as Spies, Hayes and Hacking. And the 108 percent for Superbike is one percent too lax. The one-percent solution, and a tighter cap on the size of the field would not only clean up the field, but improve race safety. And it would also enhance the quality of racing for spectators and TV viewers.

Why won't this happen? Greed. Money is the mother's milk of AMA PR and they collect vast sums of money, not only on entry fees, but also for licenses. So rather than give the factories (without whom this would be MotoST), a clean and safe track, they pander to the tail-enders. Which is puzzling, if not insane.

Thursday practice is the bane of the factories. They have a gentleman's agreement not to test, but so what? Seven of the top 10 riders in the Supersport points standings routinely test. It's as bad or worse in Superstock and Formula Xtreme. Why not exclude the top ten in points? And besides, who truly needs Thursday practice? Only those who don't know which way the track goes. And they tend not to be in the first few rows. And they are also practicing, which is different from testing, which the factories do on a regular basis and at great cost, which the tail-enders resent.

The solution to Thursday practice is to move it to Monday and Tuesday, which is how it's often done in MotoGP. This would save the factories thousands in travel costs. Testing on the same track they raced on the day before would ensure they'd be testing on a track that's as fitted with safety enhancements as the AMA is able to provide. If the slowest of the slow were eliminated, the factory riders would be less reluctant to share the track. And it should be made theirs exclusively on Tuesday. And those who claim to not profit from promoter practice could not profit a few days later. Sainthood delayed.

The tracks are getting safer. That's unquestioned. It's taken far too long, but there's a very simple reason; the riders had no voice. Some tracks, such as Infineon Raceway, have made the riders their partner for years. It will never be truly safe - space limitations won't allow it - but it is much safer than it was. And track management is among the most motorcycle-friendly and forward-thinking on the calendar

Unfortunately, there's a blight on Infineon through no fault of their own. Hideous orange traffic cones are a fixture on too many tracks. Yamaha's Ben Bostrom discovered this when an orange cone, that was on the outside of the corner, got wedged in his rear wheel after the first of two identical crashes. The argument for traffic cones on the outside of the corners is that they mark the track boundary. Which presupposes that a rider would take a wide line, say 40 feet from the apex, to square off the corner. When Neil Hodgson was first asked about the difference between World Superbike and AMA, he said, "We don't race through traffic pylons."

It's the difference between a professional race and a parking-lot gymkhana. California Speedway is the ugliest of all tracks when it comes to cones. They're everywhere: inside, outside, and sometimes on the track when they get clipped. They're wrongly used as brake markers, which should be standardized. They look ugly and amateurish, in person and on TV. Get rid of them.

Traffic cones are fixable. What about the future? There's a dangerous movement in AMA PR to dumb down the Superbike class. It goes against what the other top national series, in Britain and Japan, are doing. Given the nature of the tracks, and the increasing performance of the 1000cc bikes, you'll find very little resistance to Superstock-spec motors for the premier class. Which leaves us with the rolling hardware. Chassis modifications are a no-brainer. Aftermarket swingarms must be allowed. Same with wheels and triple clamps. Only a dingbat would tell the Dinger otherwise.

So just who is the Dinger listening to? Certainly it's not the road-race advisory board. At the moment, they're the leper in the hot tub. And this is dangerous. Because the factories spend millions of dollars and maybe someday they won't. Racing budgets come out of the advertising budget and all it will take is some ad guy to say, "No, we're going to buy World Series ads." Or Super Bowl ads. Or some other form of advertising that reaches a far larger and more diverse audience.

The advisory boards were formed in the wake of the purge of AMA Pro Racing about 17 months ago. AMA PR has only briefly had its own boss. The leadership vacuum is sucking the life out of racing. Mostly it's been run by the CEO, who should be paying attention to more pressing issues, such as membership and rider rights and land usage, rather than Harley XR750s that miraculously gain weight in AMA possession.

At the moment, the power seems to be unfairly weighted towards the AMA board of directors, an incurious group that includes one member who's also on the board of advisors of MotoST, a series that competes with the AMA Superbike Championship and is sanctioned by Roger Edmondson, who successfully sued the AMA for millions of dollars. (To be fair to Edmondson, I'm sure MotoST races are run better than AMA road races.) And MotoST has at least one other advisor whose hunger for power is well known. Only a blind man wouldn't see this as a conflict.

There can only be two explanations: The board is ignorant or the board is indifferent. Make that three: the board is complicitous. This is a world-class conflict, like a transvestite at a urinal. Do I sit down? Do I hike up my skirt? What's a girl to do?

But conflicts are inherent within the board of directors, which needs term limits worse than Congress. Every once in a while, you need to clear the bases. And for that, you need a Dinger.

July 11, 2007

Petcocks and Bostrom

Who's in charge of AMA Pro Racing? That's easy: no one. At least not according to anything you'll find on the AMA Pro Racing website. AMA CEO Rob Dingman is nominally in charge of racing, in that he's in charge of the AMA and racing falls under his purview. But as far as a stand-alone racing boss goes, that would be no one - which explains a lot.

There's a fair bit of turmoil in road racing, where the premier class is unsponsored, as is the larger of the support classes. That leaves the redundant 600cc classes, both of which continue to retain in-industry sponsors. Dirt track continues to be the Rodney Dangerfield of pro racing, a sport in which, when the AMA doesn't like what its scales tell them, they go into fat-guy mode and drive around Ohio in search of a more sympathetic scale. All while toting around a motorcycle with a chain of custody that has more fingerprints than a frat house bong.

The 2009 AMA Superbike technical rules are being hashed out as this is written. They were discussed last week during another of the super-top-secret, double-handshake conference calls, where Dick Cheney might as well have written the code of silence. The rules could be put up for public review by the time you read this, unless, like me, you're on the East Coast, in which case they'll be implemented before your *Cycle News* arrives.

Among the topics of discussion was fuel petcocks. Petcocks? Really? Is this really a problem and is it worth considering? No and no. But someone thought it merited discussion, along with similarly minor details like cams, pistons, connecting rods and crankshafts. Because we all know the way to level the playing field is spec petcocks. I'm guessing whomever thought this up had already exhausted other more relevant topics: Seat foam - what every ass needs. Decals - the same secret as real estate, location, location, location. Gas caps - saves the fruit basket from that itchy, burning feeling.

There were a few surprises on the agenda, including stock swingarms and suspension, which no one among the factory bosses had expected and no one wanted. To quote the Talking Heads' David Byrne, 'And you may ask yourself, 'Well... how did I get here?"

The current system of committees and boards and headless management is so Byzantine, archaic, and circuitous that if you tried to follow a flow chart, it'd make your GPS explode. It's meant to promote fairness, but in reality subjugates the factories, without whose support racing would not exist, to the shadows. It gives them a voice, but a secondary voice, and one that often falls on deaf ears. And in its place comes the wisdom of the board of directors, a group with very little experience in racing and particularly little knowledge of road racing. And it includes one member who recently boasted that when he arrived at the AMA, he had a hit list, and that everyone on that hit list is now gone. And this board of racing naifs could overrule American Honda's Chuck Miller, Kawasaki's Mike Preston, Yamaha's Keith McCarty, and Yoshimura Suzuki's Don Sakakura, who among them have well over a century's worth of racing experience, and an ocean of championships, with Miller winning both as a rider and a team manager.

It doesn't take long to find the road-race influence on the board of directors. Only one board member has extensive road-racing experience: John Ulrich. In addition to being a board member and former *Cycle News* employee, he's on the board of advisers of Moto-ST, he edits a magazine and website, and he runs a very good race team - one of the most successful satellite teams in the paddock.

Riders Geoff May and Martin Cardenas finished second and third at the most recent round of the AMA Supersport Championship at Miller Motorsports Park, easily the top-placing Suzukis. May was in for a podium in Superstock before an engine misfire hit. And Cardenas was among the front-runners in Formula Xtreme before finishing fifth. Kurtis Roberts told me at Infineon Raceway that it was the best team he'd ever ridden for in the United States.

But for someone in a position of power, Ulrich has taken what appears to be a cynical view of road racing. At Infineon Raceway, the team and Pirelli knew that they didn't have a rear tire that would last the entire Superbike race. But they used Saturday's Superbike race, supposedly the premier event, to test tires for Sunday's Superstock race.

"I probably won't do the whole race; I'll probably pull out after 17 laps," May said in the Infineon Superstock qualifying press conference. "I don't think the tires I'm on will actually go 28 laps. The question is if they'll go 17, do what I need to do for Superstock."

This is legal, but should it be allowed? The reason more hasn't been made of it is that May is one the most respected riders in the paddock and one who should have a factory ride. He has the confidence of his peers, who know he would do nothing to jeopardize the championship. May isn't at fault here, the system is, and anyone who exploits it. Which is why someone needs to take charge, and soon.

Whoever is put in charge of racing has to be able to make common-sense decisions based on putting on a good show at the front of the field, rather than agonizing over the tail-enders, which is the current mindset. Why the board, some of whom work for the OEMs, can't see that is troubling.

There were at least two late entries for the 40-rider AMA Supersport race in support of the Red Bull U.S. GP. *Cycle News* road-test editor and former racer Steve Atlas applied to race the Corona Honda CBR600RR that has been idle since Daytona. And Yamaha requested a spot for Ben Bostrom, whose Superstock class will be absent. In both cases, they were turned down.

"We have made great strides in improving the consistency in management and procedural decision-making this season and have precisely followed our own rules thus far," AMA road race manager Keith Kizer wrote in a letter to Mazda Raceway Laguna Seca CEO Gill Campbell. "We understand the promotional benefits of including a rider of Ben's caliber in the program or the journalistic talents of Steve Atlas, but we must stand by our original decision in order to maintain our integrity with the paddock."

Campbell wanted to see them race, but she agreed with the AMA's decision.

"For the first time, the AMA has really stood by their polices, and so I'm proud of them for that," she said. "I'm okay with it. There's been so much wishy-washy in the past."

I disagree. It's harder to make the case for Atlas than Bostrom. And the solution is simple - let Bostrom in and take the top 40 qualifiers. No one, outside of friends and family, is coming to see the guy who qualified 40th. They're coming for the stars, and Bostrom is one of them. Laguna Seca is the site of some his most memorable wins, in both AMA and World Superbike, and on both a Superbike and a 600. He's from Northern California. He's part of the show. He, and others like him, are the reason people come to races, watch races, follow races. Not for the guy finishing 40th. And the AMA needs to figure that out soon or at least put someone in the top job who understands that racing is entertainment - it's about stars, not motorcycles, and stars sell motorcycles.

Is there anyone qualified for the top-racing job? Yes, Gary Mathers, but he didn't want to answer to committees and board, so the AMA wasn't smart enough to hire him. Mathers knows how to win championships, how to lead organizations, how to motivate employees, and is well-respected in the paddock, which is why he was completely unsuitable for the job.

So instead we'll settle for second best or third best or worse. And, in the meantime, we have a misguided board, which knows little about racing, dictating orders to a downtrodden committee, which knows a lot. What's the solution? Simple: spec petcocks.

July 25, 2007

Wide Open

Can Nicky Hayden win the Red Bull U.S. Grand Prix? Of course. But so can Casey Stoner and Valentino Rossi and Dani Pedrosa. And maybe John Hopkins and Colin Edwards. Which is why it's shaping up to be the best U.S. GP yet. If everything goes well, and that's a big "if."

The three questions I heard most often at last weekend's German Grand Prix were: How's the track surface? What's the weather going to be? How old is Miguel Duhamel?

The answers are: Pristine. Look it up yourself. I don't think he knows at this point.

The results in Germany showed that Honda is finally getting serious. Or at least getting results. First and third with Pedrosa and Hayden is the high point of their otherwise dismal season. It took too long and a threat from Pedrosa to decamp before he was given a motorcycle that could win. And he's always a part or two ahead of Nicky.

"I think we still got a lot of work to do, to be honest," Hayden said after his second podium in a row.

But Stoner saw progress.

"I noticed that with Dani's and Nicky's compared to Marco's [Melandri] bike," said the championship leader, "there is a really big difference; coming onto the main straight, I could stay with Marco's bike, but with Dani's, it was a big difference from before.

"Dani's [Pedrosa] bike has got some extra engine that we haven't seen before" he later added. "Everything the lower [satellite] teams are complaining about, you could see it today on the track."

But Melandri had been effusive in his praise for HRC, thanking the factory for supplying him with an upgraded exhaust and electronics package. The Italian was able to put it to good use early in the race, but he suffered the same fate as Stoner and Hopkins.

The dominant Bridgestone tires had a mostly off day in Germany. Not entirely off; veteran Loris Capirossi proved he could still hustle around a racetrack by breaking up the Michelin hegemony. But Stoner, Melandri and Hopkins all wore out the left side of their rear Bridgestones on the left-heavy track. Stoner dropped from second to fifth and was followed home by Melandri and Hopkins. So Stoner was denied the chance to pad his points lead over Rossi. As it was, he left Germany with 32 points in hand and eight races to run.

Rossi was both lucky and unlucky: lucky in that Stoner wasn't able to maximize his points haul; unlucky in that he had a rare dry-race crash.

"I realize what could have been today, but I can't do anything about it now except try to make up for it on Sunday in America," Rossi said, which is good news for the expected 50,000 fans lining the hills of Mazda Raceway Laguna Seca.

Rossi hasn't had much luck in America, a country he's embraced, as has Stoner. In 2005, he didn't have to. The Fiat Yamaha rider controlled the championship from the start and breezed to the most recent of his seven titles. Last year he came in trailing Hayden, but a chunked tire slowed him and an overheated engine ended his race. It was one of four off results that prevented him from taking a bigger lead into the final race. And the crash in Valencia didn't help.

Rossi doesn't have to win Laguna, but he has to beat Stoner. He thinks he can. The Yamaha M1 and the Michelin tires are at the point of being competitive every weekend. It wasn't so at the beginning of the season, and Rossi was outspoken in his displeasure. As was Edwards, who has an ever longer history with the French tire maker.

New rules in place for this season limit riders to 31 tires for the weekend, 14 fronts and 17 rears, two of which are qualifiers. (Wet races have no limits.) The riders have to choose their allotment on Thursday and live with the consequences. How they select the tires is up to the individual. Some choose three different tires, and get five each. Others do the opposite: five each of three different compounds, casing, or construction. Or some mixture. In any case, it isn't uncommon for riders to get to Sunday's race with only one tire remaining - or have to spend part of practice on tires they wouldn't think of racing.

Laguna Seca will be a crap shoot for the tire boffins. The track had to be repaved after the 2006 debacle. A confluence of conditions, including sustained record heat, conspired to produce a bumpy, degrading surface.

"Last year was a disaster with the asphalt - was the worst race, worst conditions in my career," Rossi said. Stoner concurred: "I mean, last year, you know, it was like dirt track again. There was bits of stone coming up and hitting you in the face."

The resurfacing was completed nearly two months ago under the supervision of a consultant sent from Germany by MotoGP officials.

A fresh surface means the tire companies have no data. At least two companies sent technicians to Monterey to take a rubber mold of the new asphalt. The size and shape of the stones will be analyzed and the information used to produce tires. It's an inexact science, at best.

"We can ask, but even if we know what is inside of the stone, it is difficult to analyze also," Bridgestone tire boss Hiroshi Yamada said. And if it was determined that they needed completely new material, in the casing or compound, then it would take more than a month to produce.

Bridgestone produced tires for Laguna Seca last year that were good enough to put Chris Vermeulen on the pole and in front of the race for the first 16 laps. Then it went to Hayden, from Pedrosa, with Melandri third. The 2007 race will be different. Bridgestone has answers for every track. In Germany, Capirossi used a softer tire than Stoner. It worked because it gripped better and spun less than the Stoner's harder rear.

Grip is something Duhamel will have to come to grips with. The Bridgestone tires are vastly superior to the Dunlops Duhamel uses and the qualifiers are stickier than a porn-house floor. Tires are but one course of Duhamel's schooling at Laguna Seca. He'll be aboard the lightest and fastest motorcycle he's ever ridden, against many of the best riders in the world, sometimes just after wrestling what will seem like a lumbering beast, his American Honda CBR1000RR.

"Having to ride Superbikes and a Grand Prix will test the old man's fitness, I know that," Kevin Schwantz said. How old is Duhamel? Old enough for Gresini Honda team owner Fausto Gresini to nearly choke on his gnocchi when he saw a picture of the 39-year-old.

"Sure, he's not a young rider, but he's interesting," Gresini, the 46-year-old 1985 and '87 125cc World Champion, said with a smile on the pit lane in Germany. If he is older than 39 - "He was 39 when I was racing him," Randy Mamola said - he should embrace it. How many 40-, 41-, 42- or 43-year-olds can shame riders half their age?

Expectations have been raised for the Red Bull U.S. GP. Raised because SCRAMP improved what they can control: a new traffic plan, a new surface, a less crowded race schedule, more fan amenities. And raised because of little possibility of a recurrence of the freakishly scorching weather that baked last year's race.
And then there's the Indy factor. Indianapolis Motor Speedway will be hosting a round of the MotoGP, 250cc and 125cc World

Championships next September. Dorna, the GP rights holders, isn't playing Indy against Laguna Seca. The opposite is true. Dorna CEO Carmelo Ezpeleta said in Germany that he wants two healthy races in the United States. IMS knows how to put on big events. For them, MotoGP will be a snap. Now it's up to Laguna Seca to hold up its end of the deal.

August 22, 2007

Rhee-Cluse?

The most common paddock activity other than working on motorcycles is whining. About the AMA, Pro Racing in particular. It has persisted for as long as I've been trolling the pits, which is close to 35 years. It shows no signs of abating.

In my never-ending quest to do less and earn more, I offered a number of paddock and industry notables a chance to help me with this column, and to help themselves and racing, too. I asked them to come up with questions for the new AMA Pro Racing boss, Dennis Rhee, who was at Mid-Ohio, but unavailable to talk to the media. The questions could be on any topic. This, I thought, would give voice to the disenfranchised who toil behind the scenes. They would leap at the opportunity to be heard. I was wrong. There was no leaping. The response was underwhelming. I got one fully formed question, one rant that was easily shaped into a question, and one "I'll think about it." There may be a lesson in this, but it eludes me. As did Dennis Rhee at Mid-Ohio.

I got an e-mail from an industry friend, whose opinion I respect and value, when Rhee was named head of Pro Racing. It was brief and to the point. "I know Dennis Rhee. He's a good guy." Which I have no reason to doubt. Others I've spoken to have the same opinion. But I'd like to know more, as would the rest of the paddock, which is perpetually treated like mushrooms - kept in the dark and fed crap.

The rant began, "After thinking about this, I realized the reason I cannot ask an even half intelligent question is because I do not know anything about him. Where did he come from? What has he done? Does he know anything about racing? Does he know anything about motorcycle racing? Does he know anything about the business side of racing? Does he know anything about racing from a motorcycle racer's point of view? Does he know anything about racing from a team's point of view? My fear is that the answer to those questions will be no."

Some of those questions were answered in the typically mollifying AMA press release. But more should be known. Which is why, prior to Mid-Ohio, I put in a request through the proper channels that Rhee sit down with the series regulars for a chat. The response was... well, there was no response. Not a yes, not a no. Silence of the lambs. So when I discovered Rhee was at Mid-Ohio, I put the same question to AMA road-race boss Keith Kizer, who began his tenure by meeting with us last year at Mid-Ohio. That gathering had gone well and he later took us out to dinner - the best way to guarantee at least a brief period of fealty by us clearly not-underfed scribblers.

Then came the meltdown at the fall Mid-Ohio race that another free meal wasn't going to fix. But we did start out well and Kizer continues to have a good relationship with the media. And when I asked him about talking to Rhee, the response was, in short, "Give him some time."

That answer goes to the heart of the final part of the unformed question. "The AMA has a long history of poor communication with the teams and promoters. How does Dennis Rhee intend to improve the relationship between the AMA, the teams and the promoters of the events?" The answer is self-evident, but it's not Rhee's fault.

The notion that Rhee is new to the job and, therefore, unable to comment is ludicrous. Clearly, he has a wealth of knowledge about racing. Those who dealt with him last year at Mid-Ohio, where he was vice president, said he was receptive to the changes the riders wanted to make to the racetrack. He managed to convince AMA boss Rob Dingman that he was the right man for the job. And he may well be. The hope here is that he is. But we don't know. And there's no evidence that we'll know any time soon.

Kizer cited communications as his number-one issue when he was introduced last year. It remains high on the list. And yet when given the perfect opportunity to not only calm the fears of the paddock but garner good publicity, AMA PR communications dropped the ball like a leaky specimen bottle. It wasn't the first time, it won't be the last.

There is an innate distrust and fear of the media within AMA Pro Racing. It's not totally without merit. But it shouldn't be debilitating. They should work on improving communications, not preventing them. What they don't understand is that the media is merely a conduit. Yes, we as journalists care what Dennis Rhee thinks. But there are thousands, if not tens of thousands, of people throughout the Pro-Racing community whose lives will be directly impacted by what he thinks and how he acts. They deserve to know what his priorities are and how he intends to accomplish them. Ten days passed between the time of his announcement on July 24 to the start of the Mid-Ohio race weekend. Surely that was enough time to prepare to meet the press.

What I would have asked is how he plans to address the conflicts of interest in Pro Racing? The 2009 AMA Superbike rules are in the comment stage. The process, as explained to me by AMA technical and safety manager Kevin Crowther, was that the various rules committees, which deal with technical rules, vote on their individual proposals. Once approved, it moves to the six-person racing committee, which is set up with one expert from each discipline. They can't change it, they can only pass it to the AMA board of directors with an endorsement or non-endorsement and a reason why. The board of directors can then only deny the whole packet: line item vetoes aren't allowed. And it has to be a super-majority for them to send it back down.

The proposals that originally came from the board of directors were clearly influenced by someone with a vested interest in more production-based racing, which is the opposite of what most of the factories want. How did this happen? To answer that, we need only look at the structure. In their infinite wisdom, the AMA has allowed someone to be on both the racing committee and the board of directors. This might not be a problem if he wasn't a team owner, a direct beneficiary of American Suzuki, and a few other things, but he is.

But John Ulrich isn't to blame. He only has the power that is given to him, and AMA Pro Racing willingly gave him that power. If they didn't want him to be the most influential member of the food chain, they could easily have prevented it. They chose not to. So we now have a situation where the owner of a satellite team and a magazine publisher has more voice and power than the Japanese factories. AMA Pro Racing thinks this is a good idea. Does Dennis Rhee?

Yamaha road-race manager Tom Halverson gave the only complete question. It is not only relevant, but heartfelt. Halverson has been around racing a long time, seen a lot of things - not all of them pleasant. Helping dig American Honda's Miguel Duhamel out of the hay bales and air fence, which do little to protect Road Atlanta's turn 12, the most dangerous corner in racing, prompted him to ask the following:

"What does the AMA plan to do about racing at certain circuits that continue to ignore glaring safety hazards?

Motorcycle road racing is risky and dangerous; that is part of what draws us to it. But (in my personal opinion) racing around a corner at 120 mph-plus with 10 feet of runoff before a concrete wall - air fence or not - is beyond the level of what any sanctioning body should expect their racers to do.

We all know certain track owners have worked very hard, and spent a lot of money, and worked with the riders to improve safety. Others have designed circuits that are safe from the start. They all should be applauded.

But before we get complacent (again) as Miguel's incident fades from our memory, the remaining problem areas need to be fixed. Either that or we need to stop going to these circuits altogether."

Dennis?

August 29, 2007

Factory or Non-Factory?

The gang that couldn't shoot straight aimed at the wrong target and then complained about blood on the carpet. They may have hit the proper target as well, but not with the first shot and not before there were multiple fingers on the trigger. Then they didn't want to talk about it. Why would they? Better to sweep it under the blood-stained rug.

The issue was promoter practice, which at Virginia International Raceway turned into a fiasco in clear violation of AMA rule 6.6, which states, in part: "At facilities where road races are to be held, exclusive track rentals by participants, including manufacturers, teams or individuals, within 10 days preceding the first day of official practice, are not allowed. Regional race meets, promoter/racetrack organized open practice and open schools are not restricted."

The problem words are "exclusive" and "open." Thursday's promoter practice was exclusive - at least two riders were excluded - and, because of that, it wasn't open.

The excluded riders were Graves Motorsports Yamaha's Josh Herrin and Monster Kawasaki's Roger Lee Hayden, both of whom were labeled factory riders, and therefore excluded. The argument can be made that Herrin isn't a factory rider and Hayden is, but it's a silly argument.

"It's very difficult to define a factory rider," Monster Kawasaki team manager Mike Preston said in a conversation with Yamaha road-race boss Tom Halverson and Team Hammer's John Ulrich, who organized the promoter practice. He asked Ulrich, "Do you get money from Suzuki for your team? Do you get bikes from

Suzuki for your team? I'm guessing. Does Erion [Honda] get the same? Does Attack [Kawasaki] get the same? Does Jordan [Suzuki] get the same? Does MV Agusta get the same? Yes. Then how do you define it? It's your definition."

The Herrin saga began a month earlier when his crew chief, Curtis Thom, confronted AMA road-race manager Morgan Broadhead at the Red Bull U.S. Grand Prix. The discussion was specifically about VIR, and it grew heated. Team owner Chuck Graves said he nearly had to pull Thom off Broadhead. Thom's approach at VIR was purely academic. The team had no intention of practicing - they just wanted to find out if they could. They couldn't.

Broadhead next brought up the issue at Friday's riders' meeting. He admitted that everyone who participated "broke the rules." Yoshimura Suzuki's Mat Mladin shouted out, "Kick them out of the event. Until you do it, they're going to continue to do it."

"It wasn't the riders' fault, it was the promoters' fault," Broadhead said. "The penalty will be assessed to them."

More on this later.

Broadhead met afterward with Monster Kawasaki team manager Mike Preston and Yamaha team boss Tom Halverson. Ulrich later joined the conversation. Asked why Herrin couldn't participate, Ulrich replied, "Because he's a factory rider. His mechanics are based in Graves."

"He has nothing to do with the factory; he and Ben Bostrom are Graves' riders," Halverson said.

Ulrich manned up, and the editor of America's premier road-race-only publication made a startling admission: "Well, I'm completely guilty of screwing that up."

The case can be made that Ulrich screwed up with Kawasaki as well. Kawasaki's Dan Fahie approached Ulrich after Fahie had been told by a team member that Hayden wouldn't be allowed to ride. According to Fahie, he introduced himself and said he wanted to understand what had happened. What followed was a torrent of abusive language (many of the words began with the letter "f" or had that letter maybe halfway in or just before the "ing" suffix) that would make Scarface blush. That Ulrich is a member of the AMA board of directors only adds to the sordidness of the alleged behavior. Ulrich then complained to Kawasaki, saying Fahie used the word "chickens---." When I asked Fahie, he said it simply wasn't true. He was too busy dodging f-bombs. His one mistake, he admitted, was leaving John with his own f-bomb as he walked away. Anyone who knows these two knows where the truth lies.

Lies? Did someone say lies? How about mistruths? Falsehoods? Take your pick, but it was easy to find them in this wretched affair. A press release issued by Team Hammer on February 20 states, "While the factory teams often have the best riders and machines at their disposal, they also fund more than 20 days of stand-alone private testing at AMA tracks, tests that are not open to privateers."

That is probably a lie, certainly inaccurate, and conveniently vague. Is Team M4 EMGO Suzuki a factory team? Ulrich, I'm guessing, would say no. In which case the statement is a lie because he's taken part in the factory testing as recently as two weeks ago at Road Atlanta. So then his is a factory team, in which case he can't take part in his own tests. Quite the conundrum. No wonder he always looks so unhappy

The truth is that it's up to the primary organizer of the test to make the rules. Privateers have taken part in any number of tests organized by the factories over the years. The number of participants is limited because, at some point, it affects the quality of the testing. But to say privateers are flat-out banned simply isn't true.

A further statement on the various practice sessions says, "In most cases, it is the only chance these riders and teams will get to work up to speed at a particular circuit before a race weekend begins."

This is patently absurd. Any number of riders took part in the WERA event the week before the AMA race at Miller Motorsports Park. AFM's home track is Infineon Raceway. Most tracks offer either track days or club races.

All of which should be irrelevant. The AMA Superbike Championship is the pinnacle of the sport. If you're unqualified to race, don't come out. A day's practice will help, certainly, but it's not a magic bullet. The AMA goes well out of its way to punish the factory teams, who the spectators come to see and watch on television, while bending over for the less well-heeled. It's that sort of small-minded thinking out of Pickerington that will forever keep pro racing small-time.

The AMA's Morgan Broadhead made a point of telling me: "This issue is with the promoter of the event. They're willing to take care of the issue." The promoter of the event is Cameron Gray of M1 Events. (Full disclosure: Gray hired me to write the stories for the VIR program.) Gray busts his ass to put on a good weekend. His work was rewarded with a three-day crowd of 61,500. And a fine.

Gray turned the track over to Ulrich, unaware that Ulrich was breaking the rules, as written in the AMA rulebook, by excluding riders. Gray wasn't happy with the fine, but he said he had a good working relationship with Ulrich.

"I love my working relationship with John Ulrich," he said. "We've always got along great. He does a good job here with the Team Hammer deal for me. I don't think the riders should be penalized, and so who else is there to penalize?" Gray said he wouldn't ask Ulrich to help with the fine.

How much was it? No one was saying.

"It's a big number," Gray said.

And when I asked AMA road-race series director Keith Kizer, he said it wouldn't be made public. But he said the number would be determined after consulting with the new VP of racing, Dennis Rhee, and Doug Neubauer, vice president of AMA Sports and every rider's best friend. And Kizer wouldn't confirm or deny that the AMA had come to its senses and fined Ulrich $5000, which was the rumor in the paddock. Why not? Because that's the AMA way. Let's not talk about it, it'll go away. It's a bad thing. Like the drug testing at Mid-Ohio. Did the riders pass the test? We don't know. Shhhhh.

What have we learned from this sordid episode? That AMA Pro Racing - that's "Pro" racing - needs to grow a spine and ban Thursday practice, starting with the 2008 season. No promoter practice, no schools, nothing 10 days before the event, unless there's a regularly scheduled race weekend. Other sanctioning bodies shouldn't suffer because the AMA can't police its own paddock.

Testing should be further regulated, as it is in most racing series. MotoGP tests on Monday would make perfect sense and would be easy to implement and cheaper for everyone. And anyone who raced on Sunday would be allowed to test on Monday.

Will that happen? Not as long as the gang that couldn't shoot straight has a shot at it.

October 10, 2007

The Dinger Unplugged

The Dinger got so tired so quickly of the migraines from trying to fix AMA Pro Racing that he decided to blow the whole damn thing up.

In a statement in this space a few weeks back, AMA CEO Rob "The Dinger" Dingman wrote, "We are getting out of the racing-series and event-promotions business and are already actively searching for series promoters for all race disciplines."

The immediate response was disbelief. The AMA promotes races? Who knew? And since when? If I remember correctly, there were a few miserable attempts (maybe only one) to promote road races over a decade ago. Since then, not so much.

And for good reason. They're no good at it. Why? Because they're too shortsighted to see the value of the property. Which is why they're having an AMA PR fire sale. I can't wait to see the line of raging optimists bidding to pick over the carcass they've made of dirt track. No matter that it's the most exciting two-wheel racing in the world. And Supermoto, another series AMA PR has mismanaged? You could have it for a buck.

Which was exactly the offer, I'm told, that came from one interested suitor for road racing, a party that is already part of the championship and has a link-up with the bloviating huckster Steve McLaughlin and Grand Am boss Roger Edmondson. McLaughlin pined for the job of former racing boss Scott Hollingsworth; now maybe he'll get to run road racing. Edmondson ran road racing until he was wrongly excused from his job. He sued and won - more than $3 million. Edmondson back in charge? Ironical.

The dirty truth is that for years AMA PR has done an abysmal job of selling road-race series sponsorships, undervaluing the property, and either renewing or losing existing sponsorships. What isn't as well known is how many potential sponsors AMA PR turned down.

In his back-pager, The Dinger said that "success in the AMA's racing endeavors has proven elusive because the AMA has mingled its role as sanctioning body with its role as series promoter."

No, success in the AMA's racing endeavors has proved elusive because AMA PR tolerated employees who weren't qualified to polish the poles at strip clubs. There was no confusion about who was a sanctioning body and who was a series promoter when, for instance, road-race boss Keith Kizer flip-flopped on the wisdom of wet-weather racing at Mid-Ohio and nearly caused a rider boycott. Or when former road-race manager Ron Barrick refused to acknowledge that he'd screwed up the 2006 Daytona 200 by not being able to tell one red bike from another. Or Hollingsworth, Vanderslice, King, et al, allowing Buell to melt engine cases to produce the XBRR, a "legal" motorcycle, which they were convinced would be the savior of the Daytona 200 and convince the hundreds of thousands of dirty shirts to forsake Main Street for the Speedway to watch a "Harley" go four laps before puking like a bulimic on a roller coaster. How did that go? AMA PR eagerly lets Buell treat the rule book like a crackhouse urinal and then look like schmucks when Buell backs out faster than a Republican in a gay bar.

The current imbroglio over crankcase venting from the Mazda Raceway Laguna Seca season finale is a perfect example of the inadequacies of AMA PR. A few days after the race, AMA PR issued a statement condemning the riders and teams for violating the rules. The teams responded by venting their outrage, saying they'd been venting their crankcases that way all year. And they said the system had been okayed by tech boss Kevin Crowther more than once.

Wanting to get AMA PR's side of the story, I asked *Cycle News* editor Paul Carruthers to make a request to speak to Crowther through AMA spokesman Kerry Graeber. (I would have called myself, but I'd forgotten to take his cell number with me to Japan.) Graeber initially replied that Crowther was with him at the Budds Creek MXoN and was "swamped." Considering the request came on the Friday of a three-day race weekend, this was an infuriating and unacceptable reply. When Graeber asked to use *CN*'s Back Page as a giant "For Sale" sign for AMA PR, *CN* obliged, no strings attached. But to get a comment on a technical matter that casts aspersions on Suzuki's top two support teams... no, we can't have that. In the end, the answer was that it was a pending matter and there would be no comment. But it was typical of the uncommunicative AMA communications, something The Dinger has vowed to address.

The model they should look to is Dorna. Dorna is the Spanish company that holds the promotional rights to the MotoGP World Championship, among other properties. When it was revealed on the Saturday of the Japanese GP in Motegi that Dorna CEO Carmelo Ezpeleta was considering a spec-tire rule for MotoGP in 2008, a colleague put in a request to speak to him. The enthusiastic and animated CEO must not have been swamped, because he not only granted our request, made only hours earlier, but gave us half an hour of his time on the morning of the Japanese GP - the most important race on the calendar for the Japanese manufacturers. And it ended with Carmelo soliciting our opinion on the spec-tire rule. Every time I've asked to speak to Carmelo, he's obliged, and surely he has more on his plate than Dennis Rhee.

Rhee is the man everyone likes, but no one knows. At least no one in the paddock. And he's in charge of their future. When I asked prior to Mid-Ohio that he be made available to the media, it was like I was asking Britney Spears to put on panties.

The Dinger was elected earlier this year to replace Patti di Pietro, the somewhat interim CEO who suddenly and with no warning ended the AMA tenure of Hollingsworth and the Pro Racing Board. They were replaced by a collection of committees whose inner workings are more Byzantine than the CIA's. For evidence, look no further than the 2009 AMA Superbike Championship rules.

About midsummer, the road-race rules committee made a proposal that then went out to comment, then to the Pro Racing Board, then to the board of directors. When I recently asked a few team managers where it stood, the answer was, "We don't know." They thought something would happen when the board met in November, which, they said, was already too late for 2009. And if the board turns them down, the process starts over. No wonder nothing gets done. And this is the part of racing that the AMA wants to keep?

Thursday promoter practice is nothing but headaches for AMA PR. It came to a head at Virginia International Raceway, when AMA board member, magazine owner/editor, race team owner, track-day promoter - that's a lot of hats - John Ulrich got fined, along with race promoter Cameron Gray, for keeping certain riders off the track. The clear solution is to ban Thursday practice and move it to Monday. This could be done instantly. When I mentioned this to AMA road-race manager Morgan Broadhead, he acknowledged that something had to be done and that various options were being considered. A bit of advice: Don't consider - act, and take a cue from Dorna.

Ezpeleta began to consider the one tire rule at the end of June Dutch TT and acted quickly. On Saturday, he used the MotoGP website to announce that the one-tire rule was an option to restore the competitive balance of MotoGP if no other solution was found.

The matter would be voted on by all relevant parties in four weeks' time, at the Malaysian Grand Prix. If it's accepted, and it will be, the tire companies will immediately submit bids. The winning bid will be accepted a week later. The 2008 MotoGP starts about 10 days later at the Valencia tests, a few days after the season finale. Whomever wins the right to provide tires free of charge to the entire field will be expected to have enough product to supply the field. So, in a span of about 6½ weeks, MotoGP will have not only made one of its most radical ever rules changes, but it will have implemented it.

Consensus building, forward thinking, rapid response, and Valentino Rossi - these are among the reasons that MotoGP is the most popular motorcycle racing series in the world. Dorna has no interest in the AMA Superbike Championship. That's a shame, but not a surprise. Why get in bed with someone who takes months to come to a climax and by then it's too late?

As The Dinger would say, "Sorry, I've got a headache."

October 24, 2007

Stop the Insanity

The most exciting form of two-wheel motorcycle racing has been on life support for years. The schedule continues to shrink, as does the rider pool, and the number of diehards who try to keep it alive. It was only a matter of time before it succumbed to indifference and incompetence.

The end came, appropriately enough, in Las Vegas, where it wouldn't have taken Gil Grissom and his CSI team to figure out whose ham-handed fingerprints were all over the crime scene. AMA Pro Racing, those lovable rogues from Pickerington, allowed the season finale to be promoted by someone who'd never promoted a race on a track that was, by all accounts, unsuitable when last raced in 1999.

Does this happen in real sports?

The AMA Grand National Championship twins dirt-track season finale was the finale that wasn't, a non-race at Las Vegas Motor Speedway on a track made of, among other things, drywall and rocks. It wasn't dirt, it wasn't clay. It was gypsum and filler and stones and various other substances not conducive to motorcycle racing. As one old dirt-track hand put it, "They've got a multimillion-dollar facility and a two-dollar racetrack." That was one of the kinder comments I heard. Most were more scathing, the sort usually reserved for divorce lawyers, repo men, and flatulent schnauzers.

"When we were there in '97, '98 and '99, it was a piece of s--t racetrack then," a longtime sponsor told me. "It's still a piece of s--t. They don't have clay, they don't have dirt, they've got ground gypsum board. They added more stuff to the track, but they resurfaced it with the same s--t that was there before."

Vegas gave up on being a family destination years ago. It no longer wants to be Disneyland in the desert; instead, it's back to being Sin City. This is a city that's all about nightlife and gambling. But no one should be allowed to take risks with a professional series, with spectators' time and money, and certainly not with riders' lives.

In their insatiable quest to head back West - a large part of the country that has seen very little of the Grand National Series for years - AMA Pro Racing allowed a couple of first-time promoters to fumble through events. The first was in Tucson, where, by all accounts, the promoters were in over their heads. But they had a few things going for them. One was personnel, enough people to keep the program running. Another was a decent track surface, much of which they'd imported. And they also had good promotion. Chris Carr said he did more live television spots than he'd done for years. Fortunately for everyone, Kenny Coolbeth became the first rider to win both the twins and singles championship in the same year. Coolbeth rode his factory Harley to the twins championship and his Bettencourt Honda to the singles title. Why "fortunately"? Because things would have gotten ugly if they had to actually race on the Vegas half-mile.

The Vegas train wreck began when the track was given a sanction by the AMA despite an eight-year absence from the GNC calendar. In the interim, the track has gotten (for lack of a better term) taller, through the addition of some sort of gypsum, according to several people who witnessed the debacle. The promoter-who-isn't-a-promoter began watering the gypsum on Wednesday. But drywall doesn't like water. Strong winds blew through the area, negating any positive effects the water may have had. In fact, it wouldn't have made much difference.

On race day, they dragged it with tires to get the rocks out, but the top was like a crust. And once the crust broke, all that was left were giant craters. It looked like a minefield. The track was barely rideable - it definitely wasn't raceable.

According to one eyewitness, the track didn't have the sort of equipment necessary to run a dirt track. There was an attempt made to get a sweeper, but one was rented and the other was refused when it was mentioned that it was going to be used for a dirt track.

"[The track] needed to be dug up a week ahead of time and watered like hell," said one observer.

All the last-minute heroics would only have put off the inevitable.

The promoter had $80,000 of seed money and the track rental cost was $40,000. The AMA, I'm told, guaranteed the track rental. There was another $13,000 for security and ticket takers. But when it was time to let in the diehards, there were no ticket takers. There was also, I was told, a lack of corner workers.

When the riders went out for practice, they quickly discovered it was going to be a short night.

"The poor bastard doing the PA, he needs a medal," one disgruntled spectator told me. "He was being fed bulls--t left, right and center. Trying to keep people in the stands from leaving. If everybody else did the job he did, it would have been a hell of a race."

It wasn't. The riders talked about putting on an exhibition, but that would only have validated the incompetence of the promoter and the AMA. It would also probably have denied them a refund, which they were given by the befuddled promoter.

"Thirty-eight dollars to get into a race is the narrow end of the wedge," it was pointed out. "What about the $300 hotel bill, meals, gas money?" The event and the dirt-track season was officially pronounced DOA at 10:30 p.m.; R.I.P.

We are now a month removed from the announcement by AMA CEO Rob "The Dinger" Dingman that the AMA was getting out of the promotions business that they weren't in it in the first place. That the Dinger thought the AMA was in the racing-series promotions business speaks volumes about how little the Pickerington prodigies care about racing. Racing is the AMA's highest-profile activity. Done right, it brings in vast amounts of money; done wrong, it engenders vast amounts of opprobrium.

AMA CEOs aren't race people. They haven't been since Ed Youngblood. How many races, let alone dirt tracks, has the Dinger been to? Or Patti DiPietro before him? When Rob Rasor replaced Youngblood, he admitted that he wasn't up to speed on pro racing.

It should be mandatory that every AMA board member, every executive in the organization attend the Springfield Mile. Had they been there over Labor Day, they'd have felt the sport in their bones, the rumble of a pack of very low-tech but evenly matched V-twins being piloted on the razor's edge by riders racing grip to grip to the line. They'd have watched as several riders came out of the final corner with a chance to win. (When was the last time that happened in a road race or Supercross?) And they'd have seen six riders cross the line on the same second, with the very narrow victory going to Chris Carr, the warrior and champion who does more for dirt track on any given weekend than the AMA has done for years. And the margin of victory: forty-seven-thousandths of a second.

Who's going to buy dirt track? More to the point, what is there to buy? The AMA says it's still going to sanction events, which means they're still in charge of approving racetracks, which means that the Vegas fiasco won't be the last. The sport needs is to be taken away from the AMA completely. By their actions, they've proved themselves incompetent and incapable and uncaring stewards of the most pure form of American motorcycle racing.

The AMA shouldn't sell the series, they should walk away from it. Dirt track deserves better. Dirt track needs better. It needs to be run by people who care. They're out there. This is their moment. They need to seize it.

The alternative is unthinkable.

November 7, 2007

Merlyn the Magician

When Merlyn Plumlee passed away on Monday, the world lost one of its finest souls. Merlyn was special, that rare combination of humility and grace bundled with fierce determination and a talent for bringing out the best in those around him. Nowhere was this more evident than when he worked with Nicky Hayden.

Plumlee was given the task of shaping the young, former dirt tracker into a road racer. Together they won the 2002 AMA Superbike Championship before Nicky moved on to win the 2006 MotoGP World Championship. To the end, they remained close.

As did Dan Fahie, now with Monster Kawasaki but then a member of Merlyn's magical crew. As was, in a way, Dunlop's Jim Allen, who became one of Merlyn's closest friends in the paddock. And Gary Mathers, who built the title-winning team - the last to win a Superbike title for Honda.

Merlyn was diagnosed with lung cancer a little over two years ago, on the weekend we were on Phillip Island for the Australian Grand Prix. He knew the odds were long and the battle would be tough, and, in the end, this was one foe he couldn't overcome. When he died, at home with his wife, Marta, by his side, his friends had had time to consider his life in full, to celebrate his warmth and genius. Here then, a few thoughts from a few of those who were lucky enough to know him.

Fahie worked under Merlyn on the American Honda team. He's taken those lessons to Kawasaki, where he guided Roger Lee Hayden to the Supersport Championship this year.

"For me, he's been like a mentor - as much of a mentor as you can get," Fahie said. "In a sense, where, when I first started in this, I started with [Rob] Muzzy and I learned quite a bit there, but, really, my real learning took place under Merlyn. He never said 'I want things done the right way.' But he would come over and say, 'Yeah, Dano, that's the right way.' He used to use the words 'the right way,' because he wanted everything right. That was really, really important to him. And somehow, to be honest I tried to figure it out myself, somehow he was always able to get it out of me without saying it. He was very good at encouraging me; at the very least, to do things what we perceived at least was the right way. And that's what he called it. You'd make the bike right. You'd go racing right. Some people talked about Merlyn as gentleman racer. And he believed in competing the right way. That was always the way he used to put it.

"Anytime something comes up that I haven't previously thought of, which is very often, the first question I ask myself is 'What would Merlyn do now?' And then I try to go about things from there. When we're at the track and I'm trying to decide, even if I get angry with somebody, 'How would Merlyn handle this?' I try to use that as a little bit of my guideline on my way to approach a problem."

"The way that I look at it is it's terrible to see Merlyn be sick, and terrible to see it end like this. Having said all that, all you can ask is that somebody remembers, if you live 100 years, or 10 years, ain't nobody going to forget. People will, but I won't. He's left a lasting impression."

"I guess the one thing that we all have been struck with time and time again with Merlyn is his overriding sense... is that he didn't want an unfair advantage on anybody," Dunlop's Jim Allen said. "All he wanted to do was do his job the best he could do it and beat people using the resources that he had, knowing that at the same time that he wasn't placed in an unfair situation, that he was dealing with the same deck of cards everyone else had."

Allen remembered a race at Loudon, which he missed in order to attend the graduation of his daughter from college. A replacement was brought in from England and given the lay of the land, but Al Ludington, Miguel Duhamel's crew chief, basically tricked Nigel into giving him another qualifying tire or an extra tire. And when Merlyn found out about it, that's the only time - I mean Merlyn never got mad at me; I never had a disagreement with him ever - that's the only time I heard that Merlyn was furious. A lot of [what we talked about] wasn't even motorcycle stuff."

One that came to mind was a meeting they had after Allen handed out the tire-allocation sheets.

"Well, Merlyn came over to the truck one day to get his sheet at Mid-Ohio," Allen recalls. "We went through the sheet, went through all the tires, talked about all this. In the course of this, I said to him the next day, 'Merlyn, you know, we never talked about motorcycles the whole time you were in the truck.' We were in the truck for 45 minutes - we never talked about motorbikes. We talked about our business, and we talked about bicycles. For he and [me] both, it [bicycles] was a passion we both shared. Time after time, he's just an example of how you should lead your life and how you should treat people."

"Merlyn was probably one of the most organized folks I ever worked with," former American Honda race boss Gary Mathers remembers. "He'd start at the beginning of the season and he'd have a list of parts he'd need for the whole year. He knew what interval to rebuild things. He was so organized. He was pretty unassuming. If you didn't know what kind of genius he was, you'd never guess.

"One of my neatest days with him was when he was working for Rumi in Italy, running their Superbike team. He phoned me up one day, and said, 'Hi boss. I'm thinking of coming back to States. Can I come to work for you?' I said, 'When do you want to start? When you get here just give me one day and you have a job.' When I hung up the phone, I kicked back at my desk and said 'Yes!' So he came back and went to work for us and worked there ever since.

"I didn't ask him why he wanted to come back. I was just happy to get him back. He'd said that he'd had enough of being over there. I think it was a pretty tough deal. The bikes weren't that competitive. He's just one of the best people I've been around. Never heard the man complain, never. Even through this cancer.

"He used to come to me when he thought I was making a mistake and say, 'Have you thought about this?' He'd do a lot of research. When Honda decided not to get their stuff out of Japan anymore, Merlyn was the sole guy to go get things done. It's just amazing what the guy did behind the scenes."

Mathers put Merlyn in charge of Nicky Hayden when he was signed as an 18-year-old.

"For me, it was just, I was so lucky at such the right age to get to ride for him," Hayden said. "I was 18 and those are such important years, and I'd just moved up to Superbike and he helped to make sure, not only I learned, didn't just do stuff for me, made sure I understood how, why he did things with the team and how they went about things, just taught me a lot.

"I was an 18-year-old rookie. I'd like to say I just caught on so quick, but I think we got within a handful of points [388-383] of beating Mat [Mladin] that year. Really, truth is, that I was lucky just having a good team. Mathers knew how to build a team there, put a young guy in there. I definitely think he was the perfect guy at the perfect time for me.

"People talk about how Merlyn was so well mannered; he certainly loved to win. He definitely, probably better than me at keeping his emotions in check. It didn't matter what it took or the amount of work or anything else, he would get in the trenches with the boys. Just because he was the crew chief, he didn't mind putting in the hours. He definitely taught me a lot.

"A lot of people don't know it, but even after my second year in GPs when I found out my team was getting fired and my crew chief at the time was done. I tried to get Merlyn and it was actually looking pretty good. I talked to him and he had talked to the wife and it was kind of looking like it could be a go, and then kind of it as it got close to happening, someone at the HRC Racing side shut it down. At the time, I don't think they trusted me. I think they thought I was trying bring in a buddy from States. I don't think they understood what his level was."

But everyone who every worked with or knew him, certainly did. He will be missed.

December 12, 2007

Doomed?

"Every time I think racing can't get worse, it does." Those words of wisdom came from a perceptive observer and principal of the road-racing scene during last weekend's Daytona Dunlop tire test. And he's right.

Racing is doomed. At least in the United States under the current AMA administration. And the rest of the organization isn't in such great shape, either.

Those are the only logical conclusions that can be drawn after a recent radio appearance by AMA CEO Rob "The Dinger" Dingman.

The Dinger made news a while back by using this space as a giant "For Sale" sign for AMA Pro Racing. Yours for the asking is dirt track, road racing, hillclimb, and numerous other properties - maybe even Supercross. He made the point that AMA was getting out of the promotions business, which was a surprise to those who never knew the AMA was in that business. During his September interview on Pit Pass Radio, Dingman adroitly clarified - and muddied - his position.

The word he most associates with racing is "controversy." He used it four times in a span of two answers. But this was after again displaying a lack of knowledge about the AMA's place in pro racing.

[The AMA is getting] out of [the] racing series and events promotions business," the Dinger explained. "And I think a lot of people are confused by what that means. Because I think people don't necessarily understand the role that the AMA plays in professional racing."

No one more than The Dinger himself.

"I guess the best way to describe [it is that] Supercross Live Nation is our commercial partner," he continued. "They're our series promoter. They do a real good job promoting that series."

Then why is the series without a title sponsor and potentially for sale?

The Dinger continues to ignore the simple truth that the AMA has not been a series promoter - at least not in road racing - for years.

"But essentially we serve the role as both sanctioning body and series promoter," he said. "And as the sanctioning body, we make the rules and enforce the rules and provide timing and scoring and those kinds of activities at the races. And then, as the series promoter, we help to string together a number of events and promote those events as a championship series, for example, in our professional series. And that becomes difficult for us, because we're very under-resourced. We don't have the infrastructure. Everybody asks, 'Why aren't you like NASCAR?' And the immediate answer is, 'We don't have the resources of NASCAR.' Our racing department currently only consists of 27 full-time staff members. NASCAR's marketing and sales dept is much larger than that."

"[The AMA is managing] 46 various different types of racing activities," he added. "We have never been resourced to do all the things that we've tried to take on and do. One of the reasons we've not been all that successful is because we've mingled our role as sanctioning body with our role as series promoter. And I think that that has caused the motorcycle industry not to support us to the degree that they could, because of the controversy associated with us not performing either of those roles effectively."

The AMA has performed the role of sanctioning body well in some cases. There's certainly been stability in motocross and Supercross, with the exception of the occasional fuel controversy.

And the actual running of road races, and relations with track promoters, improved this year under Keith Kizer and Morgan Broadhead. The rules and committee processes, however, are a joke, with the AMA sanctioning not only racing but repellant behavior by a board member. The 2009 Superbike rules may or may not have been approved after a recent meeting in Ohio. No one at the Daytona tire test was quite sure because of the yawning silence coming out of Pickerington.

"The lack of support," the Dinger continued, "has impeded our ability to grow our membership to its full potential." Which makes little sense. The two biggest players in the industry are Harley-Davidson and American Honda. Both have membership organizations that are far more successful than the AMA, despite not offering significantly better benefits. The Harley Owners Group (H.O.G.) has more than 1 million members worldwide. The Honda Riders Club of America has about half a million members.

"One of the things that I hope will come out of this is that, like I said, once we minimize that controversy - who wants to associate their brand with a brand that's associated with controversy?" he noted. "So once I think we improve our image and improve our brand identity, it will be safe for corporations in the motorcycle industry to come to the AMA and say, 'Hey, we'd really like to do some kind of deal with you, whether it's some kind of member benefit where it's a discount.' And if we can improve our member benefits in such a way that $39 doesn't seem like a whole lot to belong to an organization that gives you $100 or $200 worth of benefits, tangible benefits, beyond the intangibles of government relations and other things, it'll enable us to grow our membership."

It's going to take more than that. AMA membership is at an all-time high of just over 290,000 members, according to Dingman. But the pool of prospective members, he said, is probably somewhere between 3 and 6 million motorcyclists - a number that is hard to define.

"Even if it's 3 million, we should hopefully penetrate deeper into that," he said. "If it's 6 million, which is probably closer to what it is, we really need to be larger than we are."

Either way, a membership of 290,000 is pathetic.

What Dingman fails to understand is that the most public face of the AMA is racing. Think of the number of AMA members, and potential AMA members, attending all the events among the 46 various disciplines. More importantly, the AMA's greatest exposure is through television. The audience numbers may not be huge, but you're still talking hundreds of thousands every weekend for much of the year. But rather than take advantage of that, The Dinger is running from it. And it's not surprising.

A very wise former dirt-track champion put it best when he said that the people who run the AMA aren't invested in racing. They don't appreciate racing, they don't understand racing, they've never lost a friend or family member to racing. They lack passion.

Racing is a passion. It's a passion for the factories - how else could a little factory like Ducati embarrass the Japanese companies in MotoGP? It's a passion for the riders, for the crews, for the fans. Without passion no one would put in the ridiculous hours it takes for a successful racing operation. These are not, in most cases, nine-to-fivers. The pooh-bahs of Pickerington are passionless. And short-sighted.

"The AMA can't be in all places at once," said the Dinger. "Our government-relations staff is similar to our racing staff. There's no way we can possibly do all the things we need to do to protect the rights of motorcyclists."

Which sounds like the most important function of the AMA isn't in great shape, either. Which is why they need the money racing generates.

Maybe they think they'll continue to generate significant income through licensing, sanctioning fees, and the sale of the various series. First they need to determine what they're selling. And despite turning racing into a "red-tag special," the potential suitors haven't been told what they're buying. Another breakdown in communication. No surprise there.

The most frequently asked question during the tire test was, "How's Morgan?" AMA road-race manager Morgan Broadhead suffered serious head injuries in a practice crash in late September at Jennings GP in Florida. The AMA put out a release or two when it happened, then nothing for a month, and only one release since. It would be unfair to suggest they don't care, but it wouldn't be unfair to wonder why they don't keep the road-race paddock informed, even if on the "Riders Only" website. (The WERA BBS is the best source.)

Morgan made a big impression with his work ethic and willingness to listen during his first year on the job, and the hope is that someday he'll be able to return. Given the seriousness of his injuries, it will take some time.

In the meantime, his job will remain open for a year, according to someone familiar with the situation. In his place, the other series' managers will cycle in and out of road racing to help out, which is just plain nutty, but not surprising. To do something more sensible might invite controversy - and we can't have that.

January 16, 2008

The Shell Game

The fire sale of AMA racing properties is blazing away, with faces old and new vying to take racing into the 21st century. But the reality is sinking in that what comes next may not be better than the muddled mess we've enjoyed all these many years. And the major Japanese manufacturers are so concerned that they're considering doing their own thing. What that means is open to interpretation. Do they start their own sanctioning body? Do they want to run all of their own championships? Will they go head to head with Live Nation for Supercross? The possibilities are endless.

The result may be that whoever buys the AMA properties may be getting the racing equivalent of a 49-cent chocolate Easter egg - pretty on the outside, empty on the inside.

Given AMA Pro Racing's abysmal stewardship of their most valuable commodity, it was not surprising that the sale was greeted with enthusiasm. Track owners and team owners alike eagerly endorsed having someone - anyone - take it out of the fumbling paws of Pickerington. Then came the initial literature and the nondisclosure agreement, and reality set in.

What AMA CEO Rob "The Dinger" Dingman and his wingman Dennis Rhee are offering is a menu of choices that puts Shanghai Jack's to shame. One from column A, one from column B, all the way to Z. Like any other hucksters, their offer is, if you want it, we got it, or we'll get it, just as long as the check clears.

The most distressing aspect is the rulebook. Anyone with about a third-grade education can see that the AMA rulebook was written to be intentionally vague. That approach comes back and bites them intermittently - remember the Buell XBRR - and is often being tweaked. And what remains is close enough not to torment any of the major players with any regularity.

The process for rules making, however, is shambolic. The committees of the various disciplines and sizes propose rules to the board of directors, a group (with the exception of the many-hatted John Ulrich) that knows nothing about racing and cannot engage in line-item vetoes. It's take it or leave it... sort of.

This time around, the board couldn't quite approve the Superbike rules package. So they invited the committee to Ohio for a game of technical checkers. When the final piece was moved, and Ulrich got what he wanted - a ban on titanium valve buckets - the rules were probably approved. Why you haven't heard about it is yet another lesson in the Byzantine methods of AMA Pro Racing.

The rules cannot officially be approved by the board of directors until the minutes from the previous meeting are approved. That won't happen until the next board meeting in Indianapolis in February. So the rules that were drafted in August don't get officially approved for six months. Any real business that operated like this would be out of business in a minute.

In the end, it's the rulebook that's causing a mixture of rebellion and consternation in the board rooms of the Japanese manufacturers.

Among the many suitors cozying up to The Dinger and his wingman is Roger Edmondson. Edmondson, you'll recall, won in excess of $3 million for being wrongfully terminated by the AMA more than a decade ago. Edmondson is the brains behind a group of investors led by Jim France, of the Daytona and NASCAR Frances. France wants everything, not just road racing. Anything else would be too chaotic. This could be the start of a whole new sanctioning body. Edmondson, who's been very successful in a number of ventures, says he's only preparing the bid that's due on

January 15 and won't be distracted from his mission to run both the Grand American sports-car series and the Moto-ST Championship. So why should there be concern?

Following his wrongful termination, Edmondson and the late Pat Murphy founded the North American Sport Bike series (NASB), a championship that had restricted weight and horsepower. You could do whatever you wanted to the bikes, as long as they made the mandated weight and power figures. Beginning in 1996, Edmondson joined forces with Formula USA, which was known for its much more liberal equipment policy. It continued to evolve before eroding into near irrelevance.

In 2006, Edmondson formed the Moto-ST Series, a twins-based, horsepower-restricted endurance championship that runs on control treaded tires. The results have been decidedly mixed. Clearly, it's not a spectator- or television-friendly series. And the season finale at Daytona drew a total of 43 entries for the three classes. But it is very popular with the riders, who get to race on the same tracks as their AMA counterparts, with the notable exception, this year, of the debacle at Iowa Speedway. Even stranger is the notion Edmondson floated at a Moto-ST riders' meeting of having a cruiser series. Does anyone really want to see Rune races? Welllll, maybe.

Edmondson certainly isn't the only principal who favors tightly controlled production racing. Scott Hollingsworth, who was fired as CEO of AMA Pro Racing nearly two years ago, is currently the chief marketing officer for the A1GP. Very simply put, it's an open-wheel IROC series - same cars, same engines, same tires. And they are but two of the possible bidders. Live Nation, which had done a fine job of promoting the AMA Supercross Championship until the recent firestorm involving out-of-country venues, is also interested in some properties. The National Promoters Group (NPG) would certainly like to keep its slice of the outdoor motocross pie, but it will have to vie with Youthstream, the promoter of the World Motocross Championships, among other things.

I've heard talk of a group of rich guys who want to buy not only the AMA series, but World Superbike as well. It will be up to the august AMA board of directors to sort through the bids. Given the secrecy surrounding the process, it's a stretch to hope there will be any transparency, as there should be for a non-profit, member-driven organization.

What happens next? Let's say someone with a bent toward production racing grabs the golden ring. And let's say that person wants horsepower limits and other restrictions that rankle the OEMs. Does anyone believe that American Suzuki, which has done the best job of developing a line of sportbikes through its racing activities, would want to race a GSX-R1000 with a cap of 170 horsepower? Or that it would embrace the notion of control ECUs or tires or fuel? Not likely. The factories and tire companies and aftermarket companies race for marketing, certainly, but also to improve the breed. Racing nearly stock motorcycles isn't what they signed on for. Which is why it would make sense for them to break away.

The manufacturers are in the driver's seat. They have the pieces that the game needs to be played. They have the bikes, they have the riders. Racing is about competition, but it's also entertainment, and entertainment thrives on personalities. The notion that anyone would run the AMA Superbike Championship without Spies and Mladin and Duhamel and the Bostroms and the Haydens is ludicrous.

It would be imprudent for the Japanese manufacturers to strike out completely on their own. Instead, they could work under the cover of the MIC, the non-profit trade association, to avoid the charges of collusion that haunted them in the 1980s. The bet on the American distributors' part is that they'd have the backing of their parent companies, which they hope would have the stomach for a protracted fight. Certainly, given the direction racing could take, they have much to lose.

Could it work? Certainly. There are some very talented people who could run a sanctioning body. Promoters... it seems there's plenty of them out there. And they may be willing to strike a deal once they find out the multimillion dollar property they thought they just bought is nothing but a shell.

January 30, 2008

Talk's Cheap

Today's episode of *Chicanery* is brought to you, like most everything else in racing, by the American distributors of the Japanese factories. Without them, there would be very little television advertising on the racing telecasts, little in the way of contingency programs, much less support for the privateers, no factory teams, little magazine advertising, and almost no road-race event sponsors. In short, a world without racing - a cold, dark, empty abyss devoid of one of life's few arguments against kissing the third rail.

And yet, the industry leaders directly responsible for the continued good health of the very racing series they've seen put on the auction block have been completely ignored by the princes of Pickerington. Must be hard for small minds to see the big picture.

Whoever takes control of racing, in its many forms, will have to deal with the factories. That may seem obvious, but it isn't, not with the current crop of kingpins in Ohio. Why the cloak and dagger society of the AMA has chosen not to engage their most valuable constituents is yet another example of the tin ear they've shown to the din coming from the paddock.

Every new boss at the AMA, regardless of his or her place in the food chain, trumpets a new era of openness and communication, then does just the opposite. Tom Lindsey, the AMA spokesman, left when AMA CEO Rob "The Dinger" Dingman arrived. Then The Dinger dismissed Bill Wood, director of communications, and cut loose Kerry Graeber, the AMA Pro Racing mouth-piece, when he shuttered the West Coast office. Since then, he's promoted Grant Parsons to the post of communications boss. Parsons, like everyone else in the Pickerington compound, likely has a bunker mentality after having seen two friends dismissed and knowing he's under The Dinger's scrutiny. The Dinger circulated a memo that, strictly interpreted, meant he wanted to know about everything that left the building. Not the best way to enhance worker productivity.

The Dinger also had a minion tell AMA Superbike media manager Larry Lawrence that he wouldn't be coming back. Lawrence wrote his AMA obituary with an impassioned plea after Wood and two others were dismissed. It would have been hard, but not impossible, for The Dinger to keep him. He could have and he should have: There is no one better and more qualified for the job than "Double L." His absence will have a negative effect on the AMA's reach into the national media, to say nothing of his immeasurable contribution to the series regulars.

If The Dinger wanted to communicate properly, he'd do it with the suits at the OEMs, not by putting his e-mail address at the end of his mission statement. And this isn't entirely about racing. The AMA's paltry membership numbers have little chance of increasing, given the current depressed market, and even less chance if they choose to alienate the factories, which are far more successful at attracting new members to their organizations.

The argument has been made that the Harley Owners Group or the Honda Riders Club of America have falsely inflated numbers. It's easy enough to do the math.

H.O.G. claims more than one million members worldwide. Each of those members was given a free membership with the purchase of their new Harley, of which about 250,000 were sold last year. Take away those numbers and you still have 750,000 members, about 2 1/2 times the AMA number.

Everyone I've spoken to in a position of upper management at not only the Japanese factories, but others as well, is baffled by The Dinger's doings. They don't disagree that someone, anyone, other than the AMA should be promoting racing - they just think they should have a say, especially over the rules making. And they're right.

The most successful form of two-wheel racing by any measure is MotoGP. Best riders, best racetracks, best television exposure, biggest crowds, and, most importantly, the most factory involvement. This comes through the Motorcycle Sport Manufacturers Association (MSMA), a group that includes the four Japanese companies and Ducati.

The MSMA is one of four crucial voices in the GP decision-making process. The others are Dorna, which owns the commercial rights; the International Road Racing Teams Association, which represents the teams; and the FIM, the sport's sanctioning body.

All four have a say in a system that has, with a few exceptions, been effective at keeping the level of racing high and the core members content.

The best road racer in the world is Valentino Rossi, even though he hasn't won the title for the past two years. No one really knows what Rossi earns, but Forbes magazine put him 11th on their 2007 list of top-paid athletes, with $30 million in total compensation. His compensation from Yamaha alone is thought to be about $18 million.

Who's the second highest paid road racer in the world? My guess would be Yoshimura Suzuki's Mat Mladin. An Australian business magazine, BRW, estimated his 2007 take as $7 million AUS, or about $6,032,000 U.S. If you think that Dani Pedrosa or Nicky Hayden or Casey Stoner or Troy Bayliss makes more than that, you'd be wrong. How much of it comes from American Suzuki? About $5 million, I'd guess - which is a huge chunk of money. But it also shows their commitment to winning. They would likely have paid Ricky Carmichael about the same when he was at the top of his game, which means that just two riders consumed a quick $10 mil. What's that worth? Six AMA Superbike titles for Mladin and four - two 250 MX, two Supercross - for Carmichael. Carmichael is considered the greatest supercross/motocross rider of all time. Mladin's wins and championship totals will never be matched. Suzuki also sponsors four of the 11 rounds of the AMA Superbike Championship.

No one is suggesting that the AMA or whoever has the deepest pockets revert to the days of non-production racing. The budgets can't support it and, besides, what's the point? The AMA Superbike Championship is one of the preeminent production-based series in the world. In terms of compensation, it's top of the list, though anyone negotiating a contract for 2008 might argue that. With sales slow in 2007, and 2008 not looking great, the OEM's have had to cut everywhere, including their racing budgets. After a few years of lackluster results, American Honda and Yamaha both went to deals that rely heavily on performance incentives. With a sea change coming in 2009, motivation shouldn't be a problem.

But you simply cannot ignore the factories if you want to maintain or improve the current level of Superbike racing in America. No one else could afford to pay the riders, support privateers, or advertise on TV. Outside-the-industry sponsorship, other than from energy drinks, is almost nonexistent, with a few notable exceptions. The Corona Honda team, which will campaign Jake Holden this year, does an excellent job of promoting their brand in local markets. They're also the title sponsor for the season ending race at Mazda Raceway Laguna Seca. And they serve the best lunch in the paddock.

American Honda vice president Ray Blank is as concerned as anyone. As the boss of the brand with the largest market share, and with a significant investment in racing, Blank is baffled.

"They [the AMA] look at it from a facet that says, 'Well, that's because we [the factories] want to be in control,'" he said. "It's not a matter of control. It's a matter of involvement, because it's critical for the continuance of our investment and I think our investment is critical for the sport. If that's taken away from us, a lot of other things go with it. It causes a big vacuum. And it's going to put us years behind. We were kind of on the upswing here for a while and I'd hate to see it go backwards."

Rather than waste this entire space on a group with little interest in or knowledge of racing, I'll use what's left on an icon who left an indelible mark.

Blank was fortunate to employ the late Merlyn Plumlee. Plumlee, for those who don't know, was a brilliant crew chief who worked with a number of road-race champions, including Nicky Hayden, Freddie Spencer, Doug Chandler, Fred Merkel and Scott Russell. He died at the end of October after a two-year battle with lung cancer.

Everyone I spoke with was of one voice; yes, he was a great mechanic, but more than that, he was a wonderful person a thoughtful, quiet soul who left those of us who were fortunate enough to know him richer from his all too brief time among us.

The Motorcycle Mechanics Institute has set up a scholarship in his name. The Merlyn Plumlee Memorial Scholarship was established to allow deserving students to study at the Motorcycle Mechanics Institute and to carry on Merlyn's philosophy of generosity, fairness and passion for the sport of motorcycle racing. Donations to the scholarship can be made through the website of the UTI Foundation (www.utifoundation.net). Given the downturn in the industry, donations may be hard to come by, but keeping his legacy alive is important and I'm confident the foundation will be gratified with the response.

Merlyn had a number of strengths. The greatest may have been communicating. He wasn't wasteful with words, which meant you listened to what he said, and he to you. The communication between rider and mechanic is crucial; without it there is no success - you might as well go ice fishing.

Maybe someone needs to send The Dinger an auger, a pole, a bucket of minnows, and a nice, comfortable stool. A few hours spent staring into an icy, dark, un-peopled void might not be a bad thing.

February 20, 2008

Time to Come Clean

Don't ever accuse AMA CEO Rob Dingman of not knowing what his peeps are up to. The "Dinger" circulated a memo this summer telling them that they are "not to send anything outside the building without my prior approval." Does that mean every e-mail? Strictly interpreted, yes, though he must be kidding. Yet on the attached routing sheet, the "Requester" was asked to submit his deadline, his direct supervisor's approval, the vice presidents approval and the approval of "The Dinger" his very own self. You would be hard-pressed to come up with a more intrusive impediment to progress or a more egregious example of micromanaging. But at least he cares about his peeps.

Dingman has a number of questions to answer when the AMA convenes its annual meeting of corporate members at this week's Indianapolis trade show. They are, in no particular order, the financial health of the organization, the rate of membership growth, the antagonism toward the American distributors of the Japanese factories, and the status of the sale of the racing properties.

Late in November, two important events happened at the Pickerington campus: First, the sudden and unexpected resignation of AMA board of directors chairman Dal Smilie in mid-November. Smilie was an AMA board member for 25 years and if the departure were amicable, he would have been given a proper send-off - a laudatory letter from Dingman and fellow board members. Instead came a two-sentence notice that didn't thank him for his years of service or lament his resignation. Someone I spoke to who contacted Smilie was told he wanted to spend more time with his family. Spending time with the family is almost always a euphemism for being shown the door. That he would suddenly leave makes little sense.

About 10 days after Smilie left, the AMA alerted one of its insurance carriers of impropriety by a board member. Rea & Associates, an Ohio accounting firm that does, among other things, forensic accounting and fraud auditing, was retained to investigate the level of impropriety. Since Smilie was the only board member to leave in November, it wouldn't be a stretch to assume he was the target of the investigation. If he wasn't the target, then who was? And what did they find? AMA membership deserves the truth. As a board member, there's little someone could do other than inflate expenses. And they would've had to be astronomical to trigger a fraud investigation. And, if it were a case of inflated expenses, who approved them? Was it Dingman or his predecessor as CEO Patti Di Pietro?

Smilie was the chairman of the board until his departure and, as such, his behavior directly affected every member of the organization. As would the disclosure of financial shenanigans by a board member, let alone the chairman of the board. The membership should demand an answer at the AMA meeting. Will it get one? Don't count on it.

If you read the minutes from AMA board meetings, you'll find they often go into executive session. This was originally done to discuss pending litigation, but has recently been abused. This comes as little surprise to even the most casual observer of the secretive and autocratic Pickerington scene.

Dingman is making little effort to make friends with the factories. They were ignored during the recent sale of AMA racing properties, while at least one prospective buyer brought the love. Dingman seems to think he doesn't need the factories. As one senior team member told me at last week's Fontana roadrace test,

"What if we didn't show up for a race? Do you think he'd care then?"

But it goes far beyond racing. The AMA cannot survive without the support of the factories and it certainly can't grow. The factories support far too many of the AMA's activities. Anyone who thinks it wise to ignore them is dingy. And yet all I heard at the test were complaints and queries, mostly about the future.

The Byzantine process that is the AMA rules-making process will culminate with the 2009 Superbike rules being "officially" approved at Indy. Teams have already begun making the changes in anticipation of the 2009 season. But what if the new series promoter decides he doesn't like the rules - that he likes racing cruisers, and likes horsepower limits, and control tires and control fuel? The AMA should mandate that the rules package, as passed, must be honored until at least 2009, if not longer.

The teams wanted to know how the races would be staffed. Will the ambitious and conciliatory Morgan Broadhead be replaced? Not exactly. Will the AMA replace the equipment that went up in flames when the road-race trailer was incinerated at a repair shop west of Columbus? Yes, in some fashion. But no one I spoke to at the test has been told for certain. As one observer said of the blaze, "Now they're really screwed. That truck had all the books for how to run the races."

Several years ago, when there was stability at the top, the AMA produced a detailed annual report and distributed it to all corporate members and to members of the AMA congress. They would also send a copy to any member who asked. The report contained the audited financial statements, membership-growth or -decline statistics, and a fairly detailed narrative about key developments and events during the year.

The basic health of the organization, such as membership and financial figures, is of interest to all AMA members, corporate and otherwise. Transparency is essential. And the fact that the opposite is happening, that a veil of secrecy and fear permeates the AMA, is not an encouraging sign.

It's not just Dingman, though he must be held accountable. The board of directors, which includes representatives from Harley-Davidson, Kawasaki, and KTM, as well as others, should push for more openness. They have the fiduciary responsibility to see that the organization is being properly run. If they know about any chicanery, it is essential that they reveal it or risk exposure for complicity. And if that does prove to be the case, they should all be thrown out. I suggest they start in reverse alphabetical order. Let's see, Ulrich, Sutton, Smith, Simpson, Reynolds, More, Long, Goldfine, Burleson. Tough one.

Is fraud the only problem at the AMA? Certainly not, especially when it comes to racing. They recently hired another vice president for racing who comes from a small sports-car organization. You must have read the release? No? Because there wasn't one, because the new era of openness and communication is pure fiction. The new VP will report to Senior VP Dennis Rhee, who knows more about racetracks than racing and isn't in the habit of sharing what he knows with the racing fraternity. Remind me, why does the AMA need more vice presidents if they're getting out of racing?

The Dinger has repeatedly disparaged racing, citing the controversy it attracts as a rationale for getting out of it. What exactly is the controversy? Is it litigation? There was, several years ago, a lawsuit brought by Roger Edmondson that cost the organization more than $3 million. The entire process, painful as it was for the principals, was completely transparent. There was another lawsuit brought when then Pro Racing CEO Scott Hollingsworth retained JamSports to promote Supercross. The settlements were eventually made out of court. Is that it? How many lawsuits have there been since then? And if so, how were they settled? If the AMA is making seven-figure payments without disclosing them to the membership, they are in violation of their responsibility.

The AMA mission statement is "to serve the interests of motorcyclists by pursuing, promoting and protecting the future of motorcycling." Did Dingman sign off on that one?

February 27, 2008

Rotten to the Core

Things are rotten in Pickerington and getting rottener. AMA CEO Rob Dingman belatedly admitted that the board may not be replete with upstanding citizens. This reluctant confession came after "The Dinger" had his hand forced by the exposure, on these pages, of financial shenanigans by a board member: The AMA alleges that former board chairman Dal Smilie was padding his expenses.

The board knew something was hinky as far back as September and hired an external auditor to go over what they believe are the cooked books in late November, about 10 days after Smilie "resigned." Nearly three months on, the auditors - for whom your membership dollars aren't paying; the AMA filed an insurance claim - continue to scour the books in search of more miscreants. The bodies are starting to pile up.

The first casualty is board member Jeff Smith, who resigned the day before last Saturday's breakfast meeting of AMA corporate board members. Didn't hear about it, you say? That would be because the new, more open, more communicative, less secretive AMA withheld the information until late Monday. Why? Maybe because it would look bad. Maybe it would look like Smith had something to do with Smilie's smiling every time he turned in an expense account that had more red flags than Tony Soprano's tax return.

In fact, Smith was involved. As the assistant treasurer of the board, Smith was in charge of approving Smilie's expenses. His resignation means one of two things: Either he was lazy - didn't he wonder why there was no decimal point somewhere on the $1500

Rooty Tooty Fresh 'n' Fruity® breakfast? - or he was complicit. The bet by his colleagues is that it's the former.

In announcing the makeup of the new board, and Smith's departure, the AMA issued a statement that was more expansive than when Smilie retreated to Montana. It said, in part, "The board passed a unanimous resolution recognizing Mr. Smith's contributions during his seven years of service as a board member and wished him well in his new endeavors."

This isn't Smith's first brush with big-buck money problems. For years, Smith, in his position as executive director of AHRMA, was entangled in lawsuits and countersuits with Team Obsolete's litigious owner Rob Iannucci that left a trail of bitterness and legal bills and little else. AHRMA's legal costs - more than $300,000 - ultimately bankrupted the vintage-racing organization and forced them into a Chapter 11 reorganization. The two parties have apparently called a truce. It's fair to say there were no winners.

With Smilie awaiting the next disclosure and Smith back in Wisconsin, the AMA board now has two vacancies that "will be temporarily filled by appointment until the next election in 2010."

The AMA Code of Regulations states: "Upon the removal, death, resignation, or lack of qualification of any director, the remaining directors may fill the vacancy at any meeting; provided, however, that if possible, any successor director shall have the same qualifications for office as the original director when elected and, where appropriate, that the successor be from the same region or be the designated representative of the same corporate member."

Who, then, should fill Smith's position? The board would be wise to choose Larry Lawrence.

Lawrence, you'll remember, is the former road-race media manager who fell on his sword after an impassioned entreaty to Dingman to reinstate two fired AMA employees. It didn't exactly work out. They're still very much fired, and their legacy may be that, under Dingman, being inflexible isn't a wise choice. And AMA Pro Racing, and the road-race paddock and press room, have lost the hardest-working and most effective media manager the AMA's ever had. With Daytona only weeks away, there's been no word of a replacement. Yet another example of the Communications Department communicating.

Lawrence began working selected road races in the early 1990s, work that earned him the job as AMA Pro Racing's communications manager for two years. When he left AMA PR, he continued working in road racing, elevating the profile of road racing and motocross in the local markets and national media for more than a decade. He also did the heavy lifting for the Motorcycle Hall of Fame and served as the election committee chairman. His insight into the inner workings of the AMA makes him the perfect choice, as does his independent voice.

Dingman dances on the board at will, and the results - and his vision for future of the organization - have not been warmly embraced.

Most of the board members know Lawrence and should enthusiastically support him, based on his passion for the AMA and his more than a decade of peerless work and stridency on behalf of the organization. Over the years, our positions regarding the AMA were at odds more than once - actually, pretty much every time - and his defense of the organization rarely wavered. Through various CEOs and road-race administrations, he was convinced they were headed in the right direction. Until recently. Is he alone? Certainly not; he's just vocal and, subsequently, recently unemployed. Which means he has plenty of time to do the board's work.

The AMA took another hit on Monday. Bill Amick, the AMA's rep on the FIM Motocross Commission, resigned. In a letter to Dingman and two FIM officials, the former employee of 30 years cited health problems "that make it impossible for me to perform at the level that I expect of myself and that you deserve."

But that wasn't the end of it.

"Equally important," the letter continued, "I will be candid and acknowledge that I have become more and more disillusioned with the manner in which the AMA has been managed in recent years. Even if I was up to the work at hand, I can no longer muster enthusiasm for the task in the light of the association's misdirection by a scandal-ridden board with a track record of ruthless meddling with its human resources and for hiring incompetents."

In referring to Dingman, Amick wrote that the AMA now "has no place for the likes of Ed Youngblood, Greg Harrison, and other quality leaders who have been fired or forced to resign so that a handful of small people can try in vain to fill a void in leadership with their inflated egos."

Amick also claimed that the "AMA's influence as a key member of the international motorcycling community has trended downward since the retirement of Ed Youngblood. Three CEOs and one interim CEO later, the AMA ranks as the FIM's number-one inside joke rather than its most influential national federation."

Harsh words, indeed, especially from someone who's served and defended the organization for most of his life. Included in that defense was a scathing critique of a column I wrote two years ago about various AMA and AMA PR blunders and the organization's secretive ways. The AMA was secretive then, and it's secretive now. Only now, it's clear that they can't run from racing fast enough. Government relations is where Dingman came from and where he'll probably return. The rest seems to be a nuisance, regardless of the fact that racing is the AMA's most visible asset.

Dingman, in discussing the state of the Pro Racing fire sale, "stressed that secrecy was a necessary part of the proceedings," according to an AMA release. Too bad a few people didn't get the memo.

At least four of the major bidders have been interviewed by *Cycle News* reporters and we've spoken privately to others. And their interest has been closely monitored by the racing community and manufacturers - those who will be most closely affected.

Road-race teams have been given a set of rules to prepare for the 2009 season. They'll be testing parts all season and a complete motorcycle in October, after the season ends. That's five months before the start of the next season. No one knows if the rules created by the road-race committees are going to be honored, and Dingman doesn't seem concerned. As a condition of the sale, he could mandate that technical rules remain in place for at least a year. That doesn't seem to be the case, and the board seems helpless to stop him.

Which is why it needs fresh blood, a dissenting voice, and more transparency. Smilie was shown the door, and Jeff Smith followed him out. The line forms to the right.

March 19, 2008

And the Winner Is...

We have a winner.

The towel "The Dinger" threw in to show that he'd give up on pro racing landed in the lap of Roger Edmondson, the once-persecuted guardian of road racing, who will use that towel to clean up the mess that just cost him and a handful of deep-pocketed friends a big pile of folding green.

Now comes the hard part.

The reaction to the sale split along predictable lines: After years of being treated like lepers, the track owners embraced Edmondson like a long-lost friend. The racing purists will need more convincing. The skepticism is deeply rooted. Reasonable people offered scenarios with no basis in fact. But there was just enough of a hint of the possibility that the pig was able to fly.

A very well-regarded former racer detailed a conspiracy theory that would make Oliver Stone pink with envy. The fix was in from the start, he said. His proof was flimsier than a toupee in a wind tunnel. What if, he said, AMA senior VP of Racing Dennis Rhee was a plant? What if he'd been hired by the Daytona group to infiltrate the AMA to get the ear of AMA CEO Rob "The Dinger" Dingman? What if he went in there to run down the value of the properties, suggest they should be sold - too controversial - then discover he knew just the right bunch of upstanding citizens to take the carcass off his hands? I mentioned this theory to Edmondson after an interview we did that appears elsewhere in this issue. It's patently absurd; Jim France doesn't do business like that, we agreed. But the fact that a reasonable person could not only envision but advance such a fantasy speaks volumes about the distrust engendered by The Dinger and his bunker buddies.

A more plausible scenario was that the RFP (request for proposal) process was a sham - that it was done as a way to placate those of us interested in transparency and fairness, while there was only one possible bidder all along. That theory was discredited by Edmondson. In a packed Friday night news conference at Daytona International Speedway, Dingman said there were 14 bidders, but that the Daytona Motorsports Group (DMG) was the only one that wanted the whole enchilada. Edmondson said the original intent was to take only road racing; only later did they see the value in the entire package, most of which they'll farm out.

I got a very insightful e-mail from a friend who never fails to present a fresh perspective. What he wrote was that when a business is acquired, the acquired party is usually tired and the new owners feel that, under their management, "which does not do dumb stuff, then the business will turn around. The AMA has essentially admitted that they do not know how to stop doing dumb stuff."

Now that they're out of the professional racing business, the AMA will fade, over time, like a bad grease stain. The model Edmondson cited for a membership body getting out of pro racing was the AAA. "Forty-one million" members, Dingman chimed in, as if that'll happen. The current pathetic membership tally is around 290,000, so the AAA doesn't have to start worrying just yet. Subtract everyone in racing who has to join, take away the life members who pay nothing, and you have a very small group of die-hards to which Dingman and his coterie can commit their full attention.

Certainly with racing off the agenda, the board of directors - a group of enablers most notable for their fecklessness and corruption - can spend more time trying to figure out why the hell they've given Dingman and his predecessors free rein and wondering what the hell he's doing. There were a number of board members in the Daytona press conference who were finding out details of the deal for the first time. They would not have been happy.

Contrast that with Edmondson - a born salesman if ever there was one, who understands the value of communication, something the AMA has never understood and will never understand. Edmondson answers his phone calls, he hands out his business cards, he meets with people, he takes their advice. He isn't afraid to admit he doesn't know everything, and he's willing to listen. But there are limits; in the end, he'll make the decisions - not a board, not a committee, but him and those around him. His first hire was a good one: Colin Fraser will run the series.

Communication is to Dingman what ass rash is to Lance Armstrong. Actually, that's unfair: Armstrong understands ass rash; The Dinger understands nothing about communication. The RFP process was swaddled in secrecy, but leaks got out and leakers were targeted. I had one prominent AMA official tell me at Daytona that he couldn't be seen with me, that he'd been accused of leaking me information. It was patently untrue, but that doesn't matter. He was the target and they'd taken aim. And besides, he was very likely a short-timer.

The onsite Pro Racing staff was gathered at 8:30 a.m. on Friday morning to be given the bad news. Dingman didn't give it, nor did Dennis Rhee. Instead, they dispatched an underling. Most of the people will be given the chance to apply for their jobs and many only work the races, so they wouldn't have to move to the DMG headquarters, which will presumably be in Daytona Beach.

Dingman has his hands full. The forensic accountants who've made the Pickerington campus a home away from home have turned up some disturbing revelations. Vendor checks - about 100 of them - meant for the AMA were sent, instead, to a post-office box, I was told by someone with knowledge of the investigation.

Whomever rented that box and collected the checks might want to call 1-800-LAWYER.

The worry in the paddock is that racing will be dumbed down with control tires and near-control motorcycles. It is a virtual certainty that the racetrack will no longer be as important a tool in developing production motorcycles. But anyone who's been watching the show for the past few years knows something had to be done if the sport hopes to attract sponsors and become a more attractive spectacle, both in person and on television. And the contrarians who argue otherwise can't possibly believe the status quo is anything but a short walk into a deep lake.

Control tires are a given, and Edmondson wants every part on every motorcycle to be available for sale. When I mentioned this to Mat Mladin, he thought it was a great idea.

"I've heard mumblings from many teams throughout the years; [most recently] the Michael Jordan Motorsports team talking: 'We need to get factory bikes, we need to get this, we need to get that,'" he said. "I really hate to be the bearer of bad news, but it doesn't matter if the bikes are the same; the best riders are still going to come to the front."

The reason the racing isn't interesting is because most of the teams aren't committed, at least not judging from their performances and the choice of riders they hire. When Mladin was on the market a few years back, the offer he got from a rival team was a quarter of what Suzuki was offering. It's no wonder they need a GPS to find the winners' circle.

The Yoshimura Suzuki team, now sponsored by Rockstar and Makita, is the best team. Try to argue with the numbers. Because they're the best team, they've developed the best motorcycle. And because of the commitment of American Suzuki and their Japanese counterparts, they're able to afford the best riders. The most coveted seat in racing is not on the Jordan Suzuki team, but the one that Ben Spies will vacate when he goes off to MotoGP next year. And the next year it'll be Mladin's seat, if he leaves. Given how much money he makes and how successful he is, you'd need a crystal ball the size of Rhode Island to see any serious future competition.

And the notion that more production-based racing will even the field is a little naive. In fact, it plays to the factories. With the best people building the bikes and the best riders riding them, and the factories able to produce the best "production" parts, the best team will always prevail. No amount of rules is going to make Eric Bostrom or Neil Hodgson or Jamie Hacking as successful as Mat Mladin or Ben Spies. Which is not a knock on those riders; they've all won National titles, and Hodgson has a World Championship.

They have to believe that on equal equipment they could compete for victories. But there's a reason Mladin has 64 Superbike wins, and it isn't just because he has the best machinery. A more reasonable question is, "Why does he have the best machinery?" It's because he's committed; driven to win, even at the advanced (for a road racer) age of 36. He's fitter now than he's ever been and lighter than he's been for years. (At least one rider's leathers looks more like the casing for a rotten sausage.) Mladin's response to all the noise he's heard all winter was on display when he decimated the field in Saturday's Superbike race. And afterward, when he mimicked playing the violin on his cooldown lap. It's because of his dedication, determination and drive that the best people in the paddock want to work with him. Winning is more fun than losing, and it pays better. It's because of that that he's among the highest-paid road racers in the world.

American road racing, as we know it, is gone forever. That isn't a bad thing. But no amount of new rules is going to suddenly even the field. For that, you need a level of commitment that doesn't exist, and that's something you can't legislate.

April 2, 2008

Many Questions

With the best of intentions, the Daytona Motorsports Group (DMG) will change the face of the AMA Superbike Championship. They'll dumb down the technical regulations, dictate an open-source policy for parts, and mandate control tires. They'll make the racing closer, more accessible, more entertaining, and safer. But safety is an issue on which they lack credibility, for one very simple reason: Daytona International Speedway is the most dangerous racetrack on the AMA calendar.

Once upon a time, the Daytona 200 meant something. It attracted the best riders on the best motorcycles, from Saarinen to Ceccotto to Agostini to Sheene to Fogarty, to say nothing of the homegrown talent - Roberts, Spencer, Rainey, Lawson, Schwantz, Russell.

That began to change in the mid-1980s, when the purpose-built Formula One machines were replaced as the premier class by the lumbering Superbikes. It also coincided with the golden era of American domination of 500cc Grand Prix racing, just after the Roberts-Spencer battles, Lawson ascendant, with Rainey and Schwantz waiting in the wings. Riders from overseas made the occasional foray to Daytona, but for the most part it ended with Carl Fogarty complaining he'd gotten a bum deal in the 1995 running of the race, won heroically from the ground up by Scott Russell.

From then on, it was just another round of the American series, with the exception of the odd appearance by an American World Superbike campaigner. Eventually they went away as well. And any notion they might come back was nixed when the track and the AMA agreed to switch the premier class again, this time to very expensive, exclusive-to-the-United-States 600cc Formula Xtreme machines.

The more prestigious-road race series were also instrumental in killing the 200. The World Superbike teams couldn't race in the 200 - tires and tech regs prevent it - and World Supersport teams didn't want to; their motorcycles wouldn't be competitive, and they had nothing to gain. No MotoGP rider would risk riding in a race that meant so little. When those series began scheduling conflicting races, the race was officially irrelevant outside the confines of the United States.

Daytona International Speedway is the most dangerous track on the American calendar by a margin that isn't measurable. Every track has a corner or two or three that's problematic; Daytona is little but danger. Racing a motorcycle - any motorcycle - on a banked track at speeds in the 180-mph range with an immovable wall only feet away is lunacy. There is no margin for error. The smallest mistake can be lethal. And the walls that cushion the blows of 3400-pound Cars of Today or Cars of Tomorrow do little other for motorcycle racers than turn them into the Riders of Yesterday. There is no way to make the current layout safe - and it could get worse.

Does anyone want to race in the rain at Daytona? Daytona is among the near majority of cracks on the calendar that aren't approved for wet racing. The others are California Speedway, Infineon Raceway, Mid-Ohio and Road Atlanta. Virginia International Raceway is on the fence; there's an issue with track sealant. Of 10 tracks, that's five nays and a maybe. During the interview we had with him, we should have asked DMG's Roger Edmondson how he would handle the wet/dry conundrum. My guess is his answer would be to upgrade the tracks to the point where they're safe in all conditions. Unfortunately, that isn't possible. Certainly not at Daytona or Fontana, or another

International Speedway Corporation property that's one of the lesser venues on the calendar. Road Atlanta in the rain is frightening. Riding on a wet Infineon Raceway is unlikely, despite years of improvements. Mid-Ohio has surface consistency and runoff issues.

Restoring the glory of the Daytona 200 means restoring the track to the days before the 600s were the premier class. No doubt the DMG would like to use the old road course and both bankings. But the tire abuse more than doubles by adding the second banking. Tires deform at speed and, coupled with the inordinate g-forces of the banking, the deformity is amplified. And doing it for most of the lap subjects tires to more heat and stress than any other track in America - if not the world. On top of which, it doubles the chance for catastrophic accidents.

It's okay to run dog-slow Moto-ST bikes on both bankings, but not proper racing motorcycles. When first asked if the new layout was safer, Rockstar Makita Suzuki's Mat Mladin did the math; riding a Superbike on one banking 15 times was less dangerous than riding a Superbike on two bankings 57 times.

My guess is that the DMG would like to attract World Supersport teams to run in the 200. Why? Beats me. Can you name two World Supersport riders? With the emphasis on more production-based racing, there's no hope that World Superbike teams would ever return. But World Supersport rules are more stringent and could be the template for the premier AMA class. And if World Supersport teams do come, the tire issue becomes paramount. If you want the non-household names of that series to puff up the field, the control tire for the United States would have to be Pirelli.

Edmondson told us in our interview that control tires would be considered.

"The tire abuses are rampant, and they've got to stop," he said.

But it's clear that he's getting bad information. Had he spoken to all the tire companies and teams, rather than taking the word of the disgruntled few, he'd have discovered the opposite. He'll certainly learn more in the coming weeks, when he travels to Los Angeles to meet with the factory teams, and later when he talks to the tire companies.

Regardless of who makes them, cost concerns mean the control slicks will almost certainly be inferior to the Dunlops that have won nearly every Superbike, Formula Xtreme, and Superstock race for as long as anyone can remember. The one-size-fits-all approach will make the motorcycles appear safer, the theory being that if you can't go as fast, you can't hit walls with as much destructive power.

The counterargument is that 600s are faster than 1000s in the corners, which is where most crashes occur. That point is hard to argue. But what about the high-profile, high-speed crash? Tires blowing up at Daytona once caused those sorts of problems, but in recent years that problem has disappeared. And they rarely happen elsewhere.

The reason they've been eliminated is that Dunlop, which had the most problems, has been relentless in improving its products. A production technique that's been in use for a few years has produced greater uniformity among the tires. These are purpose-built racing tires made in limited quantities for the best Superbike racers in America.

Could they produce these tires at a reasonable cost if they're chosen as the control tire for the 2009 series? They'd have to. But, rather than providing free product to much of the paddock, Dunlop - or Pirelli, which pays a few teams and supports others - would now charge for tires. The factories wouldn't blink, but with two riders in two classes, a team like Attack Kawasaki would suddenly be looking at a large expense.

Dunlop, like the factory teams it supports, does much of its development on the racetrack. That stops in 2009. The current method of development that has allowed Suzuki to produce the most successful line of sportbikes in history will end after this season. What they race in 2009 will be much closer to a production machine and will stay that way. The lap records set in 2008 will take years to eclipse - if they ever can be. Even today, nearly five seasons on, not all of the World Superbike lap records have been broken. Neil Hodgson still holds the official Superbike lap record of 1:35.007 from Valencia in 2003. The time was bettered by Karl Muggeridge (1:34.252) at a recent sanctioned test, but until the April 6 race, Hodgson's time still stands.

The conundrum for the DMG is the premier class - 1000cc or 600cc. If the 600cc route is taken, it would either eliminate 1000s or make them a support class. That would create a situation in which the support-class motorcycles were faster than the premier class. If 600s are the premier class, the next question would be, what are the support classes? Certainly they could include the Red Bull Rookies Cup and a less-modified 600cc class. The excitement of racing single-cylinder motocross bikes will fade quickly once cost and reliability issues are addressed. Pinning a Honda CRF450 on the Daytona banking for days on end is not a recipe for longevity.

Nor is racing at Daytona, wet or dry, 600cc or 1000cc, one banking or two. The racing may be closer, it may be more entertaining, but it can never be safe.

April 16, 2008

Good Crank, Bad Crank

On Friday, April 4, AMA Pro Racing issued two competition bulletins with new technical regulations for the 2008 AMA Superbike Championship. Rule CB31008 addressed "Modification to oil galley plugs in all classes." The rule seemed simple enough and might have gone unnoticed except for one very small detail; it was written in direct response to a board member having his motorcycle declared illegal by AMA tech inspectors following the Daytona 200.

That board member is the multi-hat wearing John Ulrich. For those who may not know, in addition to being one of the feckless enablers on the AMA board of directors, Ulrich publishes a monthly magazine devoted to road racing and owns a very well-run, professional, and successful race team. Maybe a little too successful in the eyes of the AMA tech inspectors. They discovered the crankshaft in the Suzuki GSX-R600 that Martin Cardenas rode to fourth place in the Daytona 200 was dodgy. Does that make him a cheater? I'll leave that to the semanticists. But Ulrich did pay a $2000 fine, which is appealable.

Whoever builds the team's cranks removed the oil galley plug, used a tap to thread a hole and put a cap in place. To do that, you have to remove metal, which means the crankshaft isn't as "originally homologated." That makes it illegal, regardless of anything else the team may claim about crank balancing or whether the infraction was overlooked in the past.

Rather than allow one of its own to appear deceitful, the AMA folded like a Chinese takeout menu and changed the rule. On Friday, April 4, nearly four weeks after the 200, the AMA issued a tech bulletin that states "Oil galley plugs may be modified, removed or replaced."

Will they make it retroactive to let Ulrich's team skate? Even they're not that stupid... are they?

About now you're asking yourself, "Huh, I don't remember seeing anything about this on the roadracingworld.com website or in his rag after the 200." Surely, you don't think he's going to tarnish his noble reputation by admitting to devious behavior, do you? That would be responsible journalism and there's no place for that in John's world.

And if it were any other rider who was suddenly gifted a rules revision by the AMA, Ulrich would bombard his website with an avalanche of vitriol decrying the lack of fairness and attacking the offending team.

In yet another staggering example of wanton favoritism, the offending crank was returned to the team, even though, at the time, the offense was under appeal and the AMA had yet to create a rule to protect Ulrich. I was told it was done at the request of a senior AMA staff member. If true, that person should be fired and Ulrich should be kicked off the board, unless he's admitted his guilt and just wanted the fine reduced.

A $2000 line is insignificant when you consider the penalty imposed on the Erion Honda team. When the same AMA tech inspectors, who busted the M4 EMGO team, saw the mirror finish on the crankshaft of Josh Hayes' Daytona 200-winning CBR600RR, they knew it was illegal. So did Colin Fraser, soon to be appointed director of road-race competition by Roger Edmondson. A few phone calls later and judgment was swift.

So why was one rider disqualified and the other one fined? Seems justice was not applied equally. And justice was swift. Maybe Kevin Erion needs to join the board.

Daytona Motorsports Group's Roger Edmondson, when later asked whether the punishment should have been done in Florida or Ohio, replied with this statement:

"My opinion was that, when you do these things, you need to do them in an expeditious and orderly fashion, but you need to be sure," he said. "You need to be sure. And that doesn't mean you can't be wrong. You can surely be wrong. But you need to, with all of your best capabilities, you need to make sure of what you're doing before you disqualify somebody from any race and particularly one of such a high profile."

Since it was clear that the crankshaft on the Cardenas machine was illegal, should he not have been disqualified? I'm sure Kevin Erion would pay $2000 fines all week long to get his 200 win back. Given the inconsistent application of justice, it certainly strengthens the Erion case on appeal. What once seemed implausible, that the 200 results would be changed, suddenly seems more likely.

The problem isn't entirely with Erion or Ulrich, the problem is with the AMA rulebook. Engineered to be vague and invite cynicism, criticism and condemnation, the rulebook specifies two kinds of penalties, which the AMA can impose at its discretion. Category 1 is for violations "that could potentially or effectively enhance the performance of a motorcycle used in competition." Category 2 is "All other equipment violations."

The rulebook has to be black and white, but the AMA likes gray so they can muddy the waters by asking their sleuths to debate the psyches and subtleties of engine builders. This benefits who exactly? In Daytona, it was clear who benefited.

The model to follow is the FIM, which issues press releases regarding the rulebook. They issue releases for, among other things, every new rule, every drug test, and every technical offense. They are completely transparent, which is how it should be. The

AMA is completely opaque. I'm still waiting for the AMA to release the results of the drug tests from Mid-Ohio last year.

Ulrich's hinky crank wasn't the only infraction the AMA kept quiet at Daytona. And why wasn't it revealed? The new AMA Pro Racing policy is to no longer publicize infractions outside the top three. (Cardenas had the good fortune to come in fifth, originally, then fourth when Hayes was DQed.) This from the new more open, more communicative AMA, the one that professes to be more transparent than the rose-colored glasses that AMA CEO Rob Dingman sees the world through. They can hire all the PR consultants they want, the new AMA continues to operate as a secretive society, which denies relevant information to its constituents. No wonder they can't grow the membership.

Cheating needs to be publicized if for no other reason than as a deterrent. How many of the 200 finishers knew about the crooked crank in Cardenas' bike? Precious few. And how many might have done the same thing to their cranks? No one knows. Which means had the AMA not caved by changing the rules to the benefit of Ulrich's team, other riders could have shown up at Barber with the same cheater cranks they ran at Daytona.

By its whimsical and clandestine handling of a serious equipment violation in the most high-profile race of the season, and in the faces of the new owners of their series, the AMA has once again failed its competitors and anyone associated with road racing, including the Daytona Motorsports Group. And Ulrich failed as a team owner by fielding a bike with an illegal crank. And he failed as a journalist by not publishing news clearly relevant to his readers. That's a lot of failure.

May 28, 2008

He Who Makes the Rules

The silence was broken by misinformation at Infineon Raceway. The long-awaited technical rules - being created on the elastic two- or three-week schedule - might have been announced on Sunday. Only no one told Roger.

Daytona Motorsports Group CEO Roger Edmondson said there would be no announcement on Sunday morning, two days after his director of competition said there might be. Instead, Edmondson said the rules would come this week, maybe by the time you read this.

The holdup was a wrench thrown into the works by Yamaha's race boss, Keith McCarty. Edmondson had agreed to the 2009-10 rules that the factories wanted. But on second thought, Yamaha balked. Quantity was the issue. Edmondson stipulated that each factory must guarantee four machines for the Literbike class. It was insurance that the grid wouldn't be populated by eight or nine motorcycles. At Infineon Raceway on Sunday, with the absence of the Hayden brothers - Monster Kawasaki's Roger Lee and Rockstar Makita Suzuki's Tommy - there were seven factory bikes on the grid in a field of 21. Predictably, they occupied the first seven spots, though they hadn't on Saturday.

McCarty forwarded the notion of racing the far-less-expensive Superstock-spec machines, which meant Edmondson had to take the pulse of the big four. Three responded, one didn't. But which one?

DMG director of competition Colin Fraser reluctantly implied on Friday that American Honda was the holdout. Not so, said Edmondson, who also wouldn't name names. But he did say it wasn't American Honda, which makes American Suzuki the most likely culprit. That would come as no surprise.

The Yoshimura Suzuki team, and Suzuki worldwide, has the most to lose from a more restrictive set of rules. The GSX-R line of sportbikes is what defines the company. Ever since the factory in Japan became heavily involved with the Yosh race effort, the results have soared. As has the performance of the GSX-R machines, as well as sales. Credit Mat Mladin and his crew, led by crew chief Peter Doyle. What they've done is to develop a motorcycle that both Mladin and now Ben Spies can race at a speed the rest of the field can only imagine, and one that makes a very nice streetbike, as well as being the best starting platform for a race machine. Spies' good friend Jamie Hacking finished third in both races at Infineon, but at a distance. Monster Kawasaki's Hacking knows the difficulties of developing a new motorcycle. In the absence of Roger Lee Hayden, Hacking has been forced to do all the development work on the 2008 ZX-10R. Don't expect miracles, he said.

"To pick up 15 to 20 seconds is not going to happen over the next couple weekends, that's for sure," he said. "That's going to take a lot of things."

But Kawasaki may never get the chance to close the gap. The decision on Superbike or Superstock has already been made. Edmondson said that Fraser and Bill Syfan, his deputy, were working on the specifics of the technical rules.

"I've asked for them, if possible, to have a set of rules that we can release next week," Edmondson said, without tipping his hand.

Given his aversion to heavyweight sportbikes, it's likely the Superstock rules will be adopted. But maybe not. Edmondson isn't predictable. He sprang a surprise when he not only announced the Literbike class - he had no intention of having one when he went to meet with the OEMs back in April - but agreed to implement the rules to which they agreed for two years.

That said, the future is in Daytona Superbike, he said, mainly for reasons of safety. He doesn't believe the finances make sense for the current crop of racetracks to make massive safety improvements for motorcycles only. Infineon is one of the tracks whose staff believes in motorcycle racing and has funded the safety improvements with the much larger returns from their NASCAR and NHRA weekends.

The argument that heavyweights are more dangerous that middleweights would seem self-evident: More speed equals greater danger. The counterargument is that most crashes happen in the corners, where the middleweights are faster. None of which matters. Edmondson wants a level playing field - spec tires, spec fuels, horsepower-to-weight ratios - for Daytona Superbikes, and he's the boss.

Will this make the racing closer? We'll see. But it's instructive to look to the Red Bull AMA U.S. Rookies Cup. That series runs identical machines on identical tires and fuel with a combined rider/machine weight. Are there 24 machines racing for the lead? Not yet. There were four, then three, and then one when two of the three leaders crashed out. The best race of the Infineon weekend was Formula Xtreme, a class populated by middleweight Superbikes. Erion Honda teammates Jake Zemke and Josh Hayes went head to head for the duration, with the difference being sixty-seven-thousandths of a second at the flag. The gap between them was thirteen-thousandths of a second at the previous race, at Auto Club Speedway. The Attack Kawasakis were at a distance back in third. Some might blame tires - they were on Pirellis, the Erion boys were on Dunlops - but the racing had been close in Fontana, with Larry Pegram putting his Ducati 848 into the mix... on Pirelli tires.

World Superbike is often held up as the gold standard of competition: different winners in every race, different brands on the podium, encouragement to continue. Why is that? Is it the tires? I would argue that's part of it, but there's an equally reasonable counterargument that it's talent. The depth of talent at the top of the World Superbike field is just deeper than in AMA. It certainly isn't entirely machinery. The Suzuki GSX-Rs that race in World Superbike win on occasion, but not every weekend for nearly the past two years, as Spies and Mladin have done.

Mladin said in Barber that, regardless of the rules, the results wouldn't change if the same riders were racing. In the Literbike class, I would agree. I don't think he'd win as handily in Daytona Superbike, but he doesn't have to; he said at Infineon that he wouldn't race a 600.

And whatever he races, where will he race it? With word that there was a holdout in choosing a rules package came the inevitable rumors of a breakaway series. This is preposterous. The motorcycle-racing market is too small to support two series. And even if there was the will on the part of the disgruntled manufacturers, where would they race? Most of the tracks on the current AMA calendar have links to someone on the Daytona campus, either NASCAR or Grand-Am. So where would a rival series race? Loudon? Willow Springs? Nelson Ledges? It's not going to happen.

The DMG group is here to stay. Theirs is going to be the premier road-racing series in America, even if they believe that running Moto-ST on a professional weekend is a good idea. Funny how that wasn't put up for discussion.

June 11, 2008

Success!

The combined AMA/World Superbike meeting at Miller Motorsports Park was a rousing success. The weekend crowd tally of 51,000 far exceeded anyone's expectations, the event went off without a hitch, and the racing was competitive. But the debate in the paddock wasn't as much about racing as it was about the 2009 AMA technical rules, which, it's fair to say, weren't warmly embraced. And neither were all the spectators happy, at least not the ones who had to endure the nearly three-minute lap times of the AMA riders on the 4.486-mile Full Course.

Next year's fans likely won't have to suffer the three-minute laps. Both series will run on the 3.06-mile Perimeter Course, the one the World Superbike riders rode this year and the AMA raced on the previous two years. The official reason for bipolar tracks - an unprecedented event in World Superbike - was signage: FGSports, which promotes World Superbike, wanted a clean track. The conundrum there is that the AMA riders used all but a tiny sliver of the Perimeter Course.

Everyone knows the real reason for separate tracks was tires. How would it look for the AMA regulars to lap faster on their Dunlops than the World boys on their control Pirellis? That was the comparison FGSports didn't want made. But it was certainly one that intrigued everyone in the paddock, and it was made, beginning with practice. And it would have been a great promotional tool.

As it was, it wasn't until Superpole that the World Superbike regulars on sticky rubber were able to break Ben Spies' 2-year-old single-lap record. The difference, of course, is that Spies' lap was done on a soft race tire and not a qualifier, as at least one World Superbike journalist incorrectly, though hopefully, reported. And the World Superbikes were faster than the AMA machines. The fastest World Superbike race speed was the 191.134 mph clocking of Ducati Xerox's Michel Fabrizio, who ended up third in both races. The fastest AMA speed was Neil Hodgson's 189.11 mph in Saturday's race. The difference is more stark between the winners. World Superbike double winner Carlos Checa topped out at 188.462 mph. Ben Spies' first-race top speed was 185.09 mph.

To compare race times requires some math. The AMA race is 21 laps, World Superbike is 20. But if you subtract the final lap of the 2007 Saturday AMA race, Spies' winning time was 10 seconds faster than Checa's win in this year's first race. Using the same math, Checa did beat the second race time by two seconds, though it was much hotter and the track greasier during last year's AMA race, the track had been repaved, and Spies would certainly have gone faster as well.

Never mind. The debate is over, never to be heard again. Next year's AMA Literbikes will be even more gutless wonders. With a cap of 185 horsepower in the rarefied air near the Great Salt Lake, they'll be giving away 25 horsepower to the World Superbikes. And they might be on the same tires; that's yet to be determined.

Daytona Motorsports Group sent out Daytona Superbike rules early last week and Literbike rules at the end of the week. The Literbike rules were nearly identical to the Canadian Superbike rules. The eye-catcher on the Daytona Superbike proposed machinery list was the Suzuki GSX-R750. Anyone not contractually obligated would be foolish not to choose that over a 600. It only weighs five pounds more than the GSX-R600, it would be cheaper to build, and it would be more reliable. Then came word through the paddock grapevine that it was coming off the list. Not so fast, DMG CEO Roger Edmondson said. It's not going anywhere. We'll see. Take away the GSX-R750 and the choice is the torque-happy Ducati 848.

More intriguing are the choices in Literbike. How can DMG keep a rein on electronics when the Ducati 1098R race kit comes with traction control, if you fit the race-kit ECU? Two of the machines, the BMW S1000RR and Aprilia RSV4, aren't yet for sale. And they won't be cheap, but nothing about the new rules will be.

If the intent was to keep the cost of racing down by going to a horsepower- and weight-limited series, it's a failure. The rules essentially allow open internal engine modifications, as long as the horsepower/weight number is met.

"I'm going to build an engine with pneumatic valves and a nitrous bottle in the tail section - it'll make 185 horsepower from 10,000 to 22,000," said one particularly unhappy team owner, not entirely facetiously. "It's a disaster."

The closer racing is to production, the greater the advantage to the factories. Power isn't the issue - it's torque. The factories can produce parts that aren't available to privateers. They can also produce parts that appear similar in every way to the production unit but are about as related as Ben Spies is to Ben & Jerry. The factories will find a way to make the horsepower peak well down the power range and sustain it to the red line. And the factories can dyno-test all day long. Otherwise it'll be like going to the Olive Garden during Bike Week; you'll sit around for an hour waiting for your plastic coaster to vibrate.

And what happens when they return to Miller Motorsports Park, where the altitude robs the engines of 15 to 20 percent of their power? Will they have to build special engines for that one race? Almost certainly, unless there's a provision for corrected horsepower. If not, and you want to make 185 bhp in the Tooele Valley, your Literbike engine better make well over 200 at sea level.

The line at the dyno that weekend will stretch back to Temple Square. At least for those who can afford tires.

The Japanese manufacturers are all supported by Dunlop, as are most of the top satellite teams. Pirelli supports a few of the satellite teams. What happens when they all have to pay for tires, at about $150 per? If you run both classes and Moto-ST, which will thankfully only run at about half the races, and not on the MMP AMA/WSB weekend, you're looking at a crippling tire bill. Which is not to say it won't level the playing field; it's just that the field will be leveled by propping up one end with stacks of Benjamins.

Of more concern to some riders is how they'll be perceived outside the United States. Already, a number of riders are shopping their services overseas. Will any team take a chance on a rider who's only ridden horsepower-restricted machinery? It's hard to say, since no major series uses that formula. It works in Canada, but Lou Dobbs needn't be overly concerned about waves of riders flooding over the Niagara Falls. Anecdotal evidence suggests that the World Superbike teams weren't overly impressed by the rules, and that's putting it kindly. Why would they be? They have the most competitive major series in the world. The talent pool is deep throughout the field, with a mix of veterans such as Troy Bayliss, Nori Haga and Carlos Checa battling up-and-comers such as the German Max Neukirchner and the Italian Michel Fabrizio. And now that the AMA series has unique technical rules, it'll eliminate any cooperation between the AMA and World Superbike teams.

This isn't about racing or using racing to improve the breed, it's about entertainment. It's about putting on a spectacle that can be sold to a new audience, one that doesn't yet know it will be interested in motorcycle racing, one that might be interested in other forms of racing.

"Will we have to use headlight stickers?" one rider wanted to know.

What was most intriguing about Daytona Superbike was the purse. The rider with the best performance on the day will pocket $50,000. Sounds like a lot, but race-win bonuses are more than that for the factory riders. And besides, there's a better way to have close racing. Graves Motorsports Yamaha team owner Chuck Graves said that if you want close racing, you should pay $50,000 for second. Now that's a concept everyone can embrace.

June 25, 2008

Is the Honeymoon Over?

A question of etiquette: Is it proper to have a honeymoon following a shotgun wedding? And what if the marriage hasn't been consummated? The questions become relevant as the saga of the Daytona Motorsports Group's coupling with the AMA drags on. More than three months after the first blush of love was announced with great fanfare at Daytona International Speedway, the parties are already acting more like a bickering couple. The fire sale of AMA racing properties begun by AMA CEO Rob Dingman is fast becoming a laughingstock; some of the best people in AMA Pro Racing were made redundant, and road racing is at a low point few thought possible.

"I didn't think they could make it worse than the AMA, but they have," one National Champion said to me after finishing on the podium at Road America.

Who thought we'd pine for the days of Merrill, Hollingsworth, Barrick, and Rob King? It takes something special to make that regime look good by comparison, but that's exactly what's happened.

Never in my 30-plus years of covering racing have I seen an atmosphere this toxic. This isn't idle whining, the preferred leisure-time activity of the paddock grumbler, but genuine outrage and enmity, unavoidable and passionate. It has become personal on both sides and, given recent events, threatens to get worse.

Given the horrendous stewardship of the previous regime, there was among a certain segment of the paddock, myself included, some hope that things would improve. How could they be worse? That hope was deflated at Road America for a number of reasons, many relating to safety.

What did we know of DMG's plans prior to Road America? For one, that they're taking much longer than they originally stated. The technical rules that were supposed to be out a couple of months ago are still being hashed out. Part of that can be laid at the feet of Yamaha's Keith McCarty, who suggested that guaranteeing four machines under the rules the teams had agreed upon for 2009-10 would be too expensive. So DMG CEO Roger Edmondson asked his director of competition to dumb down the rules, and that takes time. Now, rather than approving specific components, engine modifications are mostly open, as long as the peak of 185 horsepower isn't breached. Factory crew chiefs are salivating at the thought of using carbon-fiber connecting rods, titanium valves, and aluminum-beryllium pistons to build a power curve that produces 185 horsepower from 4,000 to 12,000 rpm. The costs will skyrocket far beyond anything that the 2009-10 rules would have produced, and the tilt will go even further to the factories. And time is running out to properly prepare machinery for the 2009 season.

"In just thinking about this, I think it just makes a lot of sense to continue this rules package for an additional year, because to expect all the interested parties - the riders, the teams and the manufacturers - to develop to the new specification with less than a year to do it, I don't think is reasonable. And I think most of the promoters feel that way."

That wasn't said by a wild-eyed rider, but by George Bruggenthies, the clear-thinking president and general manager of Road America, who has much to lose, including sponsorship.

American Suzuki, which sponsors Road America, has taken the hardest stance. VP Mel Harris said his factory would not race under the current rules. Is he bluffing? Angling for more open negotiations? Maybe, but it won't work. Edmondson is resolute that the rules aren't changing.

Harris' decision isn't one he could make alone. He would need the okay from his corporate bosses in Japan. Which means the Japanese are taking a stand. And if Suzuki follows through on the threat, the ramifications are wide-reaching.

If they choose not to homologate a motorcycle, and therefore not offer contingency money, there would be no Suzukis in the field. This would decimate the Literbike class. (Maybe that's the idea.) And with Suzuki sponsoring four races, promoters would also take a hit. The American distributors of the Japanese manufacturers sponsor every race, and they have a lot of power, if they choose to use it.

What happens if they all say no? No homologating motorcycles, no sponsoring of races. You'd have a field of Aprilias and BMWs and Triumphs and KTMs and Ducatis and Yamahas. Yamaha compromised its position by asking for the rules change: They have to play along.

Just as important, if the factories withdraw, who's going to buy ad time on the Speed broadcasts? How interested would Speed be in televising club racing or Moto-ST? DMG could subsidize the broadcasts, but for how long? And what sense does that make?

What these questions lead to is the belief among many that the DMG doesn't know anything about motorcycle racing. That isn't true. But it is true that they know little about racing at the factory level. Which they don't care about, because the factories won't drive this bus. Neither will the riders. The fans will, they say.

But ask the fans which bikes and riders they come to see. And ask Speed which broadcasts have the higher ratings.

With spec tires, spec fuel, and as close to spec motorcycles as possible, the riders are seeing their livelihoods threatened. Salaries will come down, as will opportunities for career advancement. What GP or World Superbike team will take a chance on a rider who's never ridden anything but a 120-horsepower 600? Or a 110-horsepower Moto-ST twin? Regardless of what you might hear to the contrary, on the world stage, the path the DMG is taking is seen as comical.

Moto-ST made its AMA debut at Road America, and if it proved anything, it was that it has no place on an AMA Superbike race weekend. This is club racing, with riders smoking on the pit wall, no pit-lane speed limit, and a level of professionalism that doesn't approach that of the AMA Superbike Championship.

It was difficult to watch at Road America knowing that the Moto-ST riders had more practice than the AMA Superbike riders, and much more than any other class, despite having fewer entries than Supersport. I base this on the last of about half a dozen schedules that circulated prior to the race - not the only example of how chaotic the organization has become. The last schedule I saw - there may have been more - showed two hours of Moto-ST practice on Friday and a 15-minute warm-up on Saturday. And many of the teams rode during Thursday's promoter practice. Superbikes had 50 minutes of practice and a 40-minute qualifying session on Friday, and a 25-minute qualifying session on Saturday. That's less than two hours total. And because of the generous track time afforded to Moto-ST, all Superbike riders were in the same qualifying session.

More than just being insulting, this is a safety issue. All of the Supersport riders were put in the same session and all of them were allowed into the race, even if they didn't get a time. This was a result of the first session being red-flagged and the second one being run in the rain. How is it that riders gain talent from not practicing?

And it was at Road America that a release was issued stating that Mid-Ohio, despite no changes having been made since the last race, was suddenly safe for racing in the wet. The release said the track had "completed updates to its motorcycle-racing-road-course facility, as requested by AMA Pro Racing." What was missing was the phrase "over the past several years," according to a follow-on statement by DMG CEO Edmondson. That no one in the employ of the DMG or AMA spotted such an obvious fallacy speaks volumes about what the riders are up against. To everyone but the AMA and DMG officials, it was a giant red flag.

Nothing has been done to address the track's most lethal areas. And the track officials steadfastly refused to meet with riders until well after expensive changes to less dangerous corners were completed. So whose fault is that?

Infineon Raceway is a perfect example of what happens when the riders and track management cooperate. Years ago, the track was blindsided when riders at a news conference suggested a boycott. The track immediately engaged the riders and spent millions on improvements to the motorcycle course and many tens of millions on the overall facility. The track still isn't safe, but the riders appreciate everything that's been done.

Mid-Ohio is the exact opposite.

A two-day test in the middle of last week confirmed what the riders believed: Nothing had been done. And they were hardened in their position that racing in the rain - because of, among other things, the surface - was not possible. The notion that the throttle goes both ways (which you will hear a lot of in the coming days, weeks and years) is ludicrous. The tracks and the sanctioning body have a responsibility to the riders to provide a safe racing environment. Asking riders to race on wet tracks at Mid-Ohio, Daytona, Fontana or Road Atlanta would cause the authorities to abrogate that responsibility. That's what happens when the sanctioning body and promoter are one and the same. This sort of thing doesn't happen in MotoGP, where the teams, the riders, the sanctioning body, and the series promoter all have a voice. That's democracy, and it works. The tracks are the best in the world, the crowds are the biggest, the riders are the best paid.

The factory riders are united in their decision to not ride in the rain at Mid-Ohio. Others will follow by example. More than one rider offered his pillion seat to any AMA or DMG official willing to sample the hazards at speed. You won't see any takers.

More than one rider has asked why they should be expected to race in the rain when the far-better-protected NASCAR Sprint Cup drivers don't. The contact patch for a pair of Superbike slicks is far less than for a quartet of Goodyear Eagles. The Car of Today makes about 850 horsepower and weighs 3.400 pounds - a power-to-weight ratio of 1 to 4. A factory Superbike makes over 200 horsepower and weighs 375 pounds (with fuel) - a power-to-weight ratio of less than 1 to 2. NASCAR drivers have sheet metal and five-way harnesses. Superbike riders have a thin layer of animal skin.

Maybe looking down the barrel of a shotgun isn't the best way to start a relationship.

July 9, 2008

Get Smart

Some very smart men are doing some very silly things that could send motorcycle racing into a death spiral from which it may never recover.

The stand-off between the Daytona Motorsports Group and the American distributors of most of the Japanese manufacturers is creeping inexorably toward the precipice of disaster. The only way out is if they come to their collective senses and realize the damage they could bring, not only to racing, but to thousands of lives.

The relationship between the DMG and the factories didn't begin well, and it has deteriorated almost from day one. The hope that the DMG would somehow be better than the AMA - and that's an impossibly low standard to meet - has yet to be realized. What the teams and riders read and hear is mostly second-hand and mostly negative; the short version is, you'll be racing dumbed-down motorcycles on unsafe tracks in inclement conditions.

Nearly four months after the sale was announced, and before it has been consummated - that should come this week - there is no rulebook, no class structure, no schedule. As American Honda boss Ray Blank said last week, "At this point, it's almost too late right now."

Mel Harris, Blank's counterpart at American Suzuki, sent a shockwave through the industry when, at Road America, he said that his company wouldn't take part under the then-proposed restricted-horsepower-and-weight rules. No Rockstar Makita Suzuki team, no Jordan Suzuki team, no homologation, no contingency. It was the kind of seismic shock that would have reverberated from L.A. to Pickerington to Daytona Beach, where Edmondson's patron Jim France would surely have noticed.

France doesn't need these headaches. The billionaire majority owner of NASCAR bankrolled Edmondson's vision because he loves motorcycles. This was a legacy move, a way to bring more credibility and respect to motorcycle racing. His father started NASCAR; his brother, by some metrics, made it the second most popular sport in America. Now it was his turn. Only it hasn't turned out that way. And it's only getting worse.

Late last week, American Honda's Ray Blank said they, too, would likely sit out next year. Suzuki's position is well known and Kawasaki would likely feel the same way. Only Yamaha has endorsed the Edmondson way, but that endorsement would have to be qualified, since there are no rules. And the rules everyone thought would be implemented appear to be changing. Again.

Edmondson had no intention of including a Literbike class when he and several of his colleagues visited Southern California in April. But he was struck by the factories' commitment to the class. Some saw this as naiveté on his part; how could they not want to showcase their showcase machines? And he was treated very badly when he arrived at American Suzuki, his first stop on the tour.

From the minute he arrived, Harris made it personal. Edmondson was throttled with his own words. What he couldn't have known was that the words he'd spoken in a *Cycle News* interview the day of the announcement were on a presentation board behind the DMG group. He couldn't have guessed that when he said, on the eve of the Daytona 200, "I do think the current Superbike series is pretty dysfunctional and probably the only one who would prefer to see the status quo is Suzuki," those words would come back to haunt him. Or that Suzuki would take offense when he said that, "As I said, school's out. New day. How's that working for everybody but Suzuki right now? And I'm not putting down Suzuki, they've done the job. They've earned their position and they're to be respected for that, but it's not my job to sell Suzukis."

He also said that "within 90 days" the factories would know the rules: "And, again, if we believe there is a new way to go, it wouldn't make sense for us to approve any rules or institute any rules that required any investment in the old rules or the old format. My inclination, without talking to anybody, would be to take a hard look at the FIM's World Superbike rules."

That isn't happening - not the rules, not the time frame. And his assertion that "this will be a dictatorship; I'm not trying to say I'm going to be the dictator - somebody will" was met with understandable resistance. As I said, an inauspicious debut.

The Literbike rules are on at least their third iteration. First came Edmondson's endorsement of the 2009-10 rules, but with a minimum of four machines from each manufacturer. That was too expensive, Yamaha thought. Edmondson countered by soliciting the opinion of the big four. Two positive responses, one negative, and one non-answer followed. What emerged was a universally panned horsepower-and-weight formula that was nearly identical to the Parts Canada Superbike Championship rules. Factory teams don't race to compete against a dyno. And they could have spent lavishly on exotic parts to reach the 185-horsepower limit. So that formula has been discarded, we think; there has been no official announcement from DMG. (The next one will likely be the completed rulebook.) Instead, the rules will closely mimic those of FIM Superstock 1000cc Cup, with a few exceptions. Engine modifications are minimal; clutch springs, a head gasket, and an exhaust pipe is the short version. Again, these haven't been officially announced, though Edmondson did confirm this was the path in a phone conversation from Brazil last week.

And the name may become "American Superbike," not to be confused with "Daytona Superbike." Does that make it the AMA Daytona/American Superbike Championship?

Regardless of how you sell it, the factories aren't buying. The hard line was solidified during a meeting at the Motorcycle Industry Council last week. What emerged was a plea from MIC president Tim Buche. What it essentially asked was, Does anybody out there have any ideas? And, if so, could you hurry it up? A new series won't happen next year. No time. Which means the premier American road-racing series will be run by the DMG. And, if Ray Blank and Mel Harris are true to their words, it will be run with precious little participation from the Japanese factories. That can't happen.

The effect of fragmentation would be disastrous. The ripple effect would extend far beyond the factory race-team mechanics who would suddenly be unemployed. The aftermarket industry - makers of shocks, exhaust pipes, leathers, helmets, bodywork - would all take a hit. The tracks, and everyone associated with the tracks, would suffer.

On the other hand, the Japanese companies are also suffering. Sales are down, workers are being laid off, buy-outs are being offered. Sitting out a year would save millions of dollars. They shouldn't be given a reason to not race.

The DMG hopes to bring road racing to a mainstream audience. That will take time, if it ever happens, which few believe. Meanwhile, the traditional fans would stay away. Given the current economic climate, very few race fans would travel long distances, pay $4 or more for a gallon of gas and inflated prices for hotels, to watch a bunch of lesser riders on mostly European sportbikes. That could be the future.

We are living in an era when, because of years of government neglect, we find ourselves with a country filled with fat SUVs, expensive gas, and no easy solutions. Except for motorcycles. The motorcycle industry has a chance to seize the moment to convert the American public to the European mindset that motorcycles are for transportation, not just recreation. But it's hard to see that message resonating when the most powerful men in the industry are playing a dangerous game of "mine's bigger than yours."

Blank said he wasn't averse to meeting with Edmondson. That's a start. One of them has to act, and all of them need to be locked into a room until a solution is found. That's the only way out of this mess.

It's clear the 2009-10 rules have to be followed, at least for the 1000s, which have to be the premier class. It's also clear that the factories don't want to be directly responsible for four of them.

At the moment, there's little incentive for privateers to spend money racing against the factories. Racing in Superbike is just a chance to hang out with the big guys. Here's an idea: Pay contingency to the top finishing nonfactory rider as if he was the winner. An example: Mladin wins, but Jordan Suzuki's Geoff May finishes sixth in Superbike. May gets the $7000 Suzuki theoretically pays to the race winner. Kawasaki doesn't currently post Superbike contingency, according to their website. But they pay $7000 for Supersport and Superstock wins. There is no regular full-time Kawasaki rider in Superbike. But with $7000 on the line for being the first ZX-10R, wouldn't someone play along? The worry about filling the field would evaporate.

Do I think that will happen? No. But if Edmondson could be convinced to accept the 2009-10 rules, the factories would have to make some kind of reciprocal concession. Their wallets aren't a bad place to start. And it would be less expensive than running a third and fourth Superbike. And it would also be cheaper than running their own series, or sitting out a year, alienating their fans, and depressing their already depressed sales. No reasonable person wants that.

What should have happened is that Edmondson should have left everything in place for a year. That was the first mistake. The next one could be even more dire.

Roger, Ray, Mel - pick up the phone. Now.

August 6, 2008

The Rules, They Are A-Changin' (Again)

When the AMA Superbike Championship resumes this weekend at the Mid-Ohio Sports Car Course, all eyes will be on the weather. As this is being written, on Monday morning, the chance of rain is slim. Which means that everyone will play along. But for how long?

The 2009 AMA Superbike Championship rules weren't met with great enthusiasm when they were announced at the combined AMA/MotoGP weekend at Mazda Raceway Laguna Seca. The teams weren't happy, though they were undeniably less unhappy than in the recent past. And the promoters I spoke to weren't happy. They continue to believe the current class structure and rules, or something very similar, should remain in place for another year. They have a product they can sell. What's next is far too speculative. And time is running out.

A few weeks before issuing the rules, Daytona Motorsports Group CEO Roger Edmondson did his second California fly-by of the OEMs. Rather than sitting down and hashing out rules, as one participant thinks should happen, Edmondson presented his proposal, listened, and then left to ruminate and consider yet more of the bad advice he seems to attract. The OEMs were under the impression that World Superbike rules would be imposed on the fastest - which is not to say premier - class. It would be called "Factory Superbike" - as opposed to "American Superbike" or "Daytona Superbike," the trifecta of confusing Superbike names.

"World Superbike" was the fourth proposal, after the original 2009-10 rules to which the manufacturers had agreed; then a weight- and horsepower-restricted class that was universally derided; and, finally, American Superbike. That wasn't the end of it.

Factory Superbikes would run the 2009-10 rules he'd proposed back in April at Barber Motorsports Park. Only now he'd wasted three months, engendered no end of ill will, and knocked back his credibility.

The 2009-10 rules will remain in place until 2011, Edmondson said, when he hopes to implement World Superbike rules. The belief is that World Superbike will dumb down at that point. Maybe they will, but no one I spoke to sees that on the horizon.

World Superbike rules are a collaboration between the FIM and FGSport. The manufacturers discuss the rules, but they do not vote on them. The FIM can propose rules, but FGSport has to agree to implement them. So unless both sides have said the rules will be tightened up, Edmondson is getting bad information, which is nothing new.

The year 2011 is a long way off. First we have to get through this weekend, then this off-season, then next year. At the moment, the manufacturers have a variety of beefs. Factory Superbike is where the best riders on the best bikes should be, but it's a class that many believe is engineered to fail. At the moment, there are 11 Superbikes on the grid, two each from Honda, Kawasaki and Yamaha, three from Suzuki, and one each from Corona Extra Honda and Jordan Suzuki.

"It's not really a race, it's an exhibition," said Yamaha race boss Keith McCarty, adding, "If you have a couple of injuries from anybody in that class, it will be a pretty grim exhibition at best."

The manufacturers should be forced to put all the best riders in one class. Yamaha should have Ben Bostrom in Superbike. Corona Extra Honda should have Jake Holden in Superbike, on a proper Superbike. Same for Geoff May at Jordan Suzuki. Clearly there are cost issues involved, but a solution must be found if that class is to be viable. And it should have two races on the weekend, like

Daytona Superbike, which the manufacturers have little time for. The bulk of the current Superbike field is made up of Superstock machines; next year they'll be called "American Superbike" and won't be allowed in Factory Superbike.

Though American Suzuki vice president Mel Harris wants two Factory Superbike races on a weekend, his counterpart at American Honda, Ray Blank, has a different view.

"In general," he said, "I don't have a negative feeling toward doubleheaders, but I do feel that single events lead up to a bigger climax."

How many climaxes will we reach? At the moment, there are 11 rounds, two of which run with world-caliber events. If the decision is made to not play second fiddle at Laguna Seca and Miller Motorsports Park, as the promoters believe will happen, that would leave nine races. And, at the moment, nine Factory Superbike races. With the motorcycle industry in a seemingly endless swoon, the days of big salaries for the top riders are dying. This will only hasten their demise.

To race American or Daytona Superbike means being subjected to dyno testing, which no one I spoke to thought was a good idea.

"I think it will be mayhem in the pits on trying to manage the testing and all those things and the variables and the inconsistencies with dynos," said Yamaha's McCarty.

One dyno operator at Road America said the dynos were calibrated once a year.

Edmondson did come to his senses on the horsepower-restricted classes by banning exotic materials. Still, that's not enough to appease the factories. They believe the class has a club-race feel and they aren't eager to play along. They want to be able to develop their machines, but not to a limit. They also want all take and very little give, which means we're closer to a resolution, but not quite there - especially on tires, which no one seems to have thought through very clearly.

Factory Superbike is open to all tire brands. Not so for the lesser classes, American and Daytona SB, each of which will run on a control tire. Consider this nightmare scenario: Since all the Factory SBs will likely run on Dunlop tires, as they currently do, what happens if Pirelli wins the contract for the other classes? And what if Rockstar Makita Suzuki and Monster Kawasaki continue to field riders in both classes? We may see Roger Lee Hayden jumping off his Dunlop-shod ZX-10R and getting on his ZX-6R with Pirellis. It's both silly and potentially unsafe. And it would make for some very awkward moments under the team canopies.

But safety is no longer the *cause célèbre* it once was. In the original discussion, Edmondson insisted that the move to 600s was because the current tracks were reaching their limits. The 2009-10 rules will slow the bikes down slightly in a straight line, but very little in the corners, where most accidents happen and where 600s can be faster than 1000s. Depending on your viewpoint, Edmondson is either being flexible or hypocritical.

On top of which, we found out late in the weekend that the FIM isn't very happy with the way the AMA sale was conducted. In an extraordinary interview with *Cycle News* correspondent Tracy Hagen that will run next week, FIM president Vito Ippolito said he explained to AMA CEO Rob "The Dinger" Dingman how critical it is when one sells the sporting and scrutineering rights.

"Frankly speaking, yes, I am very concerned," the Venezuelan said. Why the concern?

"You have to understand that the line of the sporting rights is the borderline," he said. "When you cross that borderline, you've lost everything."

What have they lost? As he said, everything. No one at the AMA is looking out for the riders, the promoters, or the fans. They've given up. They don't care. More important than maintaining sporting purity was having a fire sale and shedding 11 salaries.

The FIM is the sanctioning body for, among other series, the MotoGP World Championship. The series is promoted by Dorna, which is one party to any important decision. Another is the MSMA, the manufacturers' group that helps set the rules. Yet another is the teams' association, IRTA. This is something the American distributors of the OEMs would like to see - the proverbial four-legged stool - but won't.

Ippolito supports the sale to the DMG. "It was a good choice, I think," he said, though that doesn't temper his concerns. At the moment, the AMA has no representative on any of the FIM sporting committees.

It will get worse, possibly for road racing and certainly for Supercross, before it gets better. But that is in the future. Right now, we just have to get through Mid-Ohio.

August 13, 2008

The Future of *World* Supercross

It was as if he was waiting for someone to ask the question. In an extraordinary interview with *Cycle News* contributor Tracy Hagen, held during last Sunday's running of the Suzuka 8 Hours, FIM president Vito Ippolito revealed the FIM's plans for the AMA/FIM Supercross Championship. That the plans are what they are isn't a surprise. That he would reveal them is.

The Supercross world is about to undergo a seismic change that will reach into the executive offices of every American distributor, Japanese or not. And it could potentially have a crushing effect on the outdoor National Motocross Series.

The crux of the issue is overseas - specifically, taking the AMA/FIM SX series overseas. It was first mentioned as a throwaway line in a press release late in December announcing that AMA CEO Rob Dingman had allowed the FIM to tack its name onto the only successful Supercross series in the world. It was another press release that revived the issue.

The more recent release, headlined "Meeting between the FIM, the Japanese industry and Live Nation," was distributed on July 25. It described a Tokyo meeting between the FIM president and other FIM officials, and representatives of the four Japanese brands.

There were a number of issues discussed, none more important than Supercross. At the end of the second paragraph, it states, "Finally, the FIM will maintain its will of Motocross and Supercross being global sports, i.e., World Championships having rounds in the largest number of continents outside Europe, with riders from all continents. Moreover, Messrs [Charlie] Mancuso and [Todd] Jendro made an exhaustive presentation of the activities of Live Nation, and confirmed their intention to expand the FIM Supercross World Championship outside North America."

So when Hagen questioned Ippolito in Suzuka, it was as if someone had finally noticed and Ippolito finally had a forum to make his case.

"In the case of Supercross, the FIM is interested in having events outside of North America," Ippolito said.

That wasn't news. Live Nation had said the same. The details and timing were news.

"If we have a World Championship, it must be a real World Championship," Ippolito said. "We have to push in this direction, and Live Nation agrees that this is important. They understand and are very interested to help have rounds outside of North America."

Later he added, "For example, it will be very interesting to expand to Japan and Australia, then add one or two more rounds in other continents. We could have one or two in Europe, maybe one in Asia and one in Australia. Then we will have a new look of the championship. We hope to start adding new countries in 2010. Our target is to add four or five new countries."

The long-term Supercross contract that former AMA CEO Patti DiPietro signed allows for as many as 20 rounds. The FIM is in business to promote its World Championships, and what Dingman has allowed to happen with his fire sale is to let everything go and let Live Nation do as they please. There is no compelling reason for the AMA to have allowed the FIM to co-opt the series. Who's looking out for the riders? Who's looking out for the teams? You can't help but get the feeling that the American distributors don't understand what's about to happen, that they don't understand what the FIM and Live Nation are about to do.

The 2009 schedule has 17 rounds, with the only one outside the United States, in Toronto, Ontario, Canada. So in 2010, at least one venue will have to give up a round. It also means the season will start sooner and end later. The most likely scenario is that there will be two overseas rounds, possibly in Japan and Australia, in early December, and then the holiday break, and then the bulk of it. But where do you slip in the two European rounds? You'd want a week's break between a U.S. and European round, though it isn't essential. And it has to end in Las Vegas. Can anyone see the series finale in Madrid? So the series will run well into May, the riders and teams will be worn out, and now they've got to race the outdoors.

How many riders will be healthy? When are they supposed to heal if they do get injured? How many more riders will opt for SX-only contracts? Since Ricky Carmichael retired, how many top riders have been healthy for a complete year, Supercross and motocross?

When the idea was first floated, at the end of last year, the response wasn't universally condemned, but damn close. And it's likely to be more so given the continuing tailspin of the motorcycle industry as a whole. Maybe Monster Energy and Red Bull would want to race overseas, but who else would? Besides, the contributions of most of the team sponsors are a fraction of the overall budgets, which means that the U.S, distributors have the ultimate say. Maybe not.

The reason the FIM went straight to the Japanese was to make an end run around the American distributors.

"One of the reasons we talk with the Japanese industry is because the current teams in the Supercross World Championship are backed by American dealers and businesses," said Ippolito. "Maybe some of these teams are not interested in going out of North America. For this reason, we need to talk with the Japanese industry."

Everyone knew how cool the reception was when the idea was floated seven months ago. They knew the American bosses don't have the interest in going overseas or the budgets to do so. So if they go directly to the ultimate holders of the purse strings, maybe they have a chance. Only it doesn't work that way in all cases. Though there isn't a blanket rule, most of the American bosses have autonomy on where and when and what they race. If American Honda, for instance, doesn't want to go to Australia and Japan, they won't have to. What will force them to is that they can't afford to miss four or five rounds, regardless of where they are, if they plan on contesting the title. The only way to prevent conceding the championship is to deny support to the teams they currently help, which is all of them in one way or another. And that might be a sticky legal path that they don't want to go down.

Four or five overseas races will certainly be expensive. Back in January, Roy Janson, then with Live Nation, said Live Nation would pick up all travel costs, which is true, to a point. Some of the Japanese companies have policies that mandate business-class travel for flights over a certain length. So the cost of eight or 10 coach-class tickets to Europe or Japan, which would normally be $1,000 or $1,500, suddenly skyrockets. Will Live Nation make up the difference? Will Live Nation pay for all of the extra parts the teams will use? And if history is any judge, the weight allowance for the teams won't suffice.

The outdoors could also be damaged goods.

"[We want more U.S. riders in the] motocross World Championship, and more riders from the motocross World Championship in supercross," Ippolito said. "This is a difficult thing to do. But in my opinion, we have to think in these terms. The riders can ride in both kinds of championships. This is my goal. We have to start the Supercross World Championship at the beginning of the year and then start the motocross World Championship."

The likelihood of a crush of Americans in world MX is zero. No American has won a World Motocross Championship since Bobby

Moore won the 125cc title in 1994, and very few even try. Why should they? The money isn't nearly as good, and not everyone can adjust to the culture and lifestyle change. Supercross is an American sport and a destination for international riders and has been from the start. Belgian Roger DeCoster won the first-ever 500cc Supercross, and Dutchman Pierre Karsmakers won the 250cc Supercross (there were two classes the first two years) at Daytona in 1974.

"We don't have many [World MX] rounds outside of Europe," Ippolito also said.

Does this mean they want more rounds in the United States? And how does that impact the AMA outdoor series? When you have 20 Supercrosses and a world MX or two, how appealing is a 12-race outdoor series? There are more questions than answers, and none more important than what the Japanese think.

"Now we are waiting for some answers from the manufacturers," Ippolito said. "We don't have a target date, because we need to announce that the FIM wants to have a real World Championship. The industry will see some supercross rounds outside the United States. They have to understand that this is not a surprise. This is what we want."

September 10, 2008

Who Goes Where?

Where you decide to road race in 2009 is a question of faith. Do you have faith in Roger Edmondson, the DMG CEO who, despite a number of attempts, including Moto-ST, a sparsely attended hobbyist championship devoid of significant sponsorship, hasn't run a successful professional motorcycle series since being unfairly run out of the AMA 15 years ago? Or do you have faith in MIC boss Tim Buche, who has never run a racing series in his life and who has no promoter, no sanctioning body, no racetracks, no infrastructure and, until proven otherwise, no idea what he's been coerced into doing, who's flying on a wing and a prayer, minus the wing?

The shotgun wedding of the Daytona Motorsports Group to the American distributors of the four Japanese manufacturers was called off before the two sides could decide who'd wear the tuxedos and who'd wear the sea foam and organza. In retrospect, it never had a chance. Too many alpha males who all wanted to be the daddy and didn't much like the idea of riding bitch. These are titans of business who get their way and aren't willing to bend for a reluctant partner who doesn't share their vision of how partners should act.

So rather than counseling or cooperating or negotiating or behaving like adults, Edmondson and American Suzuki's Mel Harris and American Honda's Ray Blank tossed barbs across the transom, grown men locked in their own bitter power struggle, while hundreds - if not thousands - of the directly impacted can do nothing but watch as their livelihoods or hobbies are fractured.

It's a colossal mess with no end in sight.

The 2009 season may see parallel championships; one run by the deep-pocketed Daytona Motorsports Group and the other through the MIC and whomever they believe can create a series out of thin air. The MIC was confident of announcing the series weeks ago, before the lawyers got involved. Worries about antitrust violations and collusion have made progress slower than a Daytona Superbike.

What the MIC has at the moment is the assurance of American Honda's Ray Blank and American Suzuki's Mel Harris that they won't race in a DMG series next year, while Kawasaki and Yamaha have been less vocal. But if the MIC series has a chance to get air under the wings it currently doesn't have, Kawasaki will join them, as will Yamaha, which wouldn't want the stigma of cherry-picking the DMG series.

Their most powerful weapon is machinery. If the manufacturers are serious about running their own series, and making sure DMG has to dig deep into its own pockets to make that series viable, they will refuse to homologate and offer a contingency program for their motorcycles. This would accomplish two things: It would deny DMG a significant revenue stream - and let's not forget this is all about the money; and it would mean anyone who raced a Japanese motorcycle in the DMG series would do so with no hope of earning money from the manufacturer. But it would also deny the manufacturers the chance to do what they're in racing for in the first place: sell motorcycles.

Time is running out, but the metric on the MIC side must be adjusted. The series would struggle to be ready by Daytona, five months away. But the MIC series won't be going to Daytona; it could start a month or two later. It will certainly have less races than the 11 to 14 rounds Edmondson has proposed.

How did it come to this? There's plenty of blame to go around. It begins with AMA CEO Rob Dingman, who, more than a year ago, said: "We are not getting out of motorcycle racing. We are redefining our role so we can focus exclusively on race sanctioning as opposed to race promotion. We will partner with companies that can effectively manage racing from the commercial perspective. We will sanction racing events and provide operational staff where it is required."

That, of course, is a far cry from the truth. Yes, they still sanction some racing events - Supercross, for one - but they've given up the rulebook and the sanctioning to the DMG, a development that concerned FIM president Vito Ippolito.

Then came the bait-and-switch, but it was AMA members who got the hook and not the worm. Under false pretenses, and in violation of his own words, Dingman gave away everything that matters most.

DMG was more than happy to take the rulebook and run. Now they could create a championship without outside interference. Having one organization control the rulebook and the promotion is a bad idea.

Edmondson has been flexible, especially the big-bike class, but every proposal had a pitfall. First it was the guarantee of four machines; that didn't fly. The next was a horsepower restriction - equally reviled for being time-consuming, unnecessary, and amateurish. Anyone who's seen a Supersport race knows a horsepower restriction is not necessary, yet a dyno and scale will govern the smaller Daytona Superbikes. Literbike morphed into a near clone of the Canadian Superbike class. In turn, that gave way to American Superbike, based on FIM Superstock Cup 1000 rules. In addition, Factory Superbike, a third class run under World Superbike rules, was floated at one final fruitless meeting with many of the OEMs. American Honda's Ray Blank, for one, decided against World Superbike rules, preferring the agreed-to 2009-10 rules. But when asked if they'd support it, only one OEM responded, and it wasn't Honda. By the time it was offered, they were well on their way to their own series, and Edmondson had grown tired of trying to appease them.

Barring an unlikely peace settlement - the Arabs and Israelis have a better shot at that - the MIC will shortly put the series out to tender, and those who originally submitted bids to the AMA will dust off their folios and resubmit. The likely winner will be Hardcard Holdings, the firm whose principals are all AMA refugees. Former AMA CEO Scott Hollingsworth isn't listed on the firm's website, but he's intimately involved, along with former AMA VPs Andy Leisner and John Farris.

Despite the chronically meddlesome AMA and its board of directors, road racing enjoyed continued growth under Hollingsworth's leadership, even if he wasn't able to attract or retain sponsors. Hollingsworth left the AMA when then-AMA CEO Patti DiPietro changed the Pro Racing hierarchy in February of 2006. By then, the Superbike class had been without a sponsor for more than a year. One more class sponsor would walk away in 2006 and another in 2007, which leaves only Pro Honda Oils as an existing in-industry class sponsor. And these guys are the saviors of the sport? Already they've contacted the individual tracks.

The sanctioning-body question is more difficult. The obvious option is WERA, which is currently feuding with the AMA. But do the manufacturers want to cozy up to a club racing organization?

Considering "club racing" is how Suzuki's Mel Harris has described the DMG series, it would be, at least, ironic.

Harris isn't entirely wrong. The DMG series is for dumbed-down bikes and, eventually, dumbed-down riders. How are riders supposed to learn about machine setup when they have few options? How are mechanics supposed to learn how to tune machines when all they're doing is changing spec tires?

How this appeals to the privateers is baffling. The DMG's hope is to have 15 to 20 well-funded teams, but no one has said where the money's coming from. The only evidence we have is Moto-ST and Grand-Am. Moto-ST is hobby racing with sparse fields, very little sponsorship, and no place on professional weekend. There were a total of 24 entries, spread among three classes, for last weekend's race in New Jersey. The margin of victory in the premier class was five laps. Among the 41 total entries for the Grand-Am race, also in New Jersey, there were precious few national sponsors. Edmondson has said that about half of his field is comprised of wealthy individuals. Wealthy middle-aged hobbyists might be able to drive a race car, but they have no place on a professional motorcycle grid. Evidence of Fortune 500 companies willing to sponsor downfield riders has yet to materialize.

The DMG series is being touted as the salvation for the privateers, the under-class that has been beaten down for so long that they're eager to cozy up to anyone who might show them the least affection. But what does a privateer or a small team owner aspire to? A factory ride, of course. Privateers - serious privateers and not hobbyists - hope to get noticed, and the only way to get noticed is to race against the factories.

Every serious professional motorcycle series has the best competitors with the best support. If you're just in it for the money, go club racing. The contingencies paid by the manufacturers make it more lucrative than racing in a professional series and always have. If you're serious about racing, you want to race the best on the best machinery. Anyone who thinks otherwise is a fool, and there is no shortage of them.

Of that, I have faith.

September 24, 2008

A Glimmer of Hope

The Red Bull Indianapolis Grand Prix will long be remembered for what it did to boost the future of road racing in America. And not just because Valentino Rossi put on a masterful display in hurricane-like conditions to win the first motorcycle race at the Brickyard in 99 years. Not just because the win made him the all-time leader in the premier class with 69, coincidentally the number of the second-placed rider, Nicky Hayden, who rode valiantly with a broken foot to finish second, his best of an awful season. Not just because the 250cc GP was canceled, because the track and its surrounding areas were in no condition to hold a race, and therefore became the first GP in nearly 30 years to be canceled by weather. Not just because the crowd of more than 91,000 was the biggest to ever witness a motorcycle race in the United States, and the Indy Mile dirt-track crowd was larger than anyone could remember. Not just because it felt like a real Grand Prix, with three classes to entertain a crowd of knowledgeable Midwesterners starved for MotoGP action and sufficiently steely in their resolve to face up to Hurricane Ike.

It will also be remembered as the race that started the wheels in motion to end the impasse that has engulfed and threatened to destroy American road racing, and the return of common sense and civility to the negotiating process.

At 1:40 p.m. on Sunday afternoon, during the lull between the 125cc race and MotoGP, in the period when the 250s should have been running, Daytona Motorsports Group CEO Roger Edmondson and American Honda vice president Ray Blank did something they should have done in the months since they first sat down during Bike Week in Daytona - they talked and, more importantly, they listened.

Trying to set aside the acrimony that's enveloped the road-race community since soon after the DMG announced their plans for the future of road racing, Blank and Edmondson spent more than an hour focusing on what's best for road racing and the thousands who've been left in limbo while the manufacturers and DMG acted like petulant children.

The urgency of the mission was under-scored when the Motorcycle Industry Council announced on the eve of the Indy GP that they "Will launch a new professional road-racing series next year in the United States." Not that they might, not that they were thinking about it, not that they were spit-balling, not that they were brainstorming. They will launch a series, the clumsily named USSB Championship.

Well, it depends on what the definition of "will" is. If it's the definition any reasonably sane person would ascribe, it means the series is going forward. The MIC definition is more equivocal; they will launch a series if their members need somewhere to race that doesn't involve spec tires, spec fuel, rolling starts, swappable ECUS, and a dynamometer.

The MIC is funded by industry members who pay according to gross sales revenue. Honda has by far the largest market share, with Yamaha next, and Suzuki third. So when Honda and Suzuki needed a front for their new series, and wanted to avoid getting into a messy legal quagmire, they went to MIC President Tim Buche. Buche, who has no racing background, had little choice but to comply. The mandate was to create an entire professional racing organization out of thin air in record time. Who was paying for this? Blank himself has said that, given the current market conditions, the OEMs didn't have the spare money laying around to go on a series shopping spree.

Was it a bluff? Not really, but it certainly provided an incentive for Edmondson to get back to the bargaining table. If the manufacturers withheld support for the DMG series, if they didn't homologate motorcycles or pay contingency, if they supported a series that had a better television package, and if they had all the star riders, they'd clearly have the upper hand with their core audience.

Cycle News editor Paul Carruthers and I met with MIC President Tim Buche and Ty von Hooydonk, the former *Cycle News* associate editor who's listed as the series managing director, in the MIC suite at Indianapolis Motor Speedway. All but about 12 seconds of the more than a half-hour of conversation was off the record. What Buche would say on the record was that the MIC board was meeting on Wednesday night, September 17 "and coming out of that, we may have comment and definitive plans." The inference was that that was when the decision would be made.

Without revealing details, it's fair to say that the planning for the series was much more advanced than most people believed. It could happen, if it had to. But it won't.

Why not? A few reasons, starting with the dynamometer. The OEMs have no interest in competing in a class (Daytona Superbike) governed by a horsepower cap. It's amateurish, tedious and time-consuming, and does little to create a competitive balance. There is no good reason to alter the current Supersport rules, and Edmondson knows that. When he created the Supersport class in the early 1990s, the competition was fierce with swarms of bikes fighting for victory. A dynamometer only guarantees that the mechanics waste large parts of every race weekend hoping that the spec dyno spits out the same number as the dyno in their race shops - if they even have dynos. Or race shops.

Edmondson will have to eat a little crow on this one - "There will be a dyno," he told me by phone at VIR - but it will go down more smoothly, knowing the upside.

Kawasaki, the most sensible of this lot, has objected to the dyno from the start and the objection doubled around the time of the Miller Motorsports Park AMA/World Superbike weekend when the second (or was it the third?) proposal mandated a horsepower cap for both the middleweight and heavyweight classes. That iteration was mocked as Canada Lite, a reference to the Parts Canada Superbike Championship run by DMG director of road racing Colin Fraser. And the dyno restriction for the big bikes eventually went away. As did the use of exotic materials in the Daytona Superbike class. By then, the DMG was projecting a kind of "make it up as we go along" vibe. That was partly in response to the voice of the paddock and the dissident OEMs. But it would've done better to gather the principals in a room to hash out the details from the start.

Instead, Edmondson was taking a page from the terrorist handbook: Fly to L.A., toss a bomb in the room - World Superbike rules, no 1000cc class, 2009-2010 rules - then escape before the smoke cleared. It didn't help that he was roughed up at Suzuki, but that was the consequence of an information void.

From the time he invited *Cycle News* to Jim France's suite above Daytona International Speedway on the night of the Daytona Supercross, to the California meetings themselves, the only information in the public domain was the *Cycle News* interview.

Speaking frankly - he knows no other way - he alienated a number of his future constituents, most notably Suzuki. The wounds are still fresh. And re-opened by the disqualification of Mat Mladin for having illegal crankshafts at Virginia International Raceway.

When the appeal was denied, Suzuki rather belatedly - blame the lawyers - mounted a spirited defense of their position.

Edmondson wasn't impressed. Nor was I, but for different reasons.

AMA Special Projects Manager Bill Syfan, whose name and contact info was on the press release, refused to return phone calls seeking clarification. On the day the appeal was denied, Syfan was at a racetrack in Texas where he couldn't possibly have made an intelligent decision on the technical merits of the case. He could only have made it surrounded by a group of engineers or at least reasonably competent mechanics. And Roy Janson, DMG's director of operations, also has limited technical knowledge. Yet they were the ones involved most closely involved in the decision.

It turns out that the appeal refusal had nothing to do with the crankshafts. The appeal was denied as being "without merit" because Suzuki didn't comply with all of the items requested by the DMG when the appeal was filed. That certainly wasn't clear from the AMA press release. And it's unclear how much it will affect Suzuki's objection to the DMG.

Suzuki's Mel Harris never completely shut the door on racing with the DMG. Asked at VIR what would bring them into the fold, he said "for 2009, they could go back to all the rules and the classes we're currently doing in 2008 and come back to the table and work this thing out the way it needs to be the right way."

They did come back to the table, Edmondson and Blank, and they did make progress and they did leave with optimism. And now they need to get back to the table as soon as possible to hash out the final details. They owe it to themselves: They owe it to road racing.

Finally, men acting like men. A glimmer of hope.

October 15, 2008

Like Sands Through the Hourglass...

The 2009 AMA Superbike Championship will happen in 2009. Other than that, we don't know a whole lot about it. Rather, we're learning that everything we've heard so far is a notion, a hope, a whimsy - malleable as chewing gum, and with a similar lifespan. Time is critical, and if there's one thing that the Daytona Motorsports Group/AMA Pro Racing doesn't get, it's time.

The first set of rules came out at Barber Motorsports Park in April. Within a week, there was talk of a change - the mandated four Superbikes would cost too much - and the talk hasn't stopped. There were more changes before another set of classes was announced at the Red Bull U.S. Grand Prix in July. Factory Superbike, American Superbike, and Daytona Superbike, the Superbike trifecta of similar-looking, similar-sounding, and similarly named motorcycles would make up the field. The final rules package would follow in two weeks, around the time of Mid-Ohio, DMG CEO Roger Edmondson hoped.

It's now October, the final rules aren't set, and time marches on. As have some members of the paddock; under pressure to feed their families and pay their bills, they've been forced to look elsewhere for stability and sustenance.

But less than a month after the U.S. GP the Factory Superbike class was dead, for lack of interest. We were back to Daytona Superbike and American Superbike.

"It's past closing time here and there is clearly not sufficient support to include Factory Superbike in our program, and we won't," Edmondson said in mid-August. Asked if the rules might yet be altered, Edmondson said: "No. This is the set of rules that we're going to run our series by next year." He added, "There will be a dyno."

Not so fast - especially for Daytona Superbike, no pun intended.

The dyno is out for Daytona Superbike, which may be rebranded "Formula USA," a reminder of another failed series. The dyno is a casualty of the factories' insistence on not competing against an inanimate object. The concession was made during a meeting between Edmondson and American Honda's Ray Blank at the Red Bull Indianapolis Grand Prix.

Now comes word that Factory Superbike is coming back. This wasn't mentioned during Edmondson's meeting with the media at the AMA season finale at Mazda Raceway Laguna Seca.

Ostensibly, the gathering was to discuss the 2009 schedule. But Edmondson, as he always is, was more than willing to answer any and all questions, though the state of affairs with the factories was off limits.

Two statements stood out. The first was: "In the next few days, we'll be releasing the class structure and the rules one by one."

"Few days" being a general term. A week later, nothing's been released.

Then he added, "And I know everybody feels it's very late in the season, but I don't believe there's anything in these rules that would keep a competent team from being able to field a bike in two or three weeks."

That one got everyone's attention, or at least the attention of the people who build the bikes and know that you don't build a competitive motorcycle in two or three weeks. What it did suggest was that the rules wouldn't be significantly different from this year's and that Edmondson doesn't understand what it takes to build a racing motorcycle. Fortunately, the people who work for him do.

"We can't get fairings made in two or three weeks," one crew chief told me, and that's only one piece of the puzzle.

Who's going to be making the fairings? No one knows. All aftermarket suppliers will have to pay a homologation fee and, possibly, fund a contingency program. What will that cost? Again, no one knows. Six months after the AMA announced the anticipated sale to the DMG, and five months after the first set of rules was announced, the AMA's Bill Syfan has "begun designing the forms," Edmondson said, without grasping the absurdity of the situation. Other than not adequately explaining why Mat Mladin's appeal was denied, which takes no time, it baffles the mind why the DMG/AMA wasn't able to complete such a simple task months ago, when there was time.

Same with the classes, but now the factories have yet another set of proposals to consider, less than two months before the Daytona tire tests.

The A proposal has a Superbike class, American Superbike, Daytona Superbike without a dyno, and Sport Bike, the most expensive beginner class on two wheels. If you think sponsorship is tight in the apocalyptic world of Wall Street, try asking for half a mil so a 16-year-old in the early stages of understanding gravity can enrich whatever fairing company gets homologated, once the DMG/AMA gets around to finishing the forms.

The A Superbike could run under this year's rules, next year's rules, or World Superbike rules. The B proposal, which the factories favor, is similar, but with only one 1000cc class.

One of the big concessions on the manufacturers' side is forks. No more kit forks, only fork kits. Never mind that the forks that were being held up as an example of extravagance were anything but. Rockstar Makita Suzuki's Mat Mladin did use 2008 Showas for the early part of the season before reverting to a much older model at Infineon Raceway. (Ben Spies mostly used the new ones, though he tried the earlier models). The belief that his fork was the same as those on Nicky Hayden's Repsol Honda RC212V isn't true, according to one of the Showa technicians I spoke to. Showa is owned by Honda, so he asked, "Do you think they'd sell Mladin the same forks as Hayden uses?"

There will be no alternate gear ratios, and swingarms can't be replaced, but they can be braced.

Wheels and brakes are open, as are some engine mods. But stock pistons and rods are mandated, and that will be a mess. With similar rules, the British Superbike Series had disastrous results (unless you're a fan of spectacular engine explosions) and will move to World Superbike rules in 2009. The stock rods and pistons are a holdover from the 2009-10 rules, which were agreed to when it was thought there would be two 1000cc classes, well before the AMA decided to put Pro Racing on eBay.

The big battleground is electronics, and for that, there's no easy solution. Some new models come with different maps, including the Ducati 1098R, which has an ECU that includes traction control. The Kawasaki Ignition Management System, found on the ZX-10, is a form of traction control. Anything the DMG/AMA bans can be subverted within a model year.

What it adds up to is a proposal that's very similar to the original, which was done five months ago. Time stands still.

"He hasn't given us anything 100 percent," one crew chief said of Edmondson. "Nothing is 100 percent and we're in October. Not the tire company. Zero. We're the ones that have to put the bikes out on the track, and we have nothing."

How did it get to this? It's taken six months, but Edmondson has finally had an epiphany. He's come to realize what everyone else has known since the outset: You don't race in the United States without the factories, at least not yet. During a meeting with the private teams at Mid-Ohio, he said the future would be about the riders, not the factories. But without the factories, there are no riders, no bikes, precious little television advertising, and no racetracks.

Track promoters have played an important role in Edmondson's late-days conversion. The manufacturers sponsor nearly every race, some more generously than others, but all in good faith and with substantial support. Edmondson continues to talk about the imminent arrival of Fortune 500 companies to spread their largesse, but they're nowhere to be found in the Grand-Am series he runs.

The winner of the last round was a rich guy; he didn't list a sponsor. SunTrust, a regional bank and Fortune 500 company that also sponsors the MotoST Series (which is enough to question their judgment) sponsored the second car. Gainsco sponsored the third-placed car. Do you know what Gainsco is? No matter; they're not in the Fortune 500. Neither was the sponsor of the fourth-placed car. Fifth was another rich guy. Sixth was sponsored by Exchange Traded Gold and Mike Direct Connect. Is Ruby Tuesday in the Fortune 500? They sponsored the eighth-placed car. Mike Wiegel Helicopter Skiing, Total-R Insulation Solutions, The Media Barons, Power Plus-Porsche Performance Systems? Kodak is a Fortune 500 company. The Kodak car didn't start.

And what of the MIC? They've gone silent since soon after the Indy GP Honda, Kawasaki and Suzuki are working with the MIC to negotiate a more agreeable deal with Edmondson for a simple reason: the MIC doesn't want to run its own series, which is a good thing, because they couldn't - at least not in the short term. They might get the hang of it in time, but who has the time?

The good news is that everyone seems to be working toward a common goal and that there is a 2009 schedule with dates certain and uncertain, which means the promoters believe they'll have races. And it also means someone gave Edmondson a 2009 calendar. Now if he could only get his hands on a 2008 copy.

October 29, 2008

The Right Amount?

The inmates aren't running the asylum after all. Or if they are, they're not doing a very good job of it.

The evidence is the spec-tire era due to begin at the Valencia tests the day after this weekend's MotoGP season finale. Putting all the riders on the same tires, not just the same brand, is meant to increase safety, reduce costs, and increase competition. "Safety and cost" were mentioned three times in a release issued by Bridgestone, the only tire company to put in a bid. (In fact, the fix was in, according to racing insiders, who insist the deal was a *fait accompli* since Misano in September.)

Hiroshi Yasukawa was the Bridgestone official quoted in the release. Those who have worked with Yasukawa, Bridgestone's director of motorsports, describe him as strong-willed and unflinchingly decisive. And what he decided. along with the others (including the MSMA, the manufacturers' umbrella group) and Dorna, the series promoters, was that next year, riders will need half as many tires as they needed this year in a third as many options.

The original proposal was for each rider to have five slicks in each of two specs, front and rear - a total of 20 tires for the weekend. Bridgestone would choose the tires from seven specs developed over the winter. The specs wouldn't be vastly different. There would also be four rain tires in one spec. No intermediates, no qualifiers.

That proposal didn't sit well with the riders. Among the most outspoken was Casey Stoner, the Ducati Marlboro rider who put the 'Stones to such good effect in the 2007 MotoGP World Championship.

"The amount they have given us at the moment is stupidity," Stoner said on Friday in Malaysia. "They need to increase the tires. There needs to be a minimum of three compounds: A, B and C, soft, medium and hard. You can't just have medium-hard and hard or whatever they're choosing. What if you have a freezing cold one morning and everybody is launching it, or you have a hot afternoon and everybody is destroying tires? For me, it's all getting too complicated. It should be so easy. Nobody wants to run around on two compounds with 10 in total for each, and it will be nearly impossible to last the weekend if you're destroying tires."

Stoner spoke before the Friday afternoon safety commission meeting and before a second meeting between Valentino Rossi and Dorna boss Carmelo Ezpeleta on Saturday evening. Rossi tried to put the best face on it prior to the meeting, but there was no hiding his frustration. The deal had been agreed to by the MSMA, which includes Yamaha at the highest levels. The race team didn't have a say; neither did the riders.

"Yes, we don't have enough power," Rossi said.

That Rossi doesn't have the power is shocking. It was Rossi, after all, who a year ago at this race proposed to Ezpeleta that he be on Bridgestone tires in 2009. It was done, and the split garage was born. Ezpeleta knows Rossi is the show, and Ezpeleta will do whatever it takes for the show to go on. Dani Pedrosa - or rather his manager, Alberto Puig - used his leverage to make an extraordinary mid-season switch to Bridgestones, and a second, physical wall to go along with the virtual one already in place in the Repsol Honda garage. That gave them an edge over the Michelin riders, they hoped, but once they ceded power to Bridgestone, they were just along for the ride.

What resulted from Rossi's meeting with Ezpeleta wasn't an increase in numbers, but a change in allocation, and tires that worked over a wider range of temperatures. Now there would be eight fronts and 12 rears, both in two specs. The rain tires increased from one spec to two, four each front and rear. Each rider would get 150 tires for the six two-day winter tests - there would also be live one-day tests following certain GPs - and the manufacturers will all get an extra 100 tires to allocate as they see fit.

If, after the first few outings the number of tires isn't workable, Bridgestone will make adjustments, Rossi said.

"I am quite happy," said Rossi, trying to put the best face on it. "Also, so we don't arrive at the perfect results, but is a big, big improvement for the riders, because now the people, the organization take care about us and want to always speak with us and hear our advice. So at the end, the tire remain the same, but Bridgestone hear us, listen to us, and is ready to modify the number of the tires if have some problem. So is not a complete victory, but is not also a complete loss."

This from a rider used to dealing in complete victories.

"You know, if it becomes dangerous, I'm sure the riders won't go out, and it's going to make them [Bridgestone] look stupid and they're going to have to change," Stoner said. "But if they've given us tires that have a good, wide range of temperature and it's enough for a weekend, then I have no issues."

The second proposal was seen as a win, but how? This year, most of the riders, certainly the top ones, have tires custom-made to their specs. They choose 18 fronts and 22 rears prior to the race, plus they have rains and intermediates. How will a lower grade of tires make racing more safe? Firstly, it will slightly slow down corner speeds - the scourge statistic - and lower top speeds by preventing riders from getting drives heading onto the straights. Lap times will go up by a second or two in the short term. But Pedrosa will still be able to hit the barrier at the end of the Sachsenring's front straight if he locks up the front wheel in the rain. And John Hopkins will still be able to hit the advertising placard in Assen if it all goes wrong and the wall isn't properly protected.

How is it that costs will go down? By limiting testing. No one's paying for tires, though they may if they exceed their allocations.

And what of increasing competition? Not likely. The best riders on the best bikes will win. They'll win because they have the best crews who will be able to get to the best setups faster than the others. They have the resources to make the lesser tires work.

Stoner got it right when he said: "To be honest, it will affect other people a lot more than us, because we can work well with any package. We had some dramas destroying tires in five laps this year, but we have managed to fix this for the race. Without tires just to throw at it, it might come in handy for us."

Maybe the inmates do know what they're doing.

November 12, 2008

And the Beat Goes On

It never ends.

The catfight between the DMG-run AMA Pro Racing and the bulk of the manufacturers, under the cloak of the championship organizers-in-waiting Motorcycle Industry Council (MIC), may not be at the fever pitch it was when Roger Edmondson and Mel Harris were batting invectives back and forth like Federer and Nadal, but it's not far removed.

It hasn't gone unnoticed that the members of the MIC cartel, individually or as a group, haven't had much good to say about the proposed 2009 road-race rules, which were dropped by AMA Pro Racing on October 24. The key word is "proposed." The rules will not be released until November 20, when Edmondson and AMA CEO Rob Dingman had planned to meet with the Japanese bosses in Japan.

As a friend of mine put it, "The corporate brass at the OEs in Japan don't like to make any agreements [and probably won't] without the subsidiaries' reps present at the meetings." And the Japanese who run the subsidiaries would surely be offended that Edmondson went over their heads, "because the corporate brass will be wondering why he wants to get their blessing without the U.S. bosses in the room. Roger and Dingman obviously have no idea how the Japanese corporate machine works."

Maybe they didn't make any friends by directly contacting the Japanese companies, who would have immediately contacted their subsidiary companies here in the U.S. to get a read on the traveling salesmen. The devil being in the details, there are far too many question marks for the factories to accept the rules as they are.

Getting the U.S. distributors to agree on anything is like throwing four feral cats in a burlap bag with a ball of yarn and asking them to knit a cardigan. So if the U.S. distributors had already agreed to a set of rules, why is AMA Pro Racing throwing them away? I thought everybody liked sweaters?

The latest of many proposals, and the one that has the best chance of outliving its 28-day shelf life - from October 24 to the "final" rules package on November 20 - doesn't have many people jumping for joy, with the possible exception of Yamaha, which would gladly line up its new R1 in any form, especially Superstock, and who could blame them? Superstock machines are plenty fast and the costs are lower. The argument is easily made that there's more development in Superstock, which is closer to stock than Superbike. But the next generation of production bikes need parts that aren't on the current models, and that's not easily done with the proposed rules. And, regardless of what anyone in Daytona or Pickerington believes, spectators want fantasy. They want to see things they want, but can't have. Call it the Jessica Alba syndrome. Sure, the missus is fine, but what about taking a spin on that there model?

And even Yamaha hasn't publicly endorsed the rules. As you should read in a separate interview in the front of this issue with American Suzuki boss Mel Harris, changing the owner hasn't changed the fact that AMA Pro Racing communicates about as well as a comatose llama.

"I think there's still too many questions," American Suzuki boss Mel Harris said. "I think there's still negotiation. You may have seen an article that was saying that all the manufacturers were agreeing to race. I sent Roger [Edmondson] an e-mail saying, 'Please do not speak for Suzuki. I don't have factory authorization to say that we're racing' I said I agreed in the structure of the two classes, but I did not say that we're going to be there, because I don't have all the details to make that decision."

And yet, his race team will have about less than two weeks to prepare motorcycles for two or three riders attending the December 5-7 Daytona tire test. With the trucks having to be loaded and on the road at the end of November, it's clear that the teams will have to make any number of educated guesses. The final detailing will have to be done at the Speedway. Suzuki will have to run 2008 machinery with 2009 mods; look for 17-inch wheels, kitted forks, stock pistons and rods, and a few other specs that are mandated (at least for now) for next year.

It's also clear that the Brummies at Dunlop HQ are going to have a few sleepless nights building and air-freighting tires from their race shop in the north of England. Even more so considering the machine specs aren't entirely settled. The motorcycles that are tested in Daytona will not, in many cases, be what are raced in Daytona. Dunlop has to build DOTs for the 600s, which, if the rules remain the same, will be something below Formula Xtreme and above Supersport. And they'll run on both bankings. At night. Has anyone seen the lighting? Not yet, but there will be a night test in early December. And Superbikes, the premier class that takes a back seat to the 600s at the big dance, will run on one banking on slicks earlier in the day.

If, as is hoped, all the best riders are in the Superbike class, what does that say for Daytona SportBike? The spectacle of lesser riders, because that's what they are, racing for the biggest purse of the year, is lunacy. Would NASCAR make the Nationwide series the big show on Sunday while the Sprint Cup ran the day before? That's a rhetorical question. It's not quite like playing the World Series with AAA teams, but it's not far off.

At least two of the manufacturers won't be bothering with factory 600s. Yamaha and Honda both won 600cc championships this year and can be expected to take part, but with which riders?

And who gets to run the number-one plate: Ben Bostrom or Josh Hayes? I'd guess Bostrom, simply because Hayes has his sights set overseas. And he's not alone. Ben Spies is off to Yamaha World Superbike and others are certain to follow. World Superbike and Supersport teams know what they're going to race and where. The American teams can't say the same. Did I mention it was November?

What this means for the future isn't known. It isn't surprising that the manufacturers agreed to race in the AMA series in 2009. Next year will be different. The MIC faction will draw out their 2010 commitment as long as they can, all the while working behind the scenes to birth the championship the MIC said they would run in 2009, but won't. The streetfight continues. On a number of fronts.

Edmondson even managed to offend the promoters. It was "strongly suggested" he change the name of the premier class to anything other than Daytona SportBike and he agreed. And yet...

At least they addressed the silliness of three classes with Superbike in their names, as was once mooted. As Mel Harris said at the U.S. GP when asked what he'd be racing next year, "Superbikes."

There was Factory Superbike and American Superbike and Daytona Superbike and Red Bull Rookies Superbike and Moto-ST Superbike and Supersport Superbike. No doubt it would have prompted any number of 'Who's on first?' exchanges among the railbirds.

"What's out there now?"

"Superbikes."

"I thought they were just out there."

"They were."

"So what are these?"

"Superbikes."

"Superbikes?"

"Superbikes."

"What's next? Don't tell me."

"Superbikes."

"Why do I bother?"

The manufacturers must be asking themselves the same thing. It never ends.

December 3, 2008

Trouble and More Trouble

The AMA Superbike Championship has become a four-season debacle. What began in April as the spring of our discontent morphed into the summer of our discontent and the fall of our discontent and finally, as Richard III once famously said, the winter of our discontent.

The Shakespearean tragedy that is the shiny new AMA Pro Racing regime is heading down its own constantly changing path, with fewer and fewer willing to pay the price of the ride.

What it means is that there remains considerable uncertainty about who's going to see the ride to the end when the season begins on the first Friday of March in the new home of AMA Pro Racing - Daytona Beach, Florida.

The promise that emerged from the meeting at Indianapolis Motor Speedway between American Honda's Ray Blank and AMA PR CEO Roger Edmondson turns out to be an illusion, a false impression meant to perpetuate peace and harmony when nothing of the sort existed. And still doesn't.

The most recent evidence that all is not well can be found in the roster of riders for the Daytona Dunlop tire test. Conspicuous by their absence are American Suzuki and Kawasaki Motors. Of the two, the more revealing is Kawasaki, which has been the most moderate voice of the Big Four. Bruce Stjernstrom, the even-tempered overseer of Kawasaki's racing programs, said just over a month ago that Kawasaki was ready to go racing. But something happened to the rules that the teams had agreed to. When they were offered, in preliminary form two weeks ago, they were materially different. And the final rules were even more different, though not in any significant way. The teams believe the rules, as presented, are meant to stifle technology, and that holds no appeal.

But dumbed-down motorcycles are part of Edmondson's global vision - the one he took, along with AMA director of international affairs Rob Rasor, to Japan, where he hoped to spread the gospel to the Japanese. Only they weren't interested, at least not most of them. Honda refused to meet with him, as did Suzuki, which had asked for a specific agenda. Kawasaki referred him to the company offices in Irvine, California. The basic response was, "We don't have anything to do with you. You are not the FIM. You have no reason to be here. If the FIM wants to talk to us, we'll do that through the MSMA [Motorsports Manufacturers Association]."

They did manage to meet with Yamaha and someone from the MFJ, the Japanese equivalent of the AMA. They offered their vision of worldwide unity on rules to Yamaha, whose response was irrelevant. One out of four doesn't cut it, and that's what they might be looking at in the United States

The missteps on both sides, but especially on the AMA's side, have been impressive. Part of it is arrogance - "we paid for the thing, we've got f-you money, we're in charge, you'll do as you're told" - and part of it is bad advice. Edmondson has some very capable people on his payroll, but they are certainly being frozen out of the big-picture discussions. (When I asked one AMA PR employee about Edmondson's trip to Japan, I was told he didn't know about it.) Instead, Edmondson is getting a never-ending stream of bad advice from a number of people, many of whom have a direct interest in the outcome of his decision and have very parochial interests. Mostly he's refused to respect the factories, a mistake that's gone from ill-informed to possibly fatal.

When the Motorcycle Industry Council (MIC) announced its series for 2009 and the threat appeared legitimate, there was a flurry of activity and new rounds of phone calls. Once that fire was put out, everything went silent. If the MIC, which isn't currently capable of running a series, came around and a couple of factories said they were going that way, would there be more back-pedaling?

"[Everyone assumes] there's people talking at MIC," said one of the principals involved in talks with the MIC. "We're definitely not happy. We're disappointed. The way I look at it, they lied to us. It was a bait-and-switch. They gave us rules, they modified the rules. All of a sudden they're changing those rules and adding equipment.

"I feel like I got taken," he continued. "When they came back there around Laguna and said, 'Okay, we finally have it figured out, we need to get together,' so we're kind of looking forward, trying to be optimistic, and then they start adding and changing. He came back - this is after his meetings - and said, 'You guys have Superbike, but if you want it, you can have it my way.' Suddenly everybody woke up."

"They're going to say, 'We gave them everything they wanted: They wanted Superbike, we gave it to them. They didn't want some of the bikes on the eligible equipment list [the Suzuki GSX-R750 in particular]. They didn't want the [Ducati] 848 against 600s.' I have the proposal and there was none of this crap on it. That's not what we agreed to; that's not what you presented us with."

When this exercise began, at Daytona this past March with the announcement that shouldn't have been made, the smart thing would have been to leave everything in place for one year. That would have guaranteed the participation of all the major players while giving the new AMA time to see what they'd bought and what to do with it. Instead, Edmondson set out to re-invent the wheel, over and over and over, until what rolled down the tracks didn't look like something anyone would homologate for their motorcycles. And, along the way, the wheels rolled over the toes of far too may people, and repeatedly. So now, with the country in the worst financial straits since the Great Depression, Edmondson finds himself with a series that will have a difficult time attracting teams and fans, let alone the mythical Fortune 500 companies that are fleeing NASCAR.

The most recent sales figures show Suzuki with a 50-percent reduction in sales between October 2007 and October 2008. Honda also suffered, though not as badly, with Yamaha and Kawasaki faring the best. The factories with entry-level bikes and scooters are doing better. The big-ticket items (anything over $7,000) can't sell because people can't get financing. Is throwing $10 to 15 million at a race program the smart thing to do? Especially in a series where technology is despised and disharmony is rampant? Or would that money be better spent in other forms of advertising or rebates? It's a discussion being held at the top echelons of every motorcycle manufacturer. Why race with an organization that constantly moves the goalposts when there's no guarantee that there won't be more of the same in the future?

The same argument extends to the aftermarket world. On the final race weekend of the season, September 27 and 28 at Laguna Seca, Edmondson said this of the process of homologating aftermarket parts: "That process has started in that we have begun designing the forms, and Bill Syfan will be heading that up for us."

Let's very generously stipulate that the process began on September 27. The form was issued on November 19, a full 52 days later. This is not meant to cast aspersions on Syfan, who is among the more capable people on the AMA payroll, but just how dysfunctional does an organization have to be that it would take 51 1/2 days longer than it should to, in essence, redesign a form that already existed? Is it any wonder that nothing seems to get done and when it does, it's done badly? Redesigning a form is a job that an 8-year-old could knock off between his midmorning juice box and nap time.

Is it also any wonder that we haven't heard about a television deal? Speed can't afford to put the races on without at least two of the manufacturers. And they certainly wouldn't be interested if there was just one. No money, no ads, no TV, or, at the very least, no live TV with the big high-def truck.

As currently configured, AMA Pro Racing will be renting the Superbike teams for a year. By then, the MIC will have had a year to organize, with soon-to-be former American Suzuki boss Mel Harris working full-time as the racing czar: Could the AMA retain the teams past this season? Certainly, but they have to show the will, they have to be inclusive, and they have to engage sincerely, not just when it's expedient or to put out fires. Otherwise, this winter will be looked upon as the good old days, and the discontent will be permanent.

January 21, 2009

New Year - Same Old Story

We greet the new year with the continuing downward spiral that defines AMA Pro Road Racing.

The year 2008 ended with the news that American Honda was withdrawing for economic reasons. It was stated in a press release and reaffirmed with conviction by American Honda boss Ray Blank, but that doesn't make it so. Regardless of what is said or written in the name of Honda, perception trumps reality, and the legions of doubters outnumber the true believers. Anyone who has seen the precipitous sales slide for American Honda would have less doubt, despite Blank's oft-stated aversion to the Daytona Motorsports Group (DMG) brand of road racing. As would anyone who noticed that Honda pulled out of F1, All Japan Superbike, and the Suzuka 8 Hours, at the factory level. The foot-dragging, mind-changing, factory-disrespecting, inconsistent hierarchy in Daytona gave Honda all the cover they needed to take off a year or more.

That Honda was given the opportunity to pull out speaks to the dysfunctional negotiating practices on both sides, though the weight is heavier on the DMG side. And the shame of that is that their objectives - closer racing, lower costs, bigger crowds, better television - are noble, but they execute their strategies as well as the Detroit Lions.

Their manifest arrogance in the face of what is obvious to everyone but them - that without the factories, you don't have a series - is what continues to drive the nails deeper into the coffin they've so painstakingly constructed over the course of the last six months.

When I asked Ray Blank if Honda would have raced had the rules been settled, he replied: "That's a really hard question. We started to make a kind of combination of judgments in terms of preparation for 2009 that were more economic-based than they were rules-based."

But the reason Supercross and motocross are going forward is that they committed to those championships early on by signing riders and crews.

Had DMG and the factories negotiated in good faith and agreed to a set of rules in the spring or early summer, this would not have happened. In their quest for the results, the teams would have scooped up the best riders and crew members and the 2009 championship would be robust. Instead, it's become a worldwide laughingstock, with only one major factory (Yamaha) officially committed, unfinished technical rules, a dearth of homologated parts, promoters worried about losing their sponsorship, and a horrible television package.

To see how far the series has regressed, you need to return to Firebird Raceway in late September of 1995. That was the last time the Superbike races were shot on individual Betacams rather than live to a production truck. But now, nearly 14 years on, we're back to Betacam shoots and very little live television. (At the moment, Daytona will be live and the AMA races at Miller and Laguna Seca may be as well, if deals can be reached with the host broadcasters and sanctioning bodies.) The races will be shown either a week or two later on tape delay, but when exactly? Maybe Tuesdays at 7:30 a.m. EST, after the Ron Popeil Infomercial Spectacular and "Wrecked." But they may decide to air reruns of "Trackside" and the "Chili Bowl Midget Nationals" in that spot instead. If that happens, the races will be moved to the 2 am. EST slot, right after "The Humpy Show."

New Year - Same Old Story

As one TV insider put it. "It's a f---ed-up mess. I hope Roger [Edmondson] is really proud of that deal. He should be embarrassed."

Like everything else, this dragged on forever. When DMG CEO Roger Edmondson met the media at Mazda Raceway Laguna Seca on the final weekend in September, he said: "The television deal is on my desk. We have a disagreement over part of it, and when we solve that disagreement, we'll execute it, but it will be with Speed."

But it won't be in HD. Asked who would pay for the HD truck, Edmondson said it was "up to them to pay for the HD truck."

The television deal was agreed to during a meeting at DMG headquarters in Daytona on Monday, January 5. That it dragged on for so long means that finding reasonable time slots on a network devoted to NASCAR won't be easy. Nor will finding advertisers. By alienating the factories, who did the bulk of the advertising, and not bringing in the mythical Fortune 500 companies we've been told about, the productions have to be cheapened, as does the presentation. Maybe it's part of their secret plan to drive up live attendance: If you can't watch it live on TV, why not bring the kids to the track?! But don't plan too far ahead; the last informal poll I took suggested the number of tracks without contracts outnumbered those with.

The quixotic belief that synergy between the two- and four-wheel Daytona families would elevate road racing is the reason some of us were initially optimistic about DMG's stewardship. But those hopes have long faded, replaced by serial false steps. As this is going to press, the season-opening Daytona weekend is about seven weeks away with the trucks having to leave Southern California in six weeks. And, amazingly, the technical rules for American Superbike remain a work-in-progress.

The teams who took part in the Daytona Dunlop tire test were told that kit pistons would be allowed. But, as of today, they aren't. Which means if whoever's in charge does finally agree to make it official, the teams would have precious little time to design pistons, have them made in quantity, get them homologated, and do any serious engine testing. As one crew chief told me, "There's no f---king way we'll have our bikes ready for Daytona."

Some of the reason for that goes to parts homologation. AMA Pro Racing has committed to providing a list of aftermarket suppliers, but when one team manager asked why it hadn't been published, he was told there weren't enough commitments. Whether this is true or not, it's clear that the system is a fiasco. Teams can't build bikes because they don't know if the parts are going to be legal. And if you wait for the "list" to be circulated, you're wasting precious time getting ready to race. So the best you can do is ask your suppliers if they plan to take part and hope they follow through. A team manager and crew chief both told me they couldn't order wheels because their supplier hadn't committed. And no one in his right mind is going to order wheels, only to find out they're illegal. Given the ridiculous lateness of the process, it's clear that AMA tech inspectors have no choice but to be less vigilant than they were last year at Daytona.

What this ultimately points to is a total lack of understanding of motorcycle racing on the part of the DMG. No one with knowledge about motorcycle racing would do such an abysmal job of writing technical rules and homologating motorcycles. Not every manufacturer has homologated motorcycles. Which means you could show up at Daytona on a race-prepped machine only to find out it's a cheater. For a company that came in with the mantra of transparency, they've become increasingly opaque.

Even the wording on the homologation requirement is open to interpretation. It states: "AMA Pro American Superbike motorcycles must be street-certified for use in the United States and be available at the time of competition from U.S. retail dealers. There must be sufficient quantity available such that any person wanting to buy one for racing purposes can do so in a timely fashion." And they must be available until August 1 of the current model year.

A few questions: What does "available" mean? Does it mean available at the dealership? From the distributor? And what is "sufficient quantity"? Ducati sold out of 1098s well before August 1 of 2007, their first year of production. So would they pull the Ducatis off the grid and wipe them off the record books? A simple number - we were told 30 at the tire test - would have sufficed.

You'll find the homologation rules on the AMA Pro Racing website. That's about all you'll find. Try finding an outdoor MX schedule. Or the archives of past results. Or even the 2008 results. One of the reasons DMG bought the AMA and kept the name was the history of the sport. They were the new caretakers. They would continue the tradition of AMA Pro Racing. And, as they spiral ever downward, it's clear they have.

March 18, 2009

The Night the Lights Went Out... In Daytona

It was appropriate that for the first time ever, the Daytona Less Than 200 was run in the dark, because most of the field, the fans, and the television audience were all left in the dark.

For those of you who didn't see the nearly live Daytona LT200 - it was 55 laps, not 57, and therefore 193.05 miles - what you missed was a world-class debacle, a fiasco of the first order that proved that all the money in the world doesn't buy competence, and the Daytona LT200 was nothing if not a vivid display of incompetence that threatened the safety and lives of the riders.

Whether they wanted to or not, there was no hiding from the truth and, to his credit, AMA Pro Racing director of competition Colin Fraser didn't try. As soon as he possibly could, Fraser appeared in the media center to attempt to clarify what had happened - a fool's errand that he handled about as well as anyone could, given the scope of the debacle.

Fraser answered questions for about 17 minutes, but without the tools necessary to completely explain the various scenarios that had unfolded. There were no lap charts, no individual lap times. And, as this is being written on Monday afternoon, March 9, there still aren't. The issues involved the yellow flags, the red flag, and the pace car that he referred to 19 times as the "safety car." "Safety cars" are used in MotoGP, pace cars are used in NASCAR. The Daytona Motorsports Group is doing its best to put a four-wheel imprint on a two-wheel sport - not very successfully, judging from this weekend.

Given the lack of communication within the new AMA Pro Racing, it wasn't surprising that someone forgot to tell Colin that the blue Honda Accord his deputy Bill Syfan was driving - not very well, it would turn out - had a sticker at the top of the windshield that read "OFFICIAL PACE CAR." (About now, someone inside the Daytona Motorsports Group is ordering an "OFFICIAL PACE CAR... NOT" sticker)

In fact, the pace car not only didn't do a very good job of pacing the field or providing safety, it ruined the race. And the next time anyone suggests using a pace car, they should be stripped, covered in Alpo, and fed to toothless, geriatric beagles.

The pace car was responsible for the red flag, which meant it was responsible for the 45-minute delay and the subsequent imbroglio over the order of the single-file restart. And later it was responsible for pulling out in front of the wrong rider, which may have had an adverse affect on the outcome of the race and almost certainly screwed up the order of finish.

"I've said it before, cars and bikes don't go together - they never do," said Monster Kawasaki's fourth-place finisher Jamie Hacking, "and the result of that showed."

Hacking knows a thing or two about the perils of pace cars. The former Supersport and Superstock Champion was caught up in the pace-car accident during the 2001 Superbike race that sent Aaron Yates to the medical center and collected a number of others. That collision had begun when a Pontiac Aztek (or "asspack," as it became known) slowed on the back straight while the Superbike field was coming full throttle off the west banking. When Hacking saw the Honda Accord slow dramatically for the chicane on Friday night, he had a sense of déjà vu.

"I'm like, 'This is not going to be good,'" he thought to himself in the split second before he headed for the apron. "I thought it was going to be worse than it really was. Luckily, only one rider got in an incident there, but that could have been a really bad deal back there."

Erion Honda's Jake Zemke, the 2008 Formula Xtreme Champion, saw it coming and was hoping the others would catch on.

"And so everybody was checking up going in there, and it was happening every lap," he said. "I'm not sure why guys can't figure out, 'Okay, he's slowing down, we should probably slow down,' but it happened for, like, two or three laps before the incident. Then, obviously, there was an accident back there - it was chain reaction. Guys just hammering into each other."

Team Graves Yamaha's Tommy Aquino was acquitting himself well in his first Daytona 200 when he got collected from behind by an overeager rider who hadn't figured out that the pace car wasn't fast enough through the chicane. Aquino was mostly unhurt, but his YZF-R6 was too badly damaged to continue. Given Yamaha's one-two finish with Ben Bostrom and Josh Herrin, Aquino might have helped Yamaha with a podium sweep. Instead, he was swept off the track. And what if it had been Ben Bostrom or Josh Hayes that got clipped?

Up until that point, everything was going well. The racing was close, the pit stops were clean, the crowd was being treated to the show they'd expected. And then AMA Pro Racing just destroyed it.

If they'd learned anything since the last pace-car debacle in 2006, when then-road-race manager Ron Barrick went out without a spotter and failed to pick out the race leader, it'd be hard to prove.

Pace-car driver Bill Syfan was doing the same thing as Barrick, not catching the leaders, though it's up to race control to get him the proper information. Once a full-course yellow is ordered, the riders have to hold position. (Danny Eslick didn't get that memo and ended up being disqualified.) That leaves the pace-car driver time to find the leader, but how could he know what to do if race control didn't know what was going on?

Bostrom, and every other rider I spoke to, admitted to being confused. He was in the lead, or was he? He thought he was. Others thought he wasn't. The AMA official at the end of the pit lane didn't know what to do. Did his team work on his R6 during the red flag? Again, nothing was conclusive. But if they had worked on the bike, it wasn't their fault. AMA PR was clueless.

"Nobody knew anything," someone involved with the television broadcast told me, and he said they hadn't from the start. AMA Pro Racing never gave Speed a minute-by-minute account of when the races were going to start, which is essential if you're broadcasting live on television. And they had no idea what to do with Bostrom until they were questioned on the radio. When a member of the broadcast team asked the question, the response was, "Somebody tell TV to stay off that channel." The television crew was so concerned that they dispatched an observer to race control. Toward the end of the race, he was asked to leave. "We don't have time to deal with Speed," he was told. That won't be a problem again, since this was the only almost-live TV of the year. The Superbike race will be broadcast on March 21.

Early in the week, there were signs that DMG was turning the 200 into a NASCAR race, and it wasn't just the rolling start, which worked out well. During Wednesday's riders' meeting, Fraser got into an argument with both Bostrom and Mat Mladin about the position of the flagman. The riders wanted him on inside of the tri-oval, on the apron, in his traditional spot; MotoGP and World Superbike mandate that the flagman be on the track.

From the FIM rulebook from both World Superbike and MotoGP: "When the leading rider has completed the designated number of laps for the race, he will be shown a chequered flag by an official standing at the finish line, at track level. The chequered flag will continue to be displayed to the subsequent riders."

That regulation was prompted by an accident at a World Superbike race when the flagman was in an elevated position. This now being a NASCAR property, starter Bobby Lemming was put up in the starter's perch above the track, where the flags blended into the background, Bostrom and Mladin said.

"Do you understand the problem? Do you not understand?" Mladin asked Fraser. "Yes, Mat," Fraser replied, "and I answered the question once."

Fraser was in an untenable position, though the riders' meeting was clearly not his finest hour. Decisions are being made above him that affect his job, but which he can't question. Now DMG is trying to turn motorcycle racing into NASCAR. Nothing good will come of it. We don't need pace cars, especially ones that adversely affect the outcome of the race. And we don't need flagmen up in the air and invisible.

The reign of darkness has just begun.

April 1, 2009

Fun or Funereal?

To catalog the multitude of transgressions perpetrated by the new AMA Pro Racing on the road-race paddock would be futile. The list is long and varied and constantly growing, But if there's one thing they've done that's inexcusable, other than laying waste to their own credibility, it's that they've taken the fun out of racing.

Very few people get rich racing motorcycles. The hours are brutal, the physical demands are demanding, the return on investment is minimal. People race motorcycles, people work on racing motorcycles, people support motorcycle racing, because it's their passion, because they love it, because it's fun. But if Daytona didn't convince you, the evidence was stark at Fontana - this just isn't fun anymore.

The atmosphere in the AMA road-race paddock is funereal. The central topic of conversation isn't racing, but what's wrong with racing and how much worse it's going to get. Because, make no mistake, it continues to get worse.

That part of the Fontana weekend not spent recounting the AMA's innumerable sins from Daytona - did you know that race control didn't authorize the red flag that caused the debacle during the 200, but that it was a rogue element in the chicane? - was spent lamenting the current situation and the future.

On Saturday afternoon, AMA PR made the decision to move the Supersport race from Sunday, when it was expected to rain, to Saturday. Had they said it was because of rain, that would have been an admission that they didn't want young riders racing on a track that's barely tolerable in the dry to one that's lethal in the wet. So instead, AMA PR issued a press release in which AMA Pro president Roger Edmondson was quoted as saying, "The only class that does not have provisions for rain tires this weekend is AMA Pro Supersport, presented by Shoei, so the decision was made to run their feature at the end of today's schedule."

Completely false. Not a shred of truth to it. Dunlop, the control-tire supplier, had a truck full of rain tires for all classes and at least 200 for Supersport. That should have been enough, since each rider gets two wet fronts and two wet rears. Did I mention there were only seven riders in the Supersport race? Given the size of the field, they could have held eight wet Supersport races before the supply became an issue.

Was Edmondson ill-served by a minion who provided him with bad information? We don't know. But if there was any question, it would have been prudent to ask the question before throwing one of his partners under the tire truck. And if AMA PR is willing to treat a company that's paying a substantial sum of money like that, what hope is there for the rest of the paddock?

At the end of the weekend, Monster Attack Kawasaki's Jamie Hacking reportedly dropped a few f-bombs while making a less-than-graceful exit from the press room. For that, and for his behavior at the postrace news conference, he was suspended indefinitely. Press rooms aren't for the faint of heart, and the atmosphere would be monastic if cursing was prohibited. Hacking will miss the next round of the series at Road Atlanta, which will almost certainly guarantee that a Buell will be leading the championship. If you can't beat 'em, ban 'em. It isn't enough that they've designed a class where one machine is twice as large as the rest, has the greatest list of special allowances, and can weigh the same as the twins? Now they have to put the toughest competition, a multiple-time champion, in the docket.

Now Kawasaki has a decision to make. With Roger Lee Hayden out, is there any reason for them to drive cross country to the next round at Road Atlanta with just Leandro Mercado confirmed? Of course not. So the fans at Road Atlanta are punished by AMA PR and are denied the chance to see a successful son of the South, one less of a dwindling galaxy of stars.

Rockstar Makita Suzuki's Mat Mladin and four others were put on probation for missing a mandatory autograph session. The next time may mean a suspension. Knowing Mladin, he may make himself the test case. And why not?

What have they given to the teams or riders that helps them do their jobs? Nothing. Why should Mladin or anyone else be obligated to have to be somewhere? This is a one-way street, with money flowing south. Until they start treating the paddock like partners and not serfs, they don't deserve the respect of the riders. Had they come in amicably and offered to work together, the paddock would have responded. Instead, it's all about "you're going to do this, you're going to do that, you're not going to do this, you're not going to do that. What? You don't like it? Tough s--t. There's the door and leave."

Who would benefit from Mladin's absence? Definitely not the fans, who wouldn't get to see the greatest racer in the history of American Superbike racing.

One team owner predicted: "Suzuki will try and make Mat do the right thing so it doesn't look bad in the eyes of the public. They're not doing anything for us but taking and making our jobs more difficult to do. And not paving a good road to go to the future. I don't see them improving anything in the future. They're not helping us; why should we help them?"

The promoters, as much as anyone, deserve better. They're trying to sell a damaged commodity in a dismal economy with far too many restrictions. For instance, tracks are only allowed to give out trophies to the race winner. Second and third place get medals - the winner does also. Tommy Hayden's medal fell off its ribbon on Sunday. One winner leaned over to another and said, "I used to get these in WERA."

It's one more example of the monomaniacal compulsion to change every single aspect of motorcycle racing, to take some thing that's unique and mold it into the shape of some other series for no good reason. The pace car - in Fontana, it was a lumbering four-door that clearly wasn't made to go around corners - should be banned. What happened when the pace car came out for the mandatory three laps in Sunday's SportBike race? The fans were treated to three less laps of racing.

The rules from now on are: there are no rules. If you screw up, we'll tell you, but we won't tell you in advance. Will we race in the rain? Don't know. We'll get back to you. Racing in the rain at Fontana is insane. The daffy curbing that makes up the chicane in turn one is lethal. Hit it in the dry and you might lose your front end. In the wet, you will crash and you will hit a wall. And that simply isn't fun.

April 15, 2009

Listen to Mladin

The Kingdom of Darkness reconvened in the clay hills north of Atlanta for the first race on a proper road course. Not safe, but proper, as opposed to the road courses dropped inside the Fontucky oval and the safety-challenged World Center of Racing, where the walls are closer than your in-laws and at least as welcoming. Anyone who thought Mat Mladin had lost a step by being challenged in two of the first three races was in for a surprise. Mladin likes this layout, which is different from liking the track, which has significant safety issues in the dry and shouldn't be raced on in the wet. Just be careful how you say that.

Anyone who thinks otherwise will have been convinced by Sunday's Supersport race. A mixture of young riders and a light rain put four on the ground in short order before the race was red-flagged. That decision was of little comfort to the riders who now have to replace fairings, seats, tanks, clip-ons, etc., and who ruined perfectly good sets of leathers.

As you'll read in the coverage of the Road Atlanta race elsewhere in this issue, Mladin arrived ready to add to his tally of 12 wins. When the weekend ended, he had 14, which was more than the sum career total of the rest of the 21-rider field.

Road Atlanta is a course that rewards controlled aggression, and no one attacks a racetrack like Mladin. On top of which, his 2008 Suzuki GSX-R1000 - a little more than a month removed from a dealership warehouse - was now stiff and harsh and almost felt like a race bike. (Not coincidentally, when they were both on Michelin tires, Colin Edwards said no one else could use Valentino

Rossi's tires because they were too stiff. There's a lesson to be learned there.)

Mladin crushed the competition on Saturday to give Suzuki its 50th win in a row on a machine that was put up for sale prior to the race weekend for a mere $59,000. That amount, he accurately said, was less than Yamaha spent on its Magneti Marelli electronics.

"It's an amazing motorbike," he said. "I mean, Suzuki make amazing sportbikes. And as I said, nine championships in the last decade and a gazillion wins at the same time, it says enough."

The top four were on Suzukis, but so were four of the bottom six. As always in Superbike, most of the field was on Suzukis - 14 of the 22 riders in race one.

This presents an interesting conundrum for AMA Pro Racing. Very few things can prevent Mladin from winning every race. A crash (he fell on Sunday morning, but his team rebuilt his one race bike), a mechanical, or rain on a track he doesn't deem safe for wet racing, such as Road Atlanta or Mid-Ohio. Or for AMA Pro Racing to find a way to slow him and not the bike, which they've said they wouldn't do. Rather, they said they'd offer allowances for the other brands to close the gap. They shouldn't. As Mladin's ace crew chief Peter Doyle told me after Saturday's win, the number-one reason the streak was at 50, and is now 51, is Mladin and Spies. The second reason?

"Probably the lack of effort that the other guys have put in," he noted. "And that's not... aimed at any single person or rider, but some of the teams and the way they've gone about it and the riders they've chosen, I think that's helped our cause. I think if Troy Bayliss had been over here riding a Ducati, then we probably wouldn't have 50 wins in a row. They put some decent riders on decent motorcycles on decent teams, other people would've been winning races."

The difference between Mladin's brilliance and the sudden Buell dominance is clearly Mladin. Just as clearly, so is the 1125R. Anyone who doubts that must not have seen the Speed telecast from Fontana that was delayed two weeks and would have been more appropriately shown on the History Channel. As the field came to the line for the rolling starts, and again for one restart, Danny Eslick pinned it and left the field behind like legless turtles. Anyone who thinks that a V-twin that weighs the same and has considerably more horsepower and torque than a four-cylinder doesn't have an advantage needs to get his head out of the sand, if not elsewhere. In his first ride on a Buell, and in Daytona SportBike, Taylor Knapp nearly stole third place from Chris Peris. Knapp's previous best finish was a distant seventh in American Superbike on a Suzuki.

All this talk about average lap times is nonsense. As is the argument that Buells don't take all the top placings. Yes, it's a beast that doesn't change direction very well, but it more than makes up for it with overwhelming power. A competent rider - and Eslick is much more than competent - on an overdog is going to be hard to beat, as we've seen. Ask the riders who've had their arms pulled out of their sockets by trying to draft the Buells. (Those same riders, though, will point out that Eslick is riding it very well.) Parity is the buzzword, and in the interest of parity, they need to take away one of Buell's many gifts; the 20-pound weight allowance would be a good start.

The weather forecast for Sunday wasn't promising and, in fact, it did briefly rain. But if race officials send the Superbikes out in a soaking rain at Infineon Raceway or Mid-Ohio, that will be the end of Mladin's streak. Given the makeup of the field, a Suzuki will likely win and continue the streak. But the streak owned by Mladin and Ben Spies that started at Miller Motorsports Park in 2006 will be over.

Following his third consecutive Superpole lap - he was best by 1.6 seconds - I asked Mladin if he'd race in the rain at Road Atlanta. I knew the answer. Several years ago, I'd followed Mladin on a safety tour of Road Atlanta. The track has changed since then, notably in turn 12, but one of the worst parts, the sixth-gear back-straight kink with little comfort on the rider's right, remains.

"I don't race here in the rain, so hopefully it doesn't rain," he said, and nothing is going to change his mind. "It's no different this year to any other year. Maybe they'll run a race in the rain; I'm not too sure. But, unfortunately, it's a safety issue. Again, I'm not having a go at anyone or the track or anyone else, but the racetrack's barely up to spec for dry racing, let alone wet racing. We deal with a lot here, and there's just too many places."

"Listen, if they run a race that's fine; it doesn't bother me at all," he continued. "Obviously, some riders have already said they're going to race. It can rain. Wherever it can be torrential flooding, they want the points. If racing in the rain is all about getting points and not actually seeing the big picture and trying to protect the kids that are coming through and racing in the future and that sort of stuff, that's fine. And I understand how other teams and other riders think, and if that's their prerogative, that's their prerogative.

"Over the last decade or more - 14 years, actually, I've been here now - I've been a big safety advocate," he said. "And I don't think anybody can say that when I go out there I don't give it 100 percent, so when I get on the bike, I do my job. But at the same time, the racetracks need to improve things as we go on."

Mladin said it wouldn't take a lot to fix some of the tracks.

"And then you have a series that, by the time it happens, I'm sure, I won't be a part of anyway," he added. "But to me, to see some kid lying up against a concrete wall somewhere and I've agreed to go and race in the rain just because I want points, that doesn't sit with me - never has. It's not who I am as a human being. In the end, we're all here to race, we all race hard, but there has to be some safety built in." The mantra of the new AMA Pro Racing is that the throttle goes both ways, which implies that you don't have to go so darn fast when it's pissing rain. But when you're going through the kink at Mid-Ohio and the guy in front of you has it pinned and doesn't care whether he's remembered for leading a lap or having his name written in Sharpie on a makeshift memorial, what are you going to do?

Mladin is smart enough, and has been racing long enough, to know when and where to express his views. As does Jamie Hacking, or at least he thought he did, before he was penalized for using salty language while speaking to his wife as they left the pressroom at Auto Club Speedway. That isn't so much a free-speech issue as it is an invasion of privacy. But if the intended effect was to frighten the riders, it worked. The Kingdom of Fear was so prevalent that more than one rider with a legitimate point of view pleaded, "Please don't get me into trouble."

Rather than stifling free speech, the Kingdom of Darkness should listen to what Mladin says about track safety. Fixing the tracks would guarantee that promoters wouldn't have to worry about fans staying away, and fans wouldn't have to worry about the best riders not racing.

Will they listen to Mladin? Of course not.

May 6, 2009

Bottom Line: Go Watch!

Some guys just can't catch a break.

Take the new-and-improved AMA Pro Racing. They announced that the all-conquering Buell 1125R now has to weigh 380 pounds, up from the svelte 365, and there's a collective yawn. Well more of a "You're kidding, right?"

I was among those who thought they'd awoken from the great lumbering sleep and done the right thing. With the hard-riding Danny Eslick muscling the lumpy Rotax-powered Buell, the winner's circle suddenly had a very different look and sound. The Buell is nearly twice as big, makes more horsepower and way more torque than the Japanese fours. And, until they were told to pork up, the 1125R weighed the same as the 600s. Seemed unfair. People complained. AMA PR reacted, which isn't the same as acting, which would be difficult because the script is constantly changing, but more on that later.

Then this e-mail from a Daytona-winning team principal landed in my e-mailbox.

"Big F---ING joke! The Buells come off the racetrack at over 390 with whatever fuel is remaining. Our bikes are at 375 or maybe a little less. There is no way for us to lose 5 pounds unless we cheat!"

And this from the manager of another Supersport-winning team.

"All's we know is the Buells are weighing 390, couldn't get to claimed 385. Put them up 15 pounds, still 5 pounds lighter than they should have been." If that's to be believed, the effect on the Buells will be zero.

More amusingly, it illustrates how painfully out of touch the AMA tech wizards must have been when they created the obvious imbalance of power. They give the Buell nearly free rein when, in fact, they should have been handicapping it. It's only when the evidence of their miscalculations is manifest that they announce a penalty that's not a penalty. Don't expect anything to change.

And don't expect the gift of five pounds to the 600/fours to make any difference. Some of the bikes are under and the ones that are over can't de-girth without expensive materials.

As one denizen of the AMA Pro Racing bunker in Daytona put it, "The only effect it will have is for the media."

If AMA Pro Racing was serious, they'd take the mag wheels away from the Buells. The location of the weight is more crucial than the absolute weight. The mags makes the Buell feel lighter and accelerate harder; the outside rim is accelerating less mass, which makes it easier to turn and change direction. Mag wheels are expensive, but it's easy weight. Besides, only Buell can use them. Aprilia can use forged-aluminum wheels, but the RSV1000R is such a porker that it can't come close to the 385-pound rule for twins. How is that fair?

As one crew chief told me, "Very silly, very expensive. Weight is one of the worst things you can f--k around with, because the rules aren't flexible enough that you can make massive weight savings. You have to do it with standard parts. You're limited to where you can take weight off bikes and it's expensive."

The weight change was one of the head-scratching decisions recently made by AMA PR. More puzzling is the constantly changing promoter-practice policy. When the season began, AMA PR announced three official tests: Mid-Ohio, Infineon, and New Jersey, plus Fontana. Then Fontana became unofficial; AMA PR realized it would cost too much in manpower, time, and folding green to put it on, so they turned it over to the teams. Suzuki had the first day and Yamaha the next two.

The practice ban took money out of the pockets of a number of racetracks. Mazda Raceway Laguna Seca traditionally books about four days of preseason tests - never mind that most of it's rained or fogged out - but this year the test ban denied SCRAMP significant revenue.

The "official" Infineon test became unofficial when the AMA offered it to the manufacturers, none of whom wanted the headache of dealing with it given the restrictions, or lack thereof. So it went to the track, who did it well, as they always do.

But soon AMA PR was waffling on promoter practices. Now Thursday practice was back, but with a very strange set of rules that the promoters weren't wild about - separate paddocks for Thursday participants and AMA weekend participants, and no separate classes for everyday street riders and AMA entrants who wanted to practice on Thursday. Which means that a guy could ride his Harley in off the street and try to out-brake Mladin into Infineon's turn 12. That's something I'd pay to see.

The thinking (?) of the AMA was that none of the big teams would take part in Thursday practice if they had to set up and tear-down twice, and if their riders had to ride with street squirrels on the same track at the same time.

So a competition bulletin announced a ban on Superbike and Sportbike riders following the May 17 Infineon event. The "Track Days" are for amateurs, the bulletin said, and not for pros to test. Since the promoters have pissed off AMA PR, they've done an end run by only banning Superbike and Sportbike riders and allowing Supersport and MotoST, who they think won't mind running with the amateurs.

As one promoter told me, "For me, this is a safety issue. I don't want street riders out on the track at the same time as the pros."

The bulletin was later updated to include Road America, which wouldn't have been happy about the lost revenue. And by the time

Mid-Ohio and the others chime in, the competition bulletin will have more updates than a McDonald's sign.

The solution, of course, is to run these sessions on Monday, when the pros and amateurs could test at separate times on a track with full safety protection. Prohibiting the pros from testing does more than just deny them set-up time. It takes money out of the promoters' pockets at a time when they're desperate for anything they can get.

The promoters haven't been treated like equal partners by AMA PR. If they had, there would be AMA races on the Miller World Superbike weekend. But AMA PR's exorbitant financial demands forced Miller to rightfully show them the door and organize support races.

The economic crisis is forcing families to make hard choices, and motorcycles and motorcycle races are funded with discretionary income. Sales numbers for most brands aren't encouraging. There have been manufacturer cutbacks of race sponsorship this year, but next year, after the current contracts have out, could be even worse. And, despite vowing to make up any deficit from lost OEM backing, AMA PR has done nothing of the sort.

Which is why it's critical to go to the races. Fans across the country have vowed not to support the new AMA PR, which is understandable given their litany of missteps and misfires, and the misery they've inflicted on the paddock and the sport.

But staying away from the racetrack doesn't punish AMA PR - they'll still collect their sanctioning fee - it punishes the racetracks.

Not all tracks are owned by giant corporations that can ride out the economic storm. Road America, for one, is locally owned and run by people who are passionate about motorcycles, not some fat cats who can't see beyond the accounting ledger. It's a track that strives to provide entertainment, not just racing, and it's among the many venues coming up worthy of supporting.

Barber Motorsports Park has taken a nontraditional approach from its inception and it's worked. The natural amphitheatre is one of the best places to both watch racing and spend a day. And the museum is world class. It's one of the very few non-legacy tracks to show year-on-year growth. Infineon Raceway is owned by a big corporation, but that hasn't stopped them from spending tens of million dollars of NASCAR and NHRA money to improve rider safety and fan enjoyment.

Like Barber and Road America, Infineon works diligently to both entice new fans and pamper the regulars. Miller Motorsports Park earned the race of the year award from World Superbike in its first year. It's no surprise. No detail is too small, no request too trivial for the stall at MMP. The fact that they've anticipated most everything - with the help of the World Superbike organizers - makes the track a worthy destination for everyone, except AMA PR. And it's the only time this year most of us will get to see Ben Spies win. The following week is Road America, home to one of the best tracks and the best brats on the calendar. Then a bit of a break until the Red Bull U.S. GP at Mazda Raceway Laguna Seca, where Superbike, Sportbike, and Supersport will fill the downtime when Rossi, Stoner, Hayden, and Edwards aren't on the track.

And if you need to be convinced to go to Monterey, where the Rossi-Stoner battle turned the tide on the 2008 MotoGP World Championship, and where you can reach out and touch the riders, watch the racing from the Corkscrew, and enjoy the pleasures of Cannery Row, there is but one question: You're kidding, right?

May 20, 2009

Lies and Video Tape

A funny thing happened on the way to the dyno: AMA Pro Racing was lied to.

The irony is not lost on anyone who's watched the machinations of the new regime. But what makes it so rich was knowing who lied to them.

Following Barber Superpole qualifying, the 10 qualifying machines were rolled to a dyno at the far end of the paddock, at the invitation of AMA Pro Racing. The purpose of the exercise, as stated in an AMA PR press release, was AMA PR's "ongoing effort to maintain a competitive balance among all manufacturers" in the class. No one believed this for one very simple reason - it wasn't true.

It was done to prove to the skeptics among us that the Buell 1125R wasn't the overdog of the class, that it didn't make excessive power despite nearly twice the displacement, and that everyone who was whining about the Buell could now be compelled to shut up. But when the dyno display revealed the horsepower figure of Michael Barnes' GEICO Powersports/RMR 1125R, AMA Pro Racing officials were left speechless.

They shouldn't have been.

A visit to the Buell website claims the 1125R makes 146 bhp at 9800 rpm and 82 foot-pounds of torque at 8000 rpm. Class rules allow for, among other things, compression to be raised, cam timing to be changed, electronic upgrades, and aftermarket exhausts. So how could anyone be surprised when the Buell crossed the 150-horsepower mark on the dyno? The simple answer: That wasn't the number AMA Pro Racing had been given.

The power advantage guaranteed that the numbers wouldn't released. Had it been more in line with what they were expecting, it most certainly would have been. But the paddock being the paddock, and with the help of the press release, the numbers quickly came into focus, though whomever approved the release at AMA PR - and not someone with the slightest hint of a technical background who could talk with a straight face - insisted they were meaningless. Specifically, the release stated: "A complete listing of the dyno testing results will not be released, as raw horsepower is meaningless without an inclusion of all other variables."

Two thoughts spring to mind. The first, and most obvious, is, "Bull---t."

Horsepower is a number that everyone can relate to. When you read that a top fuel dragster makes 7000 horsepower, do you ask yourself, "Yes, but what was the elevation and humidity? And what did the dyno operator have for breakfast?"

The second thought is that they should release the other variables.

One of the team owners who witnessed the testing told me he knew the dyno operator and trusted him to be fair, though he still wasn't happy about the wear on his engine. The reason the horsepower numbers weren't released was that the Buell delivered 21 more horsepower than any other motorcycle. Second place fell to the Aprilia RSV1000R, with the Japanese fours all in the 120-horsepower range.

The more telling number is torque. At nearly 4000 more rpm, the stock Kawasaki ZX-6R makes 49.1 foot-pounds stock - 60-percent less than the Buell, and with no way of reaching it short of forced induction, which currently isn't legal. That's why you see the Buell launching off the corners ahead of the fours.

The only number that was released was the power-to-weight ratio, which pegged the Buell, without naming it, at 2.65 pounds per horsepower. That would put the porky Buell well above the allowed 380 pounds. The difference between the first and second bikes was stated at .28 pounds per horsepower, validating the belief that the Aprilia is also heavily larded, which everyone knows. (At Barber, it was lightened by the fitment of 5.5-inch aluminum wheels that were approved two days after the race.)

What makes the deception even sillier is that everyone knows how much power the Buell makes, but they also know how much it weighs, and still most riders wouldn't want to race one over the course of the season. In addition to being fat, the Buell is top-heavy and changes direction as gracefully as a drunk on a Segway. It works extremely well at certain types of tracks, and Barber, a flowing course with no long straightaways and few stop-start corners, isn't one of them. At Road America, with its three sixth-gear straights and mostly low-gear corners, the Buell should be untouchable, especially in the hands of Danny Eslick, whose style perfectly fits the Buell.

Will it balance out - the tracks that favor or punish the Buell? Hard to say, since no factory Superbike rider has ridden the new venues in New Jersey and Topeka.

During a meeting with team entrants on Thursday evening, AMA Pro Racing CEO Roger Edmondson said that Topeka was on the schedule, meaning it was no longer subject to approval, as it had been when first announced. A safety committee of a sort had visited the facility months ago for a visual inspection. But among the group was only one factory Superbike rider and one rider no longer in the AMA series. And they didn't ride the facility at speed on a race bike, which means that when the riders get there, it will be a lottery without a lot of winning tickets. Two days after the Mid-Ohio race, a test will be held at the new track in South Jersey. If the track is deemed unsafe, what are the options? The worry, according to those who have ridden it, is with one corner - a long, looping left that leads under a bridge. It may be okay... or not. And, short of altering the shape of the corner, it's unfixable.

During the same Thursday meeting at Barber, Edmondson also discussed the state of television, and what he said brought more confusion and disbelief. The claim was that ratings for the "AMA Pro Prime Time" broadcasts shown in the Saturday evening prime-time graveyard were up. There was, of course, no proof of this - only a flimsy explanation for why the numbers couldn't be revealed. If, in fact, the numbers were up, wouldn't every effort be made to trumpet them?

And if it is true that ratings are up, there will never be live television for AMA road racing. The Japanese factories won't spend the money for it. Who's going to make up for that? Buell? Aprilia? Triumph? Or the Fortune 500 companies that are going to fund the teams comprised of a racer and rent-a-racer that works so well in the Shangri-La that is Grand-Am and that Edmondson encouraged for AMA road racing? That fat rich guys who can be greased into a Grand-Am tub wouldn't be as successful on a motorcycle that weighed less than they did doesn't seem to have registered.

Given the recent history of AMA Pro Racing and how they deal with their partners - the story of how they lost the Red Bull Rookies is scandalous - only the most gullible would take Edmondson at his word. How could numbers be up for races that are shown at least a week and sometimes two weeks later? And with production values that reflect the diminished state of investment? I put this to someone who had seen the numbers, and his explanation was a shock: The ratings are up, but only marginally, and not by the 300-percent number that some nitwits are parroting. The reason he gave was that people stay home on Saturday nights - at which point I asked him what nursing home he lived in,

Not having it on Sunday frees up Speed's tube time for NASCAR programming, and if DMG is happy with their Saturday night ratings, don't expect anything to change. They're barely spending any money on that time slot, and if ratings are up, why spend all the money on television trucks with high definition?

In March of 2007, when the DMG deal was first announced, Speed offered to build an HD truck for the AMA series, but they wanted a three-year deal to amortize the cost of the truck. Like most of the deals with the DMG, this one sat on the table forever while the world around it changed. New bike sales started to slow in August, and that trend accelerated in late summer and into the fall. Honda was out; Kawasaki was out of Superbike. Had DMG come to an agreement with the factories on technical rules and a class structure in the spring or early summer, none of this would've happened. The factories would be committed, they'd be advertising, they'd demand live TV, and they'd have it.

So what does that mean? More to the point, if delaying a broadcast for a week or two increases exposure, we have to assume that Edmondson will use the model to improve his Grand-Am ratings by 300 percent by moving them to deepest, darkest Saturday night. And NASCAR can't be far behind. Imagine the anticipation that would build by delaying the broadcast of the Daytona 500 until the night of the Daytona Supercross. Fans would be going out of their minds.

Say what you want about AMA PR, but if their behavior has proved anything, it's true that numbers, unlike people, don't lie.

June 10, 2009

Cracking into Prime Time

The AMA Pro Racing drug-testing policy, though laudable, could be replaced by a much simpler method: Anyone who believes that delaying the broadcasts of road races for two weeks could result in a 300-percent ratings pop is on crack.

The amount of misinformation about the AMA Pro Prime Time television ratings in the Saturday night graveyard time slot - so popular with shut-ins, nursing home lifers, and insomniacs - is staggering. I'm told, though I personally haven't seen it, that a few crackpots are trying to propagate the laughable fallacy that the ratings are up 300 percent. To even suggest something so daft suggests ignorance as deep as a Big Gulp and the misguided belief that others would swallow it.

What I've also learned is that most people throw around the term "television ratings" without the slightest clue of what they're talking about. Here, then, is a very quick primer.

Nielsen Media Research gathers data from meters installed in the homes of "Nielsen families" in all 50 states. Additional data is gathered from diaries. Each Nielsen ratings point translates to 1,145,000 people. For instance, for the week beginning May 18, the number-one watched broadcast show in America was Wednesday's edition of "American Idol," with a 16.1 share — meaning approximately 28,838,000 viewers. (The numbers include live plus same-day DVR playback.) Tuesday's "American Idol" only generated a 13.5 share. By comparison, the top cable show for the same period was a Magic-Cavs game on TNT that generated a 5.4 share, or about 8,969,000 viewers.

If you're getting a .9 or a 1.0 for a motorcycle race, which is what the MotoGP telecasts get, you're doing well, Last year's AMA Superbike Championship events were in the .2-to-.3 range. This year's AMA Prime Time shows are below .1 - well below .1, which means that well less than 100,000 of your 306,000,000 fellow citizens are tuned in. You'll find better ratings for pay-per-view porn at Amish barn raisings.

AMA Pro Racing CEO Roger Edmondson told team principals at Barber Motorsports Park that ratings were up. Hooray! There was no evidence - only an explanation for why he couldn't provide those ratings, which no one believed. I was also told, separately, that ratings were up, and reported it - only to find out that I was wrong. It was only Daytona. Two weeks later, Edmondson told a smaller group of team principals at Infineon Raceway that ratings were down. Huh? Ratings were up for the Daytona 200 - not by 300 percent - and then began a steady but precipitous decline. Edmondson knew at Barber they weren't up.

"Does he think we don't talk to each other?" one team manager asked when told of the flip-flop.

That's the bad news. The good news is that we, all of us, have the chance to make a difference if we want to continue watching American road racing on television. And we have two very dedicated enthusiasts to thank for it.

Rick Miner is a senior vice president at Speed, but titles don't do him justice. A no-bulls--t, oversized figure, both literally and figuratively, the former New Yorker is a passionate motorcyclist who's done more than anyone alive to keep motorcycle racing on television. His partner in crime is Chet Burks, whose production company makes sure the cameras, trucks and, most importantly, personnel show up at every road race to feed a signal that Speed then sends into our houses. Burks is lower-key, though that doesn't explain the most hideous Boston Red Sox-themed Hawaiian shirt he showed up with on race day at Miller. Each credits the other and neither wants publicity, but without them there would be no AMA road racing on television. It really is that simple. That both aren't in the Motorcycle Hall of Fame (rather than the guy who invented the handlebar cupholder) is a travesty.

During Sunday's early telecast of the Miller Motorsports Park World Superbike races, Speed announced they were going back to same-day coverage. I asked Miner, "Why the change?"

"It was perfectly clear that our experiment with appointment viewing - which was clearly motivated by a need to try and cut costs in this economy - didn't work," Miner said through a slight haze of cigar smoke in his trailer in the TV compound at MMR "Racing fans, motorcycle fans, made it really clear, in no uncertain terms, that they were not happy with it. And what we need to do, as a network and as the home of motorsports in the United States, we need to respond to our fans to the extent we can and make it work. It was that simple."

The network discusses ratings every week, and after the Daytona bump, the numbers went south.

"The first AMA Pro Prime Time show, even the first delays, did well - but then the bottom fell out of it, if you will," Miner said, though he didn't have the numbers at hand. (Someone who had seen the numbers added, "The first airings were respectable, but start going out two, three weeks, they were horrendous.")

Now Speed is rapidly ramping up for same-day coverage starting at Mazda Raceway Laguna Seca. The logistics are daunting and the costs are nearly double. Try finding 30 hotel rooms for Mid-Ohio. And Speed is doing it out of pocket with no ad-sales upside, Miner said, which means no additional revenue.

"It's pure and simple a survival of AMA Pro Road Racing on television in the United States," Miner said. "This is something that it's critical that the fans support when we make this move. Because if they don't, and we don't see a vast turnaround in the economy very quickly, it's problematic. I can't say where we'd be next year."

Team managers I've spoken to are already planning for next year, as are their sponsors. The first thing they ask about is the television ratings, which is why they were encouraged when Edmondson told them they were up. If only.

The OEMs and their sponsors - Rockstar, Makita, Corona, Monster - all depend on television ratings. Racing is, among other things, a promotional tool. But if no one's watching, there's no reason to promote. And no one was watching a motorcycle race two weeks after it happened and the same night of the following race.

How we got to the well-delayed broadcasts is a story that can be laid at any number of doorsteps on both sides of the equation. The adversarial relationship that developed between most of the OEMs and DMG dragged road racing down to the point that Honda and Kawasaki withdrew as factory entities. And it could easily get worse. Already there's talk of less support for 2010 if the economy doesn't pick up. The OEMs have to see value in racing and, at the moment, with mostly paltry crowds and horrid ratings, there's very little value in putting racing rigs on the road. It's a bit chicken-and-egg.

"I'm just hoping that they come to terms with it earlier in the process," Miner said, hopefully. "I think the delay in everybody getting their act together last year was problematic for all of us."

Unfortunately, there's little we can do about CEOs hell-bent on flaunting their power to the detriment of the sport. What we can do, what me must do, is watch or at the very least record the shows, starting with Laguna Seca.

I asked Miner what 2010 looks like.

"As I said, I'm hoping the viewers support this," he reiterated. "The fans need to come out. We are rapidly approaching a date where we need to make that decision. We're not there yet, but we're definitely discussing it now. And I'm certainly hoping that the manufacturers' participation and the relationship with DMG are improving and the economy seems to be heading in the right direction. Far be it from me to make that prediction. If Alan Greenspan couldn't get it right, I'm certainly not going to get it right."

Maybe not. Here's the irony: When we vote with our remotes, it's possible we could increase the abysmal ratings by 300 percent.

Who's the crackhead now?

June 24, 2009

Mid-Term Grades

The AMA Pro Racing press release was so breathless, I couldn't contain myself. "Sixty-two motorcycles took the green flag at the Illinois State Fairgrounds for the 2009 Illinois Motorcycle Dealers Association's Springfield Mile..." it began. Wow! A 62-rider main event at Springfield. How cool is that? So I set my TiVo - I'm in Barcelona - and had the Slingbox on standby for the "green flag" at 10 p.m. European Daylight Time. This was going to be mega.

Dirt-track racing was, is, and always will be the most exciting form of two-wheel racing in the world. Viewers should have tuned into the Springfield Mile to see one hell of a show and a typically great finish. If six out of 20 riders can finish on the same second, imagine how crowded the photo finish would be with 62! Genius!

The dirt-track season is only four races old, so the jury's still out, except for the promoter who couldn't afford the increased sanctioning fee and bailed. But the road-race series passed the halfway mark at Road America, and it's time for midterm grades. The question to ask at Road America was, "How is road racing better this year?" Not surprisingly, there was little variation in the answers.

What's better is the racing in the Superbike class. Suzuki's winning streak ended at 53, though the new AMA rules should only get partial credit. Suzuki was late bringing out its 2009 GSX-R1000, and Yoshimura Racing, the best team in AMA Superbike history, had very little time to test. Rockstar Makita Suzuki's Mat Mladin had a bad day at Infineon Raceway. The front-tire choice could have been better, and he struggled - at least that was the view of the riders who passed him.

But AMA Pro Racing can take some credit, because if Mladin had his trusty Showa fork, he might have been able to adjust his way out of trouble. Instead, he had an off day and was beaten by Yamaha's Josh Hayes and three others.

In fact, after an initial barrage of dissent, the dumbed-down rules are going over fine - not least because of one intended effect: It's much cheaper to build a "Superbike."

The next day, Mladin rebounded and won, but it didn't come easily. Yamaha's Ben Bostrom gave him no rest on a track and in heat that could have produced a different result. In mixed conditions on Saturday at Road America, Mladin again showed why he's the best rider without question, riding with ruthless abandon to a dominant victory. But on Sunday, he was outgunned by Larry Pegram's 1098R Ducati, who last won a race more than 10 years ago. Pegram had the power, but he also rode flawlessly, and he deserved the win. No other track has three sixth-gear straights, and it's unlikely Pegram will repeat this season.

The Superbike class should be enhanced by the addition of Aprilia and BMW next year, but could suffer defections from some of the Japanese OEMs, who are enduring deep slides in sales and are disaffected with the path of the DMG, whom they believe would rather suck up to the lower-volume brands, who do little to promote the sport, rather than maintain the stability that grew road racing for decades.

Aside from the Superbike class, what's improved? Nothing, as far as I can tell. Lip service is given to the competitive nature of the Daytona SportBike class, but most of that can be attributed to the control Dunlop tires. M4 Suzuki's Martin Cardenas, a six-time winner, said tires were the difference between his not winning last year and this year's success. Imagine how many more races he'd have won had he been on Dunlops the past few years. Competitive balance was the lesser motivation for spec tires; the first was money.

Buell dominated the early part of the season before Cardenas began winning. The competition has been okay, but 600 racing has always been the best of the day, and this doesn't measure up to what we saw in the years 2007 and earlier. (Ben Bostrom had his way most of last season). And if the Buell was given a phony weight penalty after only three wins, what punishment would be fitting for the Suzuki, which has won twice as many and taken far more podium spots?

The television package this year was the worst in 15 years - so bad, in fact, that Speed is taking the extraordinarily generous step of doubling their production costs so that the races can be seen on the same day. Time-shifting races for two weeks turned out to be a silly idea, but one that Speed had been forced into for a variety of reasons, none of them very good.

AMA Pro Racing president Roger Edmondson's already questionable credibility took a hit when he told one group of team principals that the television ratings were up, and then two weeks later told another group the exact opposite. He told the second group that Superbike was never on the schedule for the Miller World Superbike race, but when questioned, he admitted it was.

The pace car has been poorly received, and for good reason. It was the pace car that ruined the Daytona 200. Some racers were predisposed to disliking it. Jamie Hacking was one of them, having survived a harrowing incident at Daytona several years ago. Now it will be replaced by Buell "safety & pace" bikes, a Ulysses to lead the pack and an 1125R as a sweep bike. As one rider asked, "If we couldn't see the Honda pace car at Daytona, how are we going to see a Buell?"

Common sense is among the casualties of the new regime. Corona Extra Honda's Neil Hodgson moved about an inch when he put his CBR1000RR in gear on Saturday at Road America. For that, he was given a stop-and-go penalty because, by the strict wording of the rule, he had moved forward. Did he gain an advantage? Of course not. But his race was ruined. The next day they flagged three riders, but by the time they signaled Josh Hayes, it was too late. Later that lap, he would run Michael Laverty off the track. He should have been first in. Race direction's bad decision cost Laverty a decent payday and left Celtic Racing with a parts bill they didn't deserve.

But while those lines in the rulebook are treated as gospel, others aren't. Dane Westby was given a warning for not coming straight into the pits after crashing at the end of the Barber SportBike race. The rulebook states that a rider must come in. Asked about this at the following race, an AMA official said the rider didn't have to come straight in; that it was a "gray area."

It isn't. The rule is quite clear, but the application isn't. Leaking oil on the racing line for a lap or two is far more dangerous than lurching forward an inch.

And safety is the one area that will ultimately define the regime. So far, only luck has prevented a rider boycott at any number of dodgy racetracks. That luck will run out, and when it does, AMA Pro Racing will show its true colors. Talk to them long enough about racing on clearly unsafe tracks and they'll offer the Lindsay Lohan theory on throttle application: It goes both ways. Which makes no sense to anyone who's ever raced. When it rained on the second day of last week's Mid-Ohio test, there wasn't a lot of on-track activity. Why would there be? Mid-Ohio's surface and safety margins aren't fit for wet-weather racing. If you fall on the kink on the back straight, you will hit something very hard and very quickly.

Is Heartland Park Topeka safe? We don't know. The AMA sent a safety contingent months ago. At the time, the panel included Tommy Hayden and Josh Hayes, two highly respected veterans, and three riders of more modest talent - Chris Ulrich, Dane

Westby and Cory West. (West lost his spot when he lost his AMA ride.) It's expected that only three riders at a time will take part in a track inspection.

By contrast, the MotoGP safety commission includes Valentino Rossi, Loris Capirossi, Chris Vermeulen, Casey Stoner and Dani Pedrosa, with Nicky Hayden frequently attending. What do these riders have in common? They're World Champions, one and all, which is what you want in someone who's responsible for the safety and lives of his peers.

Those who inspected Heartland Park had only the best of intentions. But they did it without Tommy Hayden, who was given just three days' notice and had a prior commitment. So if the track is homologated - and there is no indication it won't be - it will be by the consent of Hayes, because the opinions of the others, with due respect, is irrelevant.

The last time I asked a number of riders about the rider safety committee, they answered, "Is there one?" Good question. I'll ask, just as soon as I finish watching the 62-rider Springfield Mile.

July 8, 2009

The Tutor

The BlackBerry vibrated across the night stand in the darkness until it went silent. No sense answering. Had to be a wrong number.

It wasn't.

It was 7:15 a.m. where I was, in Amsterdam, but 6:15 in the British East Midlands, and Kevin Schwantz was wide awake. Why wouldn't he be?

In a world where we suffer from meddlers who, intentionally or not, are destroying the careers of young racers in the United States by focusing on the bottom line, Schwantz is doing the opposite. Since a series of injuries made racing no longer fun for him, and denied us the brilliance of his riding, Schwantz has dedicated himself to the future: helping young riders, helping Red Bull, helping Suzuki, trying to decide what to do next. His travel schedule is brutal. He spends more time in the sky than the sun.

In the past four weeks, he'd flown to the Mugello Grand Prix in the hills north of Florence, then back to the United States for Road America. The next week, he was back in southern Europe for the Catalunya GP and the test the day after, before driving south to Misano Adriatico on the Italian Adriatic for the World Superbike race.

From there, he drove to Italy's Lake Como, north of Milan, to drop off Blake Young at Ben Spies' house, the one just up the street from George Clooney's. On Tuesday he drove to Milan, flew to Atlanta, then drove to Birmingham, Alabama, for two days of the Schwantz School at Barber Motorsports Park. But he left a little early on the second day to drive back to Atlanta and hop a plane to

The Tutor

England for the World Superbike race at Donington Park, where he arrived around lunchtime on Saturday.

Schwantz is a master teacher, a master motivator, and one of motorcycling's greatest ambassadors. He doesn't criss-cross the globe because he needs the money. He doesn't do it for the adoration. He does it because he wants to make a difference and he wants to make sure others don't make the same mistakes he made.

"Last year, working with those Red Bull Rookies kids was awesome," Schwantz said; even after Red Bull pulled the plug in the United States, he still works with them internationally as often as possible. "It's one of the most rewarding things I'd done. Like I told the guys at Red Bull, I'd do it for nothing. I'm honored you're paying me."

"I'm watching the future of the sport," he continued. "I'm seeing a possible World Champion in development. For me, and from the American side of things, seeing [Ben] Spies over here, kicking World Superbike ass, and having some guys in the States who, with a little more seasoning and maturity, could possibly do the same thing, is what I'm looking out for. I'd like to see Suzuki do well, and I'd like to see us Americans do well on the World level."

Maybe it's because he didn't have someone to help him during his career. Wayne Rainey had Kenny Roberts. Schwantz had no one, but he also didn't take racing as seriously as his great rival. What he had were some of the most evil-handling motorcycles ever produced. The Suzuki RGVs of the day had blazingly fast motors, but frames that were made of string cheese. And though the Michelins were very good, they gave less warnings than the Sheboygan police department: One minute you're happily drifting both wheels, the next you've been flicked so high you can taste the airline food.

I mentioned that it seemed like he's working harder than he ever did when he raced.

"Absolutely," he said. "I've kind of let it happen, with Blake [Young] wanting to come to Barcelona for the GP and wanting to go Misano for World Superbike. I have a genuine interest in doing something for Suzuki, whether it's being the overseer for all racing worldwide or putting a MotoGP team together. I'm not sure. Every time I get on the plane to head home, I say, 'I don't want to do this.' But I think the satisfaction and the sense of accomplishment that would be there if you could turn either of these operations around to get in that dominating winning Suzuki way of things, I think would be just as rewarding as being a rider."

Blake Young is the latest rider to get Schwantz's attention. Young had never been outside the United States before going to Barcelona and Misano. He and Schwantz were in the Alstare Suzuki Brux garage when team owner Francis Batta approached and asked, "You got some young fast kid for me?"

Schwantz said: "Blake Young's pretty fast. I said Blake's pretty fast, and Fonsi [Nieto - who'd replaced the injured Max Neukirchner since the German was hurt] was standing right there. Bit of an awkward situation. But Fonsi was fine with it. He said, 'I hadn't done any riding for eight months when they called me.' There were so many ups and downs in the two days of the decision making."

They were asked on Friday morning and had to give an answer by Sunday.

"I spoke to House [Tom Houseworth, Spies' crew chief] about it, and he said, 'Are you kidding me? You're thinking about not doing it?'"

Schwantz knew Young wasn't going to win.

"It was a pretty deep group of riders, and not an easy place to come figure out as far as the track goes," he pointed out. "But at the same time, I don't think anybody expects anything, as long as you don't tear up a bunch of stuff."

Schwantz's advice was simple and direct.

"I told him all along, if you get an opportunity to get on a World Superbike... if somebody had called me I'd have jumped at the chance, even not knowing the bike, the track, the team," he said. "The more experience you get internationally, the more time you get on a bike that's got more advanced electronics than the one you're riding, I think the chance is there to improve yourself every time you get a chance to ride something like that."

So he did.

"I think more than anything," he said, "I'm an extra set of eyes out there."

Though he's more than that.

"As a racer, it's easy to get focused on one specific way," he noted. "To have somebody out there watching you and someone who has the knowledge to accomplish what I've accomplished, to have someone come in with great ideas can only help."

Early in his career, Spies would only do one fast lap at a time, and Schwantz got him to focus on six or eight or 10. With Young, he offers advice.

"You're running it in too short of a gear before getting into a corner... you've got to kind of force them a little bit more," he said. "It's so easy for a kid to say, 'That's a great idea, but not for me.' You've got to stay on top of a younger kid who's a little more fly-by. Keep reminding him, keep reminding him."

Schwantz made a suggestion that was instrumental in helping Mat Mladin win the second race at Infineon Raceway a day after Suzuki's 53-race winning streak ended.

"Each one of them is so different in their own specific way," Schwantz said. "With the knowledge Mladin has, I'll say, 'Here's what I see the other people doing, here's what I see you doing.'

"Whether it's when I used to work with an [Danny] Eslick or working with Blake, each is a little different," he added. "You have to find what helps each work and go from there. And sometimes they'll try exactly what you want and none of it will work. You've got to come up with another plan, you've got to go watch or at that point you need to quit worrying about the rider and maybe we've got a bike-setup idea."

Young wasn't sure how to get through Coppice, the fast double right leading onto the Dunlop Straight. Schwantz suggested Young could save time by leaving the Alstare Suzuki Brux GSX-R1000 in third gear, rather than shifting back to second. If Young wasn't sure, Spies sealed the deal.

"That's what I do," he said. "I keep it in third."

And now there's talk about Young doing a test in mid-July at Imola and maybe another replacement ride for Neukirchner if he's not fit for the Czech round of the series.

Young finished 25th and 17th at Donington Park, learning with every lap so that he'd be ready when he came back. It was at Donington that Spies made his MotoGP debut with Suzuki last year. On this return visit, he not only won both races - for the third time this year - but he blew away the field in race two. Now he's only 14 points from the title lead and his rival Nori Haga is in the hospital.

Schwantz spent most of his time with Spies the past four or five years, and it's paid off. Spies is the most sought-after World Superbike rider, though it's likely he'll stay where he is for another season. That work is done. But there are others.

"I guess it's, for me, seeing riders that I've worked with doing well, [that] is probably my way of being a racer now, instead of being out there," Schwantz said. "It's me helping if I can, and it's rewarding - not monetarily, just the satisfaction of doing well."

Others would be wise to learn from his example.

July 22, 2009

Safety Car Fights Way Into Top 10

AMA Pro Racing did their darndest to ruin the best-ever Red Bull U.S. Grand Prix. The MotoGP race wasn't a classic - it'd be tough to top last year's Stoner-Rossi slugfest - but the weekend itself was mostly drama-free. The weather was great, the traffic flowed, hotel gouging was slightly down, the concessions weren't flooded and neither were the porta-squats.

No, the smell that wafted over the Monterey Peninsula after Dani Pedrosa tucked away his winner's trophy was AMA Pro Racing dropping trou and leaving a flaming pile on the world stage. No wonder they don't like racing alongside professionals.

Something about bright lights and big stages brings out the best in people. But not for our friends on Fentress Boulevard in Daytona Beach. They started the season by careening the pace car through the heart of their signature event, the Daytona 200, just as the 200 was set to be remembered for making history under the lights, the lights caught fire, the lights went out, the lesser lights drove the pace car so badly that it caused a crash in the chicane, and then there were red lights and red flags. At Laguna Seca, in front of their biggest crowd, with all the industry nabobs, the Grand Prix world and the international media looking on in disbelief, they did it again. AMA PR staged one of the most staggering displays of incompetence, arrogance, and dangerous decision-making ever, a disaster so obvious and so public that they managed to piss off Nicky Hayden, and that's not easy. I've seen Hayden mad before - I was in Portugal the day Pedrosa speared him in 2006 and might have derailed his World Championship - but I've never seen him this livid. And why not? AMA Pro Racing's incompetence at something so simple as deploying the pace car could have gotten a number of riders gravely, if not fatally, injured.

When the decision to control the field was made in the Superbike race, the pace car was sent to the downside of the outside of the turn-one crest, normally taken flat stick in sixth gear. As the field came thundering over the rise, the car pulled to its left and into their path. There was a collective gasp in the press room and relief that no one had been hurt. The reason it was there, according to the AMA Pro Racing's Colin Fraser, was that it had to control the field before turn two, which is where the chaos began. Ben Bostrom's exuberance had gotten the best of him and Neil Hodgson and Larry Pegram were skittled into the gravel.

Fraser said that the proper flags were displayed from the Corkscrew to the finish line, but others weren't as sure, including the leaders. And having a nearly invisible car pull into the path of riders was a colossal, inexcusable, and possibly deadly blunder that should cost someone his job. No one at AMA Pro Racing will be punished, of course. It's the riders' fault for not seeing the flags, right? (Do we think it'll get any better at Mid-Ohio when they roll out the Buell pace and safety bike? Sure. Riders, being the generous souls that they are, will slow down to help when they see yet another Buell parked on the shoulder of the road. And, as a friend of mine asked, what happens when the pace bike crashes? Is there a plan for a backup?)

What about bringing the riders back to the pits to form up behind the pace car? That's an idea that's now bouncing around. Of course, the situation will evolve to the point where the pace car/bike/trike/Razor is not in the pit lane when the riders show up. I'd suggest using a red flag to stop the race, have the riders come back to the pits and then line up for a re-start once the track is clear. Oh wait, we already had that. I sure pity the rest of the racing world, still having to use such an old-fashioned system.

When the field was re-gridded, Bostrom was in his usual grid spot, which was a farce. The rulebook states that the rider who is "responsible for stopping a race will be placed on the restart or the finishing order in last place of the lap in which they were scored." Bostrom should also have been put to the back of the grid. And if AMA Pro Racing is alone in saying they didn't see that Bostrom caused the accident... yup, sounds about right.

In fact, they let him off on a technicality. Bostrom didn't cause the red flag, their own incompetence with the pace car did. And the pace car came out because...

Had the race not been red-flagged, Bostrom would've had to pit for the mandatory safety check, which would've put him two laps down on the field if work had to be done. And what of Pegram, the innocent victim? Because his race bike was trashed and he was forced onto his backup bike, he was put to the back of the grid. How is that fair?

There's also the question of whether all the work done on Bostrom's bike was legal. The rules are a typical shade of AMA gray.

"Mechanics may visually inspect the motorcycle for safety issues. All safety issues should be brought to the attention of AMA Pro Racing. Mechanics will be directed as to how to proceed." Maybe all the work done was related to "safety issues," but probably not.

The AMA has so little credibility that speculation was instantly raised that Yamaha was getting preferential treatment. Remember, Yamaha's the only factory who signed on to the DMG vision. When you make secret agreements with one factory, and AMA Pro Racing has been outed on that count, it's not a stretch to think it's happened again. On top of which, there was similar speculation at Daytona over whether Ben Bostrom completed the same number of laps as everyone else. He did.

None of this is meant to suggest that Yamaha did anything wrong. They know the rulebook too well and certainly wouldn't jeopardize their riders or reputation. Anything they did, rightly or wrongly, was done with the AMA's tacit approval.

If you think it's going to get better, you're wrong. AMA PR/DMG boss Roger Edmondson held a Sunday morning news conference where he'd kneecapped Gavin Trippe by taking Trippe's 450 road-racer concept and turning it into the impossible dream.

Trippe has long been an advocate of 450cc-single road racer, but everyone I spoke to in the AMA paddock thought the idea was a non-starter. These are hybrids with 450cc motocross engines that aren't built for extended high-rpm runs. The gearboxes certainly can't handle the stress of the pavement, and the backshifts and engine braking, even with the help of a slipper clutch. "After about eight hours, I toss the motor in the trash," said one rider, who trains on a 450 Supermoto bike.

Then there's the cost. Start with a $7500 motocross bike, add $1200 worth of bodywork, $2500 worth of forks, $2000 in wheels, and a couple thousand in various other parts and what do you have? An unsellable hand grenade that's slower and more expensive than a 600 and much more expensive than an entry-level street bike that a manufacturer actually sells.

Edmondson is on a fishing expedition. He wants to find someone to build 30 of these time bombs for a turn-key race series. Dad writes a big check, junior gets a bike, tires, fuel. And dad will be the one paying, because no dealer in his right mind would sponsor one of these mules.

And why would a manufacturer build a motorcycle that they don't sell? Is there any advertising value? Wouldn't they rather showcase their 600s? Or if it's going to be a spec class, why not a bike that exists? Given the coziness between the AMA and Buell,

I'm sure they could make a deal to supply a grid's worth of something that's not too fast.

Maybe Edmondson hasn't been paying attention. Maybe he hasn't noticed that bike sales are down 50-60-70 percent year to year. If a manufacturer hopes to stay out of Chapter 11, it won't be by building and selling 30 of a model that can only be ridden on Sundays. And, besides, these are the same manufacturers that Edmondson has shown little but contempt for since taking over. The ones who do all of the advertising, sponsor all the races, support most of the field.

How do you run the OEMs off, then go hat in hand asking that they build motorcycles they don't sell, while likely asking for a chunk of money to sponsor the class? And put them on a track where safety doesn't appear to be a priority and rules are manipulated like origami.

Something about that just doesn't smell right.

July 29, 2009

Rules? What Rules?

If the Buell 1125RR was any less legal, you could snort it through a hundred-dollar bill. The thing makes Bernie Madoff look legal. It makes wheelying a Fat Boy naked through Times Square with a loaded Uzi look legal. It makes the Iranian election look legal. Get the picture?

The velocity-challenged RR (or is it arf-arf?) broke cover - and a number of people's spirits - at Mid-Ohio. Among them was Rockstar Makita Suzuki's Mat Mladin, who said he'd "lost interest" in racing after finishing third on Saturday at Mid-Ohio. And after only 16 years, 82 race wins, and six (soon to be seven) championships, and serial favoritism from this year's batch of AMA PR officials. Somewhere there are legions of former AMA officials smacking their foreheads and asking, "Geez, why didn't I think of that?"

The twin-R is a purpose-built non-street-legal race bike that has been homologated as a separate model from the 1125R, which Danny Eslick rode to such good effect in both Daytona SportBike races. And the rulebook couldn't be any clearer.

"AMA Pro American Superbike motorcycles must be street-certified for use in the United States and be available at the time of competition from U.S. retail dealers." What's the difference between the RR and every other motorcycle on the approved equipment list? The rest are all street-legal.

The 1125RR isn't street-legal, and has no intention of being so. It's a race bike, or will be once they get around to fitting a re-badged Ducati Desmosedici engine, which is likely in the works and will surely be homologated as a "special allowance." Even then...

The double-R cannot be built from a single-R. The RR contains a number of chassis and motor parts that aren't separately homologated for use or included in the special allowances for the R. Which makes it even more of a separate model. It isn't like a Suzuki GSX-R1000 or Yamaha YZF-R1 that can be modified to race form with approved parts. The RR is its own beast whose inspiration comes from the R. The bodywork is completely illegal. The rulebook says it should resemble or have the similar dimensions to the original, and it does, in the same way that Jessica Simpson resembles and has the same dimensions as Homer Simpson.

And what of the rear wheel? The whisper in the paddock was that it was also illegal - it didn't look like the one in the photo Buell released - and that this was another of the back-door deals engineered to keep the few happy while laughing in the face of the rest. The RR comes with a 6-inch wheel, but Taylor Knapp discovered that the 5.75-inch wheel worked better. So they were given an allowance. Not legally, of course. But by the time you read this, it will likely be the first of many items on the "special allowances" list for the RR, along with a 1500cc engine, turbocharger, carbon-fiber bodywork - painted over, of course because carbon fiber, unlike the Er Er, is illegal - and a gas tank enclosed portable refinery unit that turns the unleaded race swill into AV gas.

The same thing happened earlier this year at Barber Motorsports Park. Aprilia wanted to use a 5.5-inch rim rather than the approved six-incher. The team raced on the smaller rim and it was later approved. That shouldn't be taken as a knock on the race team. Neither should Buell be criticized. If AMA PR is willing to bend over for them, why not? But it shouldn't have happened.

Clearly, they want Aprilia in the Superbike class. Who doesn't? But that shouldn't qualify them for star status in only their fourth race in the series.

How far they bent over for the Buell, and in which direction, is a mystery. Certainly they were aware of Buell's plans from the start. No company would embark on a project like the RR without the tender handholding from the boys in Daytona. And it's not the first time.

Who can forget Buell's last race bike? Well, most anyone who got one would like to. The XBRR, for those who don't remember, was another purpose-built race bike, but with a tragically short shelf life. The XBRR used completely different cases than the model it was allegedly based on. Sound familiar? But the claim was that Buell melted down the cases and re-formed them for the XBRR. That statement came with such furious winking from an AMA official that he completely shed his eyelashes. No doubt something like case-melting is a project for only the most serious DIY tuner who happens to have his own metal foundry and sense of humor.

But that was a different regime, which we thought we were happy to see the back of. I'm not so sure. They were incompetent and bumbling, but never this venal. Or this arrogant. The Buell 1125RR is nothing more than a big "bite me" to the rest of the paddock.

For reasons that are baffling, AMA PR is cozying up to the smaller brands while emptying their waste valves on the Japanese, for the most part.

Though the numbers aren't broken down completely, it appears that Buell has been a bright spot on the Harley balance sheet. For the six months ending June 30, Buell and MV Agusta shipments were up by 440 units from 2008, though they declined 300 in the three months ending June 30. Still, that's an improvement on Harley's 30-percent decline.

Are they putting that money back into racing? To a point. Buell offers a $5,000 contingency for winning a Daytona SportBike or Moto-GT1 race, with $3,000 for second and $2,000 for third. American Suzuki, whose sales decline is staggering, pays $7,500 to win, $5,000 for second, and $4,000 for third in American Superbike.

As if that's not enough, Suzuki supports racing as the title sponsor at Auto Club Speedway, Road Atlanta, Road America, and VIR. (All of the Japanese factories sponsor at least one race.) Given the state of their finances, how likely is it that they'll be able to afford to sponsor all four races in 2010? And will Buell or Aprilia or BMW step in if they don't? Most racetracks can't afford to race without title sponsorship, given the size of the sanction fee, and very few try.

There should be a value to the race sponsorship, but that value continues to dwindle with the behavior of AMA PR. Several riders told me there was a corner-worker shortage early in the Mid-Ohio weekend. When I mentioned this to a former AMA Pro Racing employee, the answer I got was that it was the track's "obligation to provide adequate staffing for corner workers, safety marshals as prescribed by their contract with DMG [if it even contains those details]. I suspect fewer and fewer people have an interest in coming out to stand in the rain for little or no money to watch showroom stock bikes go around in a series that has had its life sucked out of it."

The hope everywhere is that the economy will pick up and people will be able to get financing for motorcycles. And when it does, how long will it be before Yamaha or Honda or Suzuki or Kawasaki or Ducati builds the overdog that AMA PR specifically said they would ban? Months ago, one official told me that if the Yamaha YZF-R1 LE was built today, it wouldn't be homologated.

The most disappointing, though ultimately predictable, effect of the AMA PR decision-making is that it flies in the face of their original vision. They wanted affordable race bikes with a ban on unobtainable parts. Now they have a $40,000 slug (that's not my opinion; Knapp's top speed on Sunday was 162.5 mph, to 177.49 for Josh Hayes' Yamaha R1) with a very limited number of suppliers for most parts.

The shenanigans of the boys on Fentress Boulevard would be funny if they weren't so depressing. And it's certain to get worse. Makes you want to gas up the Fat Boy and strap on the Uzi. Times Square awaits.

August 5, 2009

Leadership Vacuum

By now you've seen the YouTube video of AMA tech boss Al Ludington carpet f-bombing backmarker-for-life Johnny Rock Page.[1] And by now you know that the AMA has taken away his juice box and given Ludington a time-out. What you probably don't know is that benching him isn't a very clever thing to do, even if they had to do it.

Using the standard of their excessive punishment of Monster Energy Kawasaki's Jamie Hacking, Ludington should have been fired. Hacking was severely punished and had to beg forgiveness when a private conversation he had with his wife at Fontana was overheard by a single AMA official. Compare that to the 27,000 people, as of Monday morning, who had tuned in to watch Ludington channel the profane spirits of John McEnroe and Tony Montana.

Anyone who's been in the paddock long enough knows that Ludington couldn't help himself. He didn't see a perennial backmarker. Rather, he saw someone who'd wrecked a race in a class that he'd spent all winter and most of the year trying to inject with parity, and he went a little medieval. Was his behavior out of line? Of course. But it isn't entirely his fault. If his paymasters on Fentress Boulevard had the stones to tighten the qualifying standard from 108 percent to 107 percent, they'd eliminate at least some of the blunder brigade. And if Mladin knew he could put JRP on the trailer by dropping a second off his lap time, he'd turn off his brain and throw down a lap that would make Rossi squirm.

---

[1] http://www.youtube.com/watch?v=_C42W0dyBC8

The reason that won't happen is that among the many DMG mottos is "The back gate takes care of the front gate." Another is "The throttle goes both ways." Another is "Japanese factories? We don't need no stinkin' Japanese factories!" Another is "We don't care what you think, we're going to do whatever the hell we want, even if that means homologating a Buell that is so illegal that you could end up in the slammer with a wife named Walt for transporting it across state lines." Another is "You can't spell 'damaged' without DMG." That last one might be one of mine.

The loss of back-gate revenue, even from the slowest of the slow, is something the boys in Daytona can't countenance, Quantity over quality.

Ludington's profanity-laced screed wasn't new to anyone who knows him. His language has always been colorful, but that's part of his charm. One of the many ironies of this mess is that he mostly directed that colorful language at AMA PR, before descending to the dark side.

It's also worth noting that the atmosphere of fear that permeates the paddock extends into the AMA trailer. The level of paranoia is stratospheric. Virtually all AMA road-race officials are banned from talking to the media unless they've been given prior permission. And the media has to submit questions in advance. No other motorcycle race series I know of operates likes this. Entire governments don't operate like that, though I imagine if you could get a one-on-one with North Korean dictator Kim Jung-Il, he might want to know if you were going to ask about his penchant for elevator shoes, Courvoisier, and porn.

Not that they're off base. Ludington has his favorites in the media, as does AMA Pro Racing CEO Roger Edmondson. (Hint: It's not *Cycle News*, even though *Cycle News* is the only publication and website that objectively reports on every AMA Pro Racing-sanctioned event. Without *Cycle News*, there would be no timely dirt-track or Supermoto coverage, both of which need every bit of publicity they can scrape up. *CN* also covers every motocross, Supercross, and hillclimb.) Whenever one particular website broke a story attributed to a source inside Honda, everyone at Honda, and most in the paddock, knew who leaked it.

There's no doubt JRP deserved what he got. Many think he should've gotten more than a potty-mouth lecture and a few races off. AMA PR probably didn't know he wasn't planning on going to Topeka.

When Hayes and Yates surrounded him, he should've pulled over, regardless of his endless parroting of "I held my line, I held my line." He may have had a point, but he also missed the point. No one is coming to the race to see him and no one ever will. Besides, AMA PR treats its rulebook like the Constitution: It's a living, breathing document open to interpretation, especially when it suits their purposes.

Still, rather than engage JRP, Ludington should have walked away - if he was capable of walking away, which he isn't. And the reason he got involved is partly because the leadership of the AMA is more dysfunctional than the Democratic Party.

Ludington is the most competent of all AMA officials and the most approachable. Since he doesn't, or shouldn't, get involved in operations, he has time to engage the paddock of which he was recently a part. Years of successfully pumping a never-aging Miguel Duhamel to do superhuman tasks on a Honda earned him the respect of his peers. Like his peers, he knows enough tricks of the trade that the saying "It takes a cheater to catch a cheater" is relevant. Defecting to Paranoia Central isn't held against him; quite the opposite. He may be the most competent tech boss ever (certainly in as long as anyone can remember), even if he occasionally bends the rules for underdog teams like Aprilia, Buell, and who knows who else? I know there were illegal front-end parts on at least two Suzukis at Barber, and nothing was done. Without him, the decisions coming out of Daytona would be even more mind-boggling.

Ludington got involved with JRP because he couldn't help himself, but also because it wasn't clear who was in charge. AMA Pro Racing CEO Roger Edmondson was at Mid-Ohio, but Edmondson spends a lot of time in his very nice motorhome. One rider, who owns a motorhome - maybe two - was incensed that Edmondson would bring his Prevost to the races. He shouldn't be. After his wrongful termination by the AMA in the early 1990s, followed by near-bankruptcy when the AMA tied him up in court, he worked hard to rebuild his name and career. The motorhome was well earned. Besides, if you want to hold something against him, how about that he's driven a stake through the heart of professional road racing in the United States and turned it into a worldwide laughingstock? Following the Superbike fiasco at the Red Bull U.S. Grand Prix, more than a few of my international colleagues asked, "Is it always like this?"

"No," I told them, "this is one of the better ones."

AMA Pro Road Racing managing event director Colin Fraser, who should have been in charge at Mid-Ohio, wasn't. Fraser owns the Parts Canada Superbike Championship and, instead of being at Mid-Ohio, he was at his championship's premier event at Mosport International Raceway, east of Toronto. That left someone else in charge. Who? Does it really matter? No one that anyone in the paddock had any respect for. And respect for Fraser is at an all-time low, after he'd gained some back following an ill-advised performance at the opening riders' meeting at Daytona. It was Fraser who decided to run the pace car onto the track in front of a thundering Superbike horde at Laguna Seca, and it was Fraser who vociferously defended that decision. It was as much that defense as the original botched decision that caused Fraser to lose much of the respect he had. It will take some time for him to recover that respect - if he ever does. It didn't help that he wasn't at the next race, but his priorities are clear and understandable. And, though I think the series needs a full-time race director, he should have competent staff to assist in his absence.

Lost in the fog of the JRP debacle was a much larger transgression. For what I was told were budgetary reasons, AMA PR left the dyno at home, so there was no way to police the Moto-GT class, which is horsepower-restricted. It's admirable that AMA PR thinks so highly of the Moto-GT riders that they're willing to allow them to race on the honor system. Honorable or not, a clever tuner could go into his ECU and unleash all those ponies that have been aching to run free. I guess it's just a coincidence that a Ducati won by a lap. The irony in the Ludington YouTube incident is that he's being replaced on a temporary basis by the AMA official responsible for sidelining Hacking. AMA Pro Racing vice president of competition Roy Janson overheard a private conversation between Hacking and his wife as they were leaving the news conference at Auto Club Speedway. Hacking dropped a few f-bombs that were intended only for his wife's ears. Janson heard them, made it his and the AMA's business, and suspended Hacking indefinitely and fined him $4,000 - coincidentally, the same amount Hacking had won on the weekend. The irony is that Janson's been known to unleash the occasional obscenity-filled tirade of his very own. Having witnessed it back in my Supercross days, I can assure you he can be far more entertaining than Al. What happens when someone catches one of those on videotape? Who will replace him, Ludington?

Ludington might not have put himself in that position if there was consistent leadership at AMA PR, but there's not. And there won't be anytime soon. The JRP incident is as much about AMA leadership as it is about Ludington. Or, as he so eloquently put it to JRP: "This isn't about you, dude."

And he's right.

August 19, 2009

Priorities? What Priorities?

Pop quiz: What's more harmful to a road racer: plowing into the back of a motor vehicle at full speed or getting showered by f-bombs?

In the bizarro world of AMA Pro Road Racing, the latter is the more grievous offense. For getting caught on videotape telling Johnny Rock Page what everyone has wanted to tell him for years, AMA tech boss Al Ludington was sentenced to two summer weekends by the pool, with the family, hoping the breeze from the Halifax River didn't blow the salt off the rim of his margarita.

And the punishment for sending the pace car out in front of the Superbike field, as they approached the fastest stretch of Mazda Raceway Laguna Seca, or for dropping an ambulance in front of the Daytona SportBike field at Heartland Park Topeka? Zilch. Nada. Nothing.

The worst thing that could happen to JRP is that his feelings could be hurt. The worst thing that could happen to the road racers is that they could die. I can see how AMA Pro Racing could find them indistinguishable.

After the Laguna Seca incident, which played out in full view of the MotoGP world, you would think that there would be repercussions. That someone would be disciplined. That a full apology would be issued. Just the opposite. Instead, it happened again two races later.

The Heartland Park Topeka incident didn't carry the same level of incompetence or potential damage. As the six-strong field was approaching the turn-10 downhill left near the end of the lap, the ambulance pulled onto the track from an adjacent slip road. Danny Eslick was in the pack that suddenly found it in his path.

"[Having a] however-many-ton ambulance pulling out in front of a pack of six doing 130 mph was a little bit scary there," Eslick said. "Whether the [red] flag was out, obviously we were still going. I wasn't the only one. There was four or five, six other guys going. That was a pretty scary moment."

Team Graves Yamaha's Josh Herrin, who was also in the pack, said, "It was sketchy."

The red flags had been displayed for several corners, but the stations were so far out of the riders' line of sight that no one saw them. And, as one rider pointed out, when you're racing in a pack that closely, it's kind of like a sled-dog team: You're only looking at the butt in front of you.

"There was six of us, I think, still going, and that's not the first issue I've had this weekend with flags or with vehicles being on the track," Eslick said.

Disaster could have struck in Saturday's race when a smaller pack approached the turn-13 right under waving yellow control. A corner worker was in the impact zone, not far from the track, cleaning up a fallen machine.

"That was pretty close, and there was also somebody sweeping the edge of the track for a lap or two over the last little right-hander," Eslick said when asked if he saw the corner worker in the impact zone. "Yeah, I definitely seen it, seen a bunch of lights flashing, people on the track. They were right there. There was a truck on the track the other day, too."

How much more evidence has to reach the ivory tower before they're convinced that race control is incompetent? It's clear that safety isn't near the top of the priority list. Premier parking spots for the boss's motorhome, yes… safe racetracks, not so much.

Yamaha's Josh Hayes was roundly vilified in Kansas. Part of it was justified, part was not. Hayes was the only Superbike rider willing to travel to Topeka for the express purpose of helping with track safety. Changes were made, but the track that he didn't object to wasn't close to being safe enough. Track owner Ray Irwin took it upon himself to move more than 100 yards of concrete wall, without which there would likely have been a mass boycott. And Irwin moved even more walls on Thursday night. It should never have come to that. And Irwin, and every track owner, deserves better.

In a news release prior to the event, Irwin said, "We have met or exceeded every safety issue that AMA Pro Road Racing and the AMA Pro Rider Safety Committee have raised."

Who's on the committee? No one knows. Hayes seems to be on it. Cory West, who's no longer in AMA racing, and SportBike rider Dane Westby took part in the initial track inspection because of their club experience, the key word being "club." Hayes said Chris Ulrich had a media event at the time of the second event, so he took part. With his father's website and magazine, he certainly had an outlet if he had any objections. The AMA's Bill Syfan was also there. And yet, the track, as they left it, wasn't remotely safe for racing. For dropping the ball, none of those people should be allowed anywhere near a track-inspection process for the foreseeable future. My regret is that Hayes is on that list, because what he did was noble and selfless and he had only the best of intentions, but the track was simply unacceptable.

It was unraceable until the track crew removed the 100 yards of concrete wall. It was better once the owner proactively took the wall down. And even better after the removal of a second set of walls. Still, it wasn't enough for veterans Mat Mladin and Jamie Hacking, both of whom have been active in track safety for years and both of whom stood to lose plenty. Some riders pointed out that Mladin could afford not to race because of the points lead he'd built up. That misses the point. How did he build up that points lead? And, given his bonuses, he lost a lot more than points.

Hacking, who is just now gelling with the ZX-6R and control Dunlops, doesn't have a ride for next year and his boycott may not sit well with potential employers. But, to his immense credit, he felt strongly enough to walk away. Robertino Pietri also withdrew.

The MotoGP rider-safety committee was only formalized by Valentino Rossi and Sete Gibernau after the death of Daijiro Kato in Suzuka. Now, at the end of the second year of the DMG reign, the sad state of racetrack preparedness is motivating the AMA riders to organize. Better late than never.

I asked the AMA's vice president for competition, Roy Janson, when a proper rider safety committee - that also included principals from the sanctioning body - would be announced. He couldn't give me a date, saying it would be prior to the 2010 season. That's not good enough.

Two of the final three tracks on the calendar have been found to have serious safety issues. New Jersey Motorsports Park's management has said they'll make changes, but whether those changes will satisfy the riders remains to be seen. Besides, the AMA waited too long. It wasn't until a test, which was put on by Yamaha a month and a half before the race, that the riders' voices were heard.

And why has it taken so long for the riders to be taken seriously? Because the AMA Pro Racing/DMG hierarchy is dismissive of the very people who put on the show. In a July 2008 interview with the New Hampshire Union-Leader about changes to AMA racing, and adding new venues, Edmondson said: "There's no more conservative group of people than motorcycle racers. They have a comfort zone the size of a gnat."

How comparing humans to insects benefits anyone is lost on me.

Then I got to thinking: If there was one person who could clean up this mess, it's "Super Al" Ludington. Maybe you don't agree with his methods, but his passion is clear. As a very clever friend of mine (thanks, TH) observed, imagine Al directing his wrath, not at JRP but at race control.

Ludington: "This isn't about you dude. You f--ed up the best f---ing race of the year."

Race Control: "I put a pace car on the track."

Ludington: "Dude, you don't put a pace car on the track, you get them the f--- out of the way."

Race Control: "I did the best I can."

Ludington: "Dude, you endangered the leaders and f---ed up the show. That's what you did."

Race Control: "Okay, what happens if we don't put vehicles on the track?"

Ludington: "For what? The 28th time?"

Race Control: "We don't care. We're part of it. It doesn't matter."

Ludington: "But you're not it. That's what you don't understand."

Race Control: "It's not about being it. You're part of it. You're either in it or you're not. I disagree completely."

Ludington: "Well, we'll find out. You'll probably disagree with the punishment, too."

Race Control: "Well, we sent the vehicles out, we sent the vehicles out both times."

Ludington: "See race bikes coming down the track?"

Race Control: "Yes, I saw race bikes, but I sent out the vehicles."

Ludington: "It means you don't put vehicles on the track. We had the biggest Superbike race of the year. We had six Sportbike riders in a pack. And it was shaping up until you got involved."

Race Control: "How does that mess up the show?"

Ludington: "Are you serious? You ask me, 'How did I mess up the show?' Are you serious?"

Race Control: "Absolutely."

Ludington: "You're serious. 'How did I mess up the show?' You parked two sets of riders and nearly got them killed. That's how you messed up the show. I can't even believe this."

Neither can we, Al, neither can we.

September 2, 2009

The Time Is Ripe

It is time for an intervention. It is time for the friends and family of the top ranks of the AMA Pro Road Race Series to step in and stop their destructive, addictive behavior. It is time they think twice before making decisions and statements that enrage the paddock. It is time they are told, in no uncertain terms, that they have to stop lying.

It won't be easy. They may have family, but after a year's worth of the most disastrous stewardship in the history of American road racing, they have precious few friends. And their most recent misdeeds strengthened this trend.

Competition Bulletin #2009-09 states that Thursday promoter practice would end June 8, 2009. (The practice was meant to end after the previous race, but Road America complained, so they gave them the day.) The rule was originally put into place to reduce costs. Now we have evidence that cost no longer matters.

The whispering in Virginia began on Thursday and quickly built to a crescendo. There would be a Thursday promoter practice prior to the final round of the New Jersey Motorsports Park season finale. The lie was on.

The outrage it sparked was nearly uniform, but especially vehement among those who spent around $10,000 to take part in the two-day test in New Jersey following Mid-Ohio.

When I asked an AMA Pro Racing official how this could happen, he mentioned that New Jersey was always on the books as one of the three official tests, which was true. But, I pointed out, that test happened a month earlier.

"Yeah, but not everyone could attend that test," the official told me. "Who's fault is that? Everyone was invited. That they chose not to attend is entirely on them."

More outraged were the teams who did travel to South Jersey. Two factory team bosses printed out the competition bulletin and took it to the ivory tower for an explanation. The answer they got was less than satisfying. The short answer was "We have the right do anything, any time, and if you don't like it you can piss off." In other words, "Yes, we lied to you, but if you interpret the rulebook as we do, we can lie whenever we want. We can change the rules. We can screw up. We can homologate motorcycles that are clearly not legal. We reserve the right to lie whenever and wherever, and there's precious little you can do about it. So go back to your garage to nurse your precious egos while we plan our next lie or not. We don't always plan these things. Sometimes we're just riffin'."

Such is the fear in the paddock that most of the team principals didn't want to speak on the record. One of the few who stepped forward was Monster Energy Attack Kawasaki team owner Richard Stanboli. Stanboli is a sub-contractor to Kawasaki, so when a test costs $10,000-plus, it comes out of his budget. And he wouldn't have spent the money if he knew he could have avoided it.

"It's really disappointing when you read the rules, you plan by the rules, you stick to the rules and then you find out a week or two before the next event, 'Oh by the way, we allowed one more [promoter practice],'" he said. "It's really disappointing and you really lose confidence in the system and the organization when you read bulletins upon bulletins upon bulletins about how this rule's changed, this rule's changed, and then you have the mysterious all of a sudden redirection of rules."

"I know they put little caveats in there, little disclaimers: 'We have the right to change anything we want.' But you know what?

We all plan for the long term, plan budgets around it. So now we may go out and run Thursday. We didn't plan on doing that."

The rulebook states that no one can test at a track within three days of a national event. Yamaha's Ben Bostrom and Josh Hayes raced a private R1 on Pirelli tires in a WERA endurance race the week before VIR, which would have gone over quite well at Dunlop, which has supported both for years. That they could have learned anything riding a sub-par bike on tires they don't race on, and on a track they both know well, is debatable. Larry Pegram tested on Monday at VIR, which was perfectly legal, but didn't go over well. As Stanboli said, "It shouldn't be three days. It should be a testing rule. It's a meaningless rule. So we can all test whenever we want. So we can test on Monday and race on Friday. So when we all learn the rules, we'll all just try to figure out how we can make enough money so we can up the ante. I thought the whole idea was to save money, but it hasn't saved money."

AMA Pro Racing has never had less credibility. Even in the darkest days of the previous bumbling caretakers, the feeling wasn't that they were venal, just incompetent. Colossally incompetent, but in an "aw-shucks, dang nab it" kind of way. The current caretakers make life-endangering blunders and try to justify them. They have shown a staggering inability to control the racetrack and a favoritism that coddles newcomers and alienates the established order. The end result is the Japanese factories will continue to downsize while fringe players step in for a year or two, or whenever they get bored and walk away. When AMA PR CEO Roger Edmondson meets with the principals of some of the Japanese factories at Indy this week, his reception will be less warm than it was last year, and even then it wasn't all that chummy.

Back to the test. Who benefits most? The track, for one, which stands to make a tidy profit on the day and that's a good thing. As much as I abhor the AMA flip-flopping, the track has done what appears to be a good job of quickly responding to the riders' concerns following the earlier test. Moving guardrails and building gravel pits doesn't come cheaply, but the track wanted to make sure the riders' level of comfort was elevated, if not totally satisfied. That will come with time, one hopes.

Since AMA Pro Racing is less than interested in containing costs, it might make sense to reward tracks that carry out expensive track improvements with a Thursday promoter practice. There are worse incentives. And next year a number of tracks will struggle to find sponsorship if the OEMs withdraw their backing, as is expected.

It has to be noted that New Jersey Motorsports Park should never have been put in the position of having to make wholesale improvements. If the AMA had the slightest interest in rider safety, they'd have organized a coordinated effort to inspect the track months ago. They'd have flown senior riders to the track to make detailed notes and set forth a series of deadlines. The work should have been done before the test, when the AMA pros first took to the track, and not weeks later. AMA PR certainly knew there were issues as far back as last year's Moto-ST race. Or did they? My guess is that their ability to discern safe from non-safe is tenuous, at best. And they wonder why they get beaten up with the verbal hammers wielded by riders when they get to a supposedly approved track, such as Heartland Park Topeka, which wasn't close to being fit for racing.

Who benefits other than the track? On the racing side, M4 Suzuki, one of the many teams that chose not to test. With Martin Cardenas in the thick of the championship hunt, getting a day's jump prior to qualifying can't hurt. The Buell team did travel to New Jersey for the two days, but their time wasn't focused on testing the SportBike.

The upside of the New Jersey race is that it marks the end of a depressing season. For the next six months, the teams won't have to operate in the disheartening atmosphere of the paddock. That doesn't meant the lying will stop; it won't, not without an intervention, and that's unlikely.

Unfortunately, that's no lie.

January 6, 2010

Happy New Year!

And so we bid adieu to 2009, the year we watched helplessly as the Daytona Motorsports Group used the legendary marketing acumen of the Daytona motorsports machine to transform the world's premier domestic road-race series into the world's greatest laughingstock, all without using their suddenly short arms to dig into their very deep pockets thanks to a sucker's deal with the AMA, who can no longer lay claim to being the worst caretakers of racing in America - a title many thought they'd long since retired through years of neglect, bad decisions, and financial trickery. And as bad as it was, in just a matter of months we'll be looking back fondly on 2009 as the good old days.

The 2010 season is going to be nothing short of the worst ever in the history of American road racing. It is going to suck the life out of even the most die-hard race fan. It's going to suck dry the pockets of Speed as they struggle to televise a series that fewer and fewer people care about. It's going to suck dry the promoters, because they have been burdened with the unenviable task of promoting a series devoid of interest, excitement and, most importantly, stars, which is what sports live on. And it's going to suck what little's left of U.S. Superbike racing into the blue vortex in the toilet that our friends at the DMG have created. Is it any wonder that the only two successful disciplines - Supercross and motocross - are those in which the DMG has the least involvement?

At this point, the National Superbike Championship of Burundi has more credibility. And more factory support. Honda isn't playing and, as of this writing, neither is Kawasaki. Yamaha has pulled out as a factory effort, and Suzuki has turned the reins over to Yoshimura Suzuki. Aprilia and BMW are looking for money, as is Ducati. Buell, after being wet-nursed to the championship and kept on life support by Harley-Davidson for years, was finally put out of its misery.

The apologists will say that it's the economy, and to a certain extent it is. But the sparsest AMA grids in years, if not ever, will have more to do with the policies of the DMG than those of Ben Bernanke. The AMA Superbike Championship simply has no value. There is nothing, or very little, to be gained by taking part. The value has been purposely engineered out. Clearly, money isn't the only issue. If it was, then why are all the factories gearing up for the Supercross opener? Certainly there has been some shrinkage, and KTM is out of the mix. But the core four — Yamaha, Suzuki, Honda and Kawasaki — will all back teams that show up when the gate drops at Anaheim. Their races will all be promptly televised. The outdoor Nationals are doing well and have a great TV package. Speed will air six live shows and NBC plans to air three live as well.

Don't bother trying to get a straight answer out of the DMG on the road-racing television package. At this point, I'd be surprised if even the Daytona 200 was live. (I'm told it won't be.) There is also no conceivable way that Speed can do anything but suffer seven-figure losses if they insist on same-weekend coverage, which is what we all want. Who's going to pay for it? Not Honda. Not Kawasaki. Not Buell (did they ever?). Suzuki is fighting to stay afloat, and Yamaha's parent company is looking at a $2 billion loss for fiscal 2009. The only way same-weekend coverage happens is if Jim France decides to dig deep into his pockets to pony up, which would be unprecedented.

Other than some personnel moves, which took more than a week to announce, the only news to come out of Florida was that purses had been slashed for the second year in a row. This is not a healthy trend. The purse cuts weren't officially announced: why would they be? There was nothing on the AMA Pro Racing website; the lead story is something about two-up rides, which is far more important to the collective world of road racers than knowing they'd be racing for peanuts or less. The bad news was posted on the 2010 entry form, which they turned into a policy document to announce the demise of Moto-GT.

"The Moto-GT Series is discontinued and manufacturer interest in the proposed F-450 category has not been sufficient [duh!] to allow us to include it in the 2010 program."

(The closest they came was converting a bunch of leftover 2007 Aprilia SXVs.)

You would think someone down south would have the decency to tell the Moto-GT field that they'd been euthanized. A friend of mine who raced a Buell this year had already bought spares for 2010. What's the value of spare parts for an obsolete race bike?

The fact that they didn't have the sack to announce the purse properly shows that nothing has changed, and never will as long as DMG is involved. The only announcement to come out of the fortress on Fentress was that David Atlas was now the front man, but that Roger Edmondson was still the skipper, now freed to "focus on the overall direction of AMA Pro Racing and its vision for the future." I could save him some time: The "direction" is straight into a ditch, because the "vision" is blurred by long-standing antipathy toward the factories. There is no "future."

Edmondson was noticeably absent from a fall meeting in Ohio between the AMA and DMG where, it is said, the DMG complained that they'd lost their asses and had problems with their first payment, which, it turns out, wasn't due for more than a year after the sale announcement (the sale price is rumored to be in the range of $12 million). Which means that while DMG was decimating road racing, they were doing it on credit. And it also means that they played the AMA for saps, and that all those wonderful things the AMA was going to do for the membership with the proceeds of the sale are a joke. As is the size of the membership.

In a column dated November 17, 2008, AMA CEO Rob Dingman wrote of the AMA membership being "300,000 strong." Less than 11 months later the AMA website lists membership at 246,000 - down 54,000 in less than a year and about where it was 10 years ago. This is progress? If this keeps up, they'll disappear in five years.

In an article in the house organ, Dingman complained that the AMA had lost money on Pro Racing, which is true, but only because of suspect bookkeeping. I've seen some of the numbers and I can assure you that Pro Racing made money, before the AMA guaranteed that it didn't. And if they're adamant about the losses, they should open up the books.

Don't hold your breath.

The DMG is the group that brought you rolling starts - gone. Pace car - good riddance. Superpole - outta here. TV broadcasts subjected to delayed enhancement (isn't that a commercial for 36-hour Viagra?) that delays the enjoyment for two weeks after you already know who won the race - sayonara. Threatening the staff with termination if they talked to me - a "failed experiment." The list goes on.

Having said that, it's essential that fans support the road races, or, more to the point, the racetracks. As I've said in the past, the DMG will get their sanctioning fee, regardless of the pain suffered by the promoters. Not all racetracks are owned by larger entities; most are small businesses with big worries. (As an astute friend of mine said of road racing, "Great sport, lousy business.")

So, to increase interest, and tighten up competition, the DMG has added even newer, ever more dazzling innovations. Top of the list is mandatory pit stops, but with a wrinkle: The pit crew is blindfolded. That should make the gas man the most important member of the crew. Riders will spend the first half of the race worrying about having their junk doused in unleaded and the second half with a burning sensation that brings back painful memories of Tijuana Spring Break sophomore year. Second will be selective enforcement of the technical and sporting rules to favor one team over the others. Oops, I forgot - they already do that. And finally, the top five finishers of the previous Superbike race have to give two-up rides in the next race, which means the other five starters will have a three-in-five chance for a podium finish.

So the most unlikely sentence in road racing goes from "Roger, as a seven-time AMA Superbike Champion, I want to offer you my profound and heartfelt thanks for everything you've done for the sport I've given my life to" to "And now, let's give it up for the winner of the Road America Suzuki Superbike Doubleheader, Johnny Rock..."

Aw, screw it, I can't do this anymore.

Happy New Year.

January 27, 2010

Show Me the Money

Racing is fundamentally built around two things: stars and money. Money is the mother's milk. Without money there are no stars; without stars there is no money. The 2010 AMA Professional Road Racing Jamboree, or whatever they're calling it this year, has no money and little star power - which, combined with the infighting in the halls of the Fortress on Fentress, guarantees a smashing 2010 campaign.

As this is being written, on Monday morning in an airport lounge in Milan, there was one pre-entry for the Daytona Superbike race. And he was not - nor will he ever be mistaken for - a star. The number of entries should swell, possibly reaching double digits, though the quality of the field will fall quicker than a bungee jumper. Honda and Kawasaki are gone, Yamaha is hanging on, and Suzuki is making sure the show goes on, even if they can't afford it.

The one true AMA road-racing star walked away after seeing how little regard the good ol' boys in Daytona had for the racers' safety. Whether you like him or not, Mat Mladin is a star. You don't win seven titles and 80 races without being a star. But with Suzuki selling about a third the number of bikes they sold two years ago, there was no way they could pay him what he deserved. More importantly, there is no evidence that safety will be given any greater priority this year than last, even with the game of musical chairs going on in the executive suites in Daytona. Last year they proved themselves incapable of properly running a series on any level. The most hoped-for benefit - that the NASCAR marketing machine would sweep road racing into the big time - never got out of neutral.

Now try wrapping your head around this: 2007 Formula One World Champion Kimi Räikkönen will likely be paid tens of millions of dollars not to race this year, and it makes perfect business sense.

The estimates on how much Ferrari will give the once flying Finn not to drive range from 7 to 8 million British pounds ($11,400,000 to $13,022,000), the BBC estimate, to a Spanish newspaper pumping the number up to 45 million Euros ($64,661,000) - his $51 million salary plus a tidy penalty. Ten million here, 10 million there...

Räikkönen was a disappointment after his World Championship year and Ferrari couldn't afford to keep him around. He was overshadowed by teammate Felipe Massa in 2008, the year the Brazilian missed out on the title by a single point. This year Räikkönen finished sixth.

When he signed his three-year deal to replace the retiring Michael Schumacher at Ferrari, Räikkönen was immediately catapulted into the top tier of the world's highest-paid athletes. It's generally accepted that his driving fee was $51 million per year, times three. (On the 2009 Forbes list of richest athletes, the number was put at $45 million, tying him with Michael Jordan, who retired six years ago, and Kobe Bryant. Only Tiger Woods, at $110 million, made more. I'm guessing that might change the next time the Forbes folks write about Tiger.)

Two-time F1 World Champion Fernando Alonso made his Ferrari debut at Wrooom 2010, the annual weeklong party thrown by Phillip Morris for the Marlboro Ferrari and Ducati teams high in the Italian Dolomites. The Spaniard will earn a more than healthy salary, as most drivers do in Formula One. But more important is what he brought: Banco Santander, a Spanish bank with a valuation of nearly $11 billion, signed on to back Scuderia

Ferrari for the next five years. The most breathless estimate I got, from a British F1 journalist who assured me his word was gospel, was $150 million a year. The lower end was $57,500,000 a year. Either way, it's enough to keep the team hospitality stocked with Prosecco and sangria. And if Phillip Morris withdraws after 2012, Santander gets the whole car.

Kimi Räikkönen isn't the only racer who was paid and didn't race. In 2009, John Hopkins was paid by Kawasaki after they withdrew from MotoGP... sort of. They resurfaced in the form of the Hayate team, but it wasn't a factory effort and Hopkins was under no obligation to race. Instead, he found himself on an under-funded World Superbike team that did his career no good.

Hopkins may be making his return to racing in the United States or MotoGP, or both. If he can scare up sponsorship for the team, in the form of Monster bucks, he'll return to the same team for which he rode before moving to GPs full-time in 2002. And despite seven years in Grand Prix racing, he'll return as one of the youngest riders on the depleted Superbike grid. He's only 26.

The move back to the United States would represent another example of money changing everything. Hopkins didn't set the world on fire during his Suzuki days, but no one will ever confuse the Suzuki GSV-R with a real MotoGP bike. He got as much out of the bike as was humanly possible, and when he tried to be superhuman, he ended up testing his own mortality. Hopkins' strength is also his weakness: He doesn't know when to back off. Over the past few years, he's had far too many crashes - big ones, injurious ones, bone-breaking ones - when he tried to override clearly deficient machinery. And if he tries to stay in MotoGP, it will happen again.

Hopkins may or may not race for the FB Corse team in 2010. He may or may not race the whole MotoGP season. He may or may not race as a wild card in races that don't conflict with the

AMA schedule. He may or may not race the entire AMA schedule. It's only mid-January. What's the rush?

About now you're asking, What is FB Corse and why haven't I heard about them? FB Corse is yet another vanity project that has zero chance of success in MotoGP. Remember the Ilmor? Remember Grupo Francisco Hernando? Sete Gibernau does.

The Italian team was supposed to launch in Milan on January 21. But the launch was aborted and the website is being put off until February. What they have so far is the Oral three-cylinder engine, originally designed as BMW's MotoGP weapon. But machine development is so far behind that they won't take part in the two MotoGP tests in Malaysia in February. Instead, they'll do a shake-down test at Vallelunga, outside of Rome, with 47-year-old test rider Luca Cadalora. Hopkins can't take part. He might not want to. The bike hasn't run on a racetrack in its current configuration. And he's supposed to race it against Valentino Rossi and Casey Stoner? Why?

According to an Italian journalist friend, who's in regular contact with team principal Andrea Ferrari, the bike hasn't been track-tested in a year, not since they replaced the Ferrari-type automatic transmission with a more traditional gearbox. The team will see how they stack up against the rest when they test in Qatar in March, a month before the season opener. What they'll find is that they have little hope of doing anything other than filling a spot on the sparse MotoGP grid. And to do it, they'll need money - and Hopkins is attractive, not for his on-track performance, but because he has a line to the Monster money.

Hopkins should run from this thing as fast as his beat-up body will allow him. Riding a homebuilt one-off against the best riders in the world on the best bikes in the world is a recipe for disaster. If he doesn't give it his all, he'll be criticized. If he goes as hard as he always has, he'll be back in plaster. But will he even get the chance to ride? The team thinks so. They sent word to Italian website www.bikeracing.it that Hopkins wants to race in MotoGP rather than AMA and that recent word of a possible move to the AMA series doesn't necessarily mean that it's so.

As much of a demotion as it would be, Hopkins needs to race in the United States for a year. He'll be on what has been the benchmark machine of the past seven years - the Suzuki GSX-R1000 - with a handful of parts out of the Yoshimura catalog. He may not be a star, but he has a legacy no one else on the grid can equal. He can win and he can get his confidence back. And he'll be bringing money.

His competition will come from Yamaha's Josh Hayes, the presumed front-runner, though others may step up. Blake Young should be helped by having Mladin's long-time crew chief Peter Doyle in his corner. Tommy Hayden has to win a race. Larry Pegram won three races last year, but he won't have the same support, either financially or technically, this year. There are others. The Jordan Suzuki pairing of Aaron Yates and Jake Zemke (the team could be announced any day now) should be interesting. How well will Ben Bostrom go on the Clark Racing Yamaha? Hiring much of his Yamaha crew, along with former Honda road-race boss Ron Heben, were both good moves. If he gets inspired, Bostrom could do some business. And that's about it.

Who stands to benefit most from Hopkins' arrival other than Hopper himself? The promoters. As it is, they're being asked to put on a show that increasingly fewer people want to see. They need help. They need a draw. They need John Hopkins.

I can't believe I just wrote that.

February 24, 2010

In With the New

The purge of the old DMG is nearly complete after one of the final links to former CEO Roger Edmondson left the building last week. But whether the replacements are better than the originals remains to be seen. And starting the season with so little experience, and so little communication with the teams, doesn't inspire confidence in a group whose freshman year will be remembered as a combination of ignorance and arrogance.

Edmondson is gone, though he remains a consultant. The red herring that DMG floated was that Edmondson left for health reasons. It's true that he's facing a serious health issue, though not bladder cancer, which is thankfully under control, but health had little to do with his departure. After alienating half the OEMs and running road racing into the ground, and forcing silly and ultimately reversed innovations like pace bikes and cars onto the paddock, Edmondson vacated his office, sort of. He has a contract - two years, I'm told - but to do what? Drive off the OEMs that haven't already left?

David Atlas is the new boss. Haven't heard of him? Not surprising. He's one of the other DMG principals who has remained in the background. So how did Atlas get the job? Is it because of his vast knowledge of motorcycle racing? No, it's because it fell in his lap.

The lack of knowledge about Atlas is emblematic of the AMA Pro Racing legacy of poor communications, born in Westerville, that has migrated south. One of the criticisms of Edmondson was that he was imperious, that he was disconnected from the paddock, preferring to remain secluded in his Prevost motorhome.

Atlas needs to be more engaged than his predecessor. He raised his profile by making the rounds at the Indy trade show, but missed a perfect opportunity to meet the paddock during the recent test at Auto Club Speedway. He should have been there to gather advice from team managers, crew chiefs, and riders. Instead, he's getting much of his advice from a single team owner whose agenda has always been quite clear. Atlas should know better than to listen to him, but apparently he doesn't. And until he starts to get a wider scope of opinion, the series will continue to be doomed.

Cycle News requested an interview with Atlas more than a month ago. It hasn't happened. It should. When a manager or a head coach or a CEO gets hired, the first thing any responsible organization does is make him available. Why? Because there is no better time. There is no track record. He has a clean slate. He can be introduced to the media, but more importantly, to his constituents and stakeholders through the media. Otherwise you have to ask, What's he hiding? If Atlas isn't capable of sitting down for an interview with an industry publication, which interviewed Edmondson the night the sale of Pro Racing was announced, he isn't capable of running Pro Racing. Yet further evidence of more bad advice.

The entries for Daytona are well down from last year and will be even smaller for the rest of the season. Aprilia and BMW decided not to come in, Buell went out of business, and Honda and Kawasaki decided to sit this one out. Ducati isn't supporting the series with nearly the resources it did last year. AMA Pro Racing bent over backward to accommodate Aprilia as a pretext for getting their Superbike into the field. How did that work out? Buell was given carte blanche to build a Superbike and the most liberal rules in the Sportbike field. But after hemorrhaging money forever, Harley finally pulled the plug. Many of the private teams courted BMW, who were hopeful of funding a multiple-year

Superbike effort. Their effort went south when the board vetoed the racing program and they became another of the teams looking for money, and needing more than most, since they wanted to back a turnkey operation. Kawasaki had one foot out the door last year - they handed the race team to Attack Racing - and both feet this year. American Honda's Ray Blank made it clear that the direction of DMG was keeping the biggest motorcycle company in the world out of the paddock. Refreshing honesty.

Atlas's number-one job should be to get Honda and Kawasaki back into the fold. When they're in racing, they give it the kind of support that you don't find from the smaller manufacturers. There is a reason the season opener is called the Daytona 200 by Honda. There is a reason the Infineon race was called the Kawasaki AMA Superbike Showdown. That the DMG went out of its way to support one or two bikes never made a lick of sense. And it still doesn't. Larry Pegram was incensed that they gave him a five-pound weight penalty. But doesn't he have a bit of a displacement advantage? I'm sure this could be cleared up if the AMA released Superbike dyno numbers.

Because DMG doesn't understand communications or public relations, it's hard to completely know what's going on in the Fortress on Fentress. And those who were axed are forbidden from discussing their departures. We know former race director Colin Fraser is gone, though he also has a limited contract with DMG. Paddock boss Bill Syfan was let go, along with his wife, who worked in registration. I still don't know what his sin was. Jim Wardell, who did an excellent job of running timing and scoring, as well as other IT issues, was let go. His sin was that he pointed out riders who "jumped" the start, including one repeat offender. So, rather than punishing the rider, they get rid of one of their most competent and hardest-working employees.

Marketing and media boss Ollie Dean left the company at the end of last week. Dean's legacy will be picking a fight - not a verbal spat, but an actual physical confrontation - with a race promoter. Things might have turned out differently if the promoter didn't know martial arts, but he did. And Dean was subdued, repeatedly, until he finally caught on. Roy Janson, Edmondson's right-hand man and an ace operations guy, was also given a contract.

Their replacements are trickling in, and this is where there is some hope. Dave McGrath has been hired to replace Fraser. McGrath is a solid choice, one of the most thoughtful, level-headed, even-keeled crew chiefs in the business. Before turning around Buell's program last year, he was a crew chief at American Honda. He brings instant credibility to a damaged brand. He's a great choice, but is he the right choice for the job? McGrath has never run a race, and that skill set is much different than that required for running a race team. Some of his attributes carry over, but what happens when the lights go out in the chicane? Fortunately, he'll have help. The crew on the ground, led by Beth Miller, is very good. And getting rid of the pace car/bike idiocy is a huge help. Most of the big problems - Daytona, Laguna, Topeka - were a direct result of this inane policy. My hope is that he got at least a two-year commitment and a guarantee of moving expenses to and from Daytona.

Personally, I'd have offered the job to Steve Whitelock. Whitelock is the former AMA motocross boss who, before that, was the technical chief for World Superbike. No one in America has more knowledge of how to run a race series, from top to bottom, than Whitelock. His appointment would give the series instant credibility worldwide. I suggested Whitelock to DMG management the same weekend I was asked for Al Ludington's phone number, at Miller in 2008. The response was that they wanted to hire a certain personality type best exemplified by Fraser - thoughtful, unflappable, immensely decent, and without an enemy in the world. Then they hired Ludington, who's since become a YouTube sensation, and Janson, whose temper is legendary. How's that "personality type" requirement working out? Fraser and Janson are gone, and no less a luminary and race fan than AMA CEO Rob Dingman has called for Ludington's head. Maybe he should concentrate on growing the abysmal AMA membership. Judging by the sweetheart deal he gave to the DMG, he clearly isn't great with numbers.

The purse numbers for the Daytona weekend aren't encouraging. The weekend purse is down to $225,000 from $286,000 in 2009. As strange as it sounds, it's somewhat understandable. Part of that is the economy, and part of it is that last year's purse included Moto-GT. And there is good news: The original Superbike purse, which was paltry and only paid three places, has been greatly expanded. Now it's on par with the 200 purse: Winning both legs of the Superbike race nets $20,000. It also pays down to 15th place. Whether this will continue in Fontana - Daytona always has the best purses of the year - remains to be seen. What it suggests is that someone came to his senses and realized that big bikes should be the premier class. Already there's talk of running Superbikes in the 200 in 2011. If they do, they'll need at least one tire test, which got scrapped this year because DMG didn't think it was necessary.

Likely the expanded purse is too little, too late. The original purse structure had to scare off a number of prospective Superbike entries. Why race for no money against the best riders when you can pay some of the bills by racing in a smaller class? Oddly, Sportbike is the class that's taken the greatest hit at Daytona. Last year there were 73 riders in Wednesday practice; this year there are 47 entries. Superbike is down only six, from 33 to 27 entries. Supersport is off by a third - 14 this year to last year's 19. Pre-entries for Fontana, admittedly more than a month away, are paltry.

After the embarrassment of the Pothole 500, Daytona needs a race to run smoothly, certainly more smoothly than last year's 200 debacle. If DMG wants to move past the ignorance and arrogance of the past, this would be a good place to start.

March 17, 2010

End of an Era

Dunlop road race boss Jim Allen was celebrated at a retirement party on Thursday night on the eve of his final Daytona as the head of British brand's road race team. Also being honored was Dave Watkins, the quiet giant from the home office in Manchester who designed most of the racing tires that riders in the USA and worldwide have been winning on for decades.

It isn't hyperbole to say that no single person had more influence on American road racing over the past nearly 30 years than Allen. No single person had more respect, no single person was responsible for more championships. No single person wanted to win more, nor won more, over the past nearly three decades.

Jim Allen was, and will always be, the only individual who was welcome in every garage, every semi, every pit stall. Well, almost every one. He would leave knowing more than when he arrived, but the same could be said of those he left. And they were confident that whatever they shared would remain confidential. Because in a paddock fueled by gossip, the one attribute every team valued was trust and no one was more trustworthy than Allen.

"If you go to Duhamel and say 'Mladin's using this,' well Mladin's not going to tell you anything next time. He knows that Allen blabs and he's giving away the secrets, so you don't do that stuff," Allen said. And that was difficult. Not because he had a desire to share, but because in the days before spec tires, which neither he nor Dunlop are a fan of, he wanted Dunlop to win. More than anything, Jim Allen wanted to win.

So not sending a wayward rider down the right path was "always a tricky thing, because you want all your guys to do well. You want as many Dunlop guys in the top 10 as you can get. If you've got three guys, four guys, five guys, and you've got the tires in the truck and they're on their allocation sheet, but for some reason they're not going down that road... I mean you can't say, for instance, 'Miguel's using this tire. Why don't you try it, he really likes it?' That's not fair to the Yamaha guy to say that this guy's using that tire. What you can say is, 'Have you looked at all of these? Have you looked at all the fronts? Have you tried that? What do you think of that one?' 'Well, I haven't tried that one yet.' You should get through your allocation before the end of the weekend. You can't say 'Try number X because that's the business.' It's not fair to do that. I can't take an advantage that Miguel found, for instance, by telling somebody else. And I think that gives you credibility in the long run."

But there were times when there was no choice. Some riders just never got around to trying the tires they should have. And then there were riders who would fall off again and again and never get enough time on any one tire to make an informed decision.

"Saturday night they come to you and say, 'Look, I'm in the s--t, I haven't got a clue. What should I race on?' And you say, 'Race on this or race on that.' And you don't say any more. You have to get them in the race. You can't steer them wrong and stuff. I mean, Neil, for instance, Hodgson, would take forever to make his mind up sometimes. And sometimes when he was with Ducati it was largely Ducati's fault, I think. There was just way too much on the plate for him sometimes. Once or twice, but you can't do it every race. It's not fair. But at the same time, it's your job to make sure that he gets into the race with the best setup he's got, so you always tread a fine line there."

Where there is no fine line is when you stack up Dunlop's rivalry with Michelin in the United States. Michelin was the dominant tire brand in Grand Prix racing for more than 20 years, winning nearly every 500cc World Championship, but whenever they came to the United States, they ran into a buzzsaw, and it came down to work. Allen wanted to win more than they did and he made sure that Dunlop did as well.

"I think it's related to the effort they put in," he said. "You can never take anything away from those guys. Their record, it's not impeccable, but their record is an amazing record. They have every right to be proud of it. In open competitions, they beat everybody time after time. So for sure, more than that they were the adversary.

"It must my guess is that it's related to management direction from the top. There can't have been the recognition that it's important. And the one thing I can say all the years I worked for Dunlop is the management recognized that this is our model, this is what we do, we go racing and we win and then we make the best of it by telling the world that we won."

The last time Dunlop won the 500cc World Championship was with Wayne Rainey in 1991. The man responsible was Dave Watkins. Watkins speaks so softly that it's often difficult to grasp everything he says. But when it mattered, Rainey understood Watkins.

"There was no other guy on my team on the tire side I'd rather have. I love the guy," Rainey said during a recent phone call from his home in Monterey. "He was part of team. I loved to win with him and we lost together. He always looked at the positives and he always wanted to try and learn from whatever the info I was giving him or the tires I was trying to improve. And we'd show up at the end of the year and start preseason testing and bring new tires and knew what he was working on.

"With Dave, we had a lot of good times together and a lot of hard times together, but no doubt about it, with him I always knew where I stood. Because when he knew for sure we had an issue with a tire he was never one to say, 'Check your suspension' or, 'Is your engine okay?' He was always the first one to put his hand up and say, 'We've got an issue. We'll do all we can to fix it.'"

"I really appreciated that, because tires are… probably the most important part of the bike and probably the most difficult part of the equation to sort out."

If Dunlop had one weakness, it was building too many tires. And Rainey had to do the bulk of the testing.

"Some of those tests, I can remember where we would have an easy… for a four-day test, we would have easy, seemed like front and rear tires, probably close to 200 tires to test."

Those aren't just 200 tires, those are 200 different tires and built around certain families.

"In that family, whether it was compound, you'd have to go through that, even if you didn't like the compound, if you like the stiffness of the tires or the carcass. The way that they tested them was so thorough it was five tires of one family and you'd have to go through all of them. And you had profiles and you'd have different sidewall heights and different tread thicknesses and the way the bead was laid in there and the angle of the treads and then you got the rubbers on top of that. Then you'd have to go out and put a lot of laps on them to make sure they'd last."

Rainey said there were race weekends when Watkins would say, "We want you to test these tires," and Rainey would answer, "This weekend? We want to do all those?" And Watkins would have to go back and pick the ones that would best suit him and the track and the conditions, "Normally by Sunday, he had it sorted out. He knew what was going to be the best and when he told me what he thought we should race with was normally the one we raced with.

There might have been one or maybe two races where I didn't know about his advice, what it was going to get me.

"As a rider, you always want to be able to go fast and be confident and didn't want to make a mistake. Some tires couldn't do that right away." Watkins told him, "If you can just wait a couple of laps, this is really going to be a lot better towards middle and the end." And he would always be right.

"And there would be races where he would say, 'We're not going to have what you need,' We had some tires that we didn't know if, like for Hockenheim for instance, we didn't know if the thing was going to last, and it did last and we ended up winning the race when we thought we had a problem."

One of his greatest strengths is that Watkins was never rattled and Rainey appreciated that.

"He never had a rattled look on his face, like everybody else in my camp. Win or lose, he had the same face. He never had that 'we're-in-the-crap' look. And that's good for a rider, because if you see that on a tire guy you know you're in trouble. He still calls me. There's not a lot of people, you quit racing and people that are still racing, that's their job, it's tunnel vision. But I hear from Dave a lot and I appreciate that."

No one can measure how much the paddock appreciated Jim Allen and Dave Watkins, their contribution is immeasurable. They will be missed.

April 14, 2010

Will He Return?

Mat Mladin didn't have to show up at Auto Club Speedway to make his presence felt.

Now in his first year of what could be a very short retirement, Mladin's influence is everywhere and the reason is simple - despite an unparalleled career that will never be matched, Mladin was, if not underrated, certainly underappreciated. Too often the Suzuki GSX-R1000 got the credit, not Mladin. It took Ben Spies to win the World Superbike Championship on an overmatched Yamaha for the racing world at large to realize that if Spies was that good, how good was the guy who won more races than him over the previous three years?

"To this day, people don't know how much talent Mat Mladin had." That's the opinion of Jim Allen, who recently retired after a distinguished and championship-filled career as the head of Dunlop's road-racing effort. Allen was in charge of racing for most of the past 30 years. In the course of a profile I was doing for *Sport Rider* magazine, I asked him if there was any rider who had so much talent that he could race on any tire. Mladin was his quick pick.

"The number of times that Mat Mladin out-qualified the field by a second on race tires when everybody else was using all of the qualifiers, and Mat never looked at one the whole weekend long," Allen said. "And they won't believe that. To this day, they won't believe it and it's absolutely true. And I'm not talking about once, I'm talking race after race, all season long. Somebody got close, he'd put a qualifier and then he'd be a second ahead of them again, sort of thing.

"So yeah, for sure, he'd just amaze us," Allen added. "Well, you got a pretty good idea why he'd split in three laps, because he knew when everybody else was farting around with qualifying tires, Mat was on race tires, because he knew what the race tire would do. So clearly, clearly, clearly that guy had so much talent when he was on. So that's the one that really stands out for sure."

He continued by saying that there were "riders for eras."

"I mean, an era might last a couple of years," Allen explained, "It might last five years. There're riders who'd out-qualify or outrace guys for periods of time and stuff. They'd come and they'd go. Usually those guys, as much as anything, it's a matter of everything coming together. They know that nobody else has got a chance to beat them. They know their bike is better. In Mat's case, for instance, the bike wasn't as good. He rode a 750 when other guys had 1000s."

And when I asked which crew chiefs best understood tires, it was no surprise he named Mladin's crew chief Peter Doyle first. There were others: Gary Medley, the late Merlyn Plumlee, Al Ludington.

"And it's funny, the really good guys, the good mechanics, the good crew chiefs are like the good riders, they just want to know they're being treated the same as everybody else. They don't want extras. Because they want to win, too. It's like they want to beat those guys heads-up. Merlyn, I'm sure, wanted to beat Pete Doyle; Pete Doyle wants to beat Tom Houseworth. And they don't necessarily, the good guys, the competent guys, who know their own level of talent, they don't want more than the other guys. They just want to beat them heads up."

Which is how Mladin won.

Mladin walked away healthy, wealthy, and wise while still at the top of his game. Some will argue that. He failed to win a race after Laguna Seca last year, they'll point out, which will miss the point.

Did he get suddenly slower from one race to the next or did the field get suddenly faster? Neither.

Mladin didn't win after Laguna Seca because he didn't have to. He won the first seven races and 10 of the first 12. He built up enough of a lead that he could skip two races and still win a record-extending seventh title. And if he returns next year, he'll pick up where he left off at Laguna Seca, when he still cared about winning.

Racing in the Superbike this year has been excellent, three and four riders fighting to the end and wafer-thin margins of victory. Much is being made of the suddenly competitive field, but there are forces at work that have gone unnoticed.

Jake Zemke had the distinction of being the last non-Suzuki rider to win a Superbike race when he won on the American Honda CBR1000RR at Miller Motorsports Park in 2006. He raced a Honda Superbike again in 2007, finishing third to Spies and Mladin. In 2008 he won the Formula Xtreme Championship.

There's no denying his talent. He should've been on a Superbike last year.

Zemke's win in Thursday's Daytona Superbike race was 17 seconds slower than Mladin's win in 2009, when Mladin raced a Suzuki GSX-R1000 that had been taken off a showroom floor and built to the new DMG specs in a matter of weeks. The first time Mladin rode it was at Daytona. Zemke upped the pace in Friday's Daytona Superbike race, which was only 10 seconds slower than Mladin's 2009 win.

Comparing the times from Auto Club Speedway isn't as simple. Both 2009 races were red-flagged on the first lap and timing and scoring keeps the clock running. But it's instructive to note that Mladin's time was half a second faster than this year's polesitter, Aaron Yates. Last year Mladin took the Fontana pole by nearly 1.5 seconds. There's no way that anyone will match

Mladin's performance at Road Atlanta, a track where he excelled and may again.

Blake Young has had a solid if unspectacular start to his season. He hasn't crashed and he's been on the podium. And that was at races where the Yosh team had no data on the K9, which they didn't race early last year. Young now has access to the wisdom of Peter Doyle, who moved to the young rider with Mladin's retirement.

Between last year's Australian and Malaysia GPs, I visited Mladin at his business, BikeGearWarehouse just outside of Sydney. He had plenty on his plate and didn't miss getting up early to work out. But walking away isn't always easy, especially when your phone keeps ringing.

Mladin is simply too big to ride a MotoGP machine, but he would still be a major force in World Superbike or AMA. And, if I had to bet, I would bet that he's back in the AMA paddock next year. But with whom?

Of the current players, I'd rule out Suzuki and Yamaha. And Kawasaki, whose racing department is in a state of transition, isn't a likely destination. That leaves Honda.

American Honda walked away at the end of a brutal 2009 campaign. Neil Hodgson was hurt just after Daytona and never came close to recovering full strength in his shoulder. It was a struggle for all involved just to get through the year.

The AMA Superbike series bottomed out last year and is just now starting to rebound. With the absence of Mladin, the racing is very good; middleweight racing has always been close. DMG's disastrous stewardship of the road racing has had an unintended consequence; the tracks have no money to improve safety.

Virtually every racetrack has a corner or two that needs attention. Most of the tracks have stepped up over the past several years, some more than others. But given the size of last year's crowds, and with more of the same expected this year, it isn't possible for track owners to spend more money that they don't have after being asked to sell a product that was so heavily damaged the past two years. If Mladin comes back, and the caretakers take a sudden interest in safety, they have to engage him.

    The last time American Honda won the Superbike title was in 2002 with Nicky Hayden. The 2010 season will end with an eight-year gap in championships, the longest since Fred Merkel won the first of his three consecutive Superbike titles in 1984. Could Mat Mladin make his return in 2011 on an American Honda CBR1000RR? If he does, it will be an immense undertaking, a challenge, and that may be enough to get Mladin back on the grid. And maybe then he'll be appreciated.

April 28, 2010

The Ghost of Roger

Thought you'd heard the last of Roger Edmondson? Not so fast. The former CEO of AMA Pro Racing was given a very golden parachute in a palace coup at the start of a round of dismissals that gutted the Daytona Motorsports Group. Now a "consultant," his legacy continues to cast a stain over American road racing. There were less Superbike finishers at Road Atlanta last weekend than for any race in memory, less than finish a MotoGP race. That's what happens when your arrogance drives off the factories that pay all the bills, sponsor the races, pay for the television advertising, and support racing at the grass roots. One team manager said road racing was so damaged, that he hoped it would survive.

Edmondson and his regime took over at Daytona in 2008 and immediately made their impact felt. His fingerprints were all over the decision to disqualify Josh Hayes for having an illegal crank in his Daytona 200-winning Erion Honda. Then Edmondson vowed that that would never happen again, that the rider who celebrated the victory would be otherwise punished - points, purse, etc. - but that that rider would stand as the winner. Where is Roger now that we need him?

Ironically, it was Josh Hayes who was again involved in a bad decision that showed how the new caretakers operate under pressure. Hayes jumped the start, was given a ride-through penalty, didn't serve it, then the lap he tried to serve it was negated, got lucky with a red flag, was given the pole on the re-start, went on to win the race, smiled and sprayed lots of champagne. That's what viewers saw who stayed up to watch the broadcast on Speed. It was all a mirage. A couple hours later, Blake

Young was taken on a scooter to the Yamaha transporter to collect the winner's trophy.

Hayes was rolling down the pit lane in front of the Jordan Suzuki pit when the red flag was thrown. The Jordan guys saw it and we could see it clearly from the press room, in the same tower as Timing & Scoring. Hayes was nowhere near clearing the pit lane and rejoining a green track. He couldn't have. The race had been stopped.

That's not how the AMA originally saw it. The first erroneous report given to race director Dave McGrath was that Hayes had cleared the pit lane. McGrath watched the races from pit lane, which turned out to be a mistake. He should have been in the tower, watching on TV. (Colin Fraser made the same mistake last year at Laguna Seca. Fraser was in a trailer on the inside of the track when he sent the pace car into the path of the Superbike field.) Tracks with greater aspirations have closed-circuit systems that are independent from the Speed feed. Had McGrath been in the tower, he'd have seen that Hayes was on the pit lane, both with his own eyes and on television. There would have been no doubt. Instead, the decision he made based on incompetence spawned a series of events and ill will that will last well into the season, and may be mentioned in the final reckoning, if Hayes comes up short by a few points. You can rest assured, Chuck Graves is not happy.

The living organism that is the road-racing rulebook showed its true colors again. Every year, it gets updated; and every year, it falls short. Nowhere in the rulebook does it define a ride-through penalty. The FIM rulebook on ride-throughs states that "during the race, the rider will be requested to ride-through the pit lane. Stopping is not permitted. He may then rejoin the race." Implicit is that definition is that he ride the length of the pit lane.

Without a similar definition, the AMA rulebook is open to interpretation. Is it when you leave the track? Is it when you cross the start-finish beacon? Is it when you re-join the track? No one knows and there wasn't total agreement among AMA officials, which gave Yamaha plenty of ammunition for a reversal. That didn't happen. At least not yet and probably never. Another question is whether Hayes actually served the penalty. Since scoring reverted to the end of the third lap, nothing counts from the lap he came in, except his ride-through. But if the lap doesn't count, how can the penalty?

So instead of seeing Hayes start from the back and watching Young stream to his first win, fans at the track and at home watched a guy win the race who didn't win the race. And Roger said that would never happen again.

It was an unfortunate series of events that led to the mess. Had the race not been stopped, this would have been academic. But it was, and under pressure, AMA Timing & Scoring and others, let down the field, the fans, and, most importantly, Josh Hayes and Blake Young.

Hayes would've been happy to go to the back of the grid for the re-start. He'd jumped the start, he deserved a penalty. Had he finished his ride-through, he'd have been at the back of the pack. A motivated Josh Hayes would've been a joy to watch. He certainly would've improved on the sixth-place finishing position he was given after being assessed a time penalty.

For Young, it was in some ways worse. When I told the team about the decision (AMA Pro Racing held a news conference before informing the teams) I was told he was getting a massage; in fact, he was in the shower after the massage. This wasn't the happy ending he was expecting. And he wasn't that happy.

Hayes had beaten him on the track and Young had gotten his first win, but this wasn't how he wanted it. He wanted to be on the top of the podium spraying champagne. That moment is gone forever. His first win will always have an asterisk, and, for that, he can thank AMA Pro Racing. But it's instructive to remember how this started; Hayes jumped the start. There was no denying it.

The race, though it wasn't for real, was a good one, instructive for Young. The next day, he would silence anyone who doubted he could win an outright battle. By holding off Hayes for 20 tense laps, he put himself in the mix for the championship, which continues to be the subject of debate and speculation.

Until this race, it was true that the on-track officiating was better, that the discord had been quieted. But the question has been asked, why are we doing this?

Motorcycle companies race for one specific reason, to sell motorcycles. It's that simple. Bad crowds at marginal tracks and television time slots that favor insomniacs and shift workers don't sell motorcycles. What's the five-year plan? Where is the series going? When you ask these questions, the answer you get is that they have to fix what's on the track before addressing off-track problems, a specious argument, at best, but one you get when the series promoter and sanctioning body are one and the same. The people who take care of the on-track action shouldn't have anything to do with the strategic vision. Who does?

AMA PR COO David Atlas made the rounds of the OEMs and others around the time of the race at Auto Club Speedway. He's also taken riders to dinner. He still won't do an interview with *Cycle News*, so unless we get invited to dinner, we know nothing about what he sees as the future of road racing.

There have been some hints dropped and they aren't very positive. More than once, he reportedly told people that Jim France wasn't willing to lose money forever, that he's on a short leash. Maybe France should have thought of that during the two years that Edmondson was dragging road racing into the gutter and taking the France family name down with it. If I was a billionaire, I think I'd pay a little more attention to the bottom line. But that's just me.

A good place to start is with racetracks. There continues to be opposition to Auto Club Speedway, and yet it's a fixture on the schedule, despite crowds that could fit in clown cars. Atlas knows that other tracks have problems, and he also knows he could end up with a very short series if the AMA didn't go to every track that had a significant safety or promotional issue. In talks with the factories, he showed a lack of knowledge by mentioning three tracks with little appeal for professional racers. Watkins Glen is lined with Armco and is unfixable for motorcycles. If you air-fenced the entire track, you'd have a racing surface about six-feet wide. Under no circumstances can motorcycles race there. I'd say Willow Springs is a charming dump, but I haven't been there in 10 years. I expect it's been vastly improved. Chuckwalla is in the middle of nowhere California, 46 miles from the nearest hotel. Kind of goes against the expanding into metropolitan markets mantra.

How about Miller Motorsports Park? In talks with the teams, Atlas also mentioned Miller, but I don't see it on the calendar. Meanwhile, the track just announced a purse of $40,000 for the two support races on the World Superbike card. Both races pay better than either of the AMA races at Road Atlanta and significantly more for the winner. And they're AMA sanctioned.

When World Superbike first came to Miller, they ran on a different track than the AMA. This was done to appease Pirelli, who didn't want Mat Mladin showing them up by shattering their best lap times on Dunlop tires. That fight is over. AMA Superbikes are docile compared to their world cousins, and also now ride on control tires. You could run them on the same track and the world guys would be faster. And Pirelli would be happy.

Officially, Edmondson said he didn't want to be a sideshow to World Superbike. Then came to the light the extortionate sanctioning fee he was requesting.

Even though Edmondson is gone, there's no returning to Miller. The legacy lives on.

June 23, 2010

Hall of Shame?

With the 2010 AMA Superbike season reaching the halfway point at the Suzuki Superbike Doubleheader at Road America, it's time to reflect. Of all the question marks surrounding the first AMA Superbike season since 1995 without Mat Mladin is "What kind of nitwits run the AMA Hall of Fame?"

The AMA HoF is one of the least exclusive clubs in the world. The Major League Baseball Hall of Fame in Cooperstown evokes memories of Ruth, Gehrig and Mantle. The Hall in Pickerington evokes, what? Derisive laughter.

Today's Hall of Famer is Don Castro, a fine gentleman but not a Hall of Famer. Castro won a total of one Half Mile and no championships. Nothing against Don Castro, but those aren't Hall of Fame credentials. Same goes for the late David Emde. Emde, at least, won a title, the 1977 250cc title, along with nine races. Those are not Hall of Fame credentials.

The late Randy Renfrow was on the ballot for this year's class, which is gradually getting rolled out. Renfrow won the 1983 250cc title and the final Formula One title in 1986. He won eight 250cc races, four F1 races, and one Superbike race. And even with those numbers it'd be hard to put him in the Hall. If he goes in, and he may yet - the entire class hasn't been announced - it's because he was one of the most decent, hard-working, intelligent, passionate riders ever to throw a leg over a racebike.

The AMA's Hall choices are one more example of how poorly they are at making choices. Take their racing partners. When they sold Pro Racing to the Daytona Motorsports Group, it was widely believed that the DMG would bring their vast marketing experience to bear, that the sponsors who could no longer afford NASCAR would be persuaded to throw their millions, or at least thousands, over to Superbike. That hasn't happened and it won't, because the DMG continues to have misguided priorities.

The mantra around the paddock these days is "close racing." The officials in charge of what goes on on the track have done a good job with the rules, though why they allow the Buell to continue to race remains a mystery. I went to my local Buell dealer to buy an 1125R and, guess what? There is no local Buell dealer.

Which makes this statement in the homologation form, "AMA Pro Racing American SuperBike motorcycles must be street certified for use in the United States and be available at the time of competition through U.S. retail outlets as determined by the homologating manufacturer," a little silly. Everyone talks about how close the racing is, and it is close, at least for a few riders. There were numerous photo finishes at Road America, including one that shouldn't have been. When Josh Hayes crossed the line in front of Tommy Hayden on Saturday, it was Hayden's name that went to the top. Half a world away in Italy, Nicky Hayden was watching it on live timing, as was his father, Earl, in Kentucky. "Hello darling," Earl said on Instant Messenger. "Not so fast," Nicky said, having been told the results were wrong.

The problem was simple. Hayes' transponder was on the back half of the bike. Tommy Hayden's in the nose cone. Which meant Tommy's transponder clipped the beam before Hayes, and he was given the win. Transponders should be universally placed ahead of the dash. A rule like that would have prevented the AMA from embarrassing themselves and confusing others.

Close racing is a noble goal, but the truth is, it doesn't really matter. The closest and best motorcycle racing in the United States is dirt track, which is as healthy as a syphilitic crack whore thanks to the AMA's longtime policy of wanton neglect. What else has close racing? Speedway. Ever been to a speedway race? Didn't think so. Ever seen one on TV? Me neither. In his peak years, Jeremy McGrath was winning races in bunches and by big margins. Why else would he have time to do, as a friend of mine said, "Knick-knacks." Did that kill Supercross? Just the opposite. Supercross thrived. Who came next? Ricky Carmichael. More wins by big margins. More growth. You get the picture. Formula One is the most popular form of motorsports worldwide. A close Formula One finish is defined by the first two cars finishing on the same day. And yet Fernando Alonso earns the equivalent of the U.S. national debt.

Stars and technology are what drive Formula One and any other form of motorsport. Valentino Rossi understands that more than anyone and his absence will leave a cavernous hole. Rossi grew his legend by passing riders over the last few laps, seeming to win at the last minute. The formula worked. He was a hero because he had personality and skill, was riding a cutting-edge bike, all while giving the illusion of competition. But if you had to remove one part of that equation, which would it be?

Australian Josh Waters made a big impression in his first visit to America. The reigning Aussie Superbike Champion clocked the fourth-fastest time on his first visit to Barber Motorsports Park. He did it with enthusiasm and humility and said it would be a dream come true to race in America. It's far too early to project expectations, but there's no denying he could shake up the established order. Elena Myers can also have a transformative affect on the championship, if her career is properly managed.

Martin Cardenas should be on a Superbike, but he'll have to figure out a way to stop crashing. Danny Eslick deserves a second chance on a big bike.

If the DMG has an understanding that personalities drive racing, it isn't apparent. It should be. They need only look down the hall at NASCAR, which, though it still commands huge fan loyalty, has been in slow decline for a few years.

Hall of Shame?

An April *Time* magazine article sourced Nielsen Sports as saying that "average viewership of Sprint Cup races on network television has fallen a remarkable 25 percent."

The lack of personality is one of the main causes. The most popular driver in Sprint Cup racing is Dale Earnhardt Jr. and he's rarely competitive. He hasn't won a race in two years, a 71-race streak, and he finished last season 25th in the points. Given how little they promote the sport or the riders, DMG's focus seems to be entirely on the track, which is entirely misplaced. As wonderful as it is to have close racing, does it matter if no one sees it?

Although no tracks release attendance figures, the crowds this year are a little better than last year's. When you raise the question of promotion or marketing, the answer invariably is that they have to fix what's on the track before they fix the rest.

That's a non-answer. Those two things are meant to happen on parallel tracks. The marketing department doesn't make the technical rules and the boys in tech aren't tasked to sell the sport. Their hiring of Jeff Ward, a former business partner of DMG boss David Atlas, to be the rider liaison was met with less than universal acclaim. If they wanted instant legitimacy, they would have hired Dunlop's recently retired roadrace boss Jim Allen. Jim gets along well with most everyone, including the AMA's Al Ludington and Dave McGrath, and he wouldn't stand for the DMG tarnishing his image.

Image being everything, the television images are about the same as the second half of the year, after the abysmal failure of appointment television deep on Saturday night. Chet Burks, whose company does the production on a shoestring, and Rick Miner, the Speed executive in charge, legitimately belong in the Hall of Fame for the alchemy they practice to keep racing on TV alive. But because of the feud DMG's former CEO Roger Edmondson picked with the factories, they get no support from American Honda, and this year Kawasaki walked away. It's impossible to broadcast a program in a prime-time slot without advertising support and when you have only half the major manufacturers, and no others who advertise on TV, you've got a problem.

The good folks at Miller Motorsports Park and World Superbike know a thing or two about marketing. Out of respect for the Mormons, who make up 60 percent of the population of Utah, they moved the World Superbike race to Monday. It caused a brief uproar among the European press, but they knew that the races ended too late on Sunday night to make deadlines. Besides, the first race would now be on Monday night in prime time with no competing sporting events. The reward for the bold move - a record weekend crowd of 55,000, despite no strong American rider presence.

Other than Kenny Noyes, who's lived in Spain most of his life, there isn't an American presence in Moto2. That will change at the Red Bull Indianapolis GP when Roger Lee Hayden lines up on the Moriwaki Engineering entry. American Honda's Moto2 effort is a big thumb in the eye of the DMG. The word from Honda has consistently been that they have no reason to race with the DMG. If they did, if they thought there was value in it, they would. But they don't.

Big Red will spend an enormous amount of money on this one-off race, money they could have spent fielding an AMA team. Why not cherry-pick a class they alone - it's not an option for U.S. Kawasaki or Suzuki or Yamaha - can instantly compete on equal footing. The exposure they'll get at Indy will trump anything they got last year from the Corona Extra Honda team, especially given how they're managing information.

News of the team is being carefully doled out. First came a leak to a website, then an official announcement. More is to come. Roger Lee Hayden will be announced as the rider in grand fashion and Kevin Schwantz - Shock! Horror! - will be announced as the team manager. A support race at the Red Bull Indy GP will be revealed. All in due time.

In the meantime, we anxiously await news of the next AMA Hall of Famer. Hope they have Anthony Gobert's cell number.

September 23, 2010

Happy, Happy, Happy

There's just no pleasing some people.

The good folks at the Daytona Motorsports Group have gone out of their way to put a smile on every face in the paddock. To turn those frowns upside down. To put a spring in everyone's step. They've made sensible calls on racing issues. They've stopped the favoritism in technical issues. They've addressed timing and scoring issues. As a goodwill gesture, they invited most of the paddock to the narcolepsy-inducing end of season awards banquet at the Barber Museum free of charge. In short, they're trying.

As part of the outreach program, team principals and members have convened twice. The first meeting was held for a select group at Infineon Raceway. It was productive. The most recent meeting had four times the voices and it wasn't pretty. The reason you probably didn't hear about it is that AMAPR/DMG boss David Atlas politely asks that the discussions remain private. Unfortunately, Atlas isn't aware of the Hell's Angels credo that three can keep a secret if two are dead. And when the number is in the 30's…The main topics of discussion were ECU's and testing, and there was a predictable divergence of opinion, even among some teams. Some say electronics are impossible to police, so they believe it's a lost cause. It isn't. Sophisticated electronics aren't allowed in the SuperSport class. How hard was that? Instead, there is no limit to what can be spent on electronics. You want Rossi's Magneti Marelli electronics? Not a problem. Just sign here. There are cheaper alternatives.

Testing couldn't be easier to police and needs to be. The M4 Monster Energy Suzuki and Geico Powersports/RMR Suzuki teams tested ten days before the race in South Jersey. Is it a coincidence that John Hopkins finished a season best third in Sunday's race? Or that Eslick won one race and Cardenas the other? Granted, both Eslick and Cardenas have multiple race wins this season, but it didn't hurt.

The very simple solution is to set a time period after which a rider can't test and hold firm to it, because what we're talking about isn't as much testing as practice. If the teams want to test, do it the day after the race, not the week before. And don't allow anyone to ride at the previous weekend's club race. This would require the cooperation of the track owners, some of whom schedule club events for the previous weekend.

There was a spirited discussion on the merits of both issues. Those who take a populist approach and want to make racing more inclusive for the occasional rider had one point of view, the elites thought the opposite. The discussion reached an ugly nadir when one team owner, who has a horse in the championship race, and, in front of about 30-35 team members, plus AMA officials, spewed at AMA Pro Racing's race boss Dave McGrath, "On the record, f--- you."

A quick digression. Before Al Ludington was the tech boss for AMA Pro Racing, before there was a DMG, before DMG ruined road racing, putting far too many good people out of work and hiring too many bad ones, before they were struck with the medically identifiable condition known as Wacky Ideas Syndrome - see rolling starts, pace cars, pace bikes, etc. - before their business and race practices killed attendance at race tracks nationwide, which not only put the track owners in a hole, but also made it impossible for them to find money to make safety improvements, thereby endangering the health and well-being of the riders, before they played favorites with some teams and punished others, before they made silly rules and enforced them dogmatically, before all that, Ludington considered going to work for the other AMA, the one which was incompetent in a different way, and not venal.

Ludington, who coaxed, prodded, and motivated Miguel Duhamel to his best days, didn't get the job. When I asked why, he told me, "I failed the physical. They took a back x-ray and found I had a spine."

At Auto Club Speedway last year Monster Kawasaki's Jamie Hacking was overheard making a disparaging remark to his wife. One AMA official, who has since left their employ, heard it. For that Hacking was suspended indefinitely, then forced to apologize and fined a sum which just happened to equal his weekend's winnings. What he was being punished for wasn't that profanity, but for vowing, along with Mat Mladin and Jake Zemke, not to race in the rain at the Speedway, which shouldn't even be considered. What's our hatemonger get? Nothing.

Now, what would happen if a NASCAR Sprint Cup team owner stood up at a teams' meeting and told VP of competition Robin Pemberton to eff off? Pretty good chance he'd be stricken by the hammer of Zeus. And yet, so far nothing's been done to the irritable team owner.

How can that be? How can AMAPR be so spineless as to let one of their officials be humiliated in a public forum in front of everyone who matters in the paddock? The truth is that in a very large way DMG boss David Atlas brought this on himself.

The team owner is, or was, an Atlas confidant. Atlas hasn't chosen his confidants wisely, which is why he's in this pickle. The paddock is filled with well meaning, knowledgeable people who have the best interest of racing at heart. McGrath is one of them, as is Ludington. There are others whose opinion he should solicit. Top of the list is my friend Jim Allen, who retired from a stellar career at Dunlop with his sterling reputation intact. (If Jim was still there, there wouldn't have been a surprise front tire at NJMP). No one in the history of AMA road racing was better informed. He was trusted and welcomed in every transporter, well, all but one. He followed the Hell's Angels credo, even if he didn't know it. And when the company screwed up, as they did more often than he'd have liked, he took the heat.

AMA Pro Racing's management is trying their best to be the anti-Edmondson. They're trying to be the nicer, cuddlier AMA. They want everyone to like them, to ask them to the prom, to tell them they love what they've done with their hair. They need to knock it off.

Seeking a consensus is a wise thing to do until it turns into the Tower of Babel. Soliciting the opinion of 30 or 40 people may be a nice thing, and it might satisfy the needs of the insecure to feel wanted, but it's not a very clever thing. Pick the best and the brightest and listen to them. Make a decision. And, as Eric Cartman would say, "Respect my authority!"

Ironically, trying to please everyone is what many condemned in the old AMA. That and not making decisions. These guys make decisions, rightly or wrongly, and take the heat, if there's heat to be taken. And now they have to decide whether they can accept being humiliated. If they don't, they deserve everything they get and everyone will suffer.

There's just no pleasing some people.

October 6, 2010

Secret Champions and Dirty Hogs

The final race of the AMA Pro Road Racing series at Barber Motorsports Park crowned a number of champions which the AMA did their best to keep quiet. When Martin Cardenas was celebrated for winning the title by winning the race, there was no number one plate in sight. Same for Josh Hayes. When I asked why, I was told that they would get their plates at the banquet the following night.

Huh?

The reason Suzuki and Yamaha spend millions of dollars to go racing is to win the number one plate, and sell some bikes along the way. The photo of the champion holding up the plate is a tradition that dates back to when man first walked upright. To delay the custom for more than a day, then hold it at a banquet that wasn't televised, as the podium ceremony was, and held for only members of the paddock, is so stunningly silly it defies belief. What's the harm in doing it twice? Let the factories, teams, and rider enjoy their moment in front of the fans, and SPEED, then do it again the next night, if you have to.

The good folks at Yamaha may have anticipated this. When Hayes was brought onto the podium Yamaha's Tom Halverson handed Hayes a box from UPS, a team sponsor. Inside the box was a championship t-shirt with the number '1' on the back. Hayes gladly, patiently, and goofily posed for photographers, who then sent the photos across the web, where thousands more people would see it than would see the banquet the next night.

If that sounds like the mad ravings of a curmudgeon, then so be it, but the series needs to be dragged, kicking and screaming into the 21st century and there's no indication that the Daytona Motorsports Group is up to the job.

Their current mission seems to be trying to make everyone happy on issues that have little to do with the big picture. The big tent discussion of technical rules seems admirable at first glance, but what they need to do is shrink the tent and include an elite group which has the best interests of the sport, and not just their teams, at heart. Then they need to set the rules for the next five years and be done with it. As a friend of mine pointed out, they're missing the point. "Do you think those people out there give a f--- if these bikes have 16.5 or 17 inch wheels?" What they care about is seeing stars engaged in close racing. The racing has been close this year, but where are the stars? And why aren't their stories being told?

The stars may be there if you look, but the right people aren't looking. The promotional efforts of the DMG are virtually non-existent. The media tours, where a PR person drags riders from the local TV station to the local radio station to the local newspaper, are no longer done. If they are, it's up to the individual track, which shouldn't be the case. This is free publicity, the kind the track owners crave when it comes time to fill the stands, and they're getting almost no help from the people they're paying big money to bring the circus to town.

AMAPR has a very odd relationship with publicity. They issue a press release announcing the disqualification of two Bruce Rossmeyer Daytona/RMR Racing XR1200's from the podium at New Jersey Motorsports Park, but it leaves out the most relevant details. The lack of information raised more questions than it answered. What was the infraction? When was the infraction discovered? Why was there a two week delay in announcing it? But the one question it couldn't answer was why? Why would a team which had won every race do something so blatant that would jeopardize their riders and damage the integrity of the class? Simple, because they thought they could get away with it.

Team owner Richie Morris is ultimately responsible. They were his bikes, his team. Whether he knew about it is irrelevant. If he didn't, he should immediately fire whomever was responsible and condemn the offending party. In fact, he should issue a full public apology to his riders, who lost purse money and points; the Vance & Hines organization, which has done a good job of creating a competitive class with reasonable costs; the AMA, who he insulted by thinking he wouldn't get caught; and the fans, who saw something on the track that wasn't for real. And, of course, the Bruce Rossmeyer organization, who deserve better.

Among the many things the press release didn't mention was the specific infraction, but that information was available if you asked. When the release was first issued, I made a call to the AMA Pro Racing spokesman to get more details. He didn't hesitate to tell me the Delphi EMU had been altered. What I didn't ask until later, was what had been done?

In an effort to gain an illegal advantage, the rev limiter on the EMU's was raised from 6,800 rpm to 7,200 rpm. Anyone can do this to the kit box, but the change, in electronic terms, is evident. In order to avoid getting caught, the work was farmed out to a former Harley-Davidson employee, who was convinced that he could make changes without leaving fingerprints. He couldn't. And his handiwork was apparent to the other riders on the track, as well as AMA PR, once they put the bikes on the dyno.

The crazy thing is that either it didn't help or the riders were dogging it. In the first four races of the championship, all won by RMR XR's, not once did they record the race's fastest trap speed. Most of the time they were mid-pack in a field of less than ten. The reason they won is that they had something the other teams didn't, very speedy riders.

Danny Eslick won the 2009 Daytona SportBike title by wrestling the Buell to victory. He was second to Martin Cardenas in 2010 and might have won the title had he not made running into Josh Herrin more of a priority than chasing down Cardenas. Having a bad front tire on Saturday at Barber didn't help. Jake Holden was runner-up to Eslick in two of the first three races and third in the next. When Eslick sat out the XR race in New Jersey, Holden stepped in and won. His teammate Kyle Wyman was third. Both Holden and Wyman were disqualified in New Jersey, their points and purse money rescinded.

What makes the infraction especially disappointing is that the class was created as a cheap way to go racing. You didn't have to spend thousands of dollars on electronics. You didn't have to hire an electronics wizard. You had to buy an XR1200 for under $11,000, buy the $3500 Vance & Hines AMA Spec Kit and go racing. A fully kitted race bike for under $15,000. Try that with an R6 or a GSX-R600. The purse was $10,000, split between Harley-Davidson and Vance & Hines, with the winner getting $3750, more than the winner of the American SuperBike race. Of all the classes, the XR1200 class is by far the best investment. So why so few entries?

For one the timing. The series was announced at Daytona, which was far too late for a lot of teams to gear up. (There were generally around ten bikes each weekend.) Next year should be better, if dealerships catch on to how cheaply they can go racing.

The bigger question is whether it will attract young riders. The precursor was the H-D SuperTwins class that ran from 1990-97. It was designed as the gateway for dirt trackers into road racing. That was where Ben and Eric Bostrom learned to road race. That was where Aaron Yates got his start. It was also where cheating was rampant and the class eventually died off.

Times have changed. Sixteen-year-olds don't want to ride 570 lbs. V-twins when they can ride 400 lbs. inline fours, the same motorcycle they see as a stepping stone to the premier class, American SuperBike. The solution is simple: Ride both. Twice the track time, speed up the learning curve, and make some money in the process. And your Harley sponsor and middleweight sponsor can split the travel costs.

No reason to keep quiet about that.

March 1, 2011

"Mr. Daytona"

"When I went down there, I had this confidence. It was strange. I just almost knew I couldn't be beat."

Scott Russell came to his title as "Mr. Daytona" honestly. He won the 200-miler five times, back when it meant something, back when the factories were involved, back when the best riders in the country, and some of the best in the world, thought enough to compete. And tires were the key.

Over a seven-year stretch, Russell won five times by going 100 percent of every minute of every lap and by making the most of the tires. Russell would wait until he was almost vertical before pulling the pin, a technique that made the most of the fat part of the tire, and not one every caught on.

"It wasn't like rocket science," Russell says 13 years on from his final win. "I couldn't believe the other riders couldn't figure it out back then. Just follow me. This is how we do it.

"I don't even understand it, to be honest with you. How I was able to do as well as I did and not have more heat from other riders - I can't explain."

The race that cemented his legacy was 1995. Russell famously crashed early in the race, but with a little help from the pace car was able to work his way back to the front. Russell beat Ducati's Carl Fogarty, the same Englishman he'd beaten to win the 1993 World Superbike Championship. But Fogarty wasn't the only top talent to get schooled that day.

"When you look back in '95, count the World Champions, go back and look at all the World Champions that were in that time, World Champions at the time or were going to be at one time;

there was a load of them, there was a lot of them in that particular race," he points out.

The order of finish that day was Russell, four-time World Superbike Champion Fogarty, Thomas Stevens (1991 AMA Superbike Champion), two-time World Superbike Champion Colin Edwards, three-time AMA Superstock Champion Tom Kipp, the late Yasutomo Nagai, and two-time World Superbike Champion Fred Merkel. Miguel Duhamel, who would go on to win his only AMA Superbike title in 1995, crashed out of the race.

"To be able to do that the way I did it and to beat guys with that kind of credentials, that'll be number one always for me," he said.

Russell's ability to get the most out of his rear tire wouldn't help today. With the repaving of the Speedway, Dunlop's rear tires now last twice the 15-lap race distance. "I don't know nowadays that's really a big deal with those guys with traction control and all that," he said, as well as the use of only one banking for Superbikes. "I just had a great line around that racetrack and was able to get the bike up in the middle of the tire and get going."

Asked if the run from the chicane to the finish line is the most important part of the track, Russell answered, "It's got to be, doesn't it? That's where it all goes down, man, and you gotta be in a position to make something happen, be close enough there."

Last year Russell thought, "There's no way Jake's [Zemke] going to run these guys down, gonna be able to make this work, but I'd eat those words. So definitely chicane to start-finish is the most important part of that racetrack."

Zemke won't be able to defend his Superbike sweep. Instead Russell thinks "the same old guys" will dominate the front. He names Monster Yamaha's Josh Hayes and, with the speed of the Jordan Suzukis, he "wouldn't be surprised to see a [Ben] Bostrom [in the mix] or a [Tommy] Hayden...either. Both of them seem to get around there pretty good.

"I don't know if there's a clear cut guy up front on this one. If it is, it's got to be Hayes or [Tommy] Hayden. Again, those are the two guys, I think. I think Roger's [Hayden] a question mark still for me, to be honest. This'll be a big year for him. Lot of eyes will be on him, for sure. I want him to do good.

"I'd like to see Blake [Young] up there. I like him, I like his personality, I like his fieriness. He's got to put it all together, man. He's got the right group behind him, it's just he's got some work to do still."

Russell returns to the track for the first time since 2008 when he rides a Vance & Hines XR1200 on the two-banking 3.51-mile course in Friday's XR1200 final. He wouldn't feel the same about returning to the racetrack he once owned if forced onto the shorter, 2.91-mile Superbike layout.

"I really am disappointed in the track that they've chosen to run again," he said. "That new thing for Superbikes is just no good to me."

There will never be another "Mr. Daytona." The Superbike race will never attract the world's top riders for a number of reasons - safety, cost, lack of visibility, spec tires, AMA technical rules - to say nothing of the fact that it's now a support class. There was talk at the highest levels of AMA Pro Racing of returning Superbikes to the 200 on both bankings. That could happen in 2012 if the control tire supplier, currently Dunlop, is chosen to continue beyond this season, which isn't certain. And if another company is brought in, it could set the Superbike 200 back a year or more.

"They got to go back to that track. It's just not the same," Russell said, and no one knows better than "Mr. Daytona."

March 15, 2011

The Moment

The greatest relief pitcher in the history of baseball can tell you with certainty the moment he became great. New York Yankees' closer Mariano Rivera was throwing a bullpen session in June of 1997 at Tiger Stadium when greatness was visited on him. When the ball left his hand, it did something it had never done before. The cut fastball that would confound most every hitter in the American League, and many National Leaguers during his World Series appearances was born. A deeply spiritual man, Rivera took the sudden transformation as a sign from above.

Wayne Rainey can also pinpoint the minute when his career changed. Rainey is also a deeply spiritual man, but the three-time World Champion doesn't credit divine intervention. Rather it was human error, a mistake that convinced him that if he was to join the ranks of the greats, like three-time 500cc World Champion and team owner Kenny Roberts, he had to prove himself worthy.

Rainey won a lot of races in his life - the Daytona 200, the U.S. GP three times, the Suzuka 8 Hours (when the factories put forward their best efforts, and best riders), and 24 500cc GPs. But most of that wouldn't have happened had he not made one very big mistake.

In researching a story about Rainey, I was given an account of his greatness by Dave Watkins, the quiet man who ran Dunlop's racing division for decades.

"I had the privilege to be at the track when Wayne [Rainey] became great," Watkins said over a cup of tea at his house in Sutton Coldfield, just north of Dunlop's headquarters in Birmingham, England. As Watkins remembers, Rainey was two seconds off the pace during a test for the Suzuka 8 Hours in 1988, when the team owner offered encouragement in a way only he can. "Kenny [Roberts] just said, get on the brakes f&^%-ing late," Watkins remembers Roberts saying. "Wayne was struggling in the 14s and Kenny's comments turned them into 12s after the lunch break." Watkins added, "I mean, if we said that, we'd probably get sued, but Kenny could say that."

Watkins points out that Rainey came back from the 8 Hours, which he won with Kevin Magee, and won his first Grand Prix at Donington Park the following weekend.

Roberts doesn't remember the incident, which isn't surprising since he's dispensed plenty of wisdom in the ensuing nearly 23 years. And Rainey isn't sure either.

"At that time, a quote from Kenny [Roberts] probably was pretty close to what I needed at that time at Suzuka," Rainey said. "You got to remember, when I went to Suzuka in '88, my first Grand Prix, that's when Kenny had let Randy [Mamola] go; he hired me. We didn't do a lot of testing before the championship, so I was learning how to ride the thing. I went to a circuit that I'd never been to before and I didn't realize the thing was almost four miles around…and trying to learn that. And then I remember my very first out lap was in the rain and Kevin Magee was my teammate and he had raced the 8 Hours there the year before and won the race, because he did some Herculean effort and rode the last four hours or something by himself, something crazy or something like that in the heat at Suzuka, and he won the race. So I thought in my mind, 'I'll follow Magee, because he knows where he's going.' And here I am, I got out on the track and he just disappears on the out lap. He just takes off. Of course it was in the rain. And I'm not sure where I'm going."

And the next thing he knows, Rainey's on the ground in the Spoon Curve, the signature looping left onto the Suzuka back straight.

"When you go into that corner, it's kind of deceiving because it kinda almost looks... as you enter it kinda the track goes up and then it flattens out and then as it's turning to the left it's almost like it's almost off-camber as you go into there. And then it gets flat and then you start turning again to exit onto the back straight.

"Well, I lost the front and crashed on my first out lap of my first GP race. So you can imagine what I felt like when I rode back into the pits. I remember, I ran over to the bike, I picked it up; I've got gravel everywhere. And I pick it up and I go riding back into the pits and I just went, 'Jeez, what have I done here? Man, this is not a good way to start.' And it was in the rain and it looked like it was going to rain all weekend, and of course in America we don't race much in the rain. And I remember, that one lap probably helped make me a World Champion, because I said, 'I've got to go back on this bike and I don't care if I don't know the track because it's raining and I made a mistake. Dude, you better be strong right now. This is it. If you don't do that now I'll never be able to go through adversity again racing.'"

Rainey ended up sixth in the race, beating teammate Magee, "So I was pretty happy about. But the worst part was that [Kevin] Schwantz won."

As for Roberts motivating him with profanity, Rainey laughs, "I don't really recall, because Kenny generally wouldn't tell me to brake super-deep, because Kenny didn't like that so much. But if I was braking like a grandpa, then maybe he could've said that. And that's quite possible. So, yeah, yeah, I'm sure he did. Somewhere."

March 22, 2011

Flirting With Disaster

The Daytona 200 was a manmade disaster that again graphically highlighted the sad state of AMA Pro Road Racing on a weekend when only good fortune prevented tragedy.

There's plenty of blame to go around, but ultimately it rests at the doorstep of AMA Pro Racing, which insisted on running both bankings on the most lethal racetrack on the calendar when a more sensible solution was staring them in the face.

Running on both bankings is a problem they brought on themselves in a desperate effort to cling to the past, when the race meant something, which it no longer does. They had the option of running on the single-banking Short Course, which was used for the 200 from when it was laid out in 2005 through 2008. And anyone who thinks it will ever be anything more than a round of a domestic championship is delusional. Riders have fought for and won safety improvements worldwide over the past few decades. Racing at Daytona is an insult to the many tracks, like Infineon Raceway, like Road America, like Mazda Raceway Laguna Seca, to name a few, that have been made safer. None are perfect, but they're better than they've ever been and nowhere near as dangerous as Daytona. Where else do Superbike riders fly feet from an unprotected wall at over 200 mph on the AMA's generous speed-readings? With no margin of error it's nothing but dumb luck that this year's races didn't end tragically.

It was only dumb luck that no one hit Dane Westby's Suzuki as it careened up the track after he and Josh Herrin came together on the run to the stripe. And if the Supercross track was still there, Taylor Knapp, an innocent victim of Herrin and Westby, would not have walked away. It was nothing but dumb luck that the Harley rider who wobbled himself into a high-speed crash in the tri-oval wasn't injured in a display that the XR1200s were clearly not ready for prime time at Daytona. It was only dumb luck that the entire Supersport field wasn't wiped out by the riderless Celtic Racing/Fast by Ferracci Ducati 848EVO that ghost rode all the way through the infield and crossed the track just behind race leader Tomas Puerta. Had Benny Solis not highsided out of second, with the entire pack bearing down on them, it would have been disastrous.

"It was a little bit scary seeing a bike come across the track, not really knowing, not having any way to look where it is," third-place finisher James Rispoli said, adding, "Maybe we should put some hay bales there just to catch the bikes."

And maybe AMA Pro Racing should stop trying to please everyone and make some hard calls, starting with their inane jump-start policy. Under former race director Colin Fraser, a rider was penalized if he moved at all. An involuntary twitch, a sneeze, a tic and you were convicted. It was a touch draconian. So now the AMA has gone in the complete opposite direction: It's okay to jump the start, just say you're sorry by putting your life at risk.

Monster Energy Graves Yamaha's Josh Hayes didn't just jump the start, he vaulted it, and he knew it. And he also knew that if he slowed down and let a few riders by - he wasn't sure how many - he'd save himself from a penalty. Hayes let Tommy Hayden and Blake Young past, then Roger Lee Hayden and Martin Cardenas, and then he thought to himself, "Well, you know, that's about as many I think is fair, so we'll see what happens from there."

Because of his actions under the current rules, Hayes wasn't penalized.

The last thing a rider should be thinking about at the start of a Superbike race is slowing down, but that's what Hayes was being asked to do. Fortunately, he's a very skilled rider who pulled it off with ease, as could several at the front of the field. But what if it was Triple Digit Johnny who went for the glory and blitzed the field from row seven? Do we want him calculating how much to slow down in the first turn at, say, Road America?

The self-policing rule makes sense when a rider inadvertently passes under a waving yellow, not at the start of a race. If you know you're going to be penalized when you jump it's a powerful disincentive. As it is, the riders know they can avoid a penalty by moving out of the way.

And where does the self-policing end? Team Latus Motors was given permission by AMA Pro Racing to change the motor in Jason DiSalvo's Ducati 848EVO, as the rulebook allows. An AMA official kept an eye on the work, but was the bike as safe as it would've been had it gone through tech inspection? Certainly not. And yet there it was, about to shed parts when another red flag was flown. When a team changes engines, shouldn't it be given at least a cursory inspection before being sent out? Crew chief Ronnie Sanner told me they had a "brake lever that was loose and a couple of things that were sketchy. But with the red flag, we got back in and we had 10 minutes. I just told the crew, 'I said put your hands on everything.' And we found a brake that was out of adjustment and maybe a couple of little things that maybe would've rattled loose, we were able to fix those."

Another bullet dodged. How many more are in the chamber?

April 19, 2011

The Welcome Mat

Say you've been sitting around for a few years wondering what it'd be like to race a Superbike again. Never mind that you haven't ridden one for a few years, your next birthday will be your 40th, there's less money in AMA Superbike racing than the tip jars at most Starbucks, and, to be fair, it's not like you and AMA Pro Racing are BFFs. Oh, and you had your foot cut off nearly a year ago. So, any chance you could make an impression on the AMA series in 2012?

The most successful rider in the history of AMA Superbike racing is thinking about making a comeback at an age when no rider has ever won an AMA Superbike race. Mat Mladin wants back in… maybe.

The last image of Mladin's unmatchable AMA career shows him with a big grin waving the number "1" plate following his unprecedented seventh AMA Superbike Championship at New Jersey Motorsports Park. Then he was gone.

In fact he was gone long before that. The Daytona Motorsports Group, specifically Roger Edmondson, made sure of it. The 15th round of the 2009 series, at Heartland Park Topeka, a track Edmondson put on the schedule, was so unsafe that after a few laps of Thursday promoter practice Mladin flew home (the poorly attended, poorly promoted event was taken off the schedule almost instantly). After landing back in Chino, Mladin issued a press release announcing his retirement at the end of the year. What no one could have known at the time was that his victory four weeks earlier at Mazda Raceway Laguna Seca, which would be his 82nd, would be his last. (The closest active AMA rider is Josh Hayes with

14.) The following round at Mid-Ohio would mark the beginning of the end. Following his third place in Saturday's Superbike race, he said, "That's it. Realistically, I've just lost interest, to be honest with you."

Mladin skipped the two Kansas races and crashed out of the lead in the penultimate race at New Jersey Motorsports Park. Still, he had enough of a cushion to win the title. And he nearly won his final race before a transmission gremlin stole fifth gear.

Since retiring he's been involved in his aftermarket business outside of Sydney, but he isn't as hands-on as he once was. Which means he has time to think about a comeback.

In fact, the demand for Mladin never really stopped. Ever since he left he's been courted and had serious talks with more than one team. But a return to riding, to say nothing of racing, was put on hold until he was able to fix the left ankle savaged in an ultralight accident in January 1995.

Mladin invariably politely declined to talk about the injury. But the fact that he lived with a bum ankle for 16 years, and still won at will, says something about his dedication. To fix it, surgeons had to, essentially, cut his foot off, rotate it, then screw it all back together.

The extended convalescence has been something of a blessing. If he returns in 2012 it should be to a healthier and, hopefully, less befuddled championship. Time will tell.

Retired riders have a way of fading away, and comebacks, especially delayed comebacks, are rarely successful. But Mladin made his own rules and, with the notable exceptions of World Champions Nicky Hayden and Ben Spies, didn't face a rider who could consistently beat him for the last 10 years of his career. And what he did to toughen up Hayden and Spies before they moved to a bigger stage served them well, Spies especially.

Does the championship need Mat Mladin? Yes, but it needs so much more than Mladin; promotion, a vision for the future, sensible rules, the list goes on. Could the series benefit from his presence? Unquestionably. Mladin is a very proud man and wouldn't come back if he didn't think he could win. But the fear factor's gone. No longer would the others be disheartened when he qualified on pole with a lap time they couldn't fathom. Which is another reason why his return would be compelling.

Sports thrive on personalities and Mladin is certainly one.

Regardless of what you think about him, he cannot be ignored. Which isn't to say there aren't other personalities in the series, but none have his resume and none ever will. He could be a polarizing and often misunderstood figure when he raced and his return would rejuvenate his fans and re-energize his detractors. Either way, it'd bring heat to a moribund championship that's trying desperately to make everyone like it. They allow riders to jump starts, as long as they punish themselves. And they let riders change engines, as long as they promise no parts will fall off. Makes me wonder if Josh Herrin was really suspended for a race or volunteered to sit one out.

Whoever put the 2011 calendar together needs a lesson in continuity. No one who wanted to keep the championship on the front burner would schedule a nine-week hiatus after the disastrous first race. Nothing is happening. The series is in a coma while other championships steal all the heat. Could a 40-yearold retiree change that? Hard to say, but it'd be fun to watch.

March 5, 2013

Chicanery

The final installment of Chicanery *was a blank page.*

www.ingramcontent.com/pod-product-compliance
Lightning Source LLC
Chambersburg PA
CBHW070819250426
43671CB00036B/466